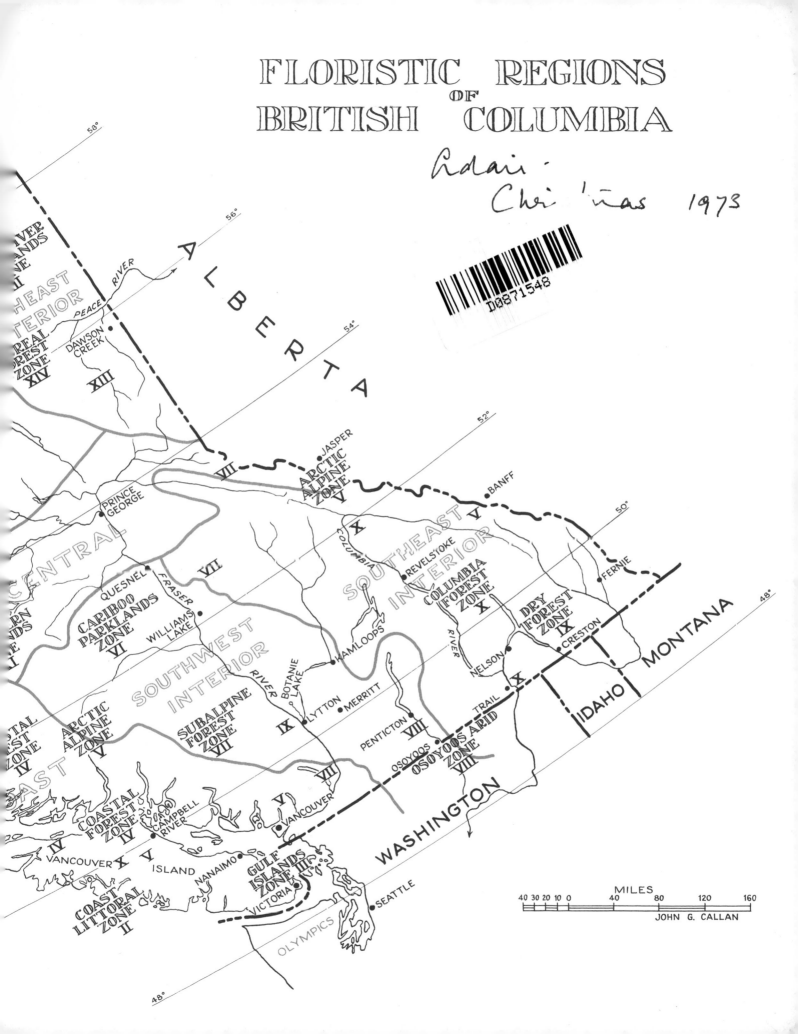

FLORISTIC REGIONS
OF
BRITISH COLUMBIA

Wild Flowers of
British Columbia

WILD FLOWERS
OF
BRITISH COLUMBIA

LEWIS J. CLARK

GRAY'S PUBLISHING LIMITED

Sidney, British Columbia, Canada

ISBN 0-88826-036-9

printed and bound in Canada by
EVERGREEN PRESS LIMITED
Vancouver, British Columbia

TO LORRAINE,

who has cheerfully accepted mud and flies in the swamps, forest
damp and desert heat, and especially the whistling storms of mountain
tops; who has out-waited the wind and watched the scudding clouds
for a burst of sunshine; who has made this book possible.

CONTENTS

LIST OF FAMILIES

LIST OF ILLUSTRATIONS

These pages list the plants illustrated, in the widely accepted sequence of *families* set forth in Engler's natural system, although for convenience the genera and species are arranged alphabetically under each family. In general this is also the sequence of appearance in this book. Only the scientific names appear in this list.

Common or English names with the scientific names, in alphabetical order, will be found in the Index at the end of the book.

Unless otherwise indicated, the illustrations are from the author's 35 mm slides.

SIZE OF PLANTS

Scale of each illustration is indicated to the right of the name, thus:

ALISMA PLANTAGO-AQUATICA   ×⅞

means that the illustration is seven-eighths as large as the original plant. The actual size of the average plant will then be a little larger than the illustration. (Similarly, the picture of ALLIUM CRENULATUM ×4 is four times life-size.)

KEY TO PRONUNCIATION

Perhaps the chief restraints to more widespread use of the scientific names of plants are uncertainty of pronunciation, and unfamiliarity with the meaning and spelling of the Latinized words. We have tried to reduce the latter difficulty by explaining the origin and roots of the generic and specific names. (In our own experience such explanations have also helped to fix these names in memory.) Hopefully, the international botanical system of pronunciation marks will reduce the former problem.

According to this system the marks ` or ´ indicate the stressed syllable in each word. They also offer a rough guide to the vowel sound, but they do not at all correspond to the well-known *grave* and *acute* marks. In general ` indicates the long form of the vowel, ´ the short form. Thus ÁLLIUM is pronounced *ahl/-ee-um;* and SMILACÌNA is approximately *smile-ah- seen/-ah.* In a very few cases the Old World pronunciation is not uniformly adopted in North America—for instance CLÉMATIS (*klem/-ah-tis*) is often, on this side of the Atlantic, *klee-may/-tis.*

mittee on Horticultural Nomenclature). But few will accept at all readily the committee's arbitrary choices, particularly since they saw fit to inflict such violence upon normal usages of the English language, as in: Rattlesnakeroot, Alpine yellowmimulus, Redosier dogwood, Mount Washington dryad (surely a provincialism, for *Dryas octopetala),* Creambush rockspirea (for *Holodiscus discolor),* or distressfully, for *Spiranthes romanzoffiana,* Continental ladiestresses! Perhaps not surprisingly, the "Standardized Plant Names" have not been widely adopted. A much better case might be made for accepting the old Indian names, where these can be precisely identified with certain plants, especially if the name was used over a wide area. We have given a number of these.

Taxonomical science is still progressing toward delimitation of that nebulous concept, the species, and problems remain, especially in some notorious genera, before the ideal situation can be realized. But for the vast majority of our plants we can be reasonably certain that valid and permanent names have been established. The accepted pronunciation of these words is indicated, together with a key explaining the pronunciation marks. Abbreviations following the names are those of the authorities responsible for that name; they need not be memorized, but the interested reader will find them listed, in Hultén as an example. No attempt has been made to find an English name for every plant, nor have we felt sufficiently presumptuous to invent names. The limited number of names in English that have been employed, are those that have enjoyed fairly wide acceptance.

In the vast area of British Columbia, which extends from the 49th parallel to the 60th (the latter being nearly 600 miles north of Amchitka in Alaska's Aleutian Islands), and from the misty Queen Charlottes 580 miles eastward to the Rockies, about 2000 species of flowering plants have been reported. Certainly many others will be found as exploration continues of the great variety of habitats between sea level and 15,300 feet (Mt. Fairweather). A large proportion of the plants described in this book range northward to Alaska and the Yukon, eastward to the Prairie Provinces, and southward to Washington, Idaho, Montana, and even Oregon and California. Hence the work should be helpful to plant-lovers of a wide area. Not included in this book are the trees or ferns (for which several excellent illustrated manuals are available), nor the horsetails, grasses, sedges, or rushes (which are of interest chiefly to specialists). We have not considered discriminating between native plants and introduced plants, many of the latter being now among our commonest species. In any case the distinction has become hazy; the European Purslane *(Portulaca oleracea),* for instance, has been with us since Samuel de Champlain mentioned seeing it established in a Huron village, in 1615.

The arrangement of families in this book is the Englerian sequence, for though some eminent botanical philosophers have suggested certain changes, there is as yet no agreement among them. However, for practical convenience of reference, we have arranged the genera within each family, and for the most part, the species within each genera, in alphabetical order. Included are about 50 percent of the species of shrubby and herbaceous flowering plants known to occur in our area. Nearly all of the more showy plants are described. Only minimal coverage has been given to the three largest families (Compositae 302, Cruciferae 112, and Leguminosae 111 known species) chiefly because of space limitations, but also because many of the species call for identification by specialists.

We have followed the authority of Hitchcock, Cronquist, Ownbey and Thompson for nomenclature of plants which occur within the coverage of their monumental work. For the taxonomy of more northern species we are greatly indebted to the scholarly work of Hultén, and of Calder and Taylor. Other major assistance has come from J. K. Henry's *Flora of Southern B.C.* (1915), and the supplement by J. W. Eastham (1947), also from Eric Garman's valuable pocket guide (1963), and the excellent monographs by Dr. T. M. C. Taylor and Dr. Adam Szczawinski. The latest available opinions have been used, but in some cases more familiar names, long in use but now displaced by application of the provisions of the International Code of Botanical Nomenclature, have been included parenthetically as synonyms.

In the descriptions an attempt has been made, particularly in the first hundred pages, to use as few technical terms as possible. However, to avoid unnecessary wordiness and loss of precision, a few such terms, all of which are explained in the illustrated glossary, have been gradually introduced. A conscious effort has been made to develop the understanding of the reader as he progresses through the book.

It is a great pleasure to acknowledge, with gratitude, assistance from many persons, not all of whom can be named here. The author is indebted to Miss M. C. Melburn, mentor to many, for encouragement, and for a large measure of enthusiasm. For the graciously offered loan of their beautiful slides (which are acknowledged in the List of Illustrations) he is indebted to Mr. and Mrs. Verne Ahier, Mr. and Mrs. T. A. Armstrong, Mr. and Mrs. Trevor Green, Mr. Kerry Joy, Miss Terese Todd, and Mrs. Jessie Woollett. From his very extensive horticultural knowledge, Mr. Ed Lohbrunner has freely contributed both support and learning. For kind assistance, especially with the Greek derivations, we wish to thank Professor George Black, of the University of Victoria, and Dr. H. G. Edinger of the department of Classics, University of British Columbia. To Dr. Marc Bell for use of the University of Victoria Herbarium, and to Dr. Adam Szczawinski, Dr. Chris Brayshaw, and Mrs. Sheila Newnham for facilities generously provided in the Provincial Herbarium, we express our thanks and appreciation. Mr. Gray Campbell, publisher, and Commander John Barclay, with the staff of Evergreen Press, have been considerate and consistently helpful. They have understood the author's affection for plants and his concern for their preservation. Particular thanks are also due to the late Mr. Ed Harrison of Evergreen Press who designed the book. The manuscript has been typed with patience and skill by Mrs. Trudy Byers. Frances and Norman Gansner have been helpful with suggestions and proofreading. Grateful acknowledgement is made to John and Gina, who have helped in many practical ways, and to Kathleen, who has given devoted and untiring assistance in checking and research.

To all of these kind people, and many others who have helped in the production of this work, we would like to express our sincere thanks.

We wish to acknowledge with gratitude Grants, which have been passed on to the public, from the Canada Council and the University of Victoria.

L.J.C.
Victoria, B.C.
January 24, 1973

"If the writer should at all appear to have induced any of his readers to pay a more ready attention to the wonders of the Creation . . . his purpose will be fully answered."

Gilbert White:
The Natural History of Selborne. (1788)

THE FLORA

 ALISMATÀCEAE. *Water Plantain Family.*

ALÍSMA PLANTÀGO-AQUÁTICA L. *Water-plantain.* [p.6]

Alisma is derived from the Celtic alis for *water*, while the Latin specific name is interpreted in the common name. The succulent leaves of this large marsh plant are usually ovate and often heart-shaped; the blades are as much as 6 inches long with fleshy stems sometimes 2 feet long. Still taller are the branching flower-stems that carry, in July or August, many small flowers. These have 3 green and persistent sepals and 3 white (sometimes pink) soon-dropped petals, centred by a cluster of green pistils and 6-9 yellow stamens.

Water-plantain occurs in shallow water or very wet pockets in fields and ditches, at low to moderate altitudes over much of North America. In British Columbia it is limited to the southern part of the Province.

But there is no reason why I should dilate at greater length upon the pleasantness and delight of acquiring knowledge of plants, since there is no one who does not know that there is nothing in this life pleasanter and more delightful than to wander over woods, mountains, plains, garlanded and adorned with flowerlets and plants of various sorts, and most elegant to boot, and to gaze intently upon them. But it increases that pleasure and delight not a little, if there be added an acquaintance with the virtues and powers of these same plants.

Leonhart Fuchs [Fuchsius]:
1542, *De historia stirpium*
(in a translation of A. Arber, 1912)

SAGITTÀRIA CUNEÀTA Sheld. *Arum-leaved Arrowhead. Wapato. Duck Potato.*

Sagittaria means *relating to arrows* with reference to the long-petiolar leaves whose blades are sagittate, i.e. shaped exactly like the pointed blades and long twin barbs of arrowheads. The specific name means *wedge-shaped*, probably descriptive of the thickened starchy tubers that grow at the ends of the rootstocks.

The Arrowheads are plants of quiet shallow sloughs, ponds, and slow streams. In late July they lift their showy white flowers above the characteristic leaves. Wapato (or wappato, or wapatoo of the Chinook jargon) was an important food for native tribes, who harvested the tubers with digging sticks or bare toes. The detached pieces rose to the surface, and were boiled or roasted. Lewis and Clark (who wintered at the mouth of the Columbia) remarked that the tubers tasted very much like roast potatoes. Ducks and geese consume the smaller tubers.

S. cuneata is a perennial of wide distribution through the Central and Northern Interior. Its flattened 6-24 inch petioles hold the leaf-blades just above, or on, the surface of the water. There is much variation in shape and size (from 3-12 inches) of the leaf-blades, or they may even be absent. In deeper water the plants produce mere ribbon-like extensions of the petioles that never reach the surface.

Flowering-stems are branched, each branch terminated by an attractive flower that has 3 green sepals and 3 snowy broadly-obovate petals. The uppermost flowers are centred by 10-20 stamens, the lowermost flowers enclose numerous pistils forming a rounded cluster. The blackish ball-head of ripened achenes that succeeds each pistillate flower provides the best means of distinguishing this species from the next. Under a 10X magnifier each achene of S. cuneata is seen to bear a short, sharp-pointed, vertical beak.

SAGITTÀRIA LATIFÒLIA Willd. *Broad-leaved Arrowhead. Wapato. Indian Potato.*
[p.6]

The specific name of this larger and more southern species means *wide-foliage*. The lobes of the "arrowhead" leaves are often (but not invariably) more widely flared (divergent) than those of *S. cuneata* (which see). However, the leaves of both species are too variable in shape and size to be very helpful in recognition. In rich soil the leaf-blades of S. latifolia may be as much as 14 inches long, but may not exceed 3 inches in less favourable circumstances. The flowers of the present species are generally larger, and may span 1¾ inches.

British Columbia records for S. latifolia are from the Fraser delta, and southern Vancouver Island.

The ripened achenes are the best distinguishing characteristic of the Broad-leaved Arrowhead. The beak is about 1/16 inch long (twice that of *S. cuneata*) and forms a horizontal projection of the upper margin of the achene (rather than a vertical point from the tip of the achene).

ARÀCEAE. *Arum Family.*

CÁLLA PALÚSTRIS L. *Water Arum. Wild Calla.*

This wildling relative of the familiar white Calla Lilies of the florist is a marsh-dweller for which new sites are constantly recorded. Indeed it appears to occur in suitably wet bogs from Quesnel north, across the width of the Province.

The name is derived from the Greek kallos, *beautiful,* and the Latin adjective meaning *of the marsh.* Calla palustris is unmistakable. Clearly it is a small (4-8 inches tall) northern cousin of *Lysichitum* (which see), but with a white spathe rather than a yellow one. The inner face of the spathe is pale green and effectively sets off the stubby spadix with its red berry-like fruit. Leaves are shiny green, 2-4 inches long, and heart-shaped (on petioles twice as long as the blades).

Pepper-hot saponins are concentrated in the "berries", but they are broken down by drying and boiling. So treated, the fruit is used by the northern natives.

LYSICHÌTUM AMERICÀNUM Hult. & St. J. *Yellow Arum. Yellow Skunk Cabbage.* [p.7]

The generic name is from the Greek words for *loose,* and for the classical *tunic,* probably with reference to the spathe in which the developing flower-stem is wrapped. Authorities are divided whether there is an Asiatic and an American species, or only one.

This is a very large tropical-looking swamp plant, whose brilliant yellow spathes illuminate the dark swamps as early as February or March. The spathe unfolds to reveal the spadix, a thick stalk bearing hundreds of small greenish flowers. Shortly the fleshy oval leaves emerge from the mud, ultimately to form huge fans. These are the largest of any plant occurring in our area. We measured one 56 inches long and 29 inches wide!

The whole plant has a smell of spring, of surging growth, that would be objectionable in a closed room but is not unpleasant in its own habitat. For the record, it does not smell at all like the mephitic spray of the skunk. Bears consume the whole plant, including the short thick rootstock, while deer occasionally browse the leaves.

This huge plant is related to the *taro,* staple food of the Polynesians. Both plants produce a stinging sensation in the mouth, due to calcium oxalate. Ages ago, however, the natives of our area discovered, as did those of the South Seas, that roasting and drying the root drove off the substance responsible for the stinging, burning taste, after which it could be ground to an edible flour.

You may look for the yellow torches of the Yellow Arum in mucky ground and swampy areas along the coast from Alaska south, and in the interior south from about the latitude of Prince George.

At the end of winter there is a season in which we are daily expecting
spring . . . Methinks the first obvious evidence of spring is the
pushing out of the swamp willow catkins . . . then the pushing up of
the skunk-cabbage* spathes . . . .

Henry David Thoreau
Journal (March 10, 1853)

*Thoreau was referring to the greenish-brown skunk-cabbage of Massachusetts
(Symplocarpus foetidus (L.) Nutt.), a plant of very similar habit.

LEMNÀCEAE. *Duckweed Family.*

LÉMNA MÌNOR L. *Lesser Duckweed.* [p.6]

This genus is one of 4 composing the family LEMNACEAE, which are believed to be
greatly reduced representatives of an ancient plant family that may have included
ancestors of our Yellow Arum, and the familiar Philodendrons. Another member of the
family is *Wolffia columbiana*, the smallest of all the flowering plants, which is only 1/16
inch long.

Lemna are free-floating water-plants consisting of a single leaf-like, flat green oval,
seldom—if ever—flowering in our area, but increasing by budding to such huge numbers
that they may form a green scum extending over acres of water. Limne (Greek) means
lake or marsh. About 8 species are distributed through temperate to tropical America
and Eurasia.

Minor means *smaller*, the plants of this species being floating, almost round
structures (thalli) a mere ¼ inch long, with one short, root-like process that may extend
as much as an inch downward into the water. The common name is appropriate, for the
masses of tiny plants are often eaten by ducks.*

Duckweed occurs in suitable ponds and lakes that are not subject to wind, from
Alaska southward. The rudimentary flowers appear (very rarely) in a fold, or cleft, on
the upper surface of the thallus. A male flower consists entirely of a single stamen, a
female flower of a solitary flask-shaped pistil.

*gold and silver fishes . . . . will also feed on
the water-plant called lemna (duck's meat). . . .

Gilbert White:
The Natural History of Selborne (1788)

LILIÀCEAE. *Lily Family.*

. . . the world
—The beauty and the wonder and the power,
The shapes of things, their colours, lights and shades . . . .

Robert Browning: Fra Lippo Lippi

This great family of about 250 genera, including more than 4000 species, is widely distributed over the earth's surface, especially in warm temperate and tropical regions. Included are many highly-prized ornamentals, and many plants of economic and historic interest. These include the Autumn Crocus *(Colchicum)* which yields colchicine, used to induce genetic mutations in other plants, and the Dragon Tree *(Dracaena)* whose resin was used by Stradivari for his violin varnish. One specimen of this slow-growing lily, gale-destroyed on Teneriffe in 1868, was locally believed to be 6000 years old!

The history of the family is very ancient, for lilies are clearly recognizable from Minoan vase paintings of Crete, dated about 1750 B.C., and present research suggests prototype lilies may be survivors from the warm period prior to the Quaternary Ice Age, i.e. about 2 million years ago.

The Latin poet Virgil called the lovely Madonna Lily "candidum," meaning *shining-white* (as distinct from "album", *dead-white*). It was introduced through the length and breadth of the known world, wherever the legionaries built permanent forts. This was not, apparently, entirely a matter of esthetic appreciation for the cool white blossoms. One of the traditional uses of the boiled bulbs was a cure for corns, so the hard-headed (and sore-footed) soldiers invariably planted the lilies to provide a convenient supply.

Members of this family have flower parts in threes (as is usual among the monocotyledonous plants) e.g. 3 sepals and 3 petals (where sepals and petals are very much alike they are sometimes referred to as *tepals*), 6 stamens (of which often 3 are short and 3 longer), and 3 divisions of the stigma corresponding to 3 divisions of the superior ovary. There is only one exception to this rule among the liliaceous genera of our area; *Maianthemum* (False Lily-of-the-valley) has its parts in fours.

ÁLLIUM. *Wild Onion.*

The characteristic taste and odour of the whitish scaly bulbs, long narrow basal leaves, and upright or nodding umbel of white to pinkish flowers will at once identify plants of this genus. The shape and covering of the bulbs are of great importance in identifying approximately 300 species that are widely distributed in the northern hemisphere.

"Alum" was Pliny's first century A.D. name for garlic. Allium was the source of the

6

T. & S. ARMSTRONG

ALISMA PLANTAGO-AQUATICA $\times$⅞ [p.1]

SAGGITARIA LATIFOLIA $\times$¼ [p.2]

LEMNA MINOR $\times$1 [p.4]

ALLIUM CERNUUM $\times$½ [p.9]

ALLIUM ACUMINATUM ×2 [p.8]

LYSICHITON AMERICANUM ×¼ [p.3]

chemists' "allyl," for it is allyl disulphide which is chiefly responsible for the odour of garlic, onions, leeks and related plants.

All of the wild onions have been extensively used, as a pleasant change from more bland vegetable foods, by early explorers and the Indians. Since the characteristic stalks and dried umbels remain late in the year, the woodsman should know that this emergency food is available with little digging. But he must be sure that both the onion odour and the whitish outer coat are present, or he runs the risk of being poisoned by Poison Camas (*Zygadenus gramineus* or *Z. venenosus*, which see) both of which have blackish outer coats but closely resemble in shape the bulbs of several Allium species.

The genus has attracted attention through many centuries. One of the most unpleasant of Chaucer's characters was the Summoner, who is perhaps symbolically characterized: "Wel loued he garlyk, onyons, and eke lekes. . . ." Early settlers in New England hung strings of onions over their doorways to ward off infections, and indeed many people today cook up a large pot of onion soup to hold a cold at bay.

ÁLLIUM ACUMINÀTUM Hooker. *Hooker's Onion.* [p.7]

Acuminatum refers to the shape of the petals, which gradually taper to a *narrow point*. They are brilliant rose, almost orchid (rarely, an albino form is seen), and very showy, since they occur in an open umbel with sometimes as many as 25 flowers. The leaves are shorter than the scape and usually 3 or 4 grow from each bulb, but they commonly wither and shrivel up before the flowers open in May or June. The plant is found in dry situations among the rocks, in southwestern British Columbia.

Archibald Menzies refers to an Allium (very probably this species) in his fascinating *Menzies' Journal of Vancouver's Voyage* (entry of June 8, 1792):

> The Shores [of Orcas Island] were almost every where steep rugged & cliffy [as the visitor of today will agree!] which made Landing difficult & the woods were in many places equally difficult of access from the rocky cliffs & chasms/with which they abounded, but I was not all displeasd at the change & general ruggedness of the surface of the Country as it producd a pleasing variety in the objects of my pursuit & added Considerably to my Catalogue of Plants.
>
> I here found another species of that *new genus* I discoverd at Village Point in Admiralty Inlet, & a small well tasted wild onion [*Allium* sp.] which grew in little Tufts in the crevices of the Rocks with a species of *Arenaria* both new. I also met with the *Lilium Canadense* [*Fritillaria lanceolata*] & *Lilium Camschatcense* [*Fritillaria camschatcensis*], the roots of the latter is the *Sarana* so much esteemd by the Kamtschadales [Aleuts] as a favorite food.

How interesting that almost two hundred years later we still find these same plants on those rugged shores!

ÁLLIUM CERNÙUM Roth. *Nodding Onion.* [p.6]

This species is distinguished by the *crook* (cernuum) in the flower-stem (scape) immediately below the flower-cluster, which causes the umbel to look downward, or nod. Two bracts enclose the flower-cluster until just before the flowers open. They are pale-pink to white. The bulb is long, gradually tapering upward, and the bulb scales are inconspicuously parallel-veined. The 2-5 leaves are slightly shorter than the scape.

Rocky or gravelly situations suit this plant, which is widely distributed and even common through lower elevations of British Columbia, except in the Queen Charlotte Islands and the far North. The rather attractive flowers appear from June to August.

Bulbs of the Nodding Onion were, and are, used as food by the Indian people. "Lillooet," in the Salish language, means "place of wild onions".

ÁLLIUM CRENULÀTUM Wieg. *Olympic Onion.* [p.23]

The Latin name refers to the crenate or *scalloped* (obscurely toothed) margins of the flowering-stem.

The bulbs resemble those of *A. cernuum* (which see) but there are usually only 2 leaves, which are longer than the scape (or flowering-stem), and the brilliant rose-purple flowers are carried in an *upright* umbel. This is an alpine plant, known only from Vancouver Island and the Olympic Peninsula. It blooms in July or August.

All the wild onion species secrete allyl disulphide, which is responsible for the characteristic smell of the bulbs and leaves. In fact one's first notice of the plants is, not infrequently, the odour arising from the bruised leaves.

ÁLLIUM GÈYERI S. Wats. var. TENÉRUM M. E . Jones. *Geyer's Onion.* [p.22]

Carl Andreas Geyer (1809-1853) was botanist with Nicollet's expedition, and collected in northern Idaho and Washington in 1844.

This rather pretty onion is very local, and has been recorded so far only from short turf meadows in Botanie Valley (north of Lytton); along the Sooke coastline of Vancouver Island, and in north central Washington. The umbels are upright, the flowers pale pink, and the leaves remain green at blooming time. The characteristic feature, however, is the bulb, which is ovoid, with a thick covering of fibrous brown scales having a rather heavy network of veins.

Also unique are the small nut-like ovate-pointed bulbils which replace some of the flowers in the umbel, and may be mistaken for unopened buds (except of course that no sepals are evident). Flowering period is June to July.

CALOCHORTUS APICULATUS ×1 [p.13]

BRODIAEA CORONARIA ×1¼ [p.12]

CALOCHORTUS MACROCARPUS ×1¼ [p.14]

ÁLLIUM SCHOENÓPRASUM L. *Wild Chives.*

The specific name is derived from schoenus, a *rush* or reed, and prason, resembling a *leek*; the plant is the ancestor of the cultivated chives, and is found around the world in the northern hemisphere.

The bulbs occur in clusters, are ovoid, and covered with papery scales that are usually white. The leaves are hollow, at least near their bases. The large, ball-shaped, compact umbel consists of numerous flowers having rose-violet to pink perianth-segments with darker veins.

The plant is found in dampish ground in northern and eastern British Columbia and into Washington. The bulbs are stored by the Eskimo for winter food.

ÁLLIUM VÁLIDUM S. Wats., reported from the head of McIntyre Creek in the Okanagan Valley, and from northern Washington, is very like *A. schoenoprasum*, but the leaves are flat or slightly keeled.

ASPÁRAGUS OFFICINÀLIS L. *Garden Asparagus.*

The generic name is derived from (*a-*) the intensive prefix, and sparasso, *to tear* (some of the species being armed with strong prickles), while officinalis means *of the apothecaries* (with reference to the inclusion of Asparagus officinalis among the numerous mediaeval lists of plants believed to have medicinal virtues).

Asparagus is known to everyone, though many who enjoy the familiar young shoots will fail to associate them with the filmy fern-like plant that has escaped from gardens all over temperate North America, particularly along the seacoast. But the tiny greenish six-cleft hanging bells of flowers will at once dispel the notion that this might be a fern, as will the presence in late summer of the bright red berries.

About 120 species originated in temperate to warm areas of the Old World.

BRODIAÈA CORONÀRIA (Salisb.) Engler. *Harvest Brodiaea. Large-flowered Brodiaea. Fool's Onion.* [p.10]

We have in our area only 1 species of this genus, named after James Brodie, a Scottish botanist who died in 1824. Until recently botanists considered a related plant (the more showy, bluish-lavender *B. douglasii* Smith) another Brodiaea, but the latter species is now named *Triteleia grandiflora* (which see). Brodiaea has only 3 fertile stamens, and 3 staminodes (lacking anthers), and leaves that have usually withered by the time the flowers open. *Triteleia* has all 6 stamens fertile, and its leaves remain green during and after flowering time.

(However, 9 other species of Brodiaea occur to the south of our area.)

Coronaria is the feminine (to agree with Brodiaea) of the Latin adjective meaning *relating to a garland*, obviously referring to the chaplet of successively opening flowers, which are striped with vivid tones of blue, purple, and violet, deliciously relieved by white at the heart of the shallow cup. Three sterile stamens add a further accent, like tiny white fans. Several narrow grass-like leaves are usually brown and shrivelled at flowering time, generally July or August. The nearly round corms, with dark-brown scaly covering, were eagerly dug by Indians and early settlers, and eaten either raw or cooked. They are reported to be very nutritious, and to have an exceptionally pleasant nut-like flavour. There is no trace of onion odour. The pretty flower-clusters, on 8 inch stems, toss in the wind on sere and withered hillsides of the southern coastal region.

Archibald Menzies, in the *Discovery* under Captain George Vancouver, landed May 28, 1792

> "on the Point near the Ship [Restoration Point, Puget Sound] where
> . . . a few families of Indians live in very Mean Huts or Sheds formd
> of slender Rafters & coverd with Mats. Several of the women were
> digging on the Point which excited my curiosity to know what they
> were digging for & found it to be a little bulbous root of a liliaceous
> plant which on searching about for the flower of it I discoverd to be
> a new *Genus* of the Triandria monogina [i.e. *Brodiaea*]. This root with
> the young shoots of Rasberries & a species of Barnacle . . . formd at
> this time the chief part of their wretched subsistance."

CALOCHÓRTUS APICULÀTUS Baker. *Three-spot Tulip.*   [p.10]

About 60 species of this fine genus of bulbous perennials are found from western Canada to Central America. In our region, we are fortunate to find 2 (or possibly 3) beautiful species. Calochortus is derived from the Greek words kallo-, *beautiful*, and chortos, *grass*, since the flowers of many species are incredibly lovely, and the leaves, that soon wither, are narrow and grass-like.

Apiculatus refers to the shape of the anthers, which taper to a *slender tip*, while the common name comes from the small, roundish, purple gland at the base of each of the 3 yellowish-white petals. Other distinguishing characteristics are the greenish-white sepals, which are shorter than the obovate petals, and the elliptical capsule which hangs downward, and has 3 ridges or wings running its length.

The plants prefer sandy soil in full sun, or open woods of conifers, in extreme southeastern British Columbia, and adjacent Montana and Washington. They bloom in June or July. Though hundreds of skilful gardeners have brought the bulbs of this, and many other species, into rockeries and borders during the last century, none of these experiments has been successful for more than a year or so. This is a great pity, for in sheer beauty some of the species challenge the popular and spectacular *Tigridia*. In fact *C. nitidus*, *C. venustus*, or our own *C. macrocarpus* (which see), are almost incredibly gorgeous.

CALOCHÓRTUS LÝALLII Baker. *Lyall's Butterfly Tulip.*

David Lyall (1817-1895) was a Scottish botanist and surgeon who collected in North America, particularly while serving with the North American Boundary Commission.

This Butterfly Tulip is a very rare plant in our area. It is similar to *C. apiculatus* (which see), but its white petals (occasionally flushed with purple) are pointed ovate, rather than obovate. The base of each petal carries a large crescent-shaped gland that is bluish-purple and very different from the small, round, purplish-black gland of *C. apiculatus*. When the capsules have ripened the two plants can be distinguished at a glance, for in the present species the capsules are held erect, but in *C. apiculatus* they are invariably bent downward.

This beautiful species of dry sagebrush and bunch-grass slopes is found occasionally near the International Boundary. But it is locally abundant in the dry country of northern Montana, and Washington east of the Cascades.

CALOCHÓRTUS MACROCÁRPUS Douglas. *Mariposa Lily.*   [p.11]

The wayfarer who first comes upon this magnificent flower while climbing the parched hillsides of the dry Interior may think it a distillation of ethereal loveliness too rare to be real. The great lavender (occasionally pink, or snowy white) caps dance like butterflies atop the slender stems. In fact, mariposa is Spanish for *butterfly*. Blooms as much as 5 inches across, the green stripe in the centre of each petal, and the pointed sepals even longer than the petals, make this species unmistakable. Macrocarpus means *large seed*.

> *I gazed awhile, and felt as light, and free*
> *As though the fanning wings of Mercury*
> *Had play'd upon my heels . . . .*

John Keats

By the time these gorgeous flowers appear in June, July, or even August at higher levels, the immediate surroundings have become dry and scorched, a setting of startling contrast for the splendid blooms. They grace dry hillsides, and benchlands, from southern British Columbia, southward, on the eastern side of the Cascades. But their numbers have seriously declined, particularly during the last decade.

Let us hope that our children, and our children's children, will continue to have the privilege, as we do, of finding and admiring in unspoiled regions the magnificent Mariposa Lilies.

CAMÁSSIA LEICHTLÍNII (Baker) S. Wats. *Great Camas. Leichtlin's Camas.* [p.23]

The generic name is Latinized "camas", very happily and properly recognized, for this was the Indian vernacular for an edible bulb. Camas was an essential and stable portion of the diet of the tribes for thousands of years before the white man came. Tribes fought over possession of particular flatlands of rich soil, where the camas in millions spread sheets of dazzling blue.

A cruel war, in the late '70's, was fought between 580 soldiers of the United States Army, and a band of 300 Nez Percé warriors under their brilliant leader, Chief Joseph. White settlers had turned their pigs to root out the bulbs in great "camas prairies", which had been for centuries essential food sources for the Indians. It is interesting to know that the natives had sedulously rogued out, during flowering time, the bulbs of Poison Camas (*Zygadenus venenosus*, which see) occurring in their prized food areas, so that they could dig the camas bulbs in those areas with confidence. The bulbs of the two plants are almost indistinguishable, but the flowers are very different (those of the poisonous plant being very much smaller, more crowded, and always creamy-white).

Digging sticks were used by the women to secure the large oval bulbs (which have dark, membranous outer scales). These bulbs were baked in ovens in the ground, and either eaten at once, or dried and stored for winter use. The Lewis and Clark expedition, on numerous occasions, was grateful for emergency supplies of camas.

The Great Camas is named after Max Leichtlin, 1831-1910, of Baden, Germany, who introduced many fine plants to horticulture.

The common name is justified, for in the wet, even mucky soils the Great Camas prefers, stems to 4 feet are not uncommon, and there is a record of 205 buds or blooms in one raceme! Six spreading tepals are uniformly spaced to form an impressive flower 2-3¼ inches in diameter. These flowers open progressively upward, from the base of the raceme and as the tepals wither, they twist tightly together. This characteristic provides a useful field distinction, for the tepals of the smaller and more common *C. quamash* (which see) shrivel *separately*.

The colour is quite variable, from palest blue to a rather intense bluish-violet. We have seen quite a number of plants with cream-coloured blooms and—once only—a lovely clear bright pink. These are generally considered colour forms only, although F. W. Gould has argued that the name C. leichtlinii should be reserved for the plant with cream-coloured flowers, and that the common blue forms should be *C. leichtlinii ssp. SUKSDÓRFII*. Though scarce in our area, the cream-flowered plant is, in the vicinity of Roseburg, Oregon, much more abundant than the blue-flowered plant.

The relatively large bulbs (about 1 inch in diameter and over 2 inches long) may be 12 inches down, and since they often occur on rocky slopes in isolated pockets of rich soil, they were less important to the Indians than the smaller bulbs of the Common Camas occurring at depths of 2-6 inches.

The Great Camas occurs in southeastern Vancouver Island (south of Nanaimo) and in coastal Washington. It blooms about a fortnight later than *C. quamash*, in late May to early June. This fine plant is abundant almost to the point of being considered a weed in south coastal gardens, but it is cultivated and highly regarded in Europe.

CAMÁSSIA QUÁMASH (Pursh) Greene. *Common Camas. Early Camas. Quamash.* [pp.22,23]

"Quamash" is just another attempt to rationalize the Indian word for the plant, as transmitted by those famed explorers, Captain Meriwether Lewis and William Clark, to Pursh (who named the plant in 1814). This was the species that, occurring in tremendous numbers, presented to the expedition the perfect appearance of a blue-water lake*. It was also a major source of food for a number of the Plains tribes.

Many authorities refer to the uneven spacing of the tepals of this species, as a means of separating it from the symmetrical arrangement found in *C. leichtlinii* (which see). While it is generally true that 5 tepals in C. quamash are somewhat grouped, leaving a larger space for the single lowermost tepal, this is not, in our observation, always valid. Not infrequently we have seen regular and irregular blossoms on the same plant. A more reliable distinction is that the uppermost of the numerous buds of *C. leichtlinii* are tightly pressed together, while those of its smaller relative tend to be well separated. But perhaps the best means of distinguishing the two is the length of the thin, pale-green bracts, that spring from the main stem at the point of attachment of each short flower-stem (or pedicel). In C. quamash the bracts are longer than the pedicels; in *C. leichtlinii*, shorter.

We have found that whitish forms of this species are very much less common than cream-coloured forms of *C. leichtlinii.*

Common Camas occurs in immense numbers in natural meadows where early spring moisture is succeeded by midsummer drought. Here, in early May, it blooms simultaneously with *Ranunculus occidentalis*, providing a spectacular carpet of blue and yellow. It occurs at low elevations in the southern portion of our area, into central Washington and Utah.

*. . . the quawmash is now in blume and from the colour of its bloom at a short distance it resembles lakes of fine clear water, so complete is this deseption that on first sight I could have swoarn it was water.

Meriwether Lewis:
Original Journals of the Lewis and Clark Expedition
(entry of June 12, 1806)

CLINTÒNIA UNIFLÒRA (Schult.) Kunth. *Queen's Cup. Blue-bead. Bead Lily.* [pp.22,26]

Clintonia was named for De Witt Clinton, governor of New York and developer of the Erie Canal. The specific name is usually apt, though occasionally one finds 2 flowers on the slender scape. There are 3 other Clintonias in North America, and 2 in eastern Asia.

Blue-bead is a plant of cold acid soils under conifers, particularly in the mountains, where its white stars illumine the damp forest floor. In favourable years the bloom will be replaced by a brilliant blue berry, startling because of its highly distinctive chroma.

Very early, from the creeping rhizomes appear pairs of upright slenderly-elliptical leaves, each pair with a 6-inch unbranched flower-stem. Like the flower-stem, the green leaves (somewhat paler below) are clothed with fine, soft, white hairs. The 6 pure white tepals are centred by 6 yellow stamens, and a pistil with 3 short stigma-lobes.

In suitable habitats in every part of British Columbia, from the beginning to end of summer according to altitude, one may expect to find the snowy flowers of the Queen's Cup. There is a fresh coolness about these plants that makes them somehow epitomize the chill pure air of mountain-woods.

DÍSPORUM HÓOKERI (Torrey) Britt. var. OREGÀNUM (Watson) Q. Jones.
Hooker's Fairy-bell. Small-flowered Fairy-bell. [p.27]

These fragile flowers of the deep woods obtain their generic name from the Greek, meaning *two seeds*, since there is a pair of seeds in each division of the ovary. About 15 species are known, chiefly from North America, with several from Asia. The leaves are thin and wilt very quickly, so the plants are best left to mature, in the fall, their rather large red berries.

Joseph Hooker (1817-1911) was one of the most colourful and talented botanists of Europe, whose travels included Antarctica (with Ross), the Himalayas, the Atlas Mountains, and the Rockies.

As one observes so frequently of plants of the shaded woods, the delicate flowers are greenish-white. The attractive leaves are prominently parallel-veined, and end in the "drip-tips" which give the observant wanderer a clue that these are plants of heavy rainfall areas. The leaves are beautifully disposed to intercept as much as possible of the pale light that filters down through the forest canopy. In late summer, the flowers yield to smoothish, red, oval berries.

Hooker's Fairy-bell occurs throughout the southern half of British Columbia, being particularly abundant on Vancouver Island and around Kootenay Lake. It blooms in May and June, and as the varietal name suggests, occurs southward to Oregon and California.

This handsome plant is quite good-natured when transplanted to the garden.

DÍSPORUM SMÍTHII (Hooker) Piper. *Large-flowered Fairy-bell.* [p.26]

This species was named after Sir J. E. Smith (1759-1828), a celebrated English botanist. It is distinguished from the more abundant *D. hookeri* (which see) by much larger, more creamy flowers, whose tepals do not curve so strongly outward. If the flowers are an inch long, it is this species.

We would make a particular plea to leave the attractive plant undisturbed, for it is already rare, and becoming increasingly so as logging proceeds apace to destroy the high shade it must have. Further, it occurs along the banks of streams, which as another consequence of logging, become so swollen during the unimpeded spring run-off that these plants, among many others, are swept away and destroyed.

You may be fortunate enough to admire this relatively rare flower in limited localities of Vancouver Island. The delicate flower-bells ring their soundless chimes in the later days of spring, and give way to brilliant orange-red berries as summer wanes.

Oh, Christ! it is a goodly sight to see
What Heaven hath done for this delicious land:
What fruits of fragrance blush on every tree!
What goodly prospects o'er the hills expand!
But man would mar them with an impious hand . . . .

George Gordon, Lord Byron:
Childe Harold's Pilgrimage

DÍSPORUM TRACHYCÁRPUM (Wats.) B. & H. *Rough-fruited Fairy-bell.*

The specific name means *rough-fruited*, for the bright orange-red berry is covered with tiny protuberances (reminiscent of the surface of the Arbutus berry). Since its range overlaps that of *D. hookeri*, (which see), one may experience considerable difficulty in separating the two, before the characteristic berries appear. The flowers are very similar, though slightly smaller for the present species, but the best distinction is the shape of the leaves. In D. trachycarpum the long slender drip-tip is replaced by an abrupt narrowing, i.e. the leaf is oval. The leaf of *D. hookeri* is usually narrowly acute, like the blade of a spear.

This species is found in the southern half of the Province, east of the Cascades, blooming between April and June.

ERYTHRÒNIUM. *Fawn Lily. Dog Tooth Violet. Adder's Tongue.*

Erythros in Greek is *red*, referring to the Eurasian species which is pinkish. The second of the common names is singularly inappropriate, for violet it is not, though some seek the dog's teeth in the shape of the perianth-segments or in the shape of the corms. Nor does the association of a snake commend itself to those who love these delicate and graceful plants. "Fawn" is suggestive of dappled coats, and the attractive brownish-purple markings on the showy leaves of some species. (This name was apparently suggested by John Burroughs.)

There are 15 distinct species, and several variants that future research may reveal as subspecies, or varieties. Except for a Eurasian species and two easterners, the centre of abundance is western North America. Many will agree with I. N. Gabrielson that ". . . of the great variety [of native bulbs] available [for garden use] my choice would, without hesitation, fall on the Erythroniums."

Four beautiful species grace the open forests or alpine slopes of our area. All push up from a long slender corm a pair of elliptical, rather succulent leaves and a slender scape bearing one, or occasionally as many as six, handsome flowers with 6 (more or less reflexed) tepals, 6 stamens, and a style that is cleft at the end into 3 stigmas.

What more felicitie can fall to creature,
Than to enjoy delight with libertie . . . .

Edmund Spenser:
Muiopotmos, or
The Fate of the Butterflie

ERYTHRÒNIUM GRANDIFLÓRUM Pursh. *Yellow Avalanche Lily. Glacier Lily.* [p.42]

The clear yellow of the Glacier Lily edges the receding snow on alpine slopes, a lovely warm note in the spring world of ice-blue and snow-white.

Grandiflorum means *large-flowered*—although *E. oregonum* (which see) better deserves that title.

This is the only yellow-flowered Erythronium of our area, so that it is easily recognized. Even in the absence of the flower, the pair of large, unmarked, broadly-elliptical leaves provide an unmistakable guide. Indeed, these served to locate the large corm, which was dug in quantities by the Indians for drying as winter food. Small rodents also store them for food, and they are eaten by both black and grizzly bear. Deer are very fond of the leaves, and especially seek out the large immature seed-pods.

The chief variation observed in the species is the colour of the anthers. On this basis Applegate, who issued a monograph on the genus in 1935, gave subspecific names for the white-anthered and yellow-anthered variations. He considered that the typical form had chocolate-red anthers. On Vancouver Island's mountains a rather dwarf form occurs, which has creamy anthers. The showiest, and commonest form of the dry Interior grows to 2 feet and has chocolate anthers, which offer a striking central accent in the clear yellow corollas. (This form occurs, apparently, only east of the Cascades.)

. . . these stars of earth, these golden flowers!

Henry Wadsworth Longfellow: Flowers

ERYTHRÒNIUM MONTÁNUM S. Wats. *White Avalanche Lily.* [p.27]

Montanum, of course, means *of the mountains*, a relationship which this beautiful lily insists upon, fiercely and finally. In the timberline parks of the Olympics and the isolated peaks of the Cascades the Avalanche Lily pushes up through the receding snow its myriad crisp-white orange-centred blooms, that toss and dance with every breeze. Transplanted to sea level with every attempt to otherwise match its former habitat, it may open pathetically a feeble, almost stemless bloom, and then pine utterly away.*

E. montanum is of very rare report in the province, and the mountain wanderer should be alert to a large white lily above a pair of unmarked, broadly-lanceolate leaves. He may be fortunate enough to extend the known range of the White Avalanche Lily in British Columbia, to date limited to Mt. Waddington, monarch of the Coast Range. Since this beautiful flower is one of the abundant glories of the Olympic Peninsula, it is not unreasonable to expect that the species may have found a foothold on some of the mountains of southern Vancouver Island.

*Since the above was written, a colony of this plant has been discovered (by Mr. Spring Harrison) not far from Port Renfrew, Vancouver Island. Here it occurs below 3000 feet. It is of the greatest interest that Mr. Verne Ahier, a very skilled gardener, reports that bulbs from this site adjust to sea level with apparent ease, under identical conditions that bring quick demise to bulbs from 6000 feet in the Olympic Mts. of Washington. The Vancouver Island form has relatively huge bulbs, that produce flower-stems graced with as many as 10 large blossoms.

> For I remember that, under the lofty turrets of Oebalia, where black
> Galesus moistens the yellow fields, I saw an old Corycian, to whom
> belonged a few [acres] of neglected land; nor was the soil rich enough
> for the plough, proper for flocks, or commodious for vines. Yet here
> among the bushes planting a few pot-herbs, white lilies, vervain, and
> esculent poppies all round, he equalled in a contented mind the
> wealth of kings . . . .
>
> Virgil: The Georgics. IV. 120

ERYTHRÒNIUM OREGÓNUM Applegate. *White Fawn Lily. Easter Lily. White Trout Lily.* [pp.30,31]

From northern Oregon (whence the specific name) through western Washington, Vancouver Island, and the extreme southern coastal mainland of British Columbia, this fine species lifts its huge white blooms above 2 handsomely mottled lanceolate leaves.

Among the floral riches of Victoria this Easter Lily has long been a feature of the magnificent spring display. But plucking the temptingly beautiful leaves dooms the bulb, and the open woodland it once carpeted has yielded to the bulldozer and the subdivision. With expanding population the White Fawn Lily must vanish from all its former haunts unless protected areas are set aside, such as Thetis Lake Nature Sanctuary (the first such sanctuary in Canada). There, through April and May, some idea of its former abundance can be observed.

Usually solitary upon its graceful stem, in pockets of richer soil doubles and trebles are common, and we have twice seen plants with 6 blooms. The reverse side of the tepals varies from yellow-green to rose-maroon, and the choice marking of the inner face, at the base of the tepals, is orange and purple, the more intense the better the exposure to light.

The White Fawn Lily is found in a variety of habitats: from woodland and high open shade, to crevices of good soil among rocks, even to open grassland. Let us ensure that our children, and our children's children, in their turn may also come to love this beautiful flower.

I wish to forget, a considerable part of
every day, all mean, narrow, trivial men . . . ,
and therfore, I come out to these solitudes . . . .

Henry David Thoreau

ERYTHRÒNIUM REVOLÙTUM Smith. *Pink Fawn Lily.* [pp.31,38]

The specific name refers to the tendency of the tepals to *recurve* or reflex, particularly after the bloom has been open a few days. The colour is sufficient to identify the species—an enchanting pink, clear and bright with exquisite white and yellow markings at the centre that perfectly set off the 6 golden stamens. Like *E. oregonum* (which see), this species has beautifully mottled leaves.

In our experience the Pink Fawn Lily prefers soil of fine sand, rather than the woody humus in which its white cousin rejoices. Thus the two species do not overlap, and E. revolutum is happiest in river valleys subject to flooding, such as those of Vancouver Island, and possibly other coastal mainland valleys, in addition to those adjacent to Kingcome Inlet.

This delightful naiad may be chanced upon in April or May. Never more than locally abundant, it must be carefully protected.

We know only one site where E. revolutum grows in an almost pure culture. This is the old flood-plain of Sutton Creek, one of the streams running into Cowichan Lake, where those who know the species only as sparsely scattered and local will rub their eyes in disbelief. Here, over a good many acres, in late May the ground is covered with an incredible carpet of hundreds of thousands of the sprightly pink blossoms. What a gift to future generations could be granted by the logging company who hold a forest management licence for this area, if as a magnanimous gesture they would establish this 40 acres as a park, and so preserve this precious, and irreplaceable legacy, for posterity.

22

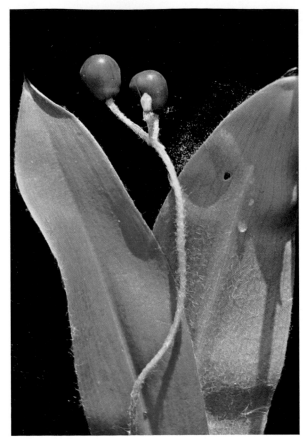

ALLIUM GEYERI var. TENERUM ×1 [p.9]

CLINTONIA UNIFLORA (FRUIT) ×1½ [p.16]

CAMASSIA QUAMASH (HABITAT) [p.16]

23

ALLIUM CRENULATUM ×1 [p.9]

CAMASSIA QUAMASH ×¼ [p.16]

CAMASSIA LEICHTLINII ×⅓ [p.15]

FRITILLÀRIA CAMSCHATCÉNSIS (L.) Ker.-Gawl. *Northern Rice-root. Indian Rice. Black Lily. Kamchatka Fritillary. Sarana. Eskimo Potato.* [p.39]

Though a number of authors state the name is derived from the Latin for chess-board, or checker-board, with reference to the checkered marking of the corolla, we have not been able to find such a derivation. The apparent source is the Latin fritillus, a *dice-box*, probably referring to the shape of the seed-capsule, or perhaps to the shape of the flower. Distributed over the north temperate zone are about 50 species, including the orange-red *F. recurva* of Oregon, and the great Crown Imperial of gardens around the world.

The type specimen of this species was credited by the mighty Linnaeus to "Canada, Camschatca". Of various spellings in the literature, the Latin genitive camschatcense is the one used by Linnaeus.

The bulbs, found an inch or two below the surface, resemble a cluster of cooked rice grains. They are, in fact, good sources of starches and sugars, and since prehistoric times have been dug in the fall, dried and powdered for winter use.

David Nelson, botanist on the *Resolution*, visited "Kamtschatka" in 1778 (shortly before Captain Cook's murder in 1779) and found the natives eating the bulbs of a plant with flowers of "an exceeding dark red colour", now thought to be the present species.

Distinction between this generally more northern plant and *F. lanceolata* (which see), in areas where the two overlap, is made more difficult by evident introgression of the two species. Typically the Northern Rice-root has less-mottled flowers, of a more uniform dark brownish-purple, and each tepal bears at the base of its inner face a waxy, dark-purple gland (which in *F. lanceolata* is greenish-yellow). The conspicuous, upright seed-capsules are rounded, and without wings.

The sturdy plants, with their very dark bells, may be found from Alaska to Washington near the coast, notably on the Queen Charlottes, more sporadically on Vancouver Island, and in a number of the more northern river valleys. They favour open spaces with a water table fairly close to the surface, and may be found in bloom from May to July.

The specimens we have seen averaged 12-18 inches tall. A good field distinction for F. camschatcensis is the flaring-mouth bell-shape of the flowers, an appearance resulting from the slight reflexing of the tepals.

FRITILLÀRIA LANCEOLÀTA Pursh. *Chocolate Lily. Mission Bell. Rice-root. Checker Lily. Skunk Lily.* [pp.39,43]

The various common names are each descriptive of some feature of this interesting perennial. Lanceolata describes the leaf shape, but this is not distinctive, nor does the lanceolate leaf help to distinguish this plant from *F. camschatcensis* (which see). Moreover, both species have brownish-purple flowers. In the present species the dark flowers are mottled with greenish-yellow, and the inner face of each tepal is marked with a conspicuous, long, greenish-yellow and sticky gland. The large upright capsules of F. lanceolata are readily recognized by 6 wing-like ridges (which are lacking in the rounded capsules of *F. camschatcensis*). A further recognition feature of the present species is that the newly-opened blossoms are *ball*-shaped (those of *F. camschatcensis* are *bell*-shaped, i.e. with tips of tepals slightly reflexed).

Though the odour is unpleasant in a closed room, the unusual flowers possess a quite extraordinary beauty when they are transilluminated by a low sun. The bract near the flower always rises in a flowing line from the curve of the pedicel, and the brilliance of the yellow anthers is enhanced by their dark setting. The *lanceolate* leaves are arranged in whorls around the lower two-thirds of the stem. The bulb (of several scales and numerous bulblets resembling grains of cooked white rice) was an important source of food for the aborigines.

Chocolate Lily is abundant in deeper pockets of soil among the rocks, at low levels on southern Vancouver Island, the Olympic Peninsula, and in the Nicola and Okanagan Valleys (into Washington). The flowering season (April-June) is generally earlier than that of *F. camschatcensis* in areas (such as central Vancouver Island) where the ranges of the two species overlap.

On southern Vancouver Island (e.g. at the mouth of Goldstream River) occurs a very vigorous form that reaches 4 feet, and bears as many as 20 blooms. This may be a polyploid. The common form is 12-18 inches high, with 1 or 2 blooms.

The flowers appear on the earth;
the time of the singing of birds is come . . . .

The Song of Solomon

FRITILLÀRIA PÙDICA (Pursh) Spreng. *Yellow Bell. Mission Bell. Yellow Fritillary. Yellow Snowdrop.* [p.39]

Pudica can be interpreted as *bashful*, conveying a pleasant image of these charming bells hanging their heads demurely. Few flowers of the southern dry Interior are known so well, or loved so much, as the Yellow Bell. Appearing as soon as the snow melts from the sagebrush flats (in March, onward to June at higher levels), the lovely flowers dramatically herald the spring.

From a small white bulb with tiny rice-like scales, the 6-inch stems carry two to six smooth, linear leaves and one, rather rarely two, campanulate blossoms about ¾ inch long, at first of an indescribably chromatic yellow, gradually becoming more orange on aging. A bonus unusual for this genus, is a pleasant scent of spring, quite distinctive. This was another of the bulbs used as food by the Indians and early explorers, and now eagerly sought by small mammals. It is suffering from thoughtless picking, over much of its range.

26

CLINTONIA UNIFLORA ×1¼ [p.16]

DISPORUM SMITHII ×1½ [p.17]

ERYTHRONIUM MONTANUM ×1¼ [p.20]

DISPORUM HOOKERI var. OREGANUM ×¾ [p.17]

LÍLIUM COLUMBIÀNUM Hanson. *Columbian Lily. Tiger Lily.* [p.50]

So many beautiful species of this genus, from all parts of the world, have been brought into our gardens, that "Lily" has become one of the best known of plant names. And that name is very familiar from the superb translation of the Authorized Version of King James:

> *Consider the lilies of the field, how they grow;*
> *they toil not, neither do they spin:*
> *And yet I say unto you, That even*
> *Solomon in all his glory was not arrayed*
> *like one of these.*

Matthew VI, 28-29

Yet the derivation of "Lily" is obscure. Professor George Black has been kind enough to compare the above passage, both in the original Greek, and in the Vulgate (Latin) translations. He points out: "Letter-for-letter transcription of the Greek words there used for 'the lilies' is ta krina. However for 'lily' early Greek had also leirion (transcribed form), and leirion—with common change of rho *(r)* to Latin *l*—is considered cognate with Latin lilium (whence comes the English lily)." Students have pointed out that lily species are not conspicuous elements in the flora of Palestine, and that the abundant scarlet *Anemone coronaria* may well have suggested the Biblical metaphor.

Of perhaps 90 species occurring in the North Temperate zone, only 2 are found in British Columbia.

This attractive lily of damp woods and open meadows is widely distributed throughout the southern half of British Columbia, except the Queen Charlotte Islands, but curiously (in view of its specific name) is least abundant in the dry valley of the Columbia. The handsome orange flowers are ornamented with numerous maroon spots. The tepals are strongly reflexed a few hours after the bud opens, and the blooms look modestly down from the top of a scape which may reach 5 feet. A particularly vigorous plant may bear nearly 30 of the striking flowers.

The blossom is at its spectacular best before the tepals curve backward to reduce the apparent size. Then the chocolate-purple anthers regally centre the brilliant corolla, which may be as much as 4¾ inches across. Whorls of 6-9, smooth, lanceolate leaves occur along the stalk.

The blooming period is June to July.

An English folk-belief that has crossed the Atlantic claims that one who smells the Tiger Lily will inevitably develop freckles!

J. W. Krutch quotes an eastern legend that a Korean Androcles removed an arrow from the foreleg of a tiger, which became devoted to him. Before the tiger died, he begged the hermit to use his magic to keep him nearby. His body became the Tiger Lily, and later, when the hermit drowned, the Lily spread over all the land, looking for him.

LÍLIUM PHILADÉLPHICUM L. *Wood Lily. Chalice-cup Lily.*   [p.51]

The specific name has been variously explained: either to the source of Linnaeus' material which was collected by his pupil, Kalm, in the vicinity of Philadelphia (Pennsylvania); from the Greek philos, *love,* plus delphos, *brother,* thought to commemorate the pharaoh Ptolemy Philadelphus; or from philos and delphicus, *loving* the Delphic *Delos,* the (anciently) wooded oracle of Apollo at Delphi, (whence the inference of inhabiting woods). This preference for open woods is repeated in one of the common names for L. philadelphicum. However in our range it also occurs—rather less often—in grassy places. The Wood Lily is the floral emblem of Saskatchewan.

The showy orange flowers look up for approbation. Like the more demure *L. columbianum* (which see), they are beautifully spotted with maroon-wine, but differ in being golden-flushed toward the centre. Indeed, in a rarely encountered form, this golden yellow entirely replaces the orange. Usually a solitary flower tops the stem; however we have seen a few plants with 5 or even 6 of the flamboyant blooms, each 5 inches across.

Unfortunately the Wood Lily is becoming rare. A host of thoughtless admirers pluck the tough stem near the ground, and in so doing remove virtually all the leaves (which occur singly or in whorls along the stem), so that even if the bulb has not been jerked from the ground, it starves.

Meanwhile the plucked flower quickly droops, and is thrown aside. Let us admire it in its natural perfection, and see that our children are trained to love it, and leave it.

This is a magnificent species.

He does not die that can bequeath
Some influence to the land he knows,
Or dares, persistent, interwreath
Love permanent with the wild hedgerows . . .
The spring's superb adventure calls
His dust athwart the woods to flame . . . .

Hilaire Belloc: Duncton Hill

LLÓYDIA SERÒTINA (L.) Reichenb. *Alp Lily.*

Edward Llwyd (1660-1709) was an early Welsh naturalist. Serotinus is, in Latin, *late,* but the implication is not obvious. We have seen this tiny plant in bloom late in August in northern British Columbia, but a number of herbarium sheets carry dates as early as the end of June. We suspect that a better explanation possibly comes from the verb sero, to join together, or *to weave together.* Linnaeus (Latinized from Carl von Linné) was an excellent Latin scholar and had no doubt collected the plant in Switzerland, when he would notice that a network of rhizomes link the bulb-like swellings from which the

Following page: ERYTHRONIUM OREGONUM ×1¼ [p.20]

ERYTHRONIUM OREGONUM (HABITAT)　　[p.20]

ERYTHRONIUM REVOLUTUM (HABITAT)　　[p.21]

narrow grass-like leaves and slender stems appear. This is the only native species of the dozen in the genus, whose centre is Europe and Asia. Many travellers from the western world have been delighted to find, in the high meadows of Switzerland and the Tirol, this familiar plant.

The pale-cream corolla is delicately pink-flushed below and purple-veined above, about ½ inch wide, and usually carried singly at the top of a slender stalk, from 2 to 6 inches tall. A few of the long narrow fleshy leaves occur along the stem, though some are basal, arising from a thick, creeping rootstock. The Alp Lily is a feature of rock-slopes in the Queen Charlotte Islands, and of high altitude meadows in northern British Columbia—and also makes sporadic occurrences in the Rockies and Selkirks. The Queen Charlotte plants are taller and larger, with greenish instead of purple venation; they have been called subspecies FLÀVA Calder & Taylor.

MAIÁNTHEMUM CANADÉNSE Desf. var. INTÈRIUS Fern. *Wild Lily-of-the-valley. Canada Mayflower.*

The generic name is derived from the Greek for *May*, plus *flower*—referring, of course, to time of flowering, but the 2 species in our area are usually as late as June or July. In fact, only a few of the plants will bloom in the crowded ground cover resulting from their running rhizomes. This is often observed on the West Coast of Vancouver Island, where acres of sterile leaves carpet the wet ground beneath the shade of Sitka Spruce. (The true Lily-of-the-valley is *Convallaria majalis*, whose familiar white bells hang downward from one side of the flower stem [they are said to be "secund"].) The flower of Maianthemum (both species) is unique in this family in having its parts in twos (2 sepals, 2 petals, a 2-chambered ovary) and fours (4 stamens). The fruit is a shiny berry, at first greenish-speckled brown, later becoming reddish. Hultén comments that the plants contain glycosides having a stimulant effect upon the heart. The genus is circumboreal, and consists of 3, or possibly 4 species.

The specific name aptly describes the distribution—from Labrador to British Columbia, and southward. Though "Canada Mayflower" literally interprets the specific name (and is given by Rickett and other authorities) it is sure to lead to confusion with the unrelated eastern *Epigaea repens*, Trailing Arbutus, widely loved as *the* Mayflower.

The handsome heart-shaped leaves of this plant slightly clasp the 4-10 inch stem, which springs from wide-creeping rhizomes. The short raceme of small whitish flowers has a delicate, though very pleasing perfume, and in the fall may produce a few spotted berries, which finally turn dull red.

This species occurs from the Selkirks eastward, and does not overlap the range of *M. dilatatum* (which see), which is confined to the Coast Range. Apart from the geographical distinction, M. canadense can be readily identified by its more abruptly tapered leaves, which have extremely short petioles.

MAIÁNTHEMUM DILATÀTUM (Wood) Nels. & Macbr. *Two-leaved False Lily-of-the-valley. Two-leaved Solomon's Seal. Deerberry.*   [pp.39,54]

Dilatatum means *spread out* or extended, but the reference is obscure; probably it applies to the pedicels or individual flower-stalks, which spread noticeably from the main stem of the raceme. The first common name, which we forbear to repeat in all its weary length, is a good argument for use of the Latin name! The last name is unspecific, since deer eat many kinds of berries in preference to these, which are in most years of sparse occurrence. And Two-leaved Solomon's Seal seems unfortunate, since we have in our area three species of *Smilacina* (which see) widely (though inaccurately) known as "Solomon's Seal(s)". Such reflections, and many similar examples in even this one family of Liliaceae, have hardened our resolve to make limited use of common names in subsequent families. Searching various texts for common names qualifies as one of the most unrewarding of pursuits, too often leading in dizzying circles until two or three or half a dozen plants have been confused. A pox on common–or uncommon–names! One is reminded of the fabled blind men, who chancing to touch different parts of an elephant, described it as a wall, a tree, a rope, a snake.

The best distinguishing characteristic of this species is the quite lengthy petiole (stem) of each leaf. The long-acuminate leaves also are distinctive, tapering gradually to a long slender point or drip-tip.

M. dilatatum, as the drip-tip might suggest, is a heavy-rainfall coastal plant of British Columbia and Washington. Calder and Taylor point out that it will not, however, tolerate moss-carpeted closed forests. It blooms rather sporadically from May through July and even later.

The scent, though faint, is very pleasant.

SMILACÌNA RACEMÒSA (L.) Desf. *False Solomon's Seal. False Spikenard.*   [p.55]

Smilacina is the diminutive of *Smilax*, an ancient Greek name apparently applied to quite another plant, not at all the Smilax of present day taxonomists. One is not impressed with the felicity of these common names, for Solomon's-seal is *Polygonatum*, and Spikenard is an Asiatic plant from which "nard", an aromatic ointment, was prepared. Not to be facetious, it is as if one could do no better after years of consideration, than "Mr. What's-his-name, not Mr. Smith, nor Mr. Jones". Smilacina is a genus of about 3 dozen species distributed in North and Central America, and Asia. They are perennials, growing from creeping rootstocks. The leaves are prominently (parallel) veined, and the small whitish flowers occur at the ends of the stems in a plumy panicle, or more open raceme. The fruit is a globular berry, orange or red, and conspicuous.

The specific name refers to the terminal *racemose* panicle of very many, creamy, small flowers, which exude a fragrance enjoyable in the woods, but rather overwhelming in a closed room. False Solomon's Seal is an impressive plant, with its bold stem-leaves providing a handsome setting for the creamy foam of flowers held 2-3 feet above the forest floor. Flowering from May into June, it produces a cluster of greenish-red berries, which late in the fall become dull purplish-red. This species occurs in damp woods across Canada, southward to California, Arizona and Georgia. S. racemosa transplants easily and provides a striking accent in a shaded part of the garden.

SMILACÌNA STELLÀTA (L.) Desf. *Star-flowered Solomon's Seal. Solomonplume. Wild Spikenard.* [p.63]

Stellata means *set with stars*, these being white ones, that are rather widely spaced in a small raceme of perhaps a dozen flowers. The 7-13 strongly-veined lanceolate leaves alternate up the unbranched stem. Since these bold leaves may be as much as 7 inches long, one anticipates much more than the relatively puny array of small flowers.

The 1-2 foot stems rise from a far-ranging rootstock, so that rather dense colonies are often seen in open places along valley bottoms. The blooms open from May to July; in the fall appear a limited number of greenish berries, that are at first prominently marked with 3 dark-purple stripes. Finally the berries turn reddish.

S. stellata is widely distributed throughout our area.

SMILACÌNA TRIFÒLIA (L.) Desf. *Trifoliate Solomon's Seal. Three-leaved Solomon's Seal.*

Though many specimens merit the specific name in having *three* stem-*leaves*, frequently only 2 or as many as 4 occur. In any case, this more northern plant is readily separated from *S. stellata* (which see), the latter having 7-13 stem-leaves. Moreover, the lower leaf surface is smooth (glabrous) in S. trifolia, finely-hairy (pubescent) in *S. stellata*. Three-leaved Solomon's Seal is a better-proportioned plant, for though the whitish flowers are small, they occur in a raceme held well above the smaller and less-numerous leaves. It is a plant of very acid sphagnum bogs north and east of Prince Rupert. There are a few records from Vancouver Island.

STENÁNTHIUM OCCIDÉNTALE A. Gray. *Mountain-bells. Bronze-bells.* [p.54]

The generic name is from the Greek steno *narrow*, plus anthos *flower*, while occidentale means *western*. The narrow bells are greenish flecked with purple, and hang gracefully downward from a grass-like stem 10-16 inches tall. The few leaves are also grass-like, growing from the base of the flower-stem.

This is a shy plant, to be encountered along the edges of shady mountain streams. Bend close, and you will be surprised by the delicious tangy perfume. Widely distributed in suitable habitats both coastal and interior, in the southern quarter of our area, Mountain-bells is never abundant. The curiously charming—though retiring—blooms appear (according to altitude) from May to August. Three other Stenanthiums are found in the east and south of this continent, and one in Asia.

When clouds are thin, and the wind is light
about the noon-tide hour
I cross the stream, through willow paths
with all around in flower.

Ch'êng Hao, 1032-1085

STREPTÒPUS AMPLEXIFÒLIUS (L.) DC. *Twisted-stalk. White Mandarin.* [p.42]

The name is descriptive of the sharply-kinked or twisted pedicels of many of the species, from the Greek streptos *twisted* plus pous *foot*, or stem. Hence, in Greek and English, Twisted-stalk is a very descriptive name, for our species have zig-zag stems, and in the case of S. amplexifolius the delicate flower-pedicels also are sharply kinked. Seven species are known, chiefly from North America, but also from Asia. They may be confused with the Fairy-bells (*Disporum*, which see).

Amplexifolius means *clasping leaf*, from the Latin amplexor, *to surround* or encircle, for the handsome ovate leaves clasp the 1-3 foot stem at each angular bend. But "twisted-stalk" applies with special emphasis as a unique and distinctive feature of the slender flower-stems (pedicels), 1 or 2 of which grow from the axil of each of the upper leaves. You may have to tilt the plant to see them clearly, and discover the extraordinary, sharp "kink" in each slim flower-stalk. The flowers are small, wide-open bells of greenish or yellowish-white, which are succeeded by much more striking orange-red, oval berries. As one might guess from its thin leaves, this is a plant of shady woods throughout the Province. It blooms in June or July. S. amplexifolius is a good-natured plant for the wild garden, where its showy fruit in late summer is very attractive.

STREPTÒPUS RÒSEUS Michx. ssp. CURVÍPES (Vail) Hult. *Simple-stemmed Twisted-stalk.* [p.54]

Roseus, of course, refers to this plant's unusual flower colour, which is rather dull *rose*-purple. The common name is useful in drawing attention to a good recognition feature of sterile plants, which are numerous. The stems are unbranched, unlike *S. amplexifolius* (which see). (The flower-peduncles in this species lack the sharp kink seen in *S. amplexifolius*.) Both these species are variable, and several varietal names have been proposed. S. roseus is nowhere abundant, but may be encountered in our area generally south of the latitude of Prince Rupert. It is found in rather open, moist woods, blooming in June and July.

STREPTÒPUS STREPTOPÒIDES (Ledeb.) Frye & Rigg. *Small Twisted-stalk.*

The specific name means *streptopus-like*, or in effect, the Streptopus species that is characteristically streptopus, a "chip off the old block". And it is indeed a small twisted-stalk, with a simple unbranched stem not over 8 inches tall. The flowers, as in *S. roseus* (which see), are rose-coloured, but of very different shape, being flat and wheel-shaped (rather than bell-shaped as in the other two species). The flower-peduncles are neither as smoothly curved as in *S. roseus*, nor as sharply bent as in *S. amplexifolius* (which see). This plant occurs in the same southern area as *S. roseus*, though it is rarer, and more alpine. Because it occurs higher, it is usually about a month later than *S. roseus*, blooming from July to August.

TOFIÉLDIA BOREÀLIS Wahlenb. *Common False Asphodel.*

The generic name commemorates Thomas Tofield (1730-1779), an early English amateur botanist. Asphodel was an immortal plant that clothed the Elysian fields; perhaps some duplicity is involved in transferring the name to a perishable plant of the New World! These are unspectacular plants with a basal fan of rush-like leaves, and a small compressed head (raceme) of very small, greenish-white to pale-purplish flowers. About 12 species occur in North and South America, and a few more in Eurasia.

Petri Andreae Matthioli, in his *Commentarii in libros sex Pedacii Dioscoridis*, 1554 (perhaps the most imposing of all the Herbals), attributes many remarkable qualities to a plant which appears to be related to this genus. Among other incredible (!) virtues ascribed to the Bog Asphodel, Matthioli states that it will cure a toothache if the ashes of the root are placed in the ear on the side of the head opposite to the offending tooth.

We have here, perhaps, an early example of psychotherapy!

Borealis refers to the wide range of this species, which is circumpolar in the arctic-alpine habitat, but extends down the spine of the Rocky Mountains in our area. *Asphodelus*, the true Asphodel, is a tall plant now supplanted in gardens by more attractive subjects. The origin of the name is given variously, but a possible explanation is from the Greek (a) *not*, and spodos *ashes*, which fits with very ancient references to the Asphodel of the Elysian fields.* Curiously, in mediaeval England, the name was distorted to Daffodil, and is now applied to the modern plant of the same name *(Narcissus)*.

In suitably acid and cold marshy meadows of the mountains, Tofieldia borealis is often locally abundant, and easily recognized from its smooth, 6-7 inch, leafless stalk, and tiny cluster of very small greenish-white flowers, in a tight head at the top of the stalk. It blooms from snow-melt in July, on through August.

"False" is one of the most common adjectives applied to plant names, perhaps in itself a reminder of the difficulty of recognition so often experienced.

*And rest at last, where souls unbodied dwell
In ever-flow'ring meads of asphodel.*

Homer: The Odyssey
(XXIV. 1. 19 of Pope's translation)

TOFIÉLDIA COCCINÈA Richardson. *Northern False Asphodel.*

Coccinea means *scarlet*, but this must be considered an overstatement. In fact the tiny flowers in an oval head are greenish tinged with purple. The plant is minute (only 1½-3 inches high) and may be further recognized by the presence of 1, or occasionally 2, very small leaves on the smooth stem. It appears to be a rare plant, being reported from a few stations chiefly in the northeastern part of our area. However, Northern False Asphodel is so easily overlooked that its rarity may be more apparent than real

TOFIÉLDIA GLUTINÒSA (Michx.) Pers. *Western False Asphodel.* [p.50]

"Glutinous" well describes the glandular sticky stem of this taller plant, which may reach 16 inches. Dan McCowan, beloved Canadian naturalist, says, "This plant, formerly humbugged and defrauded by ants whose credit was not satisfactory, found it necessary to close the shop door to these undesirable patrons by developing an unusually sticky stem. That put an end to the activities of the porch-climbing ants . . . and now the glutinous-stemmed plant does business only with bees and other insects agreeable to trade on a reciprocal basis."

The greenish-white flowers occur in a terminal cluster or raceme, and the leaves—as with other members of the genus—are basal and grass-like. The seed-capsules are much more conspicuous than the flowers, being plump and reddish-purple. Wherever open bogs are found from sea level to considerable altitudes, this common species may be encountered throughout our area. It blooms from July to August.

Following page: ERYTHRONIUM REVOLUTUM ×2 [p.21]

MAIANTHEMUM DILATATUM (FRUIT)   ×1¾
[p.33]

FRITILLARIA CAMSCHATCENSIS   ×½   [p.24]

FRITILLARIA LANCEOLATA   ×⅗   [p.24]

FRITILLARIA PUDICA   ×⅗   [p.25]

TRÍLLIUM OVÀTUM Pursh. *Large White Trillium. Western Wake-robin.* [pp.55,62]

Trillium is a genus of perhaps 25 large and showy species from North America (chiefly eastern), Japan, and the Himalayas. The name, of course, refers to the 3 leaves, sepals, petals, and thrice-cleft stigma (Latin, tres, *three*).

In our area, we have only 1 generally recognized species, though it is highly variable. Ovatum refers to the leaf shape, which is broadly *ovate*, ending in a pronounced drip-tip. The lovely white flower is regally perched above the ring of 3 leaves, which occur toward the upper end of the 12-18 inch stalk. As the flower ages, it slowly turns through pink to a wine-purple.*

Wake-robin, of course, refers to the flower's early blooming, from the beginning of April through May. Rich deep soil nourishes this luminous ornament of the damp woods, from Vancouver Island across the Province in the extreme south, extending far south of the border. The type specimen, on which Pursh established the name, was collected by Meriwether Lewis "on the rapids of the Columbia River, April 10, 1806".

Another form of the plant, an enchanting dwarf of perfect proportions, but only 1½-4 inches tall, is limited to the coastal rocks of the West Coast of Vancouver Island. Its discoverer, the late Mr. J. A. Hibberson, showed us the original specimens, growing in a rockery with sharp drainage and much crushed rock in the soil mixtures. As can be seen from the photograph of this cluster of plants, it is very choice. This form, which blooms about a fortnight earlier than T. ovatum, was designated last year, TRÍLLIUM

[p.62] HIBBERSÒNII Wiley. Other authorities may regard it as a subspecies, or possibly as a variety, or even an ecological form of T. ovatum.

> *Yet mark'd I where the bolt of Cupid fell:*
> *It fell upon a little western flower,*
> *Before milk-white, now purple with love's wound . . . .*

William Shakespeare:
A Midsummer Night's Dream

TRITELÈIA GRANDIFLÒRA Lindl. [p.62]

Until recently included in the genus *Brodiaea* (which see), there are apparently about 6 species of Triteleia scattered down the Pacific coast, from southern British Columbia to California. Triteleia are distinguished by the presence of anthers on all 6 stamens, whereas in *Brodiaea* 3 stamens only are fertile, the others modified to staminodes that resemble slim petals.

Though beautiful plants, Triteleia have not received any common name of any general recognition; two of very local application are Bluedicks (for Triteleia grandiflora) and Cluster Lilies.

Grandiflora obviously means *large-flowered*, the lovely blue-lavender tube-shaped flowers being about 1 inch long, arranged in an umbel of 5-20 blooms. The smooth stem, 2 or more feet tall, grows from a fibrous-coated corm and a pair (or more) of long, grass-like, basal leaves.

The beauty of the flower, its long-lasting qualities in water, and absence of the odour of its near relatives the onions, have contributed to a rapid decline in the species to the point that it is probably now extinct on Vancouver Island, and increasingly less common in the extreme southern dry Interior of British Columbia. Triteleia grandiflora should be rigorously protected. Though for untold centuries it survived digging by Indian tribes (who were essentially conservationists) for food, the bulldozer and plough have almost completed its rout in the span of a generation. The corm is reported by many authorities to be perhaps the tastiest of our edible "bulbs".

T. grandiflora is found in deep, rather rich soil, in open areas where it can dry out in late summer. The beautiful flowers appear over a long period of time, from late April to early July. Many will know this plant as BRODIÀEA DOUGLÀSII Wats.

TRITELÈIA HYACÍNTHINA (Lindl.) Greene. *White Triteleia. Fool's Onion.* [p.63]

With its rounded umbel of papery-textured white star-shaped flowers at the top of a slim 2-foot stem, this plant really does not look very much like a hyacinth. Needless to say, it has no onion odour, not being an *Allium*. The midvein of each of the 6 petals is strongly green, or blue, forming a pleasing accent. Unlike *T. grandiflora*, (which see), the individual flowers are not tubular but open or campanulate.

T. hyacinthina occurs quite commonly in pockets of soil that may be soggy in spring but are bone-dry by midsummer, from Vancouver Island and the adjacent Mainland coast, south to California.

If of thy mortal goods thou art bereft,
And from thy slender store two loaves
*   alone to thee are left,*
Sell one, and with the dole
Buy hyacinths to feed thy soul.

Sa'di: Gulistan

VERÁTRUM VIRÍDE Alit. ssp. ESCHSCHÒLTZII (Gray) Löve & Löve. *False Hellebore. Corn Lily. Green Hellebore (and erroneously, Skunk Cabbage). Indian Poke. Green False Hellebore.* [pp.54,66]

An interesting contradiction is afforded by the generic and first common names, vera being Latin for *truth*. The explanation, it seems, is that in ancient times Veratrum was

ERYTHRONIUM GRANDIFLORUM $\times \frac{5}{6}$ [p.19]

STREPTOPUS AMPLEXIFOLIUS (FRUIT) $\times \frac{3}{4}$ [p.35]

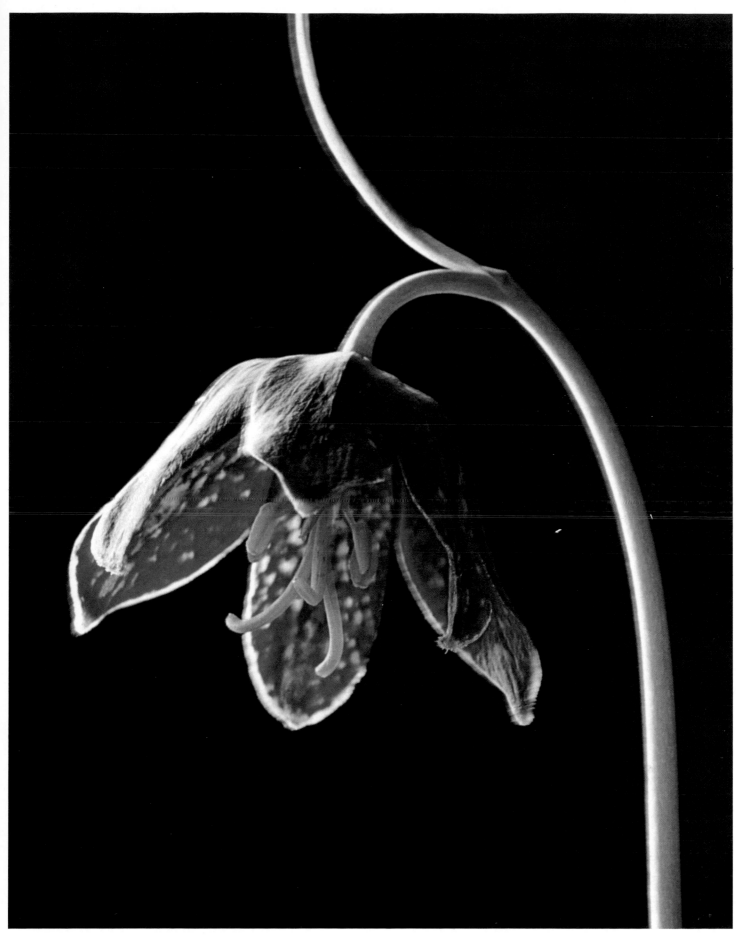

FRITILLARIA LANCEOLATA (DETAIL) ×3 [p.24]

used as the name of the true hellebore *(Helleborus)*; atrum means *black*, possibly referring to the very dark flowers of *H. niger*, or to its brownish-black rhizome.

About a dozen species are widely distributed throughout the north temperate regions, but only 1 occurs in our area.

Dioscorides, the Greek herbalist of the 1st century A.D., knew the White Hellebore, and claimed that its roots, when dried and ground, should be mixed with honey to kill mice.

This plant, Green Hellebore, is a tall coarse perennial, with very large clasping leaves that are strongly parallel-veined. One expects from such a noble plant an impressive flower, but the long much-branched panicle consists of insignificant greenish-yellow flowers. Nevertheless, the young shoots are monumental in spring, and the plant provides a statuesque accent in the wet meadows of subalpine regions.

All parts of the plant are highly poisonous when young, though after the foliage has been frosted and dried it is apparently harmless to stock. Indians used an infusion of the plant to lower the blood pressure. The plants are dried and powdered to form the garden insecticide "Hellebore".

Viride means *green*, and the varietal (or perhaps subspecific) name is after "Dr. Elsholz", a fellow voyageur with Chamisso on Kotzebue's expedition in 1815. (The name of Dr. Eschscholtz is also celebrated in the familiar California Poppy or *Eschscholtzia*, a name first mis-spelled by the Russians and since by a considerable host of gardeners!).

The common names are a sound argument for the use of the scientific name! For this and other widely distributed plants, it is rather fun to consult various flora and manuals. One will usually find in each a new and local name, some of which are used for quite another plant in other areas.

The disappointing flowers of Green Hellebore open during July-September, at the moderate altitudes it inhabits. The lusty plants occur rather widely in cold high meadows, from Alaska southward throughout our area.

In the brooks the slight grating sound of small cakes of ice . . . is full of content and promise . . . . Every rill is a channel for the juices of the meadow. Last year's grasses and flower-stalks have been steeped in rain and snow, and now the brooks flow with meadow tea . . . .

Henry David Thoreau:
Journal (March 8, 1840)

XEROPHÝLLUM TÈNAX (Pursh) Nutt. *Bear-grass. Squaw-grass. Basket-grass.*   [p.67]

Found only in North America, this is a genus of 2 or 3 species. All are large plants, whose generic name refers to harsh, *dry*, grass-like *leaves* in a dense basal clump (from which a tall unbranched stem arises to hold aloft a great plume of small white flowers).

This striking plant cannot be mistaken, for it is the only member of the Lily family in our area that is evergreen, its tall tuft of stiff grass-like leaves resembling a small-scale Pampas Grass. Tenax refers to the leaves, meaning tough or *tenacious*.

Indians dried and bleached the leaves in great quantities for use in weaving hats, capes, and baskets. Only the Rocky Mountain goat browses on the hard, sharp-edged foliage, but bear eat the softer (white) leaf-bases in early spring, and elk are fond of the rather succulent tall stems and flower-clusters.

Hundreds of small white flowers form the showy raceme, which may be held aloft 3-6 feet. At least in many parts of its range, the flowers appear only once or twice in a 10-year period; however, even the sterile leaf-clusters, 2-3 feet tall, are unmistakable. The plant grows in clay or peat soils among the mountains of southern and eastern British Columbia and adjacent Washington, and in the Olympics. The impressive flower-cluster of Xerophyllum may appear in midsummer.

ZYGÁDENUS ÉLEGANS Pursh. *Elegant Poison Camas. Mountain Death Camas.* [p.74]

Zygadenus has, one observer remarks, a venomous sound appropriate for a group of highly poisonous plants. However, the generic name is derived from the Greek zugos (*yoke*) plus aden (*gland*), descriptive of a 2-lobed nectary or gland occurring near the base of each tepal. Apparently all of the 20 species occurring in North America, and the single Asiatic species, contain highly toxic compounds which are most abundant in the membrane-covered, ovoid, tapering bulbs. Since these bulbs are difficult to distinguish from those of the edible Camas, especially *Camassia quamash* (which see), many fatalities have occurred from this confusion, particularly since native peoples commonly dug the bulbs in the hunger-time of early spring, before the appearance of the distinctive flowers. Some species of Poison Camas grow in the same prized meadows as *C. quamash*, but the Nez Percé in particular were careful to dig out and destroy Zygadenus bulbs while the blooming plants were easily told apart. The flowers are creamy-white, very much smaller than albino blooms of the Quamash, and more crowded.

Although the original spelling was Zigadenus, Zygadenus has been so widely used that it is probably academic to insist on the earlier form.

The specific name is merited, for the flowers of this species are appreciably *larger* than those of the other species of our area. They are also more impressive because borne in a more open raceme, and more striking because accented by a conspicuous, greenish, V-shaped gland. Elegant Poison Camas is a 1-3 foot plant, of higher elevations from Alaska southward into Washington. In our area, however, it does not occur west of the Cascades or Coast Mountains, being most abundant in the southeast corner of British Columbia.

Like other poisonous members of the genus Zygadenus, this species comes into bloom about a fortnight later than the edible *Camassia quamash*, in areas where both occur.

The concentration of poisonous alkaloids is lower in Z. elegans than in the other species; however since the rather succulent leaves appear before those of most plants, stock poisoning, particularly of sheep, does occur. In the rather wet meadows preferred by this species, the shallow bulbs may be readily pulled out by animals cropping the leaves. Craighead, Craighead, and Davis state 6 pounds of the green plant per hundredweight of animal (but for Z. gramineus only ½ pound per hundredweight of animal) are lethal amounts.

ZYGÁDENUS GRAMÍNEUS Rydb. *Grass-leaved Death Camas. Poison Camas.*

Gramineus describes the *grass-like* leaves of this highly toxic species. Its small creamy flowers are densely crowded in a raceme at the top of the single stem, which is seldom as much as 2 feet tall. The best distinction between this and the very similar *Z. venenosus* (which see) is the existence in the present species of a white membranous sheath or edging of the uppermost 1 or 2 stem-leaves. This species occurs in south central British Columbia, with a number of records from the extreme southeast, and a few from the lower Fraser Valley. It blooms in open meadows in late May or early June.

ZYGÁDENUS VENENÒSUS S. Wats. *Death Camas. Poison Camas.* [p.74]

Modern opinion considers this probably only a form of *Z. gramineus*, (which see) with which it is almost identical. The most reliable distinction is the presence of more than 2 stem-leaves, which lack the hyaline (membranous) sheath observed in *Z. gramineus*. The latter species also has a shorter claw at the base of each perianth-segment. The present species occurs in wet meadows, but is also found in soil pockets among rocks, and is more western in distribution, being chiefly reported from southern Vancouver Island.

These 2 species of Zygadenus occur frequently among colonies of the true Camas, *Camassia leichtlinii* or *C. quamash* (which see). Since the bulbs of the true Camas provided a staple food for some tribes, particularly of central Washington, any confusion of identification led to serious or even fatal consequences. This was the more likely to occur since the tribes came to the "camas prairies" in early spring when food was scarce, when of course the distinctive flowers of neither edible nor *poisonous* "Camas" had appeared. The dark-coated bulbs are very much alike. Some favourite "prairies" were visited by generations of hungry tribesmen, so that in course of time bulbs of the dangerous white-flowered pseudo- "Camas" were dug out and destroyed in such areas.

IRIDÀCEAE. *Iris Family.*

Rather learn and love
Each facet-flash of the revolving year.—
Red, green and blue that whirl into a white,
The variance now, the eventual unity,
Which make the miracle.

Robert Browning:
The Ring and the Book

This is a large family of 58 genera and about 1500 species, distributed over much of the earth's surface though sparsely represented in boreal regions. The chief centres are South Africa and tropical America.

The family contains many showy plants, some of which appear at first sight to be unrelated, e.g. *Crocus, Gladiolus, Tigridia,* the humble Blue-Eyed Grass, and the numerous *Iris* of our gardens. Botanically they are linked by a number of common characteristics, notably the presence of 3 stamens and an inferior ovary (i.e. an ovary placed below the calyx and corolla). The family possibly originated as an offshoot of the *Liliaceae* (which have 6 stamens and a superior ovary).

The *fleur-de-lis* of French heraldry is probably derived from the flower of *Iris pseudacorus* (which see). Orris-root, used in perfumery for its violet odour, is obtained by grinding the dried roots of *Iris florentina.*

ÌRIS

This genus of lovely flowers of perhaps 150 species (there is much disagreement about specific, subspecific and varietal status) takes its name from the classical goddess whose visible sign was the rainbow, for there are indeed Iris of every colour of the spectrum.

They are diverse also in their habitat (from dry plains to swamps), in their size, in their time of flowering, and in the nature of their roots (which range from wiry fibrous to thickened rhizomes). In some species, the 3 sepals are like the 3 petals in colour, and spread out flat on nearly the same level, but for the most part the sepals (or falls) droop downward, while the petals grow more or less upright. The style is divided into 3 flat divisions, coloured much like the petals, each division hiding a stamen. The leaves are very distinctive, being linear or sword-shaped, each growing from inside the fold of the next (i.e. the leaves are equitant), in 2 ranks.

And nearer to the river's trembling edge
There grew broad flag-flowers, purple pranked with white,

And starry river-buds among the sedge,
*   And floating water-lilies, broad and bright,*
Which lit the oak that overhung the hedge
*   With moonlight beams of their own watery light . . . .*

Percy Bysshe Shelley: The Question

ÌRIS MISSOURIÉNSIS Nutt. *Western Blue Flag.*

The specific name refers to the *Missouri* site of the type specimen.

This impressive Iris is about 2 feet tall, bearing handsome violet-blue flowers sometimes 5 inches across. It occurs near Sequim in the Olympic Peninsula, and on Whidbey Island, but generally is found east of the Cascades in zones of Bunch-grass and Sagebrush. It is very rare in British Columbia, so should not be disturbed.

Western Blue Flag is a plant of wet catch-basins, in essentially low rainfall areas. The handsome leaves grow from a thick-knotted rhizome to about the height of the stem, and are only ⅜ inch wide, or less. The round, smooth stem is usually branched, each branch commonly bearing 2 flowers. The light-blue falls (sepals) are conspicuously purple-veined, the unveined standards (petals) are uniformly deeper blue. Occasionally a mauve variation is seen, and a white form has been brought into cultivation.

The roots were employed by certain tribes in the preparation of an arrow poison claimed to have had deadly effects on human targets.

During May or early June, one may be fortunate enough to chance upon the striking blooms of this fine plant.

ÌRIS PSEUDÁCORUS L. *Yellow Flag.* [p.67]

The specific name is derived from the resemblance of the leaves (pseudo, *false*) to *Acorus calamus*, the Sweet Sedge, once much used for strewing floors. The plant is European, early introduced to this continent (where it has become invasive), and now found in our area along ditches and by stream-sides, from southern Vancouver Island and the Fraser Valley into adjacent Washington.

Gerard's (1597) *Herball* claims this plant "prospereth well in moiste medowes . . . brinkes of riuers, ponds, and standing lakes", over much of Europe. The species figures in several stories told of Clovis, fifth century king of the Franks. According to one of these, the king, when trapped in a bend of the Rhine by a superior force of Goths, was saved by noticing that Yellow Iris grew far out in the river. The plants revealed a fordable shallow, across which the Frankish forces safely retreated. This tradition may have led Louis VII, almost 700 years later, to adopt the Iris as a symbol for the forces he was gathering to attempt the Second Crusade. Thus it was called Fleur de Louis, corrupted to Fleur-de-luce, Fleur-de-lys, and finally Fleur-de-lis.

This is our only bright yellow Iris. It frequently grows from shallow water to a height of 3 feet. The flowers are usually chrome-yellow, though occasional cream forms are seen, in both cases handsomely pencilled with black. The showy blooms appear over an unusually extended period, from April to August.

A woodcut labelled ACORVS appears in the *Hortus Sanitatis*, printed at Mencz in 1485. Beautifully drawn, it almost certainly represents Iris pseudacorus L.

ÌRIS SETÒSA Pall. *Northern Flag.*   [p.78]

The specific name is from the Latin setosus or saetosus, meaning *full of bristles*, a rather extreme description of the upright standards (petals). These are small, with a narrow blade suddenly contracting to a lanceolate or awl-shaped tip. The falls are blue (rarely, purplish or white), strongly marked near the base with dark veins, and are distinctively broad and heart-shaped, reminding one almost of a Japanese Iris. The leafy bracts just below the 3-3½ inch flowers are in some forms fleshy, tinged purple, in others membranous [ssp. INTÈRIOR (Anders.) Hult.]. The thick rootstock is poisonous.

Iris setosa is the far northern representative of the genus—in fact, the type specimen was from Siberia. It is found in wet meadows and along lakeshores, in extreme northern British Columbia, and into Alaska.

SISYRÍNCHIUM. *Blue-eyed Grass.*

Sisyrinchium was a name applied by Theophrastus, about 340 B.C., to a plant allied to the Iris. The common name is misleading, for several species are yellow, others are purple.

These are grass-like tufted perennials, with (usually) winged stems, bearing small flowers which do not immediately suggest relationship with the iris. However, upon reflection, the folded leaves, the inferior ovary, and the 3 stamens joined to form with the style a central column, indicate the Iridaceae.

Authorities are in disagreement on the species, which are distinguishable on very minor characteristics, but there are probably many less "good" species than the 150 or so that have been described and named as native to North America and the West Indies.

For the most part, we are following Hitchcock et al., who "lump" a number of doubtfully valid names under a single "species of convenience" (*S. angustifolium*). Two others are well-defined, and easily recognizable, and one more is supported as a distinct entity by Calder and Taylor.

50

LILIUM COLUMBIANUM ×¼ [p.28]

TOFIELDIA GLUTINOSA ×1 [p.37]

LILIUM PHILADELPHICUM ×1 [p.29]

SISYRÍNCHIUM ANGUSTIFÒLIUM Miller. *Narrow-leaved Blue-eyed Grass.* [p.74]

The specific name means *narrow-leaved* (appropriate since they are little over ¹⁄₁₆ inch wide). This is an extremely variable species, for which a long list of species, subspecies, and varietal names have been proposed by various students. The genus badly needs a monographic study.

Under this name, Hitchcock et al. have made what appears to be a reasonable inclusion of at least 5 "species", that are dubiously distinct. Of overlapping distribution throughout the Province, from Coast to moderate elevations in the mountains, these are grassy-leaved plants with bluish, 6-tepalled flowers, that appear a little too small for the size of the leaf-tufts.

Distinctions have been made on the bases of stem-branching, relative basal-leaf to stem-length, leaf-width, absolute stem-length, proportions of the 2 bracts that enclose the developing flowers—but in a collected series all of these characteristics overlap, so that we are, it seems, dealing with extremes of a single variable species. If this position is accepted, identification is enormously simplified. In our area, apart from the much larger and purple-flowered *S. douglasii,* and the yellow-flowered *S. californicum,* it is then only needful to discriminate between the present species, and *S. littorale* (which see).

On this understanding, S. angustifolium covers a group of plants that are taller-stemmed, and narrower-leaved. The flowers are relatively smaller, averaging perhaps less than 1 inch wide, on stems often 2-4 times as long as those of *S. littorale,* and notably paler and bluer than those of the latter species. The illustration represents a specimen that is median in the group of variations.

SISYRÍNCHIUM CALIFÓRNICUM (Ker-Gawl.) Dryand. *Yellow-eyed Grass.* [p.74]

This rather variable species is instantly recognizable as the only yellow-flowered Sisyrinchium in our area. It occurs from *California,* north along the coast to Vancouver Island, and is found close to the water on lakeshores, and in coastal bogs. In British Columbia it is apparently not recorded from the mainland.

The flowers are lemon-yellow, to rather intense yellow, each of the 6 tepals being lined with 5 purplish veins. The stamens are orange-yellow and conspicuous. The blooms appear from May to July, but are strikingly matutinal, i.e. they unfold for a few hours in the morning, but wither by noon.

And this same flower that smiles to day,
Tomorrow will be dying.

Robert Herrick: Counsel to Girls

SISYRÍNCHIUM DOUGLÀSII Dietr. *Satin-flower. Purple-eyed Grass.* [pp.75,98]

Named after David Douglas, courageous plant explorer (1798-1834) of Western America, this is the reigning queen of the genus. Indeed, a rock slope covered with these sprightly bells, sensitive to every whisper of wind, is one of the floral delights of early spring.

Satin-flower is unmistakable, for it blooms as early as mid-February on Vancouver Island, and its gorgeous reddish-purple flowers are the largest of the genus (about 1½ inches across). The royal purple has its golden trove, in the shape of 3 brilliant yellow anthers. (Rarely, white, pink, or striped individuals are found.) Flowers are borne on distinct stalks (pedicels) which spring from a pair of bracts of very unequal length. The silvery-green, darker-veined leaves are usually shorter than the unbranched stem, which is 6-16 inches tall.

This plant is happiest in pockets of soil on rock slopes, or under the open shade of Garry Oaks. It is abundant on Vancouver Island, though over-picking has destroyed many colonies. Restricted to lower altitudes, Sisyrinchium douglasii occurs on both sides of the Cascades, from Kamloops into Washington, Oregon and California. The Interior form (S. INFLÀTUM of some authors) has more pointed perianth-segments, and the conjoined base of the filaments is enlarged.

> . . . *what is beautiful is a joy for all seasons,*
> *a possession for all eternity.*

Oscar Wilde: Sebastian Melmoth

SISYRÍNCHIUM LITTORÁLE Greene. *Shore Blue-eyed Grass.* [p.78]

The specific name means *of the shore*, from the Latin litoralis (also spelled littoralis).

This very variable species may represent the coastal extreme of a complex, but we follow the scholarly recognition of Calder and Taylor, and of Hultén. S. littorale occurs from the Alaska Panhandle, and Queen Charlotte Islands, at least to the vicinity of Victoria, Vancouver Island, and possibly along the adjacent coast of Washington.

Typically, this is a dwarf plant with short broad leaves, dark purplish-blue flowers with very brilliant orange-yellow centres, and a disproportionately large capsule. The tips of the tepals are cuspidate, that is, ending in an abrupt, short firm point, clearly shown in the photograph. The stem is wing-marginate and unbranched, though occasionally a small stem-leaf occurs. This is a singularly neat and compact plant, one of the most attractive of the genus.

S. littorale is found in short turf above seaside rocks, in cliff crevices, on sand beaches and river flats, and in marshes and sedge-meadows.

54

MAIANTHEMUM DILATATUM ×1 [p.33]

STREPTOPUS ROSEUS ssp. CURVIPES ×1 [p.35]

STENANTHIUM OCCIDENTALE ×1 [p.34]

VERATRUM VIRIDE ssp. ESCHSCHOLTZII ×⅓
[p.41]

SMILACINA RACEMOSA ×⅖ [p.33]

TRILLIUM OVATUM ×⅓ [p.40]

ORCHIDÀCEAE. *Orchid Family.*

. . . move along these shades
In gentleness of heart; with gentle hand
Touch—for there is a spirit in the woods

William Wordsworth:
Nutting: VI Poems of the Imagination

Botanists are agreed that the great and successful family of orchids represents a relatively primitive group, retaining many characteristics of very ancient plant forebears. Various authorities consider there may be from 430 to 610 genera, and possibly 20,000 to 35,000 species distributed all over the world, though especially numerous in the tropics. (The only rival for number of species is the Composite family, considered the most recent and most highly developed, and numbering more than 20,000 species).

One of the primitive features of existing orchids is the extraordinary abundance of seed produced by individual plants. Szczawinski reports the count of seeds in a single capsule of a tropical species (*Cycnoches chlorochilon*) undertaken—appropriately enough, in view of the astronomical number—at the Royal Greenwich Observatory; the total was 3,770,000! But such tiny seeds lack the stored food found in the seeds of more highly developed plants. Hence they depend upon a complex of favourable circumstances, including the presence of the mycelia of certain fungi, in order to germinate and survive.*

The distinctive characteristic of the orchid flower is the column, a structure formed by the fusion of some of the stamens, with the style and stigma. This is a portion of an elaborate modification of the floral parts to insure cross-pollination by insects. Numerous studies are continuing to reveal unimagined sophistication of structural, chemical, and timing devices developed by these fascinating plants to bring about vital cross-fertilization. *Angraecum sesquipedale*, from Madagascar, can only be pollinated by a single species of moth, with a proboscis or tongue more than 12 inches long!

The history of plant introductions is notably marked by a period of "orchid-mania". Even the fantastic sums spent on tulips were insignificant by comparison with the cost of the orchid collecting expeditions sent to every part of the world by rich enthusiasts of the Victorian era. So ruthless was the competition that to guarantee his "corner" on the world's supply of the charming ivory, violet, and green *Cypripedium spicerianum*, a certain professional plant-hunter in Assam took pains to exterminate the wild plants! It is interesting to recall that the first move toward preservation of any plant species was made by the governments of Assam and Burma, on behalf of the incredible Blue Orchid, *Vanda coerulea*.

Though many orchids are extraordinarily flamboyant, particularly the tropical species, most of our northern species show their kinship only in the complexity of their floral parts, for the flowers are often small and quite inconspicuous.

We have within our area perhaps 40 species, subspecies and varieties of orchids. The more spectacular ones are in grievous need of protection, increasingly so as their habitats are irrevocably altered by man's activities.

The scent produced by many species of orchids serves the purpose of attracting certain pollinator insects, often highly specific bees, wasps, flies, or moths. The scent ingredients are readily identifiable by the modern technique of gas chromatography. In this way numerous esters, and derivatives of cineole have been isolated.

*Noël Bernard, in 1904, discovered that the microscopic threads of certain fungi species must actually penetrate the seed coat before germination can occur. Shortly thereafter Dr. Lewis Knudson found that the fungus converted certain complex (and insoluble) storage starches of the seed into simpler sugars utilizable by the embryo plant. Since then the tiny seeds of orchids have been found to grow readily on agar containing sugars and other nutrients. In fact, commercial growers today use thin sections of the apical meristem (tip-growth) to multiply orchid plants, even man-created hybrids (some of which do not produce viable seed).

CALÝPSO BULBÒSA (L.) Oakes. *Fairy Slipper. Calypso. Cytherea. Deer-head Orchid. Venus Slipper. Hider-of-the-north. Pink Slipper-orchid. Lady's Slipper. False Lady's Slipper.* [pp.79,82,83]

The goddess daughter of Atlas was Calypso, whose name means *concealment*, with reference to this lovely flower's habit of hiding among the mosses of the forest floor, in the shade—essential to its existence—of high forest trees. "Bulbosa", of course, refers to the oval white pseudo-*bulb* (corm) from which grow the single, strikingly parallel-veined, ovate leaf, and the 6 inch delicate scape carrying its solitary nodding and lovely blossom. The blossom, in the windless air of the forest, delights the wanderer with its heavenly fragrance—fresh, spicy, and utterly distinctive. It is a perfume to be mentioned in the same breath with that of the *Linnaea* or Twinflower, a perfume more subtle and refined even than that of the Rein Orchid, *Habenaria dilatata* (which see).

"*. . . sweeter than the lids of Juno's eyes*
Or Cytherea's breath . . . ."

The tiny "bulb" is most tenuously fixed to the forest duff by a few thread-like fibres, which are broken with fatal effects, by the most careful attempts to pinch off the enchanting flower-stem. Further, the bulb grows only in association with certain species of fungi, so that it is virtually impossible to transplant it successfully—as many thousands of admirers can ruefully report. One must needs come reverently to its native haunts, there to admire it, and go blithely away—happy in the knowledge that others may come to enjoy it.

An unusual feature of this sole member of its genus in North America, is the appearance in late summer of the distinctive leaf, which persists through the rough weather of fall and winter, until in April (on the southern coast) the plump flower bud appears and is pushed upward by the lengthening scape. After the flower has withered the leaf slowly shrivels, and during the early summer months the plant is almost undetectable.

The 5 delicate tepals form an exquisite setting for the jewel-like lip or slipper. This may be translucent white in the Coastal form [ssp. OCCIDENTÀLIS (Holz) Calder & Taylor], or bright-yellow [ssp. BULBÒSA, Calder & Taylor] in the form occurring east of the Coast range northward to Alaska. In both forms the ground-colour is embellished with a most delicate ornamentation of sienna, purple-madder, and purple. Especially on the Saanich peninsula of southern Vancouver Island one occasionally finds the form ÁLBA, ethereally lovely and glistening white. When shape and proportion, colour and perfume are all considered, this must rank as one of the most enchantingly lovely of all our native plants.

On May 4, 1792, Archibald Menzies, naturalist with Captain George Vancouver, was anchored near the present site of Port Discovery (Washington) and, making a landing and excursion into the forest ". . . met with vast abundance of that rare plant the *Cypropedium bulbosom/* which was now in full bloom & grew about the roots of the Pine Trees in very spungy soil & dry situations." Menzies' Journal of Vancouver's Voyage, 1792.

The Fairy Slipper still comes into bloom in early May, and delights as well the heart of the modern wayfarer.

> *. . . I would wander forth*
> *And seek the woods. The sunshine on my path*
> *Was to me a friend. The swelling hills,*
> *The quiet dells retiring far between,*
> *With gentle invitation to explore*
> *Their windings, were a calm society*
> *That talked with me and soothed me.*

> William Cullen Bryant:
> A Winter Piece

CEPHALÁNTHERA AÚSTINAE (A. Gray) Heller. *Phantom Orchid.*

The generic name is from the Greek cephos, *head*, and anthos, referring to the position of the *anther* at the summit of the column. The specific name is after the American botanist R. M. Austin (1823-1919). The Phantom Orchid is a ghostly plant, palest cream to white in every part, excepting only a touch of golden-yellow in the sheltered throat of each flower.

Though an extremely rare species, Cephalanthera austinae is included in this book in the hope that more records for it will appear as an increasing number of wanderers in isolated places learn its existence and appearance. It is, of course, a saprophyte. Apparently the rhizomes, feeding upon decayed organic matter, push up the unique white stem (sometimes as much as 20 inches high) with its spectral flowers, only at intervals—occasionally as infrequently as 17 years. The erratic and rare occurrence, extraordinary appearance, beauty and delicate perfume, combine to make the finding of a Phantom Orchid a noteworthy event.

In our area there are only a few records for the last 40 years, nearly all from a small area in the lower Fraser Valley. An extremely interesting discovery by Leonard Wiley near Gresham, Oregon, revealed in an area of 5 acres no less than 865 of these plants! Alas, as is so often the case, the area was logged, then burned. Since Cephalanthera austinae is limited to the Pacific Northwest and cannot be removed to gardens, it is likely to become extinct unless protected in parks that provide its moist, coniferous forest habitat. If you are fortunate enough ever to discover it, *photograph* it. Your pleasure will be prolonged, and a very rare plant preserved!

CORALLORHÌZA MACULÀTA Raf. *Spotted Coral-root.* [p.86]

Coral-like roots interprets the generic name. However, apt as the description seems, the coral "roots" are not true roots but much-branched rhizomes, i.e. underground stems. From the rhizome arises a smooth pink or purplish stem carrying a few fleshy scales, in place of leaves, and a raceme of small yellowish or purplish flowers. These curious plants are saprophytes, that feed upon decaying organic matter in the soil, and hence have no need of chlorophyll.

Like most members of the Orchid family, the Coral-roots are becoming increasingly rare as cultivation progressively destroys their habitats. The plant-lover should not attempt to transplant Corallorhiza species to the garden, because the odd, clubbed rhizomes are associated, for their work of extracting nourishment from decayed organic materials, with a complex group of fungi found only in the natural sites.

About 15 species are generally recognized in North and South America, and 1 in Eurasia.

In the case of the present species, maculata refers to the purple *spots* conspicuous on the 3-lobed, white lip of the ½-inch flowers.

Spotted Coral-root is a striking plant of dense woodland. The smooth fleshy stems are 10-24 inches tall, with a few clasping purplish bracts in place of leaves, below a few- to many-flowered raceme of small, typically orchid-shaped flowers.

The structure of the flowers is exceptionally interesting, for they are extraordinarily adapted for cross-pollination by insects.

Three sepals and 2 of the petals are very much alike, purplish and broadly lanceolate. The bases of the 2 lowermost sepals are joined to form a curious swelling, rather amusingly called a "mentum" or chin. The remaining petal is very differently shaped, forming a broad, white lip, purple-spotted, which acts as a landing platform for insects.

The stamens and style are united to form the "column", a curved structure projecting above the lip. On the underside of the column are 2 pollen-masses or "pollinia", which dust a visiting insect. The insect's weight on the lip exposes both the nectar and the sticky stigmatic surface, to which is transferred pollen from the bloom previously visited. In this modification of the usual floral parts, the Coral-roots, like other members of the Orchid family, are exquisitely adapted for cross-fertilization.

There are further almost incredibly precise refinements of a chemical nature that control the time intervals for bending downward the pollen structures, for dehydrating the stigma surface, and for precisely altering its adhesive quality.

A very rare lemon-yellow variation occurs infrequently on Vancouver Island.

The purple plants may exist in 2 subspecies, according to Calder and Taylor. C. maculata ssp. MACULÀTA, though variable in whiteness of lip and degree of spotting, has a distinctively curved column (which is yellow beneath, with faint purple spots), a barely evident mentum, and sepals that are bent inward (not reflexed, not even widely spreading).

[pp.63,83]

C. maculàta ssp. MERTENSIÁNA (Bong.) Calder & Taylor. *Western Coral-root. Mertens' Coral-root.* (F. C. Mertens, 1764-1831, was a German botanist.) This generally more slender plant has been given specific rank by earlier botanists. It is most readily distinguished by the widely spreading sepals and petals, the distinctly pouched mentum, and the nearly straight column (which is yellow below, and unspotted). The lip is generally reddish-purple, or white with 2 large purple blotches.

Very occasionally one chances upon compact colonies of this subspecies—indeed, we have seen at least a thousand stems crowded into a hat-sized patch.

Both subspecies are found in the cool duff of coastal coniferous forests, and occasionally along the banks of shaded streams in the Central and Southern Interior, while ssp. mertensiana extends further into northern British Columbia. The blooming period is May to August, depending upon altitude.

CORALLORHÌZA STRIÀTA Lindl. *Striped Coral-root.* [p.91]

The specific name refers to the distinctive red-purple *stripes* of the lip.

Sepals and petals are purplish, as is also usually the lip, though this is occasionally yellowish or nearly white, upon which background colour the 3 vertical red-purple stripes are conspicuous. In shape the lip is quite unlike that of the other species, being slightly cupped, without lobes, and broadly elliptical.

This is the largest and showiest member of the genus. One is sometimes fortunate to chance upon the Striped Coral-root in a forest opening, when a shaft of light from behind, like a natural spotlight, transforms the blossoms into coruscating jewels.

The open raceme of 10-20 flowers, at the top of a gleaming pinkish to purplish 12-24 inch stem, appears as early as April, and as late as August. It may be found in the moist humus of the forest floor, or of shaded stream-banks. This species occurs from the south Peace River into southern Vancouver Island, Washington, Oregon, and California.

Silent flowers
Speak also
To that obedient ear within.

Onitsura

CORALLORHÌZA TRÌFIDA Chât. *Northern Coral-root.*

The specific name refers to the *three lobes* of the lip, a feature shared with *C. maculata* and *C. maculata ssp. mertensiana* (which see). But this is a smaller plant, with a yellowish stem only 4-12 inches tall. In our area Northern Coral-root is the only member of the genus having yellowish-green petals and sepals. The lip is whitish, variably or not at all spotted with magenta. It is found from north to south in our area, but not along the coast, in habitats similar to those of the other species. Indeed, in some areas of the southern Interior, one may chance upon all our Coral-roots during the course of a single day. This species blooms occasionally as early as April, but more often through the summer and late summer.

CYPRIPÈDIUM CALCEÒLUS L. var. PUBÉSCENS (Willd.) Correll. *Yellow Lady's Slipper. Yellow Moccasin Flower.* [p.90]

The name is derived from the pedilon or *slipper* of Kupris or Aphrodite, goddess of love and beauty, reputed born on the island of Cyprus. Possibly 50 species have been described from arctic to tropic conditions in Asia, Europe and America. They are distinguished from all other orchids by the presence of 2 pollen-bearing stamens, and a third sterile one which has been curiously modified to a glistening shield-like structure, arched above the fertile stamens.

Cypripedium, as just related, means *Aphrodite's slipper*; calceolus means, somewhat redundantly, *a small shoe*. One concludes that Linnaeus was more than slightly impressed by the resemblance of the beautiful, golden, pouch-like lip to a slipper, or shoe.* The variety *pubescens* was named with reference to the glandular hairs of the stem and leaves, which, particularly after the flower has withered, appear to have an irritating effect on the skin of some individuals. The name parviflórum has been suggested for a smaller-flowered northern species or subspecies, but this is probably only a variety. The Yellow Lady's Slipper is circumboreal, and over its enormous range is quite variable in size, scent, and colour of lateral petals (from yellowish, or greenish, to purplish-brown). In most forms, the lateral (side) pair of petals is spirally twisted. The inflated "pouch" in all forms is golden-yellow. Commonly a single elegant perfumed bloom is held 6-12 inches above the large, broadly lanceolate leaves, which have conspicuous parallel veins and a clasping base.

This magnificent plant is regarded by many as the most beautiful of the terrestrial orchids. Admirable indeed are the shape of the flower, the harmonious colouring, and the impressive size, but the writer confesses an even greater fascination for the exquisite *Calypso*, the Fairy Slipper.

From April to July one may encounter single specimens, or quite often, crowded clumps of the Yellow Moccasin Flower ornamenting bogs, swamps, lake and stream shores, or wet woodlands. Dr. Szczawinski found large colonies, near Summit Pass on the Alaska Highway, growing in full sun on rather dry, gravelly soil—an unexpected habitat. Cypripedium calceolus has not been reported from the coast, but otherwise

TRILLIUM OVATUM var. HIBBERSONII ×³⁄₅ [p.40]

TRILLIUM OVATUM (AGING FLOWER) ×1 [p.40]

TRITELEIA GRANDIFLORA ×1¾ [p.40]

SMILACINA STELLATA ×³/₅ [p.34]

CORALLORHIZA MACULATA SSP. MERTENSIANA
(HABITAT) ×²/₅ [p.60]

63

TRITELEIA HYACINTHINA ×1½ [p.41]

occurs sporadically throughout our area, with the exception of a gap in the central Interior.

Or, maybe, you are one of the Graces come hither, who bear the gods company and are called immortal, or else one of the Nymphs who haunt the pleasant woods, or of those who inhabit this lovely mountain and the springs of rivers and grassy meads . . . .

Homer: Homeric Hymn to Aphrodite
(translation of H. G. Evelyn-White)

*The first record of this plant appears in the *Theatrum Botanicum* (1640) by John Parkinson, Herbarist to Charles I.

CYPRIPÈDIUM MONTÀNUM Dougl. *Mountain Lady's Slipper. Moccasin Flower. White Lady's-slipper.* [p.87]

The specific name refers to this beautiful plant's usual habitat, *mountain* slopes in cool rich humus, but it also occurs in moist, or dryish open woods, at moderate altitudes.

The luminous white pouch, delicately veined with purple, and backed by dark-green or brownish-purple sepals and petals, forms a beautifully proportioned flower. It is usually solitary, at the top of a sturdy stem carrying numerous handsome leaves, which are lanceolate and clasp the stem. Rarely one sees as many as 3 of the blooms on a stem which may reach 18 or 20 inches. The lovely blossoms are delightfully fragrant. Depending upon the altitude, you may be thrilled to find the plants in bloom from May to July.

Apparently exterminated by cutting the flowers with the leafy stems (essential for nourishment of the heavy cord-like roots), or by attempts to transplant to gardens, the species is no longer known on Vancouver Island, and was never reported from the Queen Charlotte Islands. Nowhere abundant, Mountain Lady's Slipper has been collected in many areas of the southwest and southeast Interior, east of the Coast Range. This is a species urgently in need of legal protection, but the greatest hope for preserving rare plants, such as this, lies in the education of the public, to the point where people come to realize that the greatest pleasure results from admiring plants in their natural habitats.

"Wilderness is becoming one of the endangered species of environment on the planet Earth. In it is an essential that man could run out of even before he loses breathable air and rational judgment. Man has been busying himself, in the brief flash of two centuries of technological revolution, with wiping out the organic variety the world has been made of . . . . The wilderness that is home to uncounted varieties of life belongs to all those varieties, they belong to it, and man in all his colors is only one of them. As long as the wilderness endures, it will be the continuum from which new beauty can come forth, part of the natural succession that preceded man by billions of years and can be expected to survive him, however badly he impairs it before he leaves. In Wilderness is the preservation of the World, and of man."

David Brower, 1967

CYPRIPÈDIUM PASSERÌNUM Richards. *Sparrow's-egg Lady's Slipper. Franklin's Lady Slipper. Purple-spot White-slipper. Small White Lady's-slipper. Small White Northern Lady-slipper.* [p.78]

The specific name of this small-flowered northern plant means *sparrow-like*, because of the resemblance, noted during Sir John Franklin's Arctic expedition by Dr. John Richardson, of the spotted lip to the egg of a sparrow. Least showy of our three "Cyps", this plant has short stubby sepals that are greenish, the petals are whitish, and the pouch white (with the bright purple spots of the interior wall showing through faintly on the outside). More rarely, the pouch is pale-magenta. The large, clasping leaves and 10-12 inch stem are densely hairy

Sparrow's-egg Lady's Slipper may be found from June to July in the extreme north and northeast regions of British Columbia, although there are half a dozen isolated records along the line of mountains in the southeast. It occurs in sphagnum bogs, and also in gravel outwashes, and on wet talus.

EPIPÁCTIS GIGANTÈA Dougl. *Giant Helleborine.*

The generic name illustrates the misapplication of names so general prior to Linnaeus' introduction of the binary system. Theophrastus, about 340 B.C., called the totally unrelated Black Hellebore, or Christmas Rose (belonging to the Buttercup family), Epipactis. (The name derives from epipegnus, *to coagulate*, alluding to that plant's effect in curdling milk). The Helleborines are plants of Europe and Asia, of which 2 species have been introduced into North America, there to spread like weeds.

This rather showy orchid occurs in wet meadows and on stream-banks, reaching a height of nearly 5 feet where the soil is rich. The stout stem, with alternate, clasping, lanceolate leaves, carries an open raceme of 2-12 greenish or purplish flowers. The flower is about 2 inches across, with 3 rose-flushed green sepals, 2 pink to rose, purple-veined, lateral petals, and a red- and purple-veined lip. The column is short, and ornamented with a blue horn on either side.

Following page: VERATRUM VIRIDE SSP. ESCHSCHOLTZII (SHOOT) ×1½ [p.41]

IRIS PSEUDACORUS ×½ [p.48]

XEROPHYLLUM TENAX ×⅕ [p.44]

E. gigantea seems to have a predilection for hot springs, but also occurs in swamps and marshes, and along rivers, across southern British Columbia and into Washington and Idaho. It blooms from June to August.

[p.82]   EPIPÁCTIS HELLEBÓRINE (L.) Cranz. *Helleborine.* Though most reports are from southern Vancouver Island, this invasive species (smaller than E. gigantea) may be expected momentarily on the mainland of British Columbia. It reached the eastern coast from Europe in 1879, and has since been traced across the continent. Usually about a foot high, E. helleborine may reach 3 feet. The broadly ovate to lanceolate leaves are strongly parallel-veined, and become reduced toward the top of the stem to long bracts, in the axils of which the greenish-brown flowers are found. The raceme is crowded with about 2 dozen flowers, which open a few at a time from lowermost upward. They are about 1 inch across, with a greenish lip suffused with madder and rose.

The plant is in bloom from June to September, and may be found in waste places along road edges, in cool woods, as a volunteer in one's garden, and even in open fields. It is surprising to find among the aristocrats of the Orchid family an invasive, almost weedy plant.

GOODYÈRA OBLONGIFÒLIA Raf. *Large Rattlesnake Orchid. Rattlesnake Plantain.*
[pp.82,83]

Goodyer was a 17th century English botanist. In pioneer days it was believed, according to the "Doctrine of Signs", that the snakeskin markings of the leaves showed, of course, that Rattlesnake Plantain was efficacious in treatment of snake-bite. History fails to record the value of the treatment—though no doubt hardy survivors attributed recovery to the sum of the procedures employed: the poultice of these leaves, cautery, and even the internal application of frontier whisky! There are 25-30 species of rattlesnake plantains scattered over the world.

Oblongifolia refers to the shape of the leaves, which form a conspicuous rosette among the mosses of the forest floor. The very striking pattern of white lines upon the dark-green leaves is exceedingly variable. Plants growing within a few feet of each other will vary from a conspicuous white network covering the whole of the upper surface of the leaf, to a white midvein with the merest suggestion of branching. Plants with chlorophyll lacking in the strongly reticulated leaf-pattern are particularly common along the coast.

Countless strangers, upon discovering the spectacular leaves, and anticipating a bloom worthy of such a handsome rosette, have been not a little disappointed when at last the stem hoists a spike of drab greenish-white flowers.

The leaves of the Rattlesnake Orchids can be mistaken for no others; however, the distinction between our 2 species is less simple. G. oblongifolia is larger than *G. repens* (which see)—usually 10-15 inches tall, and the leaves form a distinctly flattened basal cluster. The flowers are usually arranged spirally around the upper part of the stem.

Though the 2 species overlap in the eastern half of our area from about 56° latitude southward, only G. oblongifolia is found west of the Cascades. It is particularly abundant in the Queen Charlottes and in Vancouver Island, where from June to September one may find that a few of the greenish buds have become whiter, though they never fully open.

GOODYÈRA RÈPENS (L.) R. Br. *Northern Rattlesnake Orchid. Northern Rattlesnake Plantain.*

Repens calls attention to the fleshy *creeping* rootstock of this more northern, eastern, and much smaller species. The stem is usually about 6 inches tall, and carries the greenish-white or yellowish-white flowers all on one side. The small leaves are uniformly dark-green and only occasionally form a basal rosette, being more often somewhat spaced along the stem. Toward the Alberta boundary, a form is rarely seen with leaves having a white border, due to lack of chlorophyll. However, extensive white-veining of leaves is only found in *G. oblongifolia* (which see).

Northern Rattlesnake Orchid is a plant of densely shaded woods, though it is found both in damp and rather dry areas. It is in flower from July to August.

HABENÀRIA. *Rein Orchid. Bog Orchid.*

Both scientific and common names refer to the thong-like shape of the lip and spur: like a rein (from the Latin habenas, a strap or *rein*). Though some of the Habenarias of eastern North America are very showy, all of the 8 species found in our area have small greenish or white flowers. The leaves vary from species to species and are useful in recognition, but all species have an unbranched, upright stem bearing a raceme (sometimes spike-like) whose individual flowers show the characteristic lip and column of the orchid family. The uppermost sepal and the side petals form a sort of hood over the column, and the lip has a backward tubular projection, known as the spur.

This is a large genus of perhaps 500 species, found chiefly in the warmer climatic zones of the world.

HABENÀRIA CHORÍSIANA Cham. *Chamisso's Orchid.*

The specific name honours Louis Choris (1795-1828), Russian traveller and artist.

This insignificant plant with tiny greenish flowers is considered very rare, and has been reported only from the Aleutian chain, from near Juneau, from the Queen Charlottes and from Vancouver Island. Since H. chorisiana is only about 5 inches tall and occurs in swamps and sphagnum bogs of difficult access, it may well prove less rare than overlooked. Its small size, well-spaced, tiny, fleshy flowers only ⅜ inch across, and its pair of nearly basal leaves will identify this species.

HABENÀRIA DILATÀTA (Pursh) Hook. var. LEUCOSTÁCHYS. *Tall White Bog-orchid. Fragrant White Orchid.* [pp.87,98]

Dilatata means dilated or *expanded,* and refers to the widened base (upper part) of the lip.

This stately orchid lifts its beautifully fragrant white spire as much as 3 feet above the wet surface of swamps, bogs, stream and lakeshores, or soggy meadows. In such habitats, from June to September, one may expect to discover this beautiful species throughout our area. Szczawinski considers the perfume a blend of cloves, vanilla, and syringa: others will draw different analogues. However, none who know this plant can fail to stop and admire it.

The smooth stem is clasped by rather succulent leaves, that are spear-head shaped below, but become smaller and more slender upward. Twenty or more of the gleaming white flowers, almost an inch wide, may be open at one time. The length of the spur-like projection of the lip is very variable, though Calder and Taylor can find no reason for varietal names for the extreme cases. The lip is quite distinctive—slender at its tip, it is suddenly dilated or widened near the base. The 2 yellow stamens tucked under the column enhance the whiteness of the flower.

Hultén reports that this species forms hybrid swarms with *H. convallariaefolia* (Fisch.) Lindl., in the extreme northern part of our area, and with *H. hyperborea* (L.) R. Br. (which see) throughout the Province. Such hybrids have greenish flowers.

HABENÀRIA HYPERBÒREA (L.) R. Br. *Green-flowered Bog-orchid.* [p.98]

Hyperborea from the Greek, means more than, or *beyond, the north,* for it is one of the orchids found north of the Arctic Circle. It occurs throughout our area—except in the Queen Charlotte Islands—in muskeg and peat bogs, in marshes, and along streams and lakeshores.

Habenària hyperborea is usually less than 20 inches tall, and the yellowish-green flowers are densely crowded in the raceme. Distinctive are the curved spur (about as long as the lip) and the shape of the lip, which tapers smoothly to a sharp tip. Lanceolate leaves grow up the stem but become progressively smaller upward.

The plant is in flower from June to August, depending upon the latitude and elevation.

HABENÀRIA OBTUSÀTA (Banks ex Pursh) Richards. *Blunt-leaf Rein-orchid. One-leaved Rein-orchid.* [p.99]

Obtusata refers to the characteristic *blunt* tip of the basal leaf, which is usually solitary. This small plant (rarely reaching 12 inches) is rather inconspicuous, with a few greenish-white flowers widely spaced in an open raceme. The lip and spur are about equal in length, both tapering from the base to the tip.

This hardy species is not known from the Coast but is widely distributed throughout the Interior, and especially abundant in the North. Like others of its genus, H. obtusata occurs in damp cool soils of swamps, muskegs, and dense forests of conifers.

HABENÀRIA ORBICULÀTA (Pursh) Torr. *Large Round-leaved Orchid.* [p.98]

The specific name refers to the pair of nearly *round* basal leaves, which alone will serve to identify this handsome plant. It is often 2 feet tall, and bears, in a loose raceme, up to twenty or more greenish-white flowers, which are commonly 1½ inches across. The strap-shaped lip is about 1 inch long, and the spur, which is curved and thickened toward the tip, is nearly 2 inches long.

The general appearance of the plant is refined and well-bred, a delight to the eye. H. orbiculata is locally abundant in the southern Coastal Mainland, but scarce from the Central Interior southward into Washington. Look for it in bloom from mid-June to August, in damp woods rich in humus, swamps and bogs, rarely in dry forests.

Nature's peace will flow into you as sunshine flows into trees.

John Muir, (writing in praise of
solitary walks in the
unspoiled forest) 1898

HABENÀRIA SACCÀTA Greene. *Slender Bog-orchid.*

Saccata means *sac-like* or bag-like, which well describes the completely characteristic feature of the species. This is the swollen spur—inflated toward its upper end (which points downward), often purplish, and one-third to two-thirds as long as the lip.

Slender Bog-orchid is a tall (up to 3 feet) species, common over most of our area, though less so north of the Central Interior. Its range extends into Alaska, Alberta, and Washington. The stout stem bears sheathing lanceolate leaves that become slender and acute toward the top. The flowers are well-separated, and greenish, though the petals are often purple-tipped. The lip is strap-shaped and may be purplish-brown. The habitat of H. saccata is that of most members of the genus—in wet spots. This plant blooms from June to August.

HABENÀRIA UNALASCÉNSIS (Spreng.) S. Wats. *Slender-spire Orchid. Alaska Piperia.* [p.99]

The specific name refers to the northern source of the type, the plant being circumboreal. Curiously, it appears to be extremely rare in the Northern and Northeast Interior zones, though common in the Central Interior. It is also comparatively rare along the coast, and not common in the southern part of our range.

H. unalascensis is a highly variable species in colour, length of spur, and habitat, so that it must be considered perhaps the most difficult to identify of our rein-orchids.

The plant is usually 12-18 inches tall; however, in rich soil and moist locations it may reach 36 inches. Though found along streams and in the damp humus soil of coniferous forests, Alaska Piperia is perhaps most often seen in places which by midsummer have become very dry, e.g. on rock slopes of dried-up mosses, open slopes of withered grass, on sandy or gravel outwashes. The flowers are most often greenish, but not infrequently yellowish or whitish, and the scent is variable, or absent.

Apparently we have the problem of a more than usually flexible species. Calder and Taylor, whose painstaking studies covered much more material than was available to Correll in 1950, suggest 3 *subspecies*, in place of Correll's varieties. We do not propose a detailed distinction of the subspecies, but will limit ourselves to a general statement.

This species prefers comparatively low rainfall areas, e.g. the drier east coast of the Queen Charlottes and Vancouver Island, and the arid Southwest and Southeast Interior zones. Its predilection for sites that desiccate in late summer has already been mentioned. The 1-4 lanceolate leaves generally wither in July or August, before flowering time. The lip is broadly strap-shaped and fleshy, with 3 nerves. The spur varies from as long as the lip to more than twice as long (especially in the dry southeast corner of Vancouver Island). This long-spurred extreme is associated with a lovely vanilla-like perfume. Yet the Alaskan and Albertan form, according to Hultén and to Moss, has an "unpleasant" odour. Most of the plants of shorter spur in the Central, Southwest, and Southeast Interior are, in our experience, without detectable scent. A general characteristic is some degree of twisting of the flowers, giving a somewhat disarrayed or wind-blown appearance. In the whitish-flowered specimens the midnerves are green and rather conspicuous; such plants generally show a much more densely-flowered spike than the others.

This species may give some despair to the beginning student, but at least he will find it intriguing, and will probably examine most critically (especially for scent) the plants of each new locality.

HABENÀRIA VIRÍDIS (L.) R. Br. var. BRACTEÀTA. (Muhl. ex Willd.) A. Gray.
Bracted Rein-orchid.   [p.99]

Viridis refers to the *green* colour of the flowers. This is a variety of a widely distributed Eurasian species, distinguished by the conspicuous leaf-like *bracts* that are large enough to almost hide the small greenish flowers.

These bracts, and a detail of the lip make this species, while variable, an easy one to identify. Though the greenish (sometimes bronzed) flower is small, close examination reveals the distinctive lip. Quite unlike that of any other Habenaria of our area, the lip (instead of narrowing toward the tip) becomes much broader, ending in 2 (sometimes 3) pronounced teeth.

The Bracted Rein-orchid blooms from the end of May to August, in swamps, damp woods, along stream-banks and lakeshores. It is found across the northern part of the continent, in our area most commonly in the Central Interior and Southwest Interior. It is very rare in the coastal region near Vancouver and near Victoria.

LÍSTERA BOREÀLIS Morong. *Northern Twayblade.*

M. Lister (1638-1712) was an early English naturalist. Listera are tiny and very delicate plants, quite unlike most orchids. In fact, only the closest examination of the minute flowers reveals the lip and column characteristic of the family. Two thin leaves appear on opposite sides, about halfway up the thin stem, and the very small flowers are greenish or purplish. About two dozen species are found in frigid and temperate regions of the Northern Hemisphere.

This *boreal* or northern species occurs from Alaska along mountain spurs south and east into Alberta and Idaho, though it is apparently nowhere abundant, and has never been recorded from the Coast.

The smooth stem is slightly 4-sided, rarely as much as 8-9 inches high. Just above the middle of the stem is an opposite pair of rather large, thin, oval to elliptic leaves. The tiny flowers usually number less than 12, spaced in an open raceme. They are pale yellowish-green, with petals showing a darker midvein. The lip is disproportionately long, wider at the tip (which is shallowly notched) and with a distinctive pair of minute ear-like structures at its narrowed base.

This uncommon species demands very cold, acid soil, hence is found in a limited habitat of high sphagnum bogs, and the cool shaded coniferous forests of mountain slopes. Listera borealis blooms from May to July, according to the latitude.

74

ZYGADENUS ELEGANS   ✕⅖   [p.45]

ZYGADENUS VENENOSUS   ✕½   [p.46]

SISYRINCHIUM ANGUSTIFOLIUM   ✕¾   [p.52]

SISYRINCHIUM CALIFORNICUM   ✕½   [p.52]

SISYRINCHIUM DOUGLASII $\times 3\frac{1}{4}$ [p.53]

LÍSTERA CAURÌNA Piper. *Northwest Twayblade.* [p.91]

Caurina, *of the northwest wind*, suggests this plant's distribution. It is a seldom-noticed species of the Coast, with most records from the south Mainland and Vancouver Island, and only a few from the line of the Selkirk Range.

From 4-12 inches high, the stem above the opposite pair of ovate leaves is noticeably roughened by numerous small, hair-like glands. The open raceme consists of very small greenish or yellowish flowers. Most useful in distinguishing this species is the lip, which is rounded at the tip, and has near the base a pair of tiny, sharp-pointed "teeth".

The habitat of Northwest Twayblade is wet coniferous forests, and boggy mountain slopes. In areas like the Cruickshank Canyon of Vancouver Island, where this species occurs with the much more abundant *L. cordata* (which see), the plants are distinguishable at a glance. L. caurina is much more robust, generally about twice as tall, and with leaves 2-3 times as long.

LÍSTERA CONVALLARIOÌDES (Sw.) Nutt. *Broad-leaved Twayblade.*

The specific name means *like Convallaria* (i.e. the true Lily-of-the-valley), with reference to the broadly oval leaves. It is very like *L. caurina* (which see), but stouter, and with larger flowers (the lip about ½ inch long). The lip is distinctive, with 2 minimal notches at the tip, and 2 bluntly triangular teeth near the base. Broad-leaved Twayblade is chiefly a south Coastal plant, and occurs less commonly in suitable wet mossy woods of the southwest and southeast Interior.

LÍSTERA CORDÀTA (L.) R. Br. *Heart-leaved Twayblade.* [p.91]

Cordata refers to the *heart-shape* of the leaves, a characteristic which is really not very useful in recognizing any of the Twayblades. This species, however, is readily identified by the lip, which is quite unlike that of the other species. It is deeply split almost in two, forming a pair of pointed, slender lobes, and the teeth at the base resemble a pair of buffalo horns. Two colour forms are common, and we have frequently seen on southern Vancouver Island the greenish and the purplish forms growing a few feet apart.

As Dr. Szczawinski points out, the plant is often half-submerged in moss in the densely shaded forest-floor beneath hemlock and spruce. It is common in such cold damp habitats throughout our own and adjacent areas. The tiny flowers may be seen from May to July, but a close search is needed to find the inconspicuous plant.

Sir John Lubbock, speaking of the European *Listera ovata* (very like an enlarged L. cordata), nearly a century ago pointed out that plant's astonishing adaptation for securing adhesion of the pollen masses to the hairs of insect visitors: " . . . the pollen is friable and would not of itself adhere to insects, but . . . the moment the summit of the rostellum [beak-like projection of the column] is touched it expels a large drop of viscid fluid, which glues the pollen to the insect. . . . ." He remarks that a touch, "even for instance with a human hair, is sufficient to produce this remarkable phenomenon."

MALÁXIS MONOPHÝLLOS var. BRACHYPÒDA (A. Gray) Morris & Eames. *White Adder's-mouth.*

The Greek generic name, meaning *softening*, is of uncertain application, but possibly refers to the soft, spongy texture of the swollen bulb-like corm. "Adder's-mouth" possibly refers to the appearance of the flowers, but is far-fetched when applied to our local species. There are about 250 members of the genus, chiefly of the western hemisphere.

Monophyllos is the Greek equivalent of the Latin unifolia, both meaning *one-leaved*. Most of the plants have a single leaf 2-3 inches long, with a long sheathing-stem, but we have seen in a few herbarium specimens a second smaller leaf a little higher on the stem. In fact, Anderson states there is "usually a second leaf".

White Adder's-mouth is a rare and insignificant plant of damp cool woods, bogs, and dripping wet cliffs, with a few surprising records in the mud of tidal flats. The small greenish-white, or yellowish-green flowers are sparsely arranged at the top of 8-12 inch stems. The lip is broadly heart-shaped, with the basal lobes folded round the short fleshy column.

MALÁXIS PALUDÒSA (L.) Sw. *Bog Adder's-mouth.* Paludosa is, in literal Latin, *a portion of swamp*, and the plant might be considered a fragment of wet sphagnum bogs and muskegs. However, it is an excessively rare feature of these habitats—one of the scarcest orchids of North America. The only known area in which it is reasonably abundant is Red Mud Marsh near Sandspit, Queen Charlotte Islands (Calder and Taylor).

It is even smaller and less conspicuous than *M. monophyllos* (which see); in fact, the 2-5 small, stubby leaves (which clasp the lower part of the stem) may be partly—or entirely—hidden by sphagnum moss.

The small yellowish-green flowers are well spaced along a slender 2-8 inch stem. The lip is long and narrow, slightly tapering to a rounded tip.

Quite possibly both species of Malaxis are more abundant than the scanty records suggest, and more thorough investigation of suitable habitats may yield new sites.

78

IRIS SETOSA ssp. INTERIOR $\times \frac{7}{8}$ [p.49]

V. & I. AHIER

CYPRIPEDIUM PASSERINUM $\times \frac{1}{5}$ [p.65]

SISYRINCHIUM LITTORALE $\times 2$ [p.53]

CALYPSO BULBOSA ×2¼ [p.57]

ÓRCHIS ROTUNDIFÒLIA Banks. *One-leaf Orchis. Small Round-leaved Orchis.*
[p.102]

It is fitting that the name of the family, distinguished by so many lovely plants, should be represented in our area by a solitary species of exceptional beauty. Orchis is of Greek origin, and has reference to the thick fleshy root. The specific name means, of course, *round-leaved.* About 100 species are distributed in Europe, Asia, Africa, and sparingly in North America.

There is just one leaf, nearly round (though slightly egg-shaped) and as much as 4 inches long. It cradles, at ground level, the slender 8-12 inch stem. In a spaced raceme, 2-8 white (or occasionally pale purple) flowers hover like tiny butterflies. The most conspicuous feature of the ½ to ¾ inch flower is the prominent lip, which expands to a large rounded lobe. The lip is occasionally pure white, rarely marked by 2 broad reddish-purple stripes (var. LINEÀTA Mousley), but almost always conspicuously spotted with purple. The short stout column shelters 2 pale yellow lobes of the stamen, which effectively emphasize the purple of the spots on the lip.

During June or July, in moist cold forests, bogs or swamps, the wayfarer's heart may lift with the vision of a small cluster of these delicate flowers. This dainty plant occurs along the Alaska-Yukon boundary, in the southwest Interior from Quesnel to Kamloops, and in the southern Rockies.

There is a strong temptation to pick the flower. But this will destroy it, for the feeding roots are most delicately fixed among the humus and moss. Orchis rotundifolia is not abundant anywhere, so admire it—and leave it for others to enjoy.

Look thy last on all things lovely,
Every hour. Let no night
Seal thy sense in deathly slumber
*   Till to delight*
Thou have paid thy utmost blessing;
Since that all things thou wouldst praise
Beauty took from those who loved them
*   In other days.*

Walter de la Mare: Fare Well

SPIRÁNTHES ROMANZOFFIÀNA Cham. & Schlecht. *Hooded Ladies' Tresses.*
[p.103]

Spiranthes (speira, *a spiral,* and anthos, *a flower*) refers to the spiral arrangement of the small creamy-white flowers, at the top of a 6-18 inch stem. This is a large genus of about 300 speciès, found in every continent except Africa (and of course, Antarctica).

Nikolai Rumiantzev, Count Romanzoff (1754-1826) was a Russian patron of science, and Minister of State, who sent Kotzebue to Alaska. (His name is also honoured in the genus *Romanzoffia* of the *Hydrophyllaceae* family.) The small creamy flowers, arranged with great precision in 3 spiral ranks, may suggest the appearance of neatly braided hair, hence Ladies' Tresses. That early and great English botanist William Turner, in 1562 pungently described this plant, "The floures grew very thyck together as they were writhen about the stalcke."

Several firm linear leaves are basal, but smaller ones occur up the 6-18 inch stem, finally becoming leaf-like bracts, between each flower in the dense spike. The sepals and petals remain folded over the lip and short column. Few people know that the flower has a faint, though pleasant, scent.

This is a common little orchid over our area, except in the northeast Interior. Its range extends across Canada and south to California. It is a late bloomer, in August and September. Hooded Ladies' Tresses is found in a wide variety of habitats, including dry, short-grass meadows, dry woods, marshes, sandy and gravelly beaches, and stream-sides.

 **SALICÀCEAE.** *Willow Family.*

SÀLIX ÁRCTICA Pall. *Arctic Willow* [p.110]

This creeping dwarf willow has been chosen to represent the 3 dozen or more willow species occurring in our area. They are quite notoriously "difficult", so much so that only a few specialists profess to recognize the species. Most people will be able to distinguish a willow as a "pussy-willow", at least in spring. But identification of the bewildering number of species requires microscopic study of both staminate and pistillate catkins (borne on separate plants), mature fruits, and a large, representative collection of leaves. The final blow to the keen amateur is the discovery that species (even those not closely related) frequently hybridize.

The most interesting members of the genus Salix (the name is classical Latin) are the dwarf, almost creeping species, such as *S. arctica*, *S. barrattiana* Hook. (slightly taller), *S. cascadensis* Cockerell, *S. nivalis* Hook., *S. polaris ssp. pseudopolaris* (Wahl.) Flod., *S. reticulata* L., *S. stolonifera* Cov., and *S. vestita var. erecta* Anders.

S. arctica is representative of this group. It forms mats, usually 2-4 inches high, with variably elliptical leaves usually ½ to 1 inch long. These are generally woolly when young, but the hairs are ultimately lost. Margins of leaves are entire, or obscurely notched. Pistillate catkins are relatively large—often 2 inches long, or even more. The scales that early enclose and protect the flowers are dark-brown to black, with persistent long hairs.

This species is circumboreal, and so highly variable that many varietal names have been proposed.

82

GOODYERA OBLONGIFOLIA ×²/₅ [p.68]

EPIPACTIS HELLEBORINE ×½ [p.68]

CALYPSO BULBOSA FORMA ALBA ×⅞ [p.58]

83

CALYPSO BULBOSA (VARIANT) ×2 [p.57]

GOODYERA OBLONGIFOLIA (LEAF) ×1 [p.68]

CORALLORHIZA MACULATA ssp. MERTENSIANA ×1¾ [p.60]

🌿 MYRICÀCEAE. *Wax Myrtle Family. Bayberry Family.*

MYRÌCA CALIFÓRNICA Cham. *Western Wax Myrtle.*

The genus, of about 40 species distributed chiefly in the Northern Hemisphere, probably derives its name from the Greek myrizein or myrike, meaning *to perfume,* anciently applied to a sweet-scented shrub (which may have been the tamarisk). Bayberry, source of a wax used in scented candles, is probably the best-known member of the group.

This attractive and aromatic shrub is rare with us, and seldom reaches the proportions of a small tree, as it does in the more southerly range that is suggested by its specific name.

Though occurring only occasionally in bogs and thickets along the coast as far north as Tofino, this species has been cultivated in gardens, where it is valued for its compact shape and firm evergreen foliage.

The thick leaves are considerably larger than those of *Sweet Gale* (which see), and while young they are an unusual shade of green, due to a pronounced rusty pubescence. Even when mature, both black and yellow wax glands are persistent, especially on the lower leaf-surface. These mature leaves are pointed-elliptical, generally serrate, and 2-3 inches long. The handsome Myrica californica, unlike its much more abundant northern cousin, bears both staminate and pistillate catkins on the same branch. The present species is unmistakable in winter, since the characteristic foliage is evergreen.

MYRÌCA GÀLE L. *Sweet Gale.* [p.103]

The specific name is obscure, but may have been derived from the Latin galea, a *helmet,* originally of leather. If this is correct, the term is quite descriptive of the little, stacked, brown scales of the resinous catkins. These curious brown scales conceal the stamens, which appear before any leaves are evident.

Most of us will associate the unforgettable, aromatic scent of this ubiquitous shrub with the experience of pushing boat, or canoe, through the shallow-water shrubbery that so often fringes lakes or slow stretches of rivers. As the ice moves out, and the fishing season opens, the catkins of Sweet Gale (and of Red Alder) dispense clouds of yellow pollen.

Later the 1-2 inch oblanceolate leaves unfurl, resinous and fragrant from the bright-yellow wax glands. The leaves, unlike those of *M. californica* (which see), are deciduous. Close examination shows the more scaly pistillate catkins (of some branches) are only about half as long as the staminate catkins (of other branches). Both kinds exude quantities of the scented yellow wax.

BETULÀCEAE. *Birch Family.*

CÓRYLUS CORNÙTA Marsh. var. CALIFÓRNICA (DC.) Sharp. *Hazelnut.*   [p.103]

The specific name meaning *horned,* and the generic, from korys, *a helmet,* vividly describe the helmet-like calyx enwrapping the nut fruit.

Most people know this tall shrub with its large, doubly saw-toothed, somewhat hairy leaves, and fall crop of glossy-shelled nuts, each enclosed in a hairy green covering (the basal portion of the calyx-tube). But very few know the extraordinary female flowers, which usually appear in February, long before the leaves. The pistillate flowers look like small green buds with 1-4 flaming red stigmas, whose sticky surface is ready to catch the pollen from the numerous staminate catkins. (The pollen is wind-dispersed, since there are few insects abroad at this time of year.) These male catkins are borne on the same twigs as the pistillate flowers, and somewhat resemble small alder catkins. The yellow cloud of pollen, discharged when Corylus catkins are tapped, is the first reminder of the pollen clouds to be expected from a host of less "early-bird" plants some 4-7 months later.

Jays, Clark's Nutcrackers, and Crows vie with squirrels to harvest the crop of nuts, even before they become fully ripe, so that human searchers often seek in vain. The nuts, each in its camouflage of green covering, often grow in pairs, base to base. On southern Vancouver Island, however, the shrubs almost invariably bear single nuts.

The Hazelnut is widely distributed throughout our area, and indistinct variations of the species occur from Georgia to Alaska, from Vancouver Island to Newfoundland.

> . . . *To swell the gourd, and plump the hazel shells*
> *With a sweet kernel . . . .*

John Keats: To Autumn

URTICÀCEAE. *Nettle Family.*

PARIETÀRIA PENSYLVÁNICA Muhl. *Pellitory.*

The ancient Latin name derives from paries, *a wall,* since the plant is often found growing on walls. Pensylvanicus means *of Pennsylvania,* originally from the woods

Following page: CORALLORHIZA MACULATA ×2 [p.59]

CYPRIPEDIUM MONTANUM   ×⅞   [p.64]

HABENARIA DILATATA   ×½   [p.70]

where William Penn lived. By any name this is an insignificant annual plant, with a weak stem as much as 18 inches long, that sprawls among other plants. The 1-3 inch pointed-elliptical leaves are entire and variably hairy, the upper ones carrying in their axils clusters of minute greenish flowers. These have a 4-lobed brownish perianth (sometimes centring 4 stamens, sometimes a tufted stigma, and sometimes both—all in a single cluster). The downy hairs are non-stinging, unlike those of the closely related and better known Stinging Nettle, *Urtica dioica* (which see). Pellitory occurs in southeastern B.C.

URTÌCA DIOÍCA L. var. LYÁLLII (Wats.) C. L. Hitchc. *Stinging Nettle.*   [p.342]

The generic name will be considered apt by those who have had the misfortune to brush against the Nettle's stinging hairs, and who recognize the root uro, to *burn!* The specific name, meaning that male and female flowers are borne on different plants (*dioecious*), is less descriptive. Most of the plants occurring in our area are not dioecious, but monoecious, since they bear flowers of both sexes. Botanists regard speciation of the Nettles as a particularly baffling problem.

Who does not early come to know the Stinging Nettle? This hardy plant occurs throughout our area, particularly in areas formerly cultivated. We join numerous other experimenters in reporting that young plants in spring, when boiled, provide an excellent wilderness substitute for spinach. Later, the stems develop string-like fibres, which formerly provided one of the cordage materials of native tribes.

We shall not attempt to distinguish between numerous varietal names that have been proposed, chiefly on the basis of differences in shape of leaves. All are more than adequately provided with stinging hairs! These are hollow, and arise from a small gland filled with a liquid containing formic acid.

An accidental touch breaks off the tips of the hairs, after which pressure against the skin serves to force a thin stream from the capillary hair into one's flesh. Shortly thereafter, the affected part "burns"!

Archibald Menzies, the able naturalist with Captain Vancouver, writes in his journal in the entry for June 11, 1792: "... [we] stood in for a large Bay where we came to an anchor . . . about half a mile from the Shore . . . . [and upon landing, found] the scite of a very large Village now overgrown with a thick crop of Nettles & bushes . . . along the Beach . . . we found a delightful clear & level spot cropt with Grass & wild flowers. . . ."

Have we not also, in our time, remarked on the prevalence of Urtica dioica about old Indian villages, and—like Menzies—exclaimed in delight at those flower-sprinkled bits of short turf, so characteristic of the Gulf Islands?

 # LORANTHÀCEAE. *Mistletoe Family.*

ARCEUTHÒBIUM AMERICÀNUM Nutt. *Dwarf Mistletoe.*

There are perhaps 1,000 species of Mistletoes, the majority being tropical. These are aerial parasites with branch-like, persistent leaves, and root-like haustoria, which penetrate the bark of the host plant (in our area, always *conifers*). The sticky seeds are explosively propelled several feet from the greenish berries, so that a good proportion fasten to other branches of the same or adjacent trees.

The generic name is derived from the Greek arkeuthos, *juniper,* and bios, *life,* since some species are parasitic upon juniper.

The English name is interesting, its origin being as little-known as the word itself is familiar. The roots are the German mist (used here in the diminutive form: mistel), *dung,* and the Anglo-Saxon tán, a *twig.* The connotation is probably that the seed is deposited on twigs by birds, that eat the berries, and void the undigested seeds.

Our 3 species are distinguishable only with difficulty—by employing microscopic characteristics. However, some degree of speciation may be related to the particular conifer that serves as host.

Arceuthobium americanum is believed to limit its attack to a few species of pine trees, chiefly the Lodge-pole Pine, *Pinus contorta*

The plant looks like a tuft of greenish-yellow, leathery threads, interrupted by small greenish, or brownish knobs. The leaves are reduced to barely visible scales. The rather remarkable fruit is a small bluish-green oval, which explosively expels its single sticky seed. The mucilaginous coating of the seed enables it to stick to other branches, or possibly the feet or fur of squirrels, and birds, by which it is transported considerable distances.

An obviously alien plant of this description, on branches of Lodge-pole Pine, is almost certainly this species.

ARCEUTHÒBIUM CAMPYLOPÒDUM Engelm. *Common Mistletoe.* [p.110]

The specific name means *curved stock,* with reference to the short, leathery, much-branched stems. These are orange-yellow to olive-green or brown, and the fruits are yellow to green, oval, and ultimately about ¼ inch long.

This is probably the most abundant member of the genus, attacking true fir (*Abies*), larch, spruce, juniper, pine, and hemlock.

The inconspicuous plants may most easily be detected by looking for the characteristic swellings on the branchlets of the host tree, which are caused by the "feeding-roots"—more precisely, *haustoria*—of the parasite. There is also a tendency for

CYPRIPEDIUM CALCEOLUS var. PUBESCENS ×⅞ [p.61]

91

LISTERA CAURINA ×½ [p.76]

LISTERA CORDATA ×½ [p.76]

CORALLORHIZA STRIATA ×1¼ [p.60]

the leaves of affected trees to grow in dense clusters ("Witches'-brooms") which may be visible from a considerable distance.

ARCEUTHÒBIUM DOUGLÀSII Engelm. *Douglas Fir Mistletoe.*

This species is believed to limit its attack to the Douglas Fir, *Pseudotsuga menziesii* (=*douglasii* of some authors).

The plant very much resembles *A. americanum* (which see) but the tufted branchlets are shorter in the present species, and more bluish-green. A. douglasii is not widely distributed.

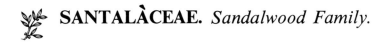 **SANTALÀCEAE.** *Sandalwood Family.*

COMÁNDRA LIVÌDA Richards. (possibly better named GEOCAÙLON LIVÌDUM (Richards) Fern.) *Red-fruited Bastard Toad-flax.* [p.110]

Greek kome, *hair*, and andros, *man*, are the roots of the name, thought to refer to the hairy bases of the stamens. The common name is puzzling, for (though there are fibres in the stems and spreading rhizomes) neither the flower nor plant, bears any resemblance to Flax (*Linum*, which see) or to Toad-flax (*Linaria*, which see). The plants are parasitic upon the roots of a variety of hosts, including *Arctostaphylos* and *Aster*.

Livida—though most will associate with "flushed" or "red"—in Latin means *bluish* or blue, probably referring to the greenish-purple calyx. There are no petals. The sepals are in the form of a shallow saucer (usually 5-lobed) that encloses a single pistil and 5 yellow stamens. Distinctive of Comandra, are the dense cobwebby bases of each stamen. This is a smaller plant (usually 4-9 inches tall) than *C. umbellata* (which see), and the flowers are chiefly solitary or few, carried in the axils of the narrowly elliptical leaves, and succeeded by bright orange-red, berry-like fruits. The thin, spreading rhizomes are reddish, and often parasitic upon other plants.

In our experience, this plant—not common—occurs in bogs, but also in moist open woods, from southern Alaska to about the latitude of Golden. Comandra livida blooms from May to August.

COMÁNDRA UMBELLÀTA (L.) Nutt. *Bastard Toad-flax.* [p.110]

Umbellata refers to the flattened clusters of pale-yellow flowers—though the arrangement is actually in cymes, rather than in *umbels*. This is a much commoner plant than *C. livida* (which see), somewhat taller, and found in drier habitats. The species varies in greyness of foliage and shape of flower, but may be readily identified (late in the year) by its harder, less pulpy fruit, which becomes blue to purplish. Another characteristic, useful in distinguishing the present species, is the much more deeply-dished (turbinate) calyx-cup, which is white to yellowish.

C. umbellata is found in wet to moist, but well-drained soils, throughout our area, though absent in the Queen Charlotte Islands, and uncommon on Vancouver Island.

We have admired at Karnak the so-called "Botanical Garden" of life-like reliefs of plants brought back by Thutmosis III (about 1465 B.C.) from his campaign in Syria. The ancient Egyptians' lively interest in the world of nature is also visible in the terraced temple of Queen Hatshepsut at Deir el-Bahari. There one can still see, portrayed with minute accuracy and obvious delight, the exotic plants (and animals) secured during the remarkable expedition to distant Punt, far-off on the east coast of Africa. In sad contrast to this early interest, many Canadians are unable to name even a dozen native plants.

 **ARISTOLOCHIÀCEAE.** *Birthwort Family.*

ASÁRUM CAUDÀTUM Lindl. *Wild Ginger.* [p.111]

The name of the genus comes from asaron, the old Greek name for one of the Old World species. These are curious and interesting plants. Some species (e.g., *A. marmorátum* with boldly mottled evergreen leaves, but native only in Washington, Oregon, and California) provide striking ground covers in gardens of Seattle, Vancouver, and Victoria.

Caudatum, from Latin cauda, a *tail*, obviously refers to the long tail-like tips of the 3 lobes of the calyx. This is the only member of the genus occurring in our area.

Because the leaves are close to the ground, and the flowers partly hidden by the humus and debris of the forest floor, this interesting plant is seldom noticed by the casual wayfarer. From a thick underground stem (rhizome) grow pairs of large, kidney-shaped, somewhat leathery leaves, whose long leaf-stalks are densely white-haired. Between the leaves, just at ground level, the very odd, rusty flowers appear. Their petals are represented by tiny scales, but the deep-cupped calyx of welded sepals is divided into 3 lobes, which are attenuated into whip-like tips, or tails, as much as 1½ inches long. Clustered in the yellowish, purple-striped bottom of the calyx-cup are 12 stamens, tightly grouped around a stubby pistil.

The calyx "flower" is a curious brownish-purple, a colour not seen by bees. From its position among the debris, one may assume the flower is pollinated by slugs, ants, millepedes, or small flies.

The whole plant has a faint odour of ginger (the ginger of commerce is the root of *Zingiber* sp., of tropical Asia), more pronounced when a rhizome is crushed.

Wild Ginger is found in moist shaded woods, from British Columbia into Washington west of the Cascades, and in northern Idaho. It has not been reported from the Queen Charlottes, but is quite common on Vancouver Island in suitable locations.

POLYGONÀCEAE. *Buckwheat Family.*

This large (and taxonomically difficult) family contains perhaps 800 species, chiefly of the North Temperate zone. Only a limited number of species will be covered in this book, for few except trained botanists will be interested enough, or sufficiently expert, to run down the names of the majority of these (often) weedy and inconspicuous plants.

The flowers are small and numerous, in densely crowded spikes (or cymes or racemes), usually greenish-white or pinkish. The flowers lack petals, but have 3 to 6 sepals. A characteristic, rather useful in recognizing members of this family, is the *sheath around the stem*, that is formed by the stipule at the base of each leaf.

Cultivated Buckwheat, Rhubarb, and the ubiquitous Silver-lace Vine (*Polygonum auberti*), are probably the best-known members of the family.

ERIÓGONUM. *Wild Buckwheat.*

The name of the genus comes from the Greek erion, *wool*, and gony, *knee* or joint. The stems of many species are divided into jointed segments, something like the stems of bamboo or other grasses, and in some of these there are woolly tufts of down at the joints; hence "woolly knees".

In this genus each of the young flowers is protected by a membranous sheath—often hairy—and usually notched into 3-10 teeth. The maturing flower is slowly pushed out of the sheath by a lengthening, slender stalk. The flower itself is also chaffy, forming a bell-shaped structure more or less completely notched into 6 segments, and enclosing 9 stamens. The whole is curiously "two-tiered".

Eriogonum is a genus of Western North America chiefly, where about 150 species have been described; of these, 8 or 9 have been reported from our area. For the most part they are plants of extremely dry habitat.

The Eriogonums are excellent bee-plants, whose nectar provides a much-admired honey.

> Every step taken into the fields, groves, and hills appears to afford new enjoyments. Landscapes and Plants jointly meet in your sight. Here is an old acquaintance seen again; there is a novelty, a rare plant, perhaps a new one . . . . When nothing new or rare appears, you commune with your mind and your God in lofty thoughts or dreams of happiness. Every pure botanist is a good man, a happy man, and a religious man.
>
> Constantine Samuel Rafinesque:
> New Flora of North America (1836)

ERIÓGONUM FLÁVUM Nutt.　[p.111]

Flavum means *yellow*; this may be pale to deep-yellow, with age sometimes becoming rose. E. flavum is an extremely variable species, with flower-stems rising 4-12 inches above a mat of grey leaves.

Typically, the leaves are at least 1¼ inches long, paddle-shaped, and densely white-haired—particularly beneath. The flowers are rank-smelling. A good 10X magnifier shows that the curious two-tiered flower (the lower involucre-cup and the upper perianth-cup) is entirely covered with fine hairs.

This common species is in bloom from early July to early September, in arid areas of southeast British Columbia.

ERIÓGONUM HERACLEOÌDES Nutt. *Umbrella Plant.*　[p.111]

The specific name means *like Heracleum*, i.e., the flattened flower-clusters are similar to those of *Heracleum lanatum* (which see), Cow Parsnip, a feature which is further emphasized in the common name.

The small cream-coloured flowers (ultimately becoming rosy) appear in compound umbels at the end of 6-16 inch stems. The leaves, forming a densely clustered mat, are silver-haired below but green above, varying from lance-shaped to linear.

The Umbrella Plant occurs on gravelly soil, from low-rainfall arid valleys to about 6000 feet on rocky ridges. In our area it is found in the Southwest and Southeast Interior zones, eastward through the Rockies into Alberta, and south into Idaho and Washington (east of the Cascades).

The open, compound umbel, and the taller stems carrying 1 or (usually) 2 whorls of stem-leaves, will sharply distinguish this species from *E. flavum* (which see).

ERIÓGONUM NIVÈUM Dougl.

Niveum refers to *snow* but the allusion is obscure, for the felted hairs covering the leaves and stems are greyish, and the flowers are not white but cream-coloured; it is not a particularly high-altitude plant, nor does it appear near snow-banks.

This is a "different-looking" Eriogonum, for instead of the usual showy umbel, the flowers are in very open cymes. The flowers appear to be haphazardly dotted, like cream-coloured buds, about the many-branched stem. The lower cup (involucre) is densely hairy and notched—apparently in two ranks—into 3 (or 4, rarely 5) teeth. The perianth-cup on its thin stalk has about 6 almost separate lobes, that are entirely without pubescence. The leaves are tufted, and variably shaped—but with stems or petioles from 1-3 times as long as the blades. They are felted with greyish hairs.

E. niveum is a plant of Sagebrush and Ponderosa Pine deserts of the Okanagan and Kootenay valleys, and southward into Washington (east of the Cascades). It may be found in bloom as late as September, or even October.

ERIÓGONUM OVALIFÒLIUM Nutt. *Oval-leaved Eriogonum.*

The *"oval-leaf"* may be broadly or narrowly ovate, on the end of a long or a short petiole, so that the leaf is not sufficiently characteristic to identify this highly variable species. Oval-leaved Eriogonum is a common and very widely distributed plant.

Commonly a plant of Sagebrush flats, it also extends upwards to alpine ridges even above timber line, in forms that become increasingly dwarfed and mat-like. Its extensive range includes the Kootenay Valley, southward on both sides of the Cascades, and into the Olympic Mountains.

A better recognition feature than the oval leaves (which may be densely silver-woolly to greenish) is the absence of leaves on the stem. Even the usual whorl of bract-like leaves immediately beneath the umbel of flowers, is lacking in this species.

The flowers are borne in a rather dense head at the top of a stem averaging perhaps 8 inches in height, occasionally 12 inches, but in alpine forms only 1½ inches. The chaffy flowers are cream to yellow, aging to pinkish or purplish. Close examination reveals that the involucral cup has 5 teeth (sometimes recurved) and that the 6 perianth-segments are cleft almost to the base, and are not at all hairy.

A very much more open inflorescence—due to *lengthened* flower-stalks—is characteristic of a plant sometimes known as E. STRÍCTUM Benth. Since plants intermediate in this and other respects are known, future study may consider these are only ecotypes of a single species. In any case, this must be considered taxonomically a very difficult species.

ERIÓGONUM UMBELLÀTUM Torr. *Sulphur Flower.* [p.114]

Umbellatum, as a specific name, calls attention to the freely-branched and open *umbel* of (usually) sulphur-yellow flowers. However, in the opinion of C. L. Hitchcock, "This is one of the most variable species in western N. Amer.," so that very few experts are able to recognize the numerous varieties for which names have been suggested. Of the 2 forms most often encountered in our area, the taller (to 12 inches) has broad basal leaves, and only 1 whorl of cauline leaves (immediately beneath the umbel), instead of 2. The flower colour is usually pale or deep yellow.

The second form is very much more dwarf, commonly less than 4 inches tall, with tighter umbels of cream or yellow, often becoming flecked with rose as they age.

A good hand-lens reveals that the involucre and perianth-cups are very like those of *E. ovalifolium* (which see), except that the rather long and round-tipped teeth of the involucral cup are almost invariably reflexed. The hairless perianth-lobes continue to elongate as the ovary develops, and may ultimately become ⅓ inch long. Leaves are usually greenish above (though occasionally somewhat woolly), and grey below (from a dense covering of hairs). But the shape of the leaves is so variable as to be of little or no use in identification of this "difficult" species.

Sulphur Flower occurs from the Cascades eastward, and from southern British Columbia southward, in dry Sagebrush habitats and up to considerable elevations.

OXÝRIA DÍGYNA (L.) Hill. *Mountain Sorrel.* [p.115]

The generic name comes from the Greek oxys, meaning *sour*, in allusion to the sharp-tasting leaves. Digyna means *two carpels* (pistil-cells).

This interesting plant, the only member of its genus, is found in Eurasia and North America (including the Arctic), in moist crevices of the mountains (to at least 12,000 feet). Mountain people value the leaves (not the root) as an antiscorbutic.

The smooth, slightly fleshy leaves, with their long petioles, are distinctive, being kidney-shaped to heart-shaped, often reddish (especially below). From the basal tuft of leaves, several stems (from 4-16 inches tall) carry crowded panicles of minute greenish flowers. These are soon succeeded by a cluster of conspicuous, reddish, broadly-winged, oval fruit, each about ⅜ inch long.

Mountain Sorrel occurs on all the mountains of our area, from Alaska south. The hiker, as he clambers over the rocks, well above timberline, readily recognizes Oxyria's cluster of broad leaves topped by panicles of reddish fruit, and perchance stops, to pluck and chew a leaf for its refreshingly sharp taste.

"If we preserved as parks only those places that have no economic possibilities, we would have no parks. And in the decades to come, it will not be only the buffalo and the trumpeter swan who need

98

SISYRINCHIUM DOUGLASII FORMA ALBA ×1
[p.53]

HABENARIA HYPERBOREA ×½ [p.70]

K. JOY

HABENARIA DILATATA var. LEUCOSTACHYS
(DETAIL) ×3 [p.70]

HABENARIA ORBICULATA ×¼ [p.71]

HABENARIA UNALASCENSIS   ×½   [p.72]

HABENARIA VIRIDIS var. BRACTEATA   ×¼ [p.73]

HABENARIA OBTUSATA   ×⅝   [p.71]

sanctuaries. Our own species is going to need them too. It needs them now."

Prof. Wallace Stegner,
from *The Marks of Human Passage* in *This Is Dinosaur,*
ed. Wallace Stegner (1955)

POLÝGONUM

The name means *many-joints* or *many-angles*, referring to the numerous joints in the stems. This large genus (about 150 species) occurs over most of the world, though more abundant in temperate regions. The species are chiefly pernicious weeds, and with few exceptions, can only be certainly identified by the botanist armed with a microscope. Few others will be interested in any but the most common, or the few showy species. Accordingly, only these will be discussed in this book.*

The leaves are usually lance-shaped, and jointed where the stipule joins the stem. The stipule wraps round the stem, forming *a sort of collar* (known as the "ocrea"), whose shape, margin, and hairiness provide important details for the identification of the species. The flowers are very small, with a perianth of undifferentiated sepals having 3-10 notches, and usually 8 stamens in two ranks of 4. There are no petals.

*For those who wish to identify others of the 25 species occurring in our area, the best reference is probably the scholarly work of Hitchcock, Cronquist, Ownbey, and Thompson, *Vascular Plants of the Pacific Northwest*, Part 2.

POLÝGONUM ACHÓREUM Blake. *Knotweed.*

The specific name, from achoris, *scurf* or dandruff, apparently refers to the overlapping scale-like leaves.

This is a very common species of dry, usually waste, ground. The prostrate stems, with characteristic "knots" or joints, form mats of oval bluish-green leaves, which are ½-1 inch long. In the axils of the leaves are found tiny flowers, with green sepals (narrowly edged with pink) forming a 5-lobed flared-mouth tube, that encloses 3 styles and 5-8 stamens.

P. achoreum occurs at low levels throughout our range, most commonly around settlements.

POLÝGONUM AMPHÍBIUM L. *Water Smartweed.* [p.115]

The specific name refers to the *amphibious* character of the plant, which has forms that are either flat-leaved and floating when growing in water, or vertical-leaved when growing on the margins of drying pools.

This perennial can be quite a striking plant in favourable wet habitats. The leaves are then large (6 inches long), oblong-lanceolate, and arranged alternately up the smooth stem. Thin wisps of roots commonly grow from the leaf-axils. The stem ends in a spike-like, tight panicle of dozens of small pinkish-red flowers. The colour is particularly conspicuous against the background of lush vegetation and blue water. Each flower has a 5-cleft perianth, and 8 stamens arranged around 2 styles.

Water Smartweed occurs in every continent save Australia, and is abundant in suitable habitats throughout lower levels of our area. The fresh pink flowers may be seen from June to September.

POLÝGONUM AVICULÀRE L. *Common Knotweed. Doorweed.*

This is a ubiquitous weed around the world, growing on very hard parched or waste soil. It is very similar to *P. achoreum* (which see), but with longer joints between the conspicuous "knots", and longer, more slender leaves. The tiny green flowers have calyx-lobes edged with white, pink, or red margins.

POLÝGONUM BISTORTOÌDES Pursh. *Mountain-meadow Knotweed. Bistort.* [p.122]

The specific name means *resembling bistorta,* a related species of the Great Plains. Bis, *twice,* and tortus, *crooked* or twisted, refer to the angularities of the stem occurring at each knot or joint. The seeds of this plant germinate while still attached to the parent stem. In due time the wind whisks the little, tailed seed-plants away, ready to set up housekeeping immediately upon reaching their new homes.

Among the grasses and flowers of alpine meadows the slender swaying plant holds up its white (or slightly pinkish) plumy cluster of small flowers. The leaves are narrow and tapered; the basal ones have long stipules; the uppermost stem ones are smaller, and stemless. The 12-24 inch flower-stems are jointed below each leaf-stipule, a characteristic of the genus. The roots are thick and knotted (whence one of the common names). These starchy roots formed an important source of food for the Eskimo, the Cheyenne and the Blackfoot, and are still sought by bears and rodents. Since the plant is widespread, and easily detected, the hiker should take note that the root, when roasted over the ashes of a campfire, is both nutritious and nut-like in taste.

SPIRANTHES ROMANZOFFIANA $\times^3/_5$ [p.80]

CORYLUS CORNUTA var. CALIFORNICA $\times 1^3/_4$
[p.85]

MYRICA GALE $\times^3/_4$ [p.84]

RUMEX ACETOSELLA $\times^1/_2$ [p.106]

Bistort's white spikes abundantly punctuate the lush assortment of flowers that follow fast upon the heels of melting snow and soon carpet the alpine meadows. It occurs in Europe, and over much of western North America (including our area from southern Alaska into Washington, in the mountains). P. bistortoides blooms from May to September.

POLÝGONUM COCCINÈUM Mühl. *Pink Knotweed.*

The specific name means *pink*. This is very similar to *P. amphibium*, (which see) but the stems are covered with short stiff hairs, and carry stem-leaves right up to the flower-spikes. The spikes are more open and longer. Pink Knotweed occurs around the margins of drying pools, commonly at low altitudes.

POLÝGONUM CONVÓLVULUS L. *Bindweed.*

The specific name directs attention both to the *convolvulus-like*, oval, arrowhead leaves, and also to the trailing or climbing habit. Almost everyone will know this weed of cultivated or waste ground. An immigrant from Europe, it is found in our area wherever settlements occur. The pale-greenish, insignificant flowers occur in the leaf-axils, as well as in small terminal racemes. The leaf shape is characteristic, and the best recognition feature.

POLÝGONUM PARONÝCHIA Cham. & Schlecht. *Beach Knotweed.* [p.115]

This is a low, shrubby, brown-stemmed plant of the seacoast, growing in gravel and sand. The firm linear leaves are often tightly rolled, to conserve moisture. White, pink-flushed flowers are clustered in the upper axils, and do not form a recognizable raceme. They are about ⅛ inch across, with a 5-notched perianth, each lobe marked with a dark centre vein. There are 8 stamens and a 3-cleft style.

Polygonum paronychia is a distinctive and interesting native member of a tedious genus that consists largely of introduced weedy plants.

The specific name means a *whitlow*, a flaw or sore at the quick of the finger nail, for which a poultice of this plant was believed efficacious. Indeed, in every culture, ancient and modern—plants have been thoroughly investigated for possible remedial values. The Chinese in very ancient times made botanical studies of a practical nature. Fragments have survived of early copies of the *Shên-nung pên ts' ao ching*, the classical herbal of Shên-nung, who reigned about 2700 B.C. This was apparently a treatise on medicinal plants. During the Dark Ages, when learning was all but extinguished in Europe, numerous local floras of impressive quality were written in China.

POLÝGONUM PERSICÀRIA L. *Lady's Thumb.*

The specific name calls attention to the leaf-shape, like that of the *peach (Prunus persica)*. These elliptic-lanceolate leaves are distinguished by a purplish, somewhat triangular mark near mid-leaf. Fancifully, this is the imprint of [Our] "lady's thumb". The branching stems grow to 3 feet, and are characterized by a fringe of bristles on the upper part of each of the "knots" in the stem. The flowers are crowded in a tight terminal cluster, and are usually pinkish-tinged.

This is yet another weedy introduction from Europe, found mostly in moist semi-waste areas, or those formerly cultivated.

POLÝGONUM SPERGULARIAEFÓRME Meisn. *Fall Knotweed.*

The specific name—of somewhat intimidating length!—means *like spergularia* (see *Spergularia rubra*).

This rather pretty species is the more welcome as it is very late-flowering, providing a touch of colour on dried-out rocky slopes, even into November and December.

The stems are very slender, somewhat sprawling, and punctuated with slim linear leaves. In cross section, the stems are not round, but sharply-angled. Though the flowers are very small, they provide bright accents. The perianth-segments are pink, with a conspicuous green mid-nerve, useful in recognition.

Fall Knotweed occurs from Vancouver Island to the Columbia River, and southward.

POLÝGONUM VIVIPÀRUM L. *Alpine Bistort.*

This 6-12 inch plant of cold lake margins, at high altitudes, is readily recognized by its numerous pinkish bulblets, which are clustered in the axils of the stem-leaves. These are dislodged by the wind, and roll to establish new plants. Hence the specific name, meaning *to bring forth live young.* The loose-clustered flowers are white, often pinkish, with long fuzzy-appearing stamens. This is a rather pretty plant.

Polygonum viviparum occurs in suitable habitats throughout our area. The thick rootstock—said to taste like almonds—is eaten in Siberia.

RÙMEX. *Dock. Sorrel.*

This is the ancient Latin name, used by Pliny for some members of the Dock tribe. There are about 125 species, chiefly of the temperate regions, many being very pernicious weeds that set enormous quantities of seeds. In the case of Sorrel, the increase is further aided by the wide-running, thread-like, yellow roots. Ten or eleven species occur in our area.

Most will be only too familiar with these ubiquitous plants—their large coarse leaves, and brownish seeds borne in long spike-like panicles. A good hand lens reveals that the tiny greenish or reddish flowers have their parts in 3's (rarely in 2's), i.e., an inner and an outer ring, each of 3 perianth-segments. In many species (generally bigger plants known as Docks), the flowers are perfect, and have both stamens and a pistil (with a 3-lobed stigma), but in some species (such as the smaller-growing Sorrels), the stamen- and pistil-bearing flowers are on different plants or on different parts of one plant. (The plants are then said to be dioecious).

Provided one has at least a 10X magnifying glass to examine the ripe fruits of the plants of this genus, identification is usually not too difficult. The leaf-shape is often helpful, but is not sufficient for accurate recognition of the species. The difficulties encountered are due to the occasional hybridization of two species. No less than 13 species have been reported in British Columbia, but we shall mention only 4.

During the Middle Ages poultices made from boiled Docks, as well as the concentrated liquid in which Docks had been boiled, were considered sovereign remedies for burns, and even for wounds. Paracelsus (1493-1541), like most of his contemporaries, thought that a beneficent Deity had provided remedies for all the ills that afflict man. But he was unique in deprecating the use of foreign medicinal herbs—since he believed that in a country where a disease arises, there nature provides a remedy. As an illustration of this principle, he pointed out that Docks invariably are found near Stinging Nettles!

RÙMEX ACETÒSA L. *Garden Sorrel.*

The specific name, meaning *acid-tasting*, suggests the reason for cultivation of this plant in some European gardens. In our area, it occurs sporadically in disturbed ground.

This species and the next are distinguished from our other members of the Dock tribe, since these alone are dioecious (see *Rumex*). Among the much more numerous staminate flowers of the long slender panicles, you will see occasional "different" flowers, which on close inspection show a number of whitish thread-like stigmas, but no stamens. The plants are 1-2 feet high with rather succulent leaves, mostly in a basal rosette. The leaves are arrowhead shaped (cf. the halberd shape of the much smaller leaves of the next species).

RÙMEX ACETOSÉLLA L. *Common Sorrel. Sour Grass.* [p.103]

This is the ubiquitous garden-weed, whose long yellow rootstocks penetrate every crevice and pocket of soil in the rockery, and in short order infiltrate the garden flower-beds. Common Sorrel is too well-known to require detailed description. The smooth, sour-tasting leaves are variably lanceolate with spreading "barbs" or lobes like mediaeval halberds. The panicle of reddish, imperfect flowers is not unattractive.

RÙMEX MARÍTIMUS L. *Golden Dock.* [p.115]

This is again a Eurasian import, now very common in wet places all over the continent. Fortunately it has not made itself at home in the mountains, but it is not limited (as the specific name suggests) to *marine* shores. The popular name is due to the over-all yellow-green aspect of the plant, which makes it stand out—even at a distance—or when growing with others of the tall species of Rumex.*

This sturdy weed is annual or biennial, usually 2-3 feet tall. The big lanceolate leaves alternate up the stems, their petioles (usually less than half as long as the blades) clasping the stem by means of the curious sheaths, that are so characteristic of this family. A field characteristic, useful in recognition of the species, is that the yellow clusters of flowers often extend from the top downward, for more than half the height of the plant. With a good magnifying glass, the details of the oddly-sculptured seeds can be studied. (These are of great assistance in distinguishing the numerous species.) Seeds of R. maritimus are notable for very long bristly spines.

RUMEX OCCIDENTÀLIS Wats., Western Dock, is often a striking plant, since leaves, stem, and especially the fruit, turn rosy-red as the summer advances. The fruit has broad net-veined valves, and completely lacks the spines of *R. maritimus* (which see). The flower-panicle is confined to the upper part of the plants, which is more slender, erect, and seldom branched. Western Dock is common in marshes and—to a lesser extent—in summer-drying meadows, from sea level to low altitudes throughout the Province.

*The interested reader is referred to the scholarly and exhaustive treatment of the genus in Part 2 of *Vascular Plants of the Pacific Northwest*, by Hitchcock, Cronquist, Ownbey, and Thompson.

CHENOPODIÀCEAE. *Goosefoot Family.*

Like the preceding family, the *Polygonaceae*, this one contains few showy plants. Nor are the 1400 species readily recognized. Generally they are plants of dry or alkaline, or marine areas, with numerous greenish flowers so small that a magnifying glass is needed to discover that they usually have 5 small, united sepals, no petals, 5 (or sometimes 1 or 2) stamens, and 2 or 3 styles.

Perhaps recognition of the plant family is made easier if one knows a few representative members, e.g. (typically) Lamb's Quarters (a *Chenopodium*, which see), cultivated spinach, familiar beet, and the fleshy *Suaeda* and *Salicornia* of our seacoasts. Only a few of the species are treated in this book.

The name is literally translated in Goosefoot, for chen is Greek for *goose*, and pous means *foot*.

ÀTRIPLEX PÀTULA L. var. OBTÙSA (Cham.) C. L. Hitchc. *Common Orache.* [p.122]

Atriplex is often confused with *Chenopodium* (which see). However, the flowers of Atriplex are monoecious in most of the species, and the female ones are enclosed by 2 bracts, while in *Chenopodium* the flowers are perfect and bractless. Perhaps the plants are most readily distinguished by their fruits: *Chenopodium* (in our species) form small round nubs, each in a shallow cup of 5 tiny sepals, but the Atriplex species of our area enclose the fruit in 2 triangular bracts. These bracts become much larger and more obvious than the Goosefoot fruits, and give the plants a distinctively interrupted appearance (as the male flowers shrivel). But both genera are notable for very small and drab green flowers, and are only included in this volume to show common and representative species.

The origin of the name is obscure, apparently being derived from ater, *black*, and plecto, *to braid*—possibly descriptive of the dark, congested flower-clusters.

The specific name is from patulus, meaning *extended* or wide-spreading, and referring to the much-branched nature of the plant. Orach or Oradhe is apparently a very old name, probably of Arabic origin—for the plants have been cultivated in Asia and Africa since remote times.

This is a highly variable weed with us—widely distributed in bare and poor ground, both inland and by the sea. The numerous branches of Common Orache may reach 2 feet. Leaves above are lanceolate, toothed, and alternate; but larger, more triangular, and opposite leaves occur below. These lower leaves are 2-3 inches long, with a few large irregular teeth that point forward. Green, inconspicuous flowers cluster in open, leafy spikes, both terminal and in the axils of the leaves. The staminate flowers have a 5-notched perianth, but the pistillate flowers, usually found lower in the spikes, have no perianth. The female flower is readily distinguished from the perfect flower of the Goosefoot by the presence of 2 lanceolate to broadly-ovate bracts, which may become

⅜ inch long, and are then conspicuous. Besides the variability in shape just mentioned, the surface of these bracts ranges from smooth to warty.

This plant is usually limited to saline or alkaline soils, and is common or weedy in Europe, and throughout temperate—and even arctic—North America. Like most of the 100 or so species of the genus, Atriplex patula survives in very dry areas, where it is browsed by domestic and wild animals.

CHENOPÒDIUM ÁLBUM L. *Lamb's Quarters. White Goosefoot.*

Greek chen, a *goose*, and pous, a *foot*, suggest a rather fanciful resemblance of the leaf-shape. Album is one of the Latin words for *white*, directing attention to the white meal of powdery scales, noticeable on the under side of the leaves. The leaf-shape may more readily suggest to some the shape of a leg of mutton. However, the leaves are quite variable—from rhombic to lanceolate in general outline, and either dentate or rather deeply lobed. In any case, the young plants provide, as we have verified, an acceptable cooked "spinach" to accompany the roast.

This is a common weed on disturbed or waste ground. The flowers, as in almost every member of this genus, are very inconspicuous; indeed they resemble nothing so much as a dense cluster of grey-green aphides! Even a 10X magnifying glass reveals few details, though with labour one can make out a fleshy perianth (deeply cleft into 5, 4, or 3 lobes) that tightly encloses a few stamens and a pistil with 2 or 3 styles.

Recognition of the 12 species of Chenopodium reported from our area is of interest only to a few specialists, so we shall not discuss them further except to mention that C. LEPTOPHÝLLUM (Moq.) Wats. is a desert species of the east side of the Cascades, C. RÙBRUM L. favours moist saline soils, and C. CAPITÀTUM (L.) Aschers. (Strawberry Blite) is a widespread immigrant from Eurasia—the only easily recognized species, because of its bright-crimson, rounded flower-masses.   [p.123]

Viability of seeds over protracted periods of time was investigated by Dr. W. J. Beal, of East Lansing, Michigan, in a series of experiments commenced in 1879. After 80 years in sealed bottles buried 18 inches below the ground, seeds of 3 out of 20 species were still capable of germination. One of the popular magazines a few years ago contained an illustrated article relating the germination of seeds of a pink-flowered Indian Lotus, that were determined by radiocarbon dating to be 1000 years old. In 1965 a Danish bog yielded seeds of *Chenopodium album*, and of *Spergula arvensis*. They were archaeologically dated at about A.D. 200, but germinated—to produce plants that proved identical with those of the same species growing today, in Denmark as in British Columbia. (Such evidence shows that plants as we know them have not changed significantly after many hundreds of generations.)

110

SALIX ARCTICA ×1 [p.81]

ARCEUTHOBIUM CAMPYLOPODUM ×¾ [p.89]

COMANDRA LIVIDA (FRUIT) ×½ [p.92]

T. & S. ARMSTRONG

COMANDRA UMBELLATA ×2 [p.93]

ERIOGONUM FLAVUM ×¼ [p.95]

ERIOGONUM HERACLEIODES ×¼ [p.95]

ASARUM CAUDATUM ×¾ [p.93]

111

SALICÓRNIA PACIFÍCA Standl. *Glasswort. Samphire.* [p.123]

The generic name is derived from sal, *salt,* plus cornu, a *horn,* from the habitat (salty marshes) and the appearance (the succulent branches stand up like stubby horns). The present species, a perennial, is abundant along the whole Pacific coastline. (Linnaeus' name, *S. virginica,* refers to an *annual* species of the east coast.)

This very familiar plant covers thousands of acres of saline mud-flats with its dense growth of 4-12 inch, soft, jointed, almost gelatinous fingers. The flowers are nearly invisible, being tiny, yellowish, and sunken in groups of 3, just above the pairs of tiny bracts that serve as leaves.

An annual species (S. EUROPÀEA L.) is very similar in appearance (though erect rather than matted), and also occurs in the same tidal flats. In addition, around alkaline

[p.563]

sloughs of the Interior, occurs another annual (S. RÙBRA A. Nels.) that is bright red.

Wort is a common Middle English word (often used as a terminal) meaning *plant* or herb; and the aptness of the prefix will be apparent to those who have noticed the peculiar translucent, glassy appearance of the massed plants, when freezing weather comes. Samphire is the "samphire" of King Lear (IV.6.15), that is, the Herbe de Saint Pierre, from sanctus, *holy,* and Petrum, *Peter.*

By any name Salicornia is relished by Geese—both Black Brant and the Honkers. In mediaeval times the plants were sometimes salted or pickled. A woodcut portraying "KALLI" appears in *De plantis aegypti* of 1592, by the Venetian Prosperi Alpini. The cut is excellent, and sufficiently detailed to recognize a species of Salicornia.

SALSÒLA KÁLI L. var. TENUIFÒLIA Tausch. *Tumbleweed. Russian Thistle.* [p.122]

Salsus, *salty,* may refer to the taste of some species, or more probably to the habitat, i.e., in alkali flats. Kali is an Arabic word for *potash,* again referring to the salty sloughs in which these plants often occur. McCowan reports that a tagged plant of this species was recovered 18 miles distant from its origin—and one may shudder to think of the number of seeds dropped by this tumbling traveller. More often the round bushes, detached from their roots, roll with the wind until caught by barbed-wire fences.

The Tumbleweed is common on drier soils of the arid southern Interior.* The many-branched stems—often reddish—grow to 4 feet in favourable circumstances, forming an almost globular bush-like plant. The leaves are alternate, ½-2 inches long, and tipped with a sharp point. Tiny green flowers occupy a depression at the base of each leaf, and are further guarded by a pair of spiny bracts. Each flower has 5 papery sepals, and produces one seed only. A large plant produces an enormous number of seeds, which are dispersed when the dried-up plant breaks away from its roots, and rolls away across the land.

This is a most unfortunate Eurasian import (introduced into South Dakota in 1877, in a consignment of flax from Europe).

*Rather surprisingly, there are a few records from southern Vancouver Island.

SUAÈDA MARÍTIMA (L.) Dumort. *Sea Blite.*   [p.122]

About 50 species, chiefly of seashore or alkaline soils, have been attributed to this genus, the name having been derived from the Arabic suwayd, for a desert species. The specific name obviously calls attention to the *maritime* occurrence of the plant, since it is found along the upper edges of tidal flats, of both the Atlantic and Pacific coasts of North America, North Africa, and Europe. Blite is Middle English (from the Latin blitum and the Greek bliton), and is applied to several herbs, probably of the present family.

Sea Blite is an insignificant and common annual, often occurring with *Salicornia* (which see). The plants are depressed to ascending; the thin leafy branches rise 6-12 inches. The leaves are smooth and linear, ½-1 inch long, fleshy, and slightly cupped. Drab, yellowish-green, tiny flowers are almost hidden in the axils of the leaves. Very little is known about the pollination of maritime plants such as this, so it would be interesting to study the subject.

In alkaline soils of the Dry Interior, a related species, S. DEPRÉSSA (Pursh) Wats. is found, scarcely distinguishable by the dilated bases (especially of the uppermost leaves).

AMARANTHÀCEAE. *Amaranth Family.*

AMARÁNTHUS RETROFLÉXUS L. *Pigweed.*   [p.123]

This is a family of about 250 species, chiefly tropical, very few of which are of any interest. The Cockscomb, *Celosia,* is the only member of the family at all familiar to gardeners.

The flowers are small and greenish, crowded in dense racemes, lacking petals, and variously provided with 0-5 stamens, and/or pistils. In short, the family is a rag-bag of unattractive, often weedy, plants.

In fact, the most interesting thing about the family is its name, and the unnatural history attached to it in ancient times. The name is from the Greek, a–, *not,* plus marainein, *to wither,* since the papery bracts persist after drying (though the stems and leaves collapse almost at once after picking).

> *Immortal Amarant, a Flour which once*
> *In Paradise, fast by the Tree of Life*
> *Began to bloom, but soon for man's offence*
> *To Heav'n removed where first it grew, there grows,*
> *And flours aloft shading the Fount of Life . . . .*

John Milton: Paradise Lost, Book III

Following page: ERIOGONUM UMBELLATUM ×1 [p.97]

OXYRIA DIGYNA ×⅕ [p.97]

POLYGONUM PARONYCHIA ×½ [p.104]

POLYGONUM AMPHIBIUM ×¼ [p.101]

RUMEX MARITIMUS ×⅓ [p.107]

115

The sonorous verse, the classical learning, are above reproach—but Milton was not botanist enough to expose the ancient sham.

Amarantus means *never-fading*. Those who know the insignificant green-flowered members of the genus, that are native to our area, as well as the more barbaric-hued *A. caudatus* of old-fashioned gardens, will recall that these plants wilt perhaps more readily than most, and will read Pliny (killed during the destruction of Pompeii and Herculaneum in A.D. 79) as more unnatural history: "There is no doubt that all the efforts of art are surpassed by the amaranth, which is, to speak correctly, rather a purple spike than a flower, and, at the same time, quite inodorous. It is a marvellous feature of this plant that it takes delight in being gathered; indeed, the more it is plucked, the better it grows.... The finest of all is the Amarantus of Alexandria, which is generally gathered for keeping; for it is a really marvellous fact, that when all other flowers have gone out, the Amarantus, upon being dipped in water, comes to life again...."

This is a stout annual weed, with root and lower stem frequently reddish. The dense racemes are chiefly terminal, sometimes axillary, and consist of dozens of small, dry, chaffy, greenish flowers, interspersed with glistening bristle-like bracts. The leaves are harshly hairy (especially below and along the veins), ovate to lanceolate, and ⅓ inch long. Pistillate and staminate flowers are borne on separate plants.

AMARÁNTHUS ÁLBUS L., *White Pigweed*, has thin *whitish* stems, with smaller, hairless, more rounded leaves, and a sprawling habit. Its flowers are entirely axillary.

The unattractive Amaranths are only included here because they have become so common and widespread, both on waste and cultivated land.

NYCTAGINÀCEAE. *Four-o'Clock Family.*

ABRÒNIA LATIFÒLIA Eschsch. *Yellow Sand Verbena.* [p.126]

Of about 25 genera occurring chiefly in the tropics or subtropics, only 1 is represented in our area. Members of this family lack petals, but in many the calyx is brightly coloured, and easily mistaken for a corolla. An interesting feature is the presence in the surface cells of the leaves, of plant crystals (raphides) which are usually visible with a 10X hand-lens.

Most gardeners will recognize the common name of the family in the Four-o'Clock (*Mirabilis species*, also called Marvel of Peru) but the most spectacular member is the *Bougainvillea*.

The generic name—from abros, *delicate* or slender—is scarcely appropriate for the sturdy species of our area, which spread their heavy stems over the sand of sea-beaches and dunes.

About 30 species have been described, chiefly from the deserts of southwestern North America. Two of these occur in our area.

The showy yellow flowers resemble those of the garden *Verbena* (of the *Verbenaceae* Family).

The Yellow Sand Verbena is a perennial, spreading its prostrate stems (of a somewhat rubbery texture) over the sand of salt-dunes as much as 3 feet in every direction. Both stems and fleshy, paired, oval *broad leaves*, are covered with sticky glandular hairs, which effectively anchor the plant by holding grains of sand, weighing as much as the plant itself. This is an interesting adaptation to its windy and insecure environment.

Cupped within 5 oval bracts, the attractive flowers, in a crowded umbel, are each rather less than ½-inch long, with a greenish-yellow tube, and brilliant, clear yellow (fading slightly orange) flared mouth that is divided into 5 lobes. The fragrance is entrancing—perhaps as sweet as that of any wild flower of our area. Those who know this plant will forever associate its unique perfume with the tang of the salt sea air.

Limited to the few yards above high tide, on sand beaches from the Queen Charlottes to California, the colourful flowers of Abronia latifolia may be encountered from June to September.

And because the breath of flowers is far sweeter in the air (where it
comes and goes, like the warbling of music) than in the hand,
therefore nothing is more fit for that delight than to know what be
the flowers and plants that do best perfume the air.

Francis Bacon: Essays: Of Gardens (1603)

ABRÒNIA UMBELLÀTA Lam. *Pink Sand Verbena.*

This was the first plant of the western coast of North America to come to the attention of the European world. The seed was collected and sent to France about 1786 by Collignon, gardener-botanist to the ill-fated la Pérouse expedition.

The specific name refers to the *clustered* terminal head of reddish-purple flowers, though the epithet is of course equally applicable to the slightly larger yellow flower-clusters of *A. latifolia* (which see). In the present species the perianth-tube (greenish with a pink flush) expands to the 5-notched flared mouth of distinct purple.

When not in flower, A. umbellata can be distinguished from *A. latifolia* by the inequality of its paired leaves, and by the pointed bracts which appear below the fruit-cluster. The seeds are very much more broadly-winged, and must have aroused much interest when first seen in France, for they are quite distinctive and unusual. The central portion is minutely hairy, but the 4-5 membranous wings, radiating from the centre, are smooth.

This second member of the genus is also a sprawling sticky-haired plant of coastal sand-dunes, with much the same—though rather more southerly—range as its congener. In our area Pink Sand Verbena is a rare plant, and the hiker along the sandy parts of our coastline should be on the alert to report any new occurrence. It has unfortunately vanished from a number of too popular sites.

🌿 PORTULACÀCEAE. *Purslane Family.*

The familiar *Portulaca grandiflora* (originally from Brazil, 1582) of sun-rich parts of our gardens, is the best-known member of this family, which contains many attractive plants of temperate zones around the world. Perhaps as many as 400 species in 16 genera are recognized, whose epicentre is undoubtedly the northwestern states of the United States. Those familiar with British plants will remember this as a very minor family limited to 3 members (all probably introduced); they will be quite unprepared for the numerous representatives that occur in such North American genera as *Lewisia, Montia, Claytonia,* and *Talinum.*

The name Porcillaca was used by Pliny nineteen hundred years ago, and is derived apparently from the Latin porto, to *bear,* and lac, juice or *sap,* since the leaves of most species are thickened and turgid with cell-sap. Purslane is the Middle English translation of the Latin name, and often appears, e.g. in Richard Hakluyt's *Voyages,* 1599 (vol. II, pt. 2, p. 109).

The family characteristics include: simple leaves (usually entire and fleshy) and regular flowers, commonly with 2 sepals and 5 petals (occasionally 2-15 or even 0). Many of the species of Portulacaceae are very showy.

CALANDRÍNIA CILIÀTA (R. & P.) DC. var. MENZIÈSII (Hook.) Macbr. *Red Maids.*
[p.126]

Of almost 100 species, chiefly found in South America, we have in our area but one charming—if diminutive—species to honour the name of Calandrini, an 18th century Swiss botanist. The specific name calls attention to the *cilia* (or hairs) found on the two unequal sepals and on the pointed leaves.

Red Maids brightens the short turf along the coast of southern B.C., and less commonly is found eastward to the Cascades, in rocky areas where the shallow soil holds spring moisture, but later dries up. In poor, impoverished ground, tiny plants may lift a single small, rose bloom only an inch above the surface, but in richer and heavier soil the succulent stems sprawl 6-8 inches through the short grass, and a flower almost ¾ inch wide appears in the axil of each of the uppermost leaves. These leaves are fleshy, entire, and lanceolate. A useful recognition feature is the increasing length of the petioles as the leaves alternate downward, until the basal leaves have petioles three times as long as the blades. The petals usually number 5—sometimes 3-7—and very occasionally are pure white. There are 5-12 stamens, with rather broad filaments, and the pistil-tip is cleft into 3 stigmas.

This is a charming little plant, to be seen in bloom from April to as late as June in some locations. Its modest charms are best appreciated from a kneeling position, appropriate in the presence of the divine handiwork represented in these small jewels.

CLAYTÒNIA LANCEOLÀTA Pursh. *Spring Beauty.* [p.123]

Spring is a relative term, for at elevations of 6000-7000 feet these modest beauties may not appear until late in July. On one occasion we saw an entire slope white with their blooms, in late August. The generic name honours John Clayton, born in 1685, a botanist who made early collections in Virginia. The specific name, as can readily be inferred, relates to the succulent, almost fleshy leaves, which are ovate to narrowly *lanceolate.*

These attractive plants grow from a small white edible corm, and may be 2-6 inches tall. (At very high altitudes they are dwarfed, and there may be only 2 of the smooth, slender leaves, whose long petioles are almost entirely below the surface of the ground. Here, on soggy slopes just emerged from the snow, the fresh green shoots point the way to buried treasure—a fact known to the grizzly bear, whose corm-digging is sometimes evident.)

The few to several ¾-1 inch flowers, in a one-sided raceme, much resemble those of several species of *Montia* (which see). On close inspection you will observe the Spring Beauty has 2 cupped sepals, and 5 petals, white to pinkish, attractively lined with deeper pink, and joined just at their bases. There are 5 stamens, which arise from the actual petal-bases, and a single pistil, whose top is cleft into 3 style-branches.

But on comparison, *Montia* species share all these characteristics. We must look further for a ready means of distinguishing them. And we find it in the fibrous roots of *Montia.* So it may be necessary to dig a few inches to the pale round *corm,* if one is to be sure the plant in question is the present species. Also, one seldom or never finds *Montia* in the extensive pure stands that are usual for the more montane Claytonia.

. . . show forth the beauty, grandeur, and all-embracing usefulness of
our wild mountain forest reservations and parks, with a view to
inciting the people to come and enjoy them, and get them in their
hearts, that so at length their preservation and right use might be
made sure . . .

John Muir, September, 1901

CLAYTÒNIA MEGARHÌZA (Gray) Parry. *Tufted Spring Beauty.*

The hiker in the Rockies may encounter, among rock crevices filled with gravel soil, another Spring Beauty, C. megarhiza. The specific name means *large rhizome,* for this plant arises not from a round corm, but rather from a fleshy, swollen taproot. In the field this beautiful plant is readily distinguished from *C. lanceolata* (which see) by its crowded tuft of many basal leaves, sometimes taller than the pink to white flowers, and quite obscuring them. These leaves are more blunt-ended than those of its relative.

This species is very much rarer than *C. lanceolata*, and the practice of removing it to gardens should be deprecated. In the rocky clefts it chooses, excavation of the taproot and its thick forks, without damage, is almost impossible. Even when removed intact to the milder, wetter climate of coastal gardens, this plant usually succumbs after a winter or two. Leave it in its stony fastness, so that others may enjoy it also, for C. megarhiza is a very attractive plant—and never so intriguing as in its magnificent mountain habitat.

LEWÍSIA COLUMBIÀNA (Howell) Robins. *Columbia Lewisia.* [p.127]

This is a genus dear to the naturalist and gardener by reason of the spectacular beauties to be found among its members. It fittingly recalls the name of Meriwether Lewis, of the Lewis and Clark Expedition, who first travelled the overland route to Oregon in 1806. As with *Delphinium, Petunia, Wistaria, Nasturtium, Geranium*, and many other plants, no English equivalent has acquired wide usage (although one species, the flamboyant *L. rediviva* (which see), is commonly called Bitter Root).

The Lewisias are perennials, with thick wrinkled roots culminating in a heavy caudex, shaped something like the foot of an elephant. From this unlikely source rises a crowded cluster of handsome tongue-like leaves, and in most species, a number of slender, branching stems carrying exquisitely delicate flowers. (In *L. tweedyii*, the supreme beauty of western Washington, these spread an elegant and impressive 3-3½ inches.) There are always 2 persistent sepals and 5-18 petals, separate and identical. Stamens may number 5-50.

Though the specific name of L. columbiana suggests that this charming mountain plant is found in the *Columbia River region*, it is also widely distributed on the highest parts of Vancouver Island and in the Olympics. It favours gravel slopes and rock crevices, or slabs covered with 6-8 inches of sharply drained soil. Especially in the last named environment, it often presents a pretty picture, with dozens of delicate flowers, ¾-1 inch wide, fluttering 4-10 inches above the low tufts of attractive succulent leaves. And how they flutter in the vagrant breezes of their airy stance! The photographer is likely to experience feelings both of enchantment, and frustration.

The flowers vary from nearly white (with subtle pink veining) to purplish-rose. They spread 7-10 identical (and separate) obovate petals, cupped within 2 persistent (and quite characteristic) sepals. These are conspicuously toothed—a feature sufficient to distinguish this plant from the rather similar *Claytonia megarhiza* (which does not overlap in range). There is some variation in the strap-shaped, thick, fleshy leaves: in some forms pointed, in others blunt-ended. Another better recognition feature is the presence—at each branching of the slender stems—of small bracts, generally toothed.

This elegant little plant is probably sufficiently common, in many sites, to justify the keen gardener in patiently excavating the long branching roots of a few specimens. But he will have to provide very sharp drainage, if he is to retain it for any length of time in the rock-garden. West of the Cascades, Lewisia columbiana is best covered with a pane of glass during our wet winters, and the Carrot Fly remains a menace (though for some reason the fly seems to victimize even more readily the more glamorous *L. tweedyii*).

Many will agree with Dr. Ira Gabrielson, who in his delightful book *Western American Alpines* writes, "In the Coastal ranges grows a rosy purple form with darker red veins and dark green leaves. This variety blooms over a longer period than any other Lewisia and is now [1932] finding its way into cultivation as L. COLUMBIÀNA var. ROSÈA. This Lewisia is the best all-round garden plant of the genus."   [p.134]

As summer winds that creep from flower to flower . . . .

Percy Bysshe Shelley:
Hymn to Intellectual Beauty

LEWÍSIA PYGMAÈA (Gray) Robins. *Dwarf Lewisia.*

On high mountain slopes from Vancouver Island through mainland B.C., and into Alaska, one may chance upon this rare and *tiny* alpine. The fleshy leaves—not much larger than a tuft of fir needles—are so easily overlooked that the species may be less uncommon than is suggested by the paucity of herbarium records.

The white—sometimes pink—flowers are only ½ inch across, and seldom open widely. They are carried singly on pedicels that are generally even shorter than the leaf-clump. The sepals are distinctly toothed, and reddish.

LEWÍSIA REDIVÌVA Pursh. *Bitter Root. Spatlum.* [p.135]

This extraordinary plant, remarkable for its spectacular flowers and adaptation to a harsh environment, is the state flower of Montana, and gives its name to the Bitter Root Mountains.

The origin of the specific name is illustrated by an anecdote. Captain Meriwether Lewis, on July 1, 1806, when the celebrated expedition he led with William Clark had reached (on their return from Oregon) a point just south of the present city of Missoula, Montana, collected a specimen of what he recognized to be a remarkable plant, and pressed it between dry papers in a botanical press. Months afterward (in Philadelphia) this completely desiccated specimen was planted, since it still showed signs of life—and proceeded to grow! Pursh was so impressed that he aptly named the new species rediviva, *restored to life.*

We would like to see the Indian name retained, just as we have seen that the native name has survived for Camas, and has even been Latinized as *Camassia* (which see). Spatlum, or Spaetlum, was even more important as a food resource to the aborigines, being more widespread and more readily kept for winter use. Bitter Root is, of course, the white man's name—for even after removal of the intensely bitter, orange-coloured, inner bark, the white interior pulp remains rather unpalatable to the European taste.

POLYGONUM BISTORTOIDES ×¼ [p.101]

ATRIPLEX PATULA var. OBTUSA ×⅘ [p.108]

SALSOLA KALI var. TENUIFOLIA ×1 [p.112]

SUAEDA MARITIMA ×1¼ [p.113]

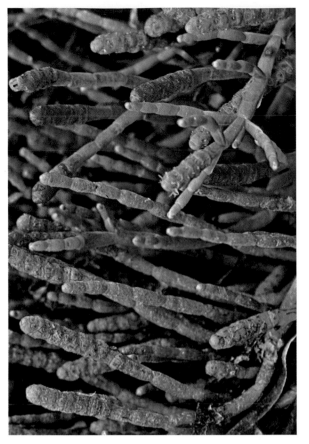

SALICORNIA PACIFICA ×1 [p.112]

AMARANTHUS RETROFLEXUS ×½ [p.113]

CLAYTONIA LANCEOLATA ×1 [p.119]

CHENOPODIUM CAPITATUM ×½ [p.109]

The reader will enjoy the interesting description of the preparation of these roots by the Indians, given by Leonard Wiley, in his valuable *Rare Wild Flowers of North America*.

Lewisia rediviva occurs—at times in vast numbers—both among the rock spurs of the high country, and the desert flats of the inter-mountain regions.

The relatively big, forked, fat rhizomes of the plant, after the first rains of waning summer, sprout a thick tuft of succulent leaves that resemble large plump fir-needles. These leaves survive the winter but begin to shrivel, and are often quite withered away by the following May, when the arid wastes are sprinkled—it seems almost overnight, miraculously—with brilliant "water-lily" blossoms—white, pink, and rose. These open only in bright sunshine, and afford a quite astounding spectacle. On dull days the spectacular waxen petals become furled, like an umbrella, within the brownish bracts and sepals, only to reappear within minutes—as if by magic—when the hot sun breaks through. The effect is breath-taking on some of the dry flats, where the plants adorn every few inches over many acres.

Each 2-inch flower (with its 12-18 petals) is solitary, carried about 3 inches above the ground, and ripens 6-20 shining brown seeds (that are spread widely when the dried capsule is broken off and rolled away by the wind). In spite of the destruction of many fields by cultivation, the lovely Bitter Root still is abundant in arid flats unsuited for irrigation, throughout the southern Dry Interior.

MÓNTIA. *Miner's Lettuce.*

Not surprisingly, since this is chiefly a North American genus, many of the approximately 50 known species occur in our area. A few of these also occur in Europe. All are characterized by the succulent stems and leaves common to the family. The roots are *fibrous*—otherwise Montia is the lowland analogue of the montane genus *Claytonia* (which see).

An unofficial—but useful—recognition feature is the white string-like bundle of conducting fibres easily pulled from the stems. All the species produce disproportionately large, shining black seeds.

Of the 12 or 13 species occurring in the region of our concern, only the most common and widespread can be considered here.

The name recognizes the Italian botanist Guiseppe Monti (1682-1760).

MÓNTIA CORDIFÒLIA (Wats.) Pax & K. Hoffm. *Heart-leaved Montia.* [p.138]

This attractive species seeks the wetness of stream-banks at lower altitudes, and small meadow-rills in the mountains. Its range is across the width of the southern portion of British Columbia, and southward.

Heart-leaved Montia has a perennial, horizontal rootstock, which pushes up—at intervals—clusters of rather thick and succulent stems, 4-12 inches high. Basal *leaves* are triangular to *heart-shaped* (whence cordifolia), noticeably thick and firm, with petioles 2-3 times as long as the blades. A single pair of opposite, unstalked, ovate leaves appear somewhat more than halfway up the tender stem. The flowers are quite large, with slightly notched petals about ¼ inch long, white, occasionally pink-striped. The running rootstock is useful in identification.

MÓNTIA LINEÀRIS (Dougl.) Greene is a very small species, with narrow, *linear* leaves. Flowers are tiny, and secund (carried on one side only of the slender stems). The plants cluster along runnels very early in the year, so that as the water dries up, and the little plants turn bright-red, they become noticeable.

MÓNTIA PARVIFÒLIA (Moc.) Greene. *Small-leaved Montia.* [p.138]

The specific name suggests the *small leaves* of this showy species. Since it is a perennial, and extends numerous slender rhizomes through the uppermost layer of forest duff, the leaf rosettes, under a cloud of pink flowers on fragile stems, may extend over several square yards. For more than 10 years we have admired a colony that bewitchingly covers the mossy top of an extensive flat rock. Toward the end of May the shaded glade is illuminated by the delicate network of pale arching stalks, spangled with a thousand flowers, pink, and of an ethereal delicacy.

The plump little basal leaves are obovate, i.e. with their greatest width nearer the tip. From each rosette arise many slim 6-12 inch stems, carrying alternate leaflets that decrease in size upward. The half-dozen flowers that cluster in each short raceme, appear relatively large (in the extreme var. FLAGELLÁRIS (Bong.) C. L. Hitchc., rather more than an inch wide). The 5 fragile petals, each accented by a long stamen, are rounded to obtusely-pointed.

MÓNTIA PERFOLIÀTA (Donn.) Howell. *Miner's Lettuce.* [p.134]

This extremely variable annual derives its specific name from the fact that the terminal pair of opposite leaves are joined along their bases, to form a shallow cup, *perforated* by the slender pedicel of the raceme of 2-20 white to pinkish, 5-petalled flowers.

The basal leaves are variable in shape, from thumb-shaped to almost diamond-shaped (rhombic-obovate) with long petioles. As usual, there are 2 sepals. The petals are slightly longer to nearly twice as long as the sepals. Variety GLAÙCA Nutt., extremely dwarf (1-2 inches tall), of a curious *greyish* hue, is found among short mosses on rocky outcrops of southern Vancouver Island. But in moist and shady situations of rich soil, the growth is lush, and the plant may reach a foot in height, and almost as much across. The best recognition characteristic of all the varieties is the connate (joined) pair of terminal leaves, which form a very distinctive saucer beneath the flower-raceme. Early

[p.134]

ABRONIA LATIFOLIA ×1⅕ [p.116]

CALANDRINIA CILIATA var. MENZIESII ×4 [p.118]

ARENARIA MACROPHYLLA ×⅘ [p.130]

ARENARIA RUBELLA ×1 [p.130]

LEWISIA COLUMBIANA ×⅘ [p.120]

miners, and other pioneers, used these leaves for "greens". We have confirmed their succulence (see also *M. sibirica*).

This is an interesting species of early spring. On dry rocky outcrops the plants of Montia perfoliata will have shrivelled, and almost vanished, by midsummer.

MÓNTIA SIBÍRICA (L.) Howell. *Western Spring Beauty. Siberian Lettuce.*   [p.134]

This species is highly variable in its wide distribution, from *Siberia,* Alaska, Vancouver Island, the Queen Charlotte Islands, to the Kootenay Lake-Arrow Lakes region. We have seen it in flower near Victoria, from March till mid-October—more than half the year.

M. sibirica vies with *M. parvifolia* (which see) as the most beautiful member of the genus occurring in our area. The ¼-¾ inch flowers open, a few at a time, along the rather elongated raceme. The 5 petals, white or pink, usually vividly lined with deeper pink, each carry a terminal notch. The tuft of fleshy, long-petioled, basal leaves have elliptical blades, usually pointed at either end. However, the blades may be nearly circular, or even strap-shaped (var. HETEROPHÝLLA Robins.). Variability includes plant-size (2-16 inches tall), foliage colour (lime-green to bronzy), and leafy succulence (variably fleshy). Some of the plants are annual; others in richer soil develop rhizomes, which persist through several winters. The succulent leaves, like those of *M. perfoliata* (which see) make a pleasant wilderness-substitute for lettuce. In the present species the opposite pair of pointed-elliptical stem-leaves have no (or very short) petioles, and they are not joined together along their bases. A further means of distinguishing Montia sibirica from other Montias, is the presence of a small, elliptical bract at the base of each of the individual flower-pedicels.

TALÌNUM OKANOGANÉNSE English. *Rock Pink.*   [p.139]

This tiny gem appears to be exceedingly rare, and is included here both because of its attractiveness, and in the hope that more stations will be reported by searchers who know its appearance. The plant was unknown to science until 1934, when one of the first two records came from Baldy Mt. in the Tranquille Range near Kamloops.

Plant-lovers should be alert to the possibility of finding this jewel on rocky slopes in the lower mountains of southern British Columbia and northern Washington. Because of its diminutive size, Rock Pink may have been overlooked, and ultimately may be found less uncommon than is indicated by the paucity of reports.

Before and after flowering, the tufts of clustered fat leaves might easily be confused with a 2-inch wide clump of *Sedum* (which see). And through the winter months, when these leaves have shrivelled away, only inch-long branchlets—apparently dead—remain to show the position of the thickened, fleshy, and perennial roots. Spring soon brings greyish-green, finger-like leaves, that are less than ½ inch long. And in late May, or at some time during the next three months (depending upon the altitude and exposure) bewitching little flowers appear on slim pedicels about 1 inch long. They are cream-coloured (flushed with yellow or pink toward their bases), slightly-cupped, and about ½ inch across. The 5 petals are slightly creased, and pointed at their tips. In the centre of the flower is a dainty cluster of about 20 stamens, surrounding a pistil with a 3-cleft style.

The generic name is the aboriginal name of a species from Senegal, while the specific name refers to *Okanogan County*, Washington. This perfectly-proportioned, miniature rock plant is choice and appealing.

 CARYOPHYLLÀCEAE. *Pink Family.*

The 2000 members of this family are nearly all annual or perennial herbs, with pairs of simple, entire, often narrow, and opposite leaves. Many have stems showing the characteristic swollen nodal-joints, familiar to every gardener, of carnations and pinks. Flowers usually have 5 sepals and 10 stamens. Petals, often 5, more rarely 4 (occasionally 0), nearly always have a narrowed base (claw) and an expanded blade.

Origin of the family name is often a subject for enquiry, since the explanation is not readily available. Caryophyllaceae is derived from the Greek karyon, *a nut,* and phyllon—*a leaf;* referring to the close-wrapped appearance of the buds, e.g. of such members as the familiar pinks.

Though no species are of economic importance, a number are showy and widely cultivated for their flowers. These include numerous *Dianthus, Gypsophila* ("Baby's Breath"), and *Lychnis chalcedonica* (the spectacular Maltese Cross). A poor relation is the irrepressible Garden Chickweed.

AGROSTÉMMA GITHÀGO L. *Corn Cockle.*

The intensely reddish-purple flowers of this Eurasian immigrant occasionally dot our fields and roadsides, demonstrating the origin of the name, from Greek agros, *a field,* and stemma, *a crown* or garland.

Corn Cockle's 2-3 foot stems (with linear, opposite leaves and oddly-spiked buds) appear almost snowy, because of the dense covering of fine white hairs. When the buds open, this hoary effect is startlingly contrasted by the gaudy purple of the 5 wide petals. The 5 sepals are joined, and felted with white pubescence for almost half their length, then suddenly separate into long thin teeth, that project well beyond the opened petals.

Agrostemma githago is one of the few weeds that have not become progressively invasive. Many will regret the decreasing abundance of this flamboyant invader. It is easily confused with *Lychnis coronaria* (which see).

In Shakespeare's day Corn Cockle must have presented a serious challenge to wheat, for he causes Biron to say, "Allons! Allons! Sow'd cockle reap'd no corn. . . ." (Love's Labour's Lost).

ARENÀRIA MACROPHÝLLA Hook. *Large-leaved Sandwort.* [p.127]

The suggested common name, though not in wide use, is given by several authorities, notably M. E. Peck. It has the possible merit of Anglicizing the scientific name, which is descriptive of the plant. Arena in early Latin meant *sand,* only later extended to the sanded "arenas" of spectacles and combat. The Sandworts (wyrt is the Old English word for *plant,* planta being a Latin word) are small tufted plants, usually with narrow, often with harsh leaves, as befits customary sun-sites in dry sand, gravel, or rock ledges. But this species is atypical, for the thin *leaves* are broadly lanceolate. Also, the leaves are carried in opposite pairs along the weakly ascending stems (rather than basally), and the plant seeks out open woodlands that are moist in springtime. The attractive small flowers show open faces of 5 white petals, backed by 5 pointed, ovate, green sepals that are variably longer or shorter than the petals. In the centre of each flower are 10 stamens and 3 styles. Arenaria macrophylla is abundant on Vancouver Island and the southern Mainland coast—rather less so in the mountains, both east and west of the Cascades.

ARENÀRIA RUBÉLLA (Wahlenb.) J. E. Smith. *Vernal Sandwort.* [p.127]

This circumpolar species, common on subalpine to alpine slopes, and also on sand or gravel river bars from Alaska south to California, is typical of a number of poorly differentiated species of our area, whose identification is often difficult even for the professional botanist.

This is a small taprooted perennial, with a tight cushion of 3-nerved, almost needle-like leaves, from which arise many 2-6 inch wiry stems carrying a few pairs of opposite, linear leaves, and a small open cyme of dainty white flowers. These have 5 pointed sepals with membranous edges, 3 nerves, and pointed tips, as well as 5 petals that may be slightly shorter to slightly longer than the sepals. Seeds are reddish-brown (whence the name rubella).

There is a distinctive, trim neatness about this aristocratic little sandwort.

CERÁSTIUM ARVÉNSE L. *Mouse-ear Chickweed.*   [p.138]

This is a difficult genus of highly variable species, the name being derived from the Greek keras, *horn,* vaguely describing the seed-capsules. A good recognition feature is the pronounced notch of the white petals, a feature that separates this genus from *Arenaria* and *Spergularia* (which see). Arvense means *field.* The pestiferous Chickweed of our gardens is STELLÀRIA MÈDIA (L.) Vill., distinguished by 3 styles. The present species has 4-5 styles and is an altogether more striking plant, with much larger flowers—in fact, the showiest of its genus.

This far-ranging and plastic species is found on coastal cliffs, river bars, and dry to moist meadowlands of the Interior (to subalpine and even alpine levels). The wayfarer comes to greet the loose grey mats, with their cheery white open faces, as old friends, upon discovering them in new and unfamiliar environments from New Mexico to Newfoundland, or even Eurasia.

The illustration will be helpful in identifying this very common plant. Though the pubescence is less in montane situations, the plants are generally conspicuous for their greyish pubescent stems and leaves. The flowers may be nearly ¾ inch wide, the 5 petals cleft about one-third of their length, and marked with greenish lines that serve as honey-guides. The 5 hairy sepals are lanceolate-pointed. There are 10 stamens.

DIÁNTHUS ARMÈRIA L. *Deptford Pink.*   [p.146]

Theophrastus, Aristotle's successor in the 4th century B.C., wrote with admiration of the Dianthus, deriving the name from Zeus (Dios is the genitive, hence *divine*) and anthos, *flower.* Two species, brought into our gardens from Europe, frequently escape and have become established locally in the southern part of our area.

This one is a rather inconspicuous little annual, slightly downy, with erect 4-12 inch stems, narrowly lanceolate leaves, and a crowded spike of small, non-scented, bright pink flowers. The toothed petals are attractively spotted, but the flower is only briefly visible—before and after flowering being hidden by the long hairy bracts. Deptford Pink is found occasionally in dry, open grassy places, flowering late in summer.

DIÁNTHUS DELTOÌDES L. *Maiden Pink*—is rather more showy. It is a greyish, somewhat matted perennial with narrow rough-edged leaves. The 6-inch flower-stems are erect, and carry a few ½-¾ inch, attractive but unscented flowers. The petals are notched, spotted, and vary in shades of pink.

HONKÉNYA PEPLOÌDES (L.) Ehrh. ssp. MÀJOR Hook. *Seabeach Sandwort.* [p.139]

Honkenya is named for Gerhard Honckeny, 1724-1805, an early German botanist. Peploides is the only species, and means *peplis-like* (the peplis was an ancient Greek cloak), since the bases of the fleshy leaves wrap round and almost hide the insignificant greenish flowers.

This sturdy plant flourishes on seabeaches down our coast, as well as along the Aleutian, Arctic, Greenland and Iceland shores. Its mats of succulent, glabrous, obovate leaves are recognizable at a distance because of their curious yellow-green colour. Thick stems trail over the sand, with numerous 4-10 inch upright shoots, whose leaves become smaller and more crowded upward. In the axils of the upper ones are tucked single flowers with 4 or 5 tiny sepals, a like number of very small greenish-white petals, and either or both, stamens (8-10) and pistil (2-6 styles).

LÝCHNIS ÁLBA Mill. *White Campion.*   [p.146]

Perhaps 3 dozen species are known from the temperate and cooler parts of the Americas. Lychnos is Greek for *lamp*, possibly from the luminous white blooms of the Night-flowering Campion (now placed in another genus, as *Silene noctiflora*). A number of these white-flowered weeds are so similar that their identification is troublesome.

Lychnis alba differs from *Silene cucubalus* (which see), *S. noctiflora*, and *S. cserei*, in a distinctive feature: it is dioecious, that is, bears staminate and pistillate flowers on separate plants. Also, the pistillate flowers in Lychnis have 5 styles (rarely 4) while the species of *Silene* usually have 3 styles.

Though a rank-growth pernicious weed, White Campion provides a showy—if too common—accent along railways and roadsides, and in hayfields, throughout the southern part of our area.

[p.138]   LÝCHNIS CORONÀRIA (L.) Desr. *Mullein Pink* (widely escaped from gardens) is often confused with similarly coloured *Agrostemma githago* (which see) but has much broader, ovate leaves, and two pointed ears about halfway up each petal.

SILÈNE. *Campion. Catchfly.*

About 400 species of this genus of the North Temperate zone have been described, quite a number being prized in the garden, e.g. the scarlet *S. californica*, lovely pink *S. hookeri*, puffed-calyx *S. suksdorfii*, and superb *S. fortunei* (from China).

The species are characterized by a more or less inflated, prominently nerved calyx-tube, and 5 petals cleft and long-clawed, with a scale and usually a very distinctive pair of auricles (like little ears, appearing about halfway up the inner face of the petal).

The name is apparently derived from the Greek sialon, *saliva*, referring to the sticky glandular hairs of the stems, that are also responsible for the name Catchfly.

SILÈNE ACAÙLIS L. var. SUBACAULÉSCENS Fern. & St. John. *Moss Campion.* [p.147]

All who come to the mountains must have seen these incredibly tight cushions, spread over the rock—like patches of moss. Almost as many will have stopped to exclaim, when the bright green mats become spangled with tight-pressed "campion" flowers of brightest rose. Acaulis means a–*(not)*, caulis, *stalked,* for indeed the ½-inch flowers do appear to be stemless.

This charming little campion, so different from lowland-dwelling members of its genus, affords a perfect illustration of adaptation to the fierce winds and high-intensity sunshine of the mountains. Thus the plant is pressed flat over the rock, with its long taproot deeply anchored in some moisture-retaining crevice, and the tiny leaves are tough, leathery, and linear. At the levels it inhabits, perhaps only 20% of the atmosphere's water-vapour is present, so the sun's actinic rays are largely unabsorbed in passing through the thinner air. Hence a small leaf area suffices to trap the needed energy. Where insects are few and harassed by incessant winds, the alpine flowers compete for their attention with flowers that are conspicuous or large (relative to the leaves), of most brilliant and visible colours, and often scented.

Silene acaulis cannot be confused with any other plant. Like nearly all cushion-plants it needs protection from those who would dig it up, and this has long been understood in places such as Switzerland, Scotland, and the Lake District of England. This beautiful and distinctive plant is circumboreal, in bloom from June to September, depending upon the altitude.

SILÈNE CUCUBÀLUS Wibel. *Bladder Campion.*

This is a noxious perennial weed, with deep roots that allow it to survive in arid exposures by the roadside and in hayfields. Like many—perhaps a majority—of our weeds, it is an immigrant from Eurasia.

The specific name cucubalus is derived from the Greek kakos, *bad,* and bolos, *a shot,* referring to an early belief that the plant was destructive to the soil.

The very *inflated* calyx-tube, conspicuously marked by a network of darker veins, is glabrous (smooth). There are 3 styles, and the flowers are perfect, that is, possess both pistil and stamens. The white flowers are freely borne and showy; but our admiration is unfortunately tinged with apprehension (and regret) when we consider how rapid has been the spread of the species (and the more desirable natives it has crowded out).

134

LEWISIA COLUMBIANA FORMA ROSEA ×³⁄₅ [p.121]

MONTIA PERFOLIATA ×½ [p.125]

MONTIA SIBIRICA ×1 [p.128]

MONTIA PERFOLIATA var. GLAUCA ×1 [p.125]

SILÈNE GÁLLICA L. *Small-flowered Catchfly.*

Linneaus' note, "Habitat in Gallia", explains the specific name. This is another weedy species of the Pacific coast introduced from the Old World, and included here because it is common and representative of several small annual species found in our area.

Silene gallica is 4-16 inches tall, strikingly hirsute, with some of the hairs longer and curiously whitened. Others are shorter, and glandular, so that the plant is very sticky. Flowers are small (less than ¼ inch), usually white but sometimes pink, and present a "pin-wheel" appearance, because the blade of each of the 5 petals is slightly twisted. Leaves are oblanceolate.

SILÈNE MENZIÈSII Hook. is lower than *S. gallica* (which see), with lanceolate leaves. Some of the small white flowers bear stamens, others on the same plant bear the pistil only. This is a leafy species, variably hairy, some varieties extremely sticky, others not so. Silene menziesii occurs in southern British Columbia, including Vancouver Island, and in Alaska. It is a native perennial.

SPERGULÀRIA RÙBRA (L.) J. & C. *Pink Sand Spurry.* [p.139]

Spargo, *to scatter*, is the root of the names *Spergula* (S. arvensis is a ubiquitous weed), and Spergularia (*like Spergula*). Though some members of the present genus are uncommon, the seeds of this little pink-flowered mat-forming weed have indeed been widely scattered, from Europe throughout the United States and Canada.

Its many stems, with bundles of ½-inch, linear, dark-green leaves, straggle over waste ground. The 5 green pointed sepals, with membranous (scarious) edges, project beyond the 5 pink obovate petals. Usually 10 stamens ring the swollen green ovary, topped with its 3 styles.

 **NYMPHAEÀCEAE.** *Water Lily Family.*

BRASÈNIA SCHRÉBERI Gmel. *Water Shield.* [p.139]

This familiar plant of shallow ponds and sluggish rivers has a world-wide distribution, though apparently it does not occur in Europe. The slender petioles (to 16 inches) connect creeping rootstocks with the floating leaves. These leaves are peltate (shield-shaped), reminiscent of the shape of a nasturtium leaf. Very characteristic is the jelly-like covering of all aquatic parts. Arising from the leaf-axils are the long peduncles, each lifting (just above the water) a small, terminal, purplish flower. Three or 4 blunt-lanceolate sepals, and 3 or 4 similar petals partly open during daylight hours, to reveal several dozen purple stamens and about half as many pistils. The flowers are curious, rather than showy, and do not appear until late in the summer.

The monotypic genus bears a name of unknown origin—possibly derived from the Latin brasenia, a *cap.* Johann C. D. von Schreber, 1739-1810, was a professor at Erlangen, in what is now West Germany.

As with *Nuphar* (which see), the broad leaves of Brasenia provide shade and shelter for fish and aquatic insects. Sometimes they are locally important as a food for ducks.

NÙPHAR POLYSÉPALUM Engelm. *Yellow Water Lily.*   [p.146]

Who does not know the ubiquitous floating pads and yellow flowers of this large aquatic plant? But many are surprised to learn that we have two species in our area. "Polysepalum" is the clue to their distinction, for this species has 7-12 broad sepals, the inner ones becoming clear bright-yellow, but *N. variegatum* (which see) has only 5 or 6. The generic name is another of the surprisingly large number of botanical names that recall the Moorish preoccupation with botany and materia medica. It derives from the Persian nenuphar, a *water lily.*

The huge, thickened rhizomes, when summer drought lowers the water levels in shallow lakes and ponds, are rooted up by black bear, and were used in times of famine by Indians. More usual was the collection and roasting of the large seeds, called Wokas. The large floating leaves effectively function to reduce over-heating of sun-warmed shallow waters. They provide resting places for a motley host, including brilliant damsel-flies and dragonflies, green frogs and ducklings—and below—myriad aquatic forms to which trout are attracted.

The great flower-cups also attract a multitude of flying insects. Structurally the flowers are of considerable interest. Usually there are 4 smaller green, and 5 large yellow sepals. The 10-18 petals are reduced to staminoidal wedges that mark off the purplish stamens in a fascinating concentric arrangement. The hugely expanded stigma, centring the rings of stamens, looks like a golden parasol, complete with radiating ribs.

The old green pond is silent;
here the hop
Of a frog plumbs the evening
stillness: plop!

Bashô

NÙPHAR VARIEGÀTUM Engelm. is very closely related to the preceding species. Indeed, E. O. Beal, in his taxonomic study of this genus (1956) makes a very good case for considering our two plants as subspecies (long isolated during the last glaciation) of

MONTIA CORDIFOLIA ✕⅘ [p.124]

MONTIA PARVIFOLIA ✕⅘ [p.125]

LYCHNIS CORONARIA ✕½ [p.132]

CERASTIUM ARVENSE ✕⅖ [p.131]

TALINUM OKANOGANENSE ×2 [p.128]

HONKENYA PEPLOIDES ssp. MAJOR ×1⅕ [p.132]

SPERGULARIA RUBRA ×1¾ [p.136]

T. TODD

BRASENARIA SCHREBERI ×⅖ [p.136]

*N. luteum**. Though the range of N. variegatum is generally more northern and eastern, that of *N. polysepalum* generally more western, the two plants overlap in our area.

The specific name probably refers to the *variety* of colouring of the 5-6 sepals, greenish outside, yellow with reddish flush within. The flowers are smaller than those of *N. polysepalum* (which see); the stamens yellow, rather than purple. Perhaps the most consistent characteristic of the present species is the flattened, sometimes even slightly-winged, petioles.

Longfellow pictures the canoe of Hiawatha as floating
> . . . *upon the river*
> *Like a yellow leaf in autumn*
> *Like a yellow water-lily.*

*An excellent woodcut of *Nuphar luteum* appears in the *Kruydtboek* of Mattias de L'Obel, printed in the year 1581.

RANUNCULÀCEAE. *Buttercup Family.*

A large family of about 1500 species divided into approximately 40 genera (of which 15 occur in our area), the Buttercups are an assorted lot. Future systematists may well consider our present arrangement should be subdivided. As it stands, the family includes many plants with a ring of similar simple petals, and also numerous ones with highly irregular specialized petals, or none. Sepals vary from 3 to 20, stamens from 5 to very many, pistils from 1 to many. Leaves are both opposite and alternate, simple and compound. The great majority of Ranunculaceae are herbs, but there are also climbing vines.

One looks hard for identifying characteristics. Most species have numerous free floral parts, spirally arranged. This is considered by botanists evidence of a very primitive stage in evolutionary development. Primitive the Buttercups may be, but it is evident by their immense numbers that they are highly successful in the eternal competition among plant species to "win a place in the sun". A non-visual characteristic is quite general in the family—an acrid juice, which contains a number of alkaloids. Some of these, as in the *Delphiniums* (Larkspurs), Monkshoods, Winter Roses (*Helleborus*), and Baneberries (*Actaea*), are poisonous. However, it is quite safe to test a single bit of leaf or stem for its bitter taste.

A large number of species are cultivated for their flowers, and quite a few have been so developed by the hybridist that many variations in shape, size, and colour have become available. Prominent among these are the graceful Columbines (*Aquilegia*), and the incredibly lovely *Clematis*. The reader will recognize native representatives also, of the cultivated *Anemone*, *Delphinium*, and *Trollius*. Peonies are closely related, but by many authorities are now placed in a separate family of their own.

The name of the family, apparently first used by Pliny, is from the diminutive of rana, *a frog*—seemingly with reference to the fact that many species are found in wet areas agreeable to little frogs!

> *There is a Flower, the lesser Celandine,*
> *That shrinks, like many more, from cold and rain;*
> *And, the first moment that the sun may shine,*
> *Bright as the sun himself, 'tis out again!*

William Wordsworth: The Small Celandine

ACONÌTUM COLUMBIÀNUM Nutt. *Monkshood.* [p.150]

The common name is both well-known and appropriate, for the conspicuous upper sepal forms a perfect hood concealing the flower's face, and the usual dark bluish-purple is sombre, and monkish. However, paler blue, and even white individuals, are occasionally seen. The generic name is very ancient, for it is one of the plants mentioned in *De materia medica* by the Greek physician Dioscorides, of the first century A.D. This variable species occurs in the area from Alaska to California; in British Columbia from Hope eastward through the mountains, including the Rockies (hence columbianum, *of the Columbia*).

This is a stately plant, sometimes 6 feet tall, its stems punctuated with handsome leaves 5-cleft (3-cleft high on the stalk), and terminated by a long, open, spike-like raceme of large (1¼ inch) dark blooms.

In spite of its height and size, Monkshood is sometimes a little difficult to find, since it grows in the dense vegetation of wet meadows, or margins of springs or brooks. The dark colour merges with the deep shadows.

The whole plant is poisonous, especially the seeds and the swollen roots, which contain two highly toxic alkaloids, aconitine and aconine. David Nelson, of Cook's Third Voyage, reported that the roots of this species (or possibly the more northern and shorter A. DELPHINIFÒLIUM*) provided the Aleuts with a deadly arrow poison.

*A. delphinifolium DC. occurs in the Rockies, from Jasper northward, and in the Queen Charlotte Islands.

ACTAÈA RÙBRA (Ait.) Willd. *Baneberry.* [p.150]

Of the half-dozen members of this genus of the North Temperate zone, only one species occurs in our area. The name comes from early Greek for the *elder-tree* (aktaia), since the large compound leaves are reminiscent of the elder leaves in shape, though not in texture. They are thin and delicate. Most of the leaves are basal, over a foot long, and 2, or even 3 times thrice-divided (ternate), the ultimate segments deeply saw-toothed.

From this handsome foliage arise 2-3 foot stems, much branched and carrying similar but smaller leaves, and crowded racemes of small white flowers. A magnifying glass is needed to distinguish 3-5 sepals, 5-10 slightly longer petals, and the usual family abundance of stamens and pistils. Both sepals and petals fall at the least touch, or even at the visit of small moths. (It has been remarked, very frequently, that plants of the deep-shaded woods are characterized by large thin leaves, and scented flowers that are white for maximum visibility, as in the present species.)

But the true beauty of this plant, which has considerable garden value, only appears in June or July when the attractive foliage sets off numerous clusters of gleaming waxy berries, in most forms *bright scarlet,* but occasionally a startling china-white. The usual colour accounts for the specific name rubra, while the white variant has been called *forma* NEGLÉCTA (Gillman) Robins. Though some authors accord specific rank to the latter, we believe that this is a case of two forms. (On one occasion we found adjacent plants—one with white, the other with red berries.)

As the common name suggests, the berries are toxic, and for that reason are not soon removed from the plants by birds. The poisonous compound protoanemonin, which paralyzes the respiratory system after ingestion of only a small amount, has been isolated from both the berries and the roots of this plant. It is of more than passing interest that the structure of this compound can be derived from that of anemonin, the characteristic toxin found in many species of the Ranunculaceae. In time the chemist may be able to provide this kind of support—or perhaps criticism—for the classification of plants as propounded by taxonomists on the basis of morphological characteristics, i.e. details of structural similarity.

ANÉMONE. *Wind Flower.*

Anemos, in Greek, means *wind,* and the name may have been derived from the wind-dispersal of the plumy seeds (achenes) of most species.

In this genus flowers are without petals, but often the sepals are coloured, and large enough to be mistaken for petals. Except for a ring of involucral leaves—like a ruff or collar just below the flowers of some species—the leaves are basal.

These are cool climate plants (often of windy, open slopes) of the Northern Hemisphere, from which about 100 species have been described. Many of these contain a poisonous alkaloid, anemonin.

ANÉMONE DRUMMÓNDII S. Wats. *Alpine Anemone.* [p.147]

This hardy mountaineer, that braves freezing winds of stony ridges, bears the name of the Scottish botanist James Francis Drummond (1851-1921).

From a firmly anchored, thick rootstock springs a tuft of short, much-divided, petioled leaves. One or two scapes rise 2-6 inches, each topped with a single inch-wide flower and interrupted—about mid-length—by a ruff of leaves similar to but smaller than the basal leaves. All parts of the plant (even the lower surfaces of the sepals) are protected by fine woolly hairs. The sepals are blunt-ended in more exposed situations, but pointed in some localities.

White above, like the nearby snow, below—the sepals reflect the blue tints of snow-shadows. The flowers are soon followed by small, rounded, densely-haired fruiting-heads, in which may be discerned a scattering of slender styles. (In some populations these styles are purplish-red, and conspicuous in the grey heads.)

Anemone drummondii is widely distributed in alpine and subalpine areas from Alaska southward.

ANÉMONE LYÁLLII Britt. *Lyall's Anemone.* [p.151]

David Lyall, naturalist and M.D., found this dainty member of the genus (apparently in 1859) along the lower Fraser River.

In early spring the slender perennial rhizomes of A. lyallii push up delicate stems 2-8 inches tall. Each stem bears (about two-thirds of the way up) 3 thin, three-foliate leaves, and (at the top) a single fragile flower about ½-¾ inch across. The delicate leaves are held flat, to capture as much as possible of the weak light filtering through the tree-canopy. Five oblong sepals, that drop at the slightest touch, are white, sometimes bluish-or purplish-tinged (especially below).

Found along the coast in southwestern British Columbia, and southward, this beautifully proportioned plant is also encountered east to the Cascades. In our experience, the favoured habitat is in light forest duff along the edges of such openings as are provided by lakes and streams.

The appealing small blooms may be seen as early as March, if the winter has been mild. By July each flower has matured a rounded head of achenes that resembles a little green blackberry.

> *. . . Down its steep verdant sides; the air*
> *Is freshen'd by the leaping stream, which throws*
> *Eternal showers of spray on the moss'd roots*
> *Of trees, and veins of turf, and long dark shoots*
> *Of ivy-plants, and fragrant hanging bells*
> *Of hyacinths, and on late anemonies,*
> *That muffle its wet banks. . . .*

    Matthew Arnold: Empedocles on Etna

ANÉMONE MULTÍFIDA Poir. *Wind Flower.* [p.147]

The specific name of this common and widely-distributed anemone means *many-cleft*, with reference to the leaves. They are several times ternately divided, and chiefly basal. These basal leaves have long, densely haired petioles, but those occurring in one or two whorls on the 8-24 inch flower-stems have very short—or no—petioles. Several stems grow rather stiffly upright, each bearing 1-3 whitish flowers that are surprisingly varied in tinting—yellowish, often pinkish, frequently bluish to purplish. The 5-9 sepals are blunt-tipped, roughly elliptical, and generally less than ½ inch long. There are no petals.

The common name refers to the achenes, each of which is embedded in a mass of fluffy hairs that air-lift the seeds over foothills and lower mountain-slopes. Tightly packed together, these hairy achenes form grey, nearly round seed-heads. Anemone multifida ranges from the arctic tundra southward through mainland British Columbia.

ANÉMONE OCCIDENTÀLIS Wats. *Western Anemone. Towhead Babies. Wind Flower.* [pp.158,159]

This is a plant typical of that fragile ecological niche, the alpine meadow. We are learning—too late for the retention of many such areas—that the incredibly floriferous, small meadows of our mountain areas are very sensitive to interference. Overgrazing (especially by domestic animals); passage of vehicles, shod horses, and even human traffic; poisoning of the various small burrowing mammals; the slightest alteration of the watertable—all these upset the delicate natural balance, and quickly destroy these priceless natural gardens. Hence road- and trail-making must be undertaken in such areas only with the greatest caution, camping cannot be permitted, and the number of hikers must be kept below certain limits, if we are to continue to enjoy such un-believable floral displays as exist today in Manning Park, the Forbidden Plateau, Mt. Revelstoke, Banff, Jasper, and a number of other areas.

In such situations this Wind Flower, in tens of thousands, opens its large, palest cream cups (often with a bluish cast on the outer faces of the sepals) soon after the snow has melted, and often when the stem has attained only a third of its ultimate 12-18 inches. The flowers contrast effectively with a ring of grey-green feathery leaves, just below the terminal bloom. However, most of the leaves (as is usually the case in this genus) are basal. Like many of its cousins, this plant secretes the poison anemonin. Stems, and long leaf-petioles alike, are silky with soft white hairs. Near the end of the short alpine summer the flowers are replaced by curious mops of plumy seeds, the "Towhead Babies". Then, true to its other name, the fall winds send the seeds, each supported by a feathery tail, blowing over the mountain passes in search of suitable homes.

Oft thou hast given them store
Of flowers—the frail-leaf'd white anemone,

Dark bluebells drench'd with dews of summer eves,
And purple orchises with spotted leaves. . . .

Matthew Arnold: The Scholar-Gipsy

ANÉMONE PARVIFLÒRA Michx. *Northern Anemone.*

This species, common from Alaska to Washington, especially in the Selkirks and the Rockies, is *few-flowered* as is implied by the specific name. A. parviflora has a definite preference for wetter soil, and along some mountain streambanks we have seen quite showy colonies arising from running rootstocks.

Each crowded, basal cluster of long-petioled, three-foliate leaves centres a 6-inch stalk, carrying a single white terminal flower, and an inch below it,—a ring of 3 deeply-cleft smaller leaves. The fragile flower is less than an inch across, its 5 or 6 white sepals usually tinged with blue, and always hairy below. It is succeeded by a whitish-grey, oval head of many woolly seeds.

During the flowering season from June to August according to the altitude, one occasionally finds blooms of Anemone parviflora that are tinted with pink, or yellow, instead of blue.

ANÉMONE PÀTENS L. var. MULTÍFIDA Pritzel. *Pasque Flower. Wild Crocus.*
[p.151]

Patens means *spreading*, possibly because the furry sepals are normally pressed together, but spread their beautiful lilac inner faces whenever the spring sun breaks through. Like the crocus of our gardens, Pasque Flower pushes its furred leaf-cluster through the cold wet ground soon after—or even before—the snow has melted. Then the beautiful flowers open and quite eclipse the few finely-divided leaves. The whole plant wears a silky white overcoat, appropriate for its early appearance. The name Pasque Flower has a religious derivation (from the Passion), since it is often in bloom at Easter-time.

With its flowers opening as much as 3 inches, in varying shades of bluish-lavender, and purple, this is the great beauty among the Anemones of our area. Rarely, a snow-white specimen is seen, with glistening hairs sometimes almost golden, and this—if the weather is kind—presents a spectacular picture. Most of the basal leaves appear after flowering (at which time the stem lengthens rapidly to as much as a foot) and each achene develops a long feathery tail, so that the aggregate looks rather like a golliwog's head.

This striking plant occurs on open slopes and prairies, at moderate to rather high altitudes, eastward from the eastern slopes of the Coast Range. Anemone patens is the State flower of South Dakota, and the official floral emblem of Manitoba.

DIANTHUS ARMERIA $\times \frac{1}{2}$ [p.131]

LYCHNIS ALBA $\times \frac{3}{5}$ [p.132]

NUPHAR POLYSEPALUM $\times \frac{1}{2}$ [p.137]

ANEMONE DRUMMONDII $\times 1\frac{1}{5}$ [p.142]

ANEMONE MULTIFIDA $\times \frac{1}{3}$ [p.144]

SILENE ACAULIS var. SUBACAULESCENS $\times 2\frac{1}{4}$ [p.133]

AQUILÈGIA BREVISTỲLA Hook. *Blue Columbine.*

Nearly 70 species of this attractive genus inhabit the mountains, and less commonly the coastal lowlands of the Northern Hemisphere. Of these we are fortunate to find 3 species in our area. Though the species are often interfertile, there is little difficulty in recognizing them.

The name derivations, both Latin and English, are unusually interesting. Though in most texts the generic name is derived from the Latin aquilla, an *eagle* (said to be suggested by the resemblance of the spurred petals to an eagle's spread talons), the ancient name was in fact apparently derived from aqua, *water,* and legere, *to collect.* Therefore aquilegus, *a water-carrier,* is an apt reference to the little drops of watery nectar found at the end of the petal-tips or spurs. Columbine, the common name, comes from columba, *a dove.* This evokes an altogether more pleasing and appropriate figure than a fierce eagle! The 5 attenuated petals then conjure up a pleasant image of doves, clustered face inward at an imagined drinking-place.

As every child knows, the showy flowers of Columbine conceal a sweet nectar in the spurs (prolongations of the 5 petals). Long-tongued bumblebees and butterflies can also reach this treasure, but the frustrated honeybees sometimes resort to burglarizing, by biting a hole into the side of the spur. So do occasional ants, but they are generally held at bay by the chevaux-de-frise of sticky, glandular guard-hairs, densely arrayed along the flower-pedicels.

The *short style,* though a useful recognition characteristic for detailed examination, is not needed in field identification. The blue sepals and creamy-yellow front portion of the petals, will readily distinguish this beautiful species, which in British Columbia is limited to the northern Rockies, but in Alberta is found rather widely in forested areas. Because the short blue spurs are bent inward, and end in enlarged nectar-glands, the resemblance is clearest in this species to five blue doves (columbae) fluttering around the pedicel with wings (the sepals) half raised. Pale-green, rather delicate leaves, blunt-lobed, and twice 3-parted, provide an attractive foil for the sprightly blossoms. The plants are commonly 1-2 feet tall, and are in bloom during the short snow-free period, in July or August.

The author can call to mind an unforgettable spectacle among the lichen-covered rocks, of cerulean-hued Mountain Bluebirds fluttering about a number of fine plants of this lovely Blue Columbine.

Edmund Spenser in *The Shepheardes Calender* (1579) lists a number of plants with names still recognizable:

> *Bring hether the Pincke and purple Cullambine,*
>   *With Gelliflowres:*
> *Bring Coronations, and Sops in wine,*
>   *worn of Paramoures.*
> *Strowe me the ground with Daffadowndillies,*
> *And Cowslips, and Kingcups, and loued Lillies. . . .*

AQUILÈGIA FLAVÉSCENS Wats. *Yellow Columbine.* [p.162]

Flavesco is the Latin verb *to make yellow*, or golden, for this species—in the perpetually moving air of its mountain retreat—nods and tosses attractive flowers suggesting that (once white) they have been dipped in clear yellow dye, variously effective in different parts.

This graceful flower of southeastern British Columbia is usually found on high rock slides and talus slopes, or in mountain meadows at high altitudes.

Hybrids—with pinkish sepals—of this species with *A. formosa* (which see) are occasionally seen, but in general this species is much more montane, so that there is rarely opportunity for hybridization. Depending upon altitude, the Yellow Columbine is in bloom between June and August.

Few wanderers in the high places of the Rockies can have failed to encounter this dainty beauty, possibly gilding its reflection in the blue waters of a mountain tarn.

AQUILÈGIA FORMÒSA Fisch. *Western Columbine.* [p.162]

Preoccupation with the political manoeuvres of our day may dispose one to a geographical interpretation of the specific name, but the student of Latin will realize that formosa means comely or *beautiful*. The epithet is apt, for this is a plant of attractive leaf-form, elegant flower-shape, and effective colour scheme. Western Columbine, from columba, *a dove* (see *Aquilegia brevistyla*) is found throughout western North America, from Alaska southward along the coast and on the lower slopes of the Coast Range—where it may be seen in bloom from May to August.

The delicate, thin leaves are three times thrice-divided and chiefly basal, on long, slender pedicels. From the cluster of leaves arise slim but wiry stems about 2 feet high. Gracefully nodding flowers have 5 sepals, coral-red, as are the short straight spurs, formed by the nectar-swollen tips of the 5 specialized petals. The petal shape is unique: spurred at one end, joined near mid-length to the floral ring of sepals, and elegantly flared above, to cradle the projecting, brush-like tuft of stamens and styles. The orange-red of the spur turns to a harmonious yellow in the expanded portion, to complete a lovely colour arrangement.

This fine plant is readily brought to the garden, where it self-seeds, to form a great attraction for butterflies and humming birds. The inward eye dwells with pleasure on recollections of Rufous Hummers, poised and darting, with blur of wings, below the Columbine blossoms.

I go to books and to nature as a bee goes to the flower,
for a nectar that I can make into my own honey.

John Burroughs: The Summit of the Years

150

ACTAEA RUBRA (FRUIT) ×½ [p.141]

ACONITUM COLUMBIANUM ×1¾ [p.141]

ANEMONE PATENS var. MULTIFIDA FORMA ALBA ×½ [p.145]

ANEMONE LYALLII ×2 [p.143]

CÁLTHA LEPTOSÉPALA DC. *Mountain Marsh Marigold.*

The Greek kalathos, a *goblet,* appears to be the source of the generic name—though it was applied by the Greeks to some unknown plant, that (like this) inhabited very wet marshy meadows. In fact, only in bud does the flower suggest a round goblet. Lepto means *thin* or narrow, both describing the creamy *sepals,* which are bluish on their outer faces. Mountain marshes, or at least wet mountain meadows, are the home of this common Marigold (or Mary's Gold, a mediaeval name for a yellow daisy sacred to the Virgin Mary).

Bright-green, fleshy leaves of this plant, oblong, wavy-edged and long-petioled, appear immediately after the snow melts, and very shortly the pale 5-12 sepalled flowers are welcomed. They span about 1½ inches, and soon drop sepals and clustered stamens, to ripen a spreading cluster of follicles, each slightly hooked at the tip.

Caltha is well-known to hikers and climbers in all the mountain regions of British Columbia.

[p.159]   CÁLTHA BIFLÒRA DC. is readily distinguished by its nearly round leaves, and the fact that its white *flowers* appear usually *in pairs.* Its range is similar to that of *C. leptosepala* (which see).

[p.159]   CÁLTHA ASARIFÒLIA DC., a species of coastal bogs and marshes, is also round-leaved i.e. like *Asarum* (which see), but with long, decumbent stems and yellow flowers.

Hark! hark! the lark at heaven's gate sings,
    And Phoebus 'gins arise,
His steeds to water at those springs
    On chalic'd flowers that lies;
And winking Mary-buds begin
    To ope their golden eyes. . . .

William Shakespeare: Cymbeline

CIMICÍFUGA ELÀTA Nutt. *Bugbane.*

This tall woodland plant affords a good illustration of the need for scientific names—for in 12 texts consulted that include this species: 7 give no common name, 3 call it Bugbane or True Bugbane, 1 Tall Bugbane, 1 False Bugbane (2 texts list it also as Black Cohosh, and 2 also as Black Snakeroot). To complete the confusion, "Bugbane" is applied variously to *Actaea rubra,* to *Trautvetteria grandis,* and to *Achlys triphylla*—quite unrelated plants. Cimicifuga clearly means Bugbane, from the Latin cimex, *a bug,* and fugo, *to drive away.* The specific name means *tall.*

Rather uncommon, Bugbane occurs in moist shady woods chiefly south of our area. The only records in B.C. are from two mountains near Chilliwack.

The very large compound leaves immediately attract attention, for they resemble 3 triple clusters of maple leaves, the whole cluster of leaflets and long stipule being 2½ feet long. The long, open racemes consist of ¼-inch white flowers, whose sepals drop at once, leaving a powder-puff of long white stamens (some with widened filaments almost like slim petals) and 1-5 beak-tipped pistils.

CLÉMATIS COLUMBIÁNA (Nutt.) T. & G. *Blue Clematis. Virgin's Bower.* [p.166]

Clematis is derived from the Greek klema, a vine-branch or *tendril*, from this plant's habit of climbing. The name is very commonly mispronounced; the accent should be on the first syllable, in which the "e" is short. Few indeed are unaware of the gorgeous Clematis varieties, among the loveliest plants of our gardens. Clematis is unique among the genera of the Buttercup Family, in having opposite leaves.

This charming—if somewhat more modest—species is practically limited to open woods and talus slopes of the *Columbia* valley. It is a good garden subject east of the Cascades, but does not long survive the wet winters of the Coast.

The leaves are 3-foliate, the leaflets pointed-ovate, the edges nearly entire to rather sharply toothed. Petals are lacking; the showy blue to purple sepals take their place. Usually 4 in number, they are lanceolate and 1½-2½ inches long, of a delicate texture attractively accented by darker veining. By August they have been replaced by a fragile mop of plume-tailed airy achenes.

Nowhere abundant, this rather delicate vine, when chanced upon, is sure to gladden the wayfarer's eye.

CLÉMATIS LIGUSTICIFÒLIA Nutt. *White Virgin's Bower. Pipestems.* [p.163]

This is a common, sturdy vine, found along creek bottoms through the dry southern Interior and—surprisingly—also on Vancouver Island, where in like situations, it occasionally clambers to the top of conifers 50 feet or more high. The specific name means that the foliage reminded Nuttall of the compound leaves of the genus *Ligusticum* of the *Umbelliferae* Family.

In fact the leaves are pinnate, usually with 5 ovate leaflets, coarsely-toothed—from nearly glabrous to lightly-clothed with long, soft, rather wavy hairs. Male and female flowers are borne separately, in small clusters, on short stems arising from the leaf-axils, in such numbers that the whole vine may be covered with their creamy abundance. On close examination you will find the pistillate flowers, too, contain numerous stamens, but they are sterile. The staminate flowers, on the other hand, show no sign of a pistil. Late in the summer the pistillate flowers give way to extravagant clouds of "old men's beards", as children call them; these are the plumy greyish tails of the achenes, by which the seeds are drifted far and wide. Occasionally one may see late blooms simultaneously with early seed plumes, since the flowering season of C. ligusticifolia is extended (from May to August end).

CÓPTIS ASPLENIFÒLIA Salisb. *Gold Thread.* [p.159]

Both generic and specific names emphasize the remarkably handsome foliage of this little plant of wet woods and bogs. Not a few collectors have brought this plant home, failed to find it in Frye, or Taylor, or any other text on ferns, speculated that they might have discovered a fern not yet described, and finally been astounded when the supposed "fern" produced flowers—curious flowers, but undeniably structures not of the world of ferns! And so the leaves must have impressed taxonomists, who in 1807 decided upon Coptis, from kopto, *to cut,* and asplenifolia, meaning with *foliage like Asplenium.* (Though the Asplenium ferns of our area have simple pinnate blades, compound ones are usual in this large genus.) The common name comes from the bright-yellow thread-like roots—which are easily observed when this dainty and good-natured plant is brought to a shady part of the garden.

The glistening leaves are firm-textured, evergreen, pinnately 5-foliate and deeply-incised—in short, like a leathery fern. The spidery flowers are pale-yellow, with 5-7 almost thread-like petals, and a like number of similar sepals, all strongly reflexed.

DELPHÍNIUM MENZIÈSII DC. *Menzies' Larkspur.* [p.166]

Six species from our area bear this ancient flower name, used by Dioscorides, Greek physician of the 1st century A.D. The derivation is from the Greek delphin, or the Latinized delphinus, meaning *dolphin,* which is explained in a 150-year old botanical dictionary "in reference to the supposed resemblance in the nectary of the plant to imaginary figures of the dolphin". Horticulturists have attempted to distinguish between annual Larkspurs, and perennial Delphiniums.

Menzies' Larkspur is the common species of the coast (though curiously, no Delphinium has been reported from the Queen Charlottes). It also occurs eastward to the Cascades. The uppermost of 5 sepals is modified into a pronounced hollow spur. The uppermost pair of petals is also produced downward into a spur, within the calyx spur, which is thus double. Only butterflies and the long-proboscis bumblebee can reach this deep nectary. The petals are ruffled, veined, and wavy-edged. Since the upper two are often white, they afford a touch of elegance in the otherwise intense azure to violet flowers.

Characteristic of this species are the following details: the roots are tuberous-clustered; the petals are shallowly notched; the lower flower-pedicels are usually much longer than the flowers.

The electric blues of the Larkspur flash from coastal bluffs and broken rock slopes in May, but those in meadows—to submontane levels—provide bright accents among the dominant whites and yellows during June and July.

DELPHÍNIUM BÍCOLOR Nutt. *Two-coloured Larkspur* is a small but showy species, inhabiting Bunch-grass and Ponderosa Pine country from Osoyoos to the Rockies.

The roots are somewhat thickened, and almost fleshy. Plants are usually 6-20 inches tall, with thickish, chiefly basal leaves that are deeply cut into overlapping wedge-shaped segments. Widely flared, the 4 lower sepals are appreciably larger than the single upper (spurred) sepal. The 2 lower petals (only shallowly-lobed) are notably large and deep-blue, but the 2 upper are small, and pale-blue (though finely pencilled with purple).

DELPHÍNIUM GLAÙCUM Wats. *Tall Delphinium.* [p.163]

Delphinium glaucum (the specific name refers to the inconspicuous *greyish-blue* bloom on the foliage) is the common species of eastern British Columbia. (It also occurs from Washington to Alaska.) In these regions, and into the Prairies above latitude 53°, this species is one of the most usual causes of stock-poisoning. Tall Delphinium is not usually in flower until mid-July.

This stately plant (to 6 feet or even more) has dark purple-blue flowers that are disappointing in size. (Perhaps we have been too long accustomed to the magnificent blooms of the many fine horticultural strains.) The flowers are carried in a long spire which extends for about 12-18 inches. Sepals are only about ½ inch long, and cupped forward, rather than flared outward. Leaves are numerous and reduced in size upward; they are deeply 5-7 lobed, and further sharply-toothed. Roots are extensive and fibrous.

Delphinine is the chief of several toxic alkaloids contained in the leaves of Delphiniums. Most losses to cattle occur in early spring, though studies indicate the lethal amount of alkaloids requires the animal to eat plants equal to about 2-3% of its body weight. Apparently cattle at times actually seek out these dangerous plants, being attracted by the flavour of the leaves. Curiously, sheep are unaffected, and have been used to eradicate the plants in restricted areas.

MYOSÙRUS MÍNIMUS L. *Mousetail.*

The common name translates the Greek mus, *mouse,* and oura, *tail,* which well describes the curious grey spike of minute flowers. This *very small* (minimus) plant is the species found at the coast, but M. ARISTÀTUS Benth., from the dry Interior, is actually smaller, both in the height of the plant, and in the length of the fruiting-spike.

Spring clay-puddles, that soon dry hard, are the favoured site for the little tufts of glabrous linear leaves, from which the mousetails stand erect, usually from 1-4 inches. The "tails" are the spike-like cluster of ripened achenes. On a casual glance, at summer's end, one might readily mistake the plant for a diminutive species of Plantain (see *Plantago*).

But in April or May one sees the Buttercup relationship in the single curious flower topping each scape. At that time a ring of 5 (less often 6 or 7) narrow sepals with long spurred bases generally encloses 4 or 5 inconspicuous slim white petals (though the petals sometimes never develop, and always drop quickly). There are 10 stamens (in M. minimus rarely 5, in M. aristatus usually 5), and a bulky cluster of crowded pistils. Ultimately, these form the "mousetail."

RANÚNCULUS. *Buttercup. Crowfoot.*

About 300 species, of colder parts chiefly of the Northern Hemisphere, are probably best known as familiar flowers of the field, though many occur in swamps, or partly submerged in lakes or streamlets. The latter kinds generated Pliny's name, meaning *littlest frog,* for they share such haunts with the amphibians. Some members of the genus, from the leaf-shape, are called Crowfoots. Every child knows the Buttercup; and in a more artless age, most children determined, by the reflection from its golden petals, that their friends did indeed, like butter! No other flower quite rivals the waxy effulgence of the Buttercup's petals.

There were Buttercups many millions of years before earliest man developed. Botanists consider that its surviving characteristics mark this as one of the most primitive of flowering plant families. Primitive the Buttercups may be, but assuredly successful—for they have spread their multitude of species and varieties across the globe. Thought-provoking is the notion that possibly the very primitiveness of the Buttercups has been a factor in their long survival and proliferation across the world. In such matters as pollination devices, they exhibit a simplicity, and lack of specialization at the opposite pole, for example, from the Orchids and the Mints. The petals lack honey-guides, and at best offer a landing platform for insects—though the nectar, in the freely exposed nectaries, may be sufficiently scented to attract the insect's attention. And both pistils and stamens are so numerous, that chances of either—or both—being touched, are excellent. Cross-fertilization does not depend upon any single group of insects. Short-tongued honeybees, or even flies and wasps, can be as effective as the long-proboscis insects, like butterflies, moths, and bumblebees.

All the species of Ranunculaceae, in greater or lesser degree, contain acrid alkaloids that usually turn grazing cattle away, which otherwise might be poisoned. Curing of hay that includes Buttercups, breaks down the poisonous Buttercup compounds so that they become innocuous.

You will find, among the wide variance of leaf-shape and size, height of plant, degree of pubescence—that make identification of many of the species difficult, two very helpful aids to identification. These are the shape and size of the *nectary,* like a little pocket at the base of each petal, and the shape of the *beak of the achene* (ripened one-seeded fruit).

Nearly 30 species occur in our area, so only a few representative members of the genus will be considered here.

Colour in flowers is a fascinating study. The principal colour compounds are the pink or red anthocyanins (which may turn to blue when the acid concentration in the cell-sap is changed), the green chlorophylls, and the yellow to orange carotenes and flavones. Certain wave-lengths of white sunlight are absorbed by the molecular structure of these compounds, and the remaining wave-lengths are reflected to the eye, which "sees" the resultant colour. But there are several other factors involved, including the structure of the cells on the surface of petals, and the presence of air in the cell-vacuoles. The latter is responsible for the scintillating "whiteness" that contributes to the brilliance of both white and (some) coloured petals. The effect is similar to that achieved by the tiny patches of white paper in a good water-colour painting.

The exceptional brilliance of Buttercup petals is also explainable in part by a layer of tapetum cells (packed with white starch granules) that lie beneath the yellow, oil-filled, epidermal cells.

"Velvety" petals (of e.g. Violets) contrast vividly with the shining Buttercup petals. Epidermal cells in the flower of the Violet present a roughened surface that reflects light in varying degrees, so that a rich depth of colour is produced. But in the Buttercup these cells are smoothly patterned, like flat tiles. There is even a sort of "varnish" layer of wax on their upper surfaces that helps to reflect light. A good microscope will reveal that the duller yellow base of each buttercup petal, near the nectary, lacks the starch grains so abundant in the tapetum layer of the outer portion of the petal.

And though the fields look rough with hoary dew,
All will be gay when noontide wakes anew
The buttercups, the little children's dower. . . .

Robert Browning:
Home-Thoughts, from Abroad

RANÚNCULUS ÁCRIS L. *Tall Buttercup.*

The specific name refers to the *acrid* juice of this, the common Buttercup that makes the fields of England golden—and is now rapidly establishing itself from Alaska to California. It is an unfortunate invader of pasturage, since the milk of grazing cattle is rendered unpalatable. Occasional fatalities among stock have been attributed to this species.

Recognition of nearly 30 species of Buttercups that occur in our area is—except in a few instances —difficult. Mature plants of this species are among the tallest of Ranunculus, not infrequently attaining 3 feet. The leaves are pentagonal in general outline, though deeply 5-7 cleft, and rather densely haired. The spreading sepals, soon falling off, are clothed with long, white, silky hairs. Petals are usually 5, about ½-inch long and a little more than half as broad, each with a smooth, obovate nectary scale at the base. If seed-heads have formed, the shape of the achenes is helpful in identification; in this species they are smooth, swollen at the base, with a marginal raised ridge, and short, straight beak that is sharply hooked only at the extreme tip.

Following page: ANEMONE OCCIDENTALIS (HABITAT)   [p.144]

159

ANEMONE OCCIDENTALIS $\times$½ [p.144]

CALTHA ASARIFOLIA $\times$½ [p.152]

COPTIS ASPLENIFOLIA $\times$⅞ [p.154]

CALTHA BIFLORA $\times$⅓ [p.152]

RANÚNCULUS AQUÁTILIS L. var. HISPÍDULUS Drew. *Water Crowfoot.* [p.167]

This *water-loving* species is one of several members of the genus that have become specialized for shallow ponds and slow-running streamlets. It is uncertain to which kind of leaf the old name Crowfoot applies, for these plants have submerged leaves that are reduced to fern-like structures (consisting merely of mid- and subsidiary veins), as well as floating leaves with very different 3-lobed blades.

But unusual as the long floating stems and two kinds of leaves appear in the Buttercup genus, the cream-coloured flowers show characteristic structures. There are 5 thin sepals, usually quickly dropped, and generally 5 unnotched petals, each with a small nectary at its base. The cluster of achenes is nearly globular.

This interesting member of the family is widely distributed over Europe and North America. It is in flower for an extended period of time, often from May until September.

As in the transition of life forms from salt to fresh water, so in the move from fresh water to land, plants necessarily led the way. About 425 million years ago primitive algae found niches ashore. These niches, in places such as river-edges and swamps, provided extensions of their aquatic environment. Here the algae evolved supporting tissues, conducting structures, and stomata for exchanging gases with the atmosphere, so that by the Carboniferous Period, about 100 million years later, lush forests of true terrestrial plants had developed.

The reader who has studied the succinct and precise characterization of such authorities as Abrams, Hitchcock, Taylor, or Szczawinski, may be interested to note the improvement in the science of plant description since Rycharde Banckes' *Herball* of 1525: "This herbe. . . men call water crowfote. This herbe hathe yelow flowres/as hathe crowfote and of the same shappe/but the leues are more departed and it hathe a longe stalke/and out of that one stalke groweth many stalkes small by the sydes. This herbe groweth in watry places."

RANÚNCULUS ESCHSCHÒLTZII Schlecht. var. SUKSDÓRFII (Gray) Benson. *Mountain Buttercup.* [p.163]

This is one of the plants whose apparent delicacy arouses our wonder, when contrasted with the savage rigour of its stormy perch, high on alpine exposures. The effect is almost as if a dainty yellow cup, set in an Elizabethan ruffle of green, had been transported from a subtropical setting. At other times, it will be seen in its thousands, just below the melting snow on a soggy alpine slope. The specific name, almost invariably mis-spelled, celebrates J. F. Eschscholtz, 1793-1831, a Russian doctor and naturalist on Kotzebue's expeditions southward from Alaska. Wilhelm Suksdorf was an authority on the flora of the State of Washington.

This is a polymorphic perennial species, many named varieties being distinguished in various parts of the plant's wide range—from the mountains of Alaska through the Rockies to California.

The stems are smooth, 2-6 inches tall, from a chiefly basal cluster of leaves. These are circular to semicircular, 3-cleft, and further deeply and coarsely toothed. The 5 yellow sepals are usually smooth, in some varieties covered with short yellow hairs, and somewhat reflexed before falling. The broad, overlapping petals are almost luminous with a colour that may owe its clear purity to the unfiltered light of high altitudes.

RANÚNCULUS FLÁMMULA L. *Creeping Spearwort.* [p.166]

The small yellow accents of this species ornament drying, muddy depressions with their *small flames* or flammula. The thin prostrate stems root at their nodes, each new plant pushing up a pair of 1-3 inch little "spear" leaves, and shortly a delicate stem, capped by the bright half-inch flower.

Further aids to identification are the small, nearly triangular nectary, the 5 sepals (about the same length as the petals, and covered with short stiff hairs below), and the achenes (which are smooth and have an almost invisibly small beak).

RANÚNCULUS GLABÉRRIMUS Hook. *Sagebrush Buttercup.* [p.167]

This perennial is widely spread through the Sagebrush and Ponderosa Pine country, where it blooms very early in the year. Soon after the thin snow has vanished, these bright yellow cups open their cheery faces to the warming sun. The specific name means *smoothest,* or very smooth, which describes the leaves. These are chiefly basal, blunt spoon-shaped, and usually entire, except for 2 notches at the tip. A more montane variety lacks these notches, the leaves being broadly lanceolate (var. ELLÍPTICUS Greene).

The plant is seldom more than 5 or 6 inches tall, and bears a number of showy, broad-petalled, waxy blooms about 1-1¼ inches wide. The nectary is quite distinctive, for it forms a deep pocket, the mouth of which is guarded by unusual, soft, white, hair-like fingers. Also unique are the oddly-crinkled brown buds.

RANÚNCULUS OCCIDENTÀLIS Nutt. *Western Buttercup.* [p.170]

This is a common species of moist well-drained soil, from Alaska to California, though limited (as the specific name suggests), to the far *west.* On the southern coast, on sun-warmed rocky slopes, the cheerful blooms may appear in early April, but the great displays of gold and blue (with *Camassia quamash,* which see) occur on the flatlands in mid-May.

AQUILEGIA FLAVESCENS ×½ [p.149]

AQUILEGIA FORMOSA (HABITAT) ×¼ [p.149]

163

CLEMATIS LIGUSTICIFOLIA (FRUIT) ×⅖ [p.153]

DELPHINIUM GLAUCUM (DETAIL) ×½ [p.155]

RANUNCULUS ESCHSCHOLTZII var. SUKSDORFII ×1¾ [p.160]

The plants average a foot in height, with leaves and stems either glabrous, or soft-pubescent. Basal leaves are deeply 3-lobed, then again 3-4 lobed and toothed, but the alternate leaves of the stem are moderately dissected, the uppermost becoming almost linear and entire. The 5 greenish (sometimes pink-tinged) sepals are characteristically spread, with the outer half sharply reflexed. The 5-8 bright petals are oblong, less than half as broad as long, and bear an obovate nectary. Achenes are variable, from short- to long-beaked, in our area.

One of the exceptional floral displays of the coastal springtime is the unforgettable carpets of Western Buttercup and Early Camas.

RANÚNCULUS RÈPENS L. *Creeping Buttercup.* [p.167]

One's admiration for this bright invader from Europe varies inversely with one's degree of involvement. Thus the gardener, battling its intrusion into his flower-beds, may be more apprehensive than appreciative. This characteristic invasiveness is indicated by the specific name, for repens means *creeping,* aptly descriptive of its insidious spread by long, decumbent branches, which root at the nodes. Bits of detached white roots also produce new plants. And seeds add their quota. Small wonder that Creeping Buttercup has extended its dominion from Atlantic to Pacific, even to Alaska, the Yukon, the Northwest Territories, and the rain-shrouded shores of the Queen Charlottes.

Any description is almost superfluous. However, most of the leaves, except in winter, are faintly marked with white, and in all seasons are covered with short white hairs. The nectary scales are wide (extending almost across the petal's base), with free edges. It must be admitted, if one is objective, that the large flowers, with their waxy brilliance, make a pretty picture against the mat of rich green leaves—in someone else's garden, of course!

RANÚNCULUS UNCINÀTUS D. Don. *Small-flowered Buttercup.*   [p.167]

Uncinatus means *hooked at the point,* a characteristic that is not unique, but very pronounced in the achenes of this species. In fact, in late summer, the ball-head of sharply hooked achenes is easily caught up by fur or fabric, and so transported. This is a tall species, its erect stems usually reaching about 2 feet in the open woodland it prefers. It is a lowland plant, very common from Alaska to California, especially west of the Cascades.

The best recognition feature is the small haphazard flowers, quite out of scale for the tall plant. There may be 1, 2, 3, 4, 5—rarely more—pale cream-yellow petals, a mere 1/16—3/16 inch long. The rounded centre of 10-30 greenish achenes is, if anything, more conspicuous than the petals. Two varieties have been named, one with nearly smooth foliage (var. UNCINÀTUS), the other heavily clothed with whitish hairs, that even extend to the achenes (var. PARVIFLÒRUS (Torr.) Benson).

THALÍCTRUM OCCIDENTÀLE Gray. *Meadow Rue.* [p.171]

Here is a rarity in a primitive family, many of whose genera display a lack of structural specialization—for this is a dioecious plant: only staminate flowers on one plant, only pistillate on another. There are no petals, and the 4-5 sepals are neither large nor conspicuous, suggesting that the species is wind-pollinated. If now we take notice of the thin leaves, precisely spread to intercept every ray of filtered light, we may anticipate with some accuracy where the plant will be found. In shade certainly, but not in the depths of the coniferous and windless forest. Then possibly it should be found among the dense growth of openings in the woods, particularly along stream-banks where some gentle airs always move? The reasoning is correct, and the tall stems (that will lift the inconspicuous flowers above the lower lush vegetation of such situations) are understandable.

It is not so easy to comprehend the advantage to a plant of avoiding self-fertilization, by the extreme measure of segregating the sexual structures on separate plants. One would think the chances of pollinating the pistils might be hazarded by isolating the two sorts of plants. Perhaps this species has, metaphorically, another trick up its sleeve, or—more precisely—at the base of its greenish sepals; for they release an odour that may be both more distinct than is apparent to the human sense, and more agreeable to insects. Since the stamens and pistils are dull purple (a colour not seen by bees) the few insect visitors are generally small flies. Close examination reveals such an abundance of small pollen-grains that our theory of wind-pollination is confirmed.

The name is one of Dioscorides'; thaliktron—applied to an ancient plant, whose identity has been lost. The specific name, of course, means western, or *of the west*. The Rue Family (*Rutaceae*) includes the citrus fruits, but also a number of plants with bitter, or even blistering taste (e.g. *Ruta graveolens,* Common Rue of the Old World). ("Rue", by a transposition of ideas, may have derived from the Middle English "rue" of Wiclif's Bible, Luke XI. 42—"But woe unto ye, Pharisees! for ye tithe mint and rue and all manner of herbs, and pass over judgment and the love of God. . . .")* We have put the matter to practical test, and can report that (like nearly every member of the Ranunculaceae) the juice is indeed acrid and bitter—sufficient to cause anyone to rue the experiment!

Members of the genus Thalictrum are difficult taxonomically, unless the mature achene is available for examination. Only the rare and tiny (2-4 inch) THALÍCTRUM ALPÌNUM L., of the six species of our area, is readily identified. T. occidentale is the common and widely-distributed species.

Thin round-toothed leaflets, twice 3-foliate, with no prominent veins, help to identify the present species. The straight lanceolate achenes are spread flat radially—or even reflexed—and are less than half as broad as long—with prominent veins and very short sticky hairs. Meadow Rue is found throughout our area, from the Coast to low altitudes in the Rockies. It is well worthwhile, and easy, to establish Thalictrum in the shady garden.

*For interest, the original version of 1380 reads: "But wo to you farisies that tithen mynte and ruwe and ech eerbe: and leuen dome & the charite of god. . . ."

166

CLEMATIS COLUMBIANA ×⅕ [p.153]

RANUNCULUS FLAMMULA ×2 [p.161]

DELPHINIUM MENZIESII ×1 [p.154]

RANUNCULUS GLABERRIMUS ×1⅗ [p.161]

RANUNCULUS UNCINATUS ×1⅖ [p.164]

RANUNCULUS AQUATILIS var. HISPIDULUS ×1 [p.160]

RANUNCULUS REPENS ×⅞ [p.164]

TRAUTVETTÈRIA CAROLINIÉNSIS (Walt.) Vail var. OCCIDENTÀLIS (Gray) C. L. Hitchc. *False Bugbane* [p.171]

The unusual name may suggest trout to wishful thinkers who note the lush abundance of this plant on stream-banks, but Trautvetteria actually honours a 19th century Russian botanist, E. R. von Trautvetter. As the specific name suggests, this is a far-ranging species, an eastern variety having been collected as early as 1788, in the area of the *Carolinas*. Our thinner-leaved, *western* (occidentalis) variety occurs in moist situations to moderate altitudes, from Vancouver Island to the Cascades. On the Coast we have occasionally seen the plant as the dominant ground cover, although few plants bloomed; so in such sites False Bugbane apparently spreads by freely-running rhizomes. The common name recalls Bugbane (*Cimicifuga elata*, which see) another apetalous plant with a mass of white stamens. (But the true Bugbane is a very much taller plant with huge, spreading, compound leaves, and an unpleasant odour efficient in keeping humans—if not insects—at bay).

In rather open woods the plants average 2 feet, but may be considerably taller in moist ditches. The large leaves (up to 10 inches across) are palmately lobed, deeply toothed, paler beneath, and covered with short, stiff, white hairs. There are no petals, and the 3-7 inconspicuous sepals are greenish, and strongly cupped. The attractiveness of the flower lies in the fluffy head of numerous white stamens. Quite hidden by the stamens—until their early dropping—are a number of pistils, which later develop into a cluster of hooked and strongly sculptured achenes.

TRÓLLIUS LÁXUS Salisb. var. ALBIFLÒRUS Gray. *Globeflower.* [p.171]

Trollius is from the German "Trollblüme", which suggests the Trolls or Goblins do not mind wet feet—for this is a genus of swamplands, usually at moderate to high altitudes. The specific name means *loose* or open, probably intended to describe the rather lax growth of this montane perennial, whose colonies appear—as the snow melts—wherever a marshy flat borders an alpine stream (from the Island, Coast, and Cascades to the Rockies—though not apparently in the Queen Charlottes (according to Calder and Taylor). When frost or rain visits its mountain home, the striking creamy flowers tent inwards like a little pink-tinged globe, whence the common name.

Lacking petals, these flowers consist of 5-10 broadly obovate, petaloid sepals, that enclose a fuzzy powder-puff of brighter yellow stamens, and many green pistils. Closer examination will show the outermost ring of stamens is modified (some authorities think these structures are the remnants of petals) into tubular-lipped staminodia that apparently secrete nectar (for we have watched the little "Blues" butterflies busily probing them, and meanwhile invoking a moment of delight for the observer). The smooth glistening leaves are handsome, and chiefly basal: they are divided into 5 lobes, then further deeply notched and toothed.

A troop of showy Globeflowers along a sparkling streamlet recalls Wordsworth's familiar lines, for the inward eye dwells with pleasure upon such recollections.

BERBERIDÀCEAE. *Barberry Family.*

ÁCHLYS TRIPHÝLLA (Smith) DC. *Vanilla Leaf. Sweet-after-death. May-leaf.*   [p.174]

We have not often listed as many as 3 common names for a species, but all are appropriate and one or more of these names are given in nearly 30 texts consulted. The generic name is pure Greek, achlys meaning *mist*, poetically descriptive of the vaporous white of the tiny flowers. They are seen to consist of a cloud of many stamens, and an inconspicuous stigma. Many of the reduced flowers (lacking both petals and sepals) cluster in each slender spire. Would that taxonomists were always so happy in their choice of names! Even the specific name is entirely apt, for the single large *leaf*, on a slender 12-inch stem, is indeed cleft quite into *three*.

This familiar and attractive plant covers large areas by means of its widely-ranging rhizomes. These extend into open areas, where mist and rain temper the sun (as along the Pacific coast) but keep to the shade of deep woods in the fiercer light of southern British Columbia. In the coastal garden Achlys is tolerant and attractive, especially in spring when the delicate leaves are unfurled to catch every beam of light. The leaves are so perfectly shingled that a fascinating variety of hues, shades, and tones of green is created by light transmitted and reflected. Country-folk formerly tied bundles of these leaves to dry, and so perfumed a room with their delicate vanilla scent.

BÉRBERIS AQUIFÒLIUM Pursh. *Tall Mahonia. Tall Oregon Grape.*   [p.170]

The generic name is derived from the Arabic "berberys", applied to one or more species of the Mediterranean coast. This is a large genus of perhaps 200 species found in disjunct areas of the Americas, Asia, Europe, and North America. Our 3 species are low shrubs of great ornamental value—B. aquifolium, in particular—being very good-natured in the garden.

David Douglas found this fine plant in the "Oregon Territory" near Fort Vancouver, at the mouth of the Columbia, in 1825. His enthusiasm was at once echoed in England when the plants became available there. For some years a plant fetched £10, at that time a very considerable sum.

Our native Berberis, unlike a majority of the species, lack sharp stem-spines. Only the toothed, leathery leaves bear mild, spinulose tips. Another characteristic is a bright-yellow inner bark, noticeable when the stems are broken. This bark was the source of one of the best yellow dyes available to the Indian people.

Tall Mahonia (named from Bernard M'Mahon, a minor early American botanist) occasionally reaches a height of 10 feet (near Duncan, Vancouver Island). It must take pride of place as one of our most attractive shrubs. The holly-like leaves appear shining or wet—whence the specific name, from aqua, *water*, and folium, *leaf*. Unlike the Holly,

RANUNCULUS OCCIDENTALIS ×½ [p.161]

MECONELLA OREGANA ×2 [p.173]

BERBERIS AQUIFOLIUM ×¾ [p.169]

TRAUTVETTERIA CAROLINIENSIS var. OCCIDENTALIS ×⅓ [p.168]

TROLLIUS LAXUS var. ALBIFLORUS ×⅗ [p.168]

THALICTRUM OCCIDENTALE ♂ ×1¼ [p.165]

however, the leaves are edged with "friendly" prickles (12-29 per leaf), and a proportion of the leaves that are 2 or 3 years old, turn brilliant tints of bronze, orange, and vermilion, before ultimately dropping. Each leaf has 5-11 firm-textured leaflets pinnately arranged. "Oregon Grape", of course, refers to the handsome clusters of dark-blue berries that are dusted with a pale powder or "bloom".

The perfumed flowers repay a closer look. You will be reminded at once of a miniature, short-trumpet daffodil. The effect is due to a ring of greenish bracts (sometimes—especially in bud—flushed with carmine), a double circle of 3 outer greenish, and 3 inner bright-yellow sepals, and finally an innermost coronet (composed of 2 circlets—each with 3 short, cleft petals of pale-lemon).

This fine plant is outstanding not only for size, leaves, and fruit but also for its quantities of beautiful yellow flowers, and for a delicious honey-like fragrance. Moreover, when we realize the fruit yields a refreshing grape-like juice (when mixed with sugar), and an excellent jelly, it becomes apparent that this ranks high among our native plants.

Berberis aquifolium is widely distributed in sunny locations throughout southern British Columbia, where from April to June, its cheerful yellow blooms gladden the beholder.

BÉRBERIS NERVÒSA Pursh. *Oregon Grape.* [p.175]

In contrast to *B. aquifolium* (which see) this might be called Low Oregon Grape, for its stem is never more than a few inches tall. From the upper end grows a cluster of exceedingly handsome leaves—firm, glossy, and mildly prickled—whose prominent venation is responsible for the specific name, nervosa meaning *veined* or sinewy.

In another respect this species is sharply distinct from its congener—its choice of habitat. Whereas *B. aquifolium* grows among rocks in full sun, B. nervosa forms a ground cover in the shade of high foliage. Characteristically, the latter species often occurs in light of such low intensity that the plants do not bloom, or produce only a few bleached and pallid flowers. But in or out of flower, the tuft of long pinnate leaves with 9-21 leaflets cannot be confused with those of any other native plant.

As might be suspected from the almost pure stands encountered under conifers, this species spreads widely by rhizomes; however, it is easy to keep within bounds, and has real merit in suitable areas of the garden. Here, and in the natural woodland where light permits, the slender spikes of deep-lemon flowers are highly decorative, and have a faint but pleasant perfume. Here also, through the winter months (though the leaves are perennial) occasional ones provide quite startling accents of positively barbaric scarlet.

Berberis nervosa is only found west of the Cascades, in southern British Columbia, and may be discovered in sporadic bloom through quite 6 months of the year.

BÉRBERIS RÈPENS Lindl. *Creeping Oregon Grape.*

This, as the specific name repens implies, is a *creeping* shrub about a foot high, which otherwise is difficult to distinguish from the more erect *B. aquifolium* (which see). It is a more eastern species, generally of southeastern British Columbia. The bluer-green, more rounded, softer-spined leaves of B. repens are further characterized by 15-43 spine-tipped teeth per leaf. If you have been sufficiently curious (and patient!) to count the spines on several leaves, you will be rewarded by a reasonable conviction that the plant under numerical investigation is not *B. aquifolium*, which has 12-29 spines, that are rather more prominent. After this dizzy experience, you may notice that the fruit of B. repens—if present—appears much darker, because the pale dusty "bloom" tends to be sparse.

 **PAPAVERÀCEAE.** *Poppy Family.*

MECONÉLLA OREGÀNA Nutt. *White Meconella.* [p.170]

California has given us the ubiquitous *Eschscholtzia* (now found in—and widely escaped from—gardens around the world). Alaska is endowed with 7 native Poppies (including the lovely *Papaver alaskanum* Hult.); but in all of British Columbia there are only 3 native members of the Papaveraceae family. And a tiny inconspicuous representative this one is; fittingly named—for Meconella is the derived diminutive of the Greek mekon, a *poppy*. It occurs in thin turf that is spring-wet, from *Oregon* and California, with its northern limit in Victoria. Meconella is one of the special treasures of Thetis Lake Nature Sanctuary, but few visitors in early spring ever notice it—a wee 2-inch plant almost invisible in the low grass and mosses—with a single white flower little more than ⅛ inch across. But before the small plants dry up and disappear (in early June), the characteristic capsule positively identifies this miniature as a true Poppy. The stem lacks, however, the milky juice familiar to us in horticultural species like the flamboyant Oriental and Iceland Poppies. The few leaves are about ¼ inch long, with entire margins. Henry remarks that the petals expand at night.

From the Edziza and Spatsisi Plateaus comes the PAPÀVER MACOÙNII Greene that resembles a low-growing Iceland Poppy, with pale-yellow inch-wide flowers.

ACHLYS TRIPHYLLA $\times$¾ [p.169]

BERBERIS NERVOSA (FRUIT) ×²⁄₅ [p.172]

CORYDALIS AUREA ×¾ [p.176]

BERBERIS NERVOSA ×½ [p.172]

FUMARIÀCEAE. *Fumitory Family.*

CORÝDALIS SCOULÉRI Hook. *Western Corydalis.*   [p.182]

Corydalis is unaltered Greek for the *crested lark*, probably because the tubular projection of the uppermost petal is, to a small degree, like a feathered crest—the fancied bird's bill being open, and the tongue represented by the joined inner petals. The specific name commemorates Dr. John Scouler, who explored the northwest coast of North America with David Douglas, in 1825. His journal makes fascinating reading.

This is a tall perennial, growing from thick rhizomes characteristic of the Fumariaceae family. The soft, hollow, smooth stems—usually partly supported by other vegetation—grow to a height of 3 or 4 feet. Each stem generally bears 3 impressive leaves (up to 16 inches long) that are thrice pinnately-divided, thin and delicate. After this preamble, the skimpy flowers, borne in a long, loose raceme, come as a distinct disappointment—for they are far too small (about an inch long) for the plant, and of a dispirited pink colour. The structure of the flower is, however, interesting. There are 2 membranous sepals, quickly dropped, and 4 petals in two pairs. The upper petal of the outer pair is hooded; the lower petal forms a lip. The tips of the inner pair are joined to provide a second hood that shelters the single 2-lobed stigma, and the double set of 3 stamens. The fat elliptical capsule is unusual, since it opens explosively at the slightest jar, and throws the seeds to a considerable distance.

The species is nowhere common, but inhabits wet shady openings—from Vancouver Island to the Cascades.

[p.175]   **CORÝDALIS AÙREA Willd.,** *Yellow Corydalis,* widely distributed over much of North America, is a much smaller plant with yellowish-white sepals and bright *golden* corolla. Its handsome blue-green much-lobed foliage attracts attention even before the brilliant flowers appear in May or June. The flower structure is similar to that of *C. scouleri* (which see) but the double hood is much shorter and round-ended. **CORÝDALIS SEMPERVÌRENS (L.) Pers.** *Pale Corydalis,* ½-2 feet, has similar blue-green foliage, but the flowers are pink with yellow tips, and the capsules are erect. It is widely distributed in open woods (including V.I.) but is not common.

DICÉNTRA FORMÒSA (Andr.) Walpers. *Western Bleeding Heart.*   [p.182]

This well-known perennial is common in moist open woods from western British Columbia southward. The spurs of the two outer petals provide the name: from the Greek dis, *twice,* and kentron, *spur.* Formosa in Latin means *beautiful,* for this is a handsome plant, clearly a small cousin of—and more modest, restrained, and to some tastes, more attractive than—the common Bleeding Heart of the garden.

The delicate foliage is exactly that greyish-green needed to set off the smoky purplish-rose of the flower-panicle, which is displayed effectively just above the leaves. The flower shape is unique, and instantly recognizable from the illustration. Dissection of a bloom reveals the 2 sepals, two sets each of a pair of oddly-shaped petals, a like arrangement of stamens, and a pistil with several lobes—that are characteristic of the family.

Dicentra formosa demands no special care in the garden, and provides a charming show from April to June. It ranges from the lowlands of the Coast eastward to the Cascades.

DICÉNTRA UNIFLÒRA Kell. of rare occurrence in southern British Columbia, is a tiny spring-blooming species, with a *solitary* white to pinkish, oddly-shaped *flower* at the top of a 2-4 inch stem. The small blossom is locally called Steer's Head, which is quite descriptive.

The leaves have unfurled all over the country . . . . Shade is
produced, and the birds are concealed and their economies go
forward uninterruptedly . . . . Myriads of little parasols are suddenly
spread all the country over, to shield the earth and the roots of the
trees from parching heat . . . .

Henry David Thoreau:
Journal, entry of June 1, 1854

 # CRUCÍFERAE. *Mustard Family.*

This huge family (about 350 genera and 2500 species) is a coherent group, clearly recognizable from the cruciform (disposed like a cross) structure of the 4 sepals and 4 petals, and from the structure of the elongated or short pod. The first characteristic is of course responsible for the name (crux, crucis, *a cross*). Nearly always there are 6 stamens, 2 being shorter and placed on opposite sides of the pistil. The naturalness of this group of plants was evident to early systematists. Even before the Christian era the Indian savant Parasara, in the *Vrikshay-ur-veda,* discussed the science of plants, and clearly recognized the present family (as the Svastika-ganiyam, a "cross" symbol to be dreadfully popularized two thousand years later). The grouping was recognized by the Aztecs, as is revealed in the Badianus Manuscript of 1552. As the "Tetradynamia", it is the only class in Linnaeus' system that has retained its integrity in modern thinking.

The family has provided many plants of agricultural importance, such as the cabbage and its kin, turnip and its kith, mustard, and many others. Also included are *Isatis tinctoria,* that provided the woad or glastum used by the early Britons, familiar Water Cress, and such garden flowers as Wallflower, *Alyssum, Aubrietia,* and *Lunaria annua* (Honesty).

These plants are rich in sulphur compounds; many also contain ascorbic acid.

The family is world-wide (a single species, *Pringlea antiscorbutica*—a revealing name—is found on remote Kerguelen Island) but most species occur in the North Temperate Zone. Some of our most persistent weeds are crucifers, notably the tenacious little Cress, *Cardamine oligosperma* (that at a touch explodes its seeds in our faces), Shepherd's Purse (*Capsella bursa-pastoris*), and the *Brassica* species that spread like a yellow carpet across neglected grain-fields.

However easy the recognition of a Crucifer may be, it is another matter entirely to determine in which of the very many genera it is classified. Hence the seed-pods (often found at the base of the spike whose upper flowers may have first attracted our attention) are almost always essential for the determination of species, and even of genera. In some of the genera extensive hybridizing takes place, so puzzling plants occur that trouble the most expert taxonomists. For this reason, and because many of the species are unattractive, only a few representatives of the Cruciferae are mentioned in this book.

BARBARÈA ORTHOCÈRAS Ledeb. *Winter Cress.* [p.182]

Barbarea is a genus of about a dozen species, named in honour of the 3rd century St. Barbara. The specific name means *straight-horn* probably with reference to the straight siliques. Several members of the genus were formerly grown for winter salads, hence the common name.

This is a rather showy, yellow-flowered plant. Its single stiff and ribbed stem may reach 2 feet, with rather numerous, pinnately-divided leaves, that are moderately reduced upward. Basal leaves are similar but larger (up to 4 inches long), with a much enlarged terminal-lobe. The clustered, small, bright-yellow flowers are typically cruciform, and soon succeeded by long straight siliques, that are sharply pointed but not prolonged into a beak. Seeds are brownish.

This biennial may be aboriginal, with a world-wide range. Like other members of the genus, Barbarea orthoceras prefers moist spots in woods and meadows.

BARBARÈA VULGÀRIS R. Br., *Yellow Rocket*, is a European import, very similar to *B. orthoceras* (which see), but with stem-leaves only lobed, not pinnately-divided, and a distinct "beak" projection at the top of the silique. Seeds are pearl-grey.

CÁKILE EDÉNTULA (Bigel.) Hook. *Sea Rocket.* [p.183]

This is a sprawling, robust, fleshy-leaved, glabrous plant of the upper portions of sea- and lake-beaches, surprisingly extensive in its growth when one realizes it is an annual. Cakile from qāqulla (Arabic) is the name apparently applied to the Mediterranean and North African plant, *Cakile maritima*. The specific name appears to derive from the Latin edo, *to eat*, but we have been unable to find any reference to aboriginal use of the plant as food. Rocket* is an early name used for a variety of crucifers.

The waxed and swollen leaves serve to store moisture during the drought of summer. They are oblong to lanceolate, coarsely and irregularly toothed. The pinkish-purple flowers of July and August fade to white, and are succeeded by conspicuous oval siliques, ribbed and distended, and almost an inch long.

*The plant with which the name was originally associated is the annual salad plant *Eruca sativa.* Eruca was early corrupted to Ruchetta by the Italians, to Roquette by the French, and finally to Rocket by the British.

CARDÁMINE PULCHÉRRIMA (Robins.) Greene. *Toothwort.*   [p.183]

Pedanios Dioskurides, now known as Dioscorides, in the first century A.D. wrote his *De materia medica,* which was for 1500 years more attentively studied than any book on botany ever written. It was the first illustrated botany, figuring about 500 plants and listing their virtues. A very precious copy, made in A.D. 512, has been found in the Imperial Library in Vienna. The drawings, after being several times hand-copied, have become so stylized that we can only guess that the originals were more life-like. But one of them is labelled "kardamon", and seems to show some cruciferous plant: this must have been the source of Gerard's name for the present genus. Pulcherrima is the superlative degree of *beautiful,* and may seem extravagant, but this species is notably attractive in this family among many insignificant and some dowdy members. There is a country wholesomeness about the little pink flowers, that is perhaps expressed in the old English name for an almost identical plant, Lady's Smock. (Many will know our plant under the older name *Dentaria tenella.*) Toothwort is a survival of the "Doctrine of Signs"; the white rounded rhizomes were thought to resemble teeth, so this was interpreted, in a homocentric era, as a sign by the Creator, that the plant ("wort" in Old English) was designed to assuage man's dental sufferings!

Moist deciduous woods of British Columbia, chiefly west of the Cascades, reveal this small pink crucifer (before the developing shrub-and tree-leaves have intercepted the light). The stems are about 8-12 inches tall, containing a cord-like string of xylem and phloem tubes. The smooth and pretty leaves are long-petiolar when basal. They change in shape upward—the lowermost being nearly round, with a few shallow notches on the outer end. The purplish sepals make a harmonious colour effect with the soft pink of the petals. Altogether this is a charming little plant which is easy in the garden, but well-mannered and never invasive.

When daisies pied and violets blue
And lady-smocks all silver white
And cuckoo-buds of yellow hue
Do paint the meadows with delight . . . .

Shakespeare: Love's Labour's Lost

DRÀBA INCÉRTA Pays.   [p.183]

Draba comes from the Greek drabe, for the Arabian Mustard (*Lepidium draba*) hence *acrid* or biting, with reference to the bitter sap of many of the 300 species that have been described. As Hultén remarks, "This genus presents many puzzling forms, permitting a variety of interpretations . . . ." Included are annuals (generally invasive weeds), biennials, and perennials (usually more choice plants of the higher mountains). Taxonomically the genus is not distinguished by any constant structural peculiarities, so that it will always afford difficult problems for the flower-lover and amateur botanist.

The specific name of the present species, incerta, meaning *uncertain*, suggests the difficulty of distinguishing this Draba.

Somewhat open tufts of this little alpine perennial consist of short stems bearing numerous, partly overlapping, firm, linear-oblanceolate leaves, whose margins are crisp with short stiff hairs. The small clumps never fail to attract the attention of the climber or hiker in the southern Cascades or Rockies, even before they bear clusters of yellow mustard-type flowers.

D. incerta is so very like *D. oligosperma* (which see), that one needs to compare the arrangement of hairs of the two species. The slightly broader leaves of D. incerta are covered with both simple and feather-shaped hairs that stand up from the surface; similar hairs of *D. oligosperma* are tight-pressed to the leaf-surface, and mostly arranged parallel with the mid-vein.

DRÀBA OLIGOSPÉRMA Hook.   [p.186]

This *few-seeded* Draba is widespread on alpine talus-slopes, and is especially frequent in the Rockies. It is a highly variable plant, generally smaller and less matted than *D. densifolia* (southern). The flowers are cream-yellow fading to whitish, carried on leafless stems about 1-3 inches tall. Leaves are pointed-linear, with a pronounced rib or keel, and bear strange hairs that repay examination under the microscope. These hairs resemble little frost-feathers, with their longer axis arranged parallel to the midrib of the leaf. The seed-capsule (silicle) is roughly elliptical and smooth to (more often) variably hairy. Identification of the numerous species of Draba occurring in our area is difficult. Another interesting species is DRÀBA LONCHOCÁRPA Rydb., found in high rocky areas from Alaska down through the Rockies, and curiously, on a few high mountains in the Queen Charlottes and Vancouver Island. Its flowers are white, its silicles longer and more slender, than those of *D. oligosperma*, and its pubescence stellate (star-shaped).

DRÀBA VÉRNA L. *Vernal Whitlow-grass.*

The specific name means *spring,* for this is one of our earliest flowers—a tiny plant blooming in March on sun-warmed rock barely covered with soil.

Very small white flowers appear scarcely to half-open, before yielding to flattened, narrowly-oval pods about ¼ inch long. These are well-separated, on slender pedicels branching from thin stems that may be from 1 inch to (rarely) 8 inches tall. The leaves are entirely basal, forming an intriguing small flat rosette. The leaf is variable in shape—but often oblong, entire to conspicuously dentate, and covered with tiny white hairs, which under the microscope are seen to be branched like the points of a star.

Earliness of appearance of this very small plant is the only reason that people notice it. Its common name arose from its supposed efficacy in treating an inflammation around the fingernail (a whitlow).

ERÝSIMUM ÁSPERUM (Nutt.) DC. *Mountain Wallflower.*   [p.187]

This splendid golden Wallflower, like its civilized relatives, is endowed with a fragrance, a fragrance that in this species reaches its apogee in the high altitude forms. We have memories of climbing upward, near the summit of Mt. Albert Edward on Vancouver Island's Forbidden Plateau—upward along a drifting trail of heavenly perfume, to kneel before our first plant. There ensconced above its rosetted leaves in a crevice of the volcanic rock, still during one of those windless lulls so rare in the mountains, a solitary spire reflected the clear brilliance of spectrum yellow.

This is a variable species. Plants we grew at the Coast from seed collected in the mountains, proved to be strictly biennial—but some populations are apparently short-lived perennials. The rather firm leaves occur in a basal rosette and also alternate up the stem. The basal leaves are oblanceolate, from nearly entire to rather sparingly dentate; the stem ones are more often nearly entire. The flowers are borne on stout pedicels in a somewhat crowded raceme, and span about an inch—or rather more. If ripened seed-pods (long siliques) can be found, they are highly characteristic, being roughly quadrangular in section and scarcely—if at all—constricted between the seeds.

This beautiful plant may be found in flower from May to August, according to altitude. The seed is not infrequently washed down from the mountain heights, to take root on sandy gravel bars along creek-beds not far above sea level. The various races of Erysimum asperum occur from southern British Columbia through most of the western states.

Erysimum is, by most authorities, derived from the Greek erusimon (eruein meaning *to draw*) apparently because, when applied as a poultice, the acrid mustard juices were thought to draw out the cause of pain. The specific name means *rough*—from the pubescence, or perhaps the toothed leaves.

ERÝSIMUM INCONSPÍCUUM (S. Wats.) MacM. *Small-flowered Rocket* is the other common Wallflower (of central and northern B.C.). Its small pale-yellow flowers

182

CORYDALIS SCOULERI ✕⅙ [p.176]

BARBAREA ORTHOCERAS ✕½ [p.178]

DICENTRA FORMOSA ✕¾ [p.176]

CAKILE EDENTULA ×²⁄₅ [p.178]

DRABA INCERTA ×¾ [p.180]

CARDAMINE PULCHERRIMA ×⅞ [p.179]

are clustered at the top of a stiff ½-2 foot stem. Leaves are linear, chiefly entire, and grey-pubescent with mostly 2-branched hairs.

HÉSPERIS MATRONÀLIS L. *Dame's Violet. Dame's Rocket.* [p.194]

This tall crucifer with its showy flowers—white through various shades of pink, purple, and violet—was brought from Eurasia in colonial days, and has become widely established along roadsides throughout North America, even to Alaska. Old names are fascinating, and this is a very old name. Aristotle's pupil Theophrastus (370-287 B.C.) apparently first used it. It is derived from the Greek hesperos, western, hence *evening*, when its fragrance is most pronounced. Pliny the Elder (who died while investigating the eruption of Vesuvius in A.D. 79) pointed out that it was cherished by Roman *matrons* (whence the specific name). This was the germ of the idea that resulted in the mediaeval "Dame's Violet". ("Violet" once meant "flower".)

The plant needs little description. In good soil it may reach 3-4 feet, the stems then being branched. The leaves and stem are finely-pubescent, with both simple and forked hairs. The scent—especially at dusk—is pleasant.

> *These I have loved . . .*
> *Rainbows; and the blue bitter smoke of wood;*
> *And radiant raindrops couching in cool flowers;*
> *And, flowers themselves, that sway through sunny hours,*
> *Dreaming of moths that drink them under the moon . . . .*

Rupert Brooke: The Great Lover

THYSANOCÁRPUS CURVÍPES Hook. *Lace-pod.* [p.194]

From a welter of small and confusing species, of many such genera as *Arabis, Brassica, Cardamine, Draba, Lepidium, Lesquerella*—not to mention that nightmare genus *Rorippa*—we have chosen to include this typical, small, and insignificant crucifer, and that for one reason only. The lacy seed-pods repay the kneeling and searching necessary to locate them, among the shallow-soil plants that crowd sunny rock-benches. The pods are responsible for the generic name: from thysanos, *fringe*, and karpos, *fruit*. Curvipes means *to cause to bend* or bow, which suggests the bending of the slender peduncles as the fruit matures.

Annual and small (usually 4-8 inches tall), with a few diminutive, alternate, lanceolate, and nearly entire leaves, and almost invisibly small, purplish-white flowers in a tight raceme, the plant escapes notice completely—until the lengthening peduncles develop the dainty, flat, round pods. But now the most blasé observer becomes intrigued by the seed-capsules as seen at close range. Often the surviving sepals are beautifully azure, and contribute to a little symphony of colour and form. The round flat pod is palest green, slightly humped over the seed at its centre, and edged like the crimped crust of a pie, with alternating green and bright rose. If you have yet to make the acquaintance of these unique silicles—hunt for them, for you are sure to be charmed.

Lace-pod is to be seen in early fruit from May to June, across the southern Province.

CAPPARIDÀCEAE. *Caper Family.*

CLEÒME SERRULÀTA Pursh. *Rocky Mountain Bee Plant.*

Cleome is a pleasant-sounding name, used by Theophrastus for a plant now unknown. He apparently coined the word from kleio, *to shut*, but the allusion is lost. This is a very fine plant of the Dry Interior, sometimes to moderate altitudes. Its showy clusters of pink flowers seem to be favoured by the bees—whence the common name. A beautiful albino form is preserved in the herbarium of the Provincial Museum (Victoria).

Though an annual, the Bee Plant may attain 4, or even 5 feet. Leaves are stalked, and have 3 even-sized, pointed-elliptical leaflets. The 4 sepals form a *notched* green cup, within which radiate 4 lanceolate petals almost ½ inch long—variously pink, purplish, or less commonly, white. There are 6 stamens, with very long pink filaments, that give the flower-cluster a fuzzy appearance. Pod-like, heavy, drooping capsules are very conspicuous, being nearly round in cross section, and long-ellipsoidal in shape.

DROSERÀCEAE. *Sundew Family.*

DRÓSERA ÁNGLICA Huds. *Long-leaved Sundew.* [p.186]

Drosera is from the Greek, meaning *dew*, descriptive of the glistening drops that trap small insects. This innovative device has apparently been widely successful in supplementing food production by the chlorophyll of these leaves, for more than 100 species of this family are spread over much of the world, particularly in Australia, North America, Europe, and Asia.

This species is widely distributed in North America, and Eurasia, including *England*, whence the specific name. In suitable bogs and swamps throughout British Columbia

186

DRABA OLIGOSPERMA ×1⅕ [p.180]

SEDUM DIVERGENS ×⅖ [p.190]

DROSERA ANGLICA ×2 [p.185]

(and north into Alaska, south into California) this remarkable plant may be encountered, sometimes in dense colonies extending over many acres. At moderate to rather high altitudes this species is perhaps more common than *D. rotundifolia* (which see). However, in some areas—as on the Forbidden Plateau of Vancouver Island—both occur, and undoubtedly hybridize.

The 2 species are at once separable, in or out of flower. D. anglica has leaf-blades at least twice, usually three or four times as long as broad, while in *D. rotundifolia* they are nearly round. Also, in the present species the basal clusters of leaves are held upright on their long petioles, rather than flat among the mosses, as in the former species.

Both species rather infrequently hoist a 6-inch leafless scape from which—all on one side—hang half a dozen dispirited whitish flowers. These open only in bright sunshine, that penetrates but seldom the mists of their marshy homes. We have patiently watched these rarely-open flowers, and observed the only visitors were mosquitoes and similar small midges and gnats—precisely the species that most often fall victim to the insectivorous leaves. If it hardly seems cricket for a plant to make "soup" from the insects that have aided it by cross-pollinating its flowers, we must reflect that in nature's scheme it is only economical to use again—even if with such brutal directness—the proteins of ephemeral insects.

Sundews are unique by virtue of their quite extraordinary leaves. Rather than repeat an account of the insect-eating mechanism of these dew-studded leaves, we shall refer the reader to the description of the following species.

One recalls the margin of a shallow mountain lake, around which massed thousands of these plants grew. The setting sun was low in front of us, so that the rays were reflected from millions of ruby beads, coruscating and flashing like a treasure trove of jewels.

Early botanists were puzzled by the unusual characteristics of the Sundew. Johann Bauhinus (generally known as Bauhin) was perhaps the most able of the 16th century systematists, yet in his *Historia plantarum universalis* (of 1651) he placed the Sundew with the ferns, mosses, fungi, and algae!

DRÓSERA ROTUNDIFÒLIA L. *Round-leaved Sundew.* [p.195]

The specific name refers to the *roundish* leaves, which, at the ends of long petioles, form a flat rosette. No one could possibly mistake a Sundew for any other native plant; this leaf-shape and habit readily distinguish the present from the previous species *D. anglica* (which see).

And what extraordinary leaves these are! The 2-8 inch flower-stalks, when they make their infrequent appearance in midsummer, are quite anticlimactic, as also are the small, drab-white, 4-5 petalled insignificant flowers. But the most casual glance is at once arrested by the unusual leaves, even though they are often partly hidden by the sphagnum and other mosses among which they grow.

Like small green frying-pans, the leaves contain chlorophyll for sun-chemistry, but

Preceding page: ERYSIMUM ASPERUM   ×1⅗ [p.181]

the sparse roots pick up from their watery surroundings very deficient amounts of minerals, and compounds of nitrogen and phosphorous. Hence the plant must make up this deficiency, and this is only possible in its wet habitat by a supplement of insect fare. (It is interesting that insectivorous plants generally, e.g. *Dionaea, Darlingtonia, Pinguicula, Sarracenia, Utricularia,* inhabit swamps and bogs.) The Round-leaved Sundew quite often grows upon old floating logs in stagnant lakes, or among the squelching mosses that ring pools in marshy terrain.

What makes the leaves so remarkable is the presence along the edges of highly modified hairs. These are gland-bearing filaments, or tentacles. Each gland secretes, and is enclosed by, a dew-drop of clear viscid fluid, tinted ruby-red by an altered derivative of chlorophyll. The colour is attractive to small crawling and flying insects, which are at once trapped. Then the tentacles bend inward, the leaf-edges curl, and the insect's juices are soon assimilated by digestive enzymes. Finally the leaf flattens, the chitinous husks of the insects blow away, and the glistening beads again appear.

Darwin,* in 1875, found that proteinaceous materials touched to the centre of the leaf quickly stimulated a response by the tentacles; inorganic materials did so only slowly, feebly, and transitorily; and rain-drops and wind had no effect. He also discovered that a fragment of human hair almost invisibly small (about 1/78,740th of a grain) would induce movement of the tentacles, as would extremely dilute solutions of many different nitrogen-containing compounds.

Wayfarers of today in suitable habitats throughout our area (in fact from Alaska south to northern California) may chance upon the Drosera, and be as intrigued by it as in their times were Linnaeus and Darwin.

*Charles Darwin in his *Insectivorous Plants* devoted over 300 pages to this plant, and suggested that a series of enzyme-triggered chemical changes produced the comparatively rapid movements of the hairs and leaf margins.

 **CRASSULÀCEAE.** *Stonecrop Family.*

SÈDUM. *Stonecrop.*

Sedum comes from Latin sedeo, *to sit,* referring to the squatty habit of these succulent plants that sit among the stones and rocks of their usual home.

There are perhaps 450 species, chiefly found in the North Temperate zone.

Dr. Fröderström in his (1936) monumental essay *The Genus Sedum L.,* comments (p. 9), "It seems as if the Crassulaceae, during their earlier development, had with few exceptions a decided tendency to spread *to the north and the east* . . . they have with a few exceptions avoided South America . . . . the whole southern half of the globe seems generally to have been forbidden territory to them."

The species have thick, fleshy leaves, well adapted to endure drought. Many are attractive, both in foliage and flower, and being good-natured, are often grown in gardens. Indeed, *Sedum spathulifolium* (which see) must be considered a first-rate garden plant—perhaps not sufficiently valued because we are too familiar with its lovely mats of many-tinted leaves, and sturdy bright yellow flowers, which ramble everywhere over rock outcrops of the Pacific coast.

Those whose acquaintance is limited to dried herbarium sheets can scarcely conjure up any reasonable impression of these plants, that cover—it seems—almost the bare stones with such an attractive crop.

SÈDUM DIVÉRGENS Wats. *Spreading Stonecrop.* [p.186]

The suggested English name is due to M. E. Peck, and is both descriptive and a translation of the specific name: however, it appears not to be in wide usage.

This is a common, rock-hugging perennial, occurring widely from rock ledges by the sea to talus and broken rock of high altitudes, from the Coast to the Cascade ranges. It can be counted upon to cheerfully spread its fleshy-leaved, rooting stems, and duly illuminate them with bright golden flower-clusters, no matter how dry and thin the garden soil, provided only that it has full sun. Sedum leaves can scarcely be confused with those of other plants, being perceptibly papillose, appearing waxed and plump to bursting point. In this species they are oval to obovate, about ¼-⅜ inch long. The leaves of the flowering stems are, for the most part, opposite. Perhaps a dozen flowers are carried in a flattened cluster at the top of each 2-5 inch erect stem. Ordinarily there are 5 pale-greenish sepals (barely joined at their bases) and about 5 bright-yellow, separate petals, that have short-pointed tips, and are spread only in hot sunshine. As usual in this genus there are twice as many stamens as petals, and the outermost ones are attached to the base of the petals. Commonly, 5 straight-beaked, buff-coloured follicles are formed, joined along their inner faces, but with the beaks, star-like—*divergent* and pointing outwards.

This is a friendly little plant, perhaps not sufficiently valued because it is so widespread and so easy to grow. The pudgy leaves in extreme drought turn reddish, and at such times especially the plant arrests one's attention.

SÈDUM LANCEOLÀTUM Torr. [p.194]

Though we have followed Hitchcock et al., in choice of this name for a common (and variable) species, it will be better known to many as *S. stenopétalum* Pursh. Fröderström, in his almost world-wide study, placed Torrey's name, lanceolatum, as a synonym for *stenopetalum*, and maintained (on distinctions which appear valid to a non-specialist) *S. douglasii* Hook. as a separate species. Hitchcock is unclear, in a final comment, whether he dismisses *S. douglasii*, or equates it with *S. lanceolatum*. To sum up, Fröderström's figure of the type *S. douglàsii* (collected by J. M. Macoun, 1902 "in British Columbia") shows a plant with follicles divergent to the point of forming a straight line. His type of *S. stenopétalum* "cultivated from seed, brought by Drummond, from the east side of the Rocky Mts., to Edinburgh and Glasgow" differs from *S. douglasii* in shape and vesture of sterile shoot, seed-shape, shape of petal, and divergency of follicles.

Essentially, both plants we have been discussing (or perhaps the 2, or more, varieties of S. lanceolatum) have a basal rosette of plump leaves, nearly to quite round in cross section. These leaves, and those that cluster tightly up the 2-6 inch flowering stems, vary from linear (most commonly) to linear-*lanceolate*, or even narrowly-ovate—the latter of course being flattened. Dark-green, sometimes dusted with a whitish farina, and generally becoming bronzed in the fall, the leaves may be smooth-surfaced, or covered with minute papilla (swellings). Rather pale-yellow flowers are clustered, in generally flattish heads. The 5 petals are variably sharp-pointed, but always distinctly separate to the base.

SÈDUM OREGÀNUM Nutt. *Oregon Stonecrop.* [p.198]

This generally southern species has worked its way along the coast, if Fröderström's opinion is accepted, northward to Vancouver Island (e.g. Mt. Helmcken), and Alaska, though Calder and Taylor did not find it in the Queen Charlottes. Since the pale-yellow, long-pointed petals (which age faintly pinkish) are joined at their bases (rather than distinct and separate as in other species), the plant is sometimes set apart in the genus *Gormania.*

The succulent foliage is most attractive, forming extensive mats of tidy rosettes—sometimes green but more often variously and richly bronzed. Flowering-stems are erect, with alternate leaves that are as fleshy as those of the sterile shoots, but not as broadly obovate. The seed-cases (follicles) are invariably erect.

This good-natured plant has attracted much attention in the garden. Though its rhizomes spread slowly it is never rampant, and in all seasons presents a tidy, well-groomed appearance.

SÈDUM RÒSEUM L. var. INTEGRIFÒLIUM (Raf.) Berger. *Roseroot.*

This variable species, in various forms, occurs on suitable scree slopes and rocky places—from Lapland, Switzerland, Wales, Ireland, North England, Scotland, and Russia, to Alaska, the Queen Charlottes, the Cascades, and the Rockies. Roseroot is the only *rose-coloured* species in our area (though most forms are rather greenish-purple). When bruised, the roots emit the fragrance of roses—hence the common name. As Hultén remarks, the leaves and young shoots are eaten raw, or boiled, by Alaskan and Siberian natives.

The 3-12 inch stems are more erect than those of other species, and crowded with flattened, fleshy leaves that are variably dentate. The flowers are crowded in flattish to rounded clusters. They are often imperfect, i.e. many have vestigial or no stamens in the pistillate flowers. Petals are rather fleshy, either blunt- or sharp-tipped, and distinct.

Good colour forms of Sedum roseum are worthwhile additions to the garden.

SÈDUM SPATHULIFÒLIUM Hook. *Broad-leaved Stonecrop.* [pp.198,199]

This is another of the 7 fine plants of this genus that brighten the rock ledges, talus slopes, and even dry Sagebrush deserts of our area. One could make an interesting collection of the native Sedums, or even (for suitable sites in the garden) of the lovely colour foliage variations of this one species. In shaded rock crevices, a distinct lime-green form occurs, in which the leaves are beautifully dusted with a silvery farina. On faces exposed to the full sun another type is locally called "Rock-rose", for many of the perfect little boutonnières develop shades of purple to deep rose-red, always centred by deliciously contrasting, smaller green leaves. Perhaps most beautiful of all are less-frequently seen variations, of ice-green most alluringly edged with shades of lavender and mauve.

All this beauty this treasure-plant possesses—besides a cast-iron constitution, complete freedom from pests, ability to creep up vertical rock faces yet never become invasive, an evergreen attractiveness; and if all this were not enough—a low-spreading canopy of brightest golden flowers that continue for a long period to gladden the grey rocks. It is a blue-print plant, one that a gardener might conjure up in his most optimistic and felicitous imagination! Yet its myriad plants scramble about the rocks and gravelly ledges, from the southern half of coastal and interior British Columbia to California. Only the peculiar perversity of man can account for the fact that this magnificent and common plant is not yet, in this country, reckoned a garden plant of outstanding quality. But the discerning few have long appreciated it, as Dr. Ira Gabrielson points out in his uniquely valuable *Western American Alpines* (of 1932)—"*S. spathulifolium,* found west of the Cascades from British Columbia to California, is not only the best of the natives [i.e. Sedums] but ranks high in comparison with any European or Asiatic yet imported into this country."

The species is easily recognized, and very constant in its characteristic features. The *leaves* are strongly flattened, and broadest beyond the mid-length, i.e. they are *thumb-shaped* (hence the name, spathulifolium). Those on the flowering stems are alternate, and often more brightly coloured than those forming the rosettes. The sepals are joined near their bases, and blunt-rounded at their tips. The mature follicles (seed-cases) are also joined at their bases, and the long-pointed tips point upward, with only the extreme tips divergent.

And beauty is not a need but an ecstasy.
It is not a mouth thirsting nor an empty hand stretched forth,

But rather a heart enflamed and a soul enchanted.
It is not the image you would see nor the song you would hear,
But rather an image you see though you close your
eyes and a song you hear though you shut your ears.

Kahlil Gibran: The Prophet

 # SAXIFRAGÀCEAE. *Saxifrage Family.*

This is a large and varied family containing many of our most prized rock plants. As most gardeners know, the name means *rock-breaker*, for typically, many species grow in such narrow crevices one might believe the roots have had some part in the formation of the cracks. The hallmark of the Saxifrages is the pair of carpels (usually visible in the 2 pistils) which may be partly united below.

The temperate and arctic regions of North America and Eurasia are home to most of the 800 species. Horticulturally valued members of the family are found in the genera *Saxifraga, Astilbe,* and *Rodgersia.*

BOYKÍNIA ELÀTA (Nutt.) Greene. *Slender Boykinia.* [p.194]

This is a pleasant plant for moist shady spots in the garden, where its pretty leaves effectively set off loose panicles of dainty white blooms all through the spring and summer. The leaves are interesting: somewhat heart-shaped but deeply 5- to 7-cleft, and further sharply dentate. Slightly glossy lower leaves have petioles that are long, but those of the stem are imperceptible. Instead, the stem-leaves bear narrow stipules, and several long brownish bristles. The 5 sepals are reddish and pointed, and joined about ⅔ of their length to form a persisting, sharply-notched cup. The 5 clawed-petals have oval blades of variable colour. A good form is a clear pink; but most common is white, fading purplish.

The English name given is advanced with small enthusiasm: it is due to M. E. Peck, and we can find it in no other text. In general, we concur with David McClintock that there is little to commend the practice of "manufacturing" an English name that is merely a translation of the Latin universal; or even less useful, one that no more than repeats the Latin. In that author's inimitable *Companion to Flowers*, speaking of the fact that most English wild plants do not possess distinctive English names in common use, he writes, "To produce such a list for all our wild plants, however, is a task of quite unbelievable difficulties, far beyond the wit even of the British Standard Institution . . . . ." We have commented on this problem at some length in the Introduction. With

194

HESPERIS MATRONALIS ×⅖ [p.184]

THYSANOCARPUS CURVIPES (FRUIT) ×1¾
[p.184]

SEDUM LANCEOLATUM ×⅗ [p.190]

BOYKINIA ELATA ×½ [p.193]

DROSERA ROTUNDIFOLIA (LEAF) ×9 [p.188]

literally dozens—in a few cases a hundred or more—common names already existing in various parts of the country for one plant, the choice becomes impossibly invidious. After all, why bother? Even if (and this will be immediately challenged by those long accustomed to apply the name to *Calypso bulbosa*, which see) we agree on Lady Slipper (or Lady's Slipper) for *Cypripedium calceolus*, those whose natural language is French (whether hailing from Quebec or Navarre) will surely not replace Sabot de Vénus with Lady Slipper, nor will those speaking German abandon their name, Frauenschu. If names like Boykinia seem "harder" than *Petunia* or *Geranium*, use will bring familiarity. Finally, to call this species Slender Boykinia may be helpful in distinguishing it from the stouter-growing *B. major*, for example, if—and only if—English is our native language. We have a name that is recognized by every ethnic group the world over: it is Boykinia elata. As has been our purpose and practice, and in the belief that association of ideas may aid recall of the proper scientific names, we point out that elata means *tall* (the slender flowering-stems reach 24 inches), and that the rather odd-sounding generic name honours Dr. Samuel Boykin (a naturalist of Georgia, U.S.A., who died in 1848).

The range of Boykinia elata is Vancouver Island (where it is quite common in suitably moist and sheltered locations) and more sparingly, eastward to the Cascades.

HEÙCHERA MICRÁNTHA Dougl. *Small-flowered Alumroot.*   [p.206]

Several of the 6 species of this genus that occur in our area hybridize, so that the variable plants are difficult to identify. The generic name is derived from Dr. Johann von Heucher, a professor of medicine at the University of Wittenberg, and the specific one means *small-flowered*. The English name refers to the astringent quality (like alum) of the thick rhizome. A familiar member of the garden flora is (originally Mexican) *H. sanguinea*, long esteemed for its pink or scarlet Coral Bells.

A favoured perch of H. micrantha is a creviced cliff face, often shaded, and sometimes looking down on sea or lake. Here it is charming, with its mist of tiny white blooms dancing on slender arched stems, above a cluster of handsome leaves. This little plant is common on Vancouver Island, and extends to the Cascades. Heuchera takes kindly to life in the garden, where its airy panicles and good nature win many admirers.

There are in our area a great many members of the "Sax" clan, that have, like this one, clusters of palmately-veined notched leaves and small pale flowers in panicles on slender scapes. Some care in studying details of structure, possibly with the help of a 10X magnifier, is needed for their identification.

The leaves of Alumroot are all basal, with long petioles 2-3 times as long as the blades, which are cordate (heart-shaped), with shallow lobes and irregular teeth. They are usually clothed with long silky whitish hairs, and the petioles are fringed with comb-like pubescence. The 5 sepals are hairy, largely joined to form a bell-shaped cup. Tiny white oval petals are 2-3 times as long as the calyx-lobes. It is important to count the stamens (5) which will at once distinguish Heuchera from *Saxifraga* and *Tiarella* (which have 10), and from *Tolmiea* (which has 3). The seed, if available, is distinctive;

it is dark brownish-purple, like a little ellipsoid hedgehog with rows of short tubercles.

HEÙCHERA GLÀBRA Willd. *Smooth Heuchera* is very similar to *H. micrantha* [p.207] though the leaves are usually broader than long, and rather more sharply-toothed. However, apparent hybrids occur, that are confusing in leaf-shape and nature of margins. The seed of H. glabra is distinctively curved—like a fat banana—paler in colour than those of *H. micrantha* and marked by fewer and longer spines. The ranges of the 2 plants overlap, but H. glabra is more northern (into the Queen Charlottes and Alaska), and more common in the Cascades.

HEÙCHERA CYLÍNDRICA Dougl. ex Hook.— is strikingly different, with much [p.199] larger flowers in a close panicle that looks thick and heavy by comparison with the open arrangement of the 2 previous species. H. cylindrica is highly variable, so that several varieties have been named—though these apparently intergrade. Generally the leaves are slightly longer than broad. Flowers are cream to greenish-yellow. The campanulate 5-lobed calyx is conspicuous, quite obscuring the shorter petals (which may be 5 or fewer in number, or even lacking). Apparently none of the forms occurs west of the Cascades, but in July the species is widespread through the southern and central Interior.

LEPTARRHÈNA PYROLIFÒLIA (D. Don) R. Br. *Pear-leaf.* [p.199]

This is a monotypic genus whose name is derived from lepto, *slender*, and arrhen, *male*, in reference to the slender filaments of the stamens, which are as much as 1½ times as long as the petals. Pyrus is the apple, quince, mountain-ash and pear, whence pyrolifolia = *pear-leaved.*

Few notice the compressed head of greenish-white flowers, but the scarlet follicles (fruits) are arresting features of alpine rills and cold meadows. So are the handsome leaves: leathery and glossy-green above, silvery-green below. They form a basal rosette, and are obovate, with pronounced teeth that point forward. A single 6-12 inch stem usually carries one or two leaves, much reduced upwards. Individual flowers in the rounded cluster are dominated by the 10 long stamens, the petals being shorter and very slender. One expects much more of such an imposing ring of basal leaves!

The bright seed-pods are a common feature of wet stream-sides in the Coastal mountains, and eastward in our area, as well as northward into Alaska.

LITHOPHRÁGMA PARVIFLÒRA (Hook.) Nutt. *Fringe-cup.* [p.206]

Greek lithos, *stone*, and phragma, *wall*, suggest a habitat we have never seen graced by this fragile little perennial. It is found over much of the Province, in grassland and Sagebrush drylands, but is most common (below rock outcrops) in the spring-wet short-turf of the southern Coast.

198

CONVOLVULUS SOLDANELLA ×½ [p.408]

SEDUM SPATHULIFOLIUM (LEAF) ×1 [p.192]

SEDUM OREGANUM ×½ [p.191]

PARNASSIA FIMBRIATA (DETAIL) ×3 [p.202]

HEUCHERA CYLINDRICA　×½　[p.197]

LEPTARHENIA PYROLIFOLIA (FRUIT)　×⅖
[p.197]

SEDUM SPATHULIFOLIUM　×⅘　[p.192]

The plant is readily recognized. Very early in the spring, from a small nubbly bulb, spring a few long-petioled leaves that are nearly round in outline, though 5-cleft almost to the base, and further triply-indented. The few 5-10 inch stems that shortly appear, usually carry 2 smaller leaves that are more narrowly-segmented, and nearly or completely sessile. By the end of March, or soon afterward, half a dozen round pink buds appear, and then unfold the delicate flowers shaped like snowflakes, but soft pink, and cupped in a 5-lobed green calyx. The 5 petals are about ⅜ inch long, usually so deeply 3-cleft they appear fringed. Both surfaces of the leaves, petioles, and flowering-stems, especially upward, are thickly covered with very small glandular hairs.

This is one of the appealing *small flowers* of our wet spring. By midsummer it has shrivelled away, and only the dormant rootstock and bulblets remain to wake again with the lengthening days.

MITÉLLA. *Mitrewort.*

The name is the Latin diminutive of mitra, a cap or *mitre*, derived—not too aptly—from the shape of the seed capsule. (For a perfect little bishop's mitre one could imagine no more perfect image than the capsule of *Tiarella*, which see).

This is a genus of a dozen species found in northwest America and northeast Asia. All are small plants with slender stems rising 6-18 inches above a basal cluster of long-petiolar, roundish, notched leaves. The five pale petals are reduced to mere branched threads appearing opposite, or alternating with, the 5 or 10 short stamens. Though tiny, these flowers are fascinating, for upon close examination they suggest jewel-work, superbly crafted of fine wire.

These little members of the Saxifrage family reveal the wisdom of a proper approach to plants—on one's knees.

> . . . *And, flower-lulled in sleepy grass,*
> *Hear the cool lapse of hours pass,*
> *Until the centuries blend and blur . . . .*
>
> Rupert Brooke:
> The Old Vicarage, Grantchester

MITÉLLA PENTÁNDRA Hook. [p.210]

The specific name means *five anthers*, a feature shared with 4 other members of the genus occurring in our area. Search of more than a dozen Floras has failed to reveal an English name of other than local usage. This is one of the more common species of Mitreworts.

This delicate inhabitant of moist and shaded places among the mountain areas of B.C., must be closely examined if its miniature beauty is to be discovered.

Mitella pentandra grows from a perennial—sometimes creeping—rootstock. In spring this produces a few somewhat heart-shaped leaves—1-2 inches long, rather deeply-toothed, with sparse, coarse hairs above and below, and a hairy petiole two to three times as long as the leaf-blade. From this basal cluster in May or June rise a number of foot-long, slender stems carrying perhaps a dozen flowers, each only ⅓ inch in diameter but as marvellously wrought as any jeweller's work in gold wire.

The 5 yellow petals, like branched threads, arise from the hypanthium (basal platform) directly opposite each of the 5 stamens. The nature lover will find much to intrigue him in the miniscule geometry of the Mitreworts, some of which have the petals inserted in the spaces between—rather than opposite—the stamens, and one (*M. nuda*, which see) that has 10 stamens (inserted both opposite to and alternate with the petals).

It has come to this,—that the lover of art is one, and the lover of nature another, though true art is but the expression of our love of nature. It is monstrous when one cares but little about trees and much about Corinthian columns . . . .

Henry David Thoreau: *Journal*, entry of Oct. 9, 1857

MITÉLLA TRIFÌDA Grah. *Three-toothed Mitrewort.* [p.211]

Trifida means *three-parted*, since the long-clawed white to lavender petals are thrice-lobed at their tips. This is a common species of shaded forests and moist mountain slopes, of the interior ranges of our area.

The plant is similar to our other species of Mitella—except in details of the flower. M. BRÉWERI A.Gray has yellowish flowers like those of *M. pentandra* (which see) but [p.207] the 5 stamens are placed *between* the lacerated petals. M. CAULÉSCENS Nutt. also has 5 stamens but they are *opposite* the greenish petals, which age purplish toward their bases. M. NÙDA L. is easily recognized by its longer, pointed calyx-lobes, and by its 10 stamens. M. OVÀLIS Greene is common from the west slopes of the Cascades to the [p.206] Coast; its leaves are longer than wide, its stamens 5, and alternate with the skimpiest petals of the genus—like thin, green wire tridents. All of these Mitreworts are intriguing.

M. trifida is thus separable in the field from the others as the only Mitella with white petals. (The lavender tint is only evident from a few feet.) The others are green to gold. All the species have a few hairy, somewhat roundish, basal leaves—always with long, pubescent petioles, and some degree of lobing or notching. All have slender scapes 6-16 inches tall, that are leafless (except for *M. caulescens*, which, as its name suggests, has 2 or 3 reduced *cauline* leaves). And all are attractive ground covers in a shaded and moist part of the garden. There the tiny flowers, like exquisitely-crafted wire jewellery, can be more readily examined.

PARNÁSSIA FIMBRIÀTA Konig. *Fringed Grass-of-Parnassus.*   [pp.198,211]

Mt. Parnassus in Greece inspired the generic name; the fimbriate or *fringed* bases of the petals, the specific one. "Grass" is a survival of an uncritical age, when the word was often equated with "plant". The broad heart-shaped leaves are not in the least reminiscent of blades of any grass.

This is the most attractive member of the genus that occurs in our area—indeed, if you have a sufficiently wet seepage in your garden, this plant can be easily and rewardingly established. The interesting creamy flowers, nearly an inch across, come in August or September, when many garden flowers are out of bloom. Parnassia fimbriata is widely distributed in wet runnels, from Alaska southward, including the Queen Charlottes.

From a short perennial rootstock the basal leaves spread their shiny heart-shaped and entire blades, at the end of smooth petioles about 2½ to 3 times as long. The 6-15 inch slender scapes have a clasping bract about halfway up, and are terminated by the showy flower. The 5 elliptical sepals are joined at their bases, and either entire or with glandular teeth. Five, spreading, creamy-white petals are clawed, and generally obovate, with 5-7 conspicuous greenish veins, and most conspicuously fimbriate with fleshy hairs near their bases. Another interesting feature is the staminodia (modified stamens): they appear like yellow accents at the base of each petal. Additionally, there are 5 fertile stamens, each with a rather large anther, and a plump 4-carpellate pistil.

The staminodia are characteristic of the genus Parnassia—and interesting structures they are. The shape of these "pseudo-stamens" is of value in recognizing the 4 species occurring in our area. The staminodia are striking in appearance: green, yellow, or orange against the white petals, usually with a number of fingers, each ending in a glistening knob. Apparently pollenizing insects are attracted because they mistake for nectaries the sham drops of honey.

PARNÁSSIA PALÚSTRIS L. *Marsh Grass-of-Parnassus.*   [p.211]

Palustris means *of marshes*, bogs, fens or stagnant water. This species occurs among squelching sphagnum along lakeshores, or the margins of springs, and in wet tundra, from Arctic America southward in the Rockies and Cascades.

Unlike *P. fimbriata* (which see), the petals of this 4-10 inch plant are not fringed along their lower portions. The single bract, less than halfway up the slim smooth stem, is usually almost as large as the long-petioled, heart-shaped, basal leaves. Five white petals are marked by a variable number of greenish veins.

Alternate with the bases of 5 fertile stamens, at the base of each of the petals, are the curious staminodia, with 6-20 or more fingers, each ending in a swollen knob that gleams in the sunshine like a real drop of nectar—though actually there is no fluid present. These false nectaries induce at least one species of fly (*Lucilia* sp.) to respond to the misleading advertisement.

SAXÍFRAGA. *Saxifrage.*

Saxifraga, with about 300 species, is the largest genus of the family, with representatives being found in the cool regions of the northern hemisphere, and along the chain of the Andes to Tierra del Fuego (where some very odd-looking members are found). The name is appropriate for these rock and mountain lovers, being derived from the Latin saxum, a *rock* or large stone, and frango, the verb *to break.*

Many of our native species are low perennials, growing from a rosette, or from a looser group of basal leaves. Most have 5 petals (generally white and often purple, orange, or yellow-spotted); all have 10 stamens.

There is an unmistakable quality of neatness and proportion about many of the species, that wins them (in spite of the small size of their flowers) a high place in the regard of most gardeners and naturalists. Indeed, these little plants have been admired for many centuries.

Thomas Johnson's editions (1633 and 1636) of Gerard's *Herball* include some woodcuts printed from blocks that were based upon ms. drawings more than 1600 years old! The original drawings (almost certainly from life) probably date back to Krateuas, of the first century before Christ. They were copied by a succession of scribes, so that it is perhaps not surprising that the representations became highly stylized. The ancients knew this. Pliny, for example, commented (Holland's translation) ". . .they that limned and drew them out, did fail and degenerat from the first pattern and originall." Thus the drawing called Saxifraga in the 9th century manuscript *Herbarium Apuleii Platonici* reveals two—and only two—useful pieces of information about the plant figured: it had opposite leaves, and the flowers were terminal on the stems.

SAXÍFRAGA AIZOÌDES L. *Yellow Mountain Saxifrage.* [p.207]

One frequently encounters the terminal "oides" meaning "like", so here *like aizoon:* Aizoon in turn was an old name for a genus of plants famed for their ability to live under almost any conditions; their name derived from aei, *always,* and zöon, *alive.* Linnaeus was apt in his choice of epithet for this sturdy little rock plant, with its fat Sedum-like leaves. He knew and admired it in Lapland and Sweden; the species also is local in northern England, Ireland, and Scotland, where the yellow petals are usually red-dotted. With us it is found in the Rockies, from Alaska to about the 49th parallel.

Loose mats of entire linear leaves, puffed with stored fluids, spread over the stones of icy streamlets in the mountains. The leaves end in an abrupt tip (mucronate), or sometimes a soft short tip. Both the basal and scapose leaves appear smooth at first notice, but will be found covered with very small, pale, fleshy hairs. The 2-4 inch upright stems are leafy, and generally bear one pale-yellow flower, about ⅜ inch wide. A pair of plump green carpels (typical of the Saxifragaceae) is usual, but as in the illustration, in this species rather often three are found. The 10 stamens have conspicuously large anthers, and the 5 linear-oblong petals are without claws, but are usually slightly ragged (erose) at their tips. The mountain rambler should be on the alert for possible orange-coloured forms of Saxifraga aizoides, or variations with orange or red spots on the petals.

SAXÍFRAGA BRONCHIÀLIS L. var. AUSTROMONTÁNA (Wieg.) G. N. Jones.
Common Saxifrage. Matted Saxifrage. [p.218]

The specific name is from bronchus, a *division* or branch, with reference to the freely branching, creeping, and rooting wiry brown stems, that result in the characteristic mat-like growth.

This is a beautiful perennial rock cover, most useful in the garden—although in time rather ugly brown patches tend to develop after the mats have spread over 2 or 3 feet. In one or another of various varieties or possibly subspecies, it is found from sea-level rocks to high alpine screes, circumboreal and southward down the mountain ranges.

The evergreen leaves, as has been suggested above, are sufficiently variable to result in plants that appear quite unlike. They may be harsh, slim-lanceloate, and sharp-tipped, with rigid stubby cilia along the margins. In other locations you will find plants with much softer thumb-shaped leaves, with much less conspicuous, smaller, softer hairs, blunt-ended with only a stubby tip. In a long succession through the summer, 2-6 inch flowering-stems rise from the dense mat of leaves. They carry a few smaller spinose leaves, and a number of branches, each terminated by a round bud, or a showy half-inch flower.

Each flower is a little picture. The oval, white to cream petals are bewitchingly dotted with a series of round spots of pure spectrum tints, graduated from tip to base in crimson, through orange, to chrome-yellow—a small symphony of colour.

SAXÍFRAGA CAESPITÒSA L. *Tufted Saxifrage.* [p.219]

The specific name means *tufted*; and what admirable little tufts of neat foliage these are!

The crowded little leaf-clusters huddle inward and show their brownish older foliage in the drought days of August, but rejoice with the first rains, and exuberantly spread three-fingered leaves of brightest green. Many 4-inch scapes push upward, usually in April, but we have seen laggard plants covered with bloom at 9000 feet, in late September, when snow might be anticipated. This accommodating rock plant is as much at home in sea-level gardens as in the high mountains of our area, or in parts of Alaska, Quebec, Lapland, Switzerland, a few niches in the Cairngorms and on Ben Nevis.

The clump of distinctive, finely glandular foliage identifies this species. Wedge-shaped, but with 3-finger divisions at the tip, the leaves are tightly bundled in little whorls. Two or three leaves, 3-lobed like those of the basal rosette, alternate up the short scape, then become simple and bract-like. One to several white flowers, spanning ½ inch (or rather less) look up from the top of the glandular scape. The calyx-cup is

SAXIFRAGACEAE

205

5-cleft about halfway. Five obovate petals may be rounded, or slightly notched at the tip; the base is usually narrowed, and sometimes slightly clawed.

Saxifraga caespitosa is a highly variable complex of forms, varieties and subspecies, but as mentioned above, the leaf-shape and growth habit will permit easy identification. The illustration is of a very dwarf and densely pubescent form occurring near Sooke Harbour, Vancouver Island.

SAXÍFRAGA FERRÙGINEA Grah. *Rusty Saxifrage.* [pp.211,222]

Rusty is the meaning of the specific name of this highly variable perennial Saxifrage. Old leaves may be purplish below, and very frequently some of the leaves in the beautiful rosettes develop rose tints, but the name probably was intended to call attention to the calyx, which is rather constantly reddish or purplish.

This pretty little plant is much admired over its wide range, from sea to alpine levels, and from Alaska southward in the Coastal and Cascade mountains, as well as on the Queen Charlottes and Vancouver Island. Rock crevices and deeper moss patches suit S. ferruginea, and we have found it easy and rewarding in the rockery.

The 1-3 inch leaves are all basal, thumb-shaped, generally with irregular, deep, but sparse teeth, always ciliate (with cilia, i.e. marginal hairs), and sometimes grey-haired, especially below. The scapes are 6-20 inches tall, very glandular-haired near the top, and strongly branching upward. Each branchlet is subtended by a small linear bract and terminated by a small white flower about ⅓ inch across. The flowers differ from the usual pattern of the genus, being irregular, i.e. with two types of petals.

On close inspection how exquisitely shaped these small flowers are! The two lower petals are unmarked and pointed-elliptical, attenuated into a long, slender base. But each of the other three petals enchantingly remind us, in chaste outline, of a Grecian vase. The incomparable line could not be improved. Two cup-marks of purest yellow are placed just so on the alabaster. A final perfect accent is provided by the plump anthers: coral before anthesis, cinnamon after.

Occasionally Saxifraga ferruginea produces clones in which the normal reproduction by seeds is supplemented by propagules (miniature plants) borne in the axils of the bracts. Our illustration shows that these daughter plants may be produced in large numbers. Readily detached by wind, they roll down-slope to suitable crevices. In this way the species is propagated even when unseasonal snow prevents seed-production.

. . . we need to put into effect, . . . for its [wilderness'] preservation, some other principle than the principles of exploitation or "usefulness" or even recreation. We simply need that wild country available to us, even if we never do more than drive to its edge and look in. For it can be a means of reassuring ourselves of our sanity as creatures, a part of the geography of hope.

Prof. Wallace Stegner: from "Wilderness Letter" in *The Sound of Mountain Water, 1969.*

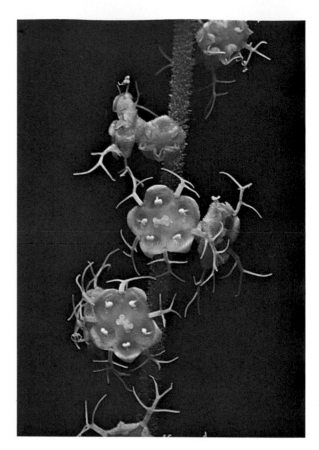

LITHOPHRAGMA PARVIFLORA ×⅜ [p.197]

MITELLA OVALIS ×9 [p.201]

HEUCHERA MICRANTHA ×⅓ [p.196]

HEUCHERA GLABRA ×⅖ [p.197]

SAXIFRAGA AIZOIDES ×1½ [p.203]

MITELLA BREWERI ×¾ [p.201]

SAXÍFRAGA INTEGRIFÒLIA Hook. *Early Saxifrage.* [p.218]

As often in this genus, Saxifraga integrifolia (which might be called *entire-leaved*) is highly variable. Its nondescript cluster of white flowers may be seen from March to midsummer, from sea level to subalpine short-turf slopes throughout our area—though not, apparently, in the Queen Charlotte Islands.

The leaves are basal, usually more or less rusty below with appressed hairs, but varying in size and notably in shape (elliptical, lanceolate, or even diamond-shaped) and in length of petiole (from longer than the blade to very short). The stout unbranched scape elongates during the rather long flowering period, and may reach 24 inches. It is almost invariably covered with red or purple glandular hairs that glisten—notably when the sun is low and behind the plant. The calyx-cup is lobed about halfway, and the lobes become reflexed. The 10 anthers may be green, yellow, orange, or—perhaps most often—red, on short filaments that barely lift them above the large ovary and 2 stubby stigmas.

SAXÍFRAGA MERTENSIÁNA Bong. *Mertens' Saxifrage.* [p.222]

This species and the next are representatives of a number of saxifrages that have a basal cluster of broad-bladed leaves and an airy, open raceme of small flowers. Mertens' Saxifrage bears the name of F. C. Mertens, 1764-1831, who was a German botanist.

This beautiful plant of wet gravel along mountain stream-banks or wet cliff-faces occurs from Alaska southward along the coast. Very succulent and smooth basal leaves are nearly round in outline, but uniformly and deeply notched. The illustration shows the curious overlapping base of the leaf-blade. The blade is 2-3 inches broad, and the petioles are usually 2 to 4 times as long as the blade. The flowers have 5 white elliptical petals, that narrow to a clawed base, 10 deciduous (soon-dropped) stamens having pink anthers and white filaments, and a pair of widely-divergent slender styles. Very conspicuous, particularly after the stamens have fallen away, is a bright yellow ring of nectaries at the base of the ovary. A characteristic feature is the reddish propagules (little plants) that replace some of the flowers. When the wind dislodges these fledgling plants they roll down the slopes and find new homes.

[p.219] SAXÍFRAGA PUNCTÀTA var. CASCADÉNSIS (Calder & Savile) Hitchc. is a similar montane species of southwestern B.C. and Washington. Its raceme is not as crowded and round in outline as that of *S. mertensiana* (which see), nor are the propagules present. Flower-stems are hairy only toward the top, the hairs being slightly curled. The white petals are rather slender (being about half again as long as broad) and taper to a claw. Stamens are persistent. The capsules are erect in this species (but hanging in *S. mertensiana*).

SAXÍFRAGA OCCIDENTÀLIS Wats. var. RUFÍDULA (Small) C. L. Hitchc.   [p.223]

Occidentalis means, of course, *western.* This complex and variable species occurs in one or another of its numerous forms from Alaska southward throughout our area, and eastward into southeastern Alberta. Possibly long isolation, due to predominantly north-south glaciation, has permitted the development of various forms in such a plastic species, notably e.g. in the Coast Mountains, eastern and western Cascades, and Rocky Mountains. But the forms are inter-fertile, and intergrade in nearly every characteristic. For this reason we have chosen to describe and figure the fairly consistent, coastal variety rufidula. The varietal epithet refers to the *reddish hairiness* of the lower leaf surface.

Usually this is a very small plant—even for a Saxifrage—with 3-5 glossy, short-petioled, 1-2 inch leaves. In this variety they are often reddish, thick, ovate and round-toothed as if from a cookie-cutter—very attractive and distinctive in the dripping rock crevices they favour. Usually a single 2-4 inch scape carries a cluster—rather flat—of small white flowers with bright-pink stamens. (In other varieties the flower-clusters are pyramidal or rounded, and in some each petal is marked with 2 yellow spots.) In the present variety the petals are unspotted but sometimes flushed purplish, with a shallow notch. The 2 green carpels are almost completely separated, straight, and tapered to a large round pistil.

This brisk little plant is sometimes in flower in early March (near the sea) but is usually about a month later.

SAXÍFRAGA OPPOSITIFÒLIA L. *Purple Saxifrage.*   [p.226]

The generic flair for variation is not lacking in this species, which is however quite unique among the saxifrages of our area, in having *opposite leaves.* It is a circumboreal—and very distinct—species occurring in tundra and alpine scree from Alaska to Newfoundland, southward through the Rockies, Selkirks and Monashee ranges, and in the Olympic mountains. Many will know it from scrambles in Scotland, and in the Swiss Alps. The best forms of Saxifraga oppositifolia are probably the most beautiful members of a genus of lovely plants.

The colour also is not found in any other Saxifrage of our area, though it is variable: from reddish-violet to a fine clear pink—almost cerise. Occasional white forms have been reported. In all forms this is a very low, matted plant, the tightly packed stems dense with overlapping opposite leaves in 4 rows. The leaves are ½-1½ inches long, without petioles, slim-pointed and entire (though the margins are fringed with stiff rigid hairs). These ciliate margins are also conspicuous on the 5 blunt lobes of the deeply-cut calyx; the lobes remain straight, or very slightly spread, but never reflexed. The beautifully crimped petals are narrowed to short broad claws. They are most attractively accented by the brownish-orange anthers. Fine plants of S. oppositifolia may be almost covered with flowers spanning a full ¾ inch—though such clones are exceptional. More

Following page: MITELLA PENTANDRA   ✕14   [p.200]

MITELLA TRIFIDA ×½ [p.201]

PARNASSIA FIMBRIATA ×¼ [p.202]

PARNASSIA PALUSTRIS ×1¼ [p.202]

SAXIFRAGA FERRUGINEA ×⅖ [p.205]

often, in the chill of alpine springtime (which may be June or even the end of July) the blooms are half this size, and appear even smaller because they do not fully expand. The illustration is of a truly superb plant. When—as in this case—the plants are growing on limestone, minute white flecks of calcium carbonate appear at the ends of the leaves.

SAXÍFRAGA TOLMIÈI T. & G.   [p.219]

We would like to have pictured a number of other saxifrages, for attractive species in our area include *S. adscéndens, argùta, cérnua*, tiny *débilis, flagellàris* with its extraordinary arching stolons, *lyálli, refléxa, rhomboìdea, tàylori* (endemic to the Queen Charlotte Islands)—and several others. Perhaps our own enthusiasm for this genus may have become visible. We shall be happy if the reader has been at all encouraged to appreciate these intriguing rock plants, to watch for the variants as well as the species, and to reflect on the floral richness of Creation.

Dr. W. F. Tolmie went as medical officer in 1832, to the Hudson Bay Company's Fort Vancouver, near the mouth of the Columbia. This extraordinary little plant that bears his name, looks as if it links the two genera *Saxifraga* and *Sedum*.

This is a true mountain dweller—from above the 6000 feet level in the southern part of its range. It inhabits crevices in slab-rock, and gritty ledges, from Alaska, through the coastal mountains (as well as Vancouver Island's Beaufort Range) to Oregon, and a few isolated refugia in the Cascades and Bitterroot Mountains.

S. tolmiei cannot be confused with any of our other native Saxifrages, but one needs to count the carpels (2, occasionally 3, very occasionally 4; 2 being the usual but not the invariable number for this genus—and not the 5 that characterize the Sedums) to be sure that it does not fit the latter genus. The whole plant forms a low leafy mat, the spatulate leaves being glabrous, entire, and less than ½ inch long—so fleshy they are almost circular in section. The erect flowering stems are 1-3 inches tall—usually glabrous but sometimes with purplish hairs, and sometimes with a few small bractlets. The saucer-shaped green, or purplish, calyx is 5-lobed nearly to the base. Five obovate white petals make a flat array spanning about ½ inch. Ten stamens ring an unusually prominent pair of carpels with outward-turning beaks.

Hitchcock, Cronquist et al. remark, "A very attractive (but not easily grown) subject for the rock garden . . . ." Even for skilled gardeners like Leonard Wiley, in Portland, and for a friend in Victoria who succeeds with the most difficult rock plants, this one has proved impossible. Apparently Saxifraga tolmiei, like *Erythronium montanum**, resists with finality attempts to transplant it from its mountain homeland.

*See footnote to *Erythronium montanum.*

TELLÌMA GRANDIFLÒRA (Pursh) Dougl. *Tall Fringe-cup.* [p.222]

Tellima is an anagram of *Mitella* (which see). Since modern scholarship places only this species in the genus, there is no "T. parviflora" (with even smaller flowers). Hence when one considers these inconspicuous fringed green flower-cups that are less than ½ inch across, the specific name seems a little—shall we say—grandiloquent. In any event this is a pleasing "Sax" relative of wet woods and stream-sides, to moderate altitudes—from Alaska south along the coast, and eastward in our area to the Cascades.

Tellima grandiflora, a perennial, seeds so copiously that the new vigorous plants often crowd out the older plant, which might lead one to believe the species an annual. The basal leaves are variable in shape, deeply notched though not lobed, and sparsely covered on both surfaces with long white hairs. These basal leaves have densely white-haired petioles 3-4 times longer than the blades. Scapes often reach 2 feet, or even more, and bear leaves that are increasingly smaller and shorter-petioled upward. The flowers are carried in a long, somewhat one-sided raceme. The cup-shaped calyx is greenish, conspicuous, and divided into 5 pointed lobes. This calyx dominates the 5 ragged skeleton petals, whose fringed ends are reflexed. Young flowers near the top of the stem have greenish-yellow petals, but the more mature flowers lower in the raceme become progressively more pink-flushed downward.

TIARÉLLA LACINIÀTA Hook. *False Mitrewort. Coolworth,* [p.227]

The generic name means *little tiara,* from the odd-shaped capsule and its persistent sepals (the tiara was the turban-like headdress of the ancient Persians). The English name also calls attention to the capsule—like a bishop's mitre or cap. "False" distinguishes this genus from the true Mitreworts, *Mitella* (which see): it must be said that the flowers and seed-cases are very different, and that of the two, the dehiscent fruit and persistent sepals of the (true) Mitrewort, far from an image of ecclesiastical head-wear—recall nothing so much as a tattered French-Canadian toque!

The specific name laciniata refers to the more *deeply-cut* leaves, that are almost the only feature distinguishing the present species from the other two occurring in our area: T. TRIFOLIÀTA L. with leaves similar in general outline but rather clearly 3-lobed to the base; and T. UNIFOLIÀTA Hook., 3-lobed less than halfway to the base. The three plants are exceedingly similar, possibly of doubtful distinction; this possibility is supported by the overlapping ranges (*T. unifoliata* may be more montane and eastern in our area), and by the fact that a deeply-cut form (or possible hybrid of T. unifoliata with T. laciniata) is found in the southeastern Selkirks and Rockies.

All are delicate perennials—of shaded damp woods—growing from slim, rather horizontal rootstocks, with a few, long-petioled, glandular-haired, basal leaves, and similar ones that decrease in size and length of petiole up the slender upright scape (usually 9-15 inches tall). A dozen or more small lacy flowers, usually in groups of 3, ornament the upper part of the scape, in an open raceme. The campanulate (bell-shaped) calyx is unevenly cleft, the upper lobe being the largest; and the 5 tiny white petals are awl-shaped, longer than the calyx-lobes. The long white filaments of the stamens are the most obvious feature of the airy little flowers. Five of these filaments are about 3 times as long as the calyx-lobes, the other five much shorter; but all are conspicuous—especially when contrasted by the orange-coloured pollen that is revealed as the anthers dehisce.

TOLMIÈA MENZIÈSII (Pursh) T. & G. *Youth-on-Age.*   [p.219]

This is a monotypic genus, named for the same Dr. W. F. Tolmie who is honoured in the specific name for *Saxifraga tolmiei* (which see). And the specific name recalls another early physician and naturalist—Dr. Archibald Menzies (a contemporary of Dr. Tolmie) who visited this coast with Captain George Vancouver's Expedition of 1790-95. Very few plants bear names signalizing two men, and since both men were M.D.'s, this plant may be unique.

Youth-on-Age is almost unique in another respect, for small buds at the base of the leaf-blades develop into aerial "daughter" plants, whence the common name, also "Pig-a-back Plant". The colour of the drab small flowers is also unusual in the Sax family: the long, toothed calyx-tube (open on one side) is greenish-purple, and the thread-like petals are chocolate-brown. But for the miniature aerial plantlets, Youth-on-Age might easily be confused with several leafy members of the Saxifragaceae.

The long-petioled, hairy, and sharply toothed leaves have blades about 2 inches long, that are similar to those of *Tiarella*, *Mitella*, and *Heuchera*. They are, however, distinct on closer examination, in possessing a pair of winged membranous stipules. The flowering stems, which are 2 feet (or even taller), carry a few reduced and shorter-stipuled leaves. Close investigation discloses 2 long and 1 short stamen, instead of the 10 stamens of *Saxifraga* and *Tiarella*.

This interesting plant is often grown in the shade garden, and even potted and brought indoors. It likes moist woodland soil—on stream-banks particularly—and occurs from Alaska south and westward—though rare east of the Cascades.

Calder and Taylor, in their valuable *Flora of the Queen Charlotte Islands*, quote a personal communication from Dr. D. B. O. Savile, "that the deep-throated, brownish, asymmetrical flowers . . . are adapted for pollination by Lepidoptera, specifically butterflies." The authors remark, "but this has not been substantiated by field observations." Since it is known that both types of bees see only the blue end of the spectrum to yellow, and that butterflies respond to yellow, orange, and especially to red; that furthermore, this is a plant of stream-banks, or at least open woods where *Lepidoptera* occur; and finally that a long-tongued insect is needed to probe the deep calyx-cup, Dr. Savile's suggestion seems reasonable. However we have had many opportunities to observe the purple to brown flowers of this plant (which is common in the Cowichan Valley of Vancouver Island, and established in our garden) but the only visitors we have ever seen are various flies (*Diptera*). Though several of the little Blue butterflies (*Lycaenopsis p. echo*) have flitted near, none ever came to these flowers. This would be an interesting question to resolve.

GROSSULARIÀCEAE. *Currant Family.*

RÌBES. *Currants and Gooseberries.*

This is yet another of the names we owe to the Arabic, ribas being the Moorish medical name for an unrelated rhubarb-like plant, *Rheum ribes* (of North Africa and Spain) which was valued for its acid properties. The genus is chiefly North American and Andean, one species being reported from Tierra del Fuego, and a few from Syria, Persia, and Afghanistan. Most familiar are the Black, Red, and White Currants, and the greenish-golden Gooseberries of the market-place. Western North America yields two beauties of the shrubbery: *R. sanguineum* (which see), the Flowering Red Currant, and *R. aureum* (which see), the Golden Currant.

About 100 species are known, with their epicentre Western North America.

Our species are realistically divided by common names into Currants, which lack spines, and Gooseberries, which are armed. Both classes have perfect regular flowers with a ring of 5 erect petals enclosed by 5 longer, and often more showy sepals, united at their bases to form a short tube, that is fused with the ovary. All have 5 stamens (alternate with the petals) and a 2-carpel 1-chamber ovary.

The queen of the genus happens to be native to our area. That curious quirk of human nature that leads us to attach great value to the rare, and in its horticultural aspect, to the difficult and "miffy" plant, too often leads many British Columbians to a lack of appreciation of this common and hardy shrub. Overseas gardeners value highly—and with justice—the spectacular *Ribes sanguineum*.

RÌBES AÙREUM Pursh. *Golden Currant.*

In dry open places in the southeastern part of our area one should be alert to the possibility of finding this quite handsome species. The calyx is a rather poor *yellow* (aureum), and its long tube yields to 5 shorter lobes.

The 5 petals are reddish or purplish, erect and very much smaller than the spreading calyx-lobes. The ripe fruit is extremely variable in colour: from yellowish, to reddish, to nearly black. All the colour variants are considered palatable, though we have not found any of them entirely pleasant. Leaves are roughly 3-lobed, about ½-2 inches long, and rather distinctively yellow-green. This leaf-colour is sufficient to make the 3-6 foot shrubs of R. aureum stand out, when growing with other shrubs on an open hillside.

RÌBES BRACTEÒSUM Dougl. *Stink Currant.*   [p.227]

This straggly shrub reaches 10 feet in rich moist soil along stream-banks, or in wet pockets of woodland, and is perhaps most easily recognized by the oppressively rank "curranty" smell of flower and foliage. The specific name derives from the very characteristic and numerous *bracts,* that are closely spaced along the rather elongated, erect flower-racemes. These bracts start out as very reduced leaves but toward the tip gradually change to slender straps.

Also helpful in recognizing this species are the very large, 5-7 lobed leaves—some as much as 8 inches wide—and the presence along the twigs, and on the lower leaf-surfaces, of many round, shining, yellowish glands. Flowers are rather inconspicuous, being greenish-white. Fruit is roughened, blue-black, and disagreeable.

Stink Currant is more abundant than a casual survey might suggest, and is found throughout the Province from Cascades to Coast.

RÌBES CÈREUM Dougl. *Squaw Currant.*

This is a common species of the eastern slopes of the Cascades. The specific name means *waxy,* the small, scarcely-lobed leaves being thickened and grey-green above, and somewhat glandular-viscid. The whitish to pinkish flowers are distinctive, since the long calyx-tube is slightly constricted just below the reflexed lobes, i.e. the shape is uniquely—for this genus—urn-shaped. The red berry looks appetizing, but the squaws must have found it rather unpalatable.

The genus is well-represented in our area, and among the numerous other members one may expect to encounter the following:

[p.230] R. DIVARICÀTUM Dougl.—especially common in the Gulf Islands, is a node-spined gooseberry with reddish-sepalled flowers having notably flared and expanded white petals, and very long, conspicuous stamens.

R. GLANDULÒSUM Grauer. *Skunk Currant,* widely distributed in wet woods and swamps of northern B.C. and Alberta, is a spineless currant with fruit (either dark red or dark purple) notably bristly from numerous stalked *glandular* hairs. The calyx is white to pinkish, and the fan-shaped petals deeper pink fading to white. The scent is very strong and unpleasant. The leaves are smooth, and 5-7 lobed, the lobes doubly serrate and acute-tipped. They turn very red in the fall.

R. HOWÉLLII Greene—a black currant with red petals, and unarmed stems; may be found in the southern Cascades.

R. HUDSONIÀNUM Richards—also unarmed, but distinctively yellow-glandular, with strong-smelling white flowers, is a montane black currant occurring from Alaska to California, especially in the Cascades.

R. INÉRME Rydb.—is a *lax* white-stemmed, single-spined gooseberry of southeast British Columbia.

R. IRRÍGUUM Dougl.—also of *wet* places of southeast British Columbia; is yet another of the numerous white- or pinkish-flowered gooseberries—this one with smooth black fruit.

R. MONTÍGENUM McClatchie—is a tiny-leaved *montane* gooseberry—again of the southern Cascades, very much like *R. lacustre* (which see).

R. OXYACANTHOÌDES L.—of the Kootenay area and the Rocky Mountains, is a smooth purple gooseberry, with greenish, tubular flowers.   [p.230]

R. TRÍSTE Pall.—widespread from Alaska to Newfoundland and southward through the Cascades; is reddish-purple, flat-flowered, with a smooth, bright red "currant".

RÌBES LACÚSTRE (Pers.) Poir. *Swamp Gooseberry. Prickly Currant.*   [p.230]

This is the smallest member of the genus occurring in our area, the very bristly shrubs attaining usually only 3-4 feet. The "gooseberry" prickles are of two kinds: some very numerous, short, and slender; others longer, stouter, in 3's and 4's where branchlets and leaf-stipules arise. The specific name calls attention to some predilection for moister woods and *stream-banks*—though we have often found it among rocky logged-over ground where conditions, at least in late summer, are very dry.

The leaves are small (about 1½ inches long and wide), 5-lobed about halfway, and further doubly-toothed. Flowers of Swamp Gooseberry are clustered in drooping racemes, and deepen from pinkish to cinnamon as they age. The flowers are noticeably flattened—like little pinkish saucers. The purple-black, slightly hairy berries resemble domestic black currants, but the taste is more bitter.

The species is found throughout our area to subalpine levels. Some forms lack the smaller spines, though the nodal ones are retained. The nectar must be particularly attractive: we cannot recall, in reasonable weather, ever having noticed a flowering bush of Ribes lacustre that was not well attended by a motley collection of insects.

RÌBES LAXIFLÒRUM Pursh. *Coast Trailing Currant.*   [p.227]

The specific name, it will occur to the observer, is rather mis-applied, for the flowers are carried erect in a raceme. It is the branches that are *lax*, for they tend to lie along the ground, reaching a man's height—or more—only in thickets where the branches are supported by other shrubs.

This is a currant species of wet woods and thickets, widely distributed from Alaska southward, though not apparently east of the Cascades.

Ribes laxiflorum can be recognized by its decumbent growth and by its 3-4 inch leaves, deeply 5-lobed and marked with a sprinkling of transparent dots or glands. The flowers appear nearly flat, the sepal-tips being pinkish- to brownish-maroon; the berries are reddish-brown, covered with glandular hairs, and unpalatable. The entire plant lacks spines.

SAXIFRAGA BRONCHIALIS var. AUSTROMONTANA
(DETAIL)   ×5   [p.204]

SAXIFRAGA INTEGRIFOLIA   ×⅗   [p.208]

SAXIFRAGA BRONCHIALIS var. AUSTROMONTANA   ×2   [p.204]

SAXIFRAGA CAESPITOSA ×1 [p.204]

TOLMIEA MENZIESII ×⅓ [p.214]

SAXIFRAGA PUNCTATA var. CASCADENSIS ×1¼ [p.208]

SAXIFRAGA TOLMIEI ×½ [p.212]

RÌBES LÓBBII Gray.   [pp.230,231]

No common name seems to have been more than locally accepted, though M. E. Peck suggests Pioneer Gooseberry, to which one might reasonably object that old-timers probably used this much less than other, more abundant and agreeably-tasting, of the wild gooseberries. Its very showy flowers will at once suggest *Fuchsia*-flowered as an epithet, but this is only a notion. The specific name recalls a plant enthusiast of California.

This is a splendid garden prospect—neat, triply prickled only at the nodes, and extremely attractive in flower and in fruit. It may be grown from cuttings taken in spring or fall.

Ribes lobbii has 3-5 lobed leaves an inch long or less, paler and more pubescent below, but viscid with sticky glands on both surfaces. The beautiful flowers hang (often in pairs) below the branches—so the shrub is best viewed from a lower level, and this should be kept in mind when siting it in the garden. The calyx is green below, flushed with red and vivid chocolate-red, and tubular; above, it becomes 5-lobed and vivid chocolate-red, the tips being strongly reflexed to reveal the ring of 5 petals which are creamy-white, often pink-tinged. The final choice accent in the flower is provided by the 5 white stamens projecting beyond the corona of petals, each tipped with a striking reddish-purple anther. The whole effect is much like a miniature *Fuchsia*.

The greenish fruit is ellipsoid, veined reddish-brown when ripe, densely covered with glandular hairs, and ornamental but unpalatable.

In flower from April to mid-June, this attractive species is never abundant in its range from Vancouver Island and the Gulf Islands, eastward to the Cascades. Ribes lobbii prefers logged-over areas, and open rocky montane slopes.

RÌBES SANGUÍNEUM Pursh.   *Flowering Red Currant.*   [p.234]

All currants are, of course, flowering, but the common name does serve to call attention to the spectacularly beautiful hanging racemes of this species. Though the specific name means *blood-red*, the colour is variable—from a blush-pink (usually in more shaded locations) to an intense and fiery carmine. Very rarely, a pearly-white form is seen. Rather than risk the loss of such a treasure by attempting to move it to the garden, a few cuttings (which root readily in sand) should be taken.

Gardeners of wide experience, taking into account its neatness of habit, good nature, and freedom from pests of all sorts, consider this one of the finest of all ornamental shrubs. The plant can be easily shaped by pruning, and indeed such pruned specimens are often lavishly covered from top to bottom with cascades of showy blooms. The display lasts for more than a month, and may begin as early as March.

This shrub's choice of locations is unusually catholic: from open woods to quite dry and exposed situations among broken rock, and from the Coast (where it is most abundant) across southern British Columbia to the Cascades. Curiously, it has not been reported from the Queen Charlotte Islands.

Out of flower, R. sanguineum is a little difficult to distinguish from several other species of Ribes, but fairly characteristic are the reddish-brown bark and irregularly 5-lobed leaves, crinkled as if cut from crêpe-paper, and both paler and more densely haired beneath. The young leaves are neatly folded, like an accordion. Nearly round, unpalatable berries are sparse, and though dark-purplish, appear palest blue because of the dense covering of bloom.

Menzies found this shrub at Redondo Bay, near Bute Inlet. A few years later David Douglas in his *Journal* wrote of this "most beautiful shrub": "This exceedingly handsome plant is abundant on the rocky shores of the Columbia...." The seeds of Ribes sanguineum that he brought back to England (in 1827) proved so valuable that this single importation alone was said to have more than paid the entire costs (£400!) of the two-year expedition.

RÌBES VISCOSÍSSIMUM Pursh. *Sticky Currant.* [p.235]

The superlative form of the Latin adjective indicates this is the *most viscid* of the currants.

The Sticky Currant is a small, unarmed, straggly shrub not often more than 6 feet tall. Stems, leaves on both surfaces, flower-calyxes, and berries are downy with both fine hairs and glandular hairs that secrete the sticky, rather pungent-smelling gum. The leaves, 5-lobed about one-third of their length, are further doubly-toothed, and usually 1½-2½ inches broad. One is struck by the conspicuous hairiness of the leaf-petioles, as well as the flower-racemes. Helpful in recognizing the species are the tubular flowers (almost ¾ inch long) grouped 6-12 in a semi-erect, rounded cluster. The greenish—sometimes purplish-tinged—calyx-lobes are fused for about half their length into a campanulate tube, and the free lobes are not reflexed. The petals are about half as long as the free calyx-lobes, and creamy-white.

The few berries are blue-black, unattractive by reason of their sticky hairiness, and unpalatable. David Douglas writes "taste musty and very disagreeable, causes vomiting".

R. viscosissimum is found in dry to moist habitats, to the limit of the timber, on open to heavily-timbered slopes, particularly in the Cascades.

HYDRANGEÀCEAE. *Hydrangea Family.*

PHILADÉLPHUS LEWÍSII Pursh. *Mock Orange. Syringa.* [p.235]

The "philadelphus" of Aristotle was a tree, now unknown. The ancient confusion is continued in the misleading name *Syringa*, which is widely used for this shrub, but of

SAXIFRAGA MERTENSIANA   ✕¾   [p.208]

TELLIMA GRANDIFLORA (DETAIL)   ✕4   [p.213]

SAXIFRAGA FERRUGINEA (DETAIL)   ✕12   [p.205]

SAXIFRAGA OCCIDENTALIS var. RUFIDULA (DETAIL) ×15 [p.209]

SAXIFRAGA OCCIDENTALIS var. RUFIDULA ×¾ [p.209]

course belongs to the unrelated Lilacs. The specific name of this striking shrub honours Captain Meriwether Lewis; the generic is said to commemorate the Pharaoh Ptolemy II Philadelphus (308-246 B.C.). By any name the Mock Orange is a handsome shrub, that each June bears a profusion of perfumed, snowy blossoms. Several observers have commented that the scent is absent in the dwarfer, somewhat less pubescent-leaved, form of the southern Dry Interior. (We have found little or no scent from bushes exposed to the blazing sun—but a detectable fragrance from those growing in partly shaded and moister gullies.) Along the southern Coast, in good soil that retains some moisture throughout the summer, specimens 10-12 feet tall are spectacular ornaments of the forest edge, and thickets by lake, stream and seashore.

The long, straight, older stems are recognizable in winter by their thin, scaling bark; by the pairs of opposite branchlets; and by the rather woody remains of the erect seed-capsules. The deciduous leaves are about 3 inches long, with 3 main veins, and a few rather pronounced edge-serrations. Usually 4 petals—oblong in general outline—enclose 30 or more stamens (uneven in length) and a single pistil. We once found a fine double form, and having failed with the cuttings attempted at the wrong time of year, returned to the stream-edge in October, to find—in the wake of logging—only a tangle of broken saplings and gouged earth.

Archibald Menzies in his journal of June 16, 1792, records that he "...landed on the opposite side of the Bay [Birch Bay], where I enjoyd much pleasure in Botanical researches, in wandering over a fine rich meadow cropt with grass reaching up to my middle, & now & then penetrating the verge of the Forest as the prospect of easy access or the variety of plants seems to invite." [Does this not recall one's own wanderings in such circumstances!] "Here I found in full bloom diffusing its sweetness that beautiful Shrub the *Philadelphus Coronarius* . . . ." [i.e. *P. lewisii* named by Pursh in 1814.]

ROSÀCEAE. *Rose Family.*

The Latin adjective roseus, rosy or *pink*, is the source of the name of this huge—in fact quite unwieldy—family. More than 3000 herbs, shrubs, and even trees have been assigned to the family, which many botanists believe should be divided, perhaps into three. Most of these plants have alternate leaves with stipules, but the fruits are various. The crushed foliage of nearly all members of the family liberates in a few minutes (from the enzymatic hydrolysis of amygdalins) benzaldehyde—readily recognized by its odour (like bitter almonds).

The family contains many plants of great economic importance—such as apples, pears, strawberries, and blackberries, and many of ornamental value—such as the Rowan, Spiraea, Hawthorn, Cotoneaster, and of course the vast tribe of Roses.

Many plants of this family lack nectaries, but produce very large amounts of pollen, which can be almost as great an inducement to visits by bees, who make from it a kind of pollen-bread used in feeding their larvae. The pink petals of roses are landing platforms—not beacons—for the bees, who can however see the bright-yellow pollen that dusts the anthers. The plants are content to achieve pollination by loss of considerable pollen to the visitors, hence they produce an excess—a fact painfully evident to those who suffer so-called "Rose-colds" in May and June.

AMELÁNCHIER ALNIFÒLIA Nutt. *Service-berry. Saskatoon.* [p.231]

The origin of the generic name is obscure. *Paxton's Botanical Dictionary* of 1849 quotes Clusius (de l'Ecluse, the Fleming who studied at the famous Medical Botanic Garden at Montpellier in 1551) as his authority that this was the Savoy name for the European Medlar. Alnifolia clearly means with *alder-like foliage.* Few children who grew up in northern B.C. or on the Prairies during the hungry thirties will forget the "Saskatoon", for they picked countless quarts of the fruit that was either eaten fresh or bottled for winter use. This was, quite literally, the only fruit that many families knew during the period of the Depression.

Five or six forms of this variable shrub have been given names, but the distinctions are difficult, and probably untenable. At the Coast the fruit is inferior in quantity, size, and sweetness, besides being much subject to attack by insects. Both eastward, and north to Alaska more useful variations occur. Normally this is a shrub 5-12 feet tall, but in rich soils the Saskatoon may develop a single trunk and attain 30 feet. The reddish-brown branches become greyish with age. The 1-2 inch leaves are alternate, and (as in all the genera of Rosaceae except *Dryas*) deciduous. They are usually glabrous, but vary from entire to sharply-toothed on the outer half, or even along the entire length. Short racemes of fragrant, showy, ¾-inch flowers are white, rarely flushed with pink. Petals are linear to oblong, and characteristically, are slightly twisted. The 5-cleft calyx withers, but is retained at the top of the mature fruit, which is a purplish pome (like a tiny dark apple). The fruit contains a number of large hard seeds, which are spread by birds.

Service-berry is one of the commonest and most widely distributed of the attractive shrubs of early summer. The fruit was important to the Indians, who pressed it into dry slabs often mentioned (and utilized) by the early explorers of the West. The famous "pemmican" was made by pounding the dry cakes with sun-dried buffalo meat and marrow-fat: it was the winter staple of most of the Plains tribes. Among the Siksika (Blackfoot) the valued bush was called "Mis-ask-wu-toomina", shortened by white settlers to "Saskatoon". Both wild and domestic game eagerly crop the twigs and foliage, so that on overgrazed range no young bushes survive.

An interesting reference to this plant occurs in *The North-West Passage by Land*, by Viscount Milton and Dr. Cheadle, in 1863:

> "The Indians brought in a plentiful supply of the poire, wild pear, or
> service berry, which we purchased for some needles and thread. This fruit

SAXIFRAGA OPPOSITIFOLIA ×4 [p.209]

TIARELLA LACINIATA ×1 [p.213]

RIBES BRACTEOSUM ×⅓ [p.216]

RIBES LAXIFLORUM ×½ [p.217]

ARUNCUS SYLVESTER ×1/10 [p.228]

227

grows on a shrub . . . with leaves resembling that of a pear-tree, but smaller, and it is said by the Hudson's Bay people that wherever it flourishes wheat will also grow to perfection. The berry is about the size of a black currant, pear-shaped, and of delicious sweetness and flavour. They are much used by the Indians on both sides the mountains, who dry them for winter use."

ARÚNCUS SYLVÉSTER Kostel. *Goatsbeard.*   [p.227]

Greek aryngos provides both the generic and common names, for it means *goat's beard* and calls attention to the large, white flower-panicles. "Sylvester" is often encountered; it means *woodland.*

This is a familiar and imposing plant, often 5-7 feet tall. The large (up to 20 inches long), tri-ternately compound leaves are composed of long-acuminate, sharply twice-dentate leaflets. They are thin, usually glabrous above, but hairy and paler green below.

The filmy cloud of creamy flowers needs close inspection to discover that the blossoms of a plant are all of one sex. The pistillate flowers are smaller, with a cluster of imperfect and undeveloped stamens around the 3 (sometimes 4 or 5) pistils. The staminate plants bear 15-20 slender stamens, and traces of vestigial pistils. The latter plants are the better choice for a shady spot in the garden, where the very attractive foliage perfectly complements the pale plumes, that appear in June or July.

Aruncus sylvester is a plant of moist woodlands, a plant that graces many a rocky creek-wall, from Alaska southward, and from the Cascades westward.

CRATAÈGUS DOUGLÁSII Lindl. *Black Hawthorn.*   [p.235]

The strong tough wood, well-known to frontiersmen, is the clue to the generic name, kratos—in Greek meaning *strength.* This is one of many plants bearing the name of that great plant explorer David Douglas, who did so much, in the 1820's, to bring to European notice many of the plants of the Pacific Northwest.

The common name makes the best comment on the general appearance of this large shrub (or perhaps small tree), for the English Hawthorn, or May, must be known by almost everybody. The fruit of the present species, however, is black. The stout, nearly straight thorns are about an inch long. Five white petals are nearly round, slightly wavy-edged. Sepals are entire or slightly toothed, triangular and reflexed, and usually slightly hairy.

Flowering in May or June, the fruit hangs on through the winter gales, and becomes an important food for hard-pressed birds. Black Hawthorn is locally abundant from the Coast, through bluffs and creek-beds of the dry Interior, across to the Rockies and northward to Alaska.

CRATAÈGUS COLUMBIÀNA Howell also occurs eastward from the Cascades in [p.235] southern British Columbia. It is distinguished by *red* fruit, and slender, slightly curved thorns up to 3 inches long.

DRỲAS DRUMMÓNDII Richards. *Drummond's Mountain Avens. Yellow Dryad.*
[p.242]

The three species of Dryas occurring in our area are much admired plants that form extensive low mats. Dryas in Latin, and in Greek, was a *wood-nymph*, but these are sun-lovers of rock ridges, talus slopes, and gravel stream-bars, chiefly of the arctic, or arctic-alpine biosphere. The specific name almost certainly refers to James Drummond, a keen Scottish naturalist, who was for many years curator of the Cork Botanic Gardens, and who died in 1863.

This plant is widespread in suitable habitats, from Alaska throughout our area—except the southern coast. A feature rare in this family is the evergreen leaves. They are striking: very dark green above, contrasting—as the alpine wind ruffles them—with the startlingly white, densely haired, lower surfaces. Leathery, deeply creased, and usually almost glossy above, the leaves have edges that are crenate and crimped downward, particularly in drought. These leaves are quite distinctive, and can be confused only with those of other Dryads. At the top of each 4-10 inch, slightly glandular, scape is a single demure flower, that never fully opens its 8-10 yellow petals. The calyx is densely covered with dark, glandular hairs.

As the brief alpine summer rushes toward snowy winter, every flower is replaced by a downy ball of elongated, plumy styles each attached to an achene which will soon blow with the winds in search of a suitable home. Then, as the hiker climbs from below, the brilliant back-light transforms each seed-head into a nimbus of dazzling silver.

Similar beautiful seed-heads decorate 2 other species of our area, which are even more attractive, since both fully expand their inch-wide flowers. DRỲAS IN-TEGRIFÒLIA Vahl, White Dryad, is a high montane species of the Rocky Mountains, from Alaska to near the 49th parallel: its *leaves* are either *entire*, or slightly crenate on the basal half only. Also with wide-open paler cream, or nearly white flowers, is DRỲAS OCTOPÉTALA L. which has crenate leaves very like those of *D. drummondii* [p.243] (which see). In spite of its name, the number of *petals* actually varies from 7 to 9—though often there are *eight*. D. octopetala is a variable plant, found in the Rocky Mountains and Selkirks of our area. Many will recognize this dryad as an old friend of the Alps, or of Snowdonia.

These three dryads are superbly adapted to the rigours of their exposed and airy homes. The tough roots are deeply anchored; the leaves are firm enough to withstand the most violent gales, and their tomentosity, as well as their tendency to curl, conserve moisture; the stems are short and use up only enough food to bring the relatively large flowers to the attention of insects; and the plumose styles, of course, permit wide dispersion of the seeds in search of suitable crevices. A more subtle adaptation is the development of root-nodules that store nitrogen, important in gritty soil that tends to be leached of nutrients by snow-melt.

RIBES LACUSTRE ×⅓ [p.217]

RIBES DIVARICATUM ×⅘ [p.216]

RIBES OXYCANTHOIDES (FRUIT) ×⅞ [p.217]

RIBES LOBBII (FRUIT) ×1 [p.220]

RIBES LOBBII   ×1   [p.220]

AMELANCHIER ALNIFOLIA   ×1   (p.225)

All three species of Dryas are potential garden plants, attractive for trim leaves, for abundant yellow or white flowers, and for long-lasting silvery seed-heads. For all this beauty they ask only full sun and sharp drainage.

FRAGÀRIA CHILOÉNSIS (L.) Duchesne. *Coastal Strawberry.*

Fragans, *fragrant*, has the same Latin root as fraga, the Roman name for strawberries—earlier strawberries (and our wild ones) being notable for their fragrance. The specific name means *of* [Isla de] *Chiloé* (Chile), for this species runs down the Pacific coast, with gaps in modern times, from Alaska to South America. Further significance of its coastal distribution is suggested by the occurrence of a subspecies in Tierra del Fuego and another in Hawaii. In places these plant colonies, linked by long stolons (runners) are sufficiently abundant to anchor the shifting sands of coastal dunes.

This is a handsome plant, not infrequently brought into gardens for its decorative value. Stiff, almost leathery leaves are shining deep-green above, silken-haired beneath, deeply creased to almost pleated along the veins. The leaves consist of 3 strongly though bluntly-toothed leaflets, and a densely white-haired long petiole. Calyx-lobes are lanceolate, and they too are silky-pubescent. Flowers average ¾ inch across (being somewhat larger, and the petals relatively broader than those of *F. virginiana*, which see); but the differences are small and inconstant, of little discriminative value unless one has both plants together.

FRAGÀRIA VÉSCA L. Wood Strawberry, of inland British Columbia, is a variable species—several varietal names being in general usage. Unlike the previous species, this is not limited to the coastal strip. Leaves of F. vesca are yellow-green and *thin*, in which they differ from the blue-green, thicker leaves of the following species. Also, in F. vesca the terminal tooth of the leaflet is larger than the adjacent ones.

Who has not turned at sight of these bright little tidbits, and who does not remember the unmatched flavour of sun-warm wild strawberries?

FRAGÀRIA VIRGINIÀNA Duchesne. *Wild Strawberry.*   [p.242]

As the specific name suggests, this species ranges to the Atlantic states, from Alaska to California, and notably throughout the British Columbia Interior, where *F. chiloensis* (which see) does not occur. It is generally thought that the domestic strawberry (which crosses with both these wildings) derives its name from the practice of placing straw around the plants to keep the fruit from contact with the soil. However, the true explanation apparently comes from the Anglo-Saxon name for the wild plants: "Streowberie" so named because the fruit "strews" (or "straws") the ground (being carried on runners that cover the ground). The name appears (as "streaberige") as early as 1265 in the household roll of the Countess of Leicester.

F. virginiana is generally distinguishable by its blue-green leaves, which are firm rather than leathery, much less deeply reticulated, and generally somewhat less hairy below than those of *F. chiloensis.* Rather useful for identification is the feature that the terminal tooth of the leaflet is noticeably *smaller* than those on either side of it. The flowers are crisply white, with petals slightly smaller and slightly narrower than in *F. chiloensis.* A keen observer of the fruits will distinguish the more deeply sunken achenes of the present species (those of *F. chiloensis* being only about one-third depressed into the surface).

"passed several of the natives Campments. A River on the North side which appeared to be navigable, we camp'd at ½ past 6 oClk P.M. plenty of Berries which the men call *poires,* they are purple bigger than a Pea, very well Tasted, some goose Berries and a few Straw berries.

Original Journal of Alexander Mackenzie
(Fri. 14th Aug. 1789)

GÈUM MACROPHÝLLUM Willd. *Large-leaved Avens.* [p.243]

Geum is derived from geyo, *to impart a relish* the shredded roots of a Mediterranean species being once so used. It is interesting to note that Hultén mentions that the rhizomes, of at least *G. rossii,* are eaten raw, usually with fat, by the Siberian Eskimo. This is a genus of about 50 species of the North Temperate to Arctic Zones. Of the 6 or 7 that occur in our region, only one (*G. triflorum,* which see) is distinctive and readily identified. Our species have pinnately-divided, basal leaves with the end segment larger than the side ones, and cauline leaves that are 3-lobed, either alternate or opposite; this generally enables distinction from *Potentilla* (which see). The magnifying glass reveals a jointed flail-like style in Geum, but a simple one-piece style in *Potentilla.*

The specific name macro, *large,* and phyllum, *leaf,* refers not to the whole leaf, but instead to the disproportionate size of the terminal leaflet, which is quite characteristic for both common varieties of our area. In fact, these are exceptional leaves, and more useful in recognition than any other detail, including the flowers, which a quick glance might easily mistake for a *Potentilla,* or even for certain species of *Ranunculus* (belonging to a different family). The basal leaves may be as much as 12 inches long, with an expanded stipular base, and many oddly-assorted toothed leaflets—odd because though generally increasing in size upward there are frequent tiny ones interposed; and curious also because the arrangement of leaflets is at first alternate, and then becomes opposite! Finally there is the very large, slightly 5-lobed, terminal leaflet. This is a unique leaf indeed, and you will find it interesting to examine. Close study of the leaves will separate this from our other yellow-flowered species: in G. ALÉPPICUM Jacq. the terminal leaflet is deeply 3-lobed; in G. CALTHIFÒLIUM Menzies it is unlobed, heart-shaped (and there are only 0-3 tiny side-leaflets); in G. RÓSSII (R. Br.) Ser. the

RIBES SANGUINEUM $\times 1\frac{4}{5}$ [p.220]

RIBES VISCOSISSIMUM   ×½   [p.221]

PHILADELPHUS LEWISII   ×¾   [p.221]

CRATAEGUS COLUMBIANA (FRUIT)   ×⅕   [p.229]

T. & S. ARMSTRONG

CRATAEGUS DOUGLASII   ×1¼   [p.228]

terminal leaflet is imperceptibly–if at all–larger than the numerous side-leaflets. G. RIVÀLE L. of wet meadows and boggy swamps has a terminal leaflet shallowly 3-lobed, but the petals are yellow to flesh-coloured and purple veined, and the sepals are purplish.

There are several stems, 12 to even 36 inches tall, with 3 different kinds of hairs, and occasional sharply toothed, 3-lobed cauline leaves. Five yellow petals, of the numerous flowers, are backed by 5 small, pointed bracteoles, alternate with 5 triangular pointed calyx-lobes. These lobes soon reflex and the petals open flat. The mass of yellow stamens drop early, exposing the developing ball-head of achenes. If you have a 10X lens, these achenes are well worth examining for their curious shape, and remarkable variety of hairs. The base of the achene is reddish and pointed-elliptical, clothed with very long hairs which point upward toward the very long style, whose tip ends in a little shepherd's crook, and then, as a further afterthought, an unexpected feather. This feather-appendage is clothed with finer whitish hairs. The third type of hairs is interspersed with the very long ones about the mid-length of the style; these are glandular (with a thin stalk and swollen tip). You will find intriguing a microscopic study of the achenes of the other species, too–possibly including those of G. SCHOFIÉLDII Calder & Taylor (endemic to the Queen Charlotte Islands). (See also these authors' scholarly treatment of the relationships of G. macrophyllum, which occurs generally throughout our area.)

GÈUM TRIFLÒRUM Pursh. *Purple Avens. Prairie Smoke.*   [p.247]

Many authorities place this "uncomfortable" member in another genus, *Sieversia*. Though hairy multi-pinnate leaves and long-tailed achenes are in the pattern of Geum, the field appearance of the flowers is very different and makes the plant readily identified. These flowers are dull purple, or pinkish; nodding rather than erect; semi-closed instead of opening flat. The pinkish petals (rarely pale-yellow veined with purple) are largely hidden by long reddish-purple bracteoles that project from the tips of the calyx-lobes. The specific name calls attention to the fact that the *flowers* almost invariably occur in *threes*.

This modest flower seldom exceeds 12 inches. Its range is limited, from moister parts of the Sagebrush country, to lower ridges of the mountains of the dry Interior–chiefly east of the Cascades. Purple Avens often blooms very early, soon after the last snow has disappeared.

HOLODÍSCUS DÍSCOLOR (Pursh) Maxim. *Ocean Spray.* [pp.243,246]

Few will be found to cavil at the common name, which evokes a perfect picture of this handsome shrub, that is festooned in late June or July with great creamy plumes.

Though most abundant within reach of salty air, Ocean Spray, in a dwarf form, or possibly subspecies, also occurs through the southern Interior.

Holodiscus (from the Greek holo-, *whole*) refers to the entire (i.e. not lobed) *disk* upon which the floral parts are placed. The specific name may be an unkind reference to the off-white or pale-cream of the flowers, or to the undeniable brown that invades the cream as the flowers wither.

No lengthy description is needed for this fine and familiar shrub, which when mature forms close clusters of stems 9-10 feet tall. The leaves are alternate, in shape somewhat like those of an alder, but much thinner and rather smaller. Hundreds of small flowers compose the large, cream-coloured panicles, whose weight is sufficient to droop the branches.

Pioneer woodsmen knew the older wood of Ocean Spray was extremely hard. We have seen a large barn constructed without nails; their place was taken by pegs of this wood. Both B. O. Mulligan and Carl English comment that this is considered by many one of our finest native shrubs. Certainly it deserves a place in any garden of moderate size.

LUÉTKEA PECTINÀTA (Pursh) Kuntze. *Partridge Foot.* [p.247]

This must be considered one of the best ground cover and foliage plants of our area. Though it inhabits moister slopes at subalpine to arctic-alpine levels, Luetkea quickly adapts to shaded parts of the garden, even near the sea. Inch-long cuttings strike readily in sand.

Only 1 species is known in the genus named for Count Lütke, famed Russian sea-captain who circumnavigated the globe in the early years of the 19th century. Pectinata means *comb-like*, referring with equal appropriateness to the deeply-toothed leaves and to the appearance of the stamens, which are united at their bases. Long placed by botanists among the *Spiraea*, this little mat-forming plant is even more puzzling to the amateur naturalist. How many, finding this plant for the first time, have found no saxifrage description to fit and believed for a while that they have "discovered" a new species! Yet its place in the Rose Family is established by a closer look, for in place of the 2 stout carpels and 5 or at most 10 stamens of the *Saxifragaceae*, here are 4, 5, or 6 slender pistils and about 20 stamens.

The crowded leaves that form the basal tufts, and continue alternately up the 4-5 inch flowering stems, are small, smooth, and 3-parted on the outer extremity, then again 3-toothed. Small white (occasionally cream or even very pale-yellow) flowers are crowded in a short raceme. (In the Queen Charlottes the flowers are usually pinkish.) Some clones show only a dozen flower-stems in a velvety green mat that may be 5 or 6 feet across, but elsewhere, as on Mt. Revelstoke, can be seen similar mats of Luetkea literally hidden by thousands of dainty racemes.

OSMARÒNIA CERASIFÓRMIS (T. & G.) Greene. *Osoberry. Indian Plum.* [p.254]

This earliest of our spring-blooming shrubs derives its name from the Greek osme, *smell,* and the generic terminal "-aronia". The specific name means *of cherry form,* which must surely refer to the leaf-shape, since the bright fruits (first orange but finally blue-purple) resemble small plums, rather than cherries. "Oso" is apparently an Indian name, but we have been unable to find any reference to aboriginal use of the bitter, though not poisonous fruit, as food.

This is a rather straggling shrub, occasionally attaining 12 feet, whose fresh green leaves are the first banners of spring, appearing after mild winters at the Coast, in February. They are 3-5 inches long, pointed-elliptical, with faintly waved margins, and of a peculiarly intense yellowish-green. Pale greenish-white flowers, in drooping racemes, appear as the leaves unfold. They are strong-smelling, some say like crushed cucumber, but perhaps most like spring and burgeoning growth. Close examination shows they are of two kinds: the staminate lacking pistils, but with three ranks of about 5 stamens each, and the pistillate, with shorter stamens whose anthers never mature (dehisce). The 5 petals are somewhat ragged, and spaced in the 5-toothed calyx-cup.

Twigs cut soon after New Year's Day and brought indoors soon spread their cool green foliage, but when the flowers open the scent is a little oppressive in the house. In June if you can find fruit-clusters that have escaped the birds, their vivid orange makes an attractive picture.

Osmaronia is found west of the Cascades, particularly along the southern Coast, and on Vancouver Island.

PHYSOCÁRPUS CAPITÀTUS (Pursh) Kuntze. *Nine-bark.* [p.246]

Physa, *bellows,* and carpus, *fruit,* explain the generic name and call attention to the inflated seed-capsules. The specific name refers to the rounded corymbs or *capitate heads* of attractive white flowers. It would be difficult to ascertain the number of layers of papery bark*, which is usually in the process of shredding.

This is a deciduous shrub of 6-12 feet, with a predilection for lake margins and stream-banks at lower altitudes, from Alaska south (on the western side of the Cascades).

The leaves are strikingly handsome, resembling 3-inch maple leaves, but glossy above and paler below, due to hairs (which the 10X magnifier reveals are star-shaped). Brown branches, and slightly reflexed calyx-lobes, also bear these stellate hairs. There are 5 white, spreading petals, very attractively centred by many stamens, which are brilliant pink before dehiscing to reveal their pollen.

East of the Cascades and in drier habitats the smaller P. MALVÀCEUS (Greene) Kuntze will be found. It is very similar to P. capitatus, but is a more notable feature in the autumn scene since its leaves turn bright russet-red.

*While Meriwether Lewis was camped in the Bitter Root Mountains he saw Physocarpus, and noted in his journal (July 2, 1806): "the wild rose, servise berry, white berryed honeysuckle, *seven bark* [the italics are ours] . . . are natives of this valley." In the present inflationary times we should not be too surprised to find the last plant promoted to Nine-bark!

POTENTÍLLA. *Cinquefoil.*

This is a large and taxonomically difficult genus, of at least 200 species, chiefly found in the northern part of the North Temperate Zone. We shall mention only a few representative species, of perhaps 25-30 found in our area. The uncertainty of the species concept is well illustrated in this group of plants. For example, *Potentilla gracilis* (which see) may be considered a fluid species comprising 6-8 variably distinct entities, some or all of which may be considered subspecies, varieties, or (by some authorities) even distinct species. Chromosome studies, investigation of fine detail (as of pollen) with the scanning electron microscope, application of the computer to analysis of variation, and the increasing knowledge of plant chemistry, all may help to provide firmer edges to that hazy notion, the species. However, in such genera as this, where hybridization and apomictic reproduction* freely occur, as well as plasticity of morphological and other features in response to soil and climatic variables, the species concept probably will remain somewhat elastic.

The name of the genus is derived from the Latin potens, *powerful,* with reference to supposed potent (medicinal) properties of certain of the species. The common name means five-leaves, which is generally descriptive of the palmate leaves. However, a few species (e.g. *P. anserina* and *P. pacifica,* which see) have pinnate leaves, very like those of *Geum.* Field distinction of the two genera is difficult. The 10X magnifier shows a characteristic kink in the jointed pistil of *Geum,* and a straight single-segment style of Potentilla. Only when plants have reached the fruiting stage is distinction easy, for Potentilla seed never has the long plumy tails of the achenes of *Geum. P. fruticosa* (which see) is a pretty subshrub, otherwise our 29 species are herbaceous annuals or perennials, usually yellow-flowered, and of varied habitat.

*apomictic reproduction—not involving a sexual process.

POTENTÍLLA ANSERÌNA L. *Silver-weed.*

Anserina means *goose,* hence *goose-down,* apparently alluding to the downy foliage. The common name refers to the shining, silver-white pubescence of the lower side of the leaves.

One hesitates to call such an attractive plant a weed; let us say it covers solid acres

[p.258]

of low wet places, apparently indifferent to fresh, alkaline, or salt conditions. This species, or the doubtfully distinct P. PACÍFICA Howell, occurs throughout our Pacific area, at lower levels. The beautiful yellow flowers are sometimes sparse, and often partly hidden by the foliage, but repay close examination. They are about ¾-1 inch broad, the five bright-yellow petals usually deeper-coloured toward the base, and variably wavy-edged. Leaves of some varieties are silvery on both faces, though usually the upper appears darker green. In *P. pacifica* the lower surface is only slightly silver-haired to almost glabrous. In all the entities the leaves (which may be 3-18 inches long) have many sharply-toothed leaflets, arranged pinnately. P. anserina spreads quickly by far-ranging stolons (creeping prostrate stems that root at the nodes).

POTENTÍLLA DIVERSIFÒLIA Lehm. *Mountain Meadow Cinquefoil.* [p.255]

This alpine to subalpine species, as its name suggests, bears *leaves of variable shape.* In fact, plants from mountain meadows differ so extremely from those found on the windswept slopes far above, that one might well believe them to be different species. The depauperate form illustrated, from the summit of Mt. Jutland, Vancouver Island, is barely 2 inches tall. The disproportionate size of this single flower is a common feature among high alpine plants. But along stream-banks at lower altitudes the stems are usually several, erect, and up to 18 inches tall, with numerous smaller flowers in an open cyme.

Leaves are diverse indeed. Generally they are 5-7 lobed, the lobes obovate in outline but deeply and rather sharply-toothed. In some forms the teeth extend almost to the mid-veins, so that a fern-like leaf is formed. Hairiness also is variable, from sparsely to densely sericeous (covered with silky hairs). Leaflets are nearly always in the range of ½ - 1¼ inches long, either greenish or greyish above and below, but not whitish. The 5 yellow petals of Potentilla diversifolia are usually twice as long as the lanceolate sepals, which are again about twice as long as the narrow bracts that alternate between the sepals.

POTENTÍLLA FLABELLIFÒLIA Hook. *Fringe-leaf Cinquefoil.* [p.247]

Flabellifolia means with *leaves like small fans.* This subalpine to alpine beauty graces wet meadows, and damp talus, throughout our area, with the exception of Queen Charlotte and Vancouver Islands.

The species is less variable—and more easily identified—than most of its relatives. The numerous basal leaves of Fringe-leaf Cinquefoil have long petioles, with 3-cleft blades. The leaflets are deeply toothed and fan-shaped, almost smooth in most forms. Five-to ten-inch stems are also usually smooth, or at most only sparingly short-haired upward. They usually bear 1 or 2 cauline leaves (that have no petioles) and a number of oval bractlets. Usually there are only 1 or 2 flowers, that spread serene yellow petals to the clear mountain sunshine. They are about 1 inch wide, or perhaps a little less. A distinctive feature, important in their beauty, is the reduction of the usual crowd of stamens to a single, spaced ring. A good form of P. flabellifolia, occasionally found, has a pale-orange spot at the base of each petal.

POTENTÍLLA FRUTICÒSA L. *Shrubby Cinquefoil.* [p.255]

Very easily recognized is this showy species, common on dry plains and subalpine slopes throughout our area and far beyond, even to Eurasia. Curiously, in Ireland, and on Helvellyn, male and female flowers are on separate plants. Fruticosa means *shrubby*, the deciduous plant forming a low, rounded bush, occasionally 3-4 feet high.

Leaves are small and greyish-green, with a short hairy petiole and 3-5 untoothed leaflets. The flowers of Shrubby Cinquefoil are intensely yellow, especially at higher levels. Petals are very broadly obovate, and almost imperceptibly notched. The seeds bear a short tuft of hairs—unique in this genus, as is the shrubby habit.

Keep a sharp look-out for specimens with very large flowers. Cuttings root readily in sand, and soon produce garden shrublets of great merit. We have seen a pale-yellow form, with numerous flowers fully 1¼ inches across. Another variation to seek has bright carmine buds, the colour being in the lower surface of the folded petals. The discovery of such "sports" lends continuing interest to one's rambles.

POTENTÍLLA GLANDULÒSA Lindl., Sticky Cinquefoil, is also variable. This is [p.246] a very common species, especially noticeable in late June and early July across the southern part of the Province. The usual form has palest yellow to cream-coloured flowers. The leaves are pinnate with 5-9 leaflets, and the stems are very often reddish. Stamens average 25-40. The numerous pistils have minutely roughened styles that are spindle-shaped.

POTENTÍLLA GRÁCILIS Dougl. *Graceful Cinquefoil. Slender Cinquefoil.* [p.254]

Graceful this plant may be, in one or all of its puzzling variations, but easily recognizable it is not! Along the Coast and inland, from Alaska south, occur many related plants that have given rise to much disagreement among botanists, as a long list of synonyms suggests. (More than 2 dozen are listed by Hitchcock et al.)

One can only describe the general features of P. gracilis. From a cluster of basal leaves with long petioles, arise one or several 16-32 inch stems, which are extensively branched upward, and bear usually 1 or 2 leaves without petioles. The basal leaves are palmate, with from 3-11 "fingers". These lobes are very diverse in shape and degree of notching, and also (as is the entire plant) in kind and quantity of pubescence. The flowers are characteristic of the genus—from pale to deeper yellow, ¾ inch or less in diameter. Some plants are partially male-sterile, with notably small stamens. Stamens usually number 20, and the slender styles are roughened only near the base.

FRAGARIA VIRGINIANA ×1 [p.232]

FRAGARIA VIRGINIANA (FRUIT) ×1 [p.232]

DRYAS DRUMMONDII ×2 [p.229]

DRYAS OCTOPETALA ×¾ [p.229]

GEUM MACROPHYLLUM ×⅘ [p.233]

HALODISCUS DISCOLOR (HABITAT) [p.236]

One is inclined to lump any Potentilla with these general characteristics under this species title. Potentilla gracilis is sufficiently common to make this procedure often satisfactory.

POTENTÍLLA HOOKERIÁNA Lehm. *Hooker's Potentilla.*   [p.255]

This dwarf perennial species honours the names of the first Director of the Royal Botanic Gardens of Kew, Sir William Jackson Hooker (1785-1865) and his even more renowned son, the great systematic botanist, Sir Joseph Dalton Hooker (1817-1911). It is an alpine species, that scarcely lifts its bright-yellow flowers above the 1-2 inch cluster of grey-haired leaves.

Hooker's Potentilla has leaves about 1 inch long, that are divided into 3 lobes, and further deeply toothed. They are densely clothed below with coarse, straight, appressed, greyish hairs (tomentose), and somewhat less densely above (so that the green of the actual upper leaf surface is visible).

This attractive small plant may be found on rocky slopes and high-altitude moraines (especially of the Rocky Mountains), also at lower levels in Alaska and Siberia.

Potentilla hookeriana is separable with difficulty from the generally whiter-haired P. NIVÈA, or from P. QUINQUEFÒLIA which is slightly taller and has 5- rather than 3-*lobed* leaves, or from P. UNIFLÒRA, distinguishable chiefly on the basis of lanate (curved and woolly) hairs. All these species have much the same range. Indeed, except for different geographical distribution, the present species overlaps most of the characteristics of a depauperate specimen of the generally coastal *P. villosa* (which see).

POTENTÍLLA PALÚSTRIS (L.) Scop. *Swamp Cinquefoil.*   [p.255]

The specific name means *of the swamp* or marsh. This is indeed a very different Potentilla—a lush plant of long smooth rhizomes, that root at every node and barely hold the pinnate leaves above the squelching mud of its watery home. The flowers, too, are unusual, with long and conspicuous greenish-purple sepals, and much shorter, skimpy, pointed, wine-red petals. The pinnate leaves are generally smooth, with 3 to usually 7, obovate leaflets, that are deeply toothed.

In suitable habitats P. palustris occurs from subalpine to sea level, from Atlantic to Pacific and from Alaska southward.

In the Middle Ages Potentilla (of one or several uncertain species) was believed to be a very potent, or powerful plant of much "virtue" in medicine. It was highly regarded by many writers, including Banckes, who introduces his *Herball* as follows:

Here begynnyth a newe mater/the whiche sheweth and treateth of
ẙ vertues & proprytes of herbes/the whiche is called an Herball.

Rycharde Banckes, London, 1525

POTENTÍLLA VILLÒSA Pall. *Hairy Cinquefoil.*   [p.259]

What a beautiful plant this is! And how easily, by comparison with some of the other species, one recognizes it. Villosa means *hairy*, the coastal plants indeed being literally silvered with long soft hairs. As usual, their purpose is to reduce transpiration and loss of moisture, for the neat round cushions of this species often cling to the merest cracks in solid rock. We have seen thriving colonies on Vancouver Island's stormy west coast, that were frequently drenched with salt-spray: possibly the hairy overcoat helps also to keep salt water from the stomata (breathing pores) of the leaves. Away from the coastal rocks P. villosa is found in the Coastal, Cascade, Selkirk, and Rocky Mountains, where it is less pubescent.

This choice perennial needs sharp drainage to succeed in the rockery, but is worth almost any amount of care. As usual, very small plants transplant best. The tri-lobed thick leaves are deeply veined and sharply toothed; the margins most beautifully outlined with silvery hairs. Striking inch-wide golden flowers are clustered low above the foliage. The petals are sharply notched, and each bears a spot of glowing orange at its base. The whole effect is admirable.

There is a pleasure in the pathless woods,
There is a rapture on the lonely shore,
There is society, where none intrudes,
By the deep Sea, and music in its roar:
I love not Man the less, but Nature more,
From these our interviews. . . .

George Gordon, Lord Byron:
Childe Harold's Pilgrimage

PRÙNUS EMARGINÀTA (Dougl.) Walpers. *Bitter Cherry.*   [p.258]

Prunus is the ancient Latin word for *plum*, while emarginata means *with a shallow notch*, i.e. at the top of the ovate leaves. Though perhaps most often seen as a straggly shrub in open woodlands of the dry Interior, at the Coast Bitter Cherry frequently attains the stature of a small tree. In broken woodland its papery bark, marked with lenticels (elliptical clusters of loose tissues), looks very cherry-like. But the small bright-red to deep-purplish fruits are sure to pucker your lips. Indeed one agrees, after recovering, that these cherries should be left for the birds.

Leaves are about 2 inches long, finely saw-edged, and become smooth with maturity. The flowers are freely borne in open bracted corymbs. They are greenish-white, not unpleasantly—if rather heavily—scented. The stamens, 10-15 in number, are long and stand conspicuously above the petals.

PRÙNUS VIRGINIÀNA L. var. DEMÍSSA (Nutt.) Torr., Choke Cherry, is a rather   [p.258]

HALODISCUS DISCOLOR (DETAIL) ×⅖ [p.236]

POTENTILLA GLANDULOSA ×½ [p.241]

PHYSOCARPUS CAPITATUS ×¾ [p.238]

GEUM TRIFLORUM $\times \frac{2}{5}$ [p.236]

LUETKEA PECTINATA $\times \frac{1}{4}$ [p.237]

POTENTILLA FLABELLIFOLIA $\times 1\frac{3}{4}$ [p.240]

similar but smaller shrub that is never tree-like. It is widespread throughout our area, from coastal to lower montane regions. Leaves of Choke Cherry are more sharply pointed than those of the Bitter Cherry, and the numerous flowers are carried in long racemes, rather than in rounded corymbs. Stamens are *bent low* (demissa) to the petals (unlike the longer ones of *P. emarginata*, which stand erect). In this variety the ripe fruit is always bluish-purple.

PÚRSHIA TRIDENTÀTA (Pursh) DC. *Greasewood. Antelope Bush.*   [p.254]

F. T. Pursh, who died in 1820, was the author of one of the best known early floras of North America. And tridentata refers to the *three teeth* (lobes) of the little, hairy, wedge-shaped leaves. This is a rigid shrub 3-9 feet tall, with inconspicuous flowers whose small yellow petals quickly drop. At first sight there is little to suggest its family affiliation.

Purshia is a desert shrub of the driest parts of the southern Interior—sometimes in areas too dry even for sagebrush. There is a great deal of nutritious oil in the woody stems, making Greasewood an excellent food for wild and domestic animals, and a first-rate fuel for the campfire. The leaves roll inward in scorching weather, exposing the greyish, densely hairy under side. Early spring brings inconspicuous, small, yellowish petals, that are almost hidden by the notched, glandular, and hairy calyx-cup. Each flower is carried stiffly alone at the end of an abbreviated shoot. The small black seeds are stored by White-footed Deer-mice in caches, that may contain 2, or even 3 pounds!

PỲRUS FÚSCA Raf. *Western Crab Apple. Pacific Crabapple.*   [p.266]

Pyrus originally referred to the *pear tree*, but pears and apples are now often placed in one genus. The specific name means *brown*, or dusky, most likely applied to the colour of the bark, which is smooth on young shrubs, becoming rough with age. Dense thickets of Crab Apple along stream-banks and swamp-edges may be almost impenetrable, because of the interlacing branches, which carry numerous, stout, spine-like spurs that are 1-2 inches long.

An earlier specific name called attention to the diverse lobes of the leaves, scarcely two of which will be exactly alike. They often turn brilliantly yellow and red in the fall, when the showy yellow fruit, sometimes red-cheeked, makes each bush spectacular. The flowers of Pyrus fusca are white, in open clusters, resembling apple blossoms, and very fragrant. They span about 1 inch, and appear in May or June.

This attractive shrub is abundant in wet woodlands of the Coast, and is also found, less commonly, on the lower slopes of the Cascades.

RÒSA. *Wild Rose.*

The roses of the northern hemisphere have been divided into considerably more than a hundred species. However natural hybridization and other factors make firm recognition difficult, and future study will in all likelihood reduce the number of species recognized. Fortunately those in our area are defined with fair clarity.

The rose has long attracted attention, from Homer's metaphor, "Rosy-fingered dawn", to surviving frescoes of rose foliage and blossoms on the palace walls of King Minos in Crete. Twelve kinds were known to Pliny in the first century A.D., and Nero is said on a single occasion to have spent the equivalent of $150,000 for the roses that were traditionally scattered at a certain phase of a banquet—after which all that occurred was "sub rosa" or secret. Today music and verse, in dozens of languages, celebrate the rose.

> *Very old are the woods;*
> *And the buds that break*
> *Out of the brier's boughs,*
> *When March winds wake,*
> *So old with their beauty are—*
> *Oh, no man knows*
> *Through what wild centuries*
> *Roves back the rose.*

> Walter de la Mare:
> All That's Past

RÒSA GYMNOCÁRPA Nutt. *Dwarf Rose.*   [p.267]

This small rose has not, apparently, received any widely recognized English name—though in some localities it is occasionally known as Dwarf or Little Rose. Its specific name means *naked fruit* (an epithet chosen by Nuttall in 1840 because of the fact—distinctive of this species among the roses of our area—that the little subglobose scarlet hips at maturity are bare, having shed their crown of short sepals).

Rosa gymnocarpa is a slender shrub, rarely as much as 4 feet tall, with thin, smooth, ovate to elliptic leaves, mostly double-serrate. In rather shaded woodland areas it spreads its dainty pink flowers, with their golden-stamen centres. The summer wayfarer stopping to admire, seldom picks the inch-wide flowers, on observing numerous slender, but effective prickles along the stems. Hence even in much-frequented areas of southern B.C., the many bright accents of the ripened hips may be seen—though a casual glance may confuse them with the similar and only slightly smaller fruit of the Red Huckleberry.

RÒSA ACICULÀRIS Lindl., Prickly Rose, like *R. gymnocarpa* (which see) is a small-flowered species with stems generally armed with a great many slender prickles. However, the hips are distinctive, for in this species the withered sepals are retained on the fruit. R. acicularis is a northern low shrub, that prefers open woods.

RÒSA NUTKÁNA Presl. *Nootka Rose.* [p.270]

This beautiful rose was first described (in 1851) from a specimen collected at *Nootka* Sound, hence the specific name.

Though some plants are armed with quite large thorns, others carry only a few small prickles. The swollen upper end of the stem (hypanthium) immediately below the sepals, may be covered with gland-tipped bristles, but is usually smooth. The strikingly handsome flowers may be as much as 3½ inches across, from light pink to deep rose. There is no good, single, recognition feature, but the species is distinguished by an aggregate of characteristics. These include the presence (usually) of a single flower at the end of each stem, and sepals with enlarged ends that are persistent. In the young fruits these sepals are carried horizontally, but later (as the roundish scarlet hips mature), vertically—in a loosely twisted crown.

The species is widely distributed in B.C., though the more heavily barbed form occurring east of the Cascades has been recognized as variety HÍSPIDA Fern.

An early morning stroll during May to July (according to the altitude) may discover the year's first Nootka Rose. Who has not then savoured the pleasure of the moment, the visual delight of the elegant buds, and the dewy freshness of the blossoms, the memorable fragrance—both of flower and foliage.

We have found this species makes sturdy and compatible stocks upon which to bud either climbing or bush varieties of cultivated roses. The hips yield a preserve or jam, of unique flavour, and provide a rich source of Vitamin C.

> *Like a rose embowered*
> *In its own green leaves,*
> *By warm winds deflowered,*
> *Till the scent it gives*
> *Makes faint with too much sweet these heavy-wingèd thieves. . . .*

Percy Bysshe Shelley: To a Skylark

RÒSA PISOCÁRPA Gray. *Clustered Wild Rose.*   [p.266]

Pisocarpa means *pea-fruited,* but the bright-red hips are quite variable, pear-shaped (usually), ellipsoidal, or nearly spherical. More characteristic is the occurrence of the flowers in clusters of 3 to 6.

This beautiful shrub does not attain quite the robust growth of *R. nutkana* (which see), and the prickles are slender, straight and few—sometimes wanting. Perhaps the best recognition feature is the almost invariable presence—on the outer surface of the persistent and narrow-waisted sepals—of numerous, fleshy, hair-like protuberances, each topped with a swollen head (said to be stipitate-glandular).

We can vividly recall, on a sunny summer morning of many years ago, our first confrontation, along the shore of a coastal lake, with the scented blossoms of a Clustered Rose that sprawled over a silver-whitened beach log. Later, the brilliant hips in lavish clumps may be admired across much of southern British Columbia.

RÒSA WOÓDSII Lindl. generally replaces *R. pisocarpa* (which see) east of the   [p.267]
Cascades. Its sepals are usually smooth, and the notches of the (often) blunt-tipped leaves are much larger and deeper than those of *R. pisocarpa.*

"The fruit when it is ripe maketh most pleasant meats and banqueting dishes, as tartes and such like. . . ."

John Gerard:
The Herball. (1633)

RÙBUS. *Bramble. Blackberry. Raspberry.*

This is a notorious genus. The species complexes are inter fertile, often apomictic (able to produce seed without pollination), and frequently polymorphic, so that in England, for example, about 400 "Brambles" have been named. We shall limit ourselves to only a few, more or less well-defined, species.

The name was used by several Roman authors, the root being the same as in ruby, meaning *red.*

"The land on this Side has quite a different appearance from that from where we entered the lake till here." [The lake was Great Slave Lake]. "The latter is but one continued View of Mountains & Islands & Solid Rock covered here & there with Moss, Shrubs & Trees, the latter quite stinted in their growth for want of Soil to nourish them; notwithstanding this barren appearance you can hardly land upon these Rocks but you will meet with gooseberries Cranberries whoilee

Berries Brow Berries Juniper Berries, Rasberries, what the Men call *Grains a Perdres* Grain a Saccacamir and what the Indians call *Pythagominan* something like a Rasberry but the last grows upon a small Stalk 1½ ft. high in wet mossy Places all those are in great plenty tho' they do not all grow in one & the same Place."

Original Journal of Alexander Mackenzie:
(Thurs. 25th June, 1789)

RÙBUS ACAÙLIS Michx. *Dwarf Raspberry.*   [p.270]

This dwarf creeping raspberry is called acaulis, or *stemless*—though it does push up each year, from its perennial rhizomes, stems 1-6 inches tall. These bear 2-5 trifoliate leaves that are further deeply notched, and a single pretty rose-red flower. Though the flowers are somewhat cupped, the petals if pressed flat will span 1 inch or more. The slim, pointed sepals are strongly reflexed. In early autumn dark-red aggregates ("berries") appear.

This attractive plant is widely distributed in suitable habitats throughout mainland B.C., and a few sites in the mountains of Vancouver Island. It ranges from tundra in the north to wet spots in the mountains southward. There are records of R. acaulis across the top of the continent to Newfoundland.

RÙBUS CHAMAEMÒRUS L. *Cloudberry.*

Rather similar in wiry creeping rootstocks and in leaf-shape to *R. lasiococcus,* this shy-blooming dwarf perennial is sharply distinguished by its dioecious character (male flowers with dwarfed pistils, female—on a different plant—with dwarfed stamens). Each flower is solitary, topping a 4-8 inch erect flower-stem. The broadly obovate petals often overlap, and the green calyx-lobes are ovate. Rounded leaves are serrate, shallowly 5-7 lobed, and leathery. The sweet fruit is soon dropped, but resembles clusters of tiny, yellowish, baked apples. Cloudberry occurs in sphagnum bogs and boggy forests northward from the latitude of northern Vancouver Island.

RÙBUS IDAÈUS L. looks very much like a domestic raspberry, though the rather small fruits are somewhat loose and crumbly, sometimes yellow when mature, as well as red. It is abundant across Canada and the northern States, and in Eurasia.

RÙBUS LASIOCÓCCUS Gray—is very similar to *R. pedatus* (which see) but has 3-(rather than 5-) lobed leaves. Its white flowers are often in pairs (rather than invariably single). Lasiococcus refers to the (minute) *hairs* covering the *red fruit.* This dwarf species occurs only in the mountains of our area, and southward.

RÙBUS LEUCODÉRMIS Dougl. *Blackcap Raspberry.*

The specific name refers to the striking *white skin* or bark of this ferociously-armed shrub. The fruit is a flattish dark-purple raspberry, possessing a unique sweet taste—not always enjoyed.

R. leucodermis is widespread throughout the Province, frequently springing up in logged and burnt-off areas.

The white flowers appear on canes of the previous year, which die back after the fruit matures. Leaflets are usually in threes, the margins irregularly and doubly saw-toothed. They are green and nearly glabrous above, but conspicuously white-pubescent below. The vicious flattened and hooked spines continue up the mainstem of the leaf.

RÙBUS PARVIFLÒRUS Nutt. *Thimble Berry.*   [p.271]

Parvus means in Latin either *few* in number or quantity, *small* in size or extent. But the beautiful blossom, with its white petals crinkled like muslin, is much the *largest* of our native species. In fact, on the west coast of Vancouver Island, blooms 1½-2 inches wide are usual. In justifying the name one could agree that only 3-5 flowers are usual in a cluster, a relatively small number in comparison with those of other species. The popular name given is more commonly employed than several others, and is probably the most appropriate. The bright-red berries conceal a very large hollow, big as a thimble.

The substance of the thin berry is small, but the flavour is very sweet. Canes are nearly if not quite without prickles, and may form dense thickets, 7 feet high, in rich damp bottomland. Smaller shrubs are common on dry hillsides, to moderate altitudes across British Columbia. Leaves of Rubus parviflorus are very large (to 10 inches long), shaped like a maple leaf, but with a soft and crinkled surface.

"On the rocky islands, and in the woods [of Nootka and Barkley Sounds]. . . . is a species of raspberry of the most delicious flavour, and far superior to any fruit of that kind we had ever before tasted. It grows on a larger bush than our European raspberry, and is free of thorns; but the fruit itself is so delicate, that a shower of rain washes it entirely away."

John Meares:
Voyages made in the Years 1788 and 1789
from China to the N.W. Coast of America (1791)

254

POTENTILLA GRACILIS var. GRACILIS ×²⁄₅
[p.241]

PURSHIA TRIDENTATA ×³⁄₅ [p.248]

OSMARONIA CERASIFORMIS ×½ [p.238]

POTENTILLA DIVERSIFOLIA ×1 [p.240]

POTENTILLA HOOKERIANA ×½ [p.244]

POTENTILLA FRUTICOSA ×⅗ [p.241]

POTENTILLA PALUSTRIS ×½ [p.244]

255

RÙBUS PEDÀTUS J. E. Smith. *Creeping Raspberry.* [p.270]

Pedatus means *footed;* the image suggested is probably that of small leaves pacing like birds' feet across the mosses. The dwarfing effect of high altitudes is dramatically evident in this mountain dweller, kin of the tall canes and shrubs of lowland raspberries. The Creeping Raspberry lifts each white flower an inch above the ground, and when the tiny fruits appear each is seen to consist of only 2 or 3, sometimes a single crimson drupelet.

The wee plants, almost hidden among the mosses, are strung together by thin wiry stolons (runners). Each plant consists of a single flowering-stem and 2 or 3 shining leaves (five-lobed and doubly-serrate, with a slim smooth petiole about twice as long as the blade). You will find a pair of prominent, brown, membranous stipules at the base of each leaf-petiole. The solitary flower is less than ¾ inch across, with 4 down-turned, toothed calyx-lobes, and 5 well-separated petals ringing a cluster of short stamens.

This is a delightful little species, that creeps close to salt water in dense hemlock-spruce forests of Alaska and the Queen Charlottes. Southward, in our area, it takes to the mountains, often above timber line. Plants from the ranges east of the Coast Range are glabrous, those of the seacoast are sparsely hairy on both surfaces. No spines or prickles are found in any of the forms of Rubus pedatus, a feature which adds to their desirability as dainty ground covers for shaded parts of the garden.

RÙBUS SPECTÁBILIS Pursh. *Salmon Berry.* [p.278]

The specific means *showy,* for the flowers are exceptional in a genus of white blooms. They are rose-coloured—very striking when unfurled against the drab background of lingering winter. A fine double form is occasionally seen. The vernacular name originated along the Columbia, where natives ate the tender, reddish shoots,* with dried salmon-roe.

The berries also were used for food. They are quite sweet, and large (about an inch in diameter), but soft, so must be eaten at once. Curiously, some of the 6-12 foot bushes bear fruit that is bright-orange when fully ripe, while others, only a few feet distant, ripen dark purplish-red fruit. Flavour is apparently identical. It would be very interesting to run chromatographic analyses of the two types.

The canes are armed with numerous short, straight prickles. Leaves are 3-foliate, and doubly-serrate, nearly smooth above, but pubescent beneath (at least along the veins).

R. spectabilis decreases in abundance from the Coast to the Cascades, to the east of which it is rare. We have flowering records (from southern Vancouver Island) in early February, and even late January.

*David Douglas in 1825 records, "They [six Indians who were with him on a difficult trip near the present Vancouver, Washington] had paddled forty miles without any sort of food except the young shoots of *Rubus spectabilis,* and water."

RÙBUS URSÌNUS Cham. & Schlecht. *Trailing Blackberry.* [p.278]

Many will entertain mixed feelings for this ubiquitous vine, perhaps influenced chiefly by the nature of their most recent encounter with it: whether a lacerating clutch around bare ankles, or a bounty of berries, finest flavoured of our native fruits. The specific name, ursinus, probably refers less to *bears'* sampling of the fruit, than to the northern distribution of the plant, under the constellation Ursa Major, the Great Bear (for this blackberry is abundant along lakeshores, and in logged-over areas, from the Central States northward, across the width of the continent).

Though even city-folk know the luscious black fruit, few people realize this species is dioecious, that is, it bears male and female flowers on separate plants. Of course, only the pistillate flowers yield berries. These flowers have many long pistils, and shorter stamens with no (or aborted) anthers. The staminate flowers of our illustration have long stamens with plump anthers, no pistils, and noticeably narrower white petals. The long trailing vines clamber over other plants as summer advances. They are liberally armed with short slender thorns, that are slightly recurved, and devastating to the incautious wayfarer.

SANGUISÓRBA SITCHÉNSIS C. A. Meyer. *Sitka Burnet.* [p.271]

The generic name is a relic of mediaeval materia medica, for the plant was used to staunch bleeding after "leeching" a patient (from sanguis, *blood*, and sorbere, to drink or *absorb*). It is a montane species, found at *Sitka*, but also southward to Oregon. Burnet is a very old name, its origins obscure. Apparently it was applied to a number of plants (e.g. *Poterium sanguisorba* L.) used in salads, and valued for their "hot" taste.

The handsome leaves are chiefly basal, as much as 12 inches long, with 9-17 leaflets arranged in pairs along the principal leaf-stem. They are thin and smooth, with a membranous stipule. Leaflets are rhombic-ovate, and strikingly toothed along the margins. Flower-stems, about 12-18 inches long, are smooth, and sometimes branched above. The flowers are tightly packed in long slim spikes, the buds at the lower end opening first, and so progressing ring-like up the spike. These whitish to greenish flowers are sometimes faintly flushed pink or purplish. A surprising feature in a family characterized by many stamens is the limitation to 4 only in this species. (In S. OCCIDENTÀLIS Nutt., also white-greenish flowered, the number of stamens is reduced to 2, and the stems are notably leafy with finely-cut, almost fern-like leaves. This species is chiefly a plant of wet bottoms, or wasteland that is wet in spring. S. sitchensis, as previously mentioned, is usually found in the mountains).

The Burnets waste no energy or substance in producing petals, nectar, or fragrance. Instead they produce millions of light pollen grains—for they are wind-pollinated.

PRUNUS EMARGINATA ✕½ [p.245]

PRUNUS VIRGINIANA var. DEMISSA ✕½ [p.245]

POTENTILLA PACIFICA ✕1 [p.240]

POTENTILLA VILLOSA ×1 [p.245]

SIBBÁLDIA PROCÚMBENS L. *Sibbaldia*   [p.279]

This *procumbent* little plant is circumboreal, commonly extending its low mats over open dry slopes of nearly all our mountains. (Sir Robert Sibbald, who died in 1722, was an early professor of medicine at Edinburgh.)

The basal leaves are 3-lobed (each lobe with 3 teeth at the tip) and white-haired on both surfaces. The ½-inch flowers have 5 minute, pale-yellow, slim petals, only about half as long as the greenish calyx-lobes. An unusual feature among the Rosaceae is the limited number of stamens, there being only 5.

Calder and Taylor comment that Sibbaldia is one of the commonest subalpine or alpine plants throughout the Cordilleran region of North America.

SÓRBUS SITCHÉNSIS Roemer. *Western Mountain Ash.*   [p.279]

This variable shrub with its white flower-clusters, and brilliant berries, was originally described from *Sitka*, Alaska. Sorbus was the early Latin name applied to one of the Mediterranean species, though in the earlier use (in Greek by Theophrastus) it seems to mean some kind of oak. Abundant as a 5-8 foot bush above 3500 feet in the mountains throughout our area, it descends to lower levels near the Coast, and may then reach 12 feet. It hybridizes with *S. aucuparia* L. (the Rowan or Mountain Ash) and much resembles that familiar tree of boulevards and gardens.

Most observers consider S. sitchensis more valuable than the familiar Rowan, chiefly because of the unrivalled colour of the berries and the less overwhelming odour of the flowers. Young twigs and buds are rusty-haired. The leaves are pinnately-compound, with 7-11 leaflets, each rather blunt-tipped, with teeth limited (in most forms) to the upper half. The small, white, fragrant flowers form slightly curved to nearly flat clusters of 15-80, usually 2-3 inches across.

[p.271]   SÓRBUS SCOPULÌNA Greene (the specific name refers to this plant's rocky habitat) is a species closely related to S. sitchensis (which see), and it, too, is most attractive in fruit. The leaves are possibly the feature most useful for separating the two species. In this case they are slimmer and sharply pointed (rather than obtuse at the tip as in *S. sitchensis*), with teeth the full length of the leaf. The pubescence is greyish (cf. reddish in the Sitka species). Flower-clusters are larger (70-200 florets) and flatter. The berries are very distinctive, being glossy bright coral-red.

Both species are spectacular when the handsome leaves turn yellow in the fall garden. The berries are eagerly sought by migrating birds. Deer as well as elk crop the young twigs, keeping the bushes compact.

SPIRAÈA BETULIFÒLIA Pall. *Birch-leaved Spiraea.*   [p.279]

Greek speira means variously *spire* or wreath. while *birch-leaved* interprets the specific name. Spireas, some of which have been called "Bridal-wreath", are familiar in the garden, and several wild species are also very showy shrubs. They are almost unique among the members of the Rosaceae, in having leaves that lack stipules.

This species is usually less than 3 feet tall. with nearly flat-topped clusters of white flowers, that are often slightly tinged lavender, or pink. The leaves are smooth. paler beneath, ovate but deeply notched. particularly toward the tips. The flattened corymbs distinguish S. betulifolia from our two species with flowers in cone-shaped trusses, and the pale colour distinguishes it from the bright-rose of *S. densiflora* (which see).

In July or August, these small shrubs bloom from sea level to about 4000 feet. They are widely distributed from the Cascades eastward.

SPIRAÈA DENSIFLÒRA Nutt., Mountain Spiraea, is a montane species, found up to 11,000 feet. It resembles *S. betulifolia* (which see). but the *dense*, flat-topped, flower clusters are a deep rose-pink. and the more compact plant seldom exceeds 1 foot in height.

SPIRAÈA DOUGLÁSII Hook. *Hardhack.*   [p.282]

Many woodsmen will assert that it is indeed very hard to hack a way through the dense growth of this common shrub. Sometimes dense thickets, 5-7 feet tall. make marshy areas almost impenetrable. The specific name is in honour of that hardy Scots botanist, David Douglas, who first brought to Europe many plants of the Pacific Northwest.

The beautiful, pink, elongate corymbs are much admired, but unfortunately turn disagreeably brown after a few days. The plant is, besides, much too invasive to consider bringing it into the garden. Leaves are nearly—or quite—glabrous in some forms, but in southern British Columbia they are generally covered below with short greyish hairs. The upper half of the leaves is sharply notched.

SPIRAÈA PYRAMIDÀTA Greene is usually 2-4 feet high, with a more open [p.271] *cone-shaped* cluster of palest pink or nearly white flowers. It is found east of the Cascades, in southern British Columbia.

LEGUMINÒSEAE. *Pea Family.*

This is an enormously successful family, about 13,000 species attesting their ability to find niches in the tropics and subtropics, in temperate and arctic climes. This habitat range accounts for variations which have required the creation of nearly 600 genera.

Members include dissimilar shrubs such as the Mimosas, and trees such as the Acacias, but some authorities elevate them to separate family status. Most of the species have papilionaceous flowers (i.e. butterfly-like flowers), and these in some systems of classification are set apart in a family, Papilionaceae. We shall, however, follow Hitchcock, Cronquist, et al., in using the more inclusive name, Leguminosae. Leguminosae means *pod-bearing.*

A great deal of repetition will be saved by pointing out that the many species of our area have highly-specialized flowers, of a more or less patterned structure. Papilionaceous flowers have 5 non-uniform petals. The uppermost is called the STANDARD, because it is usually large and showy, and stands erect to rally insects to the flowers. The 2 side-petals are WINGS; the 2 lowermost are more or less folded together, or even partially united, to form the KEEL. Inside the keel are (usually) 10 stamens, with filaments generally joined into a tube around the ovary (quite often 1 stamen is isolated). The fruit (ripened ovary) is a POD, which is variously shaped, and in most cases splits in two, releasing relatively large seeds that occur in rows. You will think that this sounds like a description of the familiar Sweet Pea, which of course is one of the family.

Most legumes have compound leaves: sometimes palmate (like a hand), sometimes pinnate (like a feather). Often a terminal leaflet is modified into a tendril, by which the plant clings to some support. A most important and characteristic feature in this family is the presence of root-nodules that contain nitrogen-fixing bacteria. Hence crops of vetch and clover are often ploughed into the soil, to act as "green fertilizers" for succeeding crops. Many species display sophisticated floral modifications to ensure cross-fertilization. These will be described in the appropriate generic descriptions.

Other members are the Peanut or Groundnut, the lovely *Wistaria* vine, Edible Peas, Beans—Broad and Bush, Soya and Pole, the ubiquitous Broom, and Gorse, Indigo (once important source of a dye), Licorice, Alfalfa, and many more. Discoveries at ancient Jericho show that the lentil (*Lens culinaris,* whose seed-shape provided our word for a camera component) was domesticated as early as 7000 B.C. and may have been used even earlier than the wheaten grasses. Also included in this enormous family is the Royal Poinciana (*P. regia,* of Madagascar originally), one of the most spectacular flowering trees of the tropics. Another is *Koompassia,* perhaps the tallest of tropical rain forest trees. It reaches 260 feet and contrasts remarkably with our Vetches and Lupines. *Cercidium* (Paloverde), and *Prosopis* (Mesquite), and *Laburnum* are members. These will be enough to demonstrate the versatility of the Leguminosae.

ASTRÁGALUS ALPÌNUS L. *Mountain Milk Vetch. Mountain Locoweed.* [p.283]

The name Astragalus is of Greek origin, but the identity of the plant has been lost. This is an enormous genus of over 2000 species. About 23 species occur in our area, and though often of local occurrence, they are rather consistent in characteristics. With some regret we have decided to picture only a single species to represent the genus. Many of the species are common, and widely distributed; furthermore quite a few have been associated in the public mind with "blind-staggers", a disease affecting horses particularly. Chemical studies however have recently proved that soils derived from certain shales contain concentrations of selenium (an element related to sulphur) that are taken up by a number of species of Astragalus and adjacent genera, and so poison grazing animals. This is the origin of the older name "Locoweed".

Members of this genus are recognized by their small pea-type flowers (white, yellow, pink or purple) and by pinnately-compound leaves. Pods are greatly varied in shape, and may suggest the wisdom of subdividing the unwieldy genus. Greek astragalos, *ankle-bone*, may refer to the pod-shape.

This *alpine* species is circumpolar, in our area most abundant in the Rockies. From perennial rootstocks arise 2-8 inch stems, bearing pinnate leaves (2-6 inches long) whose 13-23 leaflets are greenish, but hairy, and elliptical. The small flowers are pale- to deep-lilac, borne in crowded racemes. The hanging pods are brown, densely covered with black hairs.

Particularly common species of Astragalus are A. MÌSER Dougl. (with bluish-pencilled whitish flowers and narrow leaflets); and A. AGRÉSTIS Dougl.— A. DASYGLÓTTIS Fisch. (with white-winged purple flowers, and broader tip-notched leaflets).*

*Part 3 of the scholarly work by Hitchcock, Cronquist, et al., should be consulted for these and the numerous other species to be encountered in our area. See also *Oxytropis*, a closely related genus.

CÝTISUS SCOPÀRIUS (L.) Link. *Broom. Scotch Broom.* [p.283]

Beautiful, undeniably, is this immigrant shrub. Scoparius means *broom*, and there are those who have been heard to murmur darkly that they would like to see the plants swept back to Europe. As so often happens with ill-considered introductions, the golden Broom found, on this far coast, none of the checks and balances of its homeland, and literally ran wild. A sea of gold indeed, but a flood that has swamped many of our native species—a tide that shows no sign of turning.

The story of its coming to our shores has been frequently told, but it is a romantic tale and may bear repetition. Captain W. Colquhoun Grant, a dashing swordsman, late of the Royal Scots Greys, in the summer of 1849 arrived in Victoria, to find all the lands in Victoria and Esquimalt (40 square miles!) reserved by the Hudson's Bay Company (and its subsidiary company, Puget Sound Agricultural). So the doughty captain was forced to settle with his Scottish retainers at "Soke", 26 miles distant. Between summers devoted to building a fortified home and two sawmills, and growing experimental crops, he travelled widely. From the British consul in the Sandwich Islands he obtained a few seeds of the Scottish Broom. We may imagine with what nostalgia the captain planted at Sooke, 12 or 13 of these treasured seeds. Only 3 plants grew—but from them have sprung the countless thousands that annually spread a golden glory by road and hillside. The oldest reference we can find attributes the generic name to *Cythera*, one of the Ionian Islands, since Linnaeus read that one of the species was first found there.

A description is unnecessary, but the pollination and seed-scattering devices are interesting, and may not be familiar to everybody.

If one stands close to the heavily-scented bushes, it is instructive to watch the insect visitors. Here comes a fast-flying "Skipper" butterfly. But it ignores the Broom flowers in their tens of thousands, and alights on the only head of Milfoil (*Achillea millefolium*) we can see. Surely this "Blue" (*Lycaenid*)? No. But it wavers to a Buttercup—another yellow flower. (The same colour as the Broom, but this flower offers a good landing platform.) Yes, it has folded its wings upright and is walking around the open petals, its proboscis probing the little nectary purses so close to the stamens that some pollen will almost certainly stick to its hairy head and thorax. There is a buzz, and a stout bumblebee zooms down to one of the Broom flowers, its wings apparently inadequate for its heavy body garish with yellow, black and crimson.

How did it land on the bloom? Now watch closely. It was on the projecting keel, the only suitable place (since the standard and wings of the flower are held almost in a vertical plane). But with a momentary blur of wings the big insect has completed his visit, and is on an adjacent flower. And there he goes—off to the next one. (Evidently there is an advantage to the plant in clustering its flowers.) Lean a little closer. Ah! as he touched the next keel his weight pushed the halves of the keel downward, and the stamens sprang up to dust his underside. He's off again—let's pick a bloom and press down on the keel with our finger. Interesting! there are 6 short and 4 longer stamens, so the pollen was dabbed in two places for greater assurance that it would be carried to the pistil of the next flower. The pistil? Oh yes—it is curved, flattened and expanded at the sticky tip or stigma. Most important, it's much longer than even the long set of stamens; in fact it's longer than the keel. So the bumblebee certainly touched the pollen on his lower body hairs to the projecting pistil of the next bloom, even as he alighted. What a marvellously devised arrangement! How efficient in securing cross-pollination! No wonder Scotch Broom has been successful in spreading up and down the Pacific Coast. There is even a disjunct colony beside Kootenay Lake, and one may be reasonably sure it will spread further.

Have you ever stood in a clump of Broom on a hot and windless day in October? Then you will surely have heard occasionally a sharp crack, and if you persevered in tracking the sound, actually seen a blackened dry pod burst violently from top to bottom, the two halves projecting two sprays of round seeds to considerable distances.

. . . Little flower—but if I could understand
What you are, root and all, and all in all,
I should know what God and man is.

Alfred, Lord Tennyson:
Flower in the Crannied Wall

HEDÝSARUM SULPHURÉSCENS Rydb. *Yellow Loments.* [p.283]

Greek hedys, *sweet,* and aroma, *smell,* are the apparent origins of the name of this pale *sulphur-yellow* plant. It is found in the Ponderosa Pine country, especially on the eastern slope of the Cascades.

This perennial develops, from a thick woody taproot, a cluster of 12-24 inch stems, bearing pinnate leaves, and rather one-sided racemes of drooping, pale, pea-type flowers. The numerous leaflets are shaped like a slim egg, the upper parts dotted with minute transparent glands and sparse pale hairs. The plant is at once identifiable when the fruits develop. They are long, flattened pendulous pods, remarkably constricted between each of the 2-4 seeds. Such a pod is known as a loment, whence the common name.

LÁTHYRUS JAPÓNICUS Willd. var. GLÀBER (Ser.) Fern.=L. MARÍTIMUS Fries. *Beach Pea.* [p.294]

Lathyrus is a genus of about 150 species, chiefly of the North Temperate Zone. The name occurs in early Greek works, apparently derived from the augmentative la, and thoursos, *something exciting,* since the seeds were thought to have medicinal qualities. It is interesting to observe that nearly all of the greater plant families have developed species whose structures have been specialized to fit them to life on the sandy margins of the sea. For example, consider the adaptation to this environmental niche by *Honkenya peploides* in the Caryophyllaceae, *Cakile edentula* among the Crucifers, *Glehnia leiocarpa* of the Umbellifers, *Glaux maritima* in the Primulaceae, *Verbascum* sp. in the Scrophulariaceae, and *Grindelia integrifolia* among the Composites.

The Beach Pea (a replaced synonym is *maritimus, by the sea*) spreads by rhizomes that penetrate the loose sand easily, strongly anchoring the plant colony. The leaflets are leathery to withstand desiccation, and the stems are exceptionally thick and sturdy so that, in the absence of other plants on which to climb, the Pea is able to resist the unimpeded sweep of the wind.

Leaves of L. japonicus carry 6-12 glabrous leaflets. Flowers are firmly textured, quite large, and light-blue to dark-purple. The straight pod may be as much as 2½ inches long, with a usually straight, short beak. The leaf-stipules are rather distinctive: halberd-shaped, a little lop-sided, and quite as large as the leaflets (or even a little larger).

T. TODD

PYRUS FUSCA (FRUIT)   ✕⅗   [p.248]

ROSA PISOCARPA (FRUIT)   ✕½   [p.251]

PYRUS FUSCA   ✕⅗   [p.248]

ROSA GYMNOCARPA (FRUIT) ×4½ [p.249]

ROSA WOODSII ×½ [p.251]

ROSA GYMNOCARPA ×1⅕ [p.249]

LÁTHYRUS LATIFÒLIUS L. *Perennial Pea.* [p.291]

This European native has escaped from gardens and is now widely established on railway cuttings and roadsides, and most successfully, on clay banks by the sea. The specific name clearly means *broad-leaved*, and indeed, though there are only 2 leaflets per leaf, they are often 2 inches broad, and as much as 6 inches long.

This very handsome perennial quickly extends 6 or 8 feet in every direction. The flowers are very large and showy, in colour varying from white to pale-pink (or most often) clear bright rose. Leaves end in many-branched lengthy tendrils by which the Pea climbs over low bushes. Stipules have one lobe small, the other very much larger—though still a great deal smaller than the leaflets. The stems are angled and extended by long wing-like margins.

Though too vigorous for most gardens L. latifolius makes a brave show on wastelands, and its extensive root-system helps to prevent soil-slippage and erosion on steep banks.

LÁTHYRUS LITTORÀLIS (Nutt.) Endl. *Chinook Licorice. Grey Beach Pea.*

Like *L. japonicus* (which see), this is a species of seabeaches along the length of our coastline, and southward. The specific name means *of the sea shore.* One common name calls attention to the dense grey hairiness of the plants; the other, to use of the roasted roots by the Indian peoples of the Coast.

The most obvious field recognition is the general greyness of the plants. On closer approach, one notices that the leaves (with 4-8 oblong leaflets) do not terminate in a tendril, but in a sort of narrow terminal leaflet. This is quite distinctive, taken in conjunction with the beach habitat. The standard is blue to purple, the wings and keel noticeably paler, often white. When the hairy pods mature, they are very different from those of *L. japonicus*, being little over an inch long, and $\frac{1}{3}$ as wide, with a sharply recurved tip. In both species the stipules are larger than the leaflets.

Of the two sand plants this appears to be the more effectively specialized. Thus the dense pubescence may serve both to decrease transpired water loss, and to shield the leaf surface from salt spray. Further, since there are few or no other plants present on which to climb, useless tendrils have been replaced by photosynthetic appendages.

LÁTHYRUS NEVADÉNSIS Wats. = L. NUTTÁLLII Wats. *Purple Pea. Purple Nevada Pea.* [p.290]

This variable species is very common throughout our area, generally occurring in open woodland. One of the varieties does extend, as the name suggests, to *Nevada.*

Small-flowered Peas like this species are easily confused with Vetches (*Vicia,* which see). The surest way to tell them apart requires picking a flower, and pinching the keel to expose the pistil. In *Vicia* the tip of the style looks like a bottle-brush, equally hairy all round the tip; but in Lathyrus the hairs extend down the lower side only, as in a toothbrush.

L. nevadensis was long known, and will be familiar to many, as L. nuttallii. Though the leaves are tipped with single, or once-forked tendrils, the 8-30 inch plants often are more or less free-standing. Stems are angled, but not winged. The leaves have 4-10, pointed, ovate leaflets that are thin, paler beneath, smooth or very sparsely-hairy, and end in a short nubby point (mucronate). The stipules are small, with one lobe 3 times longer than the shorter (though the larger is less than one-third as long as the leaflet). The violet to purplish flowers are strongly bent upwards. The standard is usually darker than the wings or keel, and often is somewhat striped. The calyx is frequently reddish and sometimes more, sometimes less hairy, the upper teeth much shorter than the lower.

LÒTUS CORNICULÀTUS L. *Bird's Foot Trefoil.*   [p.290]

This is a European pasture plant, now widely dispersed along our roadsides, where its bright yellow flowers attract attention. The name is from the lotos of Theophrastus, but the plant he referred to is apparently the Jujube tree, *Zizyphus.* Corniculatus* means *horned,* the slim pointed pods suggesting horns. The English name, though widely used, is not entirely happy, for the leaves have five, not three leaflets, and birds of our acquaintance (with the exception of the Three-toed Woodpecker) have four toes.

These anomalous leaves are without petioles; the two pairs and the single terminal leaflets are elliptical, minutely-toothed, and hairy along the margins. The leaflets are small—less than ¾ inch long. The nearly glabrous plants are lax; they are seldom more than 8-10 inches tall and the stems are inclined to lie along the ground and root at each node. Short flower-stems bear a rounded head of flowers, resembling bright-yellow, much-enlarged clover blooms. Tucked closely under the flower-cluster is a single small bract that we suddenly realize is trefoil. The inch-long brown pods are conspicuous. They radiate from the stem-end like slender cylinders round in cross section, but pointed and slightly hooked at the tip.

LÒTUS MICRÁNTHUS Benth. *Small-flowered Lotus.* This is a much daintier [p.294] species. Native of open slopes from sea level to the mountains, it occurs westward from the Cascades. The 3-6 leaflets are only ¼-½ inch long and nearly smooth. Flowers are tiny, but worth looking at closely, for the pale-yellow petals are beautifully touched with bright-rose.

*Agnes Arber shows the obvious derivation of the woodcut of "Crow-foot Trefoile" in Johnson's (1633) edition of Gerard's *Herball.* The block must have been cut as a mirror-reversal of a vastly superior pen-drawing in Dioscoride's *Codex Aniciae Julianae* (circa A.D. 512)!

270

RUBUS ACAULIS ×³⁄₅ [p.252]

RUBUS PEDATUS ×⁷⁄₈ [p.256]

ROSA NUTKANA ×1 [p.250]

RUBUS PARVIFLORUS $\times \frac{2}{5}$ [p.253]

SANGUISORBA SITCHENSIS $\times \frac{3}{4}$ [p.257]

SORBUS SCOPULINA (FRUIT) $\times \frac{3}{5}$ [p.260]

SPIRAEA PYRAMIDATA $\times \frac{1}{3}$ [p.261]

LUPÌNUS. *Lupines.*

Lupinus is clearly derived from lupus, a *wolf,* but the allusion has been variously explained. Possibly a reference in Ovid is the correct one: since the plants often grow in poor soil, it was thought (through a confusion of cause and effect) that the plants "devoured", i.e. robbed the soil. Actually, of course, the nitrogen-fixing bacteria of the root-nodules tend to .enrich poor soil, particularly if the lush plants are ploughed in.

The lupines are taxonomically very difficult. Earlier botanists gave names to about 600 "species" but many of the features they used have since been shown to be inconstant—variable with altitude, soil, moisture, and other factors. The labours of David B. Dunn on the North American species have served to reduce the number of species by a factor of 6, while pointing out the variety of problems involved, such as glacial recessions, natural hybridization, and plasticity. We have followed his speciation, by which it appears that we have in British Columbia 27 varieties assignable to only 23 species, the majority of which occur on the south end of Vancouver Island. Some of these are rare, and very local.

Sensational stories have appeared from time to time purporting to relate the sprouting of wheat grains found in Egytian tombs. On critical examination most of these 3000-year old seeds have been found to be completely carbonized, and obviously incapable of germination. But a report in 1967, by three unimpeachable authorities, almost staggers belief. At Miller Creek, in the Yukon, during July, 1954, a mining engineer, Mr. Harold Schmidt, found in frozen silt a series of ancient burrows of rodents (later identified as those of the Collared Lemming), containing a hoard of large seeds. Out of curiosity, Mr. Schmidt bottled a few dozen, and kept them in his office. Twelve years later the seeds were sent to the National Museum of Canada. There a team headed by Dr. A. E. Porsild placed them on damp filter paper, and found 6 germinated within 48 hours, one of the resulting plants later maturing flowers. Careful investigation revealed these seeds (of a presently flourishing species, *Lupinus arcticus*) could not be less than 10,000 years old!*

*(Readers may be interested to read the original paper listed in the Bibliography under Porsild, Harington, and Mulligan.)

LUPÌNUS ARBORÈUS Sims. *Tree Lupine.* [p.294]

True, arboreus does mean *tree-like,* but in our northern latitudes this is better called a shrub, much-branched and reaching 5 or 6 feet. It is a native of California, widely introduced northward along the coast to bind the soil on steep slopes and clay banks.

The present perennial (and immigrant) species was one of the parents (with *L. polyphyllus,* which see) of the lovely Russell Hybrids that deck our perennial herbaceous borders. The bush-like growth is unique among our species, and sufficient to identify it. Lupinus arboreus is silver-haired, except for the smooth upper surfaces of the leaves.

The flowers are pale sulphur-yellow (though introgression sometimes results in pale-blue colouring).

This is a handsome shrubby Lupine.

LUPÌNUS ÁRCTICUS S. Wats. ssp. SUBALPÌNUS (Piper & Rob.) Dunn. *Subalpine Broad-leaved Lupine. Arctic Lupine.* [p.295]

Lupinus arcticus is a wide-ranging species (in part earlier called *L. latifolius*) that has been recognized under several varietal and subspecific names. As the specific name suggests, this is an arctic-alpine plant that ranges northward from the high volcanic cones of Oregon. In our area subspecies subalpinus is widely distributed, particularly in alpine meadows. Massed colonies provide sheets of colour of an intensity rivalling the mountain sky. Visitors to Mt. Revelstoke, Manning Park, Banff, and Jasper in late July and early August will recall these dazzling displays.

In the northern third of the Province there is a transition to ssp. ÁRCTICUS (with hairier leaflets and fewer stem leaves), and in southern Vancouver Island to ssp. CANADÉNSIS (Smith) Dunn (with a larger proportion of stem-leaves, and leaflets even more hairy than the other 2 subspecies).

Lupinus arcticus is a perennial, whose clumped 12-30 inch stems die back each winter to a woody base (caudex). Northern ssp. *arcticus* has most of its leaves in a basal cluster and only 2-4 cauline (on the flower-stem or scape); ssp. *canadensis* has few basal and chiefly cauline leaves. In the present subspecies all the leaves, at flowering time, originate above the ground upward along the hollow stem. This stem appears smooth to the unaided eye, and usually the upper surface of the leaflets appears glabrous, though actually finely-hairy.

Flowers of all the subspecies are variably purplish-blue, relieved by trim white accents on the outer edges of the banner petal, and on the tip of the keel that peeps out between the darker wing petals. Occasionally a pinkish individual is seen, or an albino form.

Leaflets are noticeably broad, average proportions being about ½ inch by 2 inches. At maturity the leaflets in ssp. subalpinus become blunt to rounded, with a small nub at the tip of the mid-vein (they are said to be mucronate). In the other 2 subspecies the end of the leaflet is considerably more acute.

LUPÌNUS BÍCOLOR Lindl. = L. MICRÁNTHUS Dougl. *Bicoloured Lupine.* [p.290]

The type (specimen on which the original description—in Latin—was given and the name assigned) was from seed collected by David Douglas May 23, 1825 ". . . near the Grand Rapids, Columbia River. S. [seed collected]."

This little annual is exceedingly abundant on well-drained soils near the coast of the southern half of Vancouver Island, and the Fraser River valley, southward. (L. MICRÁNTHUS has now been placed in the synonymy.) Its hairy rosettes appear soon after the New Year, and grow 2-12 inches tall, with long basal branches. The branches are terminated by close racemes of perky blue and white flowers. These have a banner that is sharply kinked backward at the mid-point. Wings and keel are blue, but the banner's blue is relieved by a wide central band, at first crisp white, later pinkish, and usually marked with a few black dots. The keel is hairy on the upper half, and its slender tip curves upward.

From April to June short-turf slopes are gay with the sprightly blue and white of this small Lupine, that affords a cool contrast to the waxy gold of *Ranunculus* sp.

LUPÌNUS DENSIFLÒRUS Benth. var. SCOPULÓRUM C. P. Smith. *Dense-flowered Lupine.* [p.302]

This is a little-known but interesting species with pale-yellow flowers.

Apparently, seed from the Californian population was brought north at an early date, for there are widely separated colonies in Washington, and along the clay cliffs of Beacon Hill Park, Victoria. Since the plant was collected at the latter site by John Macoun (1887, and probably also earlier* while engaged in the first botanical survey of this region), it is very likely that a few seeds came north, in the clothing of a Californian miner, during the Gold-rush of the sixties.

The plants are annuals, so it is clear that they have maintained themselves (possibly for more than a century) in this restricted colony. Dense-flowered Lupine grows 8-12 inches tall, with numerous compact branches, each of which bears a tuft of leaves at its summit. Stems, leaves, and calyxes are clothed with silky, white hairs. The pods are also hairy, and about ¾ inch long, with the coiled style persisting at the top.

*"During the early part of 1875 I made very extensive collections on Vancouver Island near Victoria." [One of his herbarium sheets is labelled 1887.]

Macoun's Catalogue

LUPÌNUS LYÁLLII A. Gray *Low Mountain Lupine.* [p.302]

This is a beautiful matlike perennial of alpine meadows, or dry gravelly slopes, chiefly above timber line. In our area it has been reported only from the mountains of the southern and central Interior.

The plant is silky-silvered throughout. The sturdy stems are close-pressed to the ground, with flowering stems rising 2-5 inches only. As in so many alpine plants, the flowers are conspicuously large, relative to the neat leaves—each with 5-7 leaflets (that are seldom more than ½ inch long). Commonly the leaflets are slightly folded like a V, possibly to funnel dew and rain inward to the roots. The blooms are usually compressed into a short dense raceme: they vary in colour from white to blue or violet. The banner is marked with a central stripe that may be white or pale yellow. Short stubby pods enclose 2-4 seeds that are pink or tan.

This is the choicest of the Lupines for the rockery. It is never invasive, but in wet winters on the Coast the plants need a pane of glass during winter. When growth resumes the gardener will be well repaid for this extra care.

Low Mountain Lupine bears the name of David Lyall (1817-1895), a Scotch botanist who spent much of his life in America.

LUPÌNUS POLYPHÝLLUS Lindl. *Large-leaved Lupine.* [p.302]

The stately spires of this perennial Lupine beautify wet roadside ditches and moist ground from the coast to lower levels in the mountains. It is the most lush of our species, the unbranched stems occasionally reaching 5 feet, with crowded flower-spikes at least a foot long.

The specific name means *many-leaved*, an epithet more precisely applicable to the leaflets, which vary from 9 to as many as 17. They are smooth above, but sparsely hairy below. The flowers—even from plants only a few yards apart—show a wide range of colour, from pale blue to dark violet, and purple. Close inspection shows that only the extreme tip of the keel, which is nearly always glabrous, protrudes beyond the clasped wing-petals. Pods are 1-2 inches long, and densely covered with long hairs.

Distribution is rather erratic; in our area L. polyphyllus has been recorded from the lower half of Vancouver Island, the Fraser Delta, Prince Rupert, and near Prince George. Flowering-period is mid-June to early September. The flowers turn brown as they age.

> *. . . These children of the meadows, born*
> *Of sunshine and of showers!*
>
> John Greenleaf Whittier:
> Flowers in Winter

LUPÌNUS SERÍCEUS Pursh. *Silky Lupine.* [p.290]

This highly variable Lupine is probably the commonest of our species, widespread from British Columbia to Arizona. It is most often associated with Sagebrush and *Pinus ponderosa* (Yellow Pine). The specific name is from the Latin sericus, *silk*, which describes the dense covering of long white hairs, responsible for the appearance of the leaves and stems.

Stands of this fine plant make an unforgettable picture, lapping the white boles of aspen, or the orange-red of pine trunks, like a wash of azure-blue.

From the perennial, branching crown, rise one to several erect stems 12-24 inches tall. The leaves are numerous, with 5-9 leaflets a little more than 2 inches long, and silky-pubescent on both sides. The calyx is hairy, both outside and inside. Even the basal part of the banner is hairy; and hairs line the edges of the keel. The wings, however, are glabrous. There are 4-6 ovules in the villous pod, which is 1-1½ inches long.

Darwin studied the movements of the leaves of several lupine species (among others), and commented, "That these [sleep] movements [of leaves] are in some manner of high importance to the plants which exhibit them, few will dispute who have observed how complex they sometimes are."

"lupine. . . .The earth is blued with them."

Henry David Thoreau:
Journal (June 5, 1852)

OXÝTROPIS PODOCÁRPA Gray.   [p.306]

Oxytropis (from the Greek oxys, *sharp*, and tropis, *a keel*) is very closely related to, and by some authors merged in, *Astragalus* (which see). But the beaked keel (formed from the 2 lowermost petals) is distinctive, and the absence of an above-ground stem in our 7 or 8 species, will distinguish members of this genus from the enormous number of Milk Vetches (*Astragalus*). The specific name means *stalked fruits*, these being fat reddish pods about ¾ inch long, ovoid—but pointed by the persistent style.

This pretty little alpine species can be found by diligent search on high stony ridges of the Rockies. The cluster of somewhat silver-haired, 1-2 inch leaves rises from the thickened root of this perennial. The leaves have 11-23 slim-lanceolate leaflets. The flower-stalk (peduncle) rarely exceeds the leaves in length, and bears 1 or 2 pale-purple tiny "pea" flowers that peep from the dark-purple hairy calyx.

[p.303]   OXÝTROPIS CAMPÉSTRIS (L.) DC. *Late Yellow Locoweed* which is very common throughout the Dry Interior from Lytton eastward, is often placed in the genus *Astragalus.* (It also has a number of other synonyms.) Eastham remarks this species "probably results in more losses [of livestock] than all other poisonous plants combined". A highly variable species, in our area flowers are usually pale-yellow, but locally whitish, bluish, pinkish, or purplish. The plants are much branched from the base, 8-18 inches tall, with 11-31 lanceolate leaflets that are densely silky-haired on both surfaces. Oblong-ovate pods are ½-1 inch long, with both black and white hairs. Campestris means *field-loving.*

OXÝTROPIS SPLÉNDENS Dougl. *Showy Oxytropis. Showy Locoweed.* [p.306]

In mid-July, grassy slopes near Dawson Creek are purpled with dense stands of this *attractive* species. It also occurs along the eastern slope of the Rockies from Alaska to New Mexico.

Beautiful silky leaves form a dense cluster 6-10 inches high. Very numerous leaflets are arranged in whorls of 3 to 6. They are pointed-elliptical, from ¼ to 1 inch long. The flower-stalks generally lengthen to hold the dense purple spike slightly above the mass of silvery foliage. The colour varies toward bluish or reddish, and a large patch of the plants makes a very handsome picture.

Individual flowers of Oxytropis splendens are about ½ inch long, with a densely white-haired calyx about half as long. The beak of the keel is slender and straight, or slightly curved. The pod is slim-pointed, and about ½ inch long.

TRIFÒLIUM ARVÉNSE L. *Haresfoot Clover. Rabbit-foot Clover.* [p.303]

Obvious source of the generic name is Latin tres, *three,* and folium, *a leaf.* Clover may come from "clava" or club, the triple-headed cudgel carried by Hercules. The "clover" leaf shape is seen in the familiar "clubs" of playing cards. This genus is vastly interesting, and the number of "good" species in our area numbers about 20. They are not only constant in character and easily recognized, but also display intriguing structural modifications to fit them for diverse niches in the ecosystem. Because of space limitations it is only possible to mention a few of the species, so we have chosen those less familiar. Everyone knows the Red Clover (T. PRATÉNSE L.) and the White Clover (T. RÈPENS L.); and certainly the pestiferous tiny yellow Common Trefoil (T. DÙBIUM Sibth.) is sadly familiar to anyone who takes pride in his lawns.

Identification of the Trifoliums requires careful examination of 3 principal features: first, the *leaf* shape and margin; second, details of the *calyx*; and third, whether or not there is an *involucre* (in this case the term means a whorl of united bracts that cup the flower-head).

Arvense means *of fields,* i.e. cultivated fields—for until the introduction of higher-yield species, this softly-haired 6-12 inch annual was extensively grown. It is still widespread on dry soils in England and the Continent, and has now become locally common by roadsides throughout British Columbia. T. arvense is quite distinctive, with oblong flower-heads each at the end of a short stalk, and narrow, scarcely-toothed leaves. The calyx-lobes are thin and soft, white to fawn-coloured, and much longer than the pale-pink, small, papilionaceous corolla.

278

RUBUS SPECTABILIS (FRUIT) ×³⁄₅ [p.256]

RUBUS URSINUS ♂ ×⁴⁄₅ [p.257]

RUBUS SPECTABILIS ×½ [p.256]

279

SIBBALDIA PROCUMBENS ×1⅕ [p.260]

SORBUS SITCHENSIS ×⅗ [p.260]

SPIRAEA BETULIFOLIA ×1 [p.261]

TRIFÒLIUM MÌCRODON H. & A. *Thimble Clover. Cup Clover.* [p.306]

The specific name means *small-toothed*. The aptness of the name is only appreciated when a 10X magnifier is focused on the calyx-lobes, which are seen to be not only sharp-tipped, but distinctively notched with numerous small sharp teeth. This feature, and the raised central nerve and submarginal ridge of the calyx-lobes are sufficient to determine this species.

Otherwise T. microdon is a sparsely to copiously hairy annual, seldom more than 4 inches tall, with small leaves whose leaflets are broadly obovate and deeply notched at the ends. There is a conspicuous, hairy involucre with 10-12 irregular teeth, the whole thimble-shaped (whence the common name).

This little clover is found in meadows and waste ground in southwest British Columbia, and southward.

TRIFÒLIUM SUBTERRÀNEUM L. *Burrowing Clover.* [p.307]

Though recorded in our area only during the last few years (from southern Vancouver Island), this odd European Clover is apparently becoming more widespread.

Burrowing Clover has developed a most interesting device, obviously effective in anchoring the plant to the sandy or gravelly soil in which it usually grows. (We have, however, seen it well-established in a field of wet clay soil.) Flowering-stems produced from the leaf-axils bend over until the flowers (which continue to point directly upward) have formed a sharp kink with the stem. Then as the corolla withers there is an extraordinary development of scale-like bracts of the involucre, many of which grow downward. As their tips penetrate the soil they turn outward, and like the flukes of an anchor, not only fasten the plant to the ground, but actually pull the developing fruit into the soil. Thus the common name is justified, and also the specific "subterraneum", for the seed is literally *planted in the ground.*

(The Leguminosae family displays, as in this case, a remarkable facility to adapt to particular needs. As an illustration, numerous members of this family are found in the extreme drought areas of Baja California and the arid Southwest, a habitat demanding major structural modifications.)

The Burrowing Clover has broad "shamrock"-shaped leaflets, that have conspicuous, very long white hairs along the edges, and rather shorter ones on both surfaces. Stems and flower-pedicels are also covered with white hairs. The flower-head consists of only 2 or 3 florets, which are white with a tinge of palest pink. The corolla-tube is long and slender—even longer than the strange hair-like calyx-lobes. These long calyx-lobes are green, in striking contrast to the cup portion of the calyx, which is bright-red. This is a clover of exceptional interest.

[p.307]   TRIFÒLIUM TRIDENTÀTUM Lindl. *Lance Clover.* This abundant native from May to July covers pockets of soil on the rocky hillsides of coastal British Columbia. These annual plants are glabrous throughout. Flower-heads (of few to many purple florets) are lifted 3-6 inches on branched stems, that carry sharply-pointed and notched trifoliate "lance" leaflets. Usually the corolla-lobes are tipped with white, but occasionally with darker purple. The involucre is rather distinctive, being saucer-like with sharply-toothed margins. Calyx-lobes are generally *three-toothed*, and slightly shorter than the calyx-tube.

ÙLEX EUROPAÈUS L. *Gorse. Furze.*   [p.307]

Ulex is an ancient Latin name, that was certainly applied to one of the European species several centuries B.C. Furze is the modern descendant of Old English fyrs. The word King Aelfred used in his translation of Boethius' *De Consolatione Philosophiae* (Bk. XXIII, line 3)—for furze-bushes—was fyrsas. So also is Gorse a very old word in English. In the west of Scotland one may still see, in occasional straight lines of Gorse, relics of an earlier use as hedges, and even now the prickly bush is often used by country-folk to dry the washing.

This spiny shrub is one of many similarly armed members of the Leguminosae family occurring in arid regions of the world. There is a great deal of oil in the branches, so that regardless of the obvious discomfort in cutting and bundling, it has long been used for fuel. This inflammability makes Gorse by the roadsides a hazard. Though the Furze keeps its admirers at a distance, it displays a brave show of gold through the winter months of southern coastal British Columbia.

No description is needed for this familiar shrub.

The bristling armament of plants is due to a variety of structures. Thus in *Rosa* the prickles are outgrowths of the bark, from which they break away cleanly. Rarely a petiole becomes modified to a spine. In the Crab Apple (*Pyrus fusca*) short sterile branchlets serve as spurs. The rigid furrowed spines of Ulex are modified leaves.

Earth's crammed with Heaven
And every common bush afire with God.

Elizabeth Barrett Browning:
Aurora Leigh

VÍCIA AMERICÀNA Muhl. *Wild Vetch.*   [p.303]

This is another tall purple vetch that resembles *V. sativa* (which see) but is readily distinguishable because its clusters of 4-10 flowers are not axillary, but carried on well-defined peduncles. The flowers vary from ½-1 inch in length, and are bluish-purple to reddish-purple. The leaves vary: in number of leaflets (8-14), in shape of leaflets (linear to almost oval), in texture (thin to almost leathery), and in hairiness (almost

SPIRAEA DOUGLASII   ✕⅗   [p.261]

ASTRALAGUS ALPINUS ×1 [p.263]

CYTISUS SCOPARIUS ×⅖ [p.263]

HEDYSARUM SULPHURESCENS ×⅘ [p.265]

glabrous to rather densely pubescent). Plants may reach 3½ feet in height, climbing by means of long forking tendrils. V. americana is common in open woods and thickets, particularly in coastal areas, but also occurs eastward into Alberta and northward to Alaska.

VÍCIA CRÁCCA L. *Cow Vetch.*   [p.303]

This showy purple vetch (for which at least a dozen English names are used) often festoons waste-land and roadside shrubbery with its thin stems bearing lengthy spikes of numerous, bright rosy-purple "pea" flowers. It is a Eurasian species widely naturalized over much of North America.

Vicia is the old Latin name for the plant, originally derived from vincio, *to bind together,* since the tendrils cling to other plants. Vicia is distinguishable from *Lathyrus* (see *Lathyrus nevadensis*) by the "bottle-brush" style, by stems neither angled nor winged, and by (generally) more numerous leaflets.

A perennial, Cow Vetch has clambering stems that may reach 4-5 feet. They bear 2-4 inch long leaves, made up of 12-22 slender leaflets, and ending in long branched tendrils. Stipules at the leaf-base are narrow and untoothed. The flowers are tightly packed along one side of the raceme, and hang downward. They remain semi-closed but age a deeper colour. The calyx is very unevenly notched; the upper lobes very short and triangular, the lower 2-3 times as long, slim and covered with short hairs. The pods are hairless. Also perennial, VÍCIA GIGÁNTEA Hook. climbs to 12 ft. in coastal thickets. Its leaves bear 19-29 narrow leaflets; flowers are yellowish (or purplish-tinged).

VÍCIA HIRSÙTA (L.) S. F. Gray. *Hairy Vetch.*   [p.307]

Though introduced from Europe this tiny white annual species is widespread and common in rough grassy places, chiefly along the Coast. The specific name means *hairy,* though the hairs may not be visible until a 10X magnifier is used.

Slender and completely dependent on other plants for its support, the stems of this small plant are usually 12-24 inches long. Generally not quite opposite, the 12-18 linear leaflets are squared off at the ends, except for a weak hair-like projection of the mid-vein. Tendrils are long and branched. In contrast to *V. sativa* (which see), the 1-6 flowers occur in a long-stalked spike. Though white in colour at first impression, recently-opened flowers are seen, on more careful examination, to be palest lilac. The calyx-teeth are long and slender, and nearly equal in length. The pods are downy and 2-seeded (which will distinguish this species from the very similar V. TETRASPÉRMA (L.) Moench, which has *4,* rarely 3 or 5 *seeds*).

VÍCIA SATÌVA L. *Common Vetch.*

The specific name means *cultivated*, for this plant has long been cultivated in Europe as a fodder-plant. It has now made itself at home very widely in North America.

This is a variable annual species. The leaves usually have 8-14 leaflets (that may be linear to oblanceolate to obovate), and well-developed branched tendrils. The stipules are deeply-toothed, and shaped like arrowheads. One to three flowers occur in the leaf-axils; they are without—or with the shortest possible—pedicels. The banner is strongly erect, and purplish (often with a flush of yellow near the centre) but the wings and keel are reddish-purple. Long, pointed, calyx-lobes are rather unequal and ciliate-edged. In the larger-flowered var. SATÌVA the oblanceolate leaflets are notched at the tip but with a short terminal spur (end of mid-vein); in var. ANGUSTIFÒLIA [p.310] (L.) Wahlb. *(Smaller Common Vetch)* the *leaflets* are variable but usually *linear*, again ending in a projection of the mid-vein.

 # GERANIÀCEAE. *Geranium Family.*

ERÒDIUM CICUTÀRIUM (L.) L'Her. *Stork's-bill. Filaree.* [p.310]

Erodios, in Greek, is *heron*, yet by some sort of ornithological perversity, this plant is called Stork's-bill—though the only other genus occurring in our area, *Geranium*, (which see), is reasonably enough called Crane's-bill. In any event, all three birds have long, pointed bills, and the evident intention is to draw notice to the beak-like seed-cases so characteristic of this family. The specific name is also puzzling, for it means *of Cicuta*, i.e. the toxic Water Hemlocks (*Umbelliferae*) (see Cicuta). The reference can only be to the foliage, but those who recognize both genera will find the similarity is only superficial.

This is an interesting little annual—an import from Europe—whose pretty rosettes of finely-dissected leaves are now widespread on dry ground throughout the western lowlands of North America. At intervals through almost every month in the year, short flower-stems arise from the leaf-axils to bear a few quarter-inch 5-petalled magenta flowers. These are rather inconspicuous but are shortly succeeded, following elongation of the pistil, by very striking "Stork's-bills".

The "Stork's-bill" itself rewards one's interest with a revelation of sophisticated adaptation. There are 5 plump carpels neatly tucked into grooves at the base of the "bill". From each a very long style extends upward to the tip of the "bill". Each style is straight within its groove—until wind (or a passing animal) jars the ripened fruit. You can see for yourself the sequence of events that follows, by detaching a ripened achene and its long tail. At once, in the warmth of your palm, the tail begins to twist like a corkscrew. In this way the sharply-pointed achene will normally be gimleted into the ground as the style continues to coil. Furthermore, long hairs appressed to the style when it was confined in its groove now stand out stiffly from the coils, so that they become anchored to litter on the soil's surface, and all the force of the auger is expended in twisting the seed-container downward. This is a marvellous thing to watch.

Here at my feet what wonders pass,
What endless, active life is here!

Matthew Arnold:
Lines Written in
Kensington Gardens

GERÀNIUM MÓLLE L. *Dove's-foot Crane's-bill.* [p.310]

The English name is surely an ornithological chimera, with leaves like a dove's foot and beak like a crane's! The generic name (and that of the family) comes from the Greek geranos, *a crane.* Molle means *soft,* referring to the soft white hairs that clothe this little European.

It seems harsh to call this pretty plant a weed, but it has established itself over most of North America, and is particularly abundant in moist waste ground and at the edges of lawns.

The leaves form an attractive rosette early in the spring. They are round in outline, deeply-cleft into many lobes. Flowering-stems are 3-8 inches high, with several similar though reduced leaves, and (usually) paired flowers. These are variously pinkish to purple, with 5 deeply-notched petals. The sepals are soft-haired, pointed but not bristle-tipped. There are normally 10 fertile stamens. (In the very similar G. PUSÍLLUM Burm. only 5 of the stamens develop anthers, the other 5 being sterile; the flowers are also smaller and more bluish-lilac.)

GERÀNIUM ROBERTIÀNUM L. *Herb Robert.* [p.311]

Time has left no clues to the identity of the good Robert, who may have been king or cleric, but among English country-folk the name has been associated with Robin Hood.

This hairy, rather strong-smelling annual from Europe has proved to be a very willing colonizer—particularly on the Coast. The stems are noticeably reddish, and up to 16 inches high. Fern-like leaves are 3-5 lobed, and under drought conditions also turn bright red. The pretty pink flowers are about ½ inch wide, attractively accented by 10 orange stamens and a 5-lobed pink stigma. The petals are not notched; often they are faintly lined with white.

Geranium robertianum is at home in the humus of open woods, on shingle, broken rock, and even on dry-rock walls. This aggressive immigrant blooms from April onward.

GERÀNIUM VISCOSÍSSIMUM F. & M. *Sticky Geranium.* [p.311]

This beautiful species (from dry lands east of the Cascades) is efficiently protected from pollen theft by ants or other crawling insects, for its stems, leaves, and flower-pedicels are densely covered with sticky glandular hairs. The specific name is the superlative of the Latin word for *viscid.*

Strong, branching stems, from 10-30 inches tall, bear deeply-lobed "geranium"-type leaves, that may be 4 inches across. Flowers are freely produced and handsome, being as much as 1½ inches wide and bright rosy-pink. The sepals are glandular-haired, and bristle-tipped. The petals bear short hairs near their bases, and are somewhat wavy-edged, and not notched at the tip. Not infrequently white—and occasionally deep-purple—individuals are seen.

GERÀNIUM ERIÁNTHUM DC. is a rather similar plant that ranges from [p.314] northern B.C. into Alaska. Its large deeply dissected leaves are not sticky, and its big showy flowers are mauve-violet. This species makes an attractive garden subject.

 ## LINÀCEAE. *Flax Family.*

LÌNUM PERÉNNE L. var. LEWÍSII (Pursh) Eat. & Wright. *Wild Flax.*

Widely distributed throughout western North America, this dainty blue flax prefers dry soils of prairie flats, or subalpine ridges. In our area, it is fairly common in southern and eastern parts of the Province. The specific name draws attention to the *perennial* nature of the plant, which is widely cultivated in Eurasia. Our variety, named for the overlander Captain Meriwether Lewis, differs only in stamen and pistil length.

Very slender stems, up to 20 inches high, yield with every zephyr, so that the lovely azure flowers are never still for an instant. The stems are smooth, and alternately leafy with grey-green, linear, and entire inch-long leaves. Sepals number 5—lanceolate, and membranous-edged. Unfortunately the 5 delicate petals (½-1 inch long) are fugacious, i.e. soon dropped. The shining brown seed-capsules, about ¼ inch across, contain numerous seeds that are rich in oil. (The "linseed oil" of commerce is obtained by crushing the seeds of the related annual *L. usitatissimum.*)

Flax was cultivated in very ancient times, both in Africa and Eurasia. It is portrayed in Egyptian tomb paintings as early as the 2nd Dynasty, and actual seed-capsules of flax were discovered by G. Möller in a tomb at Abusir el-Melak, that dates from about 3100 B.C. Linon, *a thread* in Greek, became in Latin, linum.

The entry of June 8, 1808, of Simon Fraser's *Second Journal* is of interest: "Wild flax is very plenty, of which the natives manufacture their thread and fishing tackle."

EUPHORBIÀCEAE. *Spurge Family.*

EUPHÓRBIA PÉPLUS L. *Petty Spurge.*

The genus, which is largely tropical and subtropical, especially in Africa, was named after Euphorbus, physician to King Juba II of Mauretania. The milky juice of *E. heptagona* was used, as late as the World War II Italian invasion, by Ethiopian warriors for an arrow-poison; many other species are known to be toxic. Even honey from *E. esula* is mildly poisonous. Best-known member of the genus is *E. pulcherrima*, the florists' spectacular "Poinsettia".

E. peplus (*cloak*, from the leafy bracts that enclose the insignificant yellow flowers) is a European introduction, now a serious weed west of the Cascades. Most gardeners know too well the 6-12 inch smooth stem, and thin, pale-green, spoon-shaped leaves with entire margins. Low on the stem they alternate, but near the tiny flowers they become opposite. The involucre has 4 tiny glands each tipped with a pair of short horns. The pistillate flowers can be distinguished by a conspicuous ¼ inch erect pistil.

Several other immigrant species of this genus are becoming troublesome weeds.

 # EMPETRÀCEAE. *Crowberry Family.*

EMPÈTRUM NÌGRUM L. *Crowberry.*

This very low evergreen plant is unmistakable because of its crow-black berries. Empetrum is a far-north plant, and an important food source to the Eskimo, but also occurs on most of our mountains. There is a curious, but apparently widespread notion in British Columbia, that the berries are toxic, or at least unsuitable for food. However, we can report, with other authors, that the juice is refreshing—although the small seeds are somewhat bitter. Nigrum means *black*, while Empetrum is derived from the Greek en, *upon*, and petros, *rock*.

The quality of blackness seems impressed on the plant, the ¼–inch leaves being swarthy green, and the curious, 3-sepal, apetalous flowers being obscure in drab brownish-purple. All the flowers bear 3 stamens, but some lack a pistil. The leaves resemble tiny fat fir-needles, and are deeply grooved beneath. They are arranged chiefly in whorls of 4 along the tough prostrate stems.

"Sat. 22 D.—The wind veered round to the Westward, still very
strong and cold as yesterday, we embarked and in 3 hours time came

to the Entrance of the *Slave Lake* under half sail with the Paddle . .
. . The wind is too strong to attempt going in the Lake, set a Net,
and camp'd for the Night, the women gathered plenty of Berries viz.
quieide Pouilles Cramberries Crow Berries, and original Berries. The
Indians killed 2 Swans 1 geese."

Original journal of Alexander Mackenzie, in his
exploration of the great river later named
after him. 1789

 **ANACARDIÀCEAE.** *Sumac Family.*

RHÚS GLÀBRA L. *Sumac.*   [p.311]

Rhus is the ancient Greek name, thought by some to have derived from rhous, *reddish*,
referring to the colour of the fruit, and perhaps also to the brilliant autumn foliage.
Sumac (also spelled Sumach) was originally summāq, an Arabian name for one of the
species. The specific name apparently refers to the *smooth* bark of this 1-10 foot shrub.

In the southern Dry Interior, especially east of the Cascades, each October finds the
Sumac in the role of a latter-day "Burning Bush", for then its large pinnate leaves turn
incandescent scarlet and flaming yellow. Probably no other native plant rivals this in
sheer intensity of colour.

But desirable as the shrub might appear, many who have brought Sumac into the
garden, have discovered with chagrin, its riotous spread by means of very long,
shallow-running roots. It should never be permitted more than a restricted pocket of soil
isolated among rocks.

This shrub is unlikely to be confused with any other. By April the bare heavy
branches have become conspicuous with large, dark-purplish, tightly-packed cones of
flower buds, visible at a great distance. Large leaves begin to develop about a month
later. The serrate-edged, pointed-elliptical leaflets usually number 7-29 to each leaf,
which may be as much as 18 inches long. Greenish-yellow flowers are only conspicuous
because so many are borne in a large tight panicle. In the fall they are succeeded by
clustered, reddish, densely-hairy fruits (drupes).

Though the reddish-brown stems, when cut, ooze a milky-resinous fluid that is acid,
few people react to this juice with irritation and inflamation of the skin. It is quite
otherwise with the sap of our two other species of Rhus.

LATHYRUS NEVADENSIS ×1¼ [p.268]

LOTUS CORNICULATUS ×⅖ [p.269]

LUPINUS BICOLOR ×1½ [p.273]

LUPINUS SERICEUS ×⅓ [p.275]

RHÙS DIVERSILÒBA T. & G. *Poison Oak.*

R. diversiloba and *R. radicans* (which see) are very similar plants, but the present species is limited in range to the Pacific Coast, where there are numerous records (though only as far north as Nanaimo and Texada Island). The best field distinction is the much less-sharply pointed leaflets of Poison Oak; in fact they are often rounded, and deeply but irregularly round-lobed (quite like oak leaves). The leaflets are in groups of 3 (or occasionally 5). A further distinction is that the lateral leaflets are sessile in the present species, but in *R. radicans* they have short petiolules. Usually the abundant flower-clusters of R. diversiloba droop downward, rather than standing erect, as with its relative. Occasionally, with suitable support, Poison Oak climbs 20 feet or even more. Both plants are quite showy in the autumn when the leaves turn bright scarlet and crimson.

Poison Oak secretes urushiol*, and is toxic in about the same degree as Poison Ivy. The flowers are fragrant, but needless to say, both plants should be examined only with caution.

*more precisely 3-n-pentadecylcatechol.

RHÙS RADÌCANS L. *Poison Ivy.*   [p.315]

This species, and the preceding, are very different in appearance to *Rhus glabra* (which see); in fact, by many authorities they have been placed in a separate genus, *Toxicodendron*, whose name suggests their toxic nature. Radicans means *rooting*, with reference to the creeping underground stolons from which the stems arise.

The deep-green, 3-leaflet leaves slightly resemble those of Ivy.

In the Dry Interior, Poison Ivy is generally erect, and may reach a height of 4-5 feet. Nearing the Coast, however, the habit is often somewhat trailing, like ivy, among the grasses, so that it may be easily overlooked—until one sits on or near the plant. Very shortly thereafter, most persons develop intense skin irritation, sometimes with hive-like swellings, and nausea. Many persons are so sensitive to the toxic oil (urushiol), that even the small amounts volatilized without decomposition, from burning the dry stems, cause severe inflammation. We witnessed a case of this sort in which the victim's eyes were tightly shut by swelling of the eyelids and forehead, half an hour after unwitting exposure to such "smoke". Some relief can be obtained by washing the affected parts with strong tea. Calamine Lotion, if available, is soothing. Persons of known sensitivity to the oil, when camping or hiking in areas where either Poison Ivy or Poison Oak (*R. diversiloba*, which see) is prevalent, should carry with them a few ounces of a concentrated solution (in 50% ethyl alcohol) of ferric chloride. Washing with soap and water, followed by several applications of this solution, diluted about 10 to 1 with water, will nearly always reduce the distressing effects. Very fortunately, neither of these dangerous plants is common. However, in certain localities, as in the vicinity of Princeton, and Fairmont Hot Springs, Poison Ivy is locally abundant, and one should always be alert for its presence.

Preceding page: LATHYRUS LATIFOLIUS   ×⅘   [p.268]

As mentioned earlier, the shiny leaves have 3 leaflets, ovate and sharp-pointed, with rounded base, and entire to coarse-toothed margins, smooth above but usually with scattered hairs below.

Numerous greenish-white flowers, in erect panicles, are borne on short peduncles, either terminal, or arising from the axils of the leaves. They are succeeded by smooth, whitish fruits (drupes), about ¼ inch in diameter.

CELASTRÀCEAE. *Staff-tree Family.*

PACHÍSTIMA MYRSINÌTES (Pursh) Raf. *False Box.*   [p.314]

The Greek is pachys, *thick*, and stigma, *stigma*, so that etymologically one might prefer the spelling Pachystima, given by many authors. However we have followed Hitchcock, Cronquist, et al. The specific name is from myrsine, the Greek word for *myrrh*. The reference then, is to the pleasant fragrance of the tiny brick-red flowers, so freely produced by this very handsome, evergreen shrub. The name False Box is appropriate, for the thick shiny leaves are reminiscent of the familiar Box (*Buxus*) of low garden-hedges.

Compact 1-3 foot bushes of Pachistima are common on rocky outcrops, from sea level to moderate altitudes, throughout British Columbia. Profusely-borne leaves are glossy bright, thick-textured, ½-1 inch long, and attractively serrate-edged. In fact so handsome are they that florists, regrettably, are now turning to the plant for foliage sprays, and professional collectors are destroying stands near the larger cities.

Tiny cruciform flowers are unusual for their reddish-mahogany colour. They are numerous in the axils of the opposite leaves.

Small seedlings of Pachistima adapt readily and provide subjects for the rockery that are both attractive and amenable.

RHAMNÀCEAE. *Buckthorn Family.*

CEANÒTHUS SANGUÍNEUS Pursh. *Buckbrush.*   [p.315]

Ceanothus is a Greek name of uncertain application used by Theophrastus for a spiny shrub, now unknown. The specific name calls attention to the *reddened* flowered-pedicels, which provide a striking contrast to the raceme of creamy bloom, becoming especially noticeable as the flowers age. As Craighead, Craighead, and Davis point out,

294

LATHYRUS JAPONICUS var. GLABER ×½ [p.265]

LOTUS MICRANTHUS ×2½ [p.269]

LUPINUS ARBOREUS ×½ [p.272]

LUPINUS ARCTICUS ssp. SUBALPINUS (HABITAT) [p.273]

this shrub provides favourite browse for deer—whence the common name. Surprisingly, the toxic glucoside saponin is found in the leaves and stem. Some writers suggest the poisonous principle is in low concentration in winter, when the shrubs are browsed; however, the absence of ill-effects is more likely due to hydrolytic breakdown of saponins during digestion. Early settlers often called this plant Soapbloom, since flowering twigs beaten in water yielded a foam. It is to be hoped that pioneer wives did not suffer ill from "dish-pan" hands with open cuts or cracks!

This open-branched deciduous shrub may reach 9 feet. It is of erratic distribution on Vancouver Island, and on both slopes of the Cascades. The branches are smooth, and usually purplish, bearing alternate leaves that have distinct petioles. The oval leaves are glandular and serrated, but thinner-textured than those of *C. velutinus* (which see). The tiny flowers are carried in a crowded panicle at the end of short, second-year branchlets. The flowers have a rather heavy scent, and wilt almost at once, so there is little temptation to pick them (though when the pedicels turn rosy the effect is quite attractive). Blooming time is June or July.

CEANÒTHUS VELÙTINUS Dougl. *Snowbrush. Sticky Laurel.*   [p.315]

One glance at the leathery and sticky-varnished leaves of this squat shrub informs the observer this is a plant adapted for arid situations. This is confirmed by the dense white pubescence on the under side of the leaves, in the typical variety, which is found in the "rain-shadow" east of the Cascades. (Variety LAEVIGÀTUS (Hook.) T. & G. lacks this hoary underside and is less varnished above; as one might guess, this is the plant of sites on Vancouver Island, the Gulf Islands, and the Coast—where the air is more humid.) The specific name means *velvety*, with reference to the lower leaf surface of the Dry Interior variety.

The bushes are covered, in July and August, with dense clusters of small flowers, that are greenish-white, rather than snowy (as might be inferred from the name Snowbrush.) Though variable, as we have seen, this species is at once distinguished from *C. sanguineus* (which see) by the fact that its leaves are evergreen. Otherwise they are similar in size and shape, but are much thicker, almost leathery. The scent is extremely heavy. We have sometimes wondered if the scent might drug the visiting bees, for it seems these hard-working visitors—who come in hundreds to linger at each bush—are noticeably less industrious than usual, and appear almost intoxicated.

RHÁMNUS PURSHIÀNA DC. *Cascara.*   [p.318]

Paxton states the generic name comes from the Celtic ram, *a tuft of branches*, but other authorities believe Rhamnus was a Greek name, applied to a plant whose identity has been lost. Frederick Pursh (1774-1820), came from Saxony to Philadelphia, where he completed his life-work *Flora Americae Septentrionalis.*

Cascara, which is limited to the Northwest Pacific coast, forms groups of erect stems that reach 15-30 feet and are noticeable in the winter woods because of their silvery-grey, almost smooth bark. This bark, from which a laxative syrup is prepared, was so persistently collected that the shrub has been exterminated in some parts of its former range. The syrup (known to pharmacists as Cascara sagrada) was, as anticipated, found also in the bark of the 3-foot Alderleaf Buckthorn (RHÁMNUS ALNIFÒLIA L'Her.), a common shrub of dry swamps in the Interior.* (The leaves of this species are smaller, and have 5-7 pairs of prominent veins, compared with 10-15 pairs on the leaves of its taller and coastal relative.)

Cascara is readily recognized in summer by its distinctive 4-inch ovate leaves with very prominent veins. The margins are fine-toothed. In the fall the inconspicuous greenish 5-petalled flowers are replaced by occasional blackish berries.

*The predictive value of taxonomy is demonstrated by this and many other cases. For example, cortisone and some precursor compounds of the molecular structures known as sex hormones, were detected by chemists in the Yam (*Dioscorea* sp.), an important food plant of the Tropics. Botanists were at once consulted to learn what plants were taxonomically related. These were tested, and almost immediately several plants were found that contained much larger amounts of the sought-for compounds.

MALVÀCEAE. *Mallow Family.*

ILIÁMNA RIVULÀRIS (Dougl.) Greene. *Mountain Hollyhock. Stream-bank Rose Mallow.* [p.319]

The derivation of Iliamna is unknown, though it may be a distorted anagram of *Malva*, a closely related genus. A possible origin is the Latin feminine noun Ilia, "the Trojan Woman", Rhea Sylvia, legendary mother of Romulus and Remus. Rivularis is the genitive, *of the brook*, for this attractive plant prefers stream-banks and runnels in the mountain meadows. In British Columbia it is only found in the southern part, but ranges from the foothills to considerable altitudes.

Mountain Hollyhock, in rich moist soil, may reach 6 feet, but 1½-3 feet is usual in drier locations. Basal, 5-7 lobed leaves resemble 2-6 inch maple or grape leaves. They decrease in size upward and often become 3-lobed, but leaf-shape is variable in the species. Under magnification, some of the leaf-hairs will be found radially forked, like tiny silver stars. The handsome flowers, in an elongated raceme, are pink, rose-purple, or nearly white, up to 2½ inches across. Pedicels are short and thick, and the calyx-lobes usually less than ¼ inch long. The club-shaped stigma is surrounded by many stamens, whose filaments are unusual, being basally united to form two concentric tubes.

This striking plant opens its beautiful flowers in a long progression from June until August.

SIDÁLCEA HENDERSÒNII Wats. *Marsh Hollyhock.* [p.314]

Coined from the names of two extraterritorial genera of the Malvaceae or Mallow Family, *Sida* and *Alcea,* Sidalcea has a pleasanter sound than most conjoined names. It is distinguished from *Iliamna* and *Sphaeralcea* (which see), which have terminal and capitate (head-shaped) stigmas, since in Sidalcea the stigma extends down the inner faces of the branched style. This pretty species is named after Dr. Louis Forniquet Henderson, 1853-1942, late professor of botany at the University of Oregon. *(Dodecatheon hendersonii* also carries his name). Many hybrid Sidalceas, such as Rose Queen and Sussex Beauty, are perhaps more popular in European than in American gardens, though the parent species are natives of western North America.

The attractive inch-wide flowers are deep-pink to reddish, borne in numerous racemes that branch from the summit of the 2-5 foot plant. Stems are nearly smooth and usually purplish. Basal leaves, on very long petioles, are about 4 inches across, nearly circular, with many shallow, rounded lobes; but the stem-leaves become smaller and shorter-petioled upward, first deeply 5-lobed, finally with 3 sharply pointed lobes. A remarkable feature is the occurrence of 3 kinds of flowers. In addition to the large 1 inch, perfect flowers (referred to above) occasional flowers in the spike-like racemes are but ½ inch wide (though perfect), and there are also similar small blooms that are imperfect, lacking anthers.

[Botanists believe that plants with several forms of flowers may mark intermediate steps in the adaptation of a plant, possibly from a self-fertilized species to one that is insect-pollinated. Thus as early as 1873 Hermann Müller pointed out (concerning two European species now occurring in our area) that *Malva rotundifolia* (now *M. neglecta* Wallr.) has a small corolla and is clearly self-pollinated, since its numerous long stigma-branches are coiled among the stamens, whereas *M. sylvestris* L., which has developed a much larger, more showy corolla (apparently the better to attract pollinating insects) keeps its stigmas erect, well above the drooping stamens.]

Sidalcea hendersonii is an interesting and showy plant found on or adjacent to tidelands from southern Vancouver Island and the Fraser Delta, southward. It is in bloom, like most of its family, through a lengthy season, usually extending from June to August end.

SPHAERÁLCEA MUNROÁNA (Dougl.) Spach. *White-leaved Globe Mallow.*

The generic name is from the Greek sphaera, a *sphere,* and *Alcea,* ancient name of a plant of the Mallow Family, with reference to the fruit, which is shaped like a 5-segmented wheel of cheese. The genus is separated on trifling anatomical distinctions from *Iliamna,* and though we have followed Hitchcock et al., perhaps a majority of authorities combine the two. (The stigma is head-shaped in both *Iliamna* and Sphaeralcea.) Two attractive species of Sphaeralcea occur in our area. S. munroana was named after General William Munro, 1818-1889, a celebrated British specialist on grasses. This showy plant is amenable to life in the rockery, where its grey-green foliage and numerous bright-pink to deep-apricot flowers attract much comment. It is happy in the driest and hottest corner, where it blooms throughout July and August. It is native to the arid plains of the southern Dry Interior, but is of rare occurrence in British Columbia.

The whole plant, like so many from low-rainfall areas, is densely clothed with short grey hairs. Under the glass these are seen to be stellate (star-shaped). The numerous stems are semi-persistent, rather floppy, and 8-24 inches long. Our two species are most readily distinguished by their leaves. In S. munroana they are roughly heart-shaped, but irregularly notched and shallowly-lobed, and from 1-2 inches long. Lower leaves have petioles longer than the blade, but the uppermost have only very short petioles. Immediately below the short, blunt-lobed, stellate calyx are 3 slim bractlets.

SPHAERÁLCEA COCCINÈA (Pursh) Rydb., *Scarlet Globe Mallow*, is a much smaller plant than S. munroana (which see), usually 4-8 inches tall, from the same hot dry valleys of the south-central and extreme south-eastern Interior. The leaves, though about the same size as those of its congener, are very different in shape, being palmately cut to the midrib, into 3-5 pointed lobes (which are generally further notched). They are grey and hairy below, but often yellow-green above. The bright flowers measure about 1¼ inches across, with 5 broad, slightly emarginate petals, that vary from yellowish-red to a curious brick-red. Usually there are no bractlets below the hairy calyx. Since the plant spreads partly by means of long rhizomes, one sees good-sized patches of S. coccinea by the roadside, especially in Alberta and Washington.

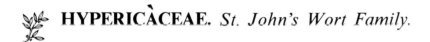 **HYPERICÀCEAE.** *St. John's Wort Family.*

HYPÉRICUM ANAGALLOÌDES C. & S. *Dwarf St. John's Wort.*   [p.318]

This diminutive native bears little resemblance to the tall foreign invaders of the Hypericum clan. H. anagalloides, an engaging little plant of wet seepages, derives its specific name from some resemblance of the small leaves to those of *Anagallis arvensis* (the Scarlet Pimpernel, which see). The St. John's Worts (Saxon wyrt = plant) were named, according to H. N. Moldenke, from the superstition that on St. John's Day, the 24th of June, the dew which fell on the plant the evening before was efficacious in preserving the eyes from disease.

Dwarf St. John's Wort in alpine situations is somewhat erect, and 1-1½ inches tall, but along stream-margins and edges of bogs at lower levels, the slender stems may be as much as 12 inches long, in which case they root at the nodes. Numerous tiny (¼-½ inch) opposite leaves are ovate, and slightly clasping, with rounded ends. They are glabrous, but a good magnifying glass reveals numerous dark, transparent dots, which are actually small glands. Pretty little coppery-yellow flowers measure about ¼ inch, or a little more. They are produced at the ends of the short stems, over a long period—often from May until August. The 5 petals, unlike those of the taller cousins *H. perforatum* and *H. formosum* (which see), are not black-dotted.

This pleasing little plant occurs in suitable habitats throughout British Columbia, though it has not so far been reported from the Queen Charlotte Islands. Dwarf St. John's Wort makes a cheerful ground cover for moist and somewhat shaded nooks in the garden.

HYPÉRICUM PERFORÀTUM L. *St. John's Wort.* [p.330]

This is a particularly "magical" plant, long thought effective in warding off a host of evil spirits and sicknesses. In rites extending back to the dawn of our history, the plants were smoked over fires kindled on the eve of St. John the Baptist's Day, June 24. Wurt or wyrt is Saxon for plant or *weed*. And weed it is, for in western North America the factors that control its abundance in Europe are modified, or missing, so that it has become rampant along thousands of roadside miles. The European beetle, *Chrysolina gemellata*, has been brought to the New World to combat this pernicious immigrant. Hopefully it will be effective. Perforatum refers to the apparent holes (actually transparent glands) noticeable along the edges of the petals, and over the leaf surfaces.

The plant is bitter, so that grazing animals avoid it unless other food is scarce. The bitterness is due to several glucosides that are phototropic, that is, suffer alteration by exposure to light—into highly toxic compounds. Thus it has been ascertained that white animals, or those with unpigmented areas, develop blisters about the mouth and eyes, some weeks after browsing the St. John's Wort. Dark animals are little affected. Dr. E. R. Jackman has reported that "sheep relish it in spring, whereas cattle shun it", so that cattle ranges are often badly invaded, while sheep ranges are nearly free of the plant. The poison appears to be cumulative in cattle and horses, with fatal outcome.

H. perforatum has a perennial taproot, and besides producing huge quantities of seeds, the plants often spread by means of short rhizomes. Hence it is very difficult to eradicate. The branched and leafy stems may attain 3 feet, and bear many-flowered, somewhat flattened clusters of the bright yellow, musk-scented flowers. These may be ¾ inch across. They are noticeable for the black spots on the petals and for the numerous clustered stamens (which are joined basally into 3 groups). Sepals are pointed-lanceolate. Leaves are variable in shape, though generally blunt-lanceolate. Held up to the light, the blade appears full of pin-pricks, and edged with black dots.

[p.314] A similar (but native) species, also perennial, is HYPÉRICUM FORMÒSUM H.B.K., that occurs in moister habitats from the Coast inland, especially at lower mountain levels. It may be distinguished by a much more open, less flat-topped inflorescence. The 5 petals are black-dotted, and the sepals are broadly oval and blunt-tipped (cf. narrowly-lanceolate, sharp-pointed sepals of *H. perforatum*, which see).

The family and generic names apparently are early Greek, derived from hyper, *above*, and icon, an *image*, the style and capsule representing a fancied figure.

VIOLÀCEAE. *Violet Family.*

VÌOLA ADÚNCA Smith. *Western Long-spurred Violet.*   [p.326]

Viola is a Latin name for several species well known to the early Romans; it should be pronounced (but seldom is) with the accent, in the Latin manner, on the first syllable. The specific name comes from aduncus, meaning *hooked*, with reference to the spurred base of the lowermost petal. In this beautiful species the spur is generally slender and long (usually more than half as long as the lowest petal), and slightly hooked at the end.

V. adunca is common from Vancouver Island to the Rockies, and variable. (Several varietal names have been proposed.) Some plants are glabrous, others densely hairy. Leaf-shape is also inconstant, though most frequently heart-shaped. The flowers are blue to deep-violet, the 3 lower petals whitish at their bases, and pencilled with purple lines that probably serve as honey-guides. Of the pencilled lower petals, the lateral pair are white-bearded, near the inner end; the style also is bearded near the tip. Keys to identification of the species are difficult: thus, stipules are said to be "more or less toothed", but actually range from entire to deeply lacerate. A reasonably consistent feature is the bearded head of the style.

No less than 16 species of Viola have been found in B.C.

A remarkable development in this genus is the elaborate nectary. This structure is a pocket formed by the joined lower portions of the filaments of the 2 lower stamens, which extends downward into the spur (itself a tube-like projection of the base of the lowermost petal). The anthers of these same 2 stamens then form an auricle, enclosing the opening to the nectary. Hence the visiting honeybee (in the case of Viola species with short spurs), or bumblebee or butterfly (in long-spurred species), led by the honey-guide pencilling, must bump the anthers as it probes for nectar. At the same time the beard-hairs of the lateral petals, and of the style, comb the pollen collected on the insect's body while visiting another plant. The arrangement is both sophisticated and efficient in securing cross-pollination. (Incidentally, the multi-faceted compound eyes of insects see edges best. This fact, and the ability of bees to detect the colour yellow, accounts for the effectiveness of the pollen-covered loop against the dark background of the violet petals, as a highly visible target for the zooming insects.)

However, the prudent Viola does not place its future entirely at the whim of visiting insects. In this genus, late in the season, remarkable "cleistogamous" (closed) flowers are produced at, or even below, ground level. These need no insect visitors, so have dispensed with petals and perfume of normal flowers. Indeed the sepals never open, and the stamens pollinate the pistil, resulting in self-fertilized viable seeds. These, like the cross-fertilized ones of spring and early summer, in due course are thrown several inches, when the curious seed-capsule explosively opens.

> . . .*Of euery sort, which in that Meadow grew,*
> *They gathered some; the Violet pallid blew,* . . . .

           Edmund Spenser: Prothalamion

302

LUPINUS DENSIFLORUS var. SCOPULORUM ×½ [p.274]

LUPINUS LYALLII ×¼ [p.274]

LUPINUS POLYPHYLLUS ×⅓ [p.275]

OXYTROPIS CAMPESTRIS ×⅖ [p.276]

TRIFOLIUM ARVENSE ×⅗ [p.277]

VICIA AMERICANA ×½ [p.281]

VICIA CRACCA ×½ [p.284]

303

VÌOLA GLABÉLLA Nutt. *Smooth Violet. Yellow Wood Violet.* [p.327]

The common name interprets the specific name, all parts of this perennial plant being *smooth* (glabrous). Viola glabella is a common species, often occurring in extensive patches, under the light shade of moist open woods. It ranges from the Coast well up into the mountains, throughout British Columbia.

The Smooth Violet is easily recognized by its yellow flowers, carried on smooth, almost succulent, leafy stems, that are often 9-12 inches tall. The thin leaves are usually heart-shaped, with serrate edges, and petioles often three times longer than the blades. Flowers are very short-spurred. The lower 3 petals are beautifully purplish-pencilled on the clear yellow. As in the purple *V. adunca* (which see) the inner parts of the 2 lateral petals, and the tip of the style, are white-bearded. The 4 upper petals are overlapped, leaving the lowermost distinctively isolated.

A pathetic commentary on the primitive use of plants for food is found in *A Botanical Study of the Stomach Contents of the Tollund Man.* Deep in the peat at Tollund in Denmark, in May 1950, was found the body of a man, preserved for more than 2000 years. There were no well-stocked Food Marts available to this early Dane. He had been able to find and eat only a few plants. About a dozen species could be identified; they included the European *Viola arvensis,* and several plants such as *Chenopodium album,* and *Rumex acetosa* (Sorrel), familiar in our area today.

VÌOLA LANCEOLÀTA L. is easily distinguished from other Violas by its unique, long, *lanceolate* leaves and small, white, purple-pencilled flowers. It occurs in bogs and very wet places.

[p.327]   VÌOLA LANGSDÓRFII (Regel) Fisch. is widespread in bogs and wet woods from Alaska southward along the coast. Heart-shaped leaves are about 2 inches long: basal ones with petioles as much as 8 inches long, but stem ones with only short petioles. Flowers are pale violet, the petals usually flushed with white but yellow at their bases. The 3 lower petals are dark-pencilled, the 2 lateral white-bearded.

[p.327]   VÌOLA NUTTÁLLII Pursh, *Yellow Prairie Violet,* is a variable species with yellow flowers, now increasingly rare in short turf along the southern coast (var. PRAEMÓRSA (Dougl.) Wats.). East of the Cascades, especially in Ponderosa Pine forest and on Sagebrush flats, occurs the var. VALLÍCOLA (A. Nels.) St. John, with less hairy leaves. The upper pair of petals is generally brownish-backed, the lower 3 are pencilled with brownish-purple. Leaves are broadly lanceolate to rhomboidal.

> *A violet by a mossy stone*
> *Half hidden from the eye!*
> *—Fair as a star, when only one*
> *Is shining in the sky.*

William Wordsworth: Lucy

VÌOLA PALÚSTRIS L. *Marsh Violet.* [p.327]

This widespread species of peaty soil in *swamps* and moist meadows, is often white-flowered (with faint purple lines on the lower three petals). But in some localities all the petals are slightly tinged with lilac (as in the form illustrated). The lateral petals are only sparsely white-bearded. Each flower caps a slender peduncle, that may be longer or shorter than the leaf-petioles.

Important in recognition of the species is the absence of true flowering-stems—the flower-peduncles and leaves both growing directly from the creeping rhizomes. The leaves are heart- to kidney-shaped, with neatly crenate edges. They are smooth, almost shining, and of a firm texture.

This is a charming small violet.

VÌOLA SEMPERVÌRENS Greene. *Evergreen Violet* [p.326]

Few wanderers in the winter woods, from the Cascades to the Coast, will have failed to notice, spread over the moss, the neat, rounded, cordate leaves of this little perennial violet. In March, onward to June, the low plants are starred with pale-yellow flowers.

This is a consistent species, easily identified. The leaves are thick and firm, neatly cut as with pinking scissors. The flowers are suffused with deeper yellow near the centre, and usually even the upper 2 petals are faintly marked with a few purple lines, but the lower 3 are always strongly pencilled. The effect is really quite charming, and this dainty species is always attractive in the garden.

Two good recognition features are the brown or purple dots which appear on the under side of older leaves, and the purplish markings on the seed-capsules (and frequently on the sepals). At the base of the lateral pair of petals are distinctive yellow beard-scales. When the woods are dry in August, careful examination in the moss at the base of the plant may reveal unusual cleistogamous flowers (see under *V. adunca).*

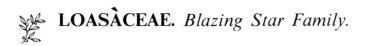

LOASÀCEAE. *Blazing Star Family.*

MENTZÈLIA LAEVICAÙLIS (Dougl.) T. & G. var. PARVIFLÒRA (Dougl.) C. L. Hitch. *Blazing Star.* [p.338]

C. Mentzel was an early German botanist who died in 1701. The specific name means *smooth-stemmed.* This is a coarse, angular biennial (or short-lived perennial) that hangs

306

OXYTROPIS PODOCARPA ×1¾ [p.276]

TRIFOLIUM MICRODON ×2 [p.280]

OXYTROPIS SPLENDENS ×⅗ [p.277]

TRIFOLIUM SUBTERRANEUM ×1 [p.28]

VICIA HIRSUTA ×1 [p.284]

TRIFOLIUM TRIDENTATUM ×1 [p.280]

ULEX EUROPAEUS ×⅓ [p.281]

307

out, on its scrawny branches, great yellow flowers of unexpected beauty. It grows in wastelands and by roadsides in desert areas of south, central, and eastern British Columbia.

Though the pale silvery stems appear smooth, usually they are rough to the touch, and the 10X glass reveals clusters of tiny barbed hairs. These same unusual hairs cover the 2-3 inch long oblong leaves, that are lobed about halfway to the midrib. During the heat of the day 3-4 inch bright golden stars dazzle the passer-by. These have 5 long, sharply pointed sepals, and 5 pointed, lanceolate petals. What appear to be 5 smaller petals interspaced, are considered by most morphologists to be modified sterile stamens (staminodia). Very conspicuous in Blazing Star is a golden puff of very many, long-filamented, normal stamens.

Of great interest is the fact that MENTZÈLIA DECAPÉTALA (Pursh) Urban & Gilg, of southern Alberta, and possibly of Southeast British Columbia, is commonly called Evening Star, since its equally large flowers open only after the sun goes down! The probable explanation is a concentration of light-energized enzymes that inhibit cellular growth, respectively in the outer or the inner faces of the petals in the two species. As a corollary, *M. laevicaulis parviflora* is pollinated by bees and butterflies, M. decapetala by moths.

 **CACTÀCEAE.** *Cactus Family.*

OPÚNTIA FRÁGILIS (Nutt.) Haw. *Brittle Prickly Pear. Brittle Cactus.* [p.330]

The origin of Opuntia is little-known, but seems to go back to *Opus*, a town in ancient Locris, one of the classical Greek states that lay east of Delphi and north of Athens. Then cacti flourished in that dry rocky area, as they do today.

The specific name calls attention to the ease with which the terminal joint is detached. This savagely-armed plant spreads its mats of fleshy jointed stems over the parched hillsides of the Dry Interior.

The Prickly Pear and its unbelievable yellow flowers are known by every child in the southern Interior. The only difficulty in recognition is the distinction between this species and *O. polyacantha* (which see), since the ranges overlap.

The cluster of pads of O. fragilis is lower than those of its cousin, and the joints are almost round in cross-section, never greatly flattened. The long spines are generally fewer in each cluster, and in the present species the filaments are most often reddish. But the huge flowers are pale- to deep-yellow, almost never aging reddish, as do those of *O. polyacantha.*

Many a child has had the misfortune to trip and fall on these spine-covered pads, and has endured the subsequent experience of submitting to extraction of the barbed thorns with the aid of pliers. But no painful memories of this sort can dim the wonder, when each July the unpromising Prickly Pears expand their quite incredible blooms.

OPÚNTIA POLYACÁNTHA Haw. *Many-spined Prickly Pear. Cactus.* [p.331]

The specific name comes from poly, *many*, and canthus, *wheel*, seemingly with reference to the numerous long spines radiating, like the spokes of a wheel, from raised pores (areoles). "Long spines many. . ." is often given in keys as distinctive of this species, but we have counted from 1 to 9 long spines in a cluster, plus 3-11 half—or less than half—as long. In *O. fragilis* (which see) the number of long spines per areole is perhaps on the average smaller, but it is not a very useful distinction.

Who does not know the symmetrical elegance of the flowers of the Prickly Pear? Blooms so fragile seem utterly improbable, when one considers the clumsy and barbed pads from which they spring.

Vestigial scale-like leaves are soon dropped, and the thickened and jointed green stems take over the function of photosynthesis, as well as support and storage. Their waxy covering, and small surface area, reduce water loss to a very low level. The ferocious spines, minutely barbed, discourage grazing animals. From the areoles arise a variety of specialized structures: long spines, short bristles, woolly pubescence, and the incredible flowers.

In this species the yellow flowers are often tinged with apricot, and may fade almost reddish. The filaments are usually yellow (cf. reddish filaments of *O. fragilis*, which see), and the areolar wool is scanty, but rusty if present. The joints of the stems are strongly flattened, and tenacious, so that even the terminal segment is not readily detached.

Though this remarkable plant occurs in the Gulf Islands and southern Vancouver Island, it seldom develops numerous flowers until the plants encounter the dry hot air of the arid Interior. There, in May and June, the Prickly Pear enlivens the drab flatlands with its quite amazing blooms.

Archibald Menzies (who sailed in 1791-95 with Captain George Vancouver) was the first botanist to set foot on the Gulf Islands—in May, 1792. His journal records that he "was not a little surprizd to meet with the Cactus Opuntia [now *Opuntia polyacantha*] thus far to the Northward, it grew plentifully but in a very dwarf state on the Eastern point of the Island which is low flat & dry sandy soil."

Frequent references to thistles in Simon Fraser's *Second Journal* (of his great trip to the sea, via the river later named after him) are explicable, we think, if by "thistle" the Prickly Pear is meant. The native species of *Cirsium* (thistles), all relatively soft-spined, would scarcely be serious impediments to the hardy voyageurs. Fraser was very ill-informed about plants, as is revealed throughout the journal. And finally, Cactus—rather than *Cirsium*—even today, is abundant along that portion of the river (north of present-day Lillooet) described in the journal entries of June 8, 6, and 9, 1808:

"Wood is scanty all over and stunted, but more pine than any other wood. Plain of small growth, with many different kinds of the willow, elder, . . . and some other I do not know. Thistles of a *deminitive growth* are so very plenty that no shoes prevents their picking the feet. . . . [the italics are ours.] La Certe and some others were sent to examine the River that we may not suddenly come upon a cascade or dangerous Rapid in this narrow gut, but I believe they did not go far, and indeed the number of hills and precipices render it not only difficult but

310

VICIA SATIVA var. ANGUSTIFOLIA ×⅞ [p.285]   GERANIUM MOLLE ×3 [p.286]

ERODIUM CICUTARIUM ×⅘ [p.285]

GERANIUM ROBERTIANUM ×³⁄₅ [p.286]

RHUS GLABRA ×¹⁄₆ [p.289]

GERANIUM VISCOSISSIMUM ×1 [p.287]

almost impossible to walk even in the Plains. Upon the tops of the hills there are so many thistles that all hands have the sole of their feet full of them, [!] and being almost continually when on shore upon rocks and stones, a pair of shoes does not last a whole day to some of us without piercing. . . . I had some trouble in coming up light, and having gone to one side of the path to see the canoes run down I got my feet full of thistles."

Our suggested identification of the "thistle" references may be accepted more readily by those who have had first-hand experience of walking in the Cactus-strewn hills of the Dry Interior.

 **ELEAGNÀCEAE.** *Oleaster Family.*

ELAEÁGNUS COMMUTÀTA Bernh. *Silver-berry.* [p.318]

This handsome shrub derives its name from elaia, *olive,* and agnos, the Greek name for the Chaste Tree (*Vitex agnus-castus*), which has similar foliage. Commutatus means *changed,* a reference apparently to the silvery appearance of both surfaces of the leaves, changed from the usual green. The dry mealy "berry" is more correctly a drupe.

No situation is too dry for this 4-12 foot bush, whose greyish-red branches are hung, in early spring, with striking silver leaves, 1-3 inches long, pointed-oval, and entire-margined. From the axils of the leaves in June and July, almost stemless, cone-shaped flowers appear in twos and threes. These are quite unique: silvered without, yellow within, and possessed of an entrancing aromatic perfume, that mingles with the Sagebrush scent. Closer investigation reveals the flower consists of a tubular calyx, whose 4 lobes flare outward. There are no petals, but 4 stamens grow from the calyx-tube, and shelter a single short style.

Very distinctive is the Silver-berry. It ranges from Alaska and the Yukon, southward in the dry Interior, and attains its best development on the slopes of narrow gullies in the scablands.

SHEPHÉRDIA CANADÉNSIS (L.) Nutt. *Soopolallie. Buffalo-berry.* [pp.318,330]

This genus of 3 species, 2 of which occur in our area, commemorates the English botanist John Shepherd, 1764-1836. The Chinook name should be retained; it is a combination of soop, *soap,* and olallie, *berry,* and is apt, because the red berry-like fruit, beaten in water, produces a pink soapy froth. The resulting pink foamy drink was much prized by the natives for its peculiar flavour—to our taste bitter, yet sweet and aromatic.

A number of the early explorers mention it. Both species of Shepherdia were grazed by the Plains Bison.

S. canadensis is an open shrub that may reach 10 feet, and is easily recognized in any season by its odd, orange-dotted, white bark, that gives the twigs a rusty appearance. In early spring, even before the leaves, the very tiny, reddish, clustered flowers appear. These are of two kinds, borne on separate shrubs. The pistillate lack even remnants of stamens, and consist only of a short pistil at the bottom of a short, 4-cleft calyx-tube, whose lobes are erect. At a casual glance the staminate flowers appear similar, but the 4 calyx-lobes are reflexed to show the 4 stamens. Thick, leathery, entire-margined, 2-inch opposite leaves develop later, and are arresting in appearance because of the dense white scurfy under side, which is conspicuously dotted with reddish scales. The general effect is rusty. The upper surface of the leaves is green and glossy; the 10X magnifier will reveal short star-shaped hairs. The fruits are shining, almost transparent, and red to orange.

Also called Buffalo-berry is SHEPHÉRDIA ARGÉNTEA (Pursh) Nutt. This is a taller, more rigid shrub, limited to the dry Interior, where it overlaps the range of the Soopolallie. Here both prefer the edges of streams, but on the Pacific Coast the Soopolallie is also found in open wooded and rocky areas. S. argentea is readily distinguished by occasional thorny spurs on the older branches, and by the silvery appearance of *both* surfaces of the leaves.

The Lewis and Clark journals contain a number of references to this shrub: "Great quantities of a kind of berry resembling a current except double the Size and Grows on a bush like a Privey, and the Size of a Damsen deliciously flavoured and makes delitefull Tarts, this froot is now ripe. (24th August 1804) . . . the Currents still abound also the Rabit berrys, which the french call graze the buff graisse de boef (24th July 1805) . . . the bush which bears the acid red berry called by the french engages *grease de buff* (buffaloe grease). . . ." (July 19, 1806).

[One might comment that bilingualism is a problem not new in the twentieth century!]

Soopolallie (Shepherdia canadensis) was one of the plants that were ashed and analyzed (by atomic absorption) in 1962-66 studies of mercury in soils (by Warren, Delavault, and Barakso). Ability to concentrate mercury was demonstrated by a number of shrubs and trees. These results indicate possible use of ash analysis of vegetation to detect environmental pollution by such toxic elements as mercury and lead.

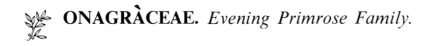

ONAGRÀCEAE. *Evening Primrose Family.*

CIRCAÈA ALPÌNA L. *Enchanter's Nightshade.* [p.339]

The only impressive feature of this physically insignificant plant, is its name. Circaea was Dioscorides' name for an unknown plant—certainly not this one—that was trans-

314

GERANIUM ERIANTHUM ×⅓ [p.287]

PACHISTIMA MYRSINITES ×⅘ [p.293]

SIDALCEA HENDERSONII ×⅓ [p.298]

HYPERICUM FORMOSUM ×⅜ [p.300]

315

CEANOTHUS SANGUINEUS ×½ [p.293]

CEANOTHUS VELUTINUS ×⅖ [p.296]

RHUS RADICANS ×½ [p.292]

ferred by Matthiolus to the present genus. The school of botanists in Paris believed this unlikely candidate was indeed the magic plant used by Circe in her attempt to enchant Ulysses. But no one can justify the name Nightshade (genus *Solanum*, which see), for the genera are poles apart.

In our area only one species is generally recognized, with intervening forms that link two very different extremes. The form illustrated is from deep-shade woods, where it is not often noticed—though abundant enough to load one's trouser-cuffs with its pear-shaped soft-hooked fruits. On gravel-bars of sun-flecked streams a compact, fleshy-leaved variant occurs, with larger pink-flushed flowers. Some form of the plant will be found in almost every region of the Province, up to moderate elevations.

Enchanter's Nightshade is a perennial with thin stems usually glabrous on the lower half, but somewhat hairy on the upper half. Leaf shape varies from nearly sagittate to pointed-ovate, with edges variously to faintly dentate.

Circaea can become a weed in shaded parts of the garden.

CLÁRKIA AMOÈNA (Lehm.) Nels. & Macbr. *Farewell-to-Spring. Summer's Darling.* [p.339]

This beautiful annual spreads its painted cups later than most plants, in fact when even the grasses are sere and yellow, hence the common names. Many will know this plant as a *Godetia*, but modern opinion suggests that presence or absence of an attenuated base ("claw") of the petals does not justify maintaining 2 separate genera. Clarkia commemorates the name of Captain William Clark, of the Lewis and Clark Expedition of 1804-1806. Amoena means *charming* or pleasing.

Highly variable are the lovely flowers, that may be single—on depauperate 3-inch individuals—or several—on the 12-inch plants that have found pockets of deeper and richer soil. One can easily appreciate how plant-breeders have been able to select for a number of cultivated forms, for scarcely two plants in a wild colony will be identical in size, or ground colour, or outer-notching of petals, or shape or colour of the markings on the petals. Perhaps a majority of plants display petal-tips more deeply-toothed than those in the illustration, and a great many have crimson to scarlet, or purplish markings near the centre of each petal. Select plants might be marked, in order to collect the seeds from the slim brown capsules in September, and to plant them at once in the garden.

The leaves are linear-lanceolate and entire, and usually 1-3 inches long. There are 4 calyx-lobes, and 4 petals that rarely are as much as 1½ inches long. Stamens are in two sets of 4, those opposite the petals being shorter, but all having purple anthers (usually yellow-tipped). The pistil has a 4-lobed stigma.

Clarkia amoena is one of the prettiest wild flowers, common on southern Vancouver Island, sparsely distributed from the Coast to the Cascades. It favours open slopes on dry hills.

[p.339] CLÁRKIA PULCHÉLLA Pursh is, perhaps, even more beautiful than *C. amoena*. It is found along the Columbia in southern British Columbia, especially around Grand Forks (where we have seen a gorgeous display). The petals are glowing pink, and deeply notched into 3 lobes.

EPILÒBIUM ANGUSTIFÒLIUM L. *Fireweed. Willow-herb.* [p.338]

In London, after the terrible fires that followed air-raids of 1943-45, the blackened ruins were covered with rosy stands of this fine flower. Indeed, in coastal British Columbia, and along the Alaska Highway, the eye is gladdened by expanses—sometimes covering thousands of acres—that glow with the incredible colour of Fireweed. One forgets, for a moment, the devastation of blackened stumps and logs they cover.

This is a genus of beautiful—but obviously invasive plants—most of which spread both by freely-produced winged seeds, and by wide-spreading rhizomes. The name is derived from the Greek epi, *upon*, and lobos, *a pod*, referring to the placement of the calyx and corolla on the top of an elongated ovary, that later becomes a slender seed-capsule. Angustifolium means *narrow-leaved*; in this species they are narrowly lanceolate, and up to 8 inches long; in fact they resemble those of such willows as the familiar Weeping Willow (*Salix babylonica*).

The erect stems are often 6 feet (occasionally 9 feet) tall, smooth, and alternate-leaved to the summit. The racemes begin to flower at the base, and become greatly elongated during the lengthy flowering season (from June to September). Everyone knows the inch-wide, rose-pink flowers. The long reddish-tinted ovary is a conspicuous feature, and even more so the very long, drooping, 4-lobed white pistil. From midsummer till after the frosts, and even when snow covers the ground, the silken parachutes with attached seeds drift through the air, turning and glinting in the sunlight.

The Indians often collected the stalks, then split them lengthwise and scraped out the glutinous sweet pith. The young leaves and new shoots were also used as a pot-herb. Deer and elk graze extensively on this plant. Many hikers will have recollections of walking through head-high stands of Fireweed, loud with the hum of bees. Fireweed honey is fragrant, dark-amber, and highly prized.

Very observant hikers may notice that the bee's activity reaches a peak about 1:00 p.m. This is the time at which production of nectar by this plant reaches a maximum. But other flowers release their nectar at other hours—a fact readily ascertained by any patient observer. Thus he will find that *Brassica* (Mustard) is most visited by bees about 9:00 a.m., but *Centaurea nigra* and *maculosa* (Knapweeds) about 11:00 a.m., *Trifolium pratense* (Red Clover) and Epilobium angustifolium, as just related, about 1:00 p.m., and *Echium vulgare* (Viper's Bugloss) about 3:00 p.m. Presumably, both bees and plants run on sun- or standard time! The extraordinary time-sense of bees has been extensively investigated since the work of K. von Frisch, begun in 1927. It is enough here to comment that the remarkable coordination between bee and flower has the obvious benefit of increasing the chances that the bees will limit themselves to visiting, and thereby pollinating, one sort of flower at a time.

[A] goodly and stately plant, hauing leaues like the greatest Willow or Ozier ... garnished with braue floures of great beautie, consisting of four leaues a piece, of an orient purple colour, hauing some threds in the middle of a yellow colour.

John Gerard: *The Herball* (edition of 1636)

318

RHAMNUS PURSHIANA ×⅖ [p.296]

HYPERICUM ANAGALLOIDES ×1 [p.299]

ELEAGNUS COMMUTATA ×½ [p.312]

SHEPHERDIA CANADENSIS (FRUIT) ×¼ [p.312]

ILIAMNA RIVULARIS   ×1¼   [p.297]

EPILÒBIUM LATIFÒLIUM L. *Broad-leaved Fireweed* [p.350]

The specific name is repeated in the common name. Though locally abundant, this more alpine species of the Cascades, Selkirks, and Rockies is much less common than *E. angustifolium* (which see). It is found on river-bars, and often on talus slopes, to considerable altitudes.

Epilobium latifolium does not increase by rhizomes but only by seeds. The clustered stems, 4-16 inches tall, bear somewhat waxy, bluish-green, lanceolate leaves, carried in pairs that are opposite (at least below). The leaves are variably entire to slightly toothed, and increase in length upward—to about 2½ inches. The 4 slim, pointed sepals are purplish, and the 4 obovate petals, rose- to pale-purple (occasionally white). The tuft of hairs topping each seed is buff-coloured.

As mountain sunlight streams across many an alpine gravel-bar, the flowers of the Broad-leaved Fireweed glow with almost incredible intensity. The fortunate wayfarer does not soon forget the spectacle.

EPILÒBIUM LÙTEUM Pursh. *Yellow Willow-herb.* [p.339]

Luteum means *yellow*, in this case a soft primrose yellow. This beautiful plant—though locally abundant—is not widespread. It occurs on the margins of creek and mountain runnels in the Coast Range, Cascades, and Selkirks. There are also a few records for Vancouver Island, but none from the Queen Charlottes.

The stems are usually simple, erect, 12-24 inches high, with hairs curiously arranged in vertical lines. The leaves are smooth (except for a few hairs along the dentate edges), pointed-oval, and 1-3 inches long. Two to ten flowers appear in the axils of the upper leaves. They face upward, on inch-long stems, and never open fully. The 4 petals are slightly notched and about the same length as the 4 slim, pointed sepals. Generally the creamy 4-lobed pistil is much longer than the 8 stamens, and is a conspicuous feature of the flower.

Yellow Willow-herb is a beautiful plant, unique in colour in a genus of pink-flowered species.

OENÓTHERA BIÉNNIS L. *Evening Primrose.* [p.343]

Theophrastus (370-287 B.C.) in his *Historiam de Plantis* and *De Causis Plantarum* (that were influential for 1800 years) used the name Oenothera. It was apparently derived from oinos, *wine*, and thera, a *catching*, since the roots were taken after meals as an incentive to wine-drinking.

The Oenotheras are a difficult group taxonomically, since the species are variable, and produce numerous hybrids and mutants. This species is an erect biennial, with leafy stems 2-4 feet tall. The plant is greyish-pubescent, the hairs being chiefly short. But some longer hairs on the lower stem and just below the flower clusters are unusual, because they have a reddish swollen base. Leaves are lanceolate, 2-7 inches long, entire to slightly toothed. The great flowers spread their softly radiant, primrose saucers as evening falls. Further to attract moth visitors, a delicate fragrance is released to drift downwind on the vagrant night airs.

From July to September, the flowers open nightly—a few at a time—from a crowded terminal bud-cluster. The 4 slim sepals enclose the pointed bud, and further extend short free ends, that are usually brilliant green and make a striking contrast with the purplish bud. They are folded right back along the pedicel as the flower opens. The broad overlapping petals are thin and delicate, up to 1 inch long. They generally age pinkish-orange to purplish.

A century ago the Dutch botanist Hugo de Vries made a name for himself, as a result of his studies of crosses between species of Oenothera, from which he formulated his theory of evolution by mutation.

OENÓTHERA PÁLLIDA Lindl. *Pink Oenothera.*   [p.350]

This surprising plant spreads pallid, or *pale*, improbably delicate flowers from the stiff, almost harsh branches of a spreading plant. It shares with Prickly Pear and Tumbleweed the most arid and desiccated flatlands. It is found in sandy or gravelly soil from New Mexico to Eastern Washington, and from Osoyoos northwestward to Spences Bridge. In our area the lovely blooms are to be seen in early June. The species is sometimes abundant locally, but it is by no means common.

Perennial rhizomes support the much branched 6-20 inch plants. Stems are sometimes smooth, but more often greyish-haired. The numerous leaves are 1-2 inches long, lanceolate, with entire to sometimes deeply-toothed margins. Though a number of authorities refer to the blooms as "vespertine", i.e. opening in the evening, we have often seen them fully expanded at noon, if thin haze or high cirrus reduces in the slightest degree the maximum intensity of the sun. But they seem to become fragrant only after sunset.

Opening white, the inch-long petals quickly become pink-edged, and soon age to soft purplish-pink. They centre the 4-cleft stigma and 8 conspicuous stamens, whose long anthers are versatile (midway balanced on the filaments). Such anthers are peculiarly effective in depositing pollen-grains upon the visiting moth. The microscope further reveals that the pollen-grains in Oenothera are loosely joined by a mesh of fine, sticky threads. Of course the fragrance, and the large pale petals help moths find the blooms.

ARALIÀCEAE. *Ginseng Family.*

ARÀLIA NUDICAÙLIS L. *Wild Sarsaparilla.*   [p.338]

Fernald states that Aralia is the Latinized form of the French Aralie, which was the Quebec habitant name for the plant (according to a French-Canadian physician, who early in the 18th century sent specimens to Tournefort at the Jardin des Plantes in Paris). Wild Sarsaparilla was once used as a substitute for Sarsaparilla (extracted from the roots of the tropical climber *Smilax*) long in vogue as a cooling summer drink. The specific name means *bare stem*, since the curious rounded flower-clusters (looking very like the flower-heads of the related ivy) are carried at the top of a naked scape. The true stem is very short and scarcely reaches the surface of the ground. From this stubby stem rise the naked 6-inch flower-scape and the taller overshadowing leaf. In wet, shaded woods of Southeastern British Columbia this large compound leaf is often conspicuous—but one needs to move it aside to discover the greenish flower-clusters.

The pleasantly fragrant, spicy roots of Aralia nudicaulis spread widely just beneath the soil surface.

OPLOPÁNAX HÓRRIDUM (J. E. Smith) Miq. *Devil's Club.*   [p.342]

Under three different genera this ferocious yet handsome shrub has retained its specific "horridum", suggesting a unanimity of opinion among many authorities. The current generic name comes from the Greek hoplon, *weapon* (the root also of the Hoplite, the heavily armed soldiers of early Greece), and *Panax*, the name of a large-leaved member of the Araliaceae, related to the Ivy. The springy stems are 4-10 feet long, often bent to the ground, the ends then rising again to an erect position. Many a hiker or forester pushing his way through the thick growth of stream-beds and wet ground, has been wounded by tripping on these procumbent stems so that the upright portions lacerated his face or hands. Every part of the stems and leaves bristles with long yellow spines. The punctures and scratches are poisoned, and soon become swollen and very painful—a fact we can ruefully confirm. "Devil's Club" is appropriate!

But this plant is beautiful too, its great 10-12 inch "maple" leaves providing handsome and effective foils for superb spikes of sealing-wax scarlet berries. In an out-of-the-way corner of the large garden Oplopanax has considerable ornamental value.

"The swampy ground was densely covered . . . with thickets of the aralea, a tough-stemmed trailer, with leaves as large as those of the rhubarb plant, and growing in many places as high as our shoulders. Both stems and leaves are covered with sharp spines, which pierced our clothes as we forced our way through the tangled growth, and made the legs and hands of the pioneers scarlet from the inflammations of myriads of punctures."

Milton & Cheadle:
The North-West Passage by Land (1865)

UMBELLÍFERAE. *Parsnip Family.*

The Umbelliferae is a family of perhaps 3000 species, rather readily identified by their aromatic foliage, sheathing petioles, and the *"umbels"* (convex or flat-topped inflorescences, the flowers on short pedicels arising from one point, with the younger flowers in the centre). But it is one thing to recognize an Umbellifer, and something vastly more difficult to place it in the proper genus. In fact unless the mature fruit (a schizocarp) is available for study with a microscope or good magnifying glass, there is very great difficulty in identifying many of the plants. In this book only representative genera and species will be described, selecting chiefly those that are showy, or those that are so dangerously poisonous that they should be known.

This thriving family has proliferated a large number of species, many of which are extremely abundant, as for instance *Daucus* (Wild Carrot) and *Heracleum* (Cow Parsnip). Part of the family's success may be attributed to the social structure of the inflorescences, in which a huge number of tiny florets are massed to make an attractive target for numerous pollinating insects. (Many of these are flower-beetles, as a minute's observation of a roadside patch of *Daucus* will show.) In this connection it is interesting to note that in this family, freshly released pollen-grains are sticky, thus helping them to hitch a ride on the hard, often smooth backs of the beetles. But after the first few hours the sticky web-like material dries up, and the small pollen-grains are then more readily wind-borne. Such species have been adapted for two alternative methods of cross-fertilization.

Though some research has been done on the relation between structural design of plants and pollination efficiency, a great deal more investigation is needed. One of the early studies, by H. Müller prior to 1890, suggested some interesting correlations. He made patient counts of the variety of insect visitors to 7 species of Umbelliferae that were selected for a range of size and conspicuousness of white flower-clusters. He found that the largest umbels (of *Heracleum*) attracted 118 species of insects, lesser umbels, smaller numbers. Thus 61 came to *Daucus*, 55 to *Perideridia*, and only 9 to *Torilis* (the smallest and least conspicuous). (One remarks that advertisers of today regrettably have learned too well the lesson of the plants, judging by the size of the billboards that line our roads.)

Müller also made one of the earliest comparisons of the spectrum of insect groups that were attracted to flowers of different families. Thus he pointed out that clustered flowers, as of the Umbelliferae (which have abundant nectar freely exposed on a flat disk surrounding the base of the pistil) and of the Compositae, which also secrete much honey (but at the base of the tubular florets) are more visited by insects than the flowers of other plant families. During the same time-interval the more accessible flowers of 10 species of Umbellifers attracted more individual insects, of a greater number of species, than came to 10 species of Composites. Also, of every 100 insects visiting e.g. the exposed honey-disks of *Daucus* (Wild Carrot): 13% were honey bees, 3% butterflies or moths, 31% flies, and 52% other orders, including beetles, wasps, ants, etc. But *Centaurea jacea* (Knapweed) with honey stored at the base of short tube-florets, attracted: 59% honeybees, 27% butterflies or moths, 12% flies, and only 2% other orders. Possibly bees prefer honey sources more exclusively available to their specialized mouth-parts, or maybe they dislike competition from the hoi polloi!

Such early work provokes modern research to obtain more significant results. For example, the flowers of *Daucus* are white (except for the purple central "target" floret) but those of *Centaurea* are purplish-blue. The effect of the colour difference needs to be evaluated, as well as differences in scent, and perhaps other factors. Resolution of results obtained when a number of parameters are involved is made much easier today, because computers are available.

ANGÉLICA DÁWSONII Wats. *Yellow Angelica.*   [p.350]

The generic name, from the Latin angelicus, *angelic*, recalls early belief in the mystical medical properties attributed to several of the species. Indeed, in Paxton's time it was Archangelica; now apparently demoted to Angelica! Sir John Dawson was a noted Canadian geologist and ethnobotanist, who died in 1899.

In moist meadows and along stream-banks, the large and handsome leaves attract attention early in the year. By mid-July, from the cluster of basal leaves a smooth and rather slender stem has risen 2 or 3 feet. The stem radiates—like the ribs of an umbrella—into a large compound umbel of very small greenish-yellow flowers. Both the basal and few stem leaves are ternately divided and twice compound (the leaflets thin, pointed-ovate, and saw-edged). Long petioles of the basal leaves become progressively shorter upward. Characteristic is a whorl of long, much-toothed, leafy bracts at the base of the umbel; however these are sometimes lacking.

This rather distinctive species occurs in eastern British Columbia, throughout Manning Park, and well to the north. At one time candied shoots of the closely related European *A. officinalis* were widely sold as an aromatic sweetmeat.

ANGÉLICA GENUFLÉXA Nutt. is a taller and very robust plant (occasionally reaching 7 feet), with white flowers. The main axis of the compound leaf (rachis) *"genuflects"* or bends sharply at the "knees" where each leaflet-pair originates. This species is common in wet thickets west of the Cascades.

ANGÉLICA LÙCIDA L. is a strictly maritime species, found in wet thickets along the coast. Formerly called COELOPLEÚRUM LÙCIDUM, it has greenish-white flowers in a large umbel that generally lacks involucral bracts. Stem-leaves are notable for their enlarged, and inflated, clasping petioles. Hultén relates that the stems and the petioles are used by the Eskimo as a wild celery, and that Siberian Eskimo inhale the fumes of the roasted root as a remedy for seasickness.

CICÙTA DOUGLÁSII (DC.) Coult. & Rose. *Water Hemlock.* [p.351]

This is one of the highly toxic species. Identification of some of the hazardous Umbellifers is so difficult that though a number are edible (to mention only the Carrot (*Daucus*), Celery (*Apium*), Parsley (*Petroselinum*), Anise (*Pimpinella*), Dill (*Anethum*), and Parsnip (*Pastinaca*), besides a number of wild species of our area) we would urge that no one attempt the experiment of eating any native or introduced plant of this family, until he can positively identify each species.

Cicuta is an ancient Latin name used by Pliny, possibly for this plant (or the equally poisonous *Conium*), and the specific name refers to the intrepid botanist David Douglas. The popular name does suggest the wet marshes and meadows favoured by the plant, but the foliage bears not the slightest resemblance to that of a hemlock tree.

This is a single-stemmed plant, reaching 3 feet, with pinnately-compound leaves along the purplish stem. The tiny flowers are greenish-white, borne in a somewhat flattened umbel made up of segregated rounded clusters. The root—if one is inclined to dig it up and cut it transversely—is quite characteristic, but the juices exuded are so violently poisonous that one must be very careful to wash the hands and knife thoroughly, and immediately. The upper part of the root is thickened just at the base of the stem, and when sectioned reveals a number of cross-partitions that divide it into many flat cells. The leaves vary up the stem. Most of them are reminiscent of the pinnate leaves of the Rowan or the Elder. The thin smooth leaflets are slimly ovate, sharp-pointed and serrate-edged. The small fruit is rounded, glabrous, with prominent corky ribs, and single oil-tubes in the intervals.

On Lulu Island, and such wet areas, cattle are occasionally killed by eating Cicuta. Almost invariably this occurs in spring, when the roots are readily pulled from the soft wet ground as animals crop the herbage. There are cases on record where cattle have died as a result of drinking seepage water from areas where their owner has bruised the roots, in digging them out to destroy. It is reported that a piece of root the size of a walnut contains enough poison (chiefly the bitter alkaloid coniine) to kill a full-grown cow.

CICÙTA BULBÍFERA L. is a smaller species—also very poisonous—found in wet meadows, or shallow (standing) water, in both lowlands and in mountain valleys. The ultimate leaf-segments are very narrowly linear. The specific name refers to swollen *bulbils* frequently borne in the axils of the upper leaves.

VIOLA SEMPERVIRENS ×2 [p.305]

VIOLA ADUNCA ×1¼ [p.301]

VIOLA GLABELLA ×2 [p.304]

VIOLA LANGSDORFII ×⅗ [p.304]

VIOLA PALUSTRIS ×⅞ [p.305]

VIOLA NUTTALLII var. PRAEMORSA ×⅗ [p.304]

CÒNIUM MACULÀTUM L. *Poison Hemlock.*   [p.351]

Most people know that an infusion of Poison Hemlock was given to Socrates in 399 B.C., upon the order of the Athenian Senate. But many pass by tall white-flowered plants, rampant in neglected plots (particularly of Vancouver and Victoria) without realizing that they are this same deadly species. Children put the most unlikely things in their mouths—even the curious, rounded, corky-ribbed fruits of Conium—and there have been fatalities resulting from blowing through whistles made from the hollow stems. So municipalities should rigorously exterminate this very dangerous European immigrant, wherever it occurs. And everyone should be able to recognize the plant.

The specific name calls attention to a feature helpful in identification, for the smooth, hollow, 6-10 foot stems are maculate (*marked*) with elongated purple spots. Conium is the Latinized form of the Greek name of this plant (koneion) used by Plato in his moving description of Socrates' trial and death (see the *Phaedo*, and the *Apologia Socratis*).

The large, ternately-compound leaves are as finely-divided as many ferns. Characteristically, they wilt within minutes of picking, or of cutting the stem. The greenish-white small flowers are borne in compound umbels. The individual florets are on slim pedicels noticeably uneven in length, from ½ to nearly 2 inches long. The microscope reveals, between the slightly wavy ribs of the fruit, numerous small oil-glands that tend to run together. The flowers have a faint but unpleasant musky odour. The highly toxic yellow oil is concentrated in the roots and fruit.

Incidentally, this is one of the few instances where we can assign an ancient name with assurance—this because there are only 2 species of the genus. One is from southern Africa; the other—which was used to execute the gentle philosopher—is this plant, anciently distributed in Europe and Asia. Now it occurs all over the world—a most undesirable introduction.

DAÙCUS CARÒTA L. *Queen Anne's Lace. Wild Carrot.*   [p.342]

The generic name is from the Greek daio, *to make hot,* alluding to some forgotten plant, apparently an Umbellifer, once native to Greece. The specific name is of course Latinized *carrot,* for the plant is the wild ancestor whose selected strains were developed into the familiar vegetable. Extremely common, this roadside biennial weed of the late summer and autumn tosses its white umbels over most of North America, and much of Eurasia, its original home.

A curious feature of the flat-topped flower-cluster is the frequent presence, in the very centre of several hundred small white florets, of a single brown, purple, or pink variant.* This is thought to represent a bull's-eye on which insects may "zero-in" for a landing.

In many parts of our area this is the most conspicuous of the late summer plants. Coarse-growing and common as it is, the finely cut "carrot" foliage and airy umbels well merit the name Queen Anne's Lace. Curiously, in Britain this name is applied to Cow Parsley (*Anthriscus sylvestris* (L.) Hoffm.), and no one knows which Queen Anne is concerned—Ann of Austria (wife of Louis XIII), or Anne (consort of James I of England, who was much interested in "simples"), or perhaps her great-granddaughter.

DAÙCUS PUSÍLLUS Michx. is a similar but smaller annual species, native west of the Cascades and southward. It is more slender and far less abundant. The bracts at the base of the small umbels are more finely divided, and lack the dry, membranous margins that are noticeable in *D. carota* (which see).

*Occasionally in reading the early herbals one is struck by the keen observation of the early botanists. Thus in Gybson's *The great herball* of 1539 we find a reference to the purple-coloured central flower in the white umbel of the Carrot: "hath a large floure,& in $\stackrel{e}{y}$ myddle therof a lytell reed prycke."

'Gerard also is very explicit: "the flowers are little, and stande upon broad spoked tufts, of a white colour, of which tuft of flowers the middle most part is of a deepe purple, the whole tuft is drawne togither when the seede is ripe, resembling a birdes nest . . . ." (*The Herball or Generall Historie of Plantes*, edition of 1597)

GLÉHNIA LEIOCÁRPA Mathias. *Beach Silver-top.* [p.351]

The common name is offered with some diffidence, since apparently it is not in wide usage. Peter von Glehn was, until 1876, curator of the St. Petersburg Botanic Garden, whence the rather strange generic name. Leiocarpa means *smooth carpels* (fruit).

This is a very unusual plant, and might be considered the entrant of the Umbelliferae family in that harsh environmental niche—sand dunes by the sea. The species has developed numerous specializations to adapt to extreme desiccation, salt-spray, and shifting sand.

Glehnia has a very extensive deep-running root system, including a stout taproot that stores reserves of water. The stem has nearly disappeared, so that the sheathing leaf-stipules are buried in the sand and serve as efficient anchors. Leaves are extraordinarily thick and leathery, waxy above and densely white-woolly beneath—all devices to reduce water loss. They are deeply tri-lobed twice over, the margins saw-toothed. The white flowers are carried in the familiar umbel, on a short, very strong woolly stalk. The fruits are striking, smooth except for a few hairs near the top, and with wing-like ribs. Their rounded shape permits them to roll before a strong wind, but their weight and pronounced ribs reduce the likelihood that they will be blown far over the sand and into the sea.

This most interesting plant is found along the coast from Kodiak Island, Alaska, to California.

330

HYPERICUM PERFORATUM ×1 [p.300]

SHEPHERDIA CANADENSIS ♀ ×⅘ [p.312]

OPUNTIA FRAGILIS ×1 [p.308]

331

OPUNTIA POLYACANTHA ×2 [p.309]

HERACLÈUM LANÀTUM Michx. *Cow Parsnip.* [p.354]

Heracleum is well named, for these are indeed plants of herculean proportions. We have seen an exceptional plant on display that measured a few inches less than 12 feet! Of about 60 species only H. lanatum is native to North America. The specific name means *woolly*. The plant is eagerly sought by domestic and wild animals, including bear, elk, and mountain-sheep; almost certainly these are better botanists than most of mankind! The thick stem sections were boiled and eaten by several native peoples, but there is perhaps too much danger to recommend the trial. The hazard is in possible confusion with the deadly *Conium maculatum* (purple-spotted stems, finely-cut foliage) or *Cicuta* species (smooth leaves somewhat pinnate, but of variable leaflet width).

This lusty perennial plant has thick, hollow stems, much branched from a single basal shoot. Though stem and leaves are usually woolly-haired, in some forms the hairs are sparse. Huge leaves spring from a large sheathing-petiole, that has 3 great leaflets, each of which may be 12 inches long. They are coarsely-toothed and palmately-lobed, their size making the plant very conspicuous. The flattened compound umbel is often 8-10 inches across; it is made up of small flowers usually greenish-white, occasionally yellowish or even pinkish. The outermost flowers have 4 deeply-notched petals that are very uneven in size. The fruits have a pleasantly aromatic odour. They are much flattened, ribbed, and marked by easily visible oil-tubes that extend downward from the tip.

Heracleum is widely distributed, often on stream-banks or moist low ground from sea level to considerable altitudes, throughout our area and indeed to Alaska and Newfoundland. In July hundreds of miles of roadsides in central and northern British Columbia are dominated by these ample white flower-clusters.

> *Leave your meadow grasses mellow,*
> > *Mellow, mellow;*
> > *Quit your cowslips, cowslips yellow . . .*
> *Quit the pipes of parsley hollow,*
> > *Hollow, hollow . . . .*

> Jean Ingelow:
> The High Tide on
> the Coast of Lincolnshire

LOMÀTIUM DISSÉCTUM (Nutt.) Math. & Const. *Chocolate Tips.* [p.354]

Lomatium is a difficult genus. In our area not less than 8 species occur, some with several varieties, but only 5 representative species will be mentioned here.

Lomatium is easily confused with *Sanicula.* In our area the fruit of the latter is bristly or scaly, and globose; in the former it is smooth (or at most, sparsely hairy at the tip) and strongly flattened. Lomatium has ternate or dissected leaves, *Sanicula* usually palmately-divided leaves.

The name comes from Greek loma, *a border*, referring to the winged or ribbed fruit of most of the species. The specific name describes the finely *dissected* foliage that is thrice-pinnate and fern-like.

This is an impressive perennial from a large woody taproot. The glabrous, hollow stems may reach 3-5 feet. The compound umbels are carried on very long stems. Flowers are usually purplish-chocolate but may be yellow. The glabrous fruit is flattened and slim-elliptical in outline, with the edge-wings narrow and corky, the face-wings (ribs) inconspicuous.

This species is an effective accent plant in the rockery. It is apparently never very common, from sea level to moderate elevations in the mountains. Its range is Vancouver Island, and both sides of the southern portion of the Cascades, where the preferred habitat is broken rock and talus, in sun or semi-shade.

LOMÀTIUM MARTINDÀLEI Coult. and Rose. *Few-fruited Hog-fennel.* [p.351]

This is a variable species, generally of fairly high altitudes in the southern Cascades, Coast Range, and especially of Vancouver Island. The handsome foliage is usually glabrous, almost entirely basal and bipinnate, with obovate segments. The leaf-petioles are thick and commonly reddish, the leaves resembling a coarse parsley. Flower-stems spring directly from the thickened root-top, and bear white, to cream, or pale-yellow umbels. The flattened fruits are very slenderly-elliptical in outline, with lateral wings and 3 ribs on each side-face. Very squat, this plant often literally hugs the ground.

L. martindalei is replaced in the Dry Interior, and eastward, by the common LOMÀTIUM MACROCÁRPUM (Nutt.) Coult. & Rose, with usually white flowers, occasionally tinged yellowish or purplish. Foliage is hairy, and often becomes purplish beneath.

LOMÀTIUM NUDICAÙLE (Pursh) Coult. and Rose. *Cous. Indian Consumption Plant.* [p.355]

The common name refers to the plant's use in the last century, to combat the white-man's tuberculosis or consumption. However, we remember a school journey in which Indian children from Lytton were bussed to Botannie Lake. As they jumped down from the bus, all the children at once pulled plants and roots of this species from the roadside, explaining that it was "Licorice, ver' good!" The bus-driver's name for it was "Indian Celery". We thought the taste was rather like a hot, spicy parsnip.

Nudicaule means *naked stem*, since the flowering stems that support the creamy-yellow umbels are naked, without leaves or bracts.

The leaves are very distinctive and readily recognized. An unusual greyish-green, they are glabrous, firm, and biternate (ternate twice). The leaflets are oblong and entire, or slightly toothed at the apex only. The little umbellets are so widely separated on very long pedicels, that one easily overlooks their common origin as parts of a spreading umbel. The fruit is narrowly elliptical and flattened, with 3 dorsal ribs and wide lateral wings. It has a delicious spicy smell, and was, in fact, often used as a spice in pioneer cooking. One remarks, however, that it is very needful not to confuse it with the fruits of *Cicuta* or of *Conium* (which see).

Dry, open, clay soils, from sea-edge to considerable elevations in the mountains, suit this lemon-coloured Umbellifer. It is found in southern British Columbia on both sides of the Cascades, to the Coast, and on the islands along the Coast.

The Indian name was Cous. Clearly the aboriginal names have priority, and should be retained whenever possible.

"Cous" referred to the thick fleshy roots of several species of Lomatium. These were ground into meal and shaped into large flat cakes. The journal of the Lewis and Clark Expedition of 1804-06 contains several records of trading beads and trinkets for cakes of Cous, or Couse, or even Cows. One such entry reads, "the noise of their women pounding the [cows] roots reminds me of a nail factory." And again, "the Cheif spoke to his people and they produced us about 2 bushels of the quawmas roots dryed, four cakes of the bread of *cows* and a dryed salmon trout." ... "The Broken Arm gave me a fiew quawmash roots as a great preasent, but in my estimation those of *Cows* is much better. I am confident they are much more healthy."

LOMÀTIUM UTRICULÀTUM (Nutt.) Coult. and Rose. *Spring Gold.* [p.355]

This is a much-loved, sprightly member of the Umbelliferae, notable for its exceedingly long season of bloom. We have a record of a plant at Thetis Lake Park, near Victoria, in bloom December 15, and thereafter it blooms in wetter shaded spots until the middle of July. So its cheerful yellow umbels long anticipate the spring, and remain until midsummer. The specific name refers to the fruit, which is a *utricle* (a small, one-seeded, thin-walled, somewhat inflated structure).

On the mosses of open rock slopes, Spring Gold very early unfolds its attractive, soft, much-dissected, fern-like leaves, and as we have seen, these are soon crowned with a short-stemmed umbel of tiny bright flowers. The flower-stems lengthen, and cauline leaves appear, as spring merges into summer, so that ultimately the 2-inch flower-heads may be 12 or 16 inches above the ground. The whole leaf-petiole is then seen to be somewhat flattened, and even winged. The flattened fruit is glabrous and elliptical, broadly winged on the edges, somewhat ribbed on the faces.

Vancouver Island and the southern Mainland west from the Cascades, rejoice in this happy plant.

Thine azure sister of the Spring shall blow
Her clarion o'er the dreaming earth, and fill

(Driving sweet buds like flocks to feed in air)
With living hues and odours plain and hill . . . .

Percy Bysshe Shelley:
Ode to the West Wind

OENÁNTHE SARMENTÒSA Presl ex DC. *Water Parsley.* [p.362]

Some species were used in Greece for perfuming wine, hence the name, from ionois, *wine,* and anthos, a *flower.* Sarmentosus means *bearing runners,* since this succulent and lax plant of marshes, sloughs, and slow streamlets, sends out roots from the nodes of its reclining stems. The leaves somewhat resemble those of parsley, though larger, softer, and coarser.

The soft stems may be a yard long, but are chiefly prostrate, sending up short weak branches. These are angularly forked, with much smaller scapose leaves at each juncture. At the ends of the branches appear loose, compound umbels of greenish-white flowers. They have a pleasant though faint fragrance. The fruits are ellipsoidal, but flattened on top, and slightly toothed. The sides are ribbed, and the cross-section is almost round, or very slightly flattened. Usually the two long styles remain, forming a "V" at the summit. The fruit is definitive, but the best field guide is the sprawling character of the plant, which is glabrous throughout.

Oenanthe is abundant in suitable wet spots near the Coast, and somewhat less common as far as the Cascades.

OSMORHÌZA CHILÉNSIS H. & A. *Sweet Cicely.* [p.355]

Osmorhiza's names, both Greek (osme, *scent,* plus rhiza, *root),* and English, are due to the sweet licorice-like odour of the crushed root. Cicely is a corruption of *Seseli,* an ancient Greek name for some sweet-scented plant whose identity has been lost. Above the fragile leaves appears a cluster of insignificant greenish-white flowers, soon succeeded by slim seeds armed with numerous hooks. Many a hiker, wearily picking these seeds from his clothing, must have wondered how the unspectacular plant came by so misleading a name. Sweet Cicely indeed!

The pale, thin leaves are twice ternate (biternate), i.e. each has 3 leaflets, which are again divided into 3 parts. As might be suggested by leaf-character and slender 2-foot stems, this perennial is a plant of windless woodlands. It is common nearly everywhere in British Columbia, and from Alaska to California; and it even reappears in *Chile* (as suggested by the specific name). In our area Sweet Cicely begins to flower as early as April.

PERIDERÍDIA GÁIRDNERI (H. & A.) Mathias. *Yampah. Wild Caraway.*   [p.362]

Heinrich Reichenbach of Dresden (1793-1879) was the author of the generic name, but its meaning has been lost. A possible origin could be from the Greek peri, *around*, and derris, a *leather coat*—which might describe the tough-coated swollen root.

This plant was well known to the Indians, who brought it to the attention of early explorers. Thus Lewis and Clark mention it frequently in their journals: "Sahcargar-weah geathered a quantity of the roots of a speceis of fennel which we found very agreeable food, the flavor of this root is not unlike annis seed . . . . those roots are very paliatiable either fresh rosted boiled or dried and are generally between thc sizc of a quill and that of a mans fingar and about the length of the latter . . . . the rind was white and thin, the body or consistence of the root was white mealy and easily reduced by pounding to a substance resembleing flour which thickens with boiling water something like flour and is agreeably flavored." This was Yampah.

"Caraway" calls attention to the close relationship to *Carum carvi*, not infrequently escaped from cultivation, and source of the much esteemed, ridged, aromatic fruits long used in "seed-cake".

The flowers of Wild Caraway might be confused with those of the ferny-leaved Wild Carrot (*Daucus carota*, which see). Both are in bloom in late summer and through the fall, and both have flat-topped compound umbels of small white flowers. But the leaves are quite different, and stems of the present species are nearly always unbranched and stiffly erect. Leaves of Perideridia consist of long slender segments, that are often dry and shrivelled by the time the white (occasionally pinkish-tinged) flowers appear. The whole plant is pleasantly aromatic, possessing a "caraway" scent that is easily recognizable when once identified. This is fortunate, for the plant could also be quite easily mistaken for the deadly poisonous *Cicuta bulbifera* (which see). However *Cicuta* prefers wet meadows and even shallow (standing) water, while Perideridia inhabits dry sites, or those that become very dry before late summer. Finally, *Cicuta bulbifera* can be recognized by the presence of swollen bulbils in the axils of a proportion of the floret-pedicels. One needs to be very certain that the plant is Perideridia before using the swollen roots for food. They are delicious either baked like miniature sweet potatoes, or fried in butter. There is general agreement that these are the best flavoured and most nutritious of the native food plants. But be sure of your identification!

SANÍCULA BIPINNATIFÌDA Dougl. *Purple Snake Root.*   [p.355]

Though Henry speculates the name may be a form of San Nicholas, it was apparently derived from the Latin sanare, *to heal*, since infusions of the European species were thought to have healing properties. The Indians of the Plains believed several species were effective for snake-bites. The specific name refers to the *twice-pinnate*, very lacerate-edged leaves.

Four perennial Sanicles occur in our area. They may be distinguished from *Lomatium* (which see), since in Sanicula the globose fruit is covered with short hooked spines (rather than simply ribbed or corky winged), and the leaves are generally palmate (instead of somewhat pinnate or tri-foliate). In this species, however, the rather thick leaves are pinnatedly-lobed. A very satisfactory identification feature, peculiar to this—among the species of our area—is a conspicuously notched rachis (main axis of the compound leaf).

Sanicula heads consist of both perfect flowers and staminate flowers. (The latter lack the 2-styled pistil characteristic of Umbelliferous flowers.) The calyx is slightly cupped, with 5 short, sharp lobes. Five incurved small petals are dark-purple. Even the pistil (on perfect flowers) and stamens are purple.

In our area this rather sombre plant is found near the sea, and on open slopes of southern Vancouver Island, and of the Mainland, east to the Cascades. Flowering time is usually June.

SANÍCULA ARCTOPOÌDES H. & A., from beaches and coastal bluffs of southern Vancouver Island, is a handsome prostrate species, with sharply-pointed leaf-segments, and a head of yellow flowers distinctively surrounded by a "ruff" of long bractlets.

SANÍCULA CRASSICAÙLIS Poepp. *Western Snake Root.* [p.363]

The specific name means *thick-stemmed*, both semi-taproot and stalks being strong and heavy. This is a common and variable species, usually yellow-flowered, but purplish in var. TRIPARTÌTA (Suksd.) H. Wolff. Apparently in our area we have tetra-, hexa-, and octoploid series.

Recognition, consequently, is rather difficult, particularly distinction from SANÍCULA GRAVEÒLENS Poepp., which has much the same range. Only the latter [p.363] occurs east of the Cascades into the Rockies, but west of the Cascades and on Vancouver Island the 2 species overlap. S. graveolens is apparently always yellow-flowered, and has twice-pinnatifid leaves (so deeply cleft as to appear pinnate). Basal leaves of typical S. crassicaulis are nearly round in general outline, though deeply and palmately 5-divided, and with margins irregularly cut into sharp teeth. (In *S. crassicaulis var. tripartita*, the basal leaves are 3-parted and even more deeply lobed, and the central division is elongated.) A tedious but good distinction is made by noting the relative abundance of perfect (pistillate) and staminate flowers in the heads. In S. graveolens the staminate flowers are the more numerous; in *S. crassicaulis* the majority are pistillate. The fruits in both species are nearly round in cross-section, and densely covered with hooked prickles, which in late autumn readily cling to cuffs and stockings.

SÌUM SUÀVE Walt. *Water Parsnip.* [p.362]

This tall water-loving Umbellifer has fibrous roots, rather than the taproot one would expect from its common name. Nor do the leaves resemble those of the parsnip. Sion

MENTZELIA LAEVICAULIS var. PARVIFLORA $\times \frac{1}{2}$ [p.305]

ARALIA NUDICAULIS $\times \frac{1}{3}$ [p.322]

EPILOBIUM ANGUSTIFOLIUM $\times \frac{1}{8}$ [p.317]

CIRCAEA ALPINA ×1 [p.313]

CLARKIA AMOENA ×⅞ [p.316]

CLARKIA PULCHELLA ×½ [p.316]

EPILOBIUM LUTEUM ×½ [p.320]

was a Greek name for an umbelliferous plant, and siw was Celtic for *water*; both may have some application. Suave means agreeable or *sweet*; the fragrance might be so described, but is almost too faint to detect. Nor should one test it for taste (we have; it is not at all sweet) for it is only too easy to mistake it for the deadly *Cicuta douglasii* (which see). So we may conclude that the naming of this plant was unhappy all around. (Incidentally, Sium has a ring of bracts at the base of the main umbel, and another of very small bractlets at the base of the final umbellets, which are lacking in *Cicuta*. And of course *Cicuta* has thickened tuberous roots with the peculiar cross-cellular spaces.)

The 2-5 feet tall, smooth stems of Sium are frequent on muddy or sandy lake shores, and in the shallow water of swampy areas from Vancouver Island to the Atlantic. The leaves are striking and unusual, glossy smooth, pinnate with lance-linear leaflets neatly toothed. Leaves low enough to dip into the water are finely fringe-edged. The large open racemes are greenish-white, occasionally pinkish. Fruit is smooth, ellipsoidal, only slightly flattened, and striated with corky ribs.

CORNÀCEAE. *Dogwood Family.*

CÓRNUS CANADÉNSIS L. *Dwarf Dogwood. Bunchberry.* [pp.363,366]

Perhaps 30 subshrubs, shrubs, and trees, are included in this genus of important ornamentals. The species are characterized by small, 4-merous flowers, crowded into tight heads, but often subtended (as by an Elizabethan collar) with 3-8 large bracts (modified leaves) that in our species are white. The cultivated Dogwoods, which include pink-flowered and variegated-foliage plants, are among the most spectacular shrubs of our gardens.

Cornu is the Latin word for *horn*, and Dr. Hitchcock advances the further interesting suggestion that it was the term applied to the ornamental knob at each end of the cylinders on which manuscripts were once rolled—an image at once calling to mind the immature inflorescence of such species as *C. nuttallii* (which see). (A friend has recognized the charm of these nubbly heads, and has used them in clever lapel ornaments centring petals of dried zonal fungi.)

The specific name indicates the Canada-wide distribution of this species, one of the most loved and ubiquitous of all our native plants. But its range is actually much wider, extending southward to New Mexico, northeastward to Greenland (and if *C. suecica* L. turns out to be only a variety, to Great Britain, Switzerland, Sweden, Norway, Russia, and Japan). Cornus canadensis is indeed a tiny replica of the great tree dogwood of the Pacific Coast, being seldom more than 7 inches tall. The bright red drupes, or "berries", that in the fall replace the insignificant true flowers, are borne in handsome clusters; hence the second common name.

Many think the circle of 4 (occasionally 3-7) pointed, cream bracts (rarely streaked or suffused with pink or purple) are petals. Actually these are modified leaves. The true flowers are tiny, perfect, and numerous, forming the close-packed centre of the "flower". Closer study shows each floret has 4 sepals, 4 purplish petals, 4 stamens, and a straight pistil. By late summer the involucral bracts have fallen, and the florets have been replaced by a tight cluster of orange-scarlet drupes, that provide startling accents on the forest floor, especially in the more open glades of wet woods.

Bunchberry survives in logged-over tracts, and is abundant enough in many areas to permit one—with clear conscience—to lift a patch of the plants, which settle down contentedly in the shady garden. In our experience, the one essential is to see that a good quantity of decaying wood is retained, through which the rootstocks may happily rove. This is one of the "Treasure" plants—attractive throughout the year, captivating through June to August, and of arresting brilliance often until Christmas, especially when the leaves become bronze and purple foils to the vermilion fruits.

Systematists are not agreed on possible recognition of local western and northern variants as C. SUÈCICA L. and C. UNALASCHKÉNSIS Ledeb. (chiefly distinguished by the presence of opposite pairs of leaves appearing below the usual whorl), but all systematists, naturalists, and simple lovers of nature are unanimous in their high regard for this charming little plant.

To him who in the love of Nature holds
Communion with her visible forms, she speaks
A various language . . . .

William Cullen Bryant: Thanatopsis

CÓRNUS NUTTÁLLII Aud. *Flowering Dogwood. Pacific Dogwood.* [p.367]

What more magnificent tribute could be paid to the memory of Thomas Nuttall (1786-1859), the first botanical explorer of great tracts of western North America? This splendid plant is the lone tree (for it often develops a single trunk and attains 60 feet) included in this book. Our explanation can only be that it is a tree-like shrub in a genus of subshrubs and shrubs, and besides, it is just too beautiful to leave out!

Protected by law, Cornus nuttallii is the provincial flower of British Columbia, attaining its finest growth along the Pacific coast as far south as California (though it extends to the western slopes of the Cascades). But no gardener need be without this lovely tree, for it grows readily from fresh seed planted in ordinary loam, to which a little loose coniferous duff has been added. Contrary to popular opinion, the small seedlings transplant well in late autumn. The young plants like the shelter of other shrubs until well established, but are then tolerant of full sun or high shade.

Dogwood is modernized from "dagwood", for the hard wood was in early days used to make "*dags*", meaning—in different parts of the coast—either skewers or wedges.

Seen against dark winter skies, the mottled grey branches seem curiously knobby with dozens of tight bud-buttons. But the branches green with spring, until in May the

342

URTICA DIOICA var. LYALLII ×½ [p.88]   DAUCUS CAROTA ×½ [p.328]

OPLOPANAX HORRIDUM (FRUIT) ×⅓ [p.322]

circles of bracts lengthen and pale, until each flower-cluster centres a ring of great creamy "petals".

By early June each tree is breath-taking—almost incredibly beautiful. Individual "flowers" in the garden in a good year have measured 6 and even 7 inches, borne so freely that at a short distance the whole tree appears white. Nor is this all. As September advances the heavily-veined, wavy-edged, elliptical leaves turn a harmonious blend of tints of plum, purple, pink, and even cerise. At the same time (the creamy bracts having fallen) the flower-heads are seen to have been replaced by clusters of drupes, all brilliant scarlet barbarically edged with orange. Then the tree is indeed an incredible sight.

Remarkably, a few trees bloom again in the fall, and it is then odd to see together both scarlet fruit and creamy "flowers". It would be interesting to determine if this clone can be vegetatively propagated to retain its double season of flowering in a variety of geographic locations.

We would like to see this native of unparalleled beauty widely planted in parks and boulevards. Our most vivid memories of it, however, will be the vision of wild trees, pale against dark conifers of forest openings or lake edges.

Accuse not Nature, she hath done her part;
Do thou but thine. . . .

John Milton: Paradise Lost

CÓRNUS STOLONÍFERA Michx. var. OCCIDENTÀLIS (T. & G.) C. L. Hitchc.
Red Osier Dogwood. Western Dogwood.   [p.370]

"Stolonifera" was suggested to Micheaux by the plant's free-spreading habit, due to natural layering of some prostrate stems, so that many upright branches appear to *grow* as from *stolons.* This common—and rather variable—shrub ranges across the northern half of the continent, from Alaska to Newfoundland. In the interior of B.C., where in wet areas it often forms nearly impenetrable thickets 6-12 feet high, it is widely—and of course quite wrongly—called "Red Willow". The bark colour (evident when the large, heavily-veined leaves have fallen) is red—sometimes very bright—so the tough, smooth canes were employed in basketry—hence the name Red Osier.

But Cornus stolonifera is a true Dogwood, as is revealed in May or June by closer examination of the flat-topped cluster of greenish-white flowers. There is no ring of showy bracts, but each floret displays the characteristic 4 small sepals, 4 spreading, pointed, oval petals, with stamens spaced flat between them, and a single, club-shaped pistil. The shrub is not conspicuous until autumn, when the red bark of the young stems links the brilliantly-coloured leaves, and the clusters of unusal drupes, that look like bluish-white berries. Then the Red Osier Dogwood rightly claims its place in a proud genus of beautiful shrubs.

Preceding page: OENOTHERA BIENNIS   ×1⅞   [p.320]

🌿 PYROLÀCEAE. *Wintergreen Family. Pyrola Family.*

PÝROLA. *Wintergreen.*

For a comment on the family Pyrolaceae, see under *Ericaceae.*

The name Pyrola refers to the similarity of the leaves of some species to those of the pear-tree (*Pyrus*). The source of oil of wintergreen is *Gaultheria procumbens* (the False Wintergreen from northeastern America), a plant closely related to our Salal.

Approximately 15 species are known, chiefly from North America and Eurasia. These are essentially plants of cool forests of conifers.

The Pyrolas are characterized as medium to low perennials with basal leaves usually thick and leathery. The unbranched flower-scapes carry terminal, rather few-flowered racemes. The nodding flowers have 5 sepals, 5 greenish to white or pinkish-purple petals, 10 stamens, and an unbranched style. The bent pistil is always large and conspicuous.

The Pyrola species of our area attract a good deal of attention, being generally pleasing in appearance, and widely distributed (though seldom abundant). Our species are evergreen.

MONÈSES UNIFLÒRA (L.) A. Gray. *Single Delight. Moneses. Wood Nymph. One-flowered Wintergreen.* [p.370]

Moneses (from monos, *single*, and hesis, *delight*) is a perfect name for this exquisite little woodlander. One winsome bloom hangs demurely from the top of a short slender stem. Unlike its near relatives the Pyrolas (indeed, many authors place this plant in that genus), Moneses holds flat—or even slightly reflexed—its triangular, waxen-white petals. The 5 pairs of stamens provide conspicuous accents in the salverform flower, which may be as much as ¾ inch wide. In the centre, rising from a large, green, five-grooved ovary, is an extraordinary pistil: straight, standing clear above the stamens, and at its summit sharply expanded, then divided into 5 upward-pointing triangular teeth. In short, the stigma is strongly reminiscent of the upper part of a chess-piece—the rook, or castle.

The leaves are roundish and basal, 1 inch or less long, with margins variably serrate to almost entire. The petioles are from one-half to nearly as long as the blades.

This charming nymph may be found in moister parts of the forest (often growing where the soil incorporates rotting wood) from sea level to perhaps 7000 feet. It occurs in such spots throughout our area, where the wayfarer—from May, even until August—will perhaps chance with pleasure upon the "Single Delight".

For his simple heart
Might not resist the sacred influence

Which, from the stilly twilight of the place,
And from the gray old trunks that high in heaven
Mingled their mossy boughs, and from the sound
Of the invisible breath that swayed at once
All their green tops, stole over him, and bowed
His spirit with the thought of boundless power
And inaccessible majesty.

William Cullen Bryant:
A Forest Hymn

PÝROLA ASARIFÒLIA Michx. *Large Wintergreen.* [p.371]

Asarifolia means that Micheaux thought the leaves resembled those of *Asarum,* Wild Ginger.

This is the largest and showiest of our Pyrolas, a very handsome plant, with its thick lustrous leaves in a basal rosette, and its 12-16 inch stem carrying 10-24 waxy pink flowers.

Due to its rambling underground stem (rhizome) with few fibrous feeding roots, it is a plant almost impossible to move into the garden. Further, it appears to rely in part on a fungus association in the decaying humus of its forest home, so it should be admired where it grows, and left for others to enjoy.

The species is not difficult to distinguish from other Pyrolas, chiefly by virtue of its size and its pink to rosy or purplish-red flowers. The half-dozen basal leaves are roundish to elliptical, about 1½-3 inches long, and with leaf-stems (petioles) at least as long as the blade. They are leathery, glossy, dark-green above and often purplish below, with edges slightly wavy (crenulate) to sparsely-and minutely-toothed (serrulate). The rather exotic-looking pink flowers, each with its strongly curved and prominent style, are about ½ inch wide. There are 5 sepals (joined at their bases), 5 separate petals (thick, waxy, and elliptical), and 10 stamens.

This alluring species is widespread, and often fairly common throughout our area (though not reported from the Queen Charlotte Islands). It blooms from late May to September, in rather damp locations, on stream-banks and in open coniferous forests, sometimes to considerable altitudes.

Now all the wood is but a murmured light
Where leaf on leaf falls softly from the height.

Henri de Regnier: Night
(translation of Seumas O'Sullivan)

PÝROLA DENTÀTA Smith. *Nootka Wintergreen.*

Dentata refers to the more or less dentate (*toothed*) leaves, which are narrower than those of *P. asarifolia* (which see), being slenderly elliptical, with the greatest width beyond the centre (i.e., they are oblanceolate). The leaves are leathery, smooth, and pale- to bluish-green without markings. The flowers, in shape, are very like those of *P. asarifolia*; however these are greenish-white to cream.

Pyrola dentata is an indistinct species—possibly only a form of *P. picta* (which see). It is apparently limited to southern Vancouver Island, a few locations in the southwest Interior, and in northern coastal and interior Washington. Nootka Wintergreen is found in coniferous forests, especially of Yellow Pine (*Pinus ponderosa*).

PÝROLA ELLÍPTICA Nutt. *Shinleaf. Wild Lily-of-the-valley.*

The specific name refers to the very broadly *elliptical* leaf, almost as rounded as that of *P. asarifolia* (which see). However, this is another species whose distinctive characteristics are obscure. Usually the leaf-petiole (stem) is shorter than the blade. A hand-lens generally reveals a collar-like enlargement just below the stigma. The flower is white, greenish-white, yellowish, or (rarely) pink-flushed.

P. elliptica is not common anywhere in our area, and is limited to the southern mainland and Vancouver Island, the central and southwestern Interior, and northern Idaho. Shinleaf is found in bloom from June to August, on dry or wet slopes, generally under some shade.

PÝROLA GRANDIFLÒRA Radius. *Arctic Wintergreen.*

The epithet *"large-flowered"* is justified—the white to pinkish, rather flat-opened blooms being more than ½ inch across.

This is a choice plant, with its relatively big flowers on a short scape from 2-6 inches tall, and its basal cluster of leathery glossy leaves, usually dark green but whitened along the veins. If this well-proportioned plant were not virtually impossible to move, it would make it a very desirable species for the rockery.

Arctic Wintergreen is, as the common name suggests, found only in the northern Interior and Alaska, being circumpolar. The northern range of Pyrola grandiflora is helpful in distinguishing it from the more southern *P. picta* (which see).

PÝROLA MÌNOR L. *Lesser Wintergreen.*

This *small* species (less than 9 inches tall) bears its white or pink ¼-inch wide flowers in a rather crowded, short raceme. The leaves are thin and dark-green, entirely basal, and with petioles equal to—sometimes longer than—the nearly round blades. Distinctive details, requiring a hand-lens, are the short straight style, and its stigma that lacks a collar, but has 5 minute lobes.

Lesser Wintergreen is found (like most Pyrolas, in the moist to rather dry humus and moss of coniferous forests) over all our area, except the Queen Charlotte Islands.

PÝROLA PÍCTA Smith. *Painted Pyrola. White-veined Wintergreen.* [p.371]

Picta or *painted*, this beautiful plant is rare in our area, being limited to Vancouver Island, and also the Kootenays westward to the Coast (in a zone generally south of Ashcroft). With its strikingly white-veined, thick, glossy leaves, and single 12-inch stem carrying 2-20 purplish-pink (or yellowish) flowers, this species never fails to attract attention. Often the leaves have a white margin as well as the white zones along the principal veins, and occasionally the lower surfaces are purplish. The plant can be identified by means of its uniquely mottled leaves.

The white areas (due to loss of chlorophyll in certain zones) are indicative of the partial parasitic character of this and some other members of the genus. In fact, the name PÝROLA APHÝLLA ("*no leaves*") has been applied to occasional plants of several species which are totally parasitic, having no leaves to produce their own food.

Painted Pyrola is a choice beauty, to be appreciated in its own natural setting.

PÝROLA SECÚNDA L. *One-sided Pyrola. One-sided Wintergreen.* [p.371]

This common plant is readily recognized, being very different from other members of the genus. The small white to greenish flowers are borne entirely *on one side* of the 4-6 inch stems, which is the meaning of the botanical term "secund". Another distinctive feature is the distribution of the leaves, which—unlike the entirely basal arrangement of other Pyrolas—occur along the lower half of the stem.

The leaves are usually pale-green (sometimes darker), of rather variable shape and serration of edges. The style, on close examination, is seen to lack a collar below the stigma, which is 5-lobed. Each of the oval petals has a pair of small rounded tubercles on the inner face, near the base.

This species is found in much the same situations as other members of the group—perhaps more often in rather moist soil of stream-banks and cold coniferous forests—to very considerable altitudes. One-sided Pyrola occurs literally throughout our area—wherever suitable habitats exist. (Alaskan and northern British Columbian plants, though, are seldom more than 3 inches tall, with thick round leaves.) Depending upon latitude and altitude, Pyrola secunda may be found in bloom from May until August, or occasionally even later.

PÝROLA VÌRENS Schweigg. = PÝROLA CHLORÁNTHA Swartz. *Greenish-flowered Wintergreen.* [p.362]

Virens means *green* and chlorantha (which may be an earlier and therefore valid name) means *green-flowered.*

This is a common species over all our area (though it does not occur in the Queen Charlottes and is most abundant in the southern Interior). P. virens looks rather like *P. secunda* (which see), but the greenish flowers are larger, and occur all round the stem—not just on one side. Also the leaves are basal only.

P. virens might be even more readily confused with *P. minor* (which see), which has a straight style. In the present species, though, the style is strongly curved—not entirely downward, but somewhat to one side. P. virens has a distinct collar below the stigma, which has 5 knobs on its upper surface.

The broadly-elliptical leaves are variable: some have their greatest width nearer the tip than the base (i.e. they are obovate), and most have the petiole longer than the blade.

# MONOTROPÀCEAE. *Indian Pipe Family.*

ALLÓTROPA VIRGÀTA T. & G. *Candy-stick. Barber-pole.* [p.374]

From the Greek allos, *other*, and tropos, *turn* or direction, the generic name indicates that young flowers face upward, but older ones turn downward (cf. *Monotropa uniflora* whose flowers are all turned in one direction: downward). Virgata, however, is Latin, meaning *striped*, with reference to the brilliant red marking of the white stem. The common names are descriptive of the general appearance of this showy plant.

The author recalls showing a visitor a fine clump of these improbable plants. It was difficult to convince him that a prankster had not been busy with red paint!

As with other members of the family* that occur in our area, this plant is a saprophyte, that grows (in association with the thread-like roots, or mycelia, of certain fungi) upon decaying plant debris among the forest litter. Since Candy-stick has no need for chlorophyll, it does not shun even the deepest shade. White, slender-pointed leaves

350

ANGELICA DAWSONII ×½ [p.324]

OENOTHERA PALLIDA ×⅖ [p.321]

EPILOBIUM LATIFOLIUM ×⅞ [p.320]

CICUTA DOUGLASII ✕⅕ [p.325]

LOMATIUM MARTINDALEI ✕⅘ [p.333]

CONIUM MACULATUM ✕⅓ [p.328]

GLEHNIA LEIOCARPA (FRUIT) ✕⅗ [p.329]

grow upward all along the sturdy stem, which may reach a height of 2 feet (but is usually less). The flowers occur in the leaf-axils of the upper half of the stem. Each flower consists of 5 white or pink sepals (about ¼ inch long) and a large, rounded, dark-red ovary, surrounded by 10 stamens.

The blooming period is extended—from May to August. Barber-pole is nowhere abundant, but occurs sporadically in the coniferous forest of southern Vancouver Island and the adjacent coast of the Mainland, including the Olympic Peninsula.

*For a comment on the Monotropaceae, see under *Ericaceae*.

. . . But here there is no light,
Save what from heaven is with the breezes blown
Through verdurous glooms and winding mossy ways.

I cannot see what flowers are at my feet,
Nor what soft incense hangs upon the boughs,
But, in embalmèd darkness, guess each sweet
Wherewith the seasonable month endows
The grass, the thicket, and the fruit-tree wild;
White hawthorn, and the pastoral eglantine;
Fast-fading violets cover'd up in leaves;
And mid-May's eldest child,
The coming musk-rose, full of dewy wine. . . .

John Keats: Ode to a Nightingale

HEMITÒMES CONGÉSTUM A. Gray. *Cone-plant. Gnome Plant.*   [p.375]

From the Greek hemi, *half*, and tomias, *sterile* or eunuch, the generic name refers to the characteristic sterility (not invariable) of one of the two paired anther-cells of each stamen. The specific name suggests the *crowded* arrangement of the pink flowers in the flattened spike. This very curious saprophytic plant, a gnome-like dweller of the shaded woods, resembles an inverted cone.

The unique floral characteristics make this the only member of its genus in the world. Indeed, Cone-plant is limited to Vancouver Island, New Denver (one record only), the Olympic Peninsula, and a few localities in Washington, Oregon, and northern California. It must rank a rare species, and the discovery of a specimen makes a very special day.

The emerging plant looks like a fungus, or like a small Cauliflower head. Shortly the mass of pinkish (or white) scale-like leaves elongates a closely scaled, club-like stem, 1-7 inches tall. At the top, densely hairy pink cups of flowers are packed together. Each has 2 to 4 linear sepals, and a bell-shaped corolla (usually 4-lobed), enclosing most often 8 stamens, and a broad, flattened yellow stigma. The flowers look upward, and are shrimp-pink (occasionally nearly white).

Hemitomes congestum is one of the oddest of the saprophytes. Its rarity demands that it be carefully protected.

HYPÓPITYS MONÓTROPA Crantz. *Pinesap. Many-flowered Indian Pipe.*   [p.378]

The name is derived from the Greek hypo, below or *beneath*, and pitys, *a pine tree*, in allusion to the plant's usual habitat. A generic name that alludes to the ecologic niche occupied by a plant, rather than to a structural detail, is most unusual; and in fact this is a rather unique plant. It is quite like Indian Pipe (*Monotropa uniflora*, which see), but has several straw-coloured flowers (rather than a single white one) on each stem. "Pinesap", like the generic name, suggests that this plant grows under pine trees, with the added idea that the shape and colour suggest congealed drippings of the resin. Monotropa means *one direction*, i.e. the flowers are all on one side of the stem.

This wide-ranging saprophyte occurs in the humus of coniferous forests throughout the southern two-thirds of our area, to California, and eastward to the Atlantic and Europe. The curious blooms (appearing in June or July) at first hang downward in a one-sided raceme, along the upper part of a 4-12 inch stem.

The stem is unbranched, but rather sparsely clothed with bract-like leaves. The entire plant is pale yellow, occasionally orange or pinkish. The campanulate flowers usually have 5 lobes toward the top of the raceme, 3 or 4 lobes toward the bottom. Most often there are 8 (but sometimes 6-10) stamens (as in *Hemitomes* which see) but unlike that plant, the pistil of Hypopitys is conspicuous, protruding beyond the petals its broad, flattened stigma. As the fleshy petals break away and the ovary swells, the flower-fragments change from a hanging to an upright position. Generally, single plants occur, rarely more than 2 or 3 stems together, whereas clumps of several dozen stems of the white Indian Pipe are frequently seen.

> *. . . Therefore am I still*
> *A lover of the meadows and the woods,*
> *And mountains; and of all that we behold*
> *From this green earth; of all the mighty world*
> *Of eye, and ear,—both what they half create,*
> *And what perceive. . . .*

William Wordsworth:
Lines Composed a Few Miles
above Tintern Abbey

354

LOMATIUM DISSECTUM ✕½ [p.332]

HERACLEUM LANATUM ✕½ [p.332]

LOMATIUM NUDICAULE ×½ [p.333]

LOMATIUM UTRICULATUM ×⅖ [p.334]

OSMORHIZA CHILENSIS ×½ [p.335]

SANICULA BIPINNATIFIDA ×⅗ [p.336]

MONÓTROPA UNIFLÒRA L. *Indian Pipe. Ghost-plant.* [p.379]

From the Greek monos and tropos, *one direction,* the generic name directs attention to the fact that the single terminal flowers are all bent downward. The specific name, of course, means *single-flowered.* The common names are descriptive of the spectral white of the plants, each like a pallid pipe with the stem stuck in the ground and the bowl turned down, as if against the rain.

Total absence of green colouring matter (chlorophyll) obviously declares the Ghost-plant a saprophyte, i.e. a plant that gets its nourishment from decaying vegetable matter.

Generally occurring in the deepest gloom of dense coniferous forests, the white clustered stems of this remarkable plant excite much interest. The 5-9 inch waxy-white, fleshy stems (which age to black) are clasped by rather spaced, scale-like leaves. The single flower capping each stem nods at first, but becomes erect as the minute seeds develop in the 5-celled superior ovary. Sepals are lacking, but there are 5 (occasionally 4-6) petals—hairy within, smooth without—that form a narrow drooping bell about an inch long, or slightly less. Inside are the stamens—usually 10—with hairy filaments and stubby anthers, and a large, shallow funnel-form stigma—with 5 lobes—that often shows in its pale gold the only touch of colour in the plant. (Very rarely, pale-pinkish, or pale-yellowish plants are seen.)

Two other species of Monotropa are known, from eastern North America and from Asia.

The whiteness of these plants makes them more easily detected, and hence improves the likelihood of their being pollinated by the few flying insects of the heavy-shade forest.

> *A wind sways the pines,*
> *And below*
> *Not a breath of wild air;*
> *Still as the mosses that glow*
> *On the flooring and over the lines*
> *Of the roots here and there.*
>
> George Meredith:
> Dirge in Woods

PTERÓSPORA ANDRÓMEDEA Nutt. *Pinedrops.* [p.375]

This tallest of our saprophytes is named from the Greek pteron, *a wing,* and sporos, *seed,* describing the unusual seed, with its very large, net-like wing at one end. The species is the only member of a genus, which does not occur outside North America. "Andromedea" refers to the Andromeda of Greek legend, daughter of Cepheus and Cassiopeia, rock-chained but rescued from the sea-monster by Perseus.

The curiously impressive, 2-3 foot stalk of Pinedrops is found in deep humus soil of coniferous forests (particularly under Hemlock and Yellow Pine). Though frequently reported from southern Vancouver Island—less commonly from the southern mainland—Pterospora andromedea has not been found in British Columbia north of the Skeena. Yet it occurs in Alaska.

The very sticky stem carries lanceolate, scale-like leaves; crowded at the base, widely-spaced near the top, where 40-60 hanging flowers form a spike-like raceme. The entire plant is yellowish- to reddish-brown, becoming rather harsh and dry, and often enduring through one—or even two—winters.

There are 5 lobes in the deeply-cleft, densely glandular-haired calyx. The corolla is urn-shaped, with 5 small lobes slightly reflexed. Usually tan to yellowish, the flowers are slightly lighter in colour than the dark stem and its modified leaves. There are 10 stamens, each with a pair of curious dagger-like awns projecting downward from the anther. The short straight pistil is topped by a flattened stigma, having a central depression.

This tall, brown, viscid plant is often overlooked, since its colour blends with the forest floor.

Because only a very small proportion of the seeds will encounter the exacting conditions necessary for germination and growth, quite astronomical numbers of seeds are produced. In a shaded forest we recall tapping a mature plant, to watch a bright myriad of the remarkable winged seeds drift through a shaft of sunlight. Beautiful under the microscope, each roundish, roughened brown seed is semi-collared by the diaphanous "sail".

ERICÀCEAE. *Heath Family.*

For winter's rains and ruins are over. . .
And time remembered is grief forgotten,
And frosts are slain and flowers begotten,
And in green underwood and cover
   Blossom by blossom the spring begins.

Algernon Charles Swinburne:
Atalanta in Calydon

Though not among the largest plant families (about 65 genera and approximately 1900 species) the Ericaceae include many plants of great interest and beauty. Notable is the magnificent tribe of about 850 Rhododendrons—centred in Asia (from Yunnan to the eastern Himalayas) but extending through the East Indies to Australia, and also found in Europe and North America. Another tribe is the Heathers, among them the Mediterranean Heather *(Erica arborea)* that attains the dimensions of a tree (whose roots provide wood for briar pipes). Yet another group contains one of our most beautiful trees, *Arbutus menziesii* or Madroño (also Madroña and Madrone), and the lovely Trailing Arbutus or Mayflower (*Epigaea repens*), floral emblem of Nova Scotia and of Massachusetts. Finally there is the large group of *Vacciniums* (Huckleberries and Blueberries), sharply distinguished by an inferior ovary.

Some authorities also include the Pyrola Family (*Pyrolaceae*) and saprophytes of the *Monotropaceae*, chiefly on the basis of a microscopic characteristic—the presence of variously shaped pores in the anther, through which the pollen escapes.

If all these tribes are included, we have a family very heterogeneous—from primitive plants with distinct petals to more advanced ones with petals united, at least at the base.

"Lumping" and "splitting" are tendencies, both of which as extremes are to be deplored. We feel that future study will probably separate the plants with an inferior ovary as *Vaccinaceae*, but probably group the non-chlorophyll genera like *Monotropa*, with *Pyrola* (compare, for instance, the general acceptance of saprophytic members among chlorophyllaceous species of the *Orchidaceae*). However for convenience, in the present treatment we have placed the saprophytes under *Monotropaceae*, other polypetalous plants under *Pyrolaceae*, and all other gamopetalous ericaceous plants, including *Vaccinium*, under *Ericaceae*. This limits *Ericaceae* to trees and medium to very woody shrubs.

The name of the family is derived from the Latin ĕrice, *Heath*, Ling, or Broom.

ANDRÓMEDA POLIFÒLIA L. *Bog Rosemary.*

*Andromeda** was, in Greek mythology, the beautiful daughter of Cepheus and Cassiopeia; the species' name means *many-leaved.*

This is a delicately attractive evergreen plant of mossy bogs, where sphagnum and acid conditions are found. In such habitats Bog Rosemary has been rather sparingly reported from Alaska southward through our area, except in the southeast Interior. It is locally abundant in the Queen Charlotte Islands, but is reported on Vancouver Island only from the extreme northern part. Blooming period is May to August.

The occasionally-branched, erect stems may be 4-30 inches high, with alternate, small leathery leaves that are narrowly-elliptic to linear in shape, and rolled downward at the edges. The lower surface is noticeably whitish. The globe-shaped pink flowers hang from long pedicels, in a small umbel at the end of each branch. The corolla is ¼-⅜ inch long, the mouth of the beautifully shaped urn being slightly flared, and five-lobed. There are 10 stamens, each with a hairy filament, and a curious anther having 2 tiny horns at the top.

Andromeda—like many others of its family—contains andromedotoxin, which lowers the blood pressure and causes breathing difficulties.

*"Andromeda" illustrates Linnaeus' frequent use of classical names. As he wrote, this plant "is always fixed on some little turfy hillock in the midst of the swamps, as Andromeda herself was chained to a rock in the sea, which bathed her feet as the fresh water does the roots of the plant."

ARCTOSTÁPHYLOS. *Bearberry*

The rather long name of this genus does not refer to the Arctic, though some of the species range far north of the Arctic Circle. Rather, arctos means *bear* (in Greek), and staphyle means *bunch of grapes*, hence Bearberry; for the rather tasteless dry berries are, in hard times, a stable source of food for bears.

These are evergreen shrubs, usually prostrate and matted (except for the erect shrubby Manzanita), with small leathery leaves, small pinkish urn-shaped flowers, and black to red, berry-like fruit.

About 45 species are known, nearly all from the west coast of North America (one being circumpolar).

ARCTOSTÁPHYLOS ALPÌNA (L.) Spreng. *Alpine Bearberry.*

This circumpolar species is known in our area only from the high Rockies of Yoho Park, and from the northern third of British Columbia, into Alaska.

It is a prostrate shrub, usually less than 6 inches high, with very noticeably shredded, papery, reddish bark. The thick firm leaves are about 1½ inches long, oval, with the greatest width nearer the tip than the base. The edges are round-toothed, the veins conspicuous. The very narrow urn-shaped flowers are pinkish, and less than ¼ inch long. The fruit is a purplish-black, drupe-like berry (containing 5 stony nutlets).

Subspecies RÙBRA (Rehd. & Wils.) Hult. is a little taller, with thinner leaves and   [p.375]
red fruits.

This is a plant of the barren peaty soil of tundra, or of alpine habitats, where it may be found in flower from May to July.

ARCTOSTÁPHYLOS COLUMBIÀNA Piper. *Manzanita.*   [p.378]

The name suggests this is a Columbian Bearberry, but it is vastly different in character from the other Bearberries. Manzanita (a Spanish name, meaning *small apples*, in allusion to the appearance of the small brown fruits) is a striking ornamental shrub to small tree. (We have seen specimens 14 feet high, with veritable trunks 6 inches in diameter.)

Its stems and branches, clothed with paper-smooth mahogany-red bark, are grotesquely branched and angled. The masses of foliage are curiously grey-green, due to a mat of grey hairs on both surfaces. The typically ericaceous, urn-shaped, pink flowers appear from May to July, and are succeeded by persistent, berry-like fruits of a unique coffee-colour.

This is a most attractive shrub of very dry, rocky outcrops, where the soil is slightly acid. When such conditions can be provided in the garden, the Manzanita can be successfully transplanted at an early age, becoming in time a choice specimen plant.

In our area A. columbiana is found on southern Vancouver Island and adjacent Gulf Islands, and on the mainland from Vancouver southward, on the western slopes of the Cascades.

ARCTOSTÁPHYLOS ÙVA-ÚRSI (L.) Spreng. *Bearberry. Kinnikinnick.*   [p.386]

Uva-ursi repeats (in Latin) the meaning of the generic name (from the Greek roots arktos, *a bear*, and staphyle, *a bunch of grapes*), so we have, literally, agreement in three languages that this is Bear-berry. The other common name is rather obscure in origin, though Haskin suggests it is of Asiatic (Indian) origin meaning mixture, that it refers to smoking mixtures, and that early fur-traders probably used Kinnikinnick to make their precious tobacco last longer. Ericolin and arbutin (both glycosides) and considerable tannin are found in the leaves and berries.

This evergreen mat-like shrub is in our area both ubiquitous and highly ornamental. It is abundant on rocky outcrops, as well as the dry floor of open woods, throughout British Columbia and indeed much further—from Labrador to Alaska, southward to the latitude of New Mexico, and also in Eurasia.

A. uva-ursi characteristically forms dense mats, sometimes many feet in diameter. The bark on the long, trailing stems is dark-brown, and somewhat shredded. The brilliant red berries, cupped by persistent, five-cleft green calyx-lobes at their bases, may be nearly ½ inch in diameter. The berries are edible, though dry and mealy. Usually the small leathery leaves are less than 1 inch long, and are generally obovate, and blunt to rounded at their tips.

Though the typical form of A. uva-ursi is easily recognized, the species produces rather puzzling hybrids, both with *A. columbiana* (which see), and with the more southern species *A. nevadensis*. The hybrids have been given various specific names (e.g. [p.386] x ARCTOSTÁPHYLOS MÈDIA Greene, which is illustrated). They are taller and more erect (to 2 feet or even more), with greyer foliage than true Kinnikinnick. Many of the forms make good garden shrubs, but none have berries of quite the brilliant vermilion displayed by true dwarf A. uva-ursi. This must rank as exceptional, among good ground covers available to the gardener.

Arctostaphylos uva-ursi would be more highly esteemed, were it not for the curious perversity that so often leads us to value a plant less, the more abundant and the better-natured it may be.

CASSÌOPE LYCOPODIOÌDES (Pall.) D. Don. *Clubmoss Mountain Heather.*

The name is from Greek mythology, Cassiopeia being the mother of Andromeda. The genus consists of 11 or 12 species of the North Temperate and Arctic zones. They are dwarf creeping shrubs, heather-like in appearance. The 4 species occurring in our area have small white (rarely pink-tinged) flowers that are more or less campanulate (bell-shaped).

The specific name means *lycopodium-like*, i.e. resembling the Lycopodiums or Clubmosses, hence the common name, which also contains a reference to the usual habitat of this dwarf plant.

Clubmoss Mountain Heather, though reported from only a few locations (on thin peat-soil) in the northern half of British Columbia, is probably less rare than the record of collections might indicate, for it is readily confused with the common *C. mertensiana* (which see).

Both are evergreen, nearly prostrate, shrubby plants with white bell-shaped flowers. Both are found in acid peaty soil of alpine slopes and crevices.

Close examination reveals the tiny scale-like leaves of the present species are irregularly ranged along the stems which are only about $1/16$ inch wide, whereas in *C. mertensiana* the stems are about $1/8$ inch wide, and the leaves are arranged in 4 distinct rows.

CASSÌOPE MERTENSIÀNA (Bong.) G. Don. *White Moss Heath. White Heather.* [p.386]

Cassiopeia was the wife of Cepheus, King of the Ethiopians. In Greek legend, her daughter was that Andromeda who was chained to the sea-rock, and rescued by Perscus. F. C. Mertens, 1764-1831, was a German botanist. The binomial requires considerable accommodation in time and ideology, but by any name this is a beautiful plant of the high mountains. White it is, a sparkling crisp white against creeping deep green stems. But this is not a true Heather (*Calluna*, or *Erica*). It is probably didactic to insist on Moss Heath, since in every alpine area of North America this plant is familiar as "White Heather".

This exceedingly common evergreen plant sprawls over rocks from timber line upward. Its growth is very slow at high altitudes, and the heather covering the boulder on which one rests, may represent the growth of 15-20 years.

The tough stems, about $1/8$ inch wide, are shingled with 4 ranks of overlapping, scale-like leaves. The snowy bells droop from slender pedicels arising near the tip of each branch. The ovate sepals are reddish, providing an effective accent for the cool white of the campanulate corollas.

Cassiope mertensiana is one of the plants inseparably associated in the mind of the hiker with unforgettable days on rock and snow, often high above the tree-line.

How divine,
The liberty, for frail, for mortal, man
To roam at large among unpeopled glens
And mountainous retirements, only trod

OENANTHE SARMENTOSA ×½ [p.335]

PERIDERIDIA GAIRDNERI ×⅖ [p.336]

SIUM SUAVE ×⅖ [p.337]

PYROLA VIRENS ×⅗ [p.349]

363

SANICULA CRASSICAULIS ×1 [p.337]

SANICULA GRAVEOLENS ×1 [p.337]

CORNUS CANADENSIS ×1 [p.340]

By devious footsteps; regions consecrate
To oldest time!

William Wordsworth:
The Excursion, Bk. IV

CASSÌOPE TETRAGÒNA (L.) D. Don. *White Mountain Heather.*

Tetragona means *four-angled*, referring to the orderly arrangement of the opposite pairs of tiny ovate leaves in 4 ranks.

The leaves are further distinguished from those of other white-flowered "Heathers" by the presence of a deep groove running the length of the lower surface. (*C. mertensiana* also has its leaves arranged in 4 ranks, but its scale-like leaves lack this characteristic groove).

This and *C. mertensiana* are the tallest of the white "Heathers", growing to about 12 inches. The leaves are tightly pressed to the stems, and the campanulate flowers hang downward in twos and threes from near the ends of each branchlet.

C. tetragona does not occur along the coast, but is found chiefly on mountains of the northern, southwestern, and southeastern Interior.

CHIMÁPHILA UMBELLÀTA (L.) Bart. var. OCCIDENTÀLIS (Rydb.) Blake. *Pipsissewa. Prince's Pine.* [p.390]

This rather pleasant-sounding name was derived by Pursh from the Greek cheima, *winter,* and philos, *loving,* so Chimaphila is nicely descriptive of these evergreen plants, whose sturdy foliage positively revels in rain or even snow.

The specific name refers to the occurrence of the striking flowers in loose semi-*umbels.* Occidentalis, of course, refers to the *western* form, found in dimly-lit coniferous forests from Alaska to California.

The odd pinkish flowers nod, each at the end of a short curved peduncle, from a smooth stem rising 4-12 inches above leaves that are arranged in one or two whorls. These leaves are an arresting feature of the plant: 1-3 inches long, narrowly obovate (i.e. having their greatest diameter nearer the tip than the base), thick, wax-glossed, and conspicuously saw-toothed. They immediately catch the eye, for there are no other leaves on the forest floor remotely like them.

Turn upward the 5-petalled inch-wide flower, and you will see that the 10 curious stamens radiate, like the spokes of a wheel, about the huge hub of the fat green ovary, capped by its sticky flat stigma.

The only insect visitors we have seen are small species of flies, though possibly at night moths come to the pale blooms, which have a pleasant faint perfume.

C. umbellata attracts much attention from those who would introduce it to their gardens, but such enthusiasts should be warned that its running rootstocks have only occasional feeding-roots, so do not respond at all kindly to transplanting.

"Pipsissewa", is an adaptation of the Cree name for the plant—pipisisikweu; the name has a charming euphony quite fitting for this curiously attractive plant. The leaves were used as a substitute for tea by both natives and early pioneers. Frequent companions through the summer are the Dwarf Dogwood (one of whose leaves appears in the illustration) and the Teaberry.

CHIMÁPHILA MENZIÈSII (R. Br.) Spreng. is a smaller plant with darker green, [p.387] less waxy, elliptical, and smaller leaves. Flowers are usually solitary, though occasionally 2 or 3 form a small umbel. Petals are usually creamy-white, sometimes pinkish. At Buttle Lake this beautiful little plant occurs with *C. umbellata*, both being in bloom in early July.

CLADOTHÁMNUS PYROLAEFLÒRUS Bong. *Copper Bush.* [p.378]

This unusual-flowered shrub derives its name from klados, *sprout*, or branch, and thamnos, *bush*. Pyrolaeflorus means *Pyrola-flowered*, because of the very long and conspicuous bent pistil that is also characteristic of members of that genus. The 5-petalled flowers are unique in colour, a kind of pale copper.

This is a monotypic genus. Cladothamnus is a 2-7 foot shrub of cool, shaded, subalpine forests and stream-banks from Alaska south, to the west of the Cascades. It is abundant right up to timber line on the Queen Charlottes, Vancouver Island, and the Coastal Range.

The deciduous leaves are notably pale green, glabrous, sometimes slightly glaucous (waxy). They are oblanceolate (with the greatest width nearer the tip than the base) and un-notched. The 5 sepals become progressively reflexed and larger as the ovary ripens, ultimately resembling small leaves. The solitary flowers are 1-1½ inches across, borne at the ends of branchlets. Stamens usually number 10, but the flower is dominated by the exceptionally large curved style, which is swollen just below the stigma.

Copper Bush is an attractive and unusual shrub.

GAULTHÈRIA OVATIFÒLIA Gray. *Western Tea-berry.* [p.391]

This flat-growing plant is smaller in all its parts, but is clearly related to *G. shallon* (which see). It is, however, restrained in its growth, and a most attractive subject for the garden. The specific name describes the shape of the 1-1½ inch, glossy and firm-textured leaves. These are paler beneath, with finely saw-toothed margins.

Small pink campanulate flowers, with flared corolla-lobes appear singly in the axils of the leaves. Though the corolla is glabrous, the calyx is covered with reddish-brown hairs. The flowers are succeeded by highly ornamental bright-red berries.

CORNUS CANADENSIS (FRUIT)   ×1⅖   [p.340]

370

MONESES UNIFLORA ×1 [p.345]

CORNUS STOLONIFERA var. OCCIDENTALIS (FRUIT) ×⅗ [p.344]

PYROLA PICTA ✕⅗ [p.348]

PYROLA SECUNDA ✕½ [p.348]

371

PYROLA ASARIFOLIA ✕⅗ [p.346]

However, we have observed that many—perhaps all—of the anthers so released have not yet dehisced, i.e. have not yet ripened sufficiently to liberate pollen through the minute longitudinal slits. It may be that the anthers are tucked in their pockets while the stigma of the same blossom is receptive, so that the arrangement is designed to prevent self-pollination. This is an interesting problem that probably requires more careful study.

There are conflicting reports on the reputed toxicity of honey derived from the nectar of these flowers. There is no doubt that the leaves and flowers contain andromedotoxin, a compound poisonous to cattle and sheep. However, Kalmia is very seldom grazed by animals when any other plants are available.

The structure of these remarkable flowers is quite fascinating.

"The standing objection to botany has always been, that it is a pursuit that amuses the fancy and exercises the memory without improving the mind or advancing any real knowledge; and where the science is carried no farther than a mere systematic classification, the charge is but too true. But the botanist that is desirous of wiping off this aspersion should be by no means content with a list of names; he should study plants philosophically, should investigate the laws of vegetation, should examine the powers and virtues of efficacious herbs, should promote their cultivation, and graft the gardener, the planter, and the husbandman, on the phytologist. Not that system is by any means to be thrown aside, without system the field of Nature would be a pathless wilderness; but system should be subservient to, not the main object of, pursuit."

Gilbert White:
The Natural History of Selborne.
Letter XL, June 2, 1778 (the same
year in which the great Linnaeus died)

LÈDUM PALÚSTRE L. ssp. GROENLÁNDICUM (Oeder) Hult. *Labrador Tea.* [p.399]

The generic name comes from ledon (*matrix*) the Greek name for a rock plant now known as *Cistus ledum*, whose foliage resembles that of our 2 species. Ledum groenlandicum is found, as might be anticipated from the subspecific name, from *Greenland* to Alaska, and southward in cold bogs and swamps (paluster = *swampy*) along the Pacific coast and inland.

This beautiful and intriguing shrub grows to a height of 1-4 feet. The remarkable evergreen leaves are carried alternately up the curiously bent stems, often appearing bunched and whorled upward. The leaves alone will identify the plant. Dotted with resinous glands, they are long-elliptical, dark glossy green above, thick and leathery, and have downward-rolled edges and extraordinary rusty-woolly lower surfaces. Such unusual leaves must have attracted the attention of the earliest "Americans", for the first explorers found the natives were making a kind of tea from an infusion of the dried and crushed foliage. Among the coureurs de bois it was common practice to extend, with this substance, their diminishing supply of precious tea.

The numerous white flowers appear in May, June or July, in showy terminal corymbs. They are about ½ inch wide, with (generally) 5 petals, and usually 5-8 long stamens, that rise like rocket-trails from the centre of each bloom.

LÈDUM GLANDULÒSUM Nutt. is very similar, except that the rusty-woolliness of the under sides of the broader, ovate leaves has been replaced with a whitish or greyish, mealy covering of numerous aromatic glands. The edges are only slightly, or not at all revolute (rolled downward). Flowers are almost identical with those of *L. groenlandicum* (which see), but nearly always have 10 stamens. The habitat is rather drier and more montane than that favoured by *L. palustre* ssp. *groenlandicum*, generally east of the Coastal Range. However, the ranges of the 2 plants overlap.

LÈDUM PALÚSTRE L. ssp. DECÚMBENS (Ait.) Hult., like subspecies *groenlandicum*, has strongly revolute leaves that are densely covered below with cinnamon-woolliness, but are much narrower (linear). Stamens usually number 10 and are hooked or curved at maturity. This is a dwarfed northern species, with the Cassiar Mountains as a southern limit. Here it is extremely common on mountain heaths and dry rocky places.

Ledol, a toxic compound that can induce cramps and paralysis, has been isolated from the leaves of all of the Ledum species. Possibly in the low concentrations of the pioneers' brew, this substance may have produced restorative effects similar to those resulting from caffeine in tea.

The attractive and aromatic Ledums make interesting accent-plants in wet parts of the rock garden. They are sometimes mistaken for small Rhododendrons.

Professors Warren and Delavault, by atomic absorption of ashed roots and stems of certain plants, have been able to detect underlying ore-bodies. Thus they have found that *Ledum groenlandicum* growing near known zinc-copper ore-bodies shows significantly high concentrations of the elements. The same researchers also found that ash of Fireweed *(Epilobium angustifolium)* growing above what was later to become the Endako open-pit operation averaged 17,000 parts per million of molybdenum, compared to 50-100 p.p.m. in ash of the same species growing in adjacent areas.

LOISELEÙRIA PROCÚMBENS (L.) Desv. *Alpine Azalea.* [p.399]

This modest mountain gem recalls the name of J. L. A. Loiseleur-Deslongchamps, 1774-1849, Parisian physician and botanist. Procumbens (meaning *trailing*) is the only member of this genus. Its dainty pink bells, above dwarf mats of tiny leaves, may be

Following page: ALLOTROPA VIRGATA ×1¼ [p.349]

HEMITOMES CONGESTUM ×1 [p.352]

ARCTOSTAPHYLOS ALPINA SSP. RUBRA ×1 [p.359]

PTEROSPORA ANDROMEDEA ×⅖ [p.356]

found high in the mountains of North America (from California to Alaska), and of Russia, Norway, and (very rarely) of the Scottish Highlands. Alpine Azalea has been found on many mountains in British Columbia, but in the Queen Charlottes, as well as near Prince Rupert, it descends to sea level bogs.

Rarely as much as 8 inches high, the wiry stems are densely clothed with smooth and leathery, entire-margined leaves only ¼ inch long. The edges are slightly revolute (rolled back); the lower surface pale and the upper dark green. Branchlets end in little clusters of bright pink (rarely, white) bells having 5-pointed lobes. There are 5 stamens, that are slightly longer than the club-topped pistil.

Softwood cuttings of this delightful rock garden subject can be rooted in sand in June.

MENZIÈSIA FERRUGÍNEA Smith. *False Azalea.*   [p.387]

The generic name honours Archibald Menzies, 1754-1842, physician-botanist with Capt. George Vancouver in his northwest explorations at the end of the 18th century. The specific name describes the *rusty* glands that cover the branches, pedicels, calyxes, and (variably) the leaves. The leaves quite closely resemble those of such garden Azaleas as *Rhododendron molle* and its hybrids. The flower, however, is a relatively inconspicuous, copper-coloured bell scarcely ½ inch long.

This is nevertheless quite an attractive shrub, particularly in autumn, when its 2½-inch, elliptical, serrate leaves display brilliant orange and crimson. It is open in growth, and reaches 6 feet in height. The very light-green leaves make the shrub easy to detect among the crowded shrubs of moist woods and mountain streambanks. It is abundant along the coast, and var. GLABÉLLA (Gray) Peck (with less glandular branches and less pointed leaves) occurs in the southeast corner of our area.

False Azalea usually has 4 calyx-lobes that are conspicuously glandular and often notched. There are 8 stamens, which do not project beyond the corolla-mouth. Fruit is an ovoid capsule.

PHYLLÓDOCE EMPETRIFÓRMIS (Smith) D. Don. *Red Mountain Heather.*   [p.399]

Phyllodoce (mellifluous name!) was a sea-nymph in early Greek mythology. Empetriformis means the leaves resemble those of *Empetrum* (*nigrum*, which see). As with *Cassiope mertensiana* (which see), it is probably idle to point out that this is not a true Heather (*Erica*, or *Calluna*). Since the time of the early explorers of our mountains, this abundant rose-coloured Heath has always been called "Red Heather".

These cheerful bells ring an invitation to high places above the timber line, to those serene and lofty slopes where peace and quiet enter our souls. Here Phyllodoce cushions the rocks with its wiry stems, that are closely ranked with persistent, stiff, needle-leaves. These are deeply grooved on the under side.

Branchlets end in a cluster of gracefully curved pedicels, each supporting a nodding, beautifully sculptured, rose-pink bell. The pedicels are reddish and covered with very short glandular hairs, particularly noticeable in an otherwise glabrous plant. The calyx-cup is 5-lobed almost to the base, and dark-red, with an intensity of colour that beautifully complements the paler hue of the corolla. Corolla-lobes roll downward within a few hours of the bud's opening. The bell-clapper is the long, projecting pistil.

The hiker or climber, who puts aside his pack-sack or pack-frame, to watch the cirrus overhead and deeply breathe the tonic air, knows well the subtle perfume of Phyllodoce.

One occasionally sees a much paler form, which in small patches (as in some parts of the Forbidden Plateau on Vancouver Island) may outnumber the usual, deep rose-coloured flowers. Very rarely an albino form is encountered. These rarities should be left, to endure where others may come to see them, for the plants seldom survive transplanting to the garden, and even if they linger, make almost no growth, and few flowers. (The very skilful may attempt to root short cuttings.)

PHYLLÓDOCE GLANDULIFLÒRA (Hook.) Coville, is a very dwarf species of [p.402] even higher altitudes (6000-10,000 feet). It is sometimes called Yellow Heather, but the curiously puckered bells are yellowish-green, so much like the foliage-colour that they are often overlooked. Glandular hairs covering the calyx and lower part of corolla are responsible for the specific name. Leaves are shorter, and broader than those of its cousin (*P. empetriformis,* which see), and very tightly compressed toward the tips of the short tough branchlets. At the inter-zones between the 2 species, one should be alert for not-infrequent hybrids, which have been called x PHYLLÓDOCE INTERMÈDIA (Hook.) Camp. They are very interesting, for one can find all degrees of transition between the wide-open rose cup of the one parent, and the tightly constricted, yellowish-green, urn-shaped flower of the other.

RHODODÉNDRON ALBIFLÒRUM Hook. *White Rhododendron.* [p.402]

Rhododendron is a magnificent genus, among whose 600-900 species and host of hybrid cultivars, are numbered many of the most prized of our garden shrubs. The late Frank Kingdon-Ward introduced many splendid species from the mountains of Burma, Assam, China, and Tibet: apparently eastern Asia is the epicentre of the genus, where bush, tree, tiny rock-inhabiting dwarfs, and even tree-dwelling epiphytic Rhododendrons, are found in great variety. The name is derived from the Greek rhodon, a *rose,* and dendron, a *tree,* though the range of colours is complete, including white, blue, purple, a host of pinks and reds, and even yellow and orange.

This is a *white-*or cream-*flowered* species, abundant in the mountains of our area, usually above 4000 feet, but descending on the West Coast of Vancouver Island (as at Muchalat Inlet) to about 800 feet. Surprisingly, it appears to be absent from the Queen Charlotte Islands. On Strata Mountain and Mt. Brooks (Forbidden Plateau), we have seen healthy and floriferous bushes growing on the limestone. This is somewhat remarkable, as Rhododendrons are known to favour acid soil. A possible explanation is

378

ARCTOSTAPHYLOS COLUMBIANA ×⅗ [p.359]

CLADOTHAMNUS PYROLAEFLORUS ×½ [p.365]

HYPOPITYS MONOTROPA ×1⅕ [p.353]

that the roots of these specimens are limited to the thin layer of duff that covers the limestone, and the duff (formed from decaying leaves) may itself be slightly acid. It is of some interest that a few of these plants showed a unique orange-yellow flush at the base of each petal.

Little description is required, for the species is very easily recognized. It is the only deciduous member of the 3 Rhododendrons occurring in British Columbia. The 2-3 elliptical leaves turn spectacular shades of bronze, orange, and crimson at the early approach of alpine snow. Branches are 2-6 feet high, with reddish hairs, and terminal (as well as axillary) saucer-shaped blooms that are ¾-1 inch wide. The 10 stamens have filaments thickly hairy on the lower half.

White Rhododendron is a memorable feature of mountain woods and open slopes, at or near the tree-line.

> We need the tonic of wildness. . . . We can never have enough of
> Nature. We must be refreshed by the sight of inexhaustible vigor, vast
> and Titanic. . . the wilderness with its living and its decaying trees,
> the thunder cloud, and the rain which lasts three weeks and produces
> freshets. We need to witness our own limits transgressed, and some
> life pasturing freely where we never wander.
>
> Henry David Thoreau: *Walden*

RHODODÉNDRON LAPPÓNICUM (L.) Wahlen. *Lapland Rosebay.* [p.402]

As pointed out by Mr. Eric H. Garman, in his valuable *Pocket Guide to the Trees and Shrubs in British Columbia*, this northern member of a normally acid-loving genus often occurs on limestone and dolomite. Dr. Szczawinski mentions its abundance around Muncho Lake and Summit Pass on the Alaska Highway, in both wet and dry habitats. Where it occurs on alpine barrens and stony heaths the soil condition is almost certainly acid. As the specific name suggests, this far-ranging species was originally described from *Lapland,* and it is also found in Russia, Greenland, and Alaska.

R. lapponicum is a very much smaller plant than our other two species, its compact and matted branches often 2 inches high, and almost never exceeding 12 inches. Close-ranked ½-1 inch leaves are oblong-elliptic; they are dark-green with rust-coloured scales (especially beneath). From 1-5 bright purple flowers appear at the ends of the short thick branchlets. They are about ½ inch across, and usually have 7-8 stamens. The resin-dotted and hairy calyx appears disproportionately small for the corolla.

Preceding page: MONOTROPA UNIFLORA   ×1⅘   [p.356]

RHODODÉNDRON MACROPHÝLLUM G. Don. *Pink Rhododendron. California Rhododendron.* [p.403]

Under conditions that permit development of a compact 4-6 foot bush, this species must rank, with the taller Flowering Dogwood, among the finest of our native shrubs. Such plants, when covered with great trusses of large pink blooms from late May to early July (depending upon altitude) can only be described as magnificent. We have seen one of several stations on southern Vancouver Island, where lack of light, and competition by conifers enclosing the wet pockets of acid soil, have combined to produce straggly branches at least 15 feet tall. Here bloom is rather sparse, and to our eyes, rather poor in colour. But along the highway in Manning Park, and into the threatened Skagit Valley, may be seen hundreds of rounded bushes bearing superb flowers. With much variation between pink and deep rose, and deeper or lighter spotting in the throat, the beautiful shrubs in some of these areas would lead the viewer to imagine himself in one of the great rhododendron gardens of the world. Even pure white albino forms have been reported.

Macrophyllum refers to the *large leaves*, which form handsome whorls to set off the spectacular flower-clusters. These shining leaves are leathery and evergreen, elliptic-oblong, and about 5 inches long. The deeply 5-lobed, campanulate corollas measure 1-2 inches across. There are 10 stamens of unequal length, with filaments that bear curious short fleshy hairs on the lower half. The reddish-brown anthers form striking accents in the rosy corollas.

Attempts to move to lowland gardens its relative, *R. albiflorum* (which see), are resented completely and with finality, but the present species is good-natured in lightly shaded parts of the garden. A friend reports good success from seed obtained (in September) from the woody inch-long capsules. However one needs, to enjoy bloom from the seedlings, patience requisite for about 7 year's anticipation. Many nurseries carry stocks of thrifty young plants that have been obtained by layering, or from cuttings—and this should be the gardener's source of supply. On no account should one dig up the wild plants. Aside from the potential hazard to a lovely native species of very limited distribution, such practice is contrary to law, for Rhododendron macrophyllum is protected by provincial statute.

VACCÍNIUM L. *Blueberry. Huckleberry. Bilberry. Cranberry. Whortleberry.*

The abundance of common names is perhaps an indication of the fact that the many species have been long known, and familiar in many regions of the English-speaking world. The Latin name is an ancient one, apparently applied to some berried shrub, which was browsed by cattle (from which the name may have derived, vacca meaning *cow*). About 200 low to tall shrubs of cold areas in the mountains of the world (except those of Australia) have been classified in this genus.

The common names in English are rather interesting. Huckleberry is an odd word; it is a corruption of the old Whortleberry, which was derived from the Anglo-Saxon wyrtil, a small shrub, which in turn is the diminutive of wyrt, or wort, that has survived in such names as Bladderwort, Butterwort, Glasswort, St. John's Wort, and many more. Bilberry (or in northern England and Scotland, Blaeberry) derives from Scandinavian roots: Danish Böllebaer, Ball-berry, and Swedish Blåbär, Blue-berry.

All Vacciniums produce many-seeded berries—blue, black, or red—that are usually of pleasant flavour. Hikers in the wet coastal or mountain regions of British Columbia are familiar with the succulent fruit of many of our 14 species. All Vacciniums have simple, alternate leaves that are deciduous, except in the evergreen, coastal species *V. ovatum* (which see), and the persistent-leaved, trailing *V. oxycoccos* (which see). All have 8-10 anthers, and a bell-shaped pink to whitish corolla, which is often 5-lobed; all are distinguished by an inferior ovary i.e. an ovary placed beneath the corolla.

The native Vacciniums are attractive and willing subjects in the garden. Perhaps the most valuable species is *V. ovatum*, with handsome evergreen leaves, numerous pretty pink flowers in spring, and blue-black berries in the fall.

"Fri. 31st July—At 5 Easterly wind and cold, plenty of whurtle Berries, Rasberries, and a berry called Poire, which grows in the greatest abundances along the Bank [of the Mackenzie River], we are much impeded in our march by Banks of Sand and small Stones, which rinders the water shallow at a distance from the shore."

Original Journal of Alexander Mackenzie (1789)

VACCÍNIUM ALASKAÉNSE Howell. *Alaska Blueberry.* [p.410]

This medium-sized bush (generally under 4 feet tall) has not been reported east of the Selkirk Range, but is of sporadic occurrence in northern British Columbia, and is abundant along the Coast, particularly of the Queen Charlottes, Vancouver Island, and *Alaska.* It grows on acid humus in wet coniferous forests.

The species is rather difficult to distinguish from *V. ovalifolium* (which see). The bronzy- to pinkish-green corolla-tubes are much pinched at the mouth, and the shallow rounded lobes do not reflex. The flowers occur singly in the leaf-axils, on ½-inch, nearly straight pedicels that are distinctively swollen, or enlarged, just below the ovaries. Leaves are egg-shaped, entire (or very slightly serrulate), and as much as 1¼ inches long. When mature they are dark-green and slightly waxy (glaucous) above, but paler below. Young twigs are slightly-angled and often yellowish-green, though sometimes reddish. The pistil in most forms protrudes distinctly beyond the corolla-mouth, but this is not invariable and frequently (as is the usual case with *V. ovalifolium*) it barely reaches the corolla-mouth.

The berry varies from bluish-black and slightly glaucous, to purplish-black and non-glaucous (i.e. with no "bloom"). A favourite with hikers and campers, the ¼-⅜ inch berries are well-flavoured.

VACCÍNIUM CAESPITÒSUM Michx. *Dwarf Blueberry. Dwarf Bilberry.* [p.410]

Caespitosum means *tufted.* This tiny shrub of high rock-ridges and swamp-edges down to sea level, is common throughout the Province. We have seen plants 1 inch high, with 1 or 2 small but deliciously sweet, blue berries.

In better soil Dwarf Bilberry may reach 6-8 inches, but the leaves (notched from tip to half-length) remain small—usually an inch long or less—and nearly always obovate. The little pink 5-lobed flowers are borne singly, on short pedicels arising from the axils of the leaves. They are bell-shaped, but slimmer in outline than those of our other Vacciniums.

Perhaps the best recognition feature at any season of the year is the mat-like habit, due to the spreading of the plant by means of running rootstocks. The twigs are usually somewhat angled, and are characteristically yellowish-green, with one or more sides distinctly reddish.

VACCÍNIUM MEMBRANÀCEUM Dougl. *Black Huckleberry. Mountain Bilberry.* [p.410]

The specific name of this tall Vaccinium, widely distributed on all our mountain slopes, calls attention to the *thin,* rather large leaves. This shrub's large black berries are considered, by general consent among hikers in the mountains, the most delicious of all. Bears and birds may be less discriminating, but are also enthusiastic about this abundant, sweet, and tangy fruit.

The 3-8 foot branches are rather open, and spreading. Somewhat angled, they are generally yellow-green and bear 2-inch, ovate leaves with attenuated sharp tips. Margins are minutely notched, pedicels very short, and surfaces not lustrous but paler beneath. Single creamy flowers (pink-flushed toward the small, reflexed lobes) are very soon replaced by greenish berries that increase to almost ½ inch in diameter. They are then nearly round, deep purplish-black, and lack the paler bluish bloom that is noticeable with most of our other species.

VACCÍNIUM MYRTILLOÌDES Michx. (= V. CANADÉNSE Kalm.) *Velvet-leaf Blueberry. Canada Blueberry.* [p.403]

Widely distributed through the Southeastern and Central Interior Zones east of the Cascades, this low bush of open and rocky woods and dry bogs bears very heavy crops of clustered blueberries. These berries are heavily covered with a bloom of pale blue, in striking contrast to the prominent black "crown" of persistent calyx-teeth. These distinctive berries make an excellent field guide to the Canada Blueberry.

Velvet-leaf Blueberry is further distinguished by the thick covering of the fine short hairs on the young twigs and the leaves. Leaves (*like those of the Myrtle*) are rather large (up to 1¾ inches long), elliptical to pointed-lanceolate, and without teeth. The whitish flowers (with pink corolla-lobes) appear in clusters of 3-6, before the leaves have fully expanded. The open corolla-tube is not at all pinched inward at its mouth, and is sharply 5-lobed.

VACCÍNIUM OVALIFÒLIUM Smith. *Oval-leaved Blueberry. Blue Huckleberry.* [p.411]

This tall Blueberry is abundant on Vancouver Island and the Queen Charlottes, and on the southern Mainland Coast. It extends up the Fraser and the Skeena valleys, but is not found again—and then only sparingly—until east of the Cascades. It is most easily recognized by its *egg-shaped leaves* (ovalifolium) and by its angular and grooved, smooth, reddish twigs.

This species gets a very early start. On the Forbidden Plateau it is usual to see the pale, pink flowers while the base of the shrub is still a foot deep in snow, and the leaves are just beginning to expand. The open bushes are usually 2-4 feet tall, but this is more than doubled in the lush wet areas of the West Coast of Vancouver Island.

The blue-black fruit is usually dusted with pale-bluish bloom. It is ¼ inch in diameter (or a little larger) and of pleasant flavour. Leaves are thin, less than 2 inches long, and entire-margined except for barely perceptible serrulations usually limited to the basal half. The single urn-shaped, 5-lobed flowers are generally somewhat less broad than long, and the style does not project beyond the corolla-mouth.

A sinister outcome of pollution of roadside vegetation has come to light as a result of analyzing the plants, by means of highly sensitive methods developed by Dr. Warren and Dr. Delavault at the University of British Columbia. In oven-dried fodder samples, (collected 840 feet from the intersection of two highways in Richmond) analyses for lead showed 545 and 5560 parts per million. Overall experience quoted by the researchers "would suggest that fodder with lead values above 100 p.p.m. dry weight might be regarded with suspicion." Other evidence reveals that part of such roadside contamination is due to lead tetraethyl present in automobile exhausts. Since lead is known to be a cumulative poison in cattle and man, the conclusion is inescapable that milk or beef from cattle fed rough hay from highway margins must be considered dangerous.

VACCÍNIUM OVÀTUM Pursh. *Evergreen Huckleberry. Shot-berry.* [p.410]

This beautiful evergreen shrub is the most distinct of our taller Vacciniums, and the most easily recognizable. Its range is nearly limited to Vancouver Island, for it does not occur on the Queen Charlottes, and its only mainland locations are near Prince Rupert, and near Vancouver.

Its ornamental foliage—unfortunately for its survival in accessible areas—is valued by florists, so that it is shipped to local (and particularly to eastern) markets by the ton. Hence, though formerly abundant near Victoria and Vancouver, Shot-berry is seldom seen close to these cities today, except in private grounds or parks. This is a very fine garden shrub, valuable in every season for its neat habit and attractive evergreen leaves. It is additionally appreciated in spring for its abundant clusters of pretty pink flowers, and in autumn for its numerous small dark berries. Perhaps the surest way to obtain a plant for the garden is to pull away, in March, or else in September, one of the outermost stems of a wild plant, being careful to see that a few fibrous roots remain attached. Pruned back and planted in moist soil with filtered sunlight, the plant can be counted upon to establish itself within a year. (Or, new-wood cuttings can be taken in July and plunged into sand-peat mixture.)

This very handsome shrub is so easily recognized that no detailed description is needed. The very firm, thick leaves are seldom more than an inch long, and pointed-*ovate* (whence the specific name ovatum). They have neatly saw-toothed margins and are dark glossy green above, paler beneath. They grow alternately along the twigs in a distinctively flat arrangement. The urn-shaped flowers appear in groups of as many as 10 (in the axils of the leaves toward the ends of the branches). They are unusual in shape, being broad-mouthed and not at all puckered. The fruit resembles black shot, and is pleasantly acid. Though small, it was so abundant that it was formerly much used by the southern Coastal tribes.

"Primitive nature is the most interesting to me. I take infinite
pains to know all the phenomena of spring, for instance, thinking that
I have here the entire poem, and then, to my chagrin, I hear that it is
but an imperfect copy that I possess and have read, that my ancestors
have torn out many of the first leaves and grandest passages, and
mutilated it in many places. I should not like to think that some
demigod had come before me and picked out some of the best of the
stars. I wish to know an entire heaven and an entire earth."

Henry David Thoreau:
(March 23, 1856)
Early Spring in Massachusetts

ARCTOSTAPHYLOS MEDIA ×½ [p.360]

ARCTOSTAPHYLOS UVA-URSI ×1¾ [p.360]

ARCTOSTAPHYLOS UVA-URSI (FRUIT) ×⅗ [p.360]

CASSIOPE MERTENSIANA ×1¼ [p.361]

CHIMAPHILA MENZIESII ✕³/₅ [p.365]

GAULTHERIA SHALLON ✕²/₅ [p.368]

GAULTHERIA SHALLON (FRUIT) ✕⁴/₅ [p.368]

MENZIESIA FERRUGINEA ✕⁴/₅ [p.376]

VACCINIUM OXYCÓCCOS L. var. INTERMÈDIUM Gray. *Bog Cranberry.*   [p.414]

Though we have followed Hitchcock et al., and (substantially) Calder and Taylor, in this nomenclature, a number of authorities (e.g. Szczawinski, Hultén) place this species in the genus *Oxycoccus.* Certainly it is very different in some structural details, and in growth characteristics, from the other shrubby Vacciniums. This one is a tiny creeping trailer of sphagnum bogs. Oxycoccos from the Greek oxys, and kokkos, means *bitter-berried,* with reference to the tart taste of the numerous, relatively large, round, white and red fruits. Cranberry was originally Crane-berry (and German Kranbeere), apparently (according to Webster) from a fanciful notion that its long, curved fruit-stalk (pedicel) resembles the neck of a crane. (Linnaeus used a Latin transliteration "oxycoccos", but a majority of modern authors—not including Hitchcock et al. —have changed the ending to the form "oxycoccus".)

Remarkable as it seems, pollen of this little species has been identified, together with that of birch and many other plants, in ancient bogs. Some of these deposits have been determined, by argon dating, to be several million years old. Little wonder that small variations have gradually developed in the circumboreal population. (For a lucid discussion of these variations the reader is referred to Calder and Taylor, or to Szczawinski.)

No lengthy description is needed of this easily-recognized plant. The slender stems creep over the sphagnum moss. They bear numerous, alternate, pointed-ovate leaves that are shining deep-green above but grey-white below. The edges of these persistent leaves are entire and revolute (rolled downward), and the length varies from ¼ to ½ inch. The small pinkish flowers, on very slender, arched pedicels, are unusual in this genus, being deeply 4-lobed rather than 5-lobed, and strongly recurved, instead of bell-shaped. Hence the 8 stamens protrude, and are very evident. Flowers are succeeded by round berries, which grow to a size quite disproportionate to the small plant, often being ½ inch in diameter. In spite of the allegation contained in the name oxycoccos, these berries are very palatable, if slightly acid. They were eagerly sought by the native peoples and the pioneers.

> "In the Vallies and low land close by the River & facing the Sun are plenty of Cranberries, can gather those of last Year & those of this upon the same Shrub, another Berry of a whitish Yellow Colour resembling a Rasberry Pathagominan & very well tasted [probably Salmon Berry, *Rubus spectabilis*] & Number of Plants & Herbs which I am not acquainted with."

Sat. July 18, 1798
Original Journal of Alexander Mackenzie
(written while exploring the great river later named after him)

VACCÍNIUM PARVIFÒLIUM Smith. *Red Huckleberry.* [p.403]

Red Huckleberry is a graceful ornament of forest openings along the Coast, and surprisingly, of a few localities around Kootenay Lake and near Revelstoke. Its slim branches, with bright, yellow-green, thin leaves, and sparkling red berries remind one of scarlet tapers in the gloom of the cathedral woods.

The specific name is inapt, for the oval, deciduous, ½-1 inch *leaves* are neither particularly *small* nor *few*. Stems permit easy recognition (even in the winter) being bright green, ridged and angled, and marked with vivid pink leaf-buds. The growth is open and airy, the slender stem usually 3-6, but occasionally 10 feet in height.

Single, inconspicuous, pinkish-yellow flowers hang like little globular urns, on short pedicels that spring from the axils of the leaves. The berries are beautiful—of a glowing semi-translucency, and bright cerise-red. They are nearly round; usually a little more than ¼ inch across; of a pleasantly refreshing acid flavour.

A favoured perch for this beautiful shrub is the top of a rotting stump, or a mouldering log. Small plants in such situations are easily removed with their long fibrous roots intact, and soon establish themselves as worthy ornamental shrubs of the shaded garden.

VACCÍNIUM SCOPÀRIUM Leiberg. *Grouseberry.* [p.414]

Scoparium means *broom*, for the close twiggy stems would make a good besom, or broom. This is a small and inconspicuous subshrub, seldom more than 10 inches high. It is strictly limited in distribution to the southeastern Interior, as far as the eastern slope of Manning Park. It is a species of the subalpine Spruce-Balsam forest, of hills and mountain slopes.

As the common name suggests, the small red fruit (also the flowers and the delicate leaves) are important in the food resources of several species of Grouse.

Slim, erect, and crowded twigs are yellowish-green and strongly angled. The pale, thin leaves are pointed-ovate, about ½ inch long, with finely-toothed margins. Tiny, single, pinkish flowers are scarcely noticeable among the clustered twigs, nor are the small red berries conspicuous. In fact they are so zealously sought by birds and small mammals that one may often search to find a single berry even in July or August, when Grouseberry is in fruit.

VACCÍNIUM VÌTIS-IDAÈA L. ssp. MÌNUS (Lodd.) Hult. *Rock Cranberry.* [p.415]

The specific name of this northern and circumboreal dwarf cranberry means the *vine of Mt. Ida* (now locally Mt. Idhi, in central Crete). Similarity of growth habit, of leaves,

Following page: CHIMAPHILA UMBELLATA var. OCCIDENTALIS   ×2 [p.364]

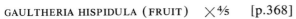

GAULTHERIA HISPIDULA (FRUIT)   ×⅘   [p.368]

APOCYNUM ANDROSAEMIFOLIUM   ×¾   [p.405]

GAULTHERIA OVATIFOLIA (FRUIT)   ×1   [p.365]

and of red fruit, often cause this little plant to be mistaken for Bearberry (*Arctostaphylos uva-ursi*, which see).

Indeed, the two plants are very much alike, and even share the same type of rocky terrain, on the needle-sprinkled floor of open Pine-woods. But Bog Cranberry is also found in the drier parts of bogs, an environment alien to Bearberry. On closer inspection the present species is seen to have much softer berries, that are juicy—if acid in flavour—rather than dry and mealy, and also leaves that are distinctively dotted with black bristly points beneath. These leathery leaves of V. vitis-idaea are ¼ to ½ inch long, dark glossy green above, paler beneath, with margins slightly revolute (rolled under). The pretty rose-pink flowers are bell-shaped, with 4 lobes, and a faint but pleasing fragrance.

This bright-berried mat-plant is abundant in the Queen Charlotte Islands, but otherwise is found east of the Cascades, particularly in the central and northern Rockies.

 # PRIMULÀCEAE. *Primrose Family.*

About 700 species, chiefly of the North Temperate and Arctic Zones, are classified in this family. A large proportion, in such genera as *Primula, Dodecatheon, Androsace, Douglasia, Trientalis*, and *Steironema*, are very beautiful plants. The Asiatic *Primula*, and European *Cyclamen* and *Soldanella*, are special treasures.

All have flowers that are regular and perfect (with both stamens and pistil), and have petals joined together in a flat or narrow tube (i.e. they are gamopetalous). Floral parts are in 5's usually, around a single style and (usually) club-shaped stigma. Leaves are opposite, or sometimes alternate, whorled or basal, but always simple, and generally entire.

ANAGÁLLIS ARVÉNSIS L. *Scarlet Pimpernel.* [p.414]

This humble little immigrant from Europe is perhaps familiar, if only by name, to readers of Baroness Orczy's novel of the French Revolution. The colour is generally salmon-red, of a quite unique and distinctive shade. Its name is derived from anagaleo, *to make happy*—or by other authorities, from ana, *again*, and agallein, *to delight**; in either case this is a pleasing small flower. But it is invasive (as suggested by arvensis, *of cultivated fields*). A common name in England is Poor Man's Weatherglass, since its flowers close when the sun is obscured. Many early works attribute medicinal virtues to this plant, e.g. Gerard affirms that "it helpeth those that be dim sighted." We also read that "the Herb Pimpernel is good to prevent witchcraft."(!)

This is a low or sprawling, glabrous annual, with squared stems, and opposite pairs of pointed, oval, entire, and unstalked leaves (occasionally whorls of leaves). Individual flowers are borne on slender stems. The calyx-cup has 5 long, lanceolate lobes, and the corolla is 5-lobed almost to the base, so that the first appearance is of separate petals. There are 5 minutely-pubescent stamens around the pistil, which develops into a fat, egg-shaped capsule.

Scarlet Pimpernel has appeared sporadically in southern British Columbia, but is quite common near Victoria and Vancouver.

> *No heart can think, no tongue can tell*
> *The virtues of the Pimpernel.*

> Old English rhyme

*Anagallis is one of the ancient generic names (see the concluding note under *Sonchus*).

DODECÀTHEON DENTÀTUM Hook. *White Shooting Star.* [p.415]

Dodecatheon. Say it: savour it. Would that all plant names were so pleasant to the ear! Dodecatheon derives from the Greek dodeka, *twelve*, and theoi, *gods*. Pliny (and much later Linnaeus) imagined, in the cluster of crowned flowers, an assembly of the Olympian deities. This is a unique member of a gracious genus—both by reason of its white colour, and by the atypical *dentate* leaves (whence the specific name). The flower-structure suggests a comet or shooting-star, the flared petals streaming backward from the conspicuous cluster of stamens.

This beautiful plant is rather rare in our area; it is reported from 4000 feet in the southern Okanagan, and in the Cascades. Dodecatheon dentatum prefers wet seepages in the mountains, where there is some shade. Given such a spot, even in the coastal garden, it is easily established and very worthwhile. However, it is so rare in our area that no attempt should be made to move the mature plants; besides, the small offsets transplant much more readily.

The big oval leaves, with their strongly-toothed margins and long petioles, form a rosette in early spring. The rootstock, through the winter, is so dead and shrivelled that one may have thought the plant lost—in fact this is usual for the other Shooting Stars also, and no doubt has led many gardeners to discard them—too soon. The flowering scapes may rise as much as 16 inches; they may have a few glandular hairs but otherwise the plant is glabrous. The 5 sepal-lobes are lanceolate; the "beak" of 5 long stamens, tight-pressed about the even longer pistil, is dark purple. The corolla-tube is creamy-yellow with a reddish-purple wavy edge; the 5 long lobes reflexed backward are creamy-white. The whole effect is cool and lovely.

DODECÀTHEON HENDERSÒNII Gray. *Broad-leaved Shooting Star.* [p.418]

Louis Forniquet Henderson (1853-1942) was an Oregon professor of botany. The best recognition feature of this beautiful Shooting Star is the basal rosette of smooth thick leaves that are strongly pressed to the ground. They are broadly oval (occasionally more thumb-shaped), narrowing to thick petioles that may be nearly as long as the blade.

The scape is usually 6-12 inches long, but in richer soil we have seen superb specimens more than 2 feet tall, with 20-22 blooms. The 5 pointed calyx-lobes are usually flecked with purple, and slightly glandular-hairy. The showy corolla is extremely variable, so that one sees in the space of a few yards individuals that are palest pink, light orchid, rose-purple, deep purple, and even (occasionally) white. In all forms there is a ring of clear yellow at the base of each lobe; and at the point where the lobes are reflexed from the tube formed by their union, a band of dark-purple. The projecting bundle of stigma and stamens is purple—so dark as to appear nearly black and make a striking complement to the corolla-lobes.

This is a well-proportioned plant of refined beauty. It is easy and admirable in the rockery, though the gardener needs to be forewarned that in August the plants shrivel to a small nub that is easily overlooked; diligent search will usually reveal a few tiny bulblets on this unpromising nubble.

Dodecatheon hendersonii graces rocky bluffs and shallow-soil meadows that have abundant moisture in spring, but dry to brick-like hardness in summer. It is found on Vancouver and the Gulf Islands (but not the Queen Charlottes), southward on the west side of the Cascades. The blooming season is mid-April to early June.

DODECÀTHEON JÉFFREYI van Houtte. *Jeffrey's Shooting Star.* [p.415]

Jeffrey's Shooting Star is a bigger plant, more lush than other Dodecatheons, and growing from a larger and more persistent rootstock. It is also a plant of much wetter habitat, frequenting seepages and stream-edges in the mountains, from Vancouver to the Cascades and Rockies, and northward into Alaska. (John Jeffrey was a botanical collector in western North America.)

This is a very distinct species. The sturdy rootstocks are connected by slender rhizomes, so that quite large clumps occur. The leaves are usually glabrous, entire or slightly wavy-edged, oblanceolate—tapering to broad petioles of variable length. Petals are generally purplish-mauve (occasionally whitish), with a white flush at the base of the lobes, and a dark-purple ring at the mouth of the tube. Most distinctive of D. jeffreyi are the very short purplish-black filaments which are almost entirely free, i.e. joined just at their bases.

Where star-flowers strew the rivulet's side—

William Cullen Bryant

DODECÀTHEON PULCHÉLLUM (Raf.) Merrill. ssp. PULCHÉLLUM = D. PAUCIFLÓRUM (Durand) Greene. *Few-flowered Shooting Star.* [p.422]

Though this plant is more often known as *D. pauciflorum*, we have deferred to the scholarly judgment of Calder and Taylor, whose studies indicate the form from the Dry Interior should be considered subspecies CUSÍCKII (Greene) Calder & Taylor, and the coastal plant (also occurring in a disjunct population in the southern Rocky Mountain Trench) as ssp. PULCHÉLLUM. The latter would include depauperate forms from the smaller drier Gulf Islands, and from the highest levels of mountains on Vancouver Island. When all this is said, this choice plant merits pulchellum, *beautiful.*

We know only a few local areas where this species grows with *D. hendersonii* (which see): normally D. pulchellum flowers 2-3 weeks later. Apparently they do not hybridize—though this has been suggested to account for a puzzling plant* which occurs on the Sooke shore-line. The 2 species are instantly separable in the field on the basis of the leaf growth: flat on the ground (and broadly ovate) for *D.hendersonii*; almost erect (and oblanceolate, usually much slimmer) for D. pulchellum. However, the present species is, as has been suggested, highly variable. The leaves may be glabrous to rather densely pubescent, they may be more ovate-lanceolate, or the whole plant may be glandular-hairy. In our area the staminal-tube is always yellow. The corolla-lobes are generally bright rose-purple, flushed with more intense colour at the base, then above this ringed with deep-yellow on which is stitched a beautiful zigzag trim of rose-purple. Pulchellum indeed! A lovely thing.

The brown seed-capsules also are very decorative. Erect at the ends of long pedicels, and cupped in the dried calyx, each elegantly sculpted slender vase is vertically lined, and topped with a flared fringe.

In one or other of its forms this species is found from coastal flats to mountain meadows, from sea level to well above timber line, and from Alaska to Mexico.

*D. LITTÓRALE Hult. may be the correct name for this striking form. The plant illustrated is from one of the Sooke coastal promontories; it appears to be a polyploid. [p.419]

DOUGLÀSIA LAEVIGÀTA A. Gray ssp. CILIOLÀTA (Constance) Calder & Taylor. *Douglasia.* [p.426]

This dwarf, matted mountaineer is apparently very rare in British Columbia—though it is to be anticipated that additional records (from other areas than Strathcona Park and the Queen Charlottes) will come as exploration continues. Douglasia is a strikingly beautiful rock plant that has so far proved difficult in cultivation.

The tight, small clumps are 1-2 inches high, with ¼ to ½-inch, narrow, pointed leaves crowded toward the ends of the clustered stems. These evergreen leaves are glossy green and usually entire-margined, sometimes with short stiff marginal hairs (i.e. they are *ciliolate*). Brilliant pink-rose to crimson flowers may be nearly ½ inch across. They are tubular, with 5 spreading lobes.

Douglasia honours David Douglas, indefatigable Scottish botanist who collected in the Pacific Coast region in the mid-1820's. Laevigata means *smooth*, referring to the nearly smooth leaves.

LYSIMÁCHIA THYRSIFLÒRA L. *Tufted Loosestrife.* [p.426]

In our area 2 members of this genus occur. The name is derived from the Greek lysis, a dissolution or *loosening*, and mache, *strife* or battle—hence also the common name. The derivation is interesting if only because we cannot guess what its origin might be. A *thyrse* is a botanical name for a contracted cylindrical (in this case) or ovoid-pyramidal, densely-flowered panicle (like a cluster of grapes).

Blooming in early summer, this is a yellow-flowered, glabrous herb of very wet places. It is common in such habitats throughout our area, and over much of North Amercia. Growing from creeping rhizomes are smooth stems as much as a yard long, mostly erect but sometimes sprawling over other plants. They bear opposite pairs of linear-lanceolate leaves up to 3 inches long, with tapered tips and entire margins. The tiny flowers are borne in dense cylindrical clusters in the axils of leaves near mid-stem—a rather unusual arrangement. Corolla-lobes, calyx-lobes, leaves and even stems are marked with small purplish-black dots. The long yellow stamens project noticeably beyond the 5 to 7-parted corolla.

LYSIMÁCHIA TERRÈSTRIS (L.) B.S.P. is a rather similar species of cranberry bogs and swamps. It has been introduced from the eastern United States, and so far is limited to southern Vancouver Island and the lower Mainland coast. This species may be readily distinguished from *L. thyrsiflora* (which see) by its terminal (rather than axial) racemes of much larger, brighter yellow flowers that have purple-streaked (instead of merely spotted) petal-lobes. Calyx-lobes usually are marked with a reddish-purple stripe on either edge. The lowermost leaves are slightly hairy on the under surface.

PRÍMULA EGALIKSÉNSIS Wormsk., choice, tiny, erect, with lilac to white deeply-notched petals, is a rare inhabitant of wet meadows along alpine streams from the Haines Cut-off and the Jasper area. Along the Rockies from Yoho to Toad River there are a few records for PRÍMULA MISTASSÍNICA Michx., with even more beautiful, larger, pink to purplish, yellow-eyed flowers.

TRIENTÀLIS LATIFÒLIA Hook. *Starflower.* [p.423]

This is a genus of 3 dainty woodlanders, 2 of which occur in our area. Their name is derived from the Latin triens, *one-third*—it seems with intent of suggesting they grow about one-third foot tall, though this is not entirely clear. Latifolia means *wide-leaved*, but the leaves are generally larger, rather than relatively wider than those of *T. europaea ssp. arctica* (which see). An occasional name is Indian Potato, with reference to the little spindle-shaped vertical root-tubers, which—though small—are abundant, starchy, and nutritious—and so were sought by the coastal tribes. But Starflower better conveys the image of this pretty little sprite of the forest.

Over most of southern and central British Columbia, Trientalis latifolia lifts its whorled 3-7 leaves at the top of a glabrous and slender stem that is 4-8 inches tall. The thin smooth leaves are broadly ovate, entire, and usually unequal in size, from 1-4 inches long. There are 6 pointed calyx-lobes, and 6 delicate pointed-lanceolate lobes of the corolla. They are cleft so nearly to the base that it is easy to believe there are 6 separate petals. Pedicels of the flowers are long and thread-like. Stamens also number 6, around a short pistil and an ovary that later develops into a most unusual white, round, dry seed-case. It has surface markings that make it look exactly like a tiny soccer football.

Starflower makes a delightful pattern on the forest floor, especially around the edges of natural openings in the trees. Fragile and dainty above their ring of delicate green leaves, the white or pale-pink flowers beguile the eye.

TRIENTÀLIS EUROPAÈA L. ssp. ÁRCTICA (Fisch.) Hult., *Northern Starflower,* is a smaller plant with leaves 2 inches long, or less, that are arranged up the length of the stem, rather than in a whorl at its summit. The flowers are white, with less sharply-pointed corolla-lobes, and the tubers are horizontal, rather than vertical as in its relative. This species also differs from *T. latifolia* (which see) in habitat (bogs and swampy places) and in range (generally more northern, into the Queen Charlottes and Alaska).

 PLUMBAGINÀCEAE. *Leadwort Family. Plumbago Family.*

ARMÈRIA MARÍTIMA (Mill.) Willd. *Sea Pink. Thrift.* [p.434]

The generic name is Latinized from the Celtic word for the plant, while the specific name obviously describes its rocky home along the *sea-coast* from Alaska to California. Hence also Sea Pink, for the rounded heads of flowers, cupped in brown papery bracts, are of every shade of pink. Thrift is a very old name, an evident allusion to the thriftiness of a plant that subsists on the merest sift of soil in the rock crevices. Occasionally the plant is found somewhat inland.

From time to time we have commented on the pollination of various plants. The Armerias afford an interesting illustration. The Armerias of the Portuguese coast have been extensively studied: the several species are distinct, very limited in area, and do not hybridize. Yet when these species were moved to England (where they flower later) inter-hybrids soon appeared. Plants established in England were hybridized by the far-ranging bumblebee, which is only abundant from late spring onward. In Portugal

399

LOISELEURIA PROCUMBENS ×¾ [p.373]

PHYLLODOCE EMPETRIFORMIS ×½ [p.376]

LEDUM PALUSTRE ssp. GROENLANDICUM ×½ [p.372]

the species flowered before the bumblebees emerged, so were pollinated by several kinds of flower-beetles that do not fly far.

Most people know these neat cushions of firm but fleshy and persistent linear leaves. Numerous tough flower-scapes are leafless, and usually about 6 inches high. The corolla is dry and papery, the better to withstand wind-whipped sea-spray. The pink cup is 5-lobed almost to the base, and bears 5 stamens arranged opposite the lobes. The 5 calyx-teeth bear short bristles above.

GENTIANÀCEAE. *Gentian Family.*

GENTIÀNA DOUGLASIÀNA Bong. *Douglas Gentian.*

Pliny the Elder in his *Historia Naturalis* (A.D. 77) relates that the king of Illyria, Gentius, discovered supposed medicinal virtues in extracts of plants of this family. The Pharmacopoeia still lists (as a tonic) Elixir of *Gentiana lutea,* a yellow-flowered species of Spain. Most of the 800 species of this family occur in the North Temperate zone, especially in alpine or arctic areas. A host of gardeners consider *G. acaulis,* native to the Alps, one of the loveliest of all rock plants.

Our only annual Gentian, Gentiana douglasiana is an attractive and compact (2-10 inch) plant of sphagnum bogs. It is an endemic species, strictly limited to the islands and mainland coastal strip of British Columbia. The ½-inch flowers are numerous, with greenish corolla-tubes having 5 flared bluish-purple lobes that are white within.

A detail, valuable in recognition of the Gentians, is the shape of the *plicae* (folds between each pair of corolla-lobes). In this species each plica is split into 2 short pointed teeth.

GENTIÀNA GLAÙCA Pallas. *Pale Gentian.*

This fairly common species is a 2-6 inch perennial of alpine meadows on the mainland. In its more attractive form the 5-lobed flowers are *glaucous* greenish-blue, and rather less than an inch long. There is also a form with greenish-yellow flowers that merge with the foliage colour. The plicae are conspicuous, and slightly pointed. Calyx-lobes are uneven in size, and blunt-tipped. There is a distinctive rosette of firm, obovate, basal leaves.

GENTIÀNA SCÉPTRUM Griseb. *Swamp Gentian.* [p.423]

This fine plant is widely distributed in meadows and boggy lake-margins of the coast, southward from Prince Rupert. The specific name suggests the sceptre-like shape of individual stems, each crowned by the infolded corolla.

The lanceolate leaves (in opposite pairs) barely clasp the 8-20 inch stem. Beautiful deep-blue flowers are 1-1½ inches long, with dark-green speckles inside. The plicae are smooth-edged folds, i.e. not toothed. The calyx is deeply 5-toothed.

As late as August—even into October—the showy cups of the Swamp Gentian provide deep-blue accents among the yellows and greens of the water's edge.

Very similar is GENTIÀNA PLATYPÉTALA Griseb., a lovely montane species restricted to the coast, from Alaska to the Queen Charlottes. In those rain-swept islands it is common, and sometimes extends down to near sea level. Its big, pale-blue chalices are white toward their bases, and very attractive. The plicae are bi-toothed, rather than entire, and the calyx-tube is distinctly split, one portion with 2, the other with 3 short stubby teeth.

Then doth thy sweet and quiet eye
Look through its fringes to the sky,
Blue—blue—as if that sky let fall
A flower from its cerulean wall.

William Cullen Bryant:
To the Fringed Gentian

GENTIANÉLLA AMARÉLLA (L.) Börner ssp. ACÙTA (Michx.) Gillett. *Northern Gentian.* [p.422]

G. amarella derives its name from the bitter alkaloids in its juices (Latin amarus, *bitter,* plus the diminutive -ella). This is a highly variable plant over its vast circumboreal range, and only a flexible description of G. amarella can be offered. The stems are single (less often considerably branched), 2-18 inches tall, and generally glabrous. Opposite leaves of the stems are pointed, but vary in width from ovate to narrowly-lanceolate; the few basal leaves are usually oblanceolate, and sometimes bear small hairs along their margins (i.e. they are ciliate). The calyx is 5-cleft nearly to the base, with lobes narrow, sharply-pointed, and slightly uneven. Corolla-tube is slender, from less than ½ inch to nearly an inch long, and cleft about half-way into 5 (rarely 4) lobes that are somewhat flared. The inner faces of the lobes are distinctively fringed with curious fleshy hairs, but the tube (from whose wall the 4-5 stamens arise) is smooth. The plant illustrated is larger and more floriferous than usual; in fact, in many areas the dwarf plants carry but one terminal flower (usually pinkish, though occasionally bluish-mauve or even white).

PHYLLODOCE GLANDULIFLORA ×1 [p.377]

V. & I. AHIER

RHODODENDRON LAPPONICUM ×⅕ [p.380]

RHODODENDRON ALBIFLORUM ×½ [p.377]

VACCINIUM MYRTILLOIDES (FRUIT) ×½ [p.383]

VACCINIUM PARVIFOLIUM (FRUIT) ×⅗ [p.389]

RHODODENDRON MACROPHYLLUM ×⅖ [p.381]

Northern Gentian prefers moist places in meadows and along stream-banks, where its inconspicuous blooms may be seen from June to the end of the summer.

This is the little annual mentioned by the much-loved old Vicar of Selborne, Gilbert White, in 1778 (Letter XLI)—"*Gentiana amarella*, autumnal gentian, or fellwort—on the Zig-zag and Hanger."

GENTIANÉLLA PROPÍNQUA (Richards.) Gillett. *Four-petalled Gentian.*

This 1-12 inch annual is widespread in mainland British Columbia. The flowers are less than an inch long, with pale-blue corollas fading to white. The corolla-tube is consistently cleft into 4, rather than 5 (pointed) lobes.

 # MENYANTHÀCEAE. *Buck Bean Family.*

FAÙRIA CRÍSTA-GÁLLI (Menzies) Makino. *Deer Cabbage.* [p.418]

Fauria will be known to many by earlier names—*Menyanthes* or *Nephrophyllidium*—now displaced by the rule of precedence. This is (like the next species) a succulent plant grazed by deer, though the rounded heart-shaped leaves are held flat on long petioles, and are not at all cabbage-like. The specific name means crest of a fowl, or *cockscomb*. This describes quite well the shape (though not the colour) of the 3 white wattles running the length of the corolla-lobes.

Fauria occurs with *Menyanthes trifoliata* (which see) in bogs, swamps, and wet runnels, usually at considerable altitudes. It has been reported from Vancouver Island, the Queen Charlottes, and the mainland coastal mountains to Alaska.

This big lush plant is glabrous. Its large, rounded leaves (often purplish beneath) have round-toothed margins, and are usually broader than long. The white flowers are about ¾ inch across, the corolla-tube deeply cleft, and the 4-5-6 lanceolate lobes held flat. As previously mentioned, they are marked with 1, or more commonly with 3, prominent crest-like ridges.

The flowers are rank-smelling, which probably accounts for the presence of numerous beetles and flies that visit, and almost certainly pollinate them.

MENYÁNTHES TRIFOLIÀTA L. *Buckbean.* [p.418]

Greek men, a *month*, and anthos, *flower*, provide the generic name with its suggestion of flower duration. The handsome fleshy leaves of the single species have 3 elliptical leaflets at the top of each long petiole, the lower end of which is much widened to form a clasping stipule. The whole plant is succulent and cropped by deer, but there is small resemblance in leaf, flower, or capsule to any species of Bean.

This is an easily recognized, and common perennial bog plant, with stout, far-spreading rootstocks. The glabrous leaves are basally clustered at the foot of a 6-12 inch flower-stem. The numerous fringed flowers are white, occasionally pink-flushed, and crowded in a short raceme. The calyx is deeply 5-6 parted, as is the corolla. The inner face of the flat corolla-lobes is covered with white hair-like projections that are very conspicuous. Some of the flowers in a single raceme have 5 stamens longer than, and almost obscuring the pistil; in others the stamens are short, so that the style is evident.

 **APOCYNÀCEAE.** *Dogbane Family.*

APÓCYNUM ANDROSAEMIFÒLIUM L. *Dogbane.* [p.391]

Greek apo, *against*, and kyon, *a dog*, is the basis of the generic and the common names. We have not been able to learn whether or not canines shun the plant! Dogbane does have a distinct sweetish odour which is more likely to attract insects—always seen in great numbers at the pink blossoms—than to repel dogs. The long and awkward specific name means *Androsaemum-leaved* (Androsaemum—from aner, *a man*, and haema, *blood*—was an early name for *Hypericum androsaemum*, which has a red juice.)

This is a tall plant (to 24 inches), with freely branched slender stems that may be glabrous or hairy. When broken they exude an acrid white juice. The opposite-paired leaves are egg-shaped, with a short pointed tip. Characteristically, the leaves droop during the heat of the mid-day.

The flowers are candy-pink bells, attractively lined with deeper pink honey-guides. Five stamens are ranked around a pistil with unusual nectaries at its base.

These 5 peg-like nectaries have inverted V-shaped openings. A visiting butterfly (very often a lordly Swallowtail, *Papilio*) can usually insert and withdraw its proboscis, and both the bee and his burly cousin, the bumblebee, are strong enough to pull away from the potential trap. But you will see, in any large patch of these plants, some flowers in which are dead flies and small moths. We have seen a Milbert's Tortoise-shell (*Nymphalis milberti*) fluttering helplessly above a Dogbane flower. Its mouth-parts had been caught in the narrowing "V". (Yes! we released the butterfly.) A 10X glass reveals the horny teeth of these small traps.

Very striking are the dry fruiting-capsules. They are pendulous, sometimes over 3 inches long, and at first sight, might remind one of the long pods of a *Vicia* or *Lathyrus* (which see). But these are follicles, that open down one side only, to release the seeds, each with a tuft (coma) of inch-long, pale-brown silky hairs.

Dogbane is abundant on dry roadsides, and has become a rather serious invader of orchards in the Dry Interior. Forms occur, especially on the Coast, that vary considerably in such characteristics as size of flower and degree to which the corolla-lobes are reflexed. In all locations the plant has a very extended period of bloom (from June to the end of September) so that it is a stable source of nectar for bees, and in fact provides a highly prized honey.

APÓCYNUM CANNABÌNUM L., *Indian Hemp,* is a plant, similar to but bigger than *A. androsaemifolium,* that reaches 5 feet. It is readily distinguished from its variable relative, for the leaves are narrower and are carried erect (rather than drooping). The flowers are white, or greenish-white, with corolla-lobes barely or not at all reflexed. Its range, like its congener, extends over the valleys and lower slopes of the United States and southern Canada.

Both plants were important to the native tribes as a source of cordage fibres, especially for fishing lines and nets. Their milky juice (latex) contains very bitter glucosides which discourage browsing animals. This is fortunate, for these compounds are toxic.

ASCLEPIADÀCEAE. *Milkweed Family.*

ASCLÈPIAS SPECIÒSA Torr. *Showy Milkweed.* [p.426]

Asklepios was the Greek god of medicine, more familiar in the Latin form as Aesculapius; powerful medicinal virtues once being attributed to the plant. Speciosa (in Latin) means *showy.* With their 2-4 foot stems and great leathery leaves these are arresting plants, even before the clustered buds open to reveal the pink flowers. Stems, broken or injured, exude quantities of the sticky latex which is responsible for the common name.

Flower parts are highly specialized, and most interesting to examine with a 10X magnifier. At first sight the "geography" of the flower is confusing, for what appear to be petals are actually hood-like outgrowths of the tube that is formed by the joined filaments of the 5 stamens. But let us trace the parts from the beginning. First there are 5 sepals, barely joined at their bases, and reflexed. They are greenish, usually tinged reddish. The petals form a tube (lobed about half its length) the lobes reddish and reflexed.

Now it is necessary to separate the parts with a needle, and look closely. Arising from the corolla-tube is another tube (column), formed from the conjoined filaments of the stamens. At the base of the column are 5 small nectariferous glands, but these are hidden by 5 pink and conspicuous erect "hoods" which also grow from the base of the column. Push one back, and inside you will see a slender curved "horn"; hood and horn overtop the anthers and the single pistil.

The purplish anthers are partly hidden by a membranous enlargement that extends downward to form 5 pairs of narrow grooves. Now a bee is ushered (first by the hoods, and then by the horns) to the top of the slippery column. Here, as it struggles to locate the source of the pleasantly-scented nectar, one or more of its feet are caught in these grooves. Then when the insect's foot is drawn up the cleft, it is forced under a delicate but sticky filament (the translator), which pulls away from the adjacent anthers two "saddle-bags" of clustered pollen grains (pollinia). So the visitor departs with one, or several, of these pairs of pollinia dangling from his feet, and inevitably brings them to the stigmatic lobes of the next blossom. This amazing complexity of structures, designed to secure cross-pollination, will recall the sophisticated devices of the Orchids, which also bundle their pollen-grains into pollinia.

In late summer Milkweed becomes still more conspicuous, as the very large seed-follicles ripen. These are usually 3-4 inches long, plump and heavy, and covered both with hairs and fleshy, curved tubercles. The follicles split on one edge only, releasing many seeds, each with a long plume of silvery hairs. On a windy day in autumn, as one watches these soar away—thousands upon thousands from half a dozen plants—it is easy to see how Asclepias has established itself in roadside ditches throughout southern British Columbia, east of the Cascades.

Dr. Kerner showed that the sharp claws of ants, attempting to reach the flowers, puncture the thin skin of the upper stems, releasing the sticky milk, which soon hardens and traps the unwanted insects.

But winged butterflies are welcome agents of pollination, and one of the most spectacular of these is the great tawny Monarch (*Anosia plexippus*), a strong-flying species well-known for its long migratory flights. Over the millenia a curious relationship has developed between the Milkweed and this butterfly. The eggs are laid on the leaves, so that the black-and-green banded larvae, feeding on them, accumulate the bitter and toxic glucosides. These glucosides are retained during and after pupation, being present in the body and also in the black gland on the hind wing of the mature insect. As a consequence the Monarch Butterfly is distasteful to birds, who have apparently inherited an instinctive revulsion, triggered by sight of the Monarch's distinctive pattern of black and white spots and bands on orange-brown. Hand-reared insectivorous birds of many species have been observed to avoid this butterfly, though taking moths and other butterflies, such as the Cabbage White (*Pieris rapae*), Pine White (*Neophasia menapia*), and Orange Tip (*Anthocharis sara*). Still more amazing, those birds denied parental instruction, ignore the edible Viceroy butterfly (*Limenitis archippus*) that has developed colouring astonishingly like that of the "protected"

Monarch. The dependence of the Monarch upon the foodplant is dramatically illustrated by the fact that Asclepias was introduced into the Sandwich Islands about 1847 or 1848: in 1850 the Monarch Butterfly appeared, and bred on those isolated islands!

 ## CONVOLVULÀCEAE. *Convolvulus Family.*

CONVÓLVULUS ARVÉNSIS L. *Field Bindweed.*   [p.426]

J. W. Thompson suggests this European, now so widely established in gardens and waste ground all over the continent, may be "the worst weed", by reason of its deep, wide-running rhizomes. The climbing habit of most of the members of the genus is conveyed by the derivation from the Latin convolvo, *to twine*; however, the present species is a squat dweller *of the fields* (arvensis). The common name bears witness to the trailing, somewhat twining stems, which are usually 6-8 inches, but in better soil may be 6 feet long.

Few gardeners are fortunate enough to lack acquaintance with this pretty but troublesome invader, which is almost impossible to eradicate.

The stems of this perennial are smooth, and bear alternate leaves of variable shape, often like a blunt-pointed and blunt-barbed spear-head. From the axil of each leaf grows a flower-stem (peduncle) that is usually longer than the leaf and carries a pair of small opposite bracts well below the flowers. The "morning-glory" flowers are usually in pairs, each with deeply 5-lobed calyx-cup, and white or creamy campanulate corolla that is creased by 5 pronounced ribs, and generally purplish-lined (at least on the under-surface).

[p.198]   CONVÓLVULUS SOLDANÉLLA L., *Beach Morning-glory,* is an aristocratic native perennial—unfortunately rather rare—found on coastal dunes. In this special environment it is immediately recognizable by its thick fleshy leaves, pinkish-purple funnel-flowers up to 2 inches across, and 2 thick bracts which clasp the calyx. It is an interesting member of the Convolvulaceae family, adapted to the rigorous environment of dry sand near the sea. It has been reported from the Queen Charlottes, Vancouver Island and Savary Island, and the southern mainland coast.

CONVÓLVULUS SÈPIUM L. var FRATERNIFLÒRUS Mack. & Bush. *White Morning-glory. Hedge Bindweed.*   [p.422]

This is a highly variable species, especially in habit, leaf shape, and hairiness, but all the forms may be described, with feeling, as beautiful—and—bad! This is yet another of the

European (and Asian) imports that have become seriously invasive weeds. Sepium is from saepes, meaning *of hedges* or fences, through and on which these vines may clamber. In fact it is much more a climber than *C. arvensis* (which see), responding with stems many yards long to good soil and coastal humidity.

This species has made itself at home across the continent, though unable to endure very low temperatures in the far north, or in the mountains. "For this," as an old farmer, transplanted from Hertfordshire used to say, "Heaven be thankit!" With such a range many variations have been observed, but though many have been named, at various levels most—or all—appear to be linked by intermediate specimens.

The flowers may be deep-pink or white, from 1½-3 inches across. Perhaps most often they are white and large—and undeniably beautiful! The leaf is often shaped like a mediaeval halberd, but is too variable to be useful in identification. A constant feature, however, is the pair of large thin pale-green bracts, immediately below the flower, so large in fact that they hide (and may be mistaken for) the calyx-lobes. The flowers are curiously twisted, both in bud and immediately following their brief morning in the sun. C. sepium, like its congener, develops a maze of thick white rhizomes that penetrate deeply, even into clay soil, and spread far and wide.

CUSCUTÀCEAE. *Dodder Family. Cuscuta Family.*

CÚSCUTA SALÌNA Engelm. *Salt-marsh Dodder.* [p.414]

This is a parasitic perennial whose orange-yellow twining stems are often seen on other plants. Research into the origin of plant names so often brings awareness of the contribution in materia medica and botany made by the Moors. In this case our generic name can be traced to the Arabic name for the plant, kashūtha. Salina means *salty*, this species nearly always parasitizing *Salicornia* (which see) of salt-marshes. The common name is from the Frisian dodd, *a bunch*, probably referring to the clustered whitish flowers.

The life history of this remarkably specialized plant illustrates the dictum "ontogeny recapitulates phylogeny". Less concisely, this means that the history of the individual summarizes the development of the race. Thus the angular seed (released when the pointed capsule splits ring-wise) contains a coiled embryo, which puts out a slender rootlet into the ground. But the ascending stem lacks chlorophyll, and in absence of a host plant, soon withers and dies. If, however, it can climb upon another plant, threadlike processes (haustoria) quickly emerge from the stem of the Dodder, and penetrate the tissues of the host, which thereafter sustains the parasite. At once the Dodder's own roots die, the orange-thread flaccid stems with their haustoria climb anti-clockwise to the top of the host plant, and then develop clustered white flowers. These have a 4-5 cleft calyx and corolla (the latter bell-shaped), a like number of

410

VACCINIUM ALASKAENSE ✕1⅕ [p.382]

VACCINIUM CAESPITOSUM (FRUIT) ✕1¼ [p.383]

VACCINIUM MEMBRANACEUM (FRUIT) ✕½ [p.383]

VACCINIUM OVATUM ✕¾ [p.385]

VACCINIUM OVALIFOLIUM (FRUIT)   ×2½   [p.384]

stamens, and 2 styles. Thus the primeval history of Cuscuta is revealed in the development of the individual plant. It evolved from ancestors with normal roots, and possibly stems containing chlorophyll, in the slow course of millennia becoming the highly specialized parasite we see today.

The botanical discrimination of the species is interesting. Its hosts are limited chiefly to members of the *Chenopodiaceae* family, less often to *Achillea* and others of the *Compositae*. The very similar CÚSCUTA EPITHÝMUM Murr. (it has thread-like rather than clubbed stigmas) attacks chiefly *Leguminosae*, notably the clovers. Perhaps we shall understand some day the factors that originally led the developing species of Cuscuta to discriminate among host plants (possibly minor variations, later gene-fixed, in the enzyme-chains involved in using the host's fluids?)

CVSCVTA is the title of a formalized illustration in the *Arnoldi de noua uilla Auicenna*, an anonymous compilation from early authors (1499). Unquestionably it represents a species of Dodder (Cuscuta).

 **POLEMONIÀCEAE.** *Phlox Family.*

The floral characteristics of this well-defined family are so constant that much repetition in the species descriptions can be avoided by a family summary.

About 265 species of the Americas and Eurasia have been described. The family is best represented in the western United States. Most of the species are herbs, although a few are shrubs or even small trees.

The flowers are gamopetalous, i.e. with petals joined in a well-developed corolla-tube, usually with 5 lobes. The lobes are most often uniform (but occasionally bilabiate in species outside our area). In this family one is advised to split a flower lengthwise (with a razor-blade) to reveal the pattern of arrangement of the 5 stamens, which arise from the upper part of the corolla tube. (The detail so revealed is most useful in identification.) The buds are usually pleated or otherwise twisted or contorted. The flowers are solitary, or more often arranged in heads or cymes, an often convex or flat-topped arrangement in which the central or terminal flower blooms earliest. Particularly distinctive, but not an obvious feature, is the pistil with its 3 carpels.

One of the few vines in the family is the familiar *Cobaea scandens* (a bat-pollinated flower). Many of the species, e.g. of *Phlox* and *Polemonium*, are very attractive widely-grown garden plants.

The family derives its name from the Greek polemos, *war*. Pliny (Roman soldier, statesman, and naturalist) states that "polemonia" was given this name from having caused a war between two kings, each of whom claimed the honour of first having discovered its medicinal virtues. The causes of some recent wars make no better sense. Incidentally, no member of the family is now used for any medicinal purpose.

COLLÒMIA GRANDIFLÒRA Dougl. *Large-flowered Collomia.* [p.435]

Greek kolla, *glue*, referring to the mucilaginous covering apparent when seeds are moistened, is the origin of the generic name. The present *large-flowered* species is often listed under *Gilia*.

This beautiful annual plant is at once noticeable for its unusual colour, a soft salmon-orange, occasionally more yellowish. The plants are generally unbranched, as much as 3 feet high, with numerous alternate, lanceolate, and entire leaves. The general impression is very like that given by *Phlox paniculata*, familiar plant of the perennial border. Indeed this Collomia makes a handsome garden plant.

When the flared tube is slit and spread apart (as recommended under *Polemoniaceae*), the distinctive stamens are easily seen. They are remarkably uneven, in length, and furthermore spring from different levels on the corolla-tube, just below the flared mouth. The mouth is cleft into 5 gently pointed lobes, which may be ½ inch long.

Collomia grandiflora has a long blooming season—from June to August. It prefers rather dry sites in open woodland, from sea level to considerable altitudes, from the Coast to the Rockies.

GÍLIA AGGREGÀTA (Pursh) Spreng. *Scarlet Gilia.* [p.427]

This genus of attractive species commemorates the 18th century Spanish botanist Felipe Luis Gil. The specific name means *clustered*, referring to the several brilliant flowers in a rather open cyme.

Scarlet Gilia is one of our most spectacular plants. The numerous tubular flowers with flared corolla-lobes are fire-cracker red, barbaric and startling in intensity. In subalpine broken rock the plants may be 4 inches tall, compact above the basal rosette of carrot-like foliage, but in open woods with richer soil, the much-branched sparse-leaved stems may reach 3 feet. The coast gardener may well covet this flame-like beauty, but though seeds germinate readily and the attractive rosettes of deeply-cut leaves look promising, they do not survive our damp winter. East of the Cascades in southern British Columbia G. aggregata is an easy biennial, well worth growing. Unfortunately this Gilia has an unpleasant smell, and wilts almost immediately after cutting.

The species is unmistakable, though a number of varieties have been named. The colour varies to yellow and even white, though the scarlet form marked with small white spots is much the most usual. If the tube is slit, the stamens will be seen to have filaments of almost uniform length inserted on the corolla-tube at a nearly constant level. The

414

VACCINIUM OXYCOCCOS var. INTERMEDIUM (FRUIT) ✕⅓ [p.388]

VACCINIUM SCOPARIUM (FRUIT) ✕⅗ [p.389]

ANAGALLIS ARVENSIS ✕1¼ [p.392]

CUSCUTA SALINA ✕⅗ [p.409]

DODECATHEON DENTATUM   ×¼   [p.393]

DODECATHEON JEFFREYI   ×⅘   [p.394]

VACCINIUM VITIS-IDAEA   ×2   [p.389]

lobes of the corolla become slender-pointed, and the tube is much longer than that of our other Gilias (¾-1¼ inches long).

This brilliant flower is not common, so it should not be picked but allowed to develop its crop of seed, so that we may continue to see its bright accent by the roadside.

LEPTODÁCTYLON PÚNGENS (Torr.) Nutt. *Spiny Phlox.*   [p.435]

This is a low, many-branched, rigid and rather dense shrub, 4-24 inches tall. It is an attractive feature of severely arid areas from Baja California to the southern Interior of British Columbia (as at the western end of Richter Pass). Tiny needle-like leaves are tightly clustered, especially toward the ends of the branchlets. The bases of the branches are grey with leaves that are dead but persistent.

Typically phlox-like, ¾ inch, whitish flowers open during the night but remain partially expanded through the day if there is any cloud cover. Buds usually are flushed with lavender, but this soon fades. The slender tube is yellowish to peach-coloured within, and about as long as the 5 corolla-lobes. The flowers—and even the foliage—possess a distinctive, sweetly aromatic fragrance.

Leptos (Greek) means *narrow,* and daktylos *a finger,* while pungens (Latin) means piercing or *sharp-pointed,* so that the scientific name accurately describes the palmately-divided spine-tipped leaves.

LINÁNTHUS BÍCOLOR (Nutt.) Greene.   [p.435]

This dainty miniature derives its name from the much larger flax-flower (Greek linon, *flax,* and anthos, *flower*). The corolla is *bicoloured,* since the yellow tube flares into pink lobes.

Linanthus bicolor is often depauperate, and so tiny that it is needful to admire the delicate trumpets from one's knees. The erect stem may be simple and an inch high, or as much as 6 inches and branched at the base. What appear to be whorls of pointed leaves are seen on closer examination to be opposite pairs of palmate leaves with 3-7 sharp fingers. These are firm, almost rigid, and covered with short stiff hairs. From the uppermost leaflet emerge clusters of slender-tubed corollas. These are purplish and hairy, in the coastal form about ½ inch long, but more than twice this length in the larger brighter-coloured variant found eastward to the Cascades. The long tube flares abruptly into 5 pointed lobes. The stamens and 3-lobed stigma project slightly from the yellow throat of the tube. Calyx-lobes are linear and almost needle-tipped.

From April to June Linanthus bicolor lifts its sweetly fragrant faces to the sun. This little annual prefers open sunny hillsides.

PHLÓX DIFFÙSA Benth. *Spreading Phlox.*   [p.438]

Phlox is itself a Greek word, meaning *flame,* descriptive of the bright flowers of this beautiful group of plants. Diffusa (Latin) means *spreading.*

This is perhaps the most widespread of 7 species occurring in our area. It is variable (e.g. in style-length) throughout its range (the mountains of British Columbia) and variants are often seen even among plants of small colonies. Within a few square yards one can find colour forms from white to pink to various shades of purple, lavender, and violet (and, let it be admitted, even a disastrous magenta); some with yellow throat, some with white, and some with delicate touches of more intense shade; forms with narrow lobes almost like wheel-spokes, and others—more attractive—with wide, even overlapping lobes, that are salverform. The illustration is of a very lovely clone.

Phlox diffusa is one of several closely related, low, mat-forming perennial species with firm, linear, opposite leaves (often sharply pointed) and with many solitary (or 2-3 grouped) flat saucer-like flowers at the branch ends. Spreading Phlox has its 5 narrow calyx-lobes covered with a spidery web of white hairs, and a corolla-tube less than twice as long as the calyx. Its mostly glabrous leaves also have arachnoid-hairy bases and margins. If you split the corolla, as we have suggested, you will find no two of the 5 short-filament stamens are attached at the same level in the throat of the tube. The 3-cleft stigma is at a level below even the lowest-placed anther. Clearly this arrangement is designed to ensure that pollen will be removed by some part of the insect visitor's head.

These dwarf tufted Phloxes are one of North America's great contributions to the rock gardens of the world. The plants need little soil or water but must have sharp drainage, for they often occur on screes or cliffs in the mountains, or in arid semi-deserts. Exceptionally choice clones of Phlox diffusa may be rooted—with a little difficulty—from new-growth cuttings, but in our experience are easier from divisions that retain some fibrous, feeding rootlets. If one can return to a selected plant after several months, layering is quite sure. In any case these special forms should be left for others to enjoy, and to perpetuate their beauty.

To encounter on rocky slopes foot-wide cushions literally covered with these beautiful flowers is a breath-catching experience.

Many will know this species as *P. douglasii,* now reduced to the synonymy.

PHLÓX CAESPITÒSA Nutt. is a similar species of the Ponderosa Pine-Sagebrush   [p.438] associes. It is slightly less compact and more erect, and the spidery web of hairs covering the calyx-lobes and leaf-bases of *P. diffusa* (which see) is replaced in this species by glandular hairs. Splitting the corolla-tube, one sees that the lowermost stamens originate below the level of the stigma.

PHLÓX ALYSSIFÒLIA Greene of extreme southeastern British Columbia has, as the name suggests (*leaves like Alyssum*) lanceolate-elliptic leaves (noticeably broader than the bristle-leaves of the two previous species). Their margins are generally white, hard, and hairy. Its flowers are larger, usually pale bluish-purple or white.

PHLÓX HÓODII Rich. has spiny leaves (often hoary) and a similar range to *P. alyssifolia* (which see). It is very densely tufted, with small white (rarely lilac) flowers. This species is abundant in southern Alberta.

418

FAURIA CRISTA-GALLI ✕ ⅘ [p.404]

MENYANTHES TRIFOLIATA ✕ ⅘ [p.405]

DODECATHEON HENDERSONII ✕ ⅗ [p.394]

PHLÓX LONGIFÒLIA Nutt. *Long-leaved Phlox.* [p.422]

The specific name refers to the *linear leaves,* which may be as much as 3 inches long, and are mostly glabrous.

This pink or white Phlox with sweetly-scented flowers, is notably taller than our other species. The upright stems may be 20 inches tall, but 8-10 inches is more usual. A distinctive feature of the rather membranous calyx-tube is the presence of stiff vertical ridges, or keels. These are especially noticeable in the buds. The flowers are large (the lobe-faces sometimes spanning 1¼ inches). The lobe-tips of the corolla arc usually slightly erose (irregular). The stamens are placed unevenly on the wall of the corolla-tube, some well below the stigma level, but others protruding from the throat.

In the southern Interior of British Columbia Phlox longifolia is an abundant perennial, found on dry plains and open rocky places up to considerable elevations.

The preservation of plants by pressing them between paper (at that time very scarce and expensive), and pasting them upon the pages of a book (a "Herbarium") apparently originated in Italy about 1550. The Herbarium of Felix Platter, eminent physician of Basle, was discovered in 1935 among the archives of the University of Bern, Switzerland. Eight folio volumes (apparently about half of the collection) contained 813 species of plants from Switzerland, Italy, France, Spain, and Egypt. One may imagine the interest with which botanists studied these specimens, most of which were still in excellent condition. The plants were collected in 1553 and 1554!

POLEMÒNIUM PULCHÉRRIMUM Hook. *Showy Jacob's Ladder.* [p.434]

As explained under Polemoniaceae (which see), polemos is the Greek word for *war.* Pulcherrimum means *very handsome.* Polemonium is a genus of beautiful perennials, with alternate pinnately-compound leaves, and cup-shaped flowers usually blue or white. Five species occur in our area. Jacob's Ladder is suggested by the numerous opposite leaflets.

P. pulcherrimum is a tufted 2-12 inch plant, with almost smooth basal leaves, each having 11-23 pointed-oval leaflets. The stems are more or less erect, sparingly branched, and with a few reduced leaves. The 5-lobed calyx and upper parts of the stems usually bear very small glandular hairs. Flowers are borne in a rather open cluster on long slender pedicels. Corollas are short-tubed, with broad lobes about as long (or up to twice as long) as the tube. When the corolla is slit lengthwise and opened out, the 5 white stamens are seen to have equally long filaments, all inserted at the same level on the short corolla-tube, and each with a tuft of soft white hairs at its base. The 3-lobed

Preceding page: DODECATHEON LITTORALE ×2 [p.395]

stigma is held a little above the anthers on a long white style. Soft lavender-blue of the corolla is relieved by a vivid orange ring at the base of the cup.

Though this, and most other Polemoniums, are malodorous, the unpleasant odour is not obvious out-of-doors; the flowers should be admired in situ.

Though on the mainland (from Alaska southward) this is a mountain species, Calder and Taylor verify Dr. Newcombe's report of its occurrence on the dry limestone cliffs of Limestone Island, Q.C.I.; a surprising locale. The flowers are blue, with noticeably long, protruding pistils, and the large leaves have numerous leaflets from ½ to 1½ inches long.

POLEMÒNIUM ACUTIFLÒRUM Willd. *Tall Jacob's Ladder,* has erect stems often attaining 2 feet, and leaves like those of *P. pulcherrimum* (which see). Corolla-lobes are somewhat *pointed,* rather than rounded, and vary from pinkish through lavender to bluish-violet. British Columbia records are central and northern. This species is very close to P. OCCIDENTÀLE Greene.

POLEMÒNIUM ÉLEGANS Greene, from the southern Cascades, is another sticky mountaineer, distinguished by its hairy-edged leaflets, that are not at all cleft, but so tightly arranged as to overlap, like shingles. Though exceedingly *beautiful,* the flowers have an unpleasant scent.

Pious and practical were the Mediaeval botanists, as is revealed in The grete Herball (whose authorship remains uncertain):

"O ye worthy reders or practicyens. . . I beseche yow take
intellygence and beholde ẙ workes & operacyns of almyghty god
which hath endewed his symple creature mankynde with the graces of
ẙ holy goost to haue parfyte knowlege and understandynge of the
vertue of all maner of herbes and trees. . . ."

[ed. 1539] The grete Herball (1526)

 **HYDROPHYLLÀCEAE.** *Waterleaf Family.*

HYDROPHÝLLUM CAPITÀTUM Dougl. *Dwarf Waterleaf.* [p.438]

Hydrophyllum means *water-leaf,* but the reference is obscure (see *H. tenuipes*). Capitatum means the inflorescence is a *head* or ball of close-packed flowers. This is an exceedingly variable perennial, but the commonest varieties are low and dwarf, var. ALPÌNUM Wats. having its stems almost entirely below the ground, and its flower-clusters just at the surface. Typically the stems of Dwarf Waterleaf are only about an inch long, the leaves extending upward a further 3-12 inches.

DODECATHEON PULCHELLUM $\times$ ⅗ [p.395]

GENTIANELLA AMARELLA $\times$ ½ [p.401]

PHLOX LONGIFOLIA $\times$ ⅘ [p.420]

CONVOLVULUS SEPIUM var. FRATERNIFLORUS
$\times$ ½ [p.408]

423

GENTIANA SCEPTRUM ×1¼ [p.401]

TRIENTALIS LATIFOLIA ×3 [p.396]

Flowers also are variable, from white to a more usual range between blue and lavender. This low plant is quite attractive, and very different in appearance from its woodland relative (*H. tenuipes* which see). The leaves rise in a cluster, on long petioles, from the shortened stem. They are obscurely pinnate (pinnatifid), with 7-11 segments, of which the upper 3 (or 5) tend to merge. The leaflets of H. capitatum are variously lobed, or (infrequently) toothed, some of the tips mucronate (ending in a little stubby point). The whole plant is loosely hairy, some of the long hairs on the calyx-lobes approaching soft spines. The rounded flower-clusters arise from short peduncles, that are much surpassed in length by the leaves. The bilobed stigma and anthers are held conspicuously above the corolla.

In rich moist soil of open meadows and slopes up to considerable altitudes, this oddly appealing plant is seen in bloom from March to July. It is limited to the southern Mainland, most often east of the Cascades.

HYDROPHÝLLUM FÉNDLERI (Gray) Heller var. ÁLBIFRONS (Heller) Macbr. is found at higher levels southward from Lytton. Fern-like leaf segments are sharply pointed, and strikingly white beneath. Calyx-lobes are marginally bristle-haired, and the flowers are white (less often purplish).

HYDROPHÝLLUM TENUÌPES Heller. *Slender Waterleaf.* [p.434]

The common name translates the generic name, from the Greek hydro-, *water*, and phyllon, a *leaf.* The meaning is obscure, though a possible explanation is that most of the species prefer wet habitats. Another explanation is that the large leaves funnel rain-water inward to the thick fleshy roots. Tenuipes means *slender-footed*, as this species (unlike most dwarf or low members of the genus) grows erect to a height of 2-3 feet.

The large (to 6 inches), nearly palmate leaves (they are described as pinni-palmately divided) attract attention before the rather dowdy flowers, which may be greenish-white to a rather washed-out purple. The single stem is generally stiffly-hairy, and bears few alternate, long-petioled, hairy leaves. These stem-leaves are almost as wide as long, the leaflets sharply and deeply toothed. The flowers are chiefly noticeable for their 5 protruding stamens and 3-cleft pistil, all more than twice as long as the cup-shaped corolla. The calyx is deeply 5-cleft, and its pointed lobes have markedly hairy margins.

Hydrophyllum tenuipes is a perennial of moist shaded woods at low elevations, from southern Vancouver Island and occasionally to the Cascades.

NEMÓPHILA PARVIFLÒRA Dougl. *Grove Lover.* [p.439]

The common name translates the Greek, nemos, *a grove*, and philein, *to love*. Most of these small-flowered relatives of the familiar edging-plant of our gardens inhabit open woodlands. (An exception is the prostrate NEMÓPHILA PEDUNCULÀTA Dougl., which is found in open meadows and moist ledges of southern Vancouver Island. Except for its growth habit it closely resembles N. parviflora.)

N. parviflora, as its name suggests, has *small flowers* scarcely more than ⅛ inch wide, and pale-lavender in colour. The sepals, weak sprawling stems, and deeply-cleft leaves bear stiff coarse hairs.

PHACÈLIA LINEÀRIS (Pursh) Holz. *Narrow-leaved Phacelia.*   [p.439]

Phacelia is a genus of about 150 species, with its centre of distribution in western North America. We shall be able to mention only two, chosen to represent the extremes of the plants found in our area. The name is drawn from the Greek phakelos, a fascicle, or close bundle, or *cluster*, with reference to the flowers crowded in an inflorescence. This species has some *linear* leaves, whence its name, but it also has 3-lobed leaves (and in any case, linear leaves are not limited to this species). Narrow-leaved Phacelia is a common annual of alkaline flats in the more arid parts of the Dry Interior*. Its big, lavender, salverform blossoms are seen from June to August.

As with most annuals, there is an almost fierce urgency to set seed, and in very arid situations depauperate plants, 2 inches high, will produce a single bloom. Normally, however, the single stem is 4-20 inches high, branched above, and sometimes bearing crowded groups of flowers in the axils of all the upper leaves. Stem, leaves, and calyx are densely fine-haired. Leaves are alternate, at first simple and linear, but developing side-lobes upward. The 5-cleft calyx is strongly hairy along the edges of the linear to spatulate lobes. Broadly campanulate, the corolla may span ¾ inch, and vary in colour from white through pale lavender to a very beautiful bluish-violet that merges into a white throat.

Phacelia linearis is a widespread and showy species.

*There are a few records from the Gulf Islands and near Victoria.

PHACÈLIA SERÍCEA (Grah.) Gray. *Silky Phacelia. Mountain Phacelia.*   [p.446]

How many climbers have been entranced by the first view of this lovely plant of mountain rock-ledges. Sericea means *silky*, from the hairs that make the basal leaf-cluster such an exquisite silky foil for the deep-purple flowers and their spectacular orange stamens.

This choice perennial graces the mountains of southern British Columbia from moderate to high elevations. The highest altitude forms seem most beautiful, by reason of their compact leaf-cluster, and a real, or fancied intensity of colour.

Leaves of Silky Phacelia are long-petioled, and irregular in their pinnate lobes, those

426

ASCLEPIAS SPECIOSA ✕²⁄₅ [p.406]

LYSIMACHIA THYRSIFLORA ✕³⁄₅ [p.396]

DOUGLASIA LAEVIGATA var. CILIOLATA ✕²⁄₅ [p.395]

CONVOLVULUS ARVENSIS ✕1 [p.408]

of the flower-stem becoming smaller, less lobed, and with shorter petioles. The dense, elongate flower-spike (properly, a thyrse) may be 4-6 inches long. Individual flowers have open-faced, campanulate corollas, whose dark colour is vividly accented by the very long violet filaments of the stamens, and their orange anthers.

ROMANZÓFFIA SITCHÉNSIS Bong. *Cliff Romanzoffia.* [p.439]

Nikolai Rumiantzev, Count Romanzoff (1754-1826) was a notable Russian patron of botany. His name is honoured by this genus of 4 beautiful species, as well as the orchidaceous *Spiranthes romanzoffiana* (which see). Sitchensis means *of Sitka,* where Eschscholtz, on the expedition sponsored by Romanzoff, discovered this exquisite little rock plant.

Moist cliffs and rock-ledges wet with snow-melt, often far above timber line, are home to this little plant that seems too delicate for such habitats. It graces such niches on all the mountain ranges of British Columbia; it is one of the regal beauties of the alpine world.

Basal leaves form a compact tuft, from which spring many slender 4-8 inch stems on which are spaced the cream-coloured cups, each with a vivid golden-orange eye. The 2-4 inch petioles of the basal leaves are at least twice as long as the blades, the blades being broadly heart-shaped, but with edges deeply and very regularly crenate-lobed. Romanzoffia sitchensis has few (often no) cauline leaves; if present they are short-petioled from near the bottom of the flower-scape. The whole plant is somewhat lax, and nearly glabrous except for short glandular hairs in the inflorescence. Calyx-lobes are oblong-linear and glabrous. Stamens have white anthers and are uneven in length, so that a few protrude just beyond the corolla-tube.

In this secluded shrine,
O miracle of grace,
No mortal eye but mine
Hath looked upon thy face.

John Bannister Tabb

ROMANZÓFFIA UNALASCHCÉNSIS Cham. (=R. TRÀCYI Jeps.) *Mist Maidens.* [p.447]

From frog-shrouded *Unalaska,* north along the coast, then south again to the misty Queen Charlottes and the stormy west coast of Vancouver Island, this remarkable Romanzoffia survives in spray-wet, rock crevices.

One would expect such high concentrations of salts must lead to disastrous exosmosis (outward movement and loss of water from the plants). But examination shows the thickened leaves are guarded by a heavy cortex, and then a waxy covering, so the sea-spray does not come into contact with the epidermal cells. Under surfaces are usually glabrous, but in a variant form are viscid-pubescent. Petioles, as in *R. sitchensis* (which see) are 2-3 times longer than the blades. The glossy blades are broader than long, with 5-8 rounded lobes. Delicate white funnel-form blossoms are in short, few-flowered racemes. Flower-stems (peduncles) are very much shorter and stronger than those of its lovely mountain relative, and the calyx-lobes are not glabrous, but short-pubescent.

The plant illustrated is wet with sea-spray. It was photographed in mid-May, in a deep rock crevice of the Sooke coast into which the sea surged, but no direct sunlight penetrated. There every seam and crack in the dark gneissic walls was crowded with the foliage tufts and bright faces of the Mist Maidens.

 BORAGINÀCEAE. *Borage Family.*

AMSÍNCKIA INTERMÈDIA Fisch. & Mey. *Fiddle-neck.* [p.446]

The rather curious generic name honours Wilhelm Amsinck, burgomaster and patron of the 19th century Botanical Garden of Hamburg. In our area occur several closely related species of these yellow- to orange-flowered and extremely bristle-haired weeds. The popular name well describes the arrangement of the small flowers in coiled or fiddle-scroll spikes. Throughout the Province, disturbed ground—especially along roadsides—is often invaded by one or more Amsinckia species.

A. intermedia has an orange-yellow corolla-tube that does not exceed ½ inch. The abundant hairs clothing the entire plant are of several kinds, and afford interesting studies under the microscope. The very stiff white ones easily penetrate the skin, and can be very irritating.

CYNOGLÓSSUM GRÁNDE Dougl. *Hound's Tongue.* [p.446]

This is the most handsome member of the genus that derives its name from the Greek kyno-, *dog,* and glossa, *tongue,* from the shape—and possibly the texture—of the leaves. Grande (Latin), *large,* is a suitable epithet, for this robust plant is 2-3 feet high, with leaf-blades up to 8 inches long, plus a petiole of equal length.

The corolla is blue to violet, ½ inch or a little more in diameter. A curious, and distinctive feature of the flowers of this family, is the presence of 5 little rounded nubs (the fornices) at the summit of the corolla-tube, opposite the corolla-lobes. In Cynoglossum these are very evident, and in this species they appear like a white, raised, almost continuous ring. If a flower is split lengthwise these fornices are seen as a row of fleshy, notched fingers, with the anthers spaced between them and slightly lower, and the simple stigma lower still. The filaments of the stamens have disappeared into the wall of the corolla-tube, so that the anthers appear to grow directly from the wall. The calyx is deeply lobed, the 5 lobes ovate and hairy.

The stems are usually glabrous, with only a few, much smaller leaves near the summit-panicle, most of the large leaves arising from the lower half. Lower surfaces of the leaf-blades and petioles are hairy, the upper faces nearly glabrous. The shape is variable, often ovate, with a pointed tip.

Hound's Tongue is easy and effective in a semi-shaded part of the garden. Perennial, from a heavy, thickened taproot, it occurs rarely in woods at low elevations in the southern Kootenay. It is an early bloomer, (sometimes in March).

CYNOGLÓSSUM BOREÀLE Fern. is a similar, though smaller species than C. grande (which see), with blue flowers less than ½ inch wide. It has a much more hairy stem, with leaves numerous to the top. Only the lowest leaves have petioles; the upper ones (being without petioles) clasp the stem. The fornices are stubby, not notched at the tip. C. boreale is a widely distributed plant (from roughly Lillooet to Revelstoke, and southward).

[p.434]   CYNOGLÓSSUM OFFICINÀLE L. is a weedy biennial immigrant from Europe, strongly established along roadsides in the southern part of the Province. The corolla is dull reddish-purple, and if split, shows short, though definite filaments on the stamens, and a style that is peg-shaped, or swollen below. The 4-clustered burs catch on clothing and hair. The plant is coarse and unattractive.

LITHOSPÉRMUM RUDERÀLE Dougl. ex Lehm. *Gromwell. Puccoon.* [p.447]

This very common plant, of open places in the Dry Interior, obtains its name from the bony nutlets, which look like mediaeval pointed helmets. Lithos is Greek for *stone,* and the more familiar word sperma, means *seed.* The meaning of the specific epithet is "growing in rubbish or a disturbed place, as along roadsides". "Puccoon" is a name applied at least 130 years ago, to any of various plants, used for staining and dyeing by the Algonkian tribes. (Another form is pakon, from pak, *blood,* also giving rise to the English word poke). At the same time "Gromwell" was in use, but it was applied to a *Sanguinaria* sp. (Bloodroot). The derivation is from the Middle English gromil or Middle French grémil, which in turn is from early French gres, sandstone, and mil, millet. Certain of the Lithospermums were used by the Indians medicinally, and in recent years they have been sources of a group of compounds related to consolidin, which may have useful analgesic properties.

This is a coarse perennial, with several very leafy stems growing 10-20 inches from a large woody taproot. Long white hairs make the stems and lower leaf surfaces hoary. The linear-lanceolate entire leaves clasp the stem. The flowers are not showy, being greenish-yellow and almost hidden in the axils of the leaves. The 5-lobed corolla is about ½ inch across. It should be split lengthwise to reveal the 5 anthers growing directly from the wall of the tube, and the slightly-clubbed pistil about as tall as the base of the anthers. The usual fornices of this family are missing, their place being taken by a ring of short glandular hairs. Rather surprisingly, the flowers are very pleasantly fragrant.

LITHOSPÉRMUM INCÌSUM Lehm., of similar range to *L. ruderale* (which see), is readily distinguished by a slim corolla-tube 3 times as long as the calyx. It is a prettier plant, the flowers more conspicuous and brighter orange-yellow, especially at the beginning of the flowering season (in May). The corolla-lobes are noticeably *irregular,* almost fimbriate.

MERTÉNSIA LONGIFLÒRA Greene. *Lungwort. Bluebells.*

F. C. Mertens, 1764-1831, was an early German botanist. This *long-flowered* species is probably the most widespread of the 5 or 6 species found in our area. Neither of the common names is generally accepted: the first belongs more properly to *Pulmonaria,* and the second will be forever associated, at least in the English mind, with spring-time carpets of *Hyacinthoides* (formerly *Scilla*) *non-scripta.* And the Scots will think of *Campanula rotundifolia* when Bluebell is mentioned. So there is good reason for general use of the Latin names of plants!

M. longiflora is an attractive plant of lower level Ponderosa Pine-Sagebrush flats in extreme southern British Columbia. It is a spring flower, its pink buds opening into attractive blue, long-tubed "bells" in April and May.

Roots are shallow tubers, almost black. The stems at 3000-4000 feet may be a mere 2 inches tall, but at lower levels average about 6-8 inches. Most of the first-year plants produce only a number of basal leaves that have appreciable petioles, and broad rounded blades. Many observers have been confused by the very different leaves of the *flowering plants,* for they are entirely cauline, without petioles, and oblong to obovate. Stems and leaves are nearly glabrous, although the lower leaf-surface may carry tight-pressed hairs. The flowers are carried in a drooping head at the top of the stem. Calyx-lobes (5) are long and pointed. The tube of the corolla is about 3 times as long as the calyx, with the 5 lobes upright (even less flared than those of its near relative, *M. oblongifolia* (which see). If the flower is slit, one can see small fornices alternating with the lobes, broad-filamented anthers that originate at the level of the fornices, and a very long pistil that overtops the anthers.

This species is described by Dr. Ira Gabrielson in *Western American Alpines*—"The first sight of a Mertensia-covered hillside is simply breath-taking in loveliness. . . ."

MERTÉNSIA OBLONGIFÒLIA (Nutt.) G. Don. On the same (or more southern) [p.450] dry slopes of the southern Interior that are the home of *M. longiflora* (which see), one may find this rarer and closely related species. Equally beautiful, M. oblongifolia is readily distinguished in the field by the fact that the flowering plants bear a number of clustered basal leaves, in addition to the leaves of the flowering stem. (Flowering plants of *M. longiflora* as a rule bear stem-leaves only.) The present species is further distinguished by more pointed leaves, flowers in which the tube is slightly shorter but the lobes more flared, and clumps of flower-stems (rather than the frequently solitary flower-stems of its cousin).

[p.451] MERTÉNSIA PANICULÀTA (Ait.) G. Don. var. BOREÀLIS (Macbr.) Williams, *Tall Lungwort* is one of several much taller species, that may reach 5 feet. Though lacking *M. longiflora's* compactness and exquisite freshness of colour, this is a handsome plant, its slender stems bending gracefully under the open raceme of pale-blue flowers. The pistil usually projects beyond the corolla, and the leaves (especially the large cordate basal ones) are nearly always covered with short, appressed hairs. Tall Lungwort is a plant of moister situations, as wet meadows and stream-banks, east of the Cascades. May sees the first flowers, but at high altitudes the blooms do not appear until August.

MYOSÒTIS LÁXA Lehm. *Forget-me-not.* [p.451]

This familiar little blue flower obtains its name from the Greek mus, *mouse,* and ous, *ear,* descriptive of the short, furred leaves of some species. Laxa means *open* or loose, which fits both the sprawling plant structure, and the long, sparsely-flowered, somewhat coiled pseudo-racemes. In older troubled times, the likeness of this flower was once embroidered on sleeves and collars of those knights who remained loyal to Henry of Lancaster. So "flower-people" preceded the 20th century!

Forget-me-nots are too well known to require any extensive description. This short-lived perennial species is soft, almost succulent, the weak stems often extending along the ground as much as 18-20 inches. The plant is essentially glabrous, though occasionally the leaves bear close-pressed stiff hairs, and the calyx apparently is always marked by short straight hairs. Frequently the buds (and occasionally the freshly opened blooms, especially in overcast weather) are pink, later turning a limpid pale-blue that is relieved by the yellow "eye". These flowers should be admired as they grow, in wet soil or shallow water, for the delicate corollas fall even as the stem is picked. Myosotis laxa is found in suitable locations at low altitudes throughout our area, and spreads its bloom over the long period from June to September. It is common in ditches and water-margins.

MYOSÒTIS SYLVÁTICA Hoffm., better known perhaps as *M. alpéstris,* is a more erect alpine species than *M. laxa* (which see). It ranges from Alaska to southern British Columbia. The flowers are delicately fragrant. At high altitudes, its blue almost rivals that of the fabulous *Eritrichium nanum,* "King of the Alps". Some of the hairs on the calyx-lobes are distinctly hooked at their tips (i.e. they are uncinate)—a good recognition feature, but one requiring a 10X magnifier.

MYOSÒTIS ARVÉNSIS (L.) Hill, chiefly of the Gulf Islands and vicinity of Victoria, has a deeply notched calyx-tube with glandular hairs. Its short pistil does not reach the level of the stamen-bases.

MYOSÒTIS DISCÒLOR Pers. is perhaps the most common species, yet it is an introduction from Europe. The buds and newly-opened corollas are yellow, later turning blue. Corolla-tube is slim, with tiny lobes never spreading flat. This is a weedy annual, not showy.

PLAGIOBÓTHRYS SCOULÉRI (H. & A.) Johnst.   [p.451]

This looks like a small white forget-me-not, this ground-hugging dwarf of spring-wet thin soil over much of the Province. In April, on windy coastal headlands, the sprawling plants often do not lift their cheerful yellow-centred white salvers more than an inch above the ground. Linear leaves, stems, and even the pointed sepal-segments are thickly hairy. The flowers yield to a cluster of 4 lanceolate rough-surfaced nutlets.

Somewhat intimidating, the generic name is derived from the Greek plagios, *placed sideways,* and bothros, *a pit* or trench, referring to the groove on the nutlet. This little plant bears the name of John Scouler (1804-71), Scottish botanist who collected extensively in western North America.

VERBENÀCEAE. *Verbena Family.*

VERBÈNA BRACTEÀTA Lag. & Rodr. *Vervain.*

No native representatives of this largely tropical family are at all comparable to the showy Verbena hybrids of our gardens. In fact, this positively dowdy plant hides even its paltry flowers in coarse leafy *bracts* that are responsible for its specfic name. Verbena is apparently of Latin origin, applied to sacred *garlands* made of an unknown plant.

This is a sprawling plant with numerous coarsely-hairy stems radiating from a taproot. Approximately opposite leaves are trifoliate and further deeply-notched, rough-pubescent throughout. At the end of each branch the leaves change to numerous long, lanceolate bracts that almost conceal ⅛ inch, drab, bluish-mauve corollas. These emerge from a bristle-haired, 5-toothed calyx-tube, that is about ⅔ as long.

This unattractive plant occurs on dry roadsides in the southern Interior.

ARMERIA MARITIMA $\times\frac{1}{2}$ [p.397]

HYDROPHYLLUM TENUIPES $\times\frac{1}{2}$ [p.424]

POLEMONIUM PULCHERRIMUM $\times\frac{1}{4}$ [p.420]

CYNOGLOSSUM OFFICINALE $\times\frac{1}{2}$ [p.430]

LEPTODACTYLON PUNGENS ×⅖ [p.416]

LINANTHUS BICOLOR ×1¼ [p.416]

COLLOMIA GRANDIFLORA ×1 [p.413]

🌿 LABIÀTAE. *Mint Family.*

Flowers of the Labiatae are highly specialized. Both sepals and petals are tubular, and lobed. The lower lip or labia (Latin *lip*) is very characteristic, and is responsible for the family name. It is variously modified, to force selected visiting insects to come into contact with the 4 (or 2) stamens and the forked pistil. The family is one of the easiest to recognize, nearly all members having the typically bilobed corolla, stems square in cross section, leaves usually opposite and simple, and nearly always dotted with glands that secrete essential oils responsible for the aromatic odour. This is very evident in members of the genus *Mentha,* or Mints, that produce a great variety of scented and flavoured oils.

About 3200 species are known, chiefly from the North Temperate Zone. Members of the Labiatae are rather noticeably scarce, or absent, in alpine areas.

Besides various kinds of Mint, and Rosemary (*Rosmarinus officinalis,* commercially grown), a number of species are valued in the flower garden, including the creeping ground cover *Ajuga,* Lavender (*Lavandula officinalis*), *Nepeta* for edging the border, *Salvia* (which includes both Garden Sage [*S. officinalis*], and the fiery scarlet *S. splendens*), besides the bright-leaved *Coleus.* (Incidentally, the frequent epithet "officinalis" in this genus shows these were once "medicinal" plants of the Herbalists.)

A concluding note throws some light on the extreme difficulty (to which frequent reference has been made in this book) of a conceptual grasp of that nebulous entity, the species. One of the long-recognized "good" species of the family, *Galeopsis tetrahit* (a weedy and successful coarse plant now found over most of the world) was actually created, or duplicated, in some famous experiments by Müntzing. He crossed two wild species (*G. pubescens* and *G. speciosa,* both having a chromosome number 16), and back-crossed the hybrid on *G. pubescens,* thereby obtaining a diploid with chromosome number of 32. The diploid appeared identical in every respect with the natural *G. tetrahit,* and readily interbred with it. The only possible conclusion is that *G. tetrahit* is a "species" which originated—possibly thousands of years ago—as a result of the natural occurrence of this crossing and back-crossing. So this must be one of the possible ways in which "species" originate.

GLECÒMA HEDERÀCEA L. *Ground Ivy. Creeping Charlie.* [p.447]

Glechon was the classical Greek name for some unknown species of *Mentha,* while the specific name in translation also accounts for the first of the common names: hederaceus in Latin means *of the ivy.* No one seems to know who Charlie was, but the running rhizomes account for the adjective.

This is a Eurasian native now well-established across North America, by moist roadsides and in wet thickets.

This low perennial, with long-petioled, pungently aromatic, and often purplish leaves, bears rather conspicuous flowers in loose whorls at the base of the leaves. The often-recommended splitting of the purple flower reveals 2 long and 2 short stamens, that bear odd split pollen-sacs on the sides of the filaments (near their upper ends). The corolla-tube is very long, expanded about halfway up, and then split into two lips—the upper 2-lobed and concave, the lower 3-lobed with the large central-lobe strongly spotted with dark-purple. The whole plant is hairy.

LÝCOPUS AMERICÀNUS Muhl. *Water Horehound.* [p.450]

Lycopus is a genus of mint-like, nearly hairless plants of very wet soils. The name is from the Greek lykos, *wolf,* and pous, *foot,* due to a fancied resemblance of the leaves (but not at all suggested by the foliage of any of our 3 species). Horehound in Europe is *Marrubium vulgare,* but the origin of the word is interesting. The original spelling was hoarhound, from *hoar* (Old English hár), the plant being covered with white, woolly down; and from hune (Anglo-Saxon) for strong-scented. Our plants are very slightly aromatic, and inconspicuously hairy.

Most outdoors people are familiar with this Lycopus, perhaps taking it for *Mentha arvensis* (which see), which often shares with it stream-banks, and gravel or sandy lakeshores. But Lycopus americanus has more deeply lobed leaves, and the flowers are white rather than lavender, and very inconspicuous in the leaf-axils. The plants form clusters, because they arise from slim rhizomes.

This species is found all across the continent, from British Columbia to Newfoundland, southward to Florida and California, so it is truly "americanus".

If the small flower is split lengthwise it is possible to see with a good magnifying glass or low-power microscope, that 2 of the 4 stamens usual in the Labiatae have aborted, only vestigial filaments remaining. The bicleft stigma is lifted on a long style to the level of the 2 functional anthers, and a ring of short hairs encircles the corolla-tube about halfway up. The corolla appears to be 4-lobed, but one of the apparent lobes is slightly notched, and is actually 2 lobes fused. The 5 calyx-lobes are sharply pointed.

LÝCOPUS UNIFLÒRUS Michx. is very similar to *L. americanus* (which see), though generally smaller and more montane, descending to sea level west of the Cascades. Its leaves are only shallowly notched, and its calyx-lobes broader, shorter, and much less sharply-pointed. There is no sign of the second pair of stamens.

The dry southern Interior plant, that tolerates alkaline shores, is LÝCOPUS ÁSPER Greene. It is exceedingly similar to *L. americanus* (which see), but larger and *coarser,* growing from a swollen rather than a slim rhizome, and with leaves that are sharply serrate only, but not deeply-lobed.

MÉNTHA ARVÉNSIS L. *Canada Mint.* [p.450]

Vast confusion surrounds the species of this genus, some authorities recognizing more than 200, others about 15. The present widespread species has a long list of apparent

438

PHLOX CAESPITOSA ×1 [p.417]

HYDROPHYLLUM CAPITATUM var. ALPINUM ×½ [p.421]

PHLOX DIFFUSA ×2 [p.417]

NEMOPHILA PARVIFLORA ×2 [p.424]

ROMANZOFFIA SITCHENSIS ×¼ [p.428]

PHACELIA LINEARIS ×2 [p.425]

439

synonyms, and will be better known to many as *M. canadénsis* L. Arvensis means *of the fields,* and Linnaeus states that in Europe it is frequent in arable fields. However, the plant is circumboreal, and in our area is found in moist soil, or sand, along streams and lakeshores. Mentha is from the Greek, one of the nymphs being *Minthe,* who was turned into a mint plant by Proserpina, in a fit of jealousy. We also have from the Greek word for incense, the Middle English tyme or thyme, now sometimes applied to the family.

The 16th century Italian herbalist Petri Andreae Matthioli quotes Galen (A.D. 130-210?), the celebrated medical writer and philosopher, that thyme "purges choler or black humour, being therefore useful to the melancholic". Though the medical aspect of this statement may be suspect, the psychology is not. Can anyone remain in ill-humour who on lake or streamshore comes upon this fragrant mint, and brings to his nostrils a few leaves, bruised, and aromatic with their special magic?

This is one of the most fragrant of the mints, a source of menthol but with traces of several aldehydes and ketones.

The 8-20 inch stems ascend from a creeping perennial rhizome; as is the rule in this family, they are square in cross section with leaves in opposite pairs. The leaves are variably glabrous or hairy, pointed oval, and sharply serrate. The axils of the middle or upper leaves bear tight, clustered balls of small flowers, light-purple, occasionally white or pinkish. A good magnifying glass is needed to study their detail, and this is necessary for positive identification. The calyx-cup is sharply 5-notched, for about ¼ of its depth. It bears both straight and knob-tipped, glandular hairs. Four equal and long stamens, and a 2-lobed pistil, project well beyond the mouth of the corolla-tube, which has 3 rounded lobes and a wider, notched one (which results from union of 2 lobes). About mid-length of the interior wall of the corolla there is a zone of long hairs.

The Mentha species secrete a variety of perfumed oils. As garden-escapes in our area, particularly near Victoria and Vancouver, one may find M. ROTUNDIFÒLIA, apple-scented; M. CITRÀTA, lemon-scented (and one of the ingredients of Eau de Cologne); M. PIPERÌTA, peppermint; M. SPICÀTA, spearmint. Various horticultural forms of these and others are known, with a number of hybrids, so that a very confusing collection results. As many woodsmen have discovered, a quick infusion of the present species makes a refreshing substitute for tea.

An Assyrian predecessor of European herbalists is known to us from incised clay tablets of the 7th century B.C. Study of these reveals that the doctors of Nineveh possessed considerable knowledge of plants and their uses. Thus HASANU (apparently a species of Thyme) was recommended for difficulty in breathing.

MONÁRDA FISTULÒSA L. var. MENTHAEFÒLIA (Grah.) Fern. *Wild Bergamot. Horse Mint.* [p.458]

This very showy flower of the central and southern Dry Interior is a purple brother of the scarlet Oswego Tea or Bee Balm (*M. didyma*) that is so well-known to gardeners.

The generic name commemorates Nicolás Monardes—or Monardez—(born a year after Columbus' great discovery), an early Spanish physician who was the author of several works on the plants of the New World. Fistulosa means *hollow*, but the application is unclear; the square stems are neither more nor less hollow than those of numerous other mints. The varietal name directs attention to the *leaves*, which are quite like those of many *Mentha* species (Mints) both in shape and because they are strongly-toothed and opposite. Bergamot originally referred to a herb of the kitchen garden whose scent was said to resemble that of a Bergamotte Orange.

Low-altitude places—open, often rocky—in July flaunt bright patches of this attractive plant. From spreading rhizomes, unbranched 18-inch stems grow stiffly erect. Each is topped by a roundish head of flowers, bright-rose, purple of varying intensity, or occasionally white. The flower-cluster is set off by a circle of large, green, leaf-like bracts. Individual flowers are about 1½ inches long, and very strongly cleft into two lips that open wide, like the gape of a fledgling bird. The lower lip, itself shallowly 3-lobed, affords a pendulous landing platform for the visiting butterfly, whose long proboscis can plumb the nectaries at the bottom of the deep corolla-tube. The long, curved, and narrow upper lip serves to hold its projecting stamens and pistil just where they will brush the head and thorax of the visiting insect.

Good colour forms of Monarda fistulosa are well worth a place in the garden, but the plants demand winter dryness, so are unlikely to succeed west of the Cascades.

PRUNÉLLA VULGÁRIS L. *Self-heal. Heal-all.* [p.459]

This spelling by Linnaeus is accepted by the International Rules of Nomenclature. However it was earlier Brunella, from the German die Bräune, *the quinsy*, for which the plant was a reputed remedy. Vulgaris means *common*, this ubiquitous plant being cosmopolitan, from sea level to moderate altitudes. Its common names witness the reputation it once possessed. Though extracts of Prunella have been studied by a number of investigators, who were encouraged by the mediaeval claims, their conclusions have been wryly stated, "The value of the Elixir appears to reside solely in the alcoholic solvent." As Rudyard Kipling nicely summed such matters:

> *"Anything green that grew out of the mould*
> *Was an excellent herb to our fathers of old."*

No detailed description of Heal-all is needed. The flowers are usually violet, but rarely one finds white individuals, or even beautiful pink ones. The flower-heads are curiously squarish in section. The calyx is generally suffused with purple. Corolla may be nearly an inch long, but in most forms is about half that length. Its upper lip is helmet-shaped, the lower is 3-lobed, of which the middle one is much the largest, and attractively fringed and decorated with white, crisped hairs. The stamens are unusual, as the filament is short-forked at the tip, one only of the forks bearing an anther.

SATURÈJA DOUGLÀSII (Benth.) Briq. *Yerba Buena.* [p.459]

This little trailing Mint is valued for the bewitching scent of its crushed leaves. Though these are evergreen, the essential oils responsible are not produced in any quantity until the winter has passed. The Greek spelling was Satureia, from earlier Arabic S'sáttar, applied to an unknown Mint. David Douglas was the Scottish farm-hand, whose intelligence and industry so impressed Sir W. J. Hooker, among others, that in 1823 at the age of 24, he was exploring the plant wonders of the far west. We have few plants with common names that recall the Spanish explorations northward from California; this one means the *good herb*. (Other Spanish names include *Chinquapin, Madroña, Mariposa.*)

Long, creeping, semi-woody stems may be a yard long. They frequently root at the internodes, and bear opposite pairs of inch-long ovate leaves, usually with a few blunt teeth. They are glabrous (or sometimes short-haired), paler below, sometimes bronzed or purpled above. From the leaf-axil, on a short pedicel with a pair of tiny bracts, a single small flower is carried. Usually white, or fading white, it is also palest blue-lavender, pink-flushed without. The tubular calyx is conspicuously striped, its 5 teeth only about one-fifth as long as the tube. Split, the corolla reveals a hairy throat, a pair of stamens with short filaments and a pair with long filaments. (Both kinds bear double anthers, which become dark crimson and make effective accents, in the pale flower.) The 3 lobes of the lower lip are wavy-edged, and almost equal in size.

Humble but esteemed, this small creeping plant prefers open, coniferous woods at lower altitudes. Yerba Buena is native to southwestern British Columbia, and blooms sparingly in June and July.

STÀCHYS CÒOLEYAE Heller. *Hedge Nettle.* [p.459]

This rather handsome, non-stinging (or "dead") magenta-flowered nettle is named after Grace Cooley, whose type specimen is dated "Nanimo, Vancouver Island, July 18, 1891". Stachys is unaltered Greek, meaning *spike*, with reference to the series of whorled flowers arranged on an ascending axis.

This robust plant is rapidly invasive from long-running rhizomes. Single stems are strongly squared and bristly-haired, reaching 3-5 feet. The oppositely-paired, ovate leaves are 3-6 inches long, coarsely crenate, and hairy on both faces. A whorl of flowers appears in the axils of the uppermost smaller leaves. The tubular flowers are about 1-1½ inches long, and (as previously mentioned) of a rather violent magenta. The calyx is shallowly notched, the lobes ending in a point sharp enough to penetrate one's skin. The bilabiate corolla shows a hooded upper lip, usually shorter than the 3-lobed lower one. There is a narrow ring of hairs within the tube, near its base. The 4 stamens carry double-anthers, and the outermost pair of stamens turn their anthers downward as they mature (dehisce).

The Hedge Nettle prefers swampy low ground, westward from the Cascades to the Coast. It has a long season in flower, from June to August.

SOLANÀCEAE. *Nightshade Family. Potato Family.*

SOLÀNUM NÌGRUM L. *Black Nightshade.*

Considerable research reveals no clear derivation for the generic name of the plant, but among others one may choose from solamen meaning *soothing* (from narcotic—or toxic!—qualities) or solor, *to comfort.* The specific epithet refers to the shiny *black* fruit, reported poisonous by some authorities, but safe by others. The puzzle is apparently resolved by Hitchcock et al., who state the immature berries are toxic but become edible at maturity "at least in some races". This evidence, and a ready confusion with undoubtedly poisonous similar black fruits of the Deadly Nightshade (*Solanum* [or *Atropa*] *belladonna* L.), suggest that children should be warned to shun the fruit.

This is a widespread annual weed, increasingly common in moist soil throughout our area. Indeed, in one or more of its numerous variations, Black Nightshade is cosmopolitan. Its yellow-centred, pale-purplish flowers appear late in summer, and are soon succeeded by egg-shaped berries—first green, then yellow, reddish, and finally black.

The variably-hairy ridged stems may clamber 2 feet, but are often prostrate. The leaves (which, like the berry, contain the bitter and toxic alkaloid solanine) are ovate, but irregular—sometimes rather notched. The flowers appear in small clusters on short flower-stems that alternate with the leaves, but do not spring from their axils. The 5 calyx-lobes are ovate, often unequal, and reflexed. The corolla has 5 lanceolate lobes. (These and the upper part of the flared tube are reflexed.) Five bright-yellow anthers form a conspicuous semi-united tube about the single pistil, which barely protrudes.

SOLÀNUM DULCAMÀRA L. (Literally sweet-bitter, but in English called *Bitter-sweet,* or *Woodbine),* is a more vine-like plant, than *S. nigrum* (which see), clambering several yards through supporting shrubbery. It has large clusters of very showy, bluish-violet flowers strikingly accented by the yellow anther-column. The fruits are bright scarlet. Bitter-sweet is a Eurasian immigrant, occurring along wet roadsides, dried creek-beds and marshy shores of southwestern British Columbia. Blooming season is May-September. [p.451]

Bring the rathe Primrose that forsaken dies,
The tufted Crow-toe, and pale Jessamine,
The white Pink, and the Pansy freakt with jet,
The glowing Violet,
The Musk-rose, and the well-attir'd Woodbine. . . .

John Milton: Lycidas

🌿 SCROPHULARIÀCEAE. *Figwort Family.*

This large family of about 200 genera and possibly 2900 species contains many treasured and popular garden flowers. Most are herbs, with a few vines and fewer trees, and several parasitic plants. They are recognized by their zygomorphic corolla, meaning a corolla that is not radially symmetrical, i.e. that has some inequality in size, form, or union of similar parts. *Labiatae* are also zygomorphic, but have a divided ovary (usually yielding 4 nutlets), whereas the Figworts have a 2-carpel 2-celled ovary. In Scrophulariaceae the sepals are united or distinct, the corolla always tubular and 2-lipped (bilabiate) but variously lobed, the stamens 2-5 but typically 4, the pistil with distinct or united stigmas. Leaves follow no definite pattern and may be either alternate or opposite.

Best known members will serve to visualize the family characteristics. They include *Antirrhinum* (Snapdragon), *Digitalis* (Foxglove), *Calceolaria,* the myriad *Penstemons, Mimulus,* the brightly painted *Castillejas,* and less typically, *Verbascum* (Mullein).

CASTILLÈJA LEVISÉCTA Greenman. *Golden Paintbrush.* [p.462]

If the euphonious generic name brings old Castile to mind, we are not so far off, for it celebrates the late 18th century Spanish botanist, Don Domingo Castillejo. Levisecta means *lightly cut,* which describes the terminal lobes of the upper leaves and bracts, which are less deeply divided than is usual in the genus. This is an extremely handsome plant, that looks as though it might have been touched with brightest yellow paint.

The "flowers" of the Indian Paintbrushes, like those of the Dogwoods, are actually coloured bracts that shelter the true blooms. It is necessary to fold back these bright, leaf-like bracts to expose the 4-cleft calyx, and long, narrow, bilabiate corolla. The upper lip, called the galea, is like a beak that almost encloses the anthers of the 4 stamens. The much reduced, stubby, lower lip's shape and size (relative to the galea) are important in recognition of the species. However, with the exception of one or two well-marked and stable species, identification of the Castilleja species is often puzzling to the expert and the specialist. This is partly due to the variability of characteristic features, but largely because numerous "hybrid swarms" exist, especially along the areas where species meet.

All our species are perennials, and all are to some degree root-parasitic, though they have chlorophyllaceous leaves. Probably about 30 "species" occur in our area, but a monographer might reduce this by a half, or possibly add a considerable number. We describe the most common kinds, having an eye for the sorts of different colours. But alas, this handy attribute is of very little value, for many yellowish species are frequently purplish, and albino forms are quite often met with. Similarly, several of the scarlet species are often rose-coloured, or crimson, or purplish, and even occasionally yellowish.

Having said this, we can suggest that a very bright-yellow Castilleja, with a galea not more than ½ the length of the corolla-tube, with lower lip only about ⅕ the galea-length, and with obtuse (not sharply pointed) calyx-lobes—begins to look like this species. If it was found west of the Cascades—especially near the sea—the chances are good that it is C. levisecta. Other characteristics then to check are: rather viscid, woolly hairs, coloured bracts about as wide as the upper leaves (with 2-6 shallow terminal lobes) and corolla about an inch long (or little less).

CASTILLÈJA SULPHÙREA Rydb., *Pallid Paintbrush* is a pale-yellow or cream-coloured species with a long hooked galea that projects beyond the coloured bracts, and has leaves lanceolate-linear and entire. It is not likely to be found far from the southeastern corner of the Province.   [p.463]

CASTILLÈJA MINIÀTA Dougl. *Common Red Paintbrush.* [pp.459,463]

It is a moot point whether this species is more common than others, without qualification of geographical area; we give Moss's name (Common Red Paintbrush) as a suggestion only, for those who are happier with an English name. Another, at least as valid, would be Scarlet Paintbrush, for miniata is derived from minium, the *scarlet-red* higher oxide of lead. But occasionally crimson specimens are seen, and even, rarely, yellow.

Castilleja miniata is widely distributed throughout our area, and is highly variable. The 8-30 inch plants may be nearly glabrous, to sticky, with long, woolly hairs. Leaves are linear to lanceolate, mostly entire, though with a few upper ones 2- or 3-lobed. The slightly-hooked tips of the galea show above the bright-coloured bracts. The calyx is deeply cleft into 2 slightly unequal parts which are then again split, the ultimate segments being linear, or slender-pointed. The galea is equal in length to the tube-part of the corolla (or about ¾ as long). The rudimentary lower lip of the corolla-tube is dark-green, and about ⅕ as long as the upper lip (galea).

This plant's splashes of barbaric colour never fail to evoke a primitive excitement. The Paintbrush hues dominate the alpine meadows, and the chromatic intensity makes visible at a great distance a patch of these plants on a lakeshore. Approach to admire it, but do not make the vain attempt to transplant it, for as mentioned under *C. levisecta* (which see), the plant is at least partially parasitic and will not long survive in the garden.

CASTILLÈJA PARVIFLÒRA Bong. (= C. OREOPÒLA Greenm.) *Rosy Paintbrush.* [p.470]

Though parviflora means *small-flowered* the term is without particular significance in this species, for which a number of varieties have been named. (C. oreopola is an older name, now displaced by the rule of precedence). Similarly Peck's suggested English name applies to some populations, but others are crimson, or white. This is the most abundant species in the high meadows of the Olympics, where thousands of summer visitors have thrilled to its brilliant display. But it is also locally abundant in Manning Park, the Peace River country, and the Rocky Mountains.

446

AMSINCKIA INTERMEDIA ×1 [p.429]

CYNOGLOSSUM GRANDE ×⅖ [p.429]

PHACELIA SERICEA ×¾ [p.425]

LITHOSPERMUM RUDERALE ×½ [p.430]

GLECOMA HEDERACEA ×⅘ [p.436]

ROMANZOFFIA UNALASCHENSIS ×1⅕ [p.428]

LYCOPUS AMERICANUS ✕1 [p.437]

MENTHA ARVENSIS ✕⅘ [p.437]

MERTENSIA OBLONGIFOLIA ✕1¼ [p.431]

MERTENSIA PANICULATA var. BOREALIS ×½ [p.432]

MYOSOTIS LAXA ×1½ [p.432]

PLAGIOBOTHRYS SCOULERI ×1 [p.433]

SOLANUM DULCAMARA ×½ [p.443]

[p.471]   LINÀRIA DALMÀTICA (L.) Mill. is a much more attractive, barely-scented, taller plant than *L. vulgaris* (which see). This fine plant may reach 4 feet. The leaves are distinctive—firm and almost leathery, pointed-ovate, clasping the strong stem. The flowers are larger (up to 1½ inches long) but of the same bright-yellow and orange. L. dalmatica is sparsely established—usually in very sandy soil—in stations across the southern part of our area. Both species of Linaria are immigrants from the Mediterranean.

MÍMULUS ALSINOÌDES Dougl. *Little Monkey Flower.* [p.475]

This bright-faced little Monkey Flower appears to have received no common name that is of any more than the most local acceptance. The genus is well-known to florists, less so to the outdoor gardener. Its name is the diminutive of mimus, a *mimic* or buffoon, from the grinning ape-like face. The specific name means *like Alsine,* a long-disused name for Minuartias, which are related to our Arenarias (see *Arenaria macrophylla*).

As soon as the spring sun has gained a little warmth, the droll faces of these tiny annuals may be spied in a sheltered rock crevice, or protected bit of short turf. Such places retain moisture just long enough for the 1-5 inch plants to bloom, and set abundant seed. And how they bloom! During their short life the tiny plants are dwarfed by beautiful golden flowers, that hold up impudent monkey faces. On inspection the limpid-yellow corolla is seen to be bilabiate: the upper lip with 2 lobes each marked by a thin purple mid-line, the lower with 3 lobes—of which the middle one is much the largest, and suffused with a more intense cadmium-yellow. Plant-lovers will find much variation in the scarlet or maroon markings on this lower lip: sometimes numerous and pin-point, sometimes fewer and larger, occasionally consolidated into a single vivid insignia. These lower lobes are lightly notched at the tip. The small leaves are variable in shape (sometimes slightly notched) and commonly purplish (at least below). The calyx-lobes are uneven and usually marked with very short white hairs.

This wee plant is altogether charming.

MÍMULUS GUTTÀTUS DC. *Common Monkey Flower.* [p.474]

A long list of synonyms attests the variability of this very beautiful Monkey Flower. The specific name means spotted or *speckled,* since the bright-yellow lower lip is variously marked with crimson or maroon.

In one form or another M. guttatus is found in seepages and wet runnels from sea level to considerable elevations throughout our area. Its showy blooms may be seen from May until late in September.

A very plastic species, it may be an annual or perennial. Impoverished plants—dwarfed by the relatively huge flowers—may be only a few inches high. But in wet and fertile soil robust plants may approach 3 feet, with succulent, hollow, squarish stems as thick as one's thumb. The leaves are variably ovate, irregularly dentate, either glabrous or soft-haired. Like the stem and leaves, the calyx is usually glabrous, but occasionally bears very short, soft pubescence. Calyx-lobes are uneven, the upper one being much larger than the others. The whole calyx swells markedly after the corolla has fallen, becoming very large and conspicuous as the seeds ripen. The showy flowers may be 1½ inches across, of a peculiarly intense gamboge-yellow. The lobes are thin and almost translucent, so that with the light behind they appear to glow with the sun's own brilliance. There is also great diversity of markings on the lower lip. We have seen a plant of Mimulus guttatus with a single crimson spot almost entirely covering the large hairy middle lobe, but usually there are many small and one larger dot, as in the illustration.

This spectacular native of western North America has been introduced and widely naturalized in Europe, where it has hybridized with several aboriginal species.

Bright patches of intense yellow far up on the faces of dripping cliffs will generally be the Common Monkey Flower. And who has not seen whole waterfalls edged with its shimmering gold, or wet pockets in alpine meadows marked with its splashes of bright colour?

MÍMULUS LEWÍSII Pursh. *Pink Monkey Flower.* [p.475]

This gorgeous Mimulus frequents stream margins at moderate to fairly high altitudes throughout our area. Mountain hikers who have marvelled at its glowing rose-pink blossoms have sought to bring young plants (or even seeds) to coastal gardens—only to be disappointed, for the plants show their unhappiness by a paucity of bloom; and sadly, after a few years, the vibrant colour degenerates to a muddy magenta. So go to the mountains to see this fine plant at its magnificent best.

Its name honours Capt. Meriwether Lewis, secretary to President Thomas Jefferson and later (with William Clark) explorer of the Far West.

M. lewisii is a perennial, with leafy stems 12 to even 30 inches tall. The whole plant is covered with sticky hairs. The handsome leaves are conspicuously veined, and variously toothed to almost entire, mostly 2-3 inches long. Calyx-lobes are sharp-pointed and almost equal. The very showy corolla may exceed 1½ inches, the slightly notched lobes being rather uniform in size. The lowermost three lobes are flushed with deeper rose along the centre line, and handsomely marked with deep yellow in the hairy throat.

MÍMULUS MOSCHÀTUS Dougl., *Musk Flower.* [p.475]

This species was introduced to English gardens about 1828 from seed collected by Douglas along the Columbia River. Today we pass by this little plant. There was a time, though, when the "Musk Plant" was grown in the "parlour" of every English cottage and castle. David Douglas and many others, have left comments about its scent, which was considered to rival that of the still-popular *Mignonette*. But as the twentieth century emerged, all over England and Europe the musk perfume began to wane. Amazingly, plants in their original home simultaneously lost their scent. The best explanation of the phenomenon may be that a genetic change occurred. We have been able to find only a barely detectable scent in hundreds of wild plants from many parts of British Columbia, Washington, and Oregon.

However pervasive or pleasant the odour may have been, M. moschatus is visually a rather trivial plant. Stems are weak, often trailing over other vegetation, and (like the ovate leaves) are densely covered with long white hairs that become rather slimy in wet weather. The flowers are long-tubed, plain yellow and with lobes more even in size, in fact the lowermost is usually the smallest in this species. The calyx does not enlarge after the corolla has dropped.

ORTHOCÁRPUS ATTENUÀTUS Gray. *Lesser Paintbrush.* [p.471]

Orthocarpus (from orthos, *straight,* karpos, *fruit,* i.e. describing the capsule) is closely allied to *Castilleja,* but the plants are smaller and the lower lip is larger, swollen, and much more prominent than the rudimentary nubs that represent the lower lip in *Castilleja.* Of approximately 25 species of western North America about 10 occur in our area. In the present common species the leaves are very attenuate (long and *slender*); the lower even linear, but the upper occasionally cleft into 2-3 very slim lobes. The erect, unbranched stems are from 4-12 inches tall.

As in the related genus, the uppermost leaves become bracts, sometimes coloured, though less vividly. In the present species these bracts are white-tipped (occasionally yellowish or purplish). The flowers are inconspicuous because of their diminutive size, but under the magnifying lens they are interesting and quite colourful. The calyx is hairy, unevenly 4-lobed, and large enough to almost hide the corolla-tube. The upper lip of the corolla (galea) is straight and beak-like, enclosing the 2 long and 2 short stamens with their odd double pollen-sacs. The lower lip is almost as long as the galea and much more conspicuous, being swollen, 3-toothed, and bright-yellow with a ring of purple spots. The teeth themselves are also purple.

This Lesser Paintbrush joins its larger brothers in April or May, on grassy slopes from southern Vancouver Island to the Cascades and southward.

[p.471]   ORTHOCÁRPUS FAUCIBARBÀTUS Gray. ssp. ALBÌDUS Keck is a showy, *white,* 3-6 inch species from the vicinity of Victoria. The 3 teeth of the lower lip are inflated to form little pouches, which touch the pointed galea. These pouches turn purplish as they age. Leaves are hairy and divided into 5-8 linear lobes.

ORTHOCÁRPUS LÙTEUS Nutt. is a rather similar plant of the Chilcotin and Cariboo, southward. As the name suggests, the flowers (considerably larger than those of *O. attenuatus,* which see) are golden-*yellow.* Leaves are very similar in shape—though hairy—and the stem also is very hairy. The calyx in this species is lobed equally. The baggy lower lip of the corolla-tube, with its 3 scarcely visible teeth, almost touches the equally-long upper lip, so that the throat is practically closed.

ORTHOCÁRPUS PUSÍLLUS Benth. is the baby of the genus—often only 1½ inches high, but in better soil attaining 6-7 inches. It is immediately spotted in the field, despite its *small* size, by the strikingly dark-purplish or wine colour developed by most of the leaves. The flowers are almost too small to see—dark chocolate with a touch of colour from the yellow anthers. It is believed they are pollinated chiefly by ants. [p.470]

PARENTUCÉLLIA VISCÒSA (L.) Car. *Yellow Bartsia.* [p.482]

This plant bears the name of Tommaso Parentucelli, curator of the Botanical Garden in Rome (later Pope Nicolas V), and the specific name refers to the *viscid* hairs of the stem, leaves, and inflorescence. Linnaeus named it Bartsia, after his friend Johann Bartsch, M.D., which accounts for its common name.

Yellow Bartsia is a semi-parasitic sticky annual, 6-15 inches high, a Mediterranean immigrant of sporadic occurrence in moist fields west of the Cascades. The crowded leaves are firm, lanceolate, unstalked, and toothed. Flowers are pale to intense yellow, about ¾ inch long and quite showy. At first sight they resemble the flowers of *Mimulus,* the lower lip being 3-lobed, but the 2 upper lobes have coalesced to form an unlobed pouch that, like the galea of *Castilleja,* encloses the 2 pairs of stamens. The 4-lobed ridged calyx increases in size after the corolla has dropped.

PEDICULÀRIS BRACTEÒSA Benth. *Wood Betony. Bracted Lousewort.* [p.483]

The rather unhappy name of this genus, from the Latin pediculus, *a louse,* is frequently interpreted to mean that the plants were once used to discourage lice; but the truth—as pointed out by that very literate authority, David McClintock—is that cattle eating lousewort were supposed to be more readily infested. The specific name refers to the sharply-pointed ovate *bracts* at the base of each flower-pedicel. Betony is a very old name, derived from one of the early Iberian tribes of Spain, the Vettones, or as Dioscorides' first century A.D. *De materia medica* spells the name, Vetonica or Betonica. Betony was once believed to be endowed with virtues to cure almost any ill. Even today in primitive southern Italy peasants eulogize with the expression, "His virtues are as the Betony's," and there the similar plant (*P. officinalis*) is cultivated in cemeteries as a charm against malign influences.

Nearly all species of Pedicularis are semi-parasitic on the roots of other plants, so even the more attractive ones are poor prospects for transplantation to the garden.

This Betony is widely distributed in open woods and wet meadows of the mountains of our area. The genus Pedicularis (of over 400 species) shows affinities with the genus

Castilleja or Paintbrushes (see *Castilleja levisecta*), both in a tendency towards parasitism, and also in the floral structure. In both Pedicularis and *Castilleja* the upper lip forms a hooded galea, that encloses the anthers of the 2 pairs of unequal stamens.

P. bracteosa produces a cluster of 2-3 foot stems, from a woody perennial caudex topping a cluster of fibrous roots and some tuberous ones (that resemble small dahlia tubers). Alternate much-dissected leaves grow chiefly from the upper part of the stems. These leaves become smaller and merely notched above, finally merging into the bracts which set off each flower in the dense spike-like raceme.

A very large number of varietal names have been proposed for numerous variants, variants that chiefly involve details of the calyx and corolla. In general, the 5 calyx-lobes are uneven (the uppermost one much the shortest), but in some varieties they are short and blunt, in others very long and pointed. The corolla is usually yellowish, often purplish; the tube nearly always purplish. The galea formed from the upper lip of the corolla is hardly (or not at all) pointed, usually rounded and cupped over the stamens. The lower lip is much shorter than the galea, toothed, and incurved to nearly close the throat.

The upper stems, and often the foliage of Pedicularis bracteosa are bronzed or purplish, so that the plants are conspicuous in the greenery of lush alpine meadows.

[p.483] PEDICULÀRIS CAPITÀTA Adams (the type is from the mouth of the Lena River, Siberia) is a typical high alpine or arctic plant: very dwarf, with a tuft of chiefly basal leaves, and a compact *head* that scarcely lifts its relatively large cream to pinkish or purplish flowers above the foliage. The pinnately-dissected leaves are further deeply cut. Pedicularis capitata occurs at elevations of 7000 feet or more, especially in the Rockies.

PEDICULÀRIS CONTÓRTA Benth., *Coiled Lousewort, Parrot's-beak,* deserves its name, the galea being curved like a shepherd's crook, and *twisted* sideways near its tip. The wide flowers are usually pale-yellow, in a distinctively long, open raceme often accounting for three-quarters of the plant's total height of 6-24 inches. The almost fern-like basal leaves are pinnate and toothed, those alternating up the stem are reduced in size upward. The calyx is smooth except for 5 raised, minutely-hairy ribs, that terminate in short, pointed lobes.

PEDICULÀRIS GROENLÁNDICA Retz. *Elephant's Head.* [p.482]

This is perhaps the finest of our Louseworts, with its impressive spike of curious red, or purple-pink flowers topping a sturdy stem that carries numerous, handsome, pinnate leaves. It seems the specimens named in 1795 were actually from Labrador rather than *Greenland,* but recently on that frigid island a tiny pocket of these plants was discovered. P. groenlandica is widely distributed throughout the mountains of our area and across the width of the continent. Its habitat is wet meadows and the edges of mountain runnels.

The glabrous perennial plants are usually 12-24 inches tall; the shorter ones are sometimes quite purplish in stem and foliage. The flowers are unmistakable, bearing a droll and evident resemblance to an elephant's head. One is actually seeing pink elephants! The trunk, of course, is the very long, tapered and upcurved galea, the drooping ears the large lateral lobes of the lower lip, and the mouth the smaller, pointed, central lobe.

One should be alert for the extraordinary flowers of this interesting plant from the latter part of June on through July.

PEDICULÀRIS ORNITHORHÝNCHA Benth., *Bird's-bill Lousewort*, gets its name [p.482] from the Greek for *bird bill*. It is found in alpine meadows of the Island, Coast, and Cascade Ranges of our area. As the name suggests, the galea of this purple-flowered species is thin and pointed, like a straight bill, the bird's head (represented by the right-angled hood) formed by the upper lip of the corolla. The lower lip is deeply 3-lobed, the lobes edged with short hairs. Calyx-lobes are erose (as if gnawed), uneven, short, and hairy. Leaves are almost entirely basal; there may be 0,1, or 2 much-reduced stem-leaves. The leaves resemble the finely-cut leaves of Milfoil (*Achillea millefolium*, which see), but in this case they are glabrous, and not infrequently purplish (especially below).

PEDICULÀRIS RACEMÒSA Dougl. *Leafy Pedicularis. Leafy Lousewort.* [p.486]

Remarkably twisted pale flowers of this Lousewort occur in twos or threes in the leaf-axils, or also in an open *raceme*, whence the specific name. Some other species however, e g *P. contorta* (which see), share this characteristic (though the flowers of many species form a compact spike or head).

This 5-24 inch perennial is included because of its wide distribution under scattered conifers, or on open slopes, at considerable altitudes across British Columbia. The flowers are not showy, being greenish-white with faint washes of yellow or purple. But they are very curiously shaped. The upper lip (galea) is hooked like a bird's claw, and strongly deflected off-centre. The lower lip is 3-lobed, the centre lobe being much smaller than the laterals and embossed by a pair of ridges. Additionally, the pedicels are frequently twisted so that the flowers are upside down. The general effect is of a colourless, strangely disorganized, and asymmetric flower.

Usually, in Leafy Lousewort many leafy stems spring from a club-like, woody caudex that tops the mass of thickened fibrous roots. The leaves are linear-oblong and regularly serrate.

PENSTÈMON DAVIDSÒNII Greene. *Beardtongue.* [p.486]

Well over 200 species of these beautiful plants are known, nearly all from western North America. Pentstemon is a spelling sometimes seen, and is closer to the Greek roots pente, *five*, and stemon, *thread* (referring to the 5 stamens), but Penstemon is the earlier and therefore the valid form. Four of these stamens are fertile, the fifth lacks an anther.

MONARDA FISTULOSA var. MENTHAEFOLIA ×1 [p.440]

PRUNELLA VULGARIS (DETAIL) ×3 [p.441]

SATUREJA DOUGLASII ×1 [p.442]

STACHYS COLLEYAE ×¾ [p.442]

CASTILLEJA MINIATA ×¼ [p.445]

Precise identification of the very numerous species already reported from our area (and others from adjacent areas north, east, and south that may yet be found in British Columbia) depends heavily upon details of the anthers of these fertile stamens, for which a microscope or 10X magnifier is required. However, most of the more common Penstemons can be recognized on the basis of growth characteristics, shape and verdure of leaf, colour and shape of flower. Details are best seen by slitting a flower lengthwise.

This common montane species of Vancouver Island and southern British Columbia was long known as *P. menziesii* Hook., but that name is illegitimate. It is one of the dwarf rock-hugging species, of which 2 varieties have been generally recognized: P. davidsonii var. MENZIÈSII (Keck) Cronqu., with scarely saw-edged leaves, and P. d. var. DAVIDSÒNII with entire leaves. The illustration is of a beautiful white variant, forma ÁLBA, from the Forbidden Plateau on Vancouver Island. (This specimen is further unusual in the frequent presence of a fourth lobe on the lower lip.) The common colour of P. davidsonii is blue-lavender to purple-lavender, though good pink forms are occasionally seen.

[p.470]

P. davidsonii forms dense evergreen mats on broken rock, the flowering-stems usually less than 4 inches tall. Leaves are thick and firm, smooth-surfaced and about ½ inch long, numerous below but becoming scarce and reduced in size above. The relatively large flowers are compactly arranged in a few-flowered raceme. Calyx is short-haired and split almost to the base, into 5 lanceolate lobes. The "palate" (mouth of the corolla-tube) is densely white-haired, and deeply grooved. A 10X glass shows the staminode or infertile stamen (like a frazzled toothbrush) bears short hairs on one side for about half its length, and the 4 purplish fertile stamens are densely covered with long hairs. The stamens are double, joined end-for-end almost in a straight line, reminiscent of the familiar peanut shell.

This very beautiful rock plant blooms soon after the snow melts, and continues till it falls again, often in September. It is equally long-blooming in the garden rockery. Good forms of Penstemon davidsonii are much admired. They may be propagated very readily by short cuttings plunged in sand, and one should always choose this method of collecting exceptional colour forms. Leave the choice Beardtongues for others to enjoy, and save yourself much "mining" of long roots deep in rock crevices, with later loss and disappointment.

PENSTÈMON FRUTICÒSUS (Pursh) Greene var. SCOULÉRI (Lindl.) Cronqu.
Shrubby Penstemon. Shrubby Beardtongue. [p.487]

This subshrubby species is described by its name, fruticosus meaning *shrub-like*. It is a variable species, but in all its forms is very beautiful. Choice forms are easily obtained for the garden by taking short cuttings, which root very readily in sand. Or even more simply, one can look for rooted prostrate branches, which grow on in their new home with scarely a check. To keep the plants attractively compact, and floriferous, they should be given gritty soil with very little food.

The plants are semi-evergreen, a proportion of the leaves usually turning reddish in the fall, and later dropping. Commonly the compact framework of branches is 6-12 inches tall. Leaves are generally without hairs, up to 2 inches long but usually shorter, generally elliptical and entire, but in var. SCOULÉRI they are much narrower, almost elliptic, and obscurely toothed. This is the variety illustrated. Flowers are relatively large (up to 2 inches long), generally blue-lavender—but so highly variable that the keen gardener should always be on the alert for exceptionally good colour forms. White, and beautiful pink specimens are seen occasionally. The lower lip of the corolla is ornamented with 2 deep folds and with long white hairs. When the corolla is slit lengthwise, the anthers (and also the filament of the half-length infertile stamen) are seen to be densely white-haired.

The wanderer in the foothills or mountains, even at 10,000 feet, may expect to find this fine plant across southern British Columbia as far as the Rockies. Brilliant displays of the Shrubby Beardtongue may be seen in July on steep road-cuts in Manning Park.

PENSTÈMON NEMORÒSUS (Dougl.) Traut. *Turtle-head.*   [p.486]

Some authorities place this rather distinctive plant in the genus *Chelone*, or *Nothochelone*, from which the common name derives (Greek chelone, a tortoise or *turtle*). The frontal aspect of the wide flat flower-tube is clearly reminiscent of the squat head of a turtle.

Turtle-head is a deciduous perennial, with many glabrous (or nearly glabrous) stems attaining 16-30 inches. The thin, strongly saw-toothed, ovate leaves occur in opposite pairs up the stems. They are from 1½-4 inches long, and ½-1½ inches wide. The handsome flowers are bluish- to pinkish-purple, both calyx and corolla covered with short glandular hairs. To our imagination the buds, rather than the opened flowers, resemble little turtle-heads. If the corolla is split longways the inside walls are seen to be glabrous, and the anthers—quite distinctively covered with long, dense wool—are very noticeable. Even the filaments are long-haired at their bases, and the staminode (infertile fifth stamen) is hairy throughout its length, which is about half the length of the fertile ones.

This species is quite common *in open woodlands* (nemorosus), especially on streambanks and lakeshores, and also in moist crevices of broken rock from sea level to considerable altitudes. Its range is from southern Vancouver Island, eastward to the Cascades, and also southward to California. The blooming period is rather late, from July to September, according to altitude.

P. nemorosus is easy in the garden, though the flowers may be rather overwhelmed by the leaves (especially in richer soil) and their colour is frequently too close to magenta to please many tastes.

PENSTÈMON OVÀTUS Dougl. *Broad-leaved Penstemon.*

This leafy deciduous species is very reminiscent of *P. nemorosus* (which see). The clasping upper leaves of the stem are described by the specific name. Unlike *P.*

Following page: CASTILLEJA LEVISECTA   ✕1⅞   [p.444]

CASTILLEJA SULPHUREA ×½ [p.445]

COLLINSIA GRANDIFLORA ×1 [p.448]

CASTILLEJA MINIATA (HABITAT) [p.445]

nemorosus this plant has basal leaves as well, and these have petioles as long as the long-*ovate* blades. Both types of leaves are sharply and conspicuously serrate.

Flowers of P. ovatus are glandular-haired on the outside, as is the case with *P. nemorosus,* but they are smaller (less than 1 inch long) and more widely flared at the mouth. The tube is magenta, the lips usually more bluish. If the tube is split, the anthers immediately distinguish the 2 plants, for in this species they are glabrous (rather than long-haired). The staminode of P. ovatus is hairy only toward the tip.

This sturdy plant is limited, in our area, to low altitudes of southern British Columbia, north to Hope and west from the Cascades. It is in bloom during the interval May-July.

PENSTÈMON PRÒCERUS Dougl. ex R. Grah. var. PRÒCERUS. *Tall Penstemon.* [p.483]

Procerus means *tall*, the scapes being 12-24 inches high. Most of the blunt to pointed-lanceolate leaves appear in opposite pairs up the stem. There is no pronounced basal rosette. The bright-blue flowers are about ½ inch long, arranged in one to several crowded whorls. This variety is a plant of low to moderate altitudes of southern mainland British Columbia.

[p.487] Generally somewhat more montane is the smaller var. TÓLMIEI (Hook.) Cronq., (2-8 inches tall). In the field it is most easily recognized by the tight, head-like arrangement (verticillaster) of the small dark flowers. At closer range the plants are seen to be somewhat tufted, with short smooth erect stems. Rosette-forming basal leaves have petioles about as long as the sharply-ovate blades, but the few stem (cauline) leaves lack petioles and are more slender. The leaves are glabrous, or nearly so. Usually the flowers are dark blue-purple, with grooved whitish throats, but occasionally in limited localities most of the plants have ochroleucous flowers; they are seldom longer than ½ inch. On minute study of the slit corolla, the lip is seen to be bearded, as is the expanded tip of the staminode or sterile stamen (which is as long as the fertile ones). The paired anthers of the latter are glabrous and form an in-line arrangement, like a peanut shell.

P. procerus var. tolmiei occurs on dry to moist rock slopes in the mountains of the Province north to Alaska, but not on Vancouver Island.

These small-flowered Penstemons are "different" rather than beautiful.

PENSTÉMON SERRULÀTUS Menzies (= P. DIFFÙSUS Dougl.) [p.486]

As suggested by the specific name, the leaves (lanceolate-ovate, entirely scapose) are *serrulate,* i.e. edged with smaller teeth than those of either *P. ovatus* or *P. nemorosus* (which see). The frontal aspect of the deep-blue to bluish-purple flowers is strikingly "taller" than the squat effect produced by the flowers of P. nemorosus. However, the best identification characteristic is the "horse-shoe" shape of the anthers. This fine 10-24 inch perennial of mountain stream-banks is not uncommon westward from the Cascades.

VERBÁSCUM THÁPSUS L. *Common Mullein.* [p.494]

The Verbascums, unlike other members of the Scrophulariaceae, have nearly regular 5-cleft corollas, not at all bilabiate. Dioscorides used the generic name, thought to be a corruption of barbascum, meaning *bearded,* perhaps in allusion to the hairy bases of the filaments, or possibly to the densely matted hairs that make foliaceous parts of some of the species appear hoary. The specific name is thought to be after Thapsus, an ancient town north of Syracuse in Sicily.

Everyone knows the tall sentinel stalks of the densely furred Mullein that line our highways and spike the dry fields of the Interior. But most people think this is a native, and are surprised to learn that it is a European import.

In the second year the strong stem surges up 5 or 6 feet from a first-year rosette of great flannel leaves. In late autumn the huge plant dies, but not before it has matured a very large number of seeds. Through the winter, and sometimes even the ensuing summer and second winter, the tough stalks rustle in the wind.

Over a period of several months, small yellow flowers open erratically up and down the tall flowering-spike. They are pleasant-smelling, and as already mentioned, atypical of the bilabiate corollas normal to the Figwort Family. The 5 lobes are nearly equal, and span ¼ - ½ inch. You will notice that the 3 upper stamens have densely yellow-haired filaments; the lower 2 have smooth (and longer) filaments. All have showy orange anthers. The club-topped pistil is prominent.

The densely matted coat of white hairs protects the rosette of leaves under the snows of winter, and in the arid heat of the biennial's second summer, effectively reduces water-loss. This great woolly plant flourished on the dry Campagna about Imperial Rome, where the long spikes were dipped in tallow and carried as torches through the streets during the Feast of Lupercalia.

VERBÁSCUM BLATTÀRIA L., *Moth Mullein,* is a similar (though smaller) biennial weed, also from Europe. But it is not woolly, being chiefly glabrous—except for sticky hairs in the inflorescence. The flowers are considerably larger than those of *V. thapsus* (which see)—usually more than an inch across—and either yellow or white. They are widely spaced on the stem, rather than densely crowded as in the more common species. Close inspection will show that all 5 filaments are covered with glandular purple hairs. The flower suggests a moth with pale-yellow wings, and a furry purple body.

V. blattaria is limited to the drier parts of the southern Interior. Moth Mullein has pleasant connotations, and conjures up mental images of soft-winged moths coming to the flowers under the pale moon. But the specific name is less poetic, being derived from blatta, a name used by several early Latin authors for an unknown insect, thought from the context to be a *cockroach.* Nevertheless, this is an attractive plant!

VERÓNICA AMERICÀNA Schwein. *Brooklime. American Speedwell.* [p.487]

A rather interesting story is hidden in the name of this genus. Saint Veronica was canonized since, according to legend, she wiped the drops of agony from the face of the Christ as He toiled with the cross toward Calvary. Her kerchief then bore the "vera iconica", *the true likeness.* However pleasing the story, most observers will experience some difficulty in linking "vera iconica" with the four-lobed face of these small blue flowers. But in mediaeval times simple folk could not dream of travelling to St. Peter's, where the sacred relic was kept, and their piety found happy expression in linking this little country flower to St. Veronica's name. Not surprisingly, the plant was then soon invested with miraculous power to heal. Even the dread "scrofula" (a form of tuberculosis) was thought healed by faith. This was the origin of Linnaeus' name for the family containing Veronica— *Scrophulariaceae.* Brooklime is an old English name involving the antique use of the verb "*to lime*" or trap birds with sticky materials; this was a plant of the soft wet mud of *brooks,* in which birds might be trapped. Also interesting is the name Speedwell (applied to all the members of the genus). It is an old English benediction to a departing guest, comparable with "God be with you" (goodbye).

This species merits its specific name for it is widespread and common throughout temperate North America. It is found in wet or swampy ground, and shows a few flowers at a time, from May through to July or even August.

There are more than 200 species of Veronica, found all over the North Temperate Zone. Many readers will remember the British Isles boast more than 2 dozen kinds; a number of these have become established in our area.

The Speedwells are easily recognized by their flattened, 4-lobed corollas, with only 2 stamens and a pistil usually clubbed at the top. The calyx is so deeply cleft that the 4 (sometimes 5) lobes may be considered as separate sepals. Leaves are opposite. Some species of Veronica are perennial, with running rhizomes; others annual, with small fibrous roots.

V. americana is a glabrous, rather lax perennial, with stems sometimes as much as 3 feet long, but usually only 6-12 inches high. All the leaves have short petioles, and are oblong or ovate, blunt-tipped, but slightly to sharply saw-edged. The flowers are borne in racemes that arise from the axils of the upper leaves. About ¼ inch wide, they are cerulean-blue, rarely pink, and have a yellowish throat. Unfortunately the corolla is fugitive and drops at the slightest touch or wind movement, so that seldom more than a few flowers are present at one time. The calyx-segments are pointed, the lowermost corolla-lobe much smaller than the other 3, and the fat capsule only faintly notched at the tip.

This is a rather pretty blue plant—of very wet places.

VERÓNICA ANAGÁLLIS-AQUÁTICA L. *Water Speedwell* of eastern British Columbia is very similar to *V. americana* (which see), and like it is found in ditches or other *wet* places. It differs in having sessile, or even clasping leaves, that are usually longer and slimmer than those of *V. americana*. The blue flowers are also smaller, about ⅕ inch across.

VERÓNICA FILIFÒRMIS Smith. *Slender Speedwell.* [p.495]

V. filiformis is admired by everyone for its lovely china-blue half-inch flowers, but feared by those who find it in their lawns. This little, prostrate, even mat-forming perennial is extraordinarily invasive. Its original home was the Caucasus, where it is not common. But introduced into Britain about the beginning of the 19th century, it soon covered the country, and bids fair to do the same in Canada and the United States. This is particularly amazing because the plant almost never sets seed! Individuals of one clone are self-sterile. Virtually all our millions of specimens are vegetatively-propagated parts of a single plant, hence cannot effectively cross-pollinate. But our lawn-mowers chop the plants into bits, which readily root—and amaze us with their rapid spread.

Undeniably beautiful it is, perhaps second only to *V. grandiflora* Gaert. of the remote Aleutian Isands. V. filiformis gets its specific name from the *thread-like* pedicels that support the lovely single flowers. These filiform stems arise from the axils of the leaves, which are short-petioled, blunt-toothed, and rounded.

From the end of April until June this species spreads solid blue sheets of intense colour over boulevards and lawns, especially in the humid Coastal Zone.

VERÓNICA SERPYLLIFÒLIA L. or *Thyme-leaved Speedwell* is widely distributed [p.495] among short grasses in North America and Europe. It is a low and compact rhizomatous perennial, with oval, shiny, untoothed (or very sparsely-toothed) leaves having no (or very short) petioles. The stems are covered with very short hairs, but the leaves are nearly (or quite) smooth. Capsules are wider than high, clearly notched, and minutely-hairy. Var. HUMIFÙSA (Dickson) Vahl. has bright-blue flowers with longer filaments, and a calyx more hairy than the leaves or stem. Var. SERPYLLIFÒLIA has paler blue to whitish flowers marked with darker lines, shorter filaments, and the calyx not more pubescent than the foliaceous parts.

VERÓNICA WORMSKJÒLDII Roem. & Schult. *Alpine Speedwell* is also known as [p.494] *V. alpina.* It is a perennial mountain species, with notably hairy stems and leaves, the calyx and flower-pedicels stickily-glandular. The corolla is about ⅓ inch wide, dark purplish-blue with even darker lines, and with the uppermost lobe appreciably wider than the other three.

 # OROBANCHÀCEAE. *Broomrape Family.*

BOSCHNIÁKIA HÓOKERI Walpers. *Poque. Ground-cone.* [p.494]

This very odd plant bears the name of a family of celebrated botanists, Sir William Jackson Hooker (1785-1865), whose name is abbreviated "Hook.", and his son Sir Joseph Dalton Hooker (1817-1911), abbreviated "Hook. f.", an equally prodigious worker. The generic name honours a Russian botanist, Boschniaki. "Poque" is the Indian name, and should, we think, be retained. Poque was used by the native peoples for food. Though substantial, the plant does not look appetizing: indeed it resembles an outsize fir cone placed upright on the soil.

It is in fact a parasite, feeding upon the roots of a number of ericaceous plants (commonly Salal), and as such lacks chlorophyll. The fleshy stem is extremely thick, with most of its 4-6 inch length beneath the surface. It carries a number of scale-like leaves that may be yellowish, brownish, or purplish. The curious flowers appear singly in the axil of each of the upper leaves or bracts.

The calyx of Boschniakia is usually irregularly 2-3 lobed, the dark firm tubular corolla 2-lipped, with the upper lip keeled and the shorter lower lip obscurely 3-lobed. Two short and two slightly longer filaments are conspicuously tufted white-hairy at their bases. The long style ends in a stigma that is variously 2-3 lobed or unlobed.

Sharp eyes are needed to mark this strange plant as it emerges in June and July from the similarly-coloured duff and litter of open slopes. Poque occurs near the coast from Alaska, southward through our area, to California.

OROBÁNCHE UNIFLÒRA L. var. PURPURÈA (Heller) Achey. *One-flowered Cancer-root. Broom-rape.*   [p.495]

This genus, of perhaps 100 species of strange root-parasites, draws its name from the Greek orobos, a *clinging plant* or vetch, and ancho, *to strangle.* This is an allusion to the fact that the plants feed on the roots of various plants. Many of the Broom-rapes consist of crowded clusters of flowers, sometimes arising from stems that have fused together; but this species (possibly the most attractive of the genus) bears a *solitary flower* (hence uniflora) at the top of a stem 2-4 inches tall. In Britain the Broom (*Cytisus scoparius* which see) is often the host, hence one of the common names. In fact, if one can trace the roots to actual juncture with the host-plant, it is often easy to identify the Orobanche species, since they are rather specific in choice of victims.

This species has been recognized under 4 varietal names, the variety PURPUREA of our area attacking usually species of *Sedum, Saxifragaceae,* or *Compositae.* In the illustration it is shown parasitic upon *Heuchera micrantha* (which see). Its curious flowers usually appear in April or May.

O. uniflora tops its short stems (which above ground bear neither leaf-remnants nor bracts) with a single purple-violet, tube-shaped flower that is quite attractive, and—rather surprisingly—possesses a faint but pleasant fragrance. Occasionally the flowers are yellowish. The 5 lobes of the corolla are almost equal in size, and all bear 3 thin dark stripes which serve as honey-guides*, a function aided by the white throat and bright orange-yellow anthers.

[p.495]   OROBÁNCHE GRAYÁNA Beck, *Clustered Cancer-root,* is parasitic on *Compositae,* especially *Grindelia integrifolia* (which see). O. grayana occurs in southern British Columbia, particularly at the Coast, where it is fairly common. The clustered whitish stems tend to merge in a stubby base which becomes brownish above, and bears several stubby bracts and numerous ragged brownish or purplish flowers. On more careful examination, one can see that the calyx-lobes are very long and slender, with short glandular hairs. The upper lip of the dark-veined corolla is split upward, the lower lip divided into 3 long and lacerate lobes. The 4 anthers are woolly with white-hairs.

OROBÁNCHE FASCICULÀTA Nutt. is very similar to *O. grayana* but parasitizes chiefly the Sagebrush, *Artemisia tridentata* (which see), occurring in the southern Dry Interior. Its flowers are nearly always purplish (rarely yellowish).

OROBÁNCHE PINÓRUM Geyer—is also similar but parasitizes chiefly coniferous tree-roots. The flowers are generally yellowish, and much less clustered than those of *O. grayana* or *O. fasciculata*. They occur along an elongated stem that surmounts the usual swollen base. This species is very rarely reported from our area.

The Orobanches are interesting and unusual plants.

*The faintest streak that on a petal lies,
May speak instruction to initiate eyes.*

William Cullen Bryant:
The Mystery of Flowers

 LENTIBULARIÀCEAE. *Bladderwort Family.*

PINGUÍCULA VULGÀRIS L. *Butterwort.* [p.498]

The name of this genus of about 30 remarkable species is the diminutive of the Latin pinguis, *fat,* with reference to the extraordinary soft, thickened leaves, whose upper surfaces appear greasy or slimy. The common name repeats this idea, wort being simply Middle English for plant. And vulgaris means *common.* However, "widespread" would be more descriptive, for though circumboreal, Butterwort is seldom abundant in the bogs and water-soaked soil of its mountain retreats.

This is our only species and it is quite unmistakable. Apart from the violet-like colour of the flower it could not be confused with any other plant. The elliptical or oblanceolate (with broadest portion nearer tip than base) leaves are entire, with short petioles making a total length of about 1-2½ inches. They form a flat rosette just above the short moss-growth, and are arresting by reason of their unusual colour—a very yellowish-green. They are still more remarkable for their insect-catching and digesting powers, for this is a carnivorous plant.

In the illustration the leaves may be seen dotted with tiny insects (largely midges) or their chitinous skeletons. Alighting on the leaves the insects have been trapped in the sticky exudate, and shortly their proteinaceous parts have been dissolved by the digestive enzymes of the plant, and absorbed. In the proteids of its insect victims the plant finds

470

CASTILLEJA PARVIFLORA ×²⁄₅ [p.445]

CASTILLEJA RHEXIFOLIA ×²⁄₅ [p.448]

PENSTEMON DAVIDSONII var. MENZIESII FORMA ALBA ×½ [p.460]

ORTHOCARPUS PUSILLUS ×1¼ [p.455]

LINARIA DALMATICA   ×¼   [p.452]

LINARIA VULGARIS   ×½   [p.449]

ORTHOCARPUS ATTENUATUS   ×1¾   [p.454]

ORTHOCARPUS FAUCIBARBATUS ssp. ALBIDUS
×⅘   [p.454]

the nitrogenous compounds essential for its growth. In this way Pinguicula survives in an uncrowded ecological niche, for the leached soils or water-soaked mosses are deficient in nitrogen.

The same or similar small ephemeral insects, also serve the plant by cross-pollinating the beautiful, deep violet-purple blossoms. These appear singly at the top of slender scapes about 2-5 inches tall. Their structure is unusual and interesting. The purple calyx is notched into 3 upper and 2 lower lobes. The corolla is shaped like a cornucopia, and appears to hang from the calyx at a point about midway of its upper edge. The pointed, spurred base of the dependent corolla-tube is nectariferous. The tube is whitish and short-haired. The mouth of the tube is strongly flared and 5-lobed, the lowest lobe being slightly the longest, and sometimes the widest. Two short, curved stamens on the floor of the tube are ready to dust the insect entering to reach the nectary, and a short pistil is waiting to receive pollen from the blossom last visited.

In elegance of form and vividness of colour Pinguicula is a charming plant. Besides, its ingenious supplementing of the food deficiencies in its marshy habitat gives the species unique interest.

Unfortunately, the vast majority of us—and not city-dwellers only—are incredibly ignorant of our plants—even the most common. In this respect we appear to be in a cultural abyss lower than that of our pioneering forefathers, and certainly below that of people of older cultures. Few indeed are the British Columbians who have ever noticed the Butterwort, and most of those would probably think it was "a funny sort of violet". In contrast, Amazon natives, Australian aborigines, and primitive dwellers of the Kalahari, in their respective environments, recognize literally hundreds of plants, and moreover, know their habitats, times of flowering and fruiting, and uses.

UTRICULÀRIA VULGÀRIS L. *Bladderwort.* [p.499]

This is another fascinating plant of the same family, that has achieved by different means than *Pinguicula* (which see) the same end, of supplementing its diet. Again it is a highly specialized plant, as is hinted in its name, from the Latin utriculus, diminutive of *bag* or pocket, referring to the small hollow bladders in which aquatic insects are trapped. This *common* species (vulgaris) has a circumboreal distribution in ponds, marshes, or even the back-waters of slow-moving streams.

Since the plant seldom announces its presence with large and showy yellow flowers (reminiscent of those of *Mimulus* which see) it is often thought to be rare. Actually none of the 3 species of our area is at all uncommon. The Bladderworts are adapted in an extraordinary degree to aquatic life. They are free-floating plants, supported by a series of remarkable "bladders", which as we shall see, serve a double function.

The true leaves of Utricularia contain chlorophyll, and photosynthesize starch with the aid of sunlight which readily penetrates the few inches of surface water in which the plants float, sustained by air in the "bladders". As is general among aquatic plants, these leaves are fimbriate (or deeply-incised into numerous slender teeth). In this genus the teeth, or to change our metaphor, the fingers radiate from a common centre or palm. Indeed they represent merely thin fringes of chlorophyllous tissue surrounding the palmate veins.

But the aquatic plant is cut off from any sources of nitrogen normally available in the soil. So the "bladders" have a second purpose. Under the microscope, or even 10X glass, they are seen to be ingeniously devised, hollow structures fitted with a valve, that is normally open. However when minute Crustaceans, or others of the tiny animalculae inhabiting pond-waters swim into the bladders, they trip certain guard-hairs, so that the valve-cover closes. The walls of the bladder then secrete digestive juices and the nitrogenous compounds in the bodies of the tiny animals are absorbed into the plant. This is a fascinating sequence to watch when a bladder-bearing leaf in a thin film of pond-water is examined on the stage of the microscope. About 25X is an ideal magnification, for the trigger-hairs can then be seen.

Sometime during the summer, from May to August, this amazing plant occasionally lifts above the water a peduncle (flowering stem) from 2-8 inches long, bearing at its summit a raceme of half a dozen or more, showy, golden, scrophulariaceous flowers. Each flower is two-lipped, the much larger lower lobe projected to form a pointed spur which curves forward beneath the lip. A "palate" or bulge on the lower lip closes the tube until the weight of a bee or bumblebee causes it to open—exposing the pair of stamens, the pistil, and of course the nectary.

The specialization of structures that adapt this small plant to its particular niche in the scheme of life must astound the thoughtful observer.

Our 3 species are most easily distinguished. U. vulgaris has the largest flowers (½ to nearly 1 inch across) and its extraordinarily pinnate leaves consist of hair-like fronds punctuated by the feeding-flotation bladders. UTRICULÀRIA INTERMÈDIA Hayne often creeps along the bottom in very shallow water. It has yellow flowers about ½ inch broad, but notably its bladders are clustered along special stems (the normal leaves consisting solely of ferny-chlorophyllaceous fronds).

UTRICULÀRIA MÌNOR L. also creeps along the bottom, but its yellow flowers are ¼ inch or less wide. U. minor, like its bigger relative *U. vulgaris* (which see), inter-mingles its bladders with the green leaf-segments.

To me the meanest flower that blows can give
Thoughts that do often lie too deep for tears.

William Wordsworth:
Ode (Intimations of Immortality,
from Recollections of Early Childhood)

MIMULUS GUTTATUS   ×1½   [p.452]

MIMULUS ALSINOIDES ×2 [p.452]

MIMULUS MOSCHATUS ×1 [p.453]

MIMULUS LEWISII ×⅖ [p.453]

PLANTAGINÀCEAE. *Plantain Family.*

PLANTÀGO MARÍTIMA L. ssp. JUNCOÌDES (Lam.) Hultén. *Sea Plantain.* [p.499]

This genus of specialized plants is world-wide in its distribution. Its name is derived from the Latin planta, the *sole* of the foot, descriptive of the leaf-shape. This *maritime* species, with some varietal or subspecific variations around the world, fringes salt-water flats of both North America and Eurasia, as well as such remote regions as Patagonia and the Galapagos Islands.

Sea Plantain's fleshy linear leaves, up to 12 inches long, are familiar to all who visit salt-marshes. Here the plant thrives even where it is daily submerged by the incoming tide. Less often the tufts find rock crevices at the sea's edge. The scapes equal or slightly surpass the upright cluster of leaves, and terminate in a long dense spike of tiny flowers. These are interesting to study with the 10X glass, especially in view of their ability to survive salt-water flooding, and even lengthy submergence in fresh or brackish water when coastal rivers rise. The durable flowers have 4 chaffy and persistent sepals, a membranous and persistent flared corolla, 4 anthers and a protruding stigma.

Perhaps less admired is the persistent PLANTÀGO LANCEOLÀTA L. *(Ribwort Plantain)* that is determined to establish itself in our lawns. Very similar, but with broad pointed-elliptical leaves, rather than lanceolate ones, is PLÀNTAGO MÀJOR *(Common Plantain),* also world-wide in distribution, but rather more often found in disturbed and [p.498] waste land or on moist roadsides. PLANTÀGO PÚRSHII R. & S., is a small silky-pubescent annual of dry plains and eroded slopes in the Dry Interior. This species has 4 stamens in the perfect flowers, and the chaffy bracts scarcely project beyond the flowers in the crowded flower-spikes.

Quite unique are the leaves of PLANTÀGO CORONÒPUS L. *(Buckshorn Plantain),* another European import. It is occasionally collected on bare ground, usually near the sea, less frequently inland on dryish sandy soil. Much smaller than the above Plantains, its specific name directs attention to the wreath or *crown* of deeply pinnate-lobed, slightly succulent leaves. The flower-spikes are typical of this genus, but the lobed leaves are quite startlingly different.

The Plantain is mentioned by Dioscorides, and also in the very earliest Anglo-Saxon "medical" writings. Apparently without any physiological effect, and certainly bland, if stringy, the Plantain was nevertheless a favourite with the herbalists*, which led Gerard as long ago as 1597 to the critical comment, "I finde in ancient writers many Good-morrowes, which I think not meete to bring into your memorie againe, as that three rootes (of the Plantain) will cure one griefe, fower another disease, six hanged about the necke are good for another maladie &c, all of which are but ridiculous toies."

*The rote of this herbe [the Plantain] is meualous good agaynst the payne of the headde, because the signe of the Ramme is supposed to be the house of the planete Mars, which is the head of the whole worlde.

Albertus Magnus: (1206-1280)
The small boke of secrets of Albartus Magnus,
of the vertues of Herbes. . . .
1525 [i.e. 1565?] edition, in English.

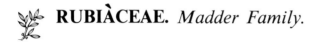 # RUBIÀCEAE. *Madder Family.*

GÀLIUM BOREÀLE L. *Northern Bedstraw.* [p.494]

Who does not know this little "Cleaver"? In British Columbia its fragrant, creamy, densely-clustered and tiny flowers haunt every lake that has a shingled shore. Galium comes from the Greek gala, *milk*, for country-folk once used the bruised plants of yellow G. VÈRUM L. to curdle milk. And boreale describes its *northern* distribution, which is indeed circumpolar, from sea level to tree-limit. Dried plants of Bedstraw (especially the Fragrant Bedstraw, cinnamon-scented *G. triflorum*) were once much used for bedding, and a pleasant mattress they must have made. Most of the numerous species of Galium occurring in our area are remembered for the tiny hooked hairs, that make their squared, lax stems and whorled leaves stick or "cleave" to one's clothing

However, the perennial G. boreale lacks these clinging hairs. Its many 8-24 inch smooth stems are square in cross section. At intervals the stem is ringed with smooth to short-haired linear leaves in fours, one from each of the flat faces. Terminal, as well as axial clusters of small, whitish, cruciform flowers appear from June onward. They are borne in such numbers that the plants of the Northern Bedstraw make an attractive sight, especially when they accent Columbine, Indian Paintbrush, and St. John's Wort of the lakeshore community.

GÀLIUM TRÍFIDUM L., widely distributed, has blunt-ended leaves in whorls, and tiny white flowers arranged singly or 2-3 on peduncles arising from the leaf-axils. The knobby fruits are smooth (without hooked hairs).

GÀLIUM TRIFLÒRUM Michx., also common, has whorled leaves ending in a sharp cusp, flowers usually in threes, and fruit bristly with hooked hairs.

CAPRIFOLIÀCEAE. *Honeysuckle Family.*

The derivation of the family name is obscure, and interesting. Caprea, a *she-goat* of certain breeds has twisted horns, whence the zodiacal sign for Capricorn. The Honeysuckles, conspicuous members of this family, climb by twisting stems; ergo, Caprifoliaceae.

Approximately 400 species are nearly all shrubs or vines, chiefly of the North Temperate Zone, or of mountain slopes in the Tropics. They have opposite leaves (that lack stipules) and bisexual flowers with parts in 5's (but *Linnaea* has 4 stamens). Many of the genera contain valued garden subjects, e.g. *Sambucus, Viburnum, Weigela,* and of course *Lonicera* (the Honeysuckles).

LINNAÈA BOREÀLIS (Gronov.) L. var. LONGIFLÒRA Torr. *Twin-flower.* [p.502]

How to write the charms of this exquisite woodlander? Perhaps in no more impressive way than to call attention to the fact, that of all the thousands of plants known to him, this was the favourite flower of the great Carolus Linnaeus. And so Fredrik Gronovius, once his benefactor in Holland, in 1737 named the monotypic genus to honour his illustrious pupil. The specific name, of course, refers to the *northern* habitat; from the forests of Sweden and Lapland (where Linnaeus admired it) around the Pole to Russia, China, Alaska, northern Canada, and Greenland. Many an Ausländer will have fond memories of this little jewel—now sadly rare, as in the pinewoods of eastern Scotland.

A number of subspecies have been proposed for forms of Linnaea borealis occurring in some of these regions, on the basis of slight variations in leaf-shape and length of corolla-tube. Our variety, with its long, slightly-flared pink trumpets, graces shaded woodlands across the continent and as far south as New Mexico. (Within the trumpet are 2 long, and 2 short stamens).

This dainty plant spreads long runners creeping over the moss, or trailing from rotting logs or stumps, from which at frequent intervals rise 2-4 inch stems. These fork at the top, each branch supporting a single trumpet—a demure, pink, rose-flushed and slender bell. Where a patch of sunlight reaches the forest floor, an elfin troupe of hundreds of these exquisite little flowers fills the still air with an incredible sweetness—surely one of the most enchanting of all plant fragrances.

If the reader finds these bewitching plants abundant in his locality, he may feel justified in moving some of the rooted runners to his garden, where—provided with light shade and a soil rich in humus—they will soon reward him with their winsome charms.

The wanderer in the summer woodland who chances upon a still company of Twin-flowers poised above their matted glossy leaves, especially near dusk when their perfume is most evident, will agree with Linnaeus that this is one of the most elegant of wildlings.

LONÍCERA L. *Honeysuckle.*

Adam Lonitzer (1528-86), an early German botanist, is remembered in the name of this genus of about 150 species, many of which are vines, chiefly found in the North Temperate Zone.

The climbers are too well-known to need lengthy description; however, we have in our area 3 shrubby species, rather less easily recognized. These three have tubular 5-notched flowers in pairs, succeeded by twin berries that are respectively black, red, and blue.

English Honeysuckle (*L. periclymenum* L.) ornaments fragrant corners of gardens around the world. Its cream-coloured blooms are highly visible at night; besides, this is the time when the scent becomes maximal. We are not surprised then to discover that this species is pollinated by moths—especially the hovering long-tongued Hawk-moths—that can reach the nectar deep in the corolla-tubes. There are no Hummingbirds in Britain (nor in most of Europe). But the New World has a host of "Hummers", so the dominant Honeysuckle species of the Pacific Coast, *L. ciliosa* (which see) has become adapted for pollination chiefly by hummingbirds. Hence the vivid orange colouring of this species, particularly attractive to these little winged jewels; and hence, too, the lack of scent, which would serve no utilitarian purpose.

LONÍCERA CILIÒSA (Pursh) DC. *Orange Honeysuckle.*   [p.499]

The *ciliate* (marginal) hairs of the paired, elliptical leaves are responsible for the specific name (see the illustration).

This is our showiest native Honeysuckle; the clusters of tubular flowers (about 1½ inches long) are vivid orange, far more striking than the well-loved English Honeysuckle. But alas, they lack entirely that species' lovely perfume. The flowers cluster in a terminal, cup-shaped leaf (actually a pair of leaves—connate—i.e. joined at their bases). You will find that the 5 stamens grow from halfway down the corolla-tube, and that their bases (as well as the adjacent parts of the tube) are pubescent. (L. DIOÌCA L., var. GLAUCÉSCENS (Rydb.) Butters, in southeastern B.C., has inch-long corollas; and L. ETRÚSCA Santi, also southern, lacks hairs inside the corolla-tube and is more deeply bilabiate than *L. ciliosa*.)

The Orange Honeysuckle is common in most parts of B.C., especially west of the Cascades, so its bright colour is frequently seen, sometimes as much as 20 feet up the small conifers on which it apparently prefers to climb. Hummingbirds and Swallowtail butterflies approve this arrangement, but the host tree is sometimes sadly repaid for its support. Quite frequently one sees young Douglas firs with tops bent sharply over, and finds the coils of the Honeysuckle have cut so deeply into the tree, that it is unable to support the pressure of wind or snow.

Fair flower, that dost so comely grow,
Hid in this silent, dull retreat,

Untouched thy honied blossoms blow,
Unseen thy little branches greet. . . .

Phillip Freneau:
The Wild Honeysuckle

LONÍCERA HISPÍDULA (Lindl.) Dougl. *Purple Honeysuckle.* [p.503]

Hispidula refers to the *stiff* and rigid bristles, which are occasionally seen on the climbing or trailing stems. More often, though, these bristles are replaced by glandular hairs, or the stems may be smooth (especially upwards).

The opposite leaves are variably pubescent or glabrous. The uppermost pair, as in L. ciliosa (which see) are joined along their bases to form a shallow cup, from which 1-3 rather long stems support clusters of wine-purple flowers (generally yellowish within). But the key to sure recognition of this rather unspectacular member of our Honeysuckles, is the presence on the lower leaves of a pair of conjoined stipules—looking like two small ears about the stem—at the point from which the leaf-petioles grow. In most years only a few berries mature; they are red, and rather juicy.

Flowering throughout the summer, the Purple Honeysuckle may be seen west of the Cascades, from B.C. south, often on dry open hillsides, where it can sprawl over broken rock or low shrubs.

LONÍCERA INVOLUCRÀTA (Rich.) Banks. *Fly Honeysuckle. Black Twin-berry.* [p.503]

The specific name calls attention to a very distinctive feature of this 3-6 foot shrub, *an involucre* of two pairs of somewhat papery bracts, that become increasingly purplish, and that serve as little ruffs to cup the 2 yellow flowers or the shining black, twin-berries that follow. Why "Fly Honeysuckle"? We have watched flies come to the very slightly scented corollas, but bumblebees and butterflies were also visitors—as also at dusk, several moths. Perhaps the two shiny black berries suggest to some a glistening fly? But common names are often trivial.

Another feature to note is the large (up to 5 inches long) leaves, prominently veined, and slightly hairy (especially beneath and on the veins). The yellow corollas, sometimes becoming slightly red-tinged, are about ¾ inch long, glandular-hairy, and divided into 5 almost equal lobes, for about half their length.

This sturdy bush occurs rather sporadically—though it is often locally abundant—from B.C. eastward to the Atlantic, and south to California, apparently seeking out damp situations and rich soil. The flowers are seen from April to the end of August (when fruit has ripened as seen in our illustration, on the lower parts of the branches).

LONÍCERA UTAHÉNSIS Wats. *Red Twin-berry.* [p.499]

This 3-6 foot shrub was described from specimens collected in *Utah*, but ranges from southern B.C. to northern California, and eastward to Alberta and Montana.

Of rather straggling growth, the grey-barked branches, (in spring) spread thin, variably-shaped leaves, against whose pale-green (in May) appear pairs of pallid cream flowers. About ¾ inch long, the tubular flower has a pronounced knob on one side of the tube-base. The top of the rather short tube is notched into five (nearly equal) lobes, about ⅓ the tube's length. Frequently one of the twin-flowers is dwarfed, so that the resulting bright-red, soft berries are very unequal in size.

Red Twin-berry is common at moderate to rather high altitudes, in the mountains.

Here also may be found the rarer and smaller shrub, LONICÈRA CAERÙLEA L., whose pale-yellow flowers are notched ½ their length, and whose fruit is *blue*-black (rarely red).

SAMBÙCUS CERÙLEA Raf. *Tree Elder. Blue Elder.* [p.503]

Nearly 20 species of Elderberries are known from all parts of the world, though in the Tropics they are limited to mountainous areas. The generic name is the classical one, known to the earliest writers, who refer to shepherds making their whistles from its hollow stems. The fruit has long been used for making jellies and wines, and is eagerly sought by birds. The seeds are reported to be somewhat toxic, producing nausea, so the fruit should be crushed and strained.

The specific name cerulea calls attention to the flat, opulent clusters of large, dark-purple berries, that are covered with a bluish, waxy covering, and thus appear pale, powdery *blue*. This is commonly a large shrub, but we have measured, at Duncan, a well-known specimen that is 14 feet high, and no less than 45 inches in circumference. The single trunk of this old "tree" has deeply furrowed, rough brown bark, that shreds off in long strips.

Like its red-fruited cousin (*S. racemosa*, which see), Blue Elder has large, pinnate leaves, but the leaflets number from 5 to as many as 11 in this species. Saw-toothed, they are more sharply-pointed (lanceolate), than those of its congener. Both plants show a predilection for moist locations and rich soil.

The Tree Elder, where it occurs near the Red-fruited Elder, is about a month later opening its heavy, flat-topped, cluster of creamy-white blooms (usually in May at the Coast). It is a more southern species, not occurring in the northern half of British Columbia, nor even in the Queen Charlotte Islands.

482

PARENTUCELLIA VISCOSA ×⅘ [p.455]

PEDICULARIS GROENLANDICA (HABITAT) ×¼
[p.456]

PEDICULARIS ORNITHORHYNCHA ×½ [p.457]

PEDICULARIS GROENLANDICA (DETAIL) ×1¼
[p.456]

PEDICULARIS CAPITATA ×1¼ [p.456]

PENSTEMON PROCERUS var. PROCERUS ×⅖ [p.464]

PEDICULARIS BRACTEOSA ×⅞ [p.455]

SAMBÙCUS RACEMÒSA L. var. ARBORÉSCENS (T. & G.) Gray. *Red-fruited Elder.* [p.506]

This impressive shrub, which may reach 15 feet, (hence the varietal name, *tree-like*), was called racemosa by Linnaeus, because the large panicles *consist of* (compound) *racemes.* The general shape of these clusters of small flowers is pyramidal or conical.

Fast-growing, pith-filled, hollow canes of the Red-fruited Elder are among the first of coastal shrubs to unfold their very large, pinnate leaves, each with a terminal leaflet and 2-3 pairs of opposite, lateral, sawtooth-edged leaflets. In April along the south coast, onward to July inland to the Cascades, the air is filled with the rather heavy fragrance, and hosts of varied insects come to the big white bloom-clusters. Toward the end of summer, the bushes become gay with bright berries, which are eagerly sought by Band-tailed Pigeons, Willow Grouse, and a multitude of smaller birds. In var. arborescens the fruit is bright scarlet, but it is black in var. MELANOCÁRPA (Gray) McMinn (a smaller shrub of the Rocky Mountains) and red, yellow, or even white in var. PÙBENS (Michx.) Koehne (a hairy-leaved small shrub of eastern B.C. and Alberta). The species complex is actually circumboreal, and well-known to most Europeans.

SYMPHORICÁRPOS ÁLBUS (L.) Blake var. LAEVIGÀTUS (Fern.) Blake. *Snowberry. Waxberry.* [p.503]

Probably the Snowberry is as well-known as the Dandelion, being wide-spread from Atlantic to Pacific, and from Alaska to California. The closely clustered berries are referred to in the generic name, from the Greek syn, *together*, phorein, *to bear*, and karpos, *fruit*. Four species occur in British Columbia, all *white*-fruited, so "albus" is not a distinctive name.

Possibly the commonest species, this familiar 3-6 foot shrub is distinguished from the other species of Snowberries on the basis of distinctions so minute they require a 10X magnifying glass. If you slit the pale-pink flower lengthwise, you will find white hairs covering the inner face of the 5 lobes of the vase-shaped corolla; a short, stubby pistil no longer than the tubular part of the corolla; and 5 short-filamented stamens growing from the tube-wall at the level of the hairy portion. SYMPHORICÁRPOS OREOPHÍLUS Gray var. UTAHÉNSIS (Rydb.) A. Nels., a more *montane* species, lacks these hairs, the lobes being smooth within. SYMPHORICÁRPOS OCCIDENTÀLIS Hook. has hairy lobes, but is sharply distinguished by a long pistil, which projects slightly beyond the mouth of the corolla-tube. This small shrub occurs in the Rockies, but only at lower elevations.

All these species have slim stems that appear smooth, but on careful examination, they are nearly always found covered with extremely small hairs—commonly blackish. All have thin leaves—2 inches long or less—sometimes entire but astonishingly variable, and usually lobed, or round-toothed, or both. Alike, the species bear small racemes of pinkish, bell-shaped flowers, about ¼ inch long. In April they are faintly perfumed, as is the delicate foliage. And in late summer all the species are ornamented with spectacular masses of hanging, soft, snow-white berries, that may be as much as ½ inch across.

The berried twigs are much used in floral arrangements with other coloured berries of the autumn. Birds turn to the bitter fruit, when hard-pressed for other food, in the diminished days of winter.

Thwaites [edit. *Original Journals of the Lewis and Clark Expeditions*] quotes an interesting letter from President Thomas Jefferson, to Madame La Comtesse de Tesse:

"Lewis's journey across our continent to the Pacific has added a number of new plants to our former stock. I have growing, which I destine for you, a very handsome little shrub of the size of a currant bush. Its beauty consists in a great produce of berries of the size of currants, and literally as white as snow, which remain on the bush through the winter, after its leaves have fallen, and make it an object as singular as it is beautiful. We call it the snow-berry bush, no botanical name being yet given to it. . . ."

Dec. 8, 1813.

SYMPHORICÁRPOS MÓLLIS Nutt. *Trailing Snowberry* is very similar, except in its manner of growth. It is a charming little trailing shrub, of the southern part of our area, that prefers crevices in broken rock. The decumbent stems often root at the nodes. Flowers are a little broader, and the filaments are longer than the anthers, (rather than the reverse proportions found in the stamens of *S. albus*, which see).

VIBÚRNUM EDÙLE (Michx.) Raf. = V. PAUCIFLÒRUM Pylaie. *High-bush Cranberry. Squashberry.* [p.506]

This classical Latin name is believed to be derived from vieo, *to tie*, because of the pliability of the branches of the European plant (*V. lantana* L.). Edule means *edible*, the brilliant red fruit (botanically a one-seeded drupe) yielding a tart but pleasing jelly, resembling that of the festive cranberry.

The High-bush Cranberry is a common, erect to straggling, opposite-leaved, 2-6 foot shrub of cold damp woods and semi-open, wooded margins of lakes and streams. It occurs sporadically throughout our area, especially toward the north, and chiefly at low levels.

There is much confusion, among various authorities consulted, on the names of the species occurring in our area, but we have followed Hitchcock, Cronquist, et al. This species is perhaps better known as *V. pauciflorum*, or Squashberry.

Mature leaves are round in outline but usually with 2 pronounced notches at the outer end, and further sharply serrate. A curious feature of these older leaves—useful in recognition—is a pair of small, ear-like teeth at the junction of the blade and petiole.

PEDICULARIS RACEMOSA (DETAIL)   ×1¾
[p.457]

PENSTEMON DAVIDSONII var. MENZIESII   ×⅓
[p.460]

PENSTEMON NEMOROSUS   ×⅗   [p.461]

PENSTEMON SERRULATUS   ×⅖   [p.464]

PENSTEMON PROCERUS var. TOLMIEI $\times \frac{3}{5}$ [p.464]

VERONICA AMERICANA $\times \frac{1}{2}$ [p.466]

PENSTEMON FRUTICOSUS var. SCOULERI $\times \frac{3}{4}$ [p.460]

Terminal leaves are pointed-lanceolate, and like the others, short-hairy beneath, especially along the larger veins. Flowers are greenish-white and tubular, arranged in flattened clusters between pairs of leaves along the stem, rather than at the ends of the branches. Flower parts are in 5's, with very short stamens not projecting beyond the mouth of the wide-flared, 5-lobed corolla-tube.

Viburnum edule bushes are easily overlooked until autumn, when they declare their presence with crimson-purpled leaves and brilliantly scarlet fruit.

VIBÚRNUM ÓPULUS L. ranges generally through damp open woods of the Central Mainland. Usually 5 or 6 feet tall, specimens twice that height are occasionally seen. The leaves are readily distinguished, being nearly glabrous, scarcely toothed but conspicuously 3-nerved, and very deeply 3-lobed (much like a *maple* leaf, hence opulus). Flat clusters of white flowers are terminal on branch ends. Each perfect central flower is very small, with short pistil, and long stamens that project beyond the lobed corolla-tube. Very different are the sterile flowers ranged round the edge of the cluster. They are nearly an inch across, with very broad, flattened lobes of the corolla, and resemble flowers of some of the garden Hydrangeas. Bright red berries of Viburnum opulus are edible, though of less than pleasing flavour.

VALERIANÀCEAE. *Valerian Family.*

PLECTRÍTIS CONGÉSTA (Lindl.) DC. *Sea Blush.* [pp.498,507]

Boon companion of Blue-eyed Mary (*Collinsia grandiflora*, which see) this delightful little plant spreads a blush of springtime colour over rock ledges above the sea, and on innumerable short-turf meadows eastward to the Cascades.

The Greek word for *plaited*, plektron, is the origin of the generic name—probably with reference to the densely *congested* inflorescence of small pink flowers. The specific name repeats this thought.

Around Victoria, Sea Blush often opens a tentative few flowers before February is out, but the inexpressibly beautiful carpets of vivid clear pink are usually at perfection during May. Not infrequently pure white specimens are seen.

The little annuals may bloom when only an inch high, but strong plants in good soil continue blooming (with occasional axial heads of flowers) until attaining possibly 18 inches. However, the rounded flower-head is usually terminal. The whole plant is glabrous, with an erect stem that is angled and usually squarish in section. The opposite pairs of slightly succulent leaves have no petioles, and are oblong, with entire margins. (Sometimes the lower leaves are oblanceolate, withering later.) A glass is needed to make out the detail of individual flowers. One looks in vain for sepals; the calyx has become obsolete. The pink corolla-tube has a short blunt spur, and is divided above into 5 lobes,

2 of which are vertical, 3 larger, widely flared and nearly horizontal. There are 3 stamens, unusual for their bluish colour, until they dehisce to expose their whitish pollen.

PLECTRÍTIS SAMOLIFÒLIA (DC.) Hoeck., with pale lavender flowers less than half as large, has now been reduced to the status of a form of *P. congesta*, though in the field it appears very unlike the typical pink form.

PLECTRÍTIS MACROCÈRA T. & G., found in southern B.C., has all 5 corolla lobes even in length, and usually white.

> "... the rural appearance"... [of Protection Island, in "Juan de Fuca's Streights"] strongly invited us to stretch our limbs after our long confined situation on board & the dreary sameness of a tedious voyage.... We found on landing ... the shore was skirted with long grass & a variety of wild flowers in full bloom, but what chiefly dazzled our eyes ... was a small species of wild Valerian [now known as *Plectritis* or *Valerianella congesta*] with reddish colord flowers growing behind the beach in large thick patches."

Archibald Menzies
(naturalist with Captain George Vancouver, 1792)

How vivid, and how familiar, the picture conjured up, of pink sheets of Sea Blush, as we read (in the Archives at Victoria) this journal entry of nearly two centuries ago!

Throw hither all your quaint enameld eyes,
That on the green terf suck the honied showres,
And purple all the ground with vernal flowres.

John Milton: Lycidas [1673 edition]

VALERIÀNA SITCHÉNSIS Bong. *Sitka Valerian.* [p.506]

The oldest reference we can find attributes the name to the Roman Valerius, who first used a tincture of the roots in medicine, but more generally the name is thought to be derived from the Latin valere, *to be in health.* Through the Middle Ages the European species, *Valeriana officinalis* (the latter means official, "having good offices" altered now in meaning and spelling to official) was highly regarded. This is the Heliotrope, familiar in gardens, of which—in an 130 year old botanical dictionary—we read: "The root affords a tincture eminently antispasmodic, prescribed with success for hysteria, excellent in habitual costiveness", which if believable, is at least somewhat baffling.

The specific name records the fact that the species was first collected at *Sitka*, by Mertens, shortly before 1833.

Like the Garden Heliotrope referred to above, this flower of moist semi-shaded nooks is perfumed—so strongly that it should be left out-of-doors. Sitka Valerian occurs along the coast, and inland to considerable altitudes in the Kootenays and the Rockies, where it may be seen in bloom from April to August.

The small flowers are clustered in rather open and nearly flat-topped arrangements, described as corymbose. Generally fading to white, they are at first very pale lavender-pink, a colour especially noticeable in the buds. The plants are somewhat lax and succulent, with squared leafy stems 12-30 inches tall. Generally glabrous, the foliage of some forms is sparsely short-haired. The leaves appear in opposite pairs up the stem, on long petioles that become progressively shorter. The blades are nearly pinnate, with 1-4 lateral pairs of "leaflets" increasing in size to a considerably larger terminal one, all with shallow and remote serrations. In Valeriana sitchensis small corolla-tubes are only slightly notched into 5 nearly equal lobes, which are much exceeded by the 3 long stamens and the even longer slim pistil.

VALERIÀNA CAPITÀTA Pall., with upper stem-leaves lacking petioles, and pale-lavender flowers clustered in a tight head, is found only in the northern half of our area.

VALERIÀNA DIOÌCA L. ssp. SYLVÁTICA (Sol.) Mey., is very widely distributed in mountain meadows. It is a smaller plant than *V. sitchensis* (which see), with a proportion of the basal leaves entire, and the smaller white flowers relatively more deeply cleft, the lobes more flared. Quite a few of the flowers lack stamens.

VALERIÀNA ÉDULIS Nutt. ex T. & G. is distinctly different. The leaves are thicker, and the yellowish-white flowers are borne in a long raceme. V. edulis occurs rarely in southeastern British Columbia, sometimes in alkaline flats.

DIPSACÀCEAE. *Teasel Family.*

DÍPSACUS SYLVÉSTRIS Huds. *Teasel.*   [p.507]

This stout European biennial appears sporadically near Vancouver and Victoria, and attracts attention with its remarkable prickly heads. Those of a related species (*D. fullonum* L.) were used by fullers to raise the nap on cloth. Dipsakos is the Greek name for *diabetes*, one of whose symptoms is a thirst for water, and dipsao means *to thirst*; the allusion, it seems, was to rain or dew accumulating in the cup-like bases of joined opposite leaves.* The coarse lanceolate leaves frequently develop odd finger-like tips. The specific name, sylvestris, *of the woods*, is inappropriate in our area, for the plants appear in open wasteland, in full sun, generally on heavy clay soil.

The harsh, angled stems (formidably prickly) often reach 5 or 6 feet. Huge terminal ovoid heads are armed with impressively sharp-spined bracts. A ring of bluish flowers gradually opens from the base of the head upward. On closer inspection the long tubular corolla of Dipsacus sylvestris is seen to be 4-lobed, with 4 protruding stamens and a shorter stigma.

*It has been suggested that such rain- or dew-filled cups serve as traps to keep ants and other crawling insects from the flowers.

KNÁUTIA ARVÉNSIS (L.) Coult. (= SCABIÒSA ARVÉNSIS L.) *Wild Scabious.* [p.507]

Though Wild Scabious is apparently an unlikely relative of the prickly Teasel (*Dipsacus sylvestris*, which see), certain botanical features show the relationship of the two plants. Knautia commemorates Christian Knaut, of Saxony, an early German physician and botanical author (1654-1716). However the genus was also called Scabiosa, source of the present common name. The derivation is from scabies, the *itch*, for which disorder a poultice of this common plant of European *fields* (arvensis) was once thought to be efficacious. The number of records in southern and central British Columbia is increasing rapidly, and the plant appears now to be well established here.

Knautia arvensis is a 1-3 foot hairy perennial, with inch-long leaves becoming progressively more pinnately-divided upward. The flattened 1-1½ inch flower-heads closely resemble those of the now-familiar annual and perennial *Scabiosa* of our gardens. Each corolla is lilac-purple and 4-lobed, emerging from a tubular calyx that has 8-12 bristle-like teeth.

 # CUCURBITÀCEAE. *Gourd Family. Cucumber Family.*

MÁRAH OREGÀNUS (T. & G.) Howell. *Bigroot. Manroot.* [p.510]

Southern British Columbia is the northern limit of this climbing perennial, that springs from a very large woody root. The generic name is the Hebrew word for *bitter*, referring to the exceedingly bitter juice of the swollen root. (Marah* is one of the very few Hebrew words encountered in the taxonomy of plants.) The plant was apparently brought northward into Canada, for it occurs at the sites of former Indian settlements in California and Oregon. The swollen fruits, like small pointed cucumbers, were probably used for food.

Large (to 8 inches long) and somewhat hairy (especially on the upper surface) palmately-lobed leaves, as well as long stems climbing by means of branched tendrils, make Bigroot easily recognizable. The white campanulate flowers are 5-8 lobed. Those in racemes contain 3 joined stamens, while those solitary in the leaf-axils are pistillate.

*The name apparently should be spelled *Mara*, since the final aspirate in Hebrew words is always omitted in Latin writing. (See note by Edward L. Greene in *Pittonia*, Feb. 15, 1887). (The earlier generic name was Echinocystis.)

 # CAMPANULÀCEAE. *Harebell Family.*

CAMPÁNULA LASIOCÁRPA Cham. *Alpine Harebell.*

This superb plant is a 2-4 inch alpine perennial. Stations in our area include Toad River, the upper Nass River, Signal Mt. and The Whistlers (Jasper), the forest lookout at McBride, and several sites in the Queen Charlottes.

Neat ¾ inch, obovate, basal leaves are sharply toothed. The few stem-leaves are more linear but just as crisply dentate. Each short stem is topped with a fine lilac-blue bell, that is relatively huge for such a small plant. (In the Queen Charlotte form the flower is as much as 1½ inches long.) The flower is much more deeply cupped (campanulate) in shape than the flattened flower of *C. piperi*, which is its southern analogue. Also, in the present species the laciniately-margined, pointed sepal-lobes clasp the corolla, instead of reflexing. Lasiocarpa means *fuzzy fruit*, a reference to the pubescent capsule.

CAMPÁNULA PÌPERI Howell, the gem of the Olympics, may possibly be found in the mountains of southern Vancouver Island—an eventuality we can hope for. It is a small and lovely crevice-plant, with firm glossy leaves that are sharply serrate, and brilliant blue (rarely white) flowers, like 5-pointed star-shaped shallow cups.

CAMPÁNULA ROTUNDIFÒLIA L. *Harebell. Bluebell.* [p.510]

This dainty but wiry little plant swings its small bells from varied perches all round the Northern Hemisphere. Crevices in arctic precipices, moist rocks sprayed by alpine streams, upland meadows, even rocks by the roadside are its homes. It is the same "Bluebell" so loved in Scotland, and in Switzerland and the Tyrol; but in England (to avoid confusion with the liliaceous *Hyacinthoides non-scripta*) it is known as "Harebell". This is a mis-spelling of Hairbell, in appropriate allusion to the hair-thin stems from which the bells depend. In the family and generic names we see the Latin campana, bell; Campanula is the diminutive—*little bell*. The specific name, when one considers the slim and sessile linear leaves of the stem, may appear inappropriate, but the blades of the basal leaves (which in dry situations may wither early) are indeed rotund in outline. They are strongly to slightly toothed, and have petioles 2 to 3 times as long as the blades. Linnaeus (who named this plant) as a professor at Uppsala, constantly passed Harebell's winter-rosettes of *rounded leaves*, which grew beside the steps to the University.

Though the buds are erect on their slender peduncles, the lovely purple-blue bells gradually swing over until they protect their nectar and pollen from the rain. This thought leads one to consider how wonderfully the flower is structured so that seed may be produced. When the campanulate corolla first expands its lobes, 5 stamens may be seen, whose filaments are broadened basally to cover the store of nectar. The anthers soon shed their minutely-hooked pollen-grains, which fall upon the numerous hairs that cover the style. The empty anthers shrivel, and the stamens wither and drop away. Then in a sequence perfected by tens of thousands of generations, the bell's clapper (the 3-lobed and clubbed stigma) becomes sticky and receptive, and the bees come crawling up the hanging bell. As they climb upward to the nectaries, the pollen-laden hairs along the style afford good footing, and of course, dust with the precious pollen-grains, the hairy legs of the bee. But the style is precisely the length of the bell's throat, so that the viscid stigma surface is positioned to remove pollen picked up by the bee's feet, during the visit to the previous flower. However, in the event that violent weather keeps the insects inactive, the maturing pistil curves and acquires its own pollen-grains. The world of nature is filled with such wonders.

In spite of its delicate appearance, the "Hairbell" is incredibly hardy, and survives the fierce alpine storms throughout our area, even into Alaska. These fragile-seeming bells so "darkly, deeply, beautifully blue" yield to the violent gale, but do not break. Perhaps this is one of the reasons for the universal affection the Harebell arouses among mountain folk everywhere. The generally montane plant descends to sea level along our coast, but never achieves there the abundant flowering mats—a foot or more across—that one sees in the Rockies. Sheep and goats avoid the foliage, since it contains bitter alkaloids. This plant is highly variable, and the enthusiast may take to his rockery, rooted portions of exceptionally large, or paler blue, or even pure white forms of Campanula rotundifolia.

A foot more light, a step more true,
Ne'er from the heath-flower dash'd the dew;
E'en the slight harebell raised its head,
Elastic from her airy tread. . . .

Sir Walter Scott:
The Lady of the Lake

CAMPÁNULA SCOULÉRI Hook. *Scouler's Harebell.* [p.511]

This is also a charming but unobtrusive Harebell, that occurs chiefly west of the Cascades. It prefers open woods, from sea level to about 5000 feet. The specific name

494

VERBASCUM THAPSUS ×¼ [p.465]

VERONICA WORMSKJOLDII ×⅘ [p.467]

GALIUM BOREALE ×1 [p.477]

BOSCHNIAKIA HOOKERI ×1 [p.467]

VERONICA SERPYLLIFOLIA var. HUMIFUSA ×2 [p.467]

VERONICA FILIFORMIS ×3/5 [p.467]

OROBANCHE GRAYANA ×3/5 [p.468]

OROBANCHE UNIFLORA var. PURPUREA ×1/3 [p.468]

commemorates Dr. John Scouler, who accompanied David Douglas in 1825, during his botanical exploration of the northwest coast of North America.

Scouler's Harebell is a 3-8 inch slender perennial, with smooth and varied alternate leaves. The basal ones are long-petioled and rounded, but higher on the stem they become more ovate, and finally lanceolate and lacking petioles. All the leaves are strongly toothed. The flowers are lavender—so pale as to appear nearly white—though the extreme tips of the long, recurved corolla-lobes are touched with more intense colour. The corolla forms a very much flatter and more open bell than that of *C. rotundifolia* (which see). Conspicuous is the very long pistil, that projects far beyond the mouth of the corolla. Though the small bloom of Campanula scouleri is not more than ½ inch across, its proportions are elegant.

LOBELIÀCEAE. *Lobelia Family.*

LOBÈLIA DORTMÁNNA L. *Water Lobelia.*   [p.510]

Lobelia is named for Matthias de L'Obel, an early French physician, who became botanist to James I, and died in London in 1616. Dortmann was a little-known Dutch apothecary. This remarkable species inhabits fine-sand and silt shore-lines of lakes and ponds in western America and northwestern Europe. Several stations in the Queen Charlottes represent its northern limit in our area, but it is locally abundant in many lakes of Vancouver Island and the adjacent Mainland. In central British Columbia L. dortmanna is replaced by the similar L. KÁLMII L. (which has broader, flatter leaves that continue up the scape, and more numerous stronger-blue flowers).

Water Lobelia's cluster of fleshy white anchor-roots produces occasional runners, as well as clumps of smooth, hollow-tubular leaves 1-3 inches long. These are normally submerged, but the slim, unbranched scape hoists—like a periscope above the water—a few spaced flowers that are ½-1 inch long. These are palest lavender-mauve, quickly fading to white. The flowers' shape readily proclaims kinship with the familiar edging Lobelia. The calyx-tube has 5 blunt-tipped lobes. The corolla is curiously inverted, with the 3-lobed (true upper) lip at the lower edge of the tube, which is about as long as these larger lobes. A few tiny bracts (but no leaves) appear on the scape. Hitchcock et al. report these scapes to 3 feet, though we have never seen them more than 10-12 inches high.

At a little distance it is quite extraordinary to see a host of these delicate flowers apparently air-borne above the surface of the water. Brilliant blue Damselflies frequently rest upon them, but the pollinating agents are probably tiny *Diptera*. The blooms are often submerged when water levels suddenly rise.

❧ COMPÓSITAE. *Composite Family.*

This is the largest family of flowering plants, some of whose nearly 20,000 species are found in every type of habitat in every corner of the world. The majority are herbs, although some shrubs, trees, and even climbing species are included.

The number of species of great economic importance is smaller than might be expected for such a gigantic family. Perhaps most familiar are the huge Sunflower, *Helianthus annuus* (which see), selected strains of which are grown quite extensively for the oil expressed from the seeds, and its smaller cousin *H. tuberosus*, so-called Jerusalem Artichoke (but actually a North American native) esteemed for the delicately-flavoured roots. Another artichoke entirely, is the giant, thistle-like Globe Artichoke (*Cynara scolymus*), whose immature flower-heads are steamed or boiled. *Lactuca sativa* is seldom allowed to show its typically "composite" flower-heads; it is the Lettuce so extensively cultivated. Many thousands of acres in India are devoted to culture of *Carthamus tinctorius*, whose flowers provide a brilliant yellow dye.

More familiar to gardeners is the host of members of the Compositae tribe, that are cultivated for their beautiful flowers. They include Michaelmas Daisies and China Asters (*Callistephus*), *Cosmos* and *Chrysanthemum*, *Dahlia* and *Zinnia*. Florists' "Cineraria" is *Senecio cruentus*, while *S. keniodendron* is the remarkable Tree Groundsel of Mt. Kilimanjaro. The Sagebrush of the Dry Interior, and *Leontopodium alpinum*, "Edelweiss" of the Alps and Himalayas, are both Composites. So is the extraordinary Vegetable Sheep, *Haastia pulmonaris*, of New Zealand.

The variety and degree of specialization of such species suggests that the Compositae represents the most advanced plant family of the Dicotyledons. This conclusion is also supported by the extraordinary abundance of many of the members. Such abundance is largely the outcome of highly efficient adaptations to secure fertilization of the seed.

Characteristic of the family is the grouping of a number of individual flowers on a common receptacle, with an encircling ring of bracts that protects the flowers as they mature. The flower-head may contain hundreds of individual florets, so that insect visitors easily pollinate large numbers of pistils, and immense quantities of seed are produced. The seed (achene) is well provided with storage food, and often bears a feathery pappus by which it may be parachuted far and wide. As has been suggested, nearly all Composites are insect-pollinated; however, Wormwood and Sagebrush (*Artemisia sp.* which see) and Ragweed (*Ambrosia artemisiifolia*, and *A. trifida*, chiefly of the eastern part of the North American continent) are wind-pollinated, and so produce enormous numbers of pollen-grains (to the distress of "hay-fever" victims).

In addition to the clustering of flowers in a flower-head, the Compositae are further characterized by a number of structural peculiarities. Chief of these is an extraordinarily effective arrangement of the pistil and 5 stamens, that prevents self-pollination (unless as a last resort when, for example, bad weather at high altitudes has prevented visitation by insects, the plants are forced to genetically less desirable self-fertilization, so that viable seed may be produced).

This arrangement consists in fusion of the anthers of the stamens into a hollow tube, enclosing the immature pistil. The filaments remain separate. The anthers release their pollen into the central tube, from which it is pushed by the piston-like action of the

PLANTAGO PURSHII ×1 [p.476]

PLECTRITIS CONGESTA ×⅞ [p.488]

PINGUICULA VULGARIS ×1 [p.469]

T. & S. ARMSTRONG

UTRICULARIA VULGARIS ✕⅖ [p.472]

PLANTAGO MARITIMA ssp. JUNCOIDES ✕⅓ [p.476]

LONICERA UTAHENSIS ✕1¼ [p.481]

LONICERA CILIOSA ✕½ [p.479]

lengthening pistil. The (non-fertile) exposed surfaces of the pistil are usually short-haired, so as to more efficiently brush the pollen-dust upward and outward. A great variety of insects are drawn to the compound flower-heads, attracted both by the copious supply of pollen (from which for example, the honeybee makes "bee-bread" to feed its larvae), and by the nectar, which is so freely produced (from a ring around the base of the style) that it rises high in the corolla-tube and can be reached by even the shortest-tongued visitors. During all this time the receptive stigmatic surfaces of the pistil are kept tightly pressed together. Only after the pollen of a particular floret has blown away, or has been transported by insects to other more mature florets on other flower-heads, are the stigmatic surfaces exposed, by the spreading of the forked tip of the style.

Since the florets are so closely packed together, sepals to protect each one have become unnecessary, and have become modified into mere scales at the top of the achene, or often into long hairs (pappus), sometimes plumose, which then serve to air-lift the seed. The petals have been modified into a slender tube that encases the essential stamens and pistil. But in many kinds of Composites the corolla-tube has been further modified to serve another purpose. In some genera all of the corollas have been split part way, and flattened out, as well as elongated, into a kind of strap. These are called rays, or ray-florets. But in about four times as many of the genera, only the outermost ring of florets are strap-flowers, whose rays then act as bright banners to attract insects to the entire compound flower-head. Sometimes these ray-florets lack stamens, and even pistils, being wholly specialized as attention-getters, or advertisers, in which case the central or tubular "disk-florets" are entrusted with the vital stamens and pistils. A few species lack even marginal ray-florets. Perhaps this is the supreme asset of the Compositae: association of their flowers in something like a social organization designed for the maintenance of the species. A very large percentage have yellow flowers, or yellow ray-florets, having long anticipated our traffic engineers in discovering that this is the colour most visible, apparently to a majority of insects, as well as to human eyes. Small wonder that this family almost monopolizes the floral scene in late summer and fall.

In our treatment of the family it has been possible only to include representative species of the larger or more showy genera. We suggest that readers interested in determining the names of the very numerous other species of Compositae, should refer to the two keys in Part 5 of the great work by Hitchcock, Cronquist, Ownbey, and Thompson, *Vascular Plants of the Pacific Northwest*. The keys make use of such characteristics as: flowers all ray-florets (ligulate) or only the marginal ones ligulate, presence or absence of pistils in the marginal florets, type of pappus, and shape and arrangement of bracts that enclose the involucre (flower-head).

> *And the dead leaves lie huddled and still,*
> *No longer blown hither and thither;*
> *The last lone aster is gone;*
> *The flowers of the witch-hazel wither;*
> *The heart is still aching to seek,*
> *But the feet question 'Whither?'*

Robert Frost: Reluctance

ACHILLÈA MILLEFÒLIUM L. *Milfoil. Yarrow.*   [p.510]

Achilles, of the vulnerable heel, is the name-source of this alphabetically first genus of the great family of Composites. And the leaf or foil (French feuille) may not be divided a thousand times, but it is very much dissected. Degree of dissection is extremely variable, and is the basis of several subspecific and varietal names. However, this was one of the plants included in the now classic studies by J. Clausen, on the effects of climate upon plant structures. He was able to show that leaf-fringing of plants altered in a few years when they were transplanted from the mountains to the coast, and *vice versa*. Yarrow is an old Scottish name, after the parish of Yarrow on the little river of the same name.

This aromatic perennial is known throughout the Northern Hemisphere. Its flat-topped cluster of small white (sometimes pinkish) flowers may be found from April to October, or even through most of the winter, at the Coast.

These flower-heads will be seen to consist of two kinds of flowers. The ray-flowers ringing each cluster have a conspicuous 2-notched lip at the top of the tube, whereas the tube of the disk-flowers is evenly notched to form 5 short teeth. If the corollas are plucked off, you can see they grow from a sort of platform (the receptacle) on which are many short, chaffy scales. In ssp. LANULÒSA (Nutt.) Piper the *long-woolled* leaf segments are so numerous that they give the ferny leaf a third dimensional "thickness".

The widespread but scarcely invasive Achillea millefolium prefers dry locations, from sea level to considerable altitudes.

ADENOCAÙLON BÍCOLOR Hook. *Path-finder Plant. Silver Green.*   [p.518]

The common names emphasize the sharp contrast between this plant's *two colours* (bicolor)—the green upper surface and the silvery white-haired lower surface of the large leaves. As the stroller in semi-shaded or open woods looks backward, his trail is marked by the white pattern of leaves he has disturbed. The tall stem (1-3 feet) bears glandular hairs above, whence the name, from the Greek aden, *gland*, and kaulos, *stem*.

The large leaves (4-6 inches long) appear out of proportion to the meagre whitish flowers, that are sparsely distributed near the top of the slender stem. On reflection however, one comes to realize the shaded habitat calls for a large, photosynthesizing leaf area, and the absence of wind makes long and wide and very thin leaves feasible. Butterflies and bees are not attracted to the dimly lit areas, so the Path-finder Plant must rely on small flies, which can be attracted by odour. Hence none of the plant's energy need be dissipated in producing large and showy petals. Instead it is important for the plant to produce quantities of hooked achenes, that may hitch a ride on infrequent passing animals, and so disseminate the seed. On very close examination the outer tubular florets in the head, about 4-8 in number, are found to be pistillate; the ripened achenes of these are elongated and covered with tiny but efficient hooked hairs.

LINNAEA BOREALIS var. LONGIFLORA ×2¼ [p.478]

LONICERA HISPIDULA   ×⅞   [p.480]

LONICERA INVOLUCRATA (FRUIT)   ×⅞
[p.480]

SAMBUCUS CERULEA   ×½   [p.481]

SYMPHORICARPOS ALBUS var. LAEVIGATUS
(FRUIT)   ×1   [p.484]

These achenes radiate from the involucral hub like the spokes of a wheel. The staminate flowers occupy the central part of the flower-head.

Adenocaulon bicolor is a plant of the southern part of our area. It is common in suitably moist woods from sea level to limited altitudes.

ANÁPHALIS MARGARITÀCEA (L.) B. & H. *Pearly Everlasting.*   [p.518]

This attractive and common composite, with its crisp white papery flowers, bears a euphonious but obscure name. The generic name Anaphalis may have been invented by Linnaeus as an approximate anagram of the nearly related genus *Gnaphalium* (which derives from knaphalon, a *tuft of wool*). As with Sylvia, we might ask, who is Margaret? But there is no romantic story. The word "margaritaceus", means *pearly*, of pearls. The popular name is descriptive, and apparently used over most of the plant's wide range of North America, eastern Asia, and parts of Europe. The plants are often dried for winter ornament, hence "everlasting". Thoreau called this the artificial flower of the September pastures. The pearly effect is due to the whitened tips of the chaffy bracts, which closely surround the tiny yellow clustered florets.

Across the length and breadth of our area, this is a highly variable species. The subalpine variety is especially attractive, being even more woolly, and much more compact than the lowland plants. The plants do not usually bloom until July, but the enduring flowers may be seen above the snows of winter.

Usually Pearly Everlasting grows 1-2 feet tall, from a perennial rhizome. The stem is erect and unbranched, densely white-woolly, as are the numerous, sessile, 2-4 inch, linear-lanceolate leaves that alternate up its entire length. Though the flower-heads are generally crowded in a flattened cluster, in the Dry Interior a variety is seen with much more open heads of drab buff-coloured florets. Commonly the leaves are covered with white wool below, less so above. A good glass is needed to make out the details of the tiny flowers. The ring of whitened bracts is conspicuous. Enclosed by them are tubular staminate flowers, with a non-functioning pistil reduced to a thread-like style. Or there may be much narrower-tubed pistillate flowers, with a divided style. Both of these flower-types occur together in some few plants, but generally the pistillate and staminate flowers are found on separate plants.

If care is taken to choose only pure-pistillate flowered plants (thereby preventing rampant spread) this bright-faced little wildling will provide bloom in the garden long after most flowers are past.

ANTENNÀRIA RÒSEA Greene. *Pink Pussy-toes.*   [p.578]

Perhaps 19 species of Antennaria occur in our area. Due to geographic and ecological variation, and non-sexual reproduction of numerous clones, definition of the species (with rare exceptions) is very difficult. They are white-woolly perennials, with generally simple and entire leaves, some of which form a basal tuft. Antennaria rosea is unique in a genus of whitish or buffy flowers, for its pretty *rosy* bracts (though they age whitish, and occasionally never develop the typical pink colour). In this species the bracts are blunt-pointed, not round-tipped as in *A. umbrinella.* The generic name alludes to the fancied resemblance of the pappus of the staminate flowers to the *antennae* of insects. Pink Pussy-toes is common in British Columbia, especially in the Dry Interior, where it sometimes climbs to moderate altitudes. Montane plants are commonly more intense pink.

ANTENNÀRIA UMBRINÉLLA Rydb. *Pale Everlasting.* [p.511]

This species is representative of small alpine members of the genus, being almost indistinguishable from *A. ALPÌNA* (L.) Gaertn., or from a white *A. rosea* Greene (which see). A. umbrinella is common at moderate to quite high elevations in most parts of Canada. The specific name is the diminutive of the Latin umbrinus, *umber*, probably alluding to the colour of the involucral bracts.

A. umbrinella in its dwarf mat-forming habit, and persistently grey-woolly foliage, is almost identical with *A. rosea.* The bracts of the involucre are round-tipped, whereas those of the still higher-level *A. alpina* are sharply-pointed, and those of the more lowland *A. rosea* are blunt-pointed. Bracts in the present species vary from brown, to yellowish, to grey-green—at the base; and from pale-brown to grey-white at the tip. Flower-heads are nearly always, as in the specimen illustrated, creamy-white.

Pale Everlasting is an attractive little species in the coterie of plants that brighten rock ledges and crevices in our storm-swept mountains.

ÁNTHEMIS ARVÉNSIS L. *Field Chamomile.* [p.519]

Greek anthemon means *flower,* so the allusion is, apparently, to the numerous white blooms, that appear in long succession throughout the summer and fall. This European invader of *fields* (arvensis) and waste places is widely distributed at lower levels in our area.

The leaves of Anthemis arvensis are alternate and much dissected. "Flowers" (of course flower-heads) are quite large, averaging about an inch wide. Each ray-floret, with its long white strap, has a functional pistil. The disk-florets are bright yellow tubes notched at their tips. Both kinds grow from a cone-shaped receptacle which bears numerous chaffy scales. The "flower" is slightly odorous, unlike ÁNTHEMIS CÒTULA L. which is very strongly and unpleasantly scented. A. TINCTÒRIA L. has bright yellow ray-flowers.

Chamomile (also spelled Camomile) Tea, was brewed from the European, more dwarf, and pleasantly aromatic species *A. nobile* (L.) Allioni. It was long esteemed as a tonic and blood-purifier.

506

VIBURNUM EDULE ✕²⁄₅ [p.485]

VALERIANA SITCHENSIS ✕¹⁄₅ [p.489]

SAMBUCUS RACEMOSA var. ARBORESCENS (FRUIT) ✕¹⁄₂ [p.484]

DIPSACUS SYLVESTRIS $\times$ ⅖ [p.490]

KNAUTIA ARVENSIS $\times$ ⅞ [p.491]

PLECTRITIS CONGESTA (HABITAT) [p.488]

ÁRCTIUM MÌNUS (Hill) Bernh. *Lesser Burdock.* [p.518]

The hooked burs of this widespread coarse weed (originally from Eurasia) have been playthings of children for a very long time. Who knows how much this prank has assisted in the centuries-long spread of this plant?.

The rough involucre, with its dense coat of black hooked bracts, is probably responsible for the generic name, from the Greek arktos, *a bear.* This great plant may reach 4½ feet in height, and almost as much across. The very large leaves are somewhat triangular, and as much as 24 inches long.

All the flowers are tubular and perfect, the corolla purplish. The inflorescences typically are arranged in cone-shaped semi-racemes, and the individual heads are about 1 inch or less thick. ÁRCTIUM LÁPPA L., the *Great Burdock,* is even larger, reaching 6, 7, or even 8 feet, with gigantic leaves, and heads fully 1½ inches wide, that are arranged in a cluster flatter than the rounded clusters of its relative. A. lappa is not as common as *A. minus,* but both Eurasian pests are now established throughout most of North America. In British Columbia the Great Burdock is infrequent at the Coast.

Some of the very early botanical illustrations show details of surprising realism. LAPPA (Burdock) in Brunfels' *Herbarum vivae eiconeb* [sic] (1530-40) is depicted with one leaf withered, two more accidentally broken, and several damaged by insects!

ÁRNICA. *Arnica.*

About a dozen species of the beautiful, yellow, perennial flowers of Arnica enrich our area, and reach their finest development in the mountains. The generic name is thought to be derived from the Greek arnakis, a *lamb's skin,* because in this genus the involucral bracts are often woolly.

Recognition of the species of Arnica requires careful dissection of the small flowers, with the aid of a 10X magnifier. A stereoscopic microscope of about the same power is not very expensive, and will greatly facilitate, or encourage, detailed examination of plant structures, which will be found of fascinating interest.

One looks first for a yellow or orange head with both disk- and ray-flowers. (In our area ÁRNICA PÁRRYI Gray generally lacks ray-flowers.) Next a razor blade should be used to slice the flower-head lengthwise. Now the pappus (see the Glossary, or the *Compositae* Family) can be studied. In Arnica the pappus consists wholly or partly of hair-like bristles. Having thus narrowed down the search, one checks to see if the stem (cauline) leaves are opposite (rarely, the smallest and uppermost ones are somewhat alternate). We are then fairly sure the specimen belongs to the genus Arnica. (Arnica may be confused with *Senecio.*)

ÁRNICA ALPÌNA (L.) Olin. *Alpine Arnica.*   [p.519]

In Arnica alpina the solitary stems rise a mere 2-8 inches and bear only a single head. Leaves are entire or very nearly so, slenderly-lanceolate, and (like stem and inflorescence) densely hoary with glandular hairs (knobbed at the top) as well as long woolly hairs. Though bent downward at first, the mature heads are later held stiffly erect: they generally measure less than an inch across. There are usually 9-12 rays that are strongly but unevenly notched.

This little plant with its sturdy golden flowers inhabits the wind-swept rocks of our higher *mountains.* In one of several variations Alpine Arnica is circumboreal. Arnica alpina ssp. ATTENUÀTA (Greene) Maguire is taller, and generally has 3 flower heads, and longer, more tapered leaves.

> ". . . with the view of encouraging. . . that love of natural history
> from which I myself have derived so much happiness."
>
> Sir John Lubbock:
> British Wild Flowers (1893)

ÁRNICA CORDIFÒLIA Hook. *Heart-leaved Arnica.*   [p.522]

This is probably our most showy Arnica, with splendid heads spanning 1½ to a measured 3¼ inches. The pappus is white, or nearly so, with very small barb-like projections. The *leaves* are *heart-shaped* (except at the top of the scape), sometimes entire but more often deeply toothed. Several varieties have been named. In general this species is seldom found west of the Cascades.

ÁRNICA DIVERSIFÒLIA Greene. *Vari-leaved Arnica.*

In the taxonomic sense this is a "poor" species, the name applied (for convenience) to a complex group of apparent hybrids involving *A. amplexicaulis, A. cordifolia, A. latifolia,* and *A. mollis.* A comprehensive text such as Hitchcock, Cronquist, Ownbey, and Thompson, or L. Abrams (see Bibliography) should be consulted for details on these species. In any case, A. diversifolia is a convenient label for a group of Arnicas, that provide vivid splashes of sunshine colour in alpine meadows, and in openings among the dwarf timber near tree-line. The *leaves,* as the specific name suggests, are *variable,* even on the same plant.

The stems are tufted or individual, from 6-24 inches tall, and from nearly smooth to somewhat glandular-hairy. The basal leaves are usually heart-shaped with rather broad,

MARAH OREGANUS   ×⅞   [p.491]

CAMPANULA ROTUNDIFOLIA   ×⅖   [p.492]

ACHILLEA MILLEFOLIUM   ×½   [p.501]

LOBELIA DORTMANNA   ×⅘   [p.496]

ANTENNARIA UMBRINELLA ×¼ [p.505]

CHRYSOTHAMNUS NAUSEOSUS ×⅕ [p.525]

CAMPANULA SCOULERI ×2¼ [p.493]

slightly-winged petioles. About 3 or 4 pairs of smaller leaves without petioles occur up the scape. All the leaves are somewhat toothed, but they vary from glabrous to sparsely glandular-hairy. Usually Vari-leaved Arnica has heads that often do not open flat. The pappus is buff-coloured and rather plumy.

[p.519]   ÁRNICA FÚLGENS Pursh, *Shining Arnica,* is common throughout the Dry Interior. Sharply distinct from the previous Arnicas, this is a densely grey-pubescent plant. Though in poor ground sometimes 4 inches high, it is usually three times as tall. Fulgens means *shining,* possibly because the yellowish-orange flowers appear so bright against the greyish foliage. Flowers are usually solitary on long peduncles. Lanceolate leaves have entire margins.

[p.523]   ÁRNICA LATIFÒLIA Bong. *Broad-leafed Arnica* is a very common species that occurs throughout our area. The flowering-heads are generally smaller than those of *A. cordifolia* (which see), and have fewer and narrower ray-florets, but both species are mutable. The leaves too, are exceedingly variable, some of them (on most plants) having rounded rather than pointed tips. Generally leaves of both species, especially the most basal ones, are somewhat heart-shaped, but in the field the larger mid-scape leaves of A. latifolia help to distinguish it. The pappus is white and barbellate (with short stiff hairs).

ÁRNICA MÓLLIS Hook.   [p.523]

Mollis means *soft* or gentle, possibly applied to the leaves, which are generally (but not definitively) thin and flexible.

This bright-yellow Arnica is once again a variable species, widespread in moist spots to high altitudes but only occasional, especially on Vancouver Island, near sea level. A. mollis is, in general, a small plant, usually about 6 inches in height. The shape of the leaves is ovate to lanceolate but apparently never cordate, the edges entire to (more often) irregularly dentate. The involucral bracts are pointed, and nearly always glandular near their tips but long-haired basally. Pappus is distinctly tawny, and somewhat plumose.

We have a vivid recollection of dark spray-wet sills of slate in the midst of a tumbling West Coast stream, on which perched dozens of clusters of this gay little Arnica, vivid bits of colour flashing in the morning sunlight.

ARTEMÍSIA TRIDENTÀTA Nutt. *Common Sagebrush.*   [p.530]

Artemisia* was the wife of Mausolus, whose tomb at Halicarnassus was one of the Seven Wonders of the ancient world. This species, whose familiar bushes are such a characteristic feature of the Dry Interior landscape, has most of its leaves (at least those low on the branches) neatly tipped with *three lobes*, whence "tridentata". Perhaps the most nostalgic recollection of the arid lowlands is the fresh perfume of the Sagebrush.

The number of species of this very difficult genus, that occur in our area, is probably greater than 16. Distinctions are blurred, so that even careful study of a plant may result in nothing more precise than that it is close to such and such a species. We have included only a few of the most common.

Ambitious but ignorant stock raisers, by overgrazing hundreds of thousands of acres in the cattle country of the Dry Interior, have profoundly altered the flora of these vast areas. In such circumstances Sagebrush is one of the plants that move in to replace other more valuable plants and grasses—particularly on soils of volcanic origin. The species extends southward, but in Alberta is rare, only occurring in the extreme southeast. The gnarled, grey-green, 2-5 foot branches of Sagebrush, with their shredded bark and wedge-shaped, 3-notched, grey leaves are a familiar sight in arid regions of the Province. Some of the uppermost leaves are often un-notched, but all are thickly covered above and below with short, grey, tightly compressed hairs.

The tiny flower-heads are without peduncles. Growing in an open panicle-like arrangement, each flower-head contains 3-5 (up to 8 in higher-altitude forms) brownish-yellow flowers, that have both a pistil and 5 minute stamens. One expects from the rather attractive and interesting foliage something better than these small and dowdy flowers. Sagebrush does not come into bloom until mid-September. But the much more showy yellow flowers of Rabbit Brush (*Chrysothamnus nauseosus*, which see), whose bushes generally intermingle with those of the Sagebrush, appear in early August, or late July.

*. . . but there is one name which I cannot omit that of Artemisia. It seems to me a most strange and interesting thing that she—a woman—should have taken part in the campaign against Greece. . . . Her own spirit of adventure and manly courage were her only incentives. . . . not one of the confederate commanders gave Xerxes sounder advice than she did.

Herodotus: The Histories, Bk. VII
(5th century B.C.)

ARTEMÍSIA CAMPÉSTRIS L. *Cut-leaf Wormwood.*

This is a circumboreal species, with numerous varieties. Campestris means *of the plains.* Generally found in sandy areas, sometimes near the sea, this plant is almost inodorous. In the first year the plant develops a basal rosette of long-petioled, much-divided leaves. The stem that develops the following year may be 6 to 36 inches tall, and bears—increasingly upward—less divided, and shorter-petioled leaves, until those in the spike-like cluster of flower-heads are simple and linear. All the leaves are variously hairy to nearly glabrous. In the same way the involucre may be smooth, or densely white-tomentose (covered with matted woolly hairs). If a microscope is available the species can be distinguished by the flower details. The outermost flowers have a well-developed pistil with 2-branched stigma, and a conspicuous ovary. But the inner flowers have a wizened ovary, and shrunken, usually rudimentary style.

ARTEMÍSIA FRÍGIDA Willd. *Pasture Wormwood. Pasture Sage.* [p.530]

Frigida means *of cold regions,* this beautiful, silvered subshrub ranging to northern Alaska and northern Siberia. It occurs widely through the Dry Interior, often in mixed stands with Rabbit Brush (*Chrysothamnus nauseosus,* which see) and Common Sagebrush (*A. tridenta,* which see). The present species is at once distinguished from other Artemisias by its small size (under 20 inches), graceful stems, and silvered feathery foliage. The Sage fragrance of this species is, perhaps, the most pleasant of all the Artemisias.

The perfumed leaves are densely white-haired on both surfaces, and two or three times thrice-split into almost hair-like divisions. Flower-heads are pale yellow, and clustered towards the ends of the semi-erect branchlets. The flowers of Pasture Sage are all fertile, but so small that a good glass or microscope is needed to make out their details. The receptacle is very convex, and covered with tiny hairs.

ARTEMÍSIA SUKSDÓRFII Piper. *Wormwood.* [p.530]

Southern British Columbia, especially near the Coast, is the home of this stout perennial. Its sturdy stems often reach 5 feet in clay pockets on rocky shores, rather less in the upper parts of sandy beaches. Wormwood looks something like a Golden Rod (*Solidago* which see) with greenish (rather than yellow) flower-heads. The specific name honours Wilhelm Suksdorf, 1850-1932, who was one of the foremost collectors of the northwest flora.

Strong, clustered stems are very erect and unbranched, often reddish. The broadly-lanceolate leaves occur alternately up the stem, and may be 5 inches long. They are variously saw-edged to nearly entire, strikingly white-hairy below, but green and nearly glabrous above. Very small flower-heads occur in small panicles in the axils of the upper leaves, but chiefly in a large, elongated, terminal raceme. With a powerful glass it is possible to see that each head contains 5-10 tiny greenish flowers, about two-thirds of these being pistillate. The receptacle is hairless.

Artemisia suksdorfii is quite a handsome plant, attracting attention from its size, the green and silver appearance of the leaves, and its pleasant aromatic scent.

ÁSTER. *Aster. Michaelmas Daisy.*

In North America there may be about 300 species of Aster, many of which hybridize freely, so that the amateur who would like to identify an Aster in hand, is likely to sympathize with the American botanist Asa Gray (1810-1888)—"Never was so rascally a genus! . . . [they] may reduce me to blank despair!"

The name, Michaelmas Daisy, dates from 1582, when the adoption by Christendom of Pope Gregory XIII's revised calendar caused Michaelmas Day (September 29) to fall 10 days earlier, at which date many of the garden forms have come to full flower. In English, Latin and Greek, aster means *a star,* whose radiating rays suggest the ray-flowers of most members of the genus.

In identification, all parts of the plant, including the root, must be studied. Foliage character, presence or absence of ray-flowers, details of the pappus (modified calyx, often hairlike, at the summit of the achene or fruit), and of the involucral bracts that surround the flower-head—all must be considered for the closest match with the descriptions in such a reference text as Hitchcock, Cronquist et al. At least 22 species (many of them variable) are known to occur in our area so that positive identification in some cases is extremely difficult. We can only consider a few representative species.

Aster is not always easily distinguished from *Erigeron* (which see). In the field Erigerons look like thinner-rayed Asters. On closer examination Erigerons are found to have 50 or more ray-florets, and 1 (or 2) series of nearly equal involucral bracts. But Asters have 10-50 florets, and several series of unequal bracts.

Like the great majority of Composites, Asters bloom later than most plants. They are generally at their best in late August or September, and often linger into November.

When daisies go, shall winter time
Silver the simple grass with rime;
Autumnal frosts enchant the pool
And make the cart-ruts beautiful. . . .

Robert Louis Stevenson:
The House Beautiful

ÁSTER ALPÌNUS L. ssp. VIERHÁPPERI Onno. *Mountain Aster.*

This is an arctic-alpine and circumboreal species. It forms a small, compact plant, usually 4-6 inches high, that is hairy throughout. Leaves are oblanceolate and blunt-ended. Flower-heads are terminal and solitary, and relatively large for the small plant (about 1 inch across). The rays are violet, lavender, bluish, or white. Pappus is scarcely double, having only a few short outer hairs. Records for this little mountaineer are from the Rockies, particularly in the north.

ÁSTER CILIOLÀTUS Lindl. (= A. LINDLEYÁNUS T. & G.).

This is perhaps the most common tall purple Aster east of the Cascades. It is variable, and widespread. The stiff stems rise from long, creeping rhizomes. The 2- to 5-inch lower leaves are broadly-lanceolate, with a winged petiole, but these leaves often wither before flowering time. Upward the leaves become narrower, though the petioles remain winged. Finally, those leaves from whose axils the flower-peduncles rise, are sessile and much less toothed, or even entire. Involucral bracts are pointed-slender and smooth, with sparsely firm-haired edges. (Ciliolatus means *hair-like*). They are rather chaffy, except for a green midrib and sharp green tip. Flower-heads are numerous, about an inch across, with blue-violet rays and reddish-purple disk-florets. Achenes are smooth.

ÁSTER CONSPÍCUUS Lindl. *Showy Aster.*   [p.530]

Conspicuous indeed is this fine Aster, when in late July, or August, its splendid blooms dominate open woodlands in the mountains. The Showy Aster is one of the Aster species that are easily and certainly identified. It occurs widely from Princeton and Spences Bridge, eastward into the Rockies.

This is an erect plant 18-36 inches high, with a rough and hairy stem. Leaves, especially about mid-stem, are very large—as much as 6 inches long. They are ovate and usually saw-toothed, rather rough to the touch, both above and below, because of numerous tiny papillae. (More succinctly, both surfaces are scabrous.) These big distinctive leaves have no (or the shortest possible) petioles. Involucres of the flower-heads bear several rows of overlapping glandular bracts, which have papery bases and spreading pointed green tips. In A. conspicuus, ray-flowers number between 12 and 35, the rays themselves being a beautiful bluish-violet, and about ½-¾ inch long.

ÁSTER PÁNSUS (Blake) Cronq. = A. MULTIFLÒRUS var. PÁNSUS Blake. *Tufted White Prairie Aster.* [p.519]

Bearing very numerous small white-rayed "flowers," this species is abundant in sandy soil, especially above the margins of alkaline ponds in the southern Dry Interior. Linear, entire, greyish leaves crowd the much-branched stems. Involucral bracts (in about 3 ranks) are green, with tips generally turned outward.

ÁSTER SUBSPICÀTUS Nees. (= A. DOUGLÀSII Lindl.) (= probably A. FOLIÀCEUS Lindl. in DC.). *Douglas Aster.* [p.531]

The abundance of synonyms evidences the difficulty of recognition.

This is another tall (20-40 inches) purple Aster that is variable and widespread. It is very common along the seashore, on stream-banks, roadsides or in open woods. Douglas Aster in one form or another ranges from the Coastal islands pretty much throughout British Columbia, and even further northward and southward. The material is so diverse that description becomes difficult, but the numerous variants appear to merge, so that it appears we have here a highly variable species, rather than a complex of related species.

Stems are greenish or purplish, variously pubescent to glabrous, but generally slim. Leaves are usually numerous, entire to slightly toothed (chiefly about the middle), thin to firm, oblanceolate below but becoming lanceolate upward. Lower leaves often wither early, but generally have short petioles which disappear upward, most upper leaves being sessile (with leaf-base directly attached to main stem). Heads are about an inch or a little broader, with blue-purple to rosy-purple rays. Disk-flowers are yellowish to reddish. The involucral bracts are firm, with roughened margins, and most often have a brownish or yellowish base. The pappus on ripe achenes is often reddish-tinged. Achenes are rough-surfaced.

The flower-heads of this and other species attract an enormous number of insects, notably bumblebees and butterflies. The Asters make a large contribution to the colourful scene in the "season of mists and mellow fruitfulness".

BALSAMORHÌZA SAGITTÀTA (Pursh) Nutt. *Balsam-root.* [pp.534,535]

The common name literally interprets the Greek balsamon, *balsam,* and rhiza, *root.* (The woody, perennial taproot is aromatic). The specific name describes the great leaves, *shaped like arrowheads,* with blades 12 inches long and 6 inches wide, and petioles even longer than the blades. They form impressive tufts on the slopes, admirable complements to the ample yellow flower-heads, which in May often gild entire hillsides.

From the cluster of leaves, numerous 10-30 inch stems rise—each surmounted by a single showy head that often spans 4 inches. A few small leaves are usual on each stem. The brilliant yellow ray-flowers, in the bright spring sunshine, almost dazzle the eye. The very numerous disk-flowers are also yellow. This showy species is unmistakable, with its large grey and silver, entire-edged leaves, and usually woolly-haired involucre.

Balsam-root was an important food-plant for the tribes of the arid Interior. They ate the young tender shoots, and roasted both the thick resinous roots and the abundant oily seeds. Deer, elk, mountain sheep, and domesticated stock all graze this plant.

BALSAMORHÌZA DELTOÌDEA Nutt., *Northwest Balsam-root* is a very similar plant of open places on southern Vancouver Island. The leaves are green, and lack the silvery undersides of its relative from the Sagebrush and Bunch-grass country.

ADENOCAULON BICOLOR $\times \frac{1}{8}$ [p.501]

ANAPHALIS MARGARITACEA $\times \frac{1}{2}$ [p.504]

J. WOOLLETT

ANTENNARIA ROSEA $\times \frac{1}{4}$ [p.504]

ARCTIUM MINUS $\times \frac{1}{2}$ [p.508]

ANTHEMIS ARVENSIS $\times \frac{3}{5}$ [p.505]

ARNICA ALPINA $\times \frac{1}{2}$ [p.509]

ASTER PANSUS $\times \frac{2}{5}$ [p.516]

ARNICA FULGENS $\times \frac{1}{2}$ [p.512]

BÉLLIS PERÉNNIS L. *English Daisy.* [p.531]

This irrepressible little white Daisy of our lawns and fields can be seen in flower on the southern Coast, every month of the year. The illustration shows a plant photographed in Victoria on January 31! The Daisy and the Dandelion are probably the two best-known of all flowers. Originally Eurasian, the English Daisy is now well-established in northern U.S.A. and southern Canada, though in British Columbia it is rarely found east of the Coast Range.

No description is necessary. Not infrequently one finds nearly double forms, in which there are one or several additional rows of ray-florets. Very often the rays are pink, or purple flushed, especially at the tips, and below. Robert Burns sang of the "Wee, modest, crimson-tippit flow'r". These ray-flowers are pistillate, but the yellow disk ones are perfect, having both stamens and pistil. Pappus is usually wanting, although sometimes represented by a few short bristles.

The euphonious generic name comes from the Latin bellus, *pretty,* while perennis calls attention to the *perennial* character of this plant. As is rather generally known, Daisy is a corruption of "day's eye", from the sun-resemblance of the yellow disk and radiating rays. (Chaucer, in line 184 of the *Prologue to the Legend of Good Women* wrote "The dayes-yë or elles the yë of day".)

This little flower for many centuries has been considered the epitome of rural simplicity, a favourite subject for poets from Burns to Wordsworth and Tennyson.

There grew. . .
   Daisies, those pearled Arcturi of the earth,
The constellated flower that never sets. . . .

Percy Bysshe Shelley:
The Question

Bright Flower! *for by that name at last,*
When all my reveries are past,
I call thee. . .
That breath'st with me in sun and air,
Do thou, as thou art wont, repair
My heart with gladness, and a share
   Of thy meek nature!

William Wordsworth:
To the Same Flower [The Daisy]

BÌDENS CÉRNUA L. *Beggar-ticks. Bur Marigold.* [p.531]

Bidens means *two teeth.* The pappus at top of the flattened achenes is modified into 2-4 sharp barbed teeth or spikes, which readily hitch a ride on the outdoorsman's socks or trouser-cuffs, whence also the name Beggar-ticks. Cernua means *drooping* or nodding—the flower-heads soon turn downward.

A fast-growing annual, Bidens cernua seeks wet ditches or the shallows by lake or stream, and soon reaches 2-3 feet. The plant is glabrous or slightly rough-surfaced (scabrous), much branched and leafy. Pointed-ovate to slim-lanceolate leaves lack petioles, and have sharply- to sparingly-serrated margins. The yellow flowers generally have 6-8 rather broad rays, but these are sometimes lacking. When present the ray-flowers are neutral, that is, lack both stamens and pistil. Disk-flowers are very numerous and perfect, appearing brown except for the yellow stamens. The involucral bracts are of two kinds: an outer row of long, pointed, greenish ones, that are reflexed, and an inner rank of brown membranous ones, that are faintly dark-striped, and remain erect. The numerous achenes, when ripe, form a prickly ball.

CENTAURÈA MACULÒSA Lam. *Spotted Knapweed.*   [p.531]

Centaurea is a genus of unattractive, immigrant weeds, often purplish-flowered and somewhat resembling small thistles. The only attractive member is the familiar Corn-flower or Bachelor's Button, *C. cyanus.* The name of the genus is easily confused with *Centaurium,* quite unrelated small plants of the Gentian family. Both names apparently derive from the Centaur called Chiron, who was thought to have used a potion of an unknown plant to heal the wound in his foot, made by the arrow of Hercules. Maculosa means *spotted,* suggested by the black markings on the bracts of the involucre. The common name is a corruption of Knopweed; knop (or knob) in Chaucerian English dating from the 14th century, meant a protuberance, or bump (as in the King James translation of Exodus XXV: 31, 33, 36). The reference apparently is to the knob-like buds which punctuate the thin branches.

As suggested above, none of the 7 or 8 species is native. Most are invasive and some, such as *C. rèpens* L. and *C. nìgra* L. (which see), very persistent weeds. Spotted Knapweed is now widely dispersed on roadsides of central southern British Columbia.

A biennial, or sometimes short-lived perennial, its scraggly stems and narrowly pinnate leaves are felted with grey hairs. The plant may reach 5 feet, but about half that height is more usual. Numerous branches each end in a knob-like dark bud. These open in a long succession from June to October. Florets are all tubular (i.e. this is a "discoid" flower) but the outer ones are longer, deeply cut, and purplish-tipped (occasionally white). The flattened achenes nearly always are ringed with pointed hairs $^1/_{16}$ inch long. The involucral bracts are worthy of microscopic study; in fact they are the single best feature for discriminating between the Centaurea species. In C. maculosa they are tightly imbricated (shingled), and strongly marked with dark vertical lines. All the involucral bracts are pale-green and black-tipped—the upper ones long and slender—the middle and lower abruptly narrowed, and conspicuously margined near the tip with coarse comb-like teeth.

CENTAURÈA DIFFÙSA Lam., a *much-branched* annual, or occasional biennial, has similar finely-divided, grey, felted leaves, but smaller flowers that are usually cream-coloured (though not infrequently purplish). The involucral bracts are distinctive, being

Following page: ARNICA CORDIFOLIA ✕1 [p.509]

ARNICA LATIFOLIA $\times \frac{1}{4}$ [p.512]

ARNICA MOLLIS $\times \frac{3}{5}$ [p.512]

ARNICA MOLLIS (HABITAT) [p.512]

pale-green and fringed with several buff-coloured teeth, of which the terminal one is ⅛ inch long, spine-sharp and outward-pointing.

CENTAURÈA NÌGRA L. *Black Knapweed.* The names call attention to the inch-wide, notably black, rather squat inflorescence. Bracts, except the leafy innermost, are tipped with black star-shaped fringes.

CENTAURÈA RÈPENS L. *Russian Knapweed,* is a perennial, with creeping blackish roots. Flower-heads are fading purplish, above a characteristic pale fat involucre. The bracts are broad and smooth, with rounded spineless tips.

CHAENÁCTIS DOUGLÀSII (Hook.) H. & A. *Hoary Chaenactis.* [p.534]

Chaenactis derives from the Greek chaino, *to gape,* and aktis, *ray,* describing the flared mouth of the florets. This variable 4-20 inch biennial is locally common on the arid plains of the southern Dry Interior. The erect plants are early covered with white hairs, though this vesture decreases with age. Deeply bipinnate leaves are basal and also alternate up the stems. Flower-heads are ½-¾ inch broad, with a single rank of blunt-tipped, glandular-haired, involucral bracts. The florets are all discoid and perfect, with protruding stamens. Achenes are short-pubescent, and topped by 10-16 chaffy pappus-scales. The hoary plants attractively complement flesh-coloured (fading whitish) flowers.

CHRYSÁNTHEMUM LEUCÁNTHEMUM L. *Ox-eye Daisy.* [p.534]

The genus is widely-known, notably from the work of generations of skilled hybridizers in Japan. The name comes from the Greek "chrysanthemon", which in turn was a composite of chrysos, *gold,* and anthos, *flower.* But the total name was not one of Linnaeus' happiest, for it involves a contradiction, or at least betrays indecision: a *white-flowered* golden-flower! "Chrysanthemum" has a mellifluous quality, but "leucanthemum" after it is just too much. So we turn with relief to the common name—a daisy like the great fringed eye of an ox.

An incredibly prolific plant, this beautiful Eurasian invader whitens countless pastures of temperate North America. In June, about the vacation-time, when children tumble out of the schools, millions upon millions of Ox-eye Daisies come into flower.

Then butterflies, bees, flies, and all manner of winged creatures accept the invitation signalled by the shining white rays. On the sturdy upturned faces they find easy landing places, as well as rings of ray-flowers that consecutively liberate their pollen and nectar, over a period of many weeks. Small wonder then, that huge quantities of seeds are formed, and the species continues its colonization. This was one of 4 parents of the popular Shasta Daisy developed by the late Luther Burbank.

Over the shoulders and slopes of the dune
I saw the white daisies go down to the sea,

A host in the sunshine, a snow-drift in June...

Bliss Carman: Daisies

CHRYSÓPSIS VILLÒSA (Pursh) Nutt. *Golden Aster.* [p.535]

The generic name results from linking the Greek chrysos, *gold,* and opsis, *aspect*; hence Golden Aster. Villosa means *soft-haired,* the foliage appearing greyish-green from the pubescence.

This perennial is quite variable, sometimes rather erect and 20 inches tall, but more often somewhat sprawling and 4-5 inches high. The lower leaves wither early, becoming inconspicuous. Upper leaves are alternate, entire, and strap-shaped. Bright yellow flower-heads are about 1 inch across, and consist of a ring of 10-25 pistillate ray-florets, enclosing many disk-florets that have both stamens and pistil. The pappus is double: an inner ring of long, off-white hairs, and a shorter set. Involucral bracts are neatly imbricated (lapped). They are pubescent, slender and pointed; the innermost bracts are longest.

This little plant, of dry plains in the southern Interior, endures summer drought cheerfully. It seems to prefer sandy soil in full sun, and in such situations Chrysopsis villosa is sometimes quite abundant.

CHRYSOTHÁMNUS NAUSEÒSUS (Pall.) Britt. *Rabbit Brush.* [p.511]

The generic name means *golden-crowned,* from the conspicuous, orange-yellow flowers that tip the wiry stems, while the specific name refers to the heavy scent (which is strong but not at all *nauseating*). This abundant shrub of the Dry Interior provides winter browse for jackrabbits (hence the common name) as well as for deer and mountain sheep. Pure stands of Rabbit Brush invade poor soils from which grasses have largely vanished, due to overgrazing by domestic stock.

A local name is False Goldenrod, which conveys a rough impression of the plant's appearance. Numerous stems average perhaps 2 feet, but this is a variable species and exceptional plants attain 6 feet. The much-branched twigs are thin and wiry, closely covered with grey-white felted hairs. The numerous, linear leaves may be similarly felted, or only sparsely haired. Heads are usually 5-flowered. The non-ligulate (discoid) flowers have about 5 rows of bracts in the involucre: all these flowers are perfect and have white, hair-like pappus.

Chrysothamnus nauseosus blooms in late July (more than a month earlier than Common Sagebrush, *Artemisia tridentata*) at which time hundreds of acres are annually covered with its golden flower-heads.

CHRYSOTHÁMNUS VISCIDIFLÒRUS (Hook.) Nutt. is a similar but smaller plant than *C. nauseosus,* collected near Osoyoos and in the Columbia Valley. The twigs are nearly smooth, with only occasional stiff hairs, and the leaves are usually twisted and slightly viscid. Involucres are also often *sticky,* but the amount and kind of pubescence is variable.

CICHÒRIUM ÍNTYBUS L. *Blue Sailors. Chicory.* [p.542]

Cichorium is the Latinized spelling of the Egyptian name that was applied, almost certainly, to this species. As early as 1539 the English scholar Sir Thomas Elyot mentions "cikorie or suckorie". This European immigrant has been cultivated for many years, both for its leaves and roots. The blanched leaves are the "barbe-de-capucin", esteemed in France for winter salads. The roots are sliced, roasted, and ground as an additive to coffee. Europeans familiar from an early age with chicory-flavoured coffee consider as improvements the added colour, bitterness, and body. The specific name is repetitive, the Latin poet Vergil referring to endive, or *succory,* as intibus, intybus, or intubus.

This may be the only plant of our area that can be instantly recognized by colour alone. The big flower-heads are dandelion-shaped but of an extraordinary, and unique, cerulean blue (whence one of the common names, Blue Sailors). Occasionally albino forms are seen.

The coarse, stiff, and rigid branches may be 2-5 feet high, with a few small, lanceolate leaves, from whose axils the flower-stems develop. (The stems, when cut, exude an acrid, milky juice.) Basal leaves are quite different, up to 10 inches long and shaped very much like those of the familiar Dandelion *(Taraxacum officinale,* which see). Flower-heads consist entirely of ray-flowers, all of which are perfect, i.e. bear both stamens and pistil. The flower-heads fold inward (in effect closing) about noon—or earlier if the day turns dark. The effect is striking, for a vivid blue patch by the roadside becomes so quickly extinguished that one may find difficulty in relocating the plants.*

This sturdy weed (originally of Europe and the Near East) is now common on waste ground, over much of North America, particularly west of the Cascades. Cichorium intybus is in bloom from July to October.

*This time-sense in plants needs much more investigation. We do know that nectar is yielded, for example, by the Chicory flowers only between 7 a.m. and noon, and also that certain individual honeybees will go infallibly to these flowers only during the five hours specified. Though the sun continues to shine, the flowers nevertheless close at noon. Both bees and flowers keep standard time!

CÍRSIUM Mill. *Thistle.*

The name is apparently derived from the Greek kirsos, *a swollen vein,* for which Thistles were reputed to be a remedy. More realistically, the roots and peeled stems of these unlikely plants (particularly of *C. edule* and *C. foliosum* which see) provide valuable and palatable food in emergency. They were so used by several Indian tribes. Additionally, thistledown provides an excellent tinder, and can be ignited by the flint of a gas-lighter, or cigarette-lighter that is out of fuel.

Cirsium formerly was *Carduus,* a name now limited to European species distinguished on the (perhaps weak) basis of an unbranched or simple pappus, instead of the branched plumy pappus of Cirsium. The species are difficult to distinguish, partly because natural hybridization occurs.

Thistles as a group are readily recognized—though many laymen are surprised to learn that perhaps as many as 200 species of Cirsium are known, all native to the Northern Hemisphere.

CÍRSIUM ARVÉNSE (L.) Scopoli. *Creeping Thistle. Canada Thistle.*

Arvense means *of cultivated fields,* which is, alas too descriptive. Unlike the Spear Thistle, *Cirsium vulgare* (which see), and our native Thistles that favour roadsides and wasteland, this Eurasian invader is not discouraged by cultivation. In fact, its creeping rhizomes may be cut and broken by the harrow, only to increase and spread a very noxious pest. "Canada Thistle" though in common use is, of course (one might say like many English names), quite inappropriate—the species being native to Europe, Asia, and North Africa.

Cirsium arvense is unique among Thistles found in our area, in that most of the plants are dioecious, i.e., pistillate and staminate flowers occur on different individuals. Both kinds of flowers are pink-purple (or occasionally white), sweet-scented, and much smaller (½ - ¾ inch) than the flower-heads of other thistles. The plants are 2-5 feet high (rather ferociously prickly in var. HORRÍDUM Wimm. & Grab., which is generally widespread in our area). Only the lowermost bracts of the involucre end in weak fleshy spines—the rest are spineless. With the aid of a 10X magnifier, one may determine that the plumy white pappus is longer than the corolla-tube in pistillate flowers, but shorter than the tube in staminate flowers.

This very troublesome weed has increased its range rapidly in the last two decades, and is now ubiquitous in our area—wherever ground is cultivated.

CÍRSIUM ÉDULE Nutt. *Edible Thistle.* [p.542]

The specific name calls attention to the *edible* quality of this native species; however, it is not unique among Thistles as an emergency food plant.

This is a biennial usually, since most of the plants die after blooming in their second year. The thick succulent stems become slender upward, and may reach a height of 6 feet. The deeply toothed leaves are sparsely white-haired on both surfaces, with moderate spines along the margins and tip. The involucre, which is 1-1½ inches high, provides the most useful recognition features. Its bracts do not overlap like shingles, but stand out in every direction from a thick, felted ball of cobwebby hairs. The bracts are slender, and gradually taper to a soft spine. The flowers are showy reddish-purple. On close examination, the pistil is seen to protrude as much as ½ inch beyond the corolla-tube.

As with *C. foliosum* (which see), the taproot and lower stem, when peeled, provide a pleasantly-flavoured emergency food. This should be known to woodsmen, for the Edible Thistle is easily found in isolated regions of wet meadows, and openings in moist woods, to quite high levels in the mountains. Its blooming period is extended (from July to September) so that it is easily discovered by the lost wayfarer. C. edule occurs west of the Cascades, from northern British Columbia into Washington.

CÍRSIUM FOLIÒSUM (Hook.) DC. *Leafy Thistle.*

The specific name means *leafy,* which directs attention to the characteristically long, slender leaves that at least crowd, or usually overtop the flowers.

This handsome native is a conspicuous plant of mountain meadows, with its densely leafy stem rising stiffly erect from 1 to 4 feet. The succulent stem is almost without taper. The flower-heads are 1-1½ inches wide, whitish to pale-pink, and are usually almost hidden by a cluster of slightly-toothed linear leaves growing upward from just below the flowers. The spines are soft and not formidable. A web of fine hairs gives the entire plant a whitish, or greyish-green appearance.

Closer examination shows the broad bracts of the involucre are nearly smooth—the lower ones ending in a short spine, the upper in a soft, expanded, and fringed tip.

This Thistle is a favoured food of deer, elk, and bear. The peeled stem has a sweet delicate taste, providing a wilderness substitute for celery. The root also can be boiled.

C. foliosum is in bloom from June to early August, depending upon the altitude. It occurs in cool, wet, mountain meadows east of the Cascades, from the southern Yukon to California. It is rare in our area.

Butterflies come in numbers to sip the nectar of the crowded flowers, and in so doing cross-fertilize the plants.

CÍRSIUM HÓOKERIANUM Nutt. *Hooker's Thistle. White Thistle* [p.542]

Named by Nuttall after the great botanist Sir William J. Hooker, this North American Thistle is generally hoary with dense white hairs, though in older plants the pubescence may become less abundant.

Hooker's Thistle appears to be a short-lived perennial in our area. The flowers are creamy-white, and the heads measure almost 2 inches across. Bracts of the inflorescence overlap slightly, and are somewhat less densely cobweb-haired than those of *C. edule* (which see). The present species can be distinguished by observing that the spine-tipped bracts all point upward toward the florets, instead of in every direction. The leaves of C. hookerianum are also much less deeply-toothed than those of *C. edule.*

In middle to late summer this bold plant may be seen in bloom in moist bottom-land and pockets of deeper soil, to moderate altitudes throughout our area, chiefly east.

CÍRSIUM UNDULÀTUM (Nutt.) Spreng. *Wavy-leaf Thistle.* [p.542]

The specific name refers to the rather pronounced *wavy edge* of the prickle-marginate leaves. However, this is not an adequate—or satisfactory—distinguishing characteristic.

Wavy-leaf Thistle is a tall biennial plant (occasionally to 7 feet) with stems thinly to densely covered with white hairs. The leaves are much more deeply-toothed than those of either *C. foliosum* or *C. hookerianum* (which see), though scarcely as deeply-indented as those of *C. edule.* They are woolly-white on both sides, but in older leaves the upper surface becomes nearly smooth. The flower-heads are 1½-3 inches broad, and pale-lavender to pinkish.

The bracts of the involucre provide the best means of identification. They are numerous, and imbricate (overlapped like shingles). All save the innermost have a raised darker gland along the back. The outermost end in a long spine; the innermost in a long chaffy tip. Though most often rather densely white-haired, the involucre is occasionally almost without pubescence.

This is a plant of the dry prairies and roadsides of southern British Columbia, northern Washington and Oregon east of the Cascades. Like others of the Cirsium tribe, C. undulatum is often in bloom for a lengthy period, from May to September.

CÍRSIUM VULGÀRE (Savi) Airy-Shaw. *Bull Thistle. Spear Thistle.* [p.543]

The specific name means *common,* and unfortunately this introduction from Eurasia has become a very common roadside weed from Alaska southward and eastward. The English names quoted—from a large number—refer to the size and vigour of this bold plant, and to its almost impregnable armour of sharp prickles.

In fact, this species is distinguished from all the others of our area, by the presence of prickles on the *upper surface* of the leaves, as well as along the edges. Another good identifying characteristic is the extension of the leaf-bases, as prickled wings, downward along the stems. The showy purple to magenta flowers of C. vulgare are usually about 1½ inches across. Every bract of the involucre ends in a long sharp spine. The plants are biennials, and push the formidable stem 2-5 feet upward from the rosette of prickly leaves formed during the first year of growth.

Though many will deplore the spread of this weedy plant, few will have failed to admire the reddish-purple blooms, with their attendant butterflies.

ARTEMISIA FRIGIDA ×½ [p.514]

ARTEMISIA SUKSDORFII ×⅖ [p.514]

ARTEMISIA TRIDENTATA ×⅖ [p.512]

ASTER CONSPICUUS ×⅖ [p.516]

ASTER SUBSPICATUS ×²⁄₅ [p.517]

BELLIS PERENNIS ×³⁄₅ [p.520]

BIDENS CERNUA ×½ [p.520]

CENTAUREA MACULOSA ×²⁄₅ [p.521]

CONÝZA CANADÉNSIS (L.) Cronqu. *Horse-weed.* [p.543]

This annual weed was long classified in the genus *Erigeron.* As the specific name suggests, the plant's distribution is *Canada-wide.* (The species is one of the relatively few native plants that we have —unintentionally—exported, e.g. to the United States and also to Europe, where it has become a nuisance.)

Most authorities derive the name from the Greek konops, *a flea,* and Pliny apparently applied the name Conyza to some kind of Fleabane. Horses seem to relish the plant. With us it is most abundant in the Sagebrush and Bunch-grass country.

Horse-weed grows stiffly erect to as much as 4 feet, with a great many short branchlets arising from the axils of each of the upper leaves. The branchlets bear numerous very small heads. Leaves are numerous, entire, and alternate. The lower ones (which soon wither) are slimly-oblanceolate; the upper ones are linear, sharply pointed, and become more nearly sessile upward. Leaves and stems vary from nearly hairless to rather copiously hirsute. Ray-florets are dingy-white, and barely surpass the involucral bracts in length. Pappus is short and scanty.

CÓTULA CORONOPIFÒLIA L. *Brass Buttons.* [p.543]

Greek kotyle, a *little cup,* is Latinized in the generic name. In fact, the bright yellow "Brass Buttons" also suggest a small cup turned face down. The specific name (from the Latin corono, to *surround,* or enclose in a circle), describes the garland-like leaves.

The origin of this cheerful small invader of our tidal flats is interesting, for its home is South Africa. It has achieved the long journey to the west coast of North America—even to Vancouver Island, the Queen Charlottes, and southern Alaska. About 50 species of the genus have been described, nearly all from the Southern Hemisphere. C. coronopifolia is the only one occurring in our area.

From 2-10 inches high, the sprawling branches commonly root at the nodes. The whole plant is glabrous, with unstalked, long-lanceolate, variously toothed or entire leaves, that are thick and succulent. The ½ inch, round flower-heads are aromatic and rayless. Involucral bracts are rounded at the apex, membranous-bordered, and arranged in 2 rows. There is no pappus. Unusual in this family is the 4-toothed (rather than the almost invariable 5-toothed) corolla of the tiny disk-flowers.

CRÈPIS CAPILLÀRIS (L.) Wallr. *Smooth Hawksbeard.* [p.543]

In our area are found about a dozen of these Hawksbeards, rather like aristocratic relatives of that bane of our lawns, the Fall Dandelion, *(Leontodon autumnalis,* which see). This genus derives its name from the Greek krepis, a boot or *sandal,* possibly from the deeply-cut leaves, which may suggest the thongs of a sandal. A great many genera of the *Compositae* Family are more than superficially similar, so that determination of the genus to which an unknown yellow-flowered Composite belongs, is often a matter of considerable doubt. One looks first to see if all the florets are ray-flowers, that both inner and outer florets have stamens as well as pistils, and that the juice is milky. The list of possible genera for our "dandelion" type flower has now been reduced to 11. Looking further, one checks that the pappus consists of simple separate hairs, and that the seed (achene) is almost smooth, and nearly round in cross-section. Now we know our plant belongs in one of *Agoseris, Crepis, Hieracium,* or *Microseris.* The pappus is white, which rules out *Hieracium* (in which the pappus is brownish or greyish). The heads are not solitary, nor the involucral bracts in several rows, so it cannot be *Agoseris* or *Microseris;* therefore we have come to the conclusion our plant must be a *Crepis.*

We have chosen Crepis to illustrate the use of a key, which is almost a necessity in such huge families as *Compositae, Cruciferae,* and *Umbelliferae*—at least until one has learned to recognize with certainty a few species in each of the genera. Then, and only then, one can say, "This looks like a Crepis—now which species is it?"

C. capillaris is the commonest member of the genus, an introduced annual (occasionally biennial in habit) only too familiar in our fields, but also widely dispersed in open ground, particularly west of the Cascades. The branched stem is 4-30 inches tall, generally smooth but with some very short stiff hairs, at least on the lower part. Leaves are both basal (extremely varied in shape and lobing, but always toothed) and stem or cauline (the uppermost lanceolate and sessile with characteristically long, pointed ears or auricles). All the leaves bear numerous short, stiff hairs that are usually yellowish. The involucral bracts (arranged in a single row) are sharply pointed, and covered with short glandular hairs, as well as some simple black ones. The flower-heads are numerous, and small (about ½ inch long). C. capillaris probably refers to the longer black *hairs* of the involucral bracts.

CRÈPIS ATRABÁRBA Heller ssp. ORIGINÀLIS Babc. & Stebb. *Slender Hawksbeard* [p.535]

Atrabarba, *black-bearded,* refers to the involucral bracts, distinguished by a line of stubby black bristles. This many-stemmed yellow-flowered perennial is conspicuous in June on the dry open benchlands of southern British Columbia, eastward to the Prairies. The stems are nearly glabrous, branched only at the top, and each branchlet is terminated by a flower-head about ¾ inch broad. Leaves are chiefly basal, and deeply pinnate-divided into very slender lobes. The numerous Hawksbeards derive their name from a fancied likeness of the thread-like pappus of the (usually) greenish achenes to the bristle-hairs about the beak of a hawk.

CRÈPIS OCCIDENTÀLIS Nutt. occurs widely through the Dry Interior. It is representative of a number of sturdy perennial species. The plant is densely grey-haired in early summer, though later often becoming hairless. Usually, the rather broad involucral bracts bear a few stiff, black hairs among the more numerous whitish hairs.

CHAENACTIS DOUGLASII   ×¼   [p.524]

CHRYSANTHEMUM LEUCANTHEMUM   ×⅕
[p.524]

BALSAMORHIZA SAGITTATA (HABITAT)   [p.517]

BALSAMORHIZA SAGITTATA ×⅕ [p.517]

CREPIS ATRABARBA ssp. ORIGINALIS ×⅓ [p.533]

CHRYSOPSIS VILLOSA ×⅖ [p.525]

CROCIDIUM MULTICAULE ×1 [p.536]

Achenes are most often green, though occasionally brownish. The bright yellow flowers usually span more than 1 inch. Big basal leaves are a good field-mark for C. occidentalis, being often 6-8 inches long, handsomely and strikingly incised with deep notches and irregular teeth.

CROCÍDIUM MULTICAÙLE Hook. *Goldstars.*   [p.535]

The generic name is a diminutive of the Greek krokys, a loose thread or *nap of wool*, referring to the fuzzy cluster of white hairs in the axils of the scapose leaves. The genus has only one species, which is quite variable. Multicaule means *many stems*; however, a depauperate form, found along the sandy eastern coast of Vancouver Island, invariably consists of a single stem.

This is a fragile little yellow daisy which (unlike the majority of the Composites) blooms very early in the year—generally March or early April. It brightens sandy plains along the coast from Vancouver Island south to California, and less frequently, cliff ledges at rather low elevations inland along the river valleys.

A slender stem rises 2-5 inches from a small ground-hugging rosette. The basal leaves are fleshy, with a short petiole about ½-1 inch long, and a spoon-shaped (spatulate) blade. The coastal form has smooth or entire leaves, those of the interior are more or less coarsely toothed. The opposite cauline leaves, occurring along the lower part of the stem, are scarcely more than linear bracts, but each carries a tuft of snowy hairs at its juncture with the stem. Goldstar's solitary flowers nod in bud, then face the sun with a ring of 5-13 bright yellow ray-florets enclosing a mass of disk-flowers. The flower is ½-1 inch across. Crocidium multicaule has a single row of 8-12 smooth bracts, reddish-brown to pale-green, and slenderly triangular in shape.

> . . .—*hark!*
> *'Tis the early April lark,*
> *Or the rooks, with busy caw,*
> *Foraging for sticks and straw.*
>
> John Keats: Fancy

ERÍGERON. *Fleabane.*

Erigeron is a huge genus of at least 200 species, most of which occur in northwestern North America. About 30 species are found in our area, many being attractive and interesting. Regretfully, space considerations limit us to brief mention of 9 of these.

Erigerons are frequently confused with Asters (see discussion under *Aster*). Except at high altitudes, Erigerons are flowers of the spring and early summer; Asters of late summer and fall. More precisely, Erigerons are distinguished by involucral bracts that are almost uniform in length, and arranged in a single ring (or in a few cases, two slightly overlapping rings). By contrast, the bracts of Asters are commonly shingled (imbricate), the inner ones appreciably longer than the outer, and often paper-like (chaffy) except for a green (sometimes leafy) tip. A quick field check that is often useful: in most Erigerons the rays are more numerous, and narrower, than in Asters.

Erigeron is derived from the Greek eri, *spring,* and geron, *an old man;* terms that are variously explained as referring either to the hair-tufted seed-heads produced early in the year, or to the hoariness of some of the spring-flowering species. Fleabane is very old; a name surviving from a time when it was thought that bundles of the plants, brought into the house, would discourage fleas.

ERÍGERON ÁCRIS L. is a circumpolar species, a rather tall Fleabane with numerous clustered flower-heads. It is a biennial, or short-lived perennial. Leaves are oblanceolate below, lanceolate and somewhat reduced above. Unlike the leaves of *E. annuus* (which see), they are entire, not toothed. Leaves and stems are hairy, especially toward the lower part of the plant, and the involucral bracts are usually hairy and glandular. These bracts are green (or purplish), the inner ones noticeably longer and attenuate. Distinctive is the presence of 2 kinds of pistillate florets: the outer with short white or pinkish rays, the inner without rays. Enclosed by these rings of pistillate flowers are the numerous (yellow) perfect disk-flowers. In E. acris these are exceeded in length by the usually tawny (sometimes white) pappus.

ERÍGERON ANNÙUS (L.) Pers. is also a tall species, chiefly *annual,* abundant (even weedy) in fields and waste-ground. It is widespread at low elevations in the southern part of our area, and over much of southern Canada and the United States. It may reach 5 feet and bears numerous, coarsely and sharply toothed leaves that are noticeably bristly-ciliate near their bases. Generally the whole plant is hirsute, with long, spreading hairs. Pappus of the ray-flowers lacks the 10-15 fragile hairs of the disk-flowers, but retains the few short scales. Ligules of the ray-flowers are white, rarely bluish.

ERÍGERON COMPÓSITUS Pursh. *Cut-leaf Fleabane.*

Compositus means *well-arranged,* referring to the neat growth-pattern of the species.

This is a highly fluid species, with many of the variations assigned varietal names. All of them are attractive low or even dwarf plants of rocky or sandy habitats, from Greenland to Alaska, and southward to northern California. Blooming in May near sea level, at high altitudes the flowers follow upon the heels of late-melting August snow.

Cut-leaf Fleabane is a low perennial, with tufts of foliage lifting numerous 2-8 inch stems, each crowned by a single flower-head. Foliage is almost entirely basal, and varies from densely woolly to almost glabrous. Stem-leaves are few to none. Involucral bracts are covered with glandular and spreading hairs. Ray-flowers are white, or pinkish, or bluish—or in some varieties, absent.

E. c. var. COMPÓSITUS has basal leaves deeply 3-lobed three or four times over.

[p.547]   E. c. var. TRÍFIDUS (Hook.) Gray, is an exceedingly compact form, from high altitudes in the mountains. Its small, densely hairy leaves are usually *3-lobed.* Relatively large, broad-rayed flower-heads are carried just above the tight cushion of leaves, on stems only 1-2 inches long. This is a fascinating variety.

[p.550]   E. c. var. DISCOÌDEUS Gray, is common in the Dry Interior at moderate altitudes. Its leaves are only sparsely short-haired, once ternate (composed of 3 subdivisions); its flower-stems are usually 6-9 inches tall. The solitary flowers are generally without rays, consisting only of a circle of yellow disk-florets. Occasionally plants bear a row of short ray-florets, nearly always white.

Erigeron compositus is so widespread that the hiker or climber almost anywhere in the Dry Interior, or in the Coastal mountains, may expect to see the bright open faces of one or other of its varieties.

ERÍGERON LINEÀRIS (Hook.) Piper.   [p.546]

This beautiful, golden, perennial species is abundant among the Sagebrush of southern British Columbia, and up to moderate elevations in the mountains. Its name is derived from the slightly fleshy, long and *linear* leaves, which are almost entirely basal.

Large yellow flower-heads usually span an inch, or a little more. Nearly always they are solitary, on a 2-12 inch stem. Leaves, stems, and involucral bracts are covered with short grey hairs. (The involucral bracts sometimes also have glandular hairs). With a 10X magnifying glass it is possible to see that each achene (seed) is topped by a tuft of white hairs and also a few short, chaffy scales.

More abundant at higher levels, is ERÍGERON AÙREUS Greene, *Golden Fleabane,* with bright *yellow* flower-heads almost identical with those of *E. linearis* (which see). The leaves of the two species are, however, quite different. The basal leaves of E. aureus are much broader, with almost rounded to obovate blades, and long petioles; there are usually also a few reduced cauline leaves. Involucral bracts are sparsely—to densely—covered with woolly hairs, and are generally purplish, at least at their tips. Achenes, as with *E. linearis,* have both hairs and a few, small, outer scales.

Both these handsome yellow-flowered species are attractive additions to the rockery. They have the merit of blooming through much of the summer, demanding only full sun and sharp drainage.

ERÍGERON PEREGRÌNUS (Pursh) Greene. *Tall Purple Fleabane. Mountain Daisy. Aster Fleabane.*

Peregrinus means exotic, or *foreign.* The connotation is obscure, but may suggest that the sumptuous purplish-blue blossoms appear almost alien to the cloud-swirled rock fastnesses in which they are found. (The species was long known as *E. salsuginòsus* (Rich.) Gray, but E. peregrinus has botanical precedence.)

Erigeron peregrinus is a common and variable species, some of the forms descending to moist meadows at moderate elevations. Our bright-coloured plants, with nearly glabrous foliage, are known as subspecies CALLIANTHÈMUS (Greene) Cronqu. The high-altitude form, less than 8 inches tall, with very small cauline leaves, and ample blunt-tipped basal ones, is var. SCAPÒSUS (T. & G.) Cronqu. The larger, subalpine var. [p.546] ANGUSTIFÒLIUS (Gray) Cronqu. has narrower, more pointed leaves, and may reach 2 feet in height, like var. CALLIANTHÈMUS (which is the most abundant of the [p.546] varieties). This last has wider basal leaves, usually broadly obovate, and rather large, ovate stem-leaves.

These attractive perennials have pointed, generally green, long involucral bracts. The larger varieties of Aster Fleabane sometimes have more than one flower-head on a sparingly-branched stem, but most are solitary. The pappus consists of 20-30 hairs, sometimes with a very few, tiny scales.

This engaging plant accepts cheerfully a move to the well-drained rockery. Erigeron peregrinus seems to hold its vivid colour exceptionally well at sea level.

So fair, so sweet, withal so sensitive,
Would that the little Flowers were born to live,
Conscious of half the pleasure which they give;
That to this mountain-daisy's self were known
The beauty of its star-shaped shadow, thrown
On the smooth surface of this naked stone!

William Wordsworth:
Poems of Sentiment and Reflection XLII

ERÍGERON PHILADÉLPHICUS L. *Pink Fleabane.* [p.547]

The structure of this tall pink Fleabane is very unlike that of the dwarf montane species, such as *E. compositus* (which see).

Pink Fleabane may behave as an annual, flowering and withering in one year, but usually is biennial, or apparently sometimes survives 3 or 4 years. Within this life span it may be 8 inches high, or 36 inches. Basal leaves are about 2-2½ inches long, oblanceolate, and variously toothed to deeply lobed, or even entire. A number of scarcely smaller cauline leaves alternate up the stem, and either have no petioles (i.e. they are sessile), or actually wrap around the stem. Leaves and stem are sometimes nearly smooth, but generally show long, spreading hairs. Flower-heads are usually numerous, each having a very large number of ray-florets, with ligules that are extremely narrow, and vary in colour from deep pink to almost white. The seeds bear a white pappus of 20-30 hairs.

This is a widespread species, whose fragile-appearing flower-heads first show in May, and in shaded open woodlands, linger until fall. E. philadelphicus particularly favours moist roadside ditches, and stream-banks. (For the derivation of philadelphicus, see *Lilium philadelphicum.*)

ERÍGERON PÙMILUS Nutt. [p.550]

Pumilus means *dwarf*, though this species is not as low-growing as several other Erigerons. It is a perennial, often bushy in appearance, since it is much branched. An abundant plant of dry Sagebrush country, E. pumilus opens its very numerous, many-rayed flower-heads from May to July. The rays may be white, or more rarely pinkish, or bluish.

    The stems are from 2-16 inches tall, covered (like the leaves and the involucre) with spreading hairs. Some glandular hairs also occur on the stems, especially under the flower-heads. Basal leaves are narrowly oblanceolate and entire; the cauline similar, though usually decreasing in size upward. The hairy bracts are narrowly lanceolate, green with a brownish midrib. Pappus is double—the inner consisting of 7-25 long hairs, the outer of very small scales.

ERÍGERON SPECIÒSUS (Lindl.) DC. *Showy Erigeron.*

Speciosus, or *showy*, well describes the big, brightly coloured "flowers" of this handsome species. The plants may be 8-30 inches tall, and in rich well-watered soil the flower-heads may span 2 inches, though usually rather less. Each head bears 65-150 ray-florets, vividly purplish-blue (although occasionally white-rayed individuals are seen). The big flowers, in loose clusters, make brilliant accents in open woods and rocky hillsides, at moderate elevations in the mountains. The species is common east of the Cascades, but rare toward the Coast.

    Stems of Showy Erigeron are erect and unbranched, generally rising in clusters from short heavy rootstocks. Like the leaves, they are usually glabrous (smooth). Lower leaves are stalked, upper not. The upper leaves are decreased in size. Leaf-blades are long-lanceolate and entire, usually with hairs along the margins (i.e. they are ciliate), and sometimes also along the main veins on the lower surface. Involucral bracts are numerous, with spreading tips. These bracts bear both short glandular, and some longer simple hairs. Achenes are usually 2-nerved, sometimes 4-nerved.

ERIOPHÝLLUM LANÀTUM (Pursh) Forbes. *Woolly Sunflower.* [p.551]

Eriophyllum (from the Greek erion, *wool*, and phyllon, *leaf*) is a small genus of low "sunflowers". Lanatum (*woolly*) is the only species occurring in our area; the name further emphasizes the woolly hairs that cover the entire plant.

    This striking perennial reflects the sun's colour on rocky ledges of the southern Coast region. From May until August end, Woolly Sunflower opens numerous 2-inch flowers above a compact, 6-12 inch cluster of deeply-lobed to pinnately-divided hoary leaves.

The first rains tend to remove some of the woolly covering from the upper leaf surfaces.

Involucral bracts are single-ranked, with tips variously blunt to acute. Ray-florets normally number about 12, but are sometimes wanting. Achenes are glabrous, or nearly so, with a few uneven but short pappus scales.

Eriophyllum lanatum is a very worthwhile and "easy" subject for the rockery, where small pockets of thin sandy soil will ensure trim and compact growth.

FRANSÈRIA CHAMISSÒNIS Less. *Sand-bur.*

Franseria (from Antony Franser, an 18th century Spanish physician and botanist) was once classed in the genus *Ambrosia*. The specific name of this thick-leaved sturdy plant of shifting sand beaches, recalls the name of Adelbert Ludwig von Chamisso, German poet-naturalist, who visited Alaska in the ship Rurik in 1816 and 1817. The apt common name draws attention to harsh burs, with 2-4 rows of strong prickles, that assault bare feet rather painfully.

A big, sprawling perennial plant, the Sand-bur anchors itself in the sand with a number of buried branches, and protects its leaves and stems with a silvery coat of tight-pressed hairs. Thick leaves may be of two shapes, so different that many have believed two distinct species occur in this habitat. Var. CHAMISSÒNIS has ample diamond-shaped leaf-blades, merely shallow-toothed and silvery-grey, while var. BIPINNATISÉCTA Less. has greener leaves so deeply bisected and toothed, that they are almost skeletonized. Yet the varieties overlap geographically in some areas, as in different parts of Long Beach, on the west coast of Vancouver Island. It would be very interesting to discover if there is a correlation between leaf-shape and the micro-climate in which the two varieties (or possibly forms) occur. It may be significant that the most northerly population (that of the stormy, heavy-rainfall beaches of the Queen Charlotte Islands) consists entirely of the plants with bipinnate-dissected leaves. The plant illustrated is of this form (from Parksville, Vancouver Island).

[p.551]

Flowers are disappointing—small and drab, though numerous. They form a tight terminal raceme, and also occur in smaller clusters in the axils of the upper leaves. All are turned strongly downward. Some plants bear chiefly pistillate florets, others chiefly staminate. (This variation is not apparently related to the two extremes of leaf form.) The more staminate florets will usually be found in the terminal raceme, while the axillary flower-heads contain mostly pistillate florets. The large brown burs of Franseria are quite conspicuous toward the end of summer.

GAILLÁRDIA ARISTÀTA Pursh. *Brown-eyed Susan. Gaillardia.* [p.547]

Rare indeed is a generic name that derives from a first, or Christian name. In this case the flower's name honours Gaillard de Marentonneau, a French botanist. Aristata means

542

CICHORIUM INTYBUS ×½ [p.526]

CIRSIUM EDULE ×⅕ [p.527]

CIRSIUM HOOKERIANUM ×⅖ [p.528]

CIRSIUM UNDULATUM ×⅖ [p.529]

CIRSIUM VULGARE ×½ [p.529]

CONYZA CANADENSIS ×¼ [p.532]

COTULA CORONOPIFOLIA ×½ [p.532]

CREPIS CAPILLARIS ×⅖ [p.532]

bearded, alluding to the numerous bristles that cover the receptacle, and become evident when the ripened seeds have fallen. There are a number of common names of local usage, including the descriptive Brown-eyed Susan, but Gaillardia is apparently much the best-known.

This perennial is one of our most handsome wild flowers. It is found on open hillsides and less dry portions of flat prairie, never climbing high into the mountains. Those who live in the southern Dry Interior know it well. From June to September its striking golden blooms, with their orange-brown centres, make vivid patches of colour in the grey and dusty landscape.

Brought into the garden, Gaillardia aristata has excited the comment that it is more attractive than the larger-flowered horticultural varieties—possibly because it displays better balance between leaf, stem, and flower. Especially if the soil is rather lean, the plant maintains a distinctive well-bred look.

The stems are seldom branched, about 10-24 inches tall, and like the leaves, somewhat grey-haired. Leaves are oblanceolate in outline; the basal ones entire and tapering to a stalk, the stem-leaves variously-notched and stalkless. The splendid terminal flower-heads may span as much as 3 inches. Ray-flowers are very broad (almost wedge-shaped) with strongly 3-cleft tips. Good forms can be found, with an orange—or sometimes a purplish—flush extending outward from the base of the rays. Disk-flowers also are variable in colour: rarely yellow, often orange-brown, sometimes purple. After the ray-florets drop, the arched receptacle continues to develop until the disk-florets form a nearly globular head, with the involucral bracts strongly reflexed. The achenes are topped with a pappus of 6-10 lanceolate-pointed bristly scales.

GRINDÈLIA INTEGRIFÒLIA DC. *Gum Weed.* [p.551]

This sturdy plant of the wind-lashed, spray-swept coast, honours David Grindel, 1776-1836, a Russian botanist. The specific name means *entire-leaved,* which describes the uppermost stem-leaves, but not the basal ones, which are almost invariably toothed. The common name comes at once to mind when the flower-heads begin to develop, for they are nearly hidden by an exudate of sticky white latex.

[p.551] This very common plant is found along the coast, from Alaska south to Northern California. It is extremely variable, particularly in length of ray-flowers. The maritime salt-marsh form, var. MACROPHÝLLA (Greene) Cronq., is particularly showy, with impressively large flower-heads, as much as 2½ inches across. Away from the immediate vicinity of the sea-spray, the rays are usually broader and shorter.

The milky appearance of the immature flower-heads at once distinguishes the Gum Weeds. These flower-heads later develop bright-yellow ray-florets and disk-florets, in sunflower fashion. This species in all its variants is readily distinguished from other members of the genus by the fact that although some of the sticky tips of the green involucral bracts point "every-which-way", most of them point upward. "Flowers" are numerous on the robust 1-2½ foot plants. Blooming from June well into November, Gum

Weed is perhaps the most conspicuous plant of the coastal scene for the latter half of the year.

GRINDÈLIA SQUARRÒSA (Pursh) Dunal, is the species of the southeastern Dry Interior. It is a shorter-lived perennial than *G. integrifolia* (which see) and in fact sometimes behaves as a biennial. The flower-heads are smaller, only rarely spanning 1½ inches. The involucral bracts are all strongly reflexed, with the possible exception of the innermost row.

> *No warmth, no cheerfulness, no healthful ease,*
> *   No comfortable feel in any member—*
> *No shade, no shine, no butterflies, no bees,*
> *   No fruits, no flow'rs, no leaves, no birds—*
> *   November!*

Thomas Hood: No!

HELIÁNTHUS ANNÙUS L. *Common Sunflower.*   [p.554]

This great plant (found beside roadsides, particularly in the Dry Interior) extends far southward, and was cultivated for centuries before Columbus came to the New World. Wild strains seldom exceed 7 feet, nor the ripened flower-heads 5 inches in diameter, but modern cultivated strains far surpass these dimensions. (Today the oil expressed from the achenes has become important since it contains a large proportion of poly-unsaturated fatty acids.)

The generic name has Greek roots: helios, *sun,* and anthos, *flower.*

Few who drive Interior roads in late summer can have failed to note these tall Sunflowers. Stems and 6-12 inch pointed-ovate leaves bear hairs stiff enough to puncture one's skin. The yellow or brownish disk-flowers are arranged upon a broad, nearly flat receptacle. Conspicuous green bracts around the receptacle are hairy and ovate, with a long, pointed tip that is ciliate (fringed with marginal hairs).

Extensive root systems penetrate deeply and spread widely in search of the food elements and water needed to develop, in *one year's* (annuus) growing season, a plant so huge. Let us hope the species does not fall victim to the unfortunate (and, we think, short-sighted) practice of spraying herbicides along our road margins.

> [The Sunflower or] hearbe of the Sunne it is a strange flower, for it casteth out the greatest Blossomes and the moste particulars that euer haue been seene, for it is greater then a greate Platter or Dishe, and hath diuers coloures. . . it sheweth maruelleus faire in Gardens.
>
> —John Frampton (in his 1596 translation of Nicolas Monardes' *Joyfull newes Out of the New-found Worlde. Wherein are declared, the rare and singuler vertues of diuers Herbs, Trees, Plantes, Oyles & Stones. . . . Englished by John Frampton Marchant (London)*

ERIGERON PEREGRINUS var. CALLIANTHEMUS ×½ [p.539]

ERIGERON LINEARIS ×1 [p.538]

ERIGERON PEREGRINUS var. SCAPOSUS ×⅖ [p.539]

ERIGERON COMPOSITUS var. TRIFIDUS ×1¼
[p.538]

ERIGERON PHILADELPHICUS ×⅖ [p.539]

GAILLARDIA ARISTATA ×⅖ [p.541]

HIERÀCIUM ALBIFLÒRUM Hook. *White-flowered Hawkweed.*   [p.554]

Hieracium is a gargantuan genus, with about 800 recognized "species". The name is from hierax, *a hawk*—indeed, it was once believed that the fantastic vision of hawks was sharpened by their supposed addiction to these plants. Certainly the eye of a hawk is needed to distinguish between the host of species. We can only describe two reasonably clear-cut species, and for the rest, comment simply that these are generally yellow-flowered plants showing clear affinities with *Crepis, Lactuca, Leontodon,* and *Taraxacum.* From all these genera that have flower-heads entirely composed of ray-flowers, this one is separable with some difficulty on the following considerations: the pappus consists of unbranched hairs and is tawny (sordid, i.e. not white); the (usually) leafy stems bear several flower-heads; the achenes are neither beaked nor flattened, but round in cross section.

The present species is rather distinctively *white-* or cream-*flowered,* whence al-biflorum. It is a tall perennial, common in lower woodlands from Coast to Rockies. Stems are usually 1-2½ feet tall, long-haired below, sometimes nearly glabrous above. Lower leaves are stalked, more or less hairy, oblanceolate, and either entire or sparingly denticulate; upper leaves become sessile, as well as much smaller and less hairy. Involucral bracts are blackish-green, sometimes glandular-hairy near their bases.

Very often associated with the similar-statured, but yellow-flowered *Madia sativa* (which see), Hieracium albiflorum blooms through July and August, in woodlands west of the Cascades.

HIERÀCIUM AURANTIÀCUM L. *Orange Hawkweed.*   [p.554]

This brilliant Hieracium is named aurantiacum, literally *orange-red.* It is a European weed, introduced into one's garden with peril, since it spreads rapidly by winged seeds and also by creeping rhizomes.

In England this showy plant is sometimes cultivated in gardens, and is known as Fox and Cubs, a name nicely descriptive of the clustered small plants arising from the abundant runners, and of the densely furred herbage. Involucral bracts are clothed with long blackish hairs. The colour of the ray-flowers is distinctive, so no further description is needed.

The invasion of North America by Orange Hawkweed affords yet another illustration of the fact that when removed from a long-established equilibrium in its native land, a species often becomes rampant. In Switzerland, where a system of checks and balances has developed, this is a relatively uncommon plant. Too many parallels come to mind: it is sufficient to mention only the English Starling on this continent, or the Rabbit in Australia. Man in his ignorance tampers too often perilously with nature.

HYPOCHAÈRIS RADICÀTA L. *Cat's Ear.*

This familiar lawn-pest bears bright "dandelion" flowers that are easily confused with those of *Leontodon autumnalis,* (which see). Rays of the outermost florets are greenish-grey beneath, but those of *Leontodon* are often streaked reddish beneath. Leaves of Cat's Ear are generally hairier and less deeply incised. Achenes of Cat's Ear are "beaked," i.e. separated from the tuft of pappus hairs by a slim "waist". When the achenes have blown away, the exposed receptacle is seen to bear a number of peg-like scales (which are lacking in *Leontodon*).

LACTÙCA BIÉNNIS (Moench.) Fern. *Tall Blue Lettuce.* [p.554]

This Eurasian immigrant is now weedy in moist roadside ditches and waste ground, at lower altitudes throughout British Columbia. Its generic name comes from the Latin lac, *milk*, also (as used by Ovid) the milky sap of plants. As is generally known, this characteristic white juice exudes from the cut stems of all Lactuca, including the cultivated Lettuce, *L. sativa* L. It is quite amazing that a *biennial* plant like this can lift its tree-like stem 7-12 feet, within two short growing seasons. We have several times measured plants nearly 13 feet tall.

Though the plants are generally smooth throughout, one sometimes finds hairs on the midribs of the lower surface of the leaves. These notched and deeply-lobed leaves may be very large (up to 16 or 18 inches long). Very many dull-bluish flower-heads on slender pedicels appear in succession all through the summer and fall. Occasionally the ray-flowers are white, or pale yellow. The flower-heads are composed entirely of ray-florets, all of which have both stamens and pistil. Involucral bracts are green, pointed, and close-pressed (imbricate).

Four other species occur in our area, of which only LACTÙCA CANADÉNSIS L. achieves the astonishing height of *L. biennis* (which see). The flowers are usually yellow, rarely blue, but this is an unreliable criterion. To establish the identity of the Lettuces, one needs a microscope to study the achenes (seeds). In *L. biennis* the seed has no "beak" before branching out into the numerous buff-coloured hairs of the pappus, and the seed itself has several prominent lines, or nerves, that run lengthwise over the surface. In L. canadensis there is but one nerve on either face of the flattened seed, which is further distinguished by a short beak.

LACTÙCA MURÀLIS (L.) Fresen. is also yellow-flowered, but has achenes that are distinctively reddish-brown. This is an all too successful invader of our gardens. Before pulling up this slender Lettuce, a moment's examination of the leaves is worth-while. Basal leaves have a long petiole that is not at all clasping. A few inches higher on the stalk the petioles have become winged, with clasping ear-like stipules. Still higher the petiole-wings have broadened to rival the notched terminal blade, and near the flower-cluster the blade has disappeared—the broad, pointed petiole now terminating in stipules that quite enclose the stem, like a collar. Few plants display a greater variety of leaf-shapes.

ERIGERON PUMILUS   ✕ ⅕   [p.540]

ERIGERON COMPOSITUS var. DISCOIDEUS   ✕ ⅖   [p.538]

LEONTODON NUDICAULIS   ✕ ½   [p.552]

MATRICARIA MATRICARIOIDES   ✕ 1⅕   [p.553]

ERIOPHYLLUM LANATUM   ×1¼   [p.540]

FRANSERIA CHAMISSONIS var. BIPINNATISECTA
×⅖   [p.541]

GRINDELIA INTEGRIFOLIA   ×½   [p.544]

GRINDELIA INTEGRIFOLIA var. MACROPHYLLA
×½   [p.544]

LACTÙCA PULCHÉLLA (Pursh) DC. seldom exceeds 3 feet and bears very *showy,* blue flowers, larger than those of L. biennis (which see). Its achenes have a short thick beak, and several vertical ridges.

LACTÙCA SERRIÒLA L. has yellow flowers, and is distinguished by long prickly hairs on stem and leaves, and by multi-lined achenes with a very long slender beak. (The spelling L. SCARIÒLA is considered illegitimate.)

LÁPSANA COMMÙNIS L. *Nipplewort.* [p.555]

This is a Eurasian weed, all too *common* in gardens, fields, and roadsides, though apparently shunning woodlands. It belongs to a small genus named from the Greek lampsane, apparently a name for an unrecognizable crucifer figured by Dioscorides, who derived the name from lapazo, *to purge.*

Nipplewort is an upright annual, reaching 5 feet in good garden soil. The stem is hairy below, but nearly smooth above, carrying numerous thin, ovate leaves, about 2-5 inches long. The leaf-margins are wavy to deeply-toothed. Pale-yellow flower-heads are very numerous, and small. These heads consist of about a dozen ray-florets. Achenes are smooth, curved, and bear no pappus. Usually there are only 5-8 thin, green involucral bracts.

LEÓNTODON AUTUMNÀLIS L. *Fall Dandelion. August-flower.*

This European weed is now common around Victoria and Vancouver. The name is from the Greek leon, *lion,* and odous, *a tooth,* obviously with reference to the deeply incised leaves. Both specific and common names suggest this is chiefly a *fall-blooming* species.

Unlike the Common Dandelion *(Taraxacum officinale,* which see) the Fall Dandelion has a stem, which is branched upward. The stem is smooth, 6-24 inches tall, and carries a number of small scale-like bracts just below the flower-heads. The bright yellow flower-heads are sheltered by 2 rows of green involucral bracts—the inner long and narrow, the outer much shorter. The brownish achenes are directly topped by buff-coloured plumy pappus hairs. Fall Dandelion is easily confused with Cat's Ear *(Hypochaeris radicata,* which see) both having non-milky stems.

[p.550] LEÓNTODON NUDICAÙLIS (L.) Merat, is a similar plant (also from Europe). In this less common species the *stems are naked* (nudicaulis) i.e. lacking the small bracts of its relative. Also the (unbeaked) achenes are of 2 kinds; the outermost bearing only very minute scales, the central ones topped with plumose hairs plus a sparse fringe of shorter bristles.

Leontodon nudicaulis also is frequent in lawns and boulevards, as well as in disturbed or waste-ground, especially along the southern Coast. The illustration is of a depauperate form, from sand-dunes near the sea.

LUÌNA HYPOLEÙCA Benth. *Silver-back.* [p.555]

The name of this small group of beautiful rock plants is an anagram of *Inula,* a Eurasian genus. Hypoleuca, meaning *pale or whitish beneath,* describes the leaves, which are green above but strikingly silver-haired beneath, appearing white when the wind ruffles the foliage.

The flower colour is almost enough to identify the plant—a very unusual creamy-buff. Clustered 6-14 inch stems bear numerous alternate, sessile, elliptic, and entire (rarely few-toothed) leaves about 1-1½ inches long. Thick and firm, with vividly contrasting dark-green and silver-white, they are very handsome. Flower-heads are carried upright in clusters at the summit of the stems. There are no ray-flowers. Sparse-haired, lanceolate involucral bracts form a single row, enclosing 10-20 disk-florets. Pappus consists of white bristles above the hairy achenes.

Luina hypoleuca is a beautiful mountain plant, often growing in cracks on sheer rock faces. It is found in the Cascades and Coast Ranges, and on Vancouver Island.

MÀDIA SATÌVA Mol. Sagg. *Chilean Tarweed.*

Almost invariable companion—in dry woods—of the White-flowered Hawkweed (*Hieracium albiflorum,* which see) is this yellow-flowered plant of similar stature. Chilean Tarweed ranges into South America, where the Chilean name (*Madi*) accounts for the scientific name. In Chile, Madia sativa was once *sown* (sativa) in fields for the highly nutritious oil that was expressed from the seeds. Abundant also in California, the seeds of this species provided the Indians with readily stored food for winter use.

The flower-heads of Chilean Tarweed expand their yellow ray-florets at night, and look dispirited in sunlight when the rays are partially collapsed. But the strong and very distinctive smell of the plants is obvious in hot sunlit patches of the autumn woods. It is a peculiar odour—reminiscent of cut Rhubarb—and immediately recognizable when the source has once been identified.

The 2-3 foot plants are so common that the hiker's clothes often become sticky with the viscid gum brushed from the glandular hairs of leaves, stem, and inflorescence. One notices the plants because they are cluttered by white parachute-seeds of other Composites. This annual is taller and more robust than several smaller species of Madia that occur in British Columbia.

MATRICÀRIA MATRICARIOÌDES (Less.) Porter. *Pineapple Weed.* [p.550]

This lowly weed is instantly recognizable by the "pineapple" scent of its crushed flowers. Since it is widespread in waste—especially trodden—places, the distinctive odour often

HELIANTHUS ANNUUS $\times \frac{1}{4}$ [p.545]

HIERACIUM ALBIFLORUM $\times \frac{1}{5}$ [p.548]

LACTUCA BIENNIS $\times \frac{1}{6}$ [p.549]

HIERACIUM AURANTIACUM $\times \frac{1}{2}$ [p.548]

LAPSANA COMMUNIS ×²⁄₅ [p.552]

PETASITES PALMATUS ×⅓ [p.556]

LUINA HYPOLEUCA ×½ [p.553]

RUDBECKIA HIRTA ×⅕ [p.557]

announces its presence when the ground-hugging plant has been overlooked. The generic name is derived from the Latin matrix, *mother*, plus caria, *dear*, and was applied by the herbalists to this plant, and several others of the Chamomile clan (see *Anthemis arvensis*) that were believed to have medicinal virtues. The specific name repeats the idea, in a sort of closed-circle thinking, since the terminal, -oides, means *like*, i.e. Matricaria. More explicitly then, this is a Matricaria that looks like a Matricaria. Fortunately, it is not often that we encounter scientific names like this.

Pineapple Weed is a small annual, with much-branched, smooth, and sprawling stems, and numerous fern-like, finely-cut leaves. Flower-heads are conical and rayless, composed of very small, 4-notched, yellow disk-florets. Involucral bracts are broadly-oval, with chaffy margins. Pappus is reduced to an insignificant crown of tiny scales.

MATRICÀRIA MARÍTIMA L. is a nearly scentless herb, usually of saline places and along the *seashore*. It is sharply distinguished by its white ray-florets. Curiously, its yellow disk-florets are nearly always 5-toothed, whereas those of *M. matricarioides* (which see) are almost invariably 4-toothed. It is a taller plant—from 4 inches to as much as 24 inches tall—with less finely-divided foliage than its relative.

PETASÌTES PALMÀTUS (Ait.) Gray. *Colt's Foot.* [p.555]

Petasites derives from the Greek petasos, a *broad-brimmed hat,* which describes the wide basal leaves. (For speciation we have chosen to follow the scholarly treatment of Hultén, and of Calder and Taylor, rather than our usual authority, Hitchcock, Cronquist, et al.) Palmatus (from the large *hand-shaped* leaves) is then the Colt's Foot species illustrated—a common plant of woodlands at lower altitudes.

Most Composites bloom late in the year, but the Colt's Foot pushes its thick stem through the ground at the beginning of March, sometimes while snow still lingers. Soon the rapidly lengthening shoot displays a heavy, flattened cluster of purplish (sometimes white, rarely yellow) flower-heads. These are of two kinds, the staminate soon withering. The pistillate-heads usually have a few short ray-florets. By early summer they are succeeded by clusters of achenes whose radiating pappus recall a very large, but flattened, Dandelion "puff". Soon after the appearance of flowering-stems, stout leaf-shoots emerge. They are folded in an extraordinary manner, with the hairy lobes reflexed, at an early stage evoking the metaphor of the little foot of a colt. By mid-summer the flower-shoots have withered, and the great fan-leaves have reached their full size—commonly a foot wide, or even more. The big umbrellas are white-haired below, deeply 5-7 lobed at least ½ of their width (the lobes further toothed) and the blades are carried flat on the tops of strong petioles about 18-24 inches long.

Since individual stems bearing flower-heads rise from points along the creeping rhizomes distinct from the buds that originate leaves, and since the flowers have often shrivelled before the leaves reach their full development, many woodsmen fail to associate the two.

PETASÌTES FRÍGIDUS (L.) Fries, is a more northern and alpine plant than *P. palmatus* (which see), with palm-shaped to triangular leaves merely toothed, rather than lobed. It is very short and sturdy, with thick, heavy stems. Flowering stems carry relatively large, sheathing, bract-like leaves.

PETASÌTES NIVÀLIS Greene, is a coastal to rather cordilleran species, with leaves lobed about ⅓ or ¼ of their width. In Manning Park this species apparently forms hybrid swarms with *P. frigidus* (which see), which is very similar.

PETASÌTES SAGITTÀTUS (Banks) A. Gray, of wet seepages from Alaska to Labrador—but in our area limited to the lowlands—is immediately distinguishable by its leaves. These are, as the name suggests, shaped like *an arrowhead* as much as 10 inches long. The margins are usually sharply toothed.

Palaeomagnetic studies prove that about 65 million years ago, North America was joined to Eurasia through present-day Labrador and Greenland. But the westward drift of our continent isolated the Cenozoic ancestors of flowering plants that—millions of years earlier—had diversified as representative of the families that we know today. Hence many of our species, such as *Linnaea borealis, Empetrum nigrum, Rubus chamaemorus, Petasites frigidus,* are very ancient, and explicably circumboreal in distribution.

RUDBÉCKIA HÍRTA L. *Black-eyed Susan. Cone-flower.* [p.555]

We seem to have a plethora of dark-eyed Susans (see e.g. *Gaillardia aristata*). Cone-flower is a name applied also (and more appropriately) to RATIBÌDA COLUM-NÍFERA (Nutt.) Woot. & Standl. (This latter plant, of our extreme southern Dry Interior, is tall and showy. Its disk-florets are arranged on an inch-long, slender, thimble-shaped receptacle, and its broad yellow ray-florets are reflexed).

The generic name Rudbeckia recalls a pleasant bit of history. The young Linnaeus, as an impoverished student, was taken into the household of the Professor of Botany at Uppsala, Olaf Rudbeck. The kindly old professor found a tutoring job for the ragged and hungry young man, and later launched him on his remarkable career (initially as a plant collector in Lapland). Many years later, when Linnaeus had carved an immortal name in science, he honoured his old benefactor by naming the genus of attractive plants, Rudbeckia. Hirta means *hairy,* the entire plant being rough-haired.

This attractive yellow "sunflower" occurs sporadically in the southern half of our area, including a few records from Vancouver Island. This is apparently an introduced species, its centre of distribution being the central states of the United States of America.

Rudbeckia hirta is our only member of the genus. The plants prefer dry situations, and grow 12-30 inches high. With us the species is apparently a biennial. The alternate leaves are elliptical to lanceolate, long-stalked at the base of the stem, becoming shorter-stalked and finally sessile upward. Showy single "flowers" are often 3 inches across. The bright-yellow ray-florets are effectively accented by the rounded, central boss of almost black disk-flowers. Very often the rays are flushed with orange, particularly near their bases. There is no pappus, but the surface of the curved receptacle is chaffy.

J. WOOLLETT

SAUSSUREA DENSA $\times \frac{1}{3}$ [p.560]

SENECIO CYMBALARIOIDES $\times \frac{1}{3}$ [p.560]

SENECIO JACOBAEA $\times \frac{1}{2}$ [p.561]

SENECIO SYLVATICUS $\times \frac{1}{4}$ [p.561]

SENECIO TRIANGULARIS ×⅓ [p.561]

SOLIDAGO CANADENSIS var. SALEBROSA
×⅖ [p.564]

SOLIDAGO SPATHULATA ×⅖ [p.565]

SONCHUS ARVENSIS ×⅓ [p.565]

Hairy involucral bracts are slenderly pointed, and become strongly reflexed as the flower-head matures.

SAUSSÙREA DÉNSA (Hook.) Rydb. *Saw-wort. Purple Hawkweed.* [p.558]

Named after Horace Bénédict de Saussure (1740-1799), famed Swiss botanist, geologist, and early alpinist, this sturdy mountain dweller attracts attention, soon after the snow has melted, with its large, densely furred, and compact leaf-cluster. Then its *crowded* foliage wrapped around the stubby stem and its dark flower-buds merit the specific name, densa. Soon coarse, roughly saw-edged leaves unfold, and the thick stem lengthens to 4 or 8 inches as the terminal flower-head matures.

The "flowers" look like tight balls of wool, from which protrude dark-purple disk-florets. There are no ray-flowers. The sturdy plant looks well-equipped to face the chill alpine winds. One is somehow surprised, on leaning closer, to discover a pleasant fragrance.

Saussurea densa is found at medium to high altitudes, particularly in the Rockies. It occurs also in Manning Park, and Henry quotes a record from Mt. Benson, V.I. New records for this conspicuous plant will be of interest.

SENÈCIO CYMBALARIOÌDES Nutt. [p.558]

Senecio is derived from senex, *an old man,* since the receptacle lacks bristles or hairs—like a bald head! Cymbalarioides, *like cymbals,* possibly refers to the shape of the lower leaf-blades. The leaves vary in an extraordinary degree upwards: from ones resembling a notched frying-pan, through feather-shaped and deeply notched, to upper leaves that are entire and pointed-lanceolate, or even linear. The first 2 variations have long petioles, the upper none. Nor is the application of cymbalarioides clear—for the name is applied to a complex of probably 7 intergradational subspecies.* This title of convenience may be applied to variable but attractive plants found from Alaska southward, in open woods and subalpine slopes.

The exceptionally variable foliage may be light-green, or in stations relatively close, dark-purple. Leaves and stem are generally thickish and quite succulent. Higher altitude plants may have a single terminal head, but at lower levels there are usually several. Though ray-flowers are sometimes absent, the flower-heads are generally large (to more than an inch across), and showy (bright-yellow or nearly orange). Involucral bracts are broad—in some forms smooth, in others pubescent. Achenes are smooth.

Senecio cymbalarioides is an eye-catching plant, often noticed. Regretfully we must omit more than a dozen other perennial species that occur in our area.

*The interested student will find valuable the scholarly discussion by Calder and Taylor.

Two ubiquitous annuals—both European imports—are SENÈCIO VULGÀRIS L, *Common Groundsel,* altogether too well-known to gardeners, and SENÈCIO SYLVÁ- TICUS L., a plant that chooses woodlands, especially near the Coast. S. sylvaticus is the taller plant (attaining 3 feet). Both species have irregularly notched leaves, but those of the rural species are longer, more pointed, and greyer. Also, the bracts forming the outermost ring of its involucre lack the black tips that are so characteristic of urban S. vulgaris. [p.558]

SENÈCIO JACOBAÈA L. *Tansy Ragwort.* [p.558]

Once again, this is a pernicious immigrant from Europe, now increasing rapidly in waste ground, and along roads, and railways.

Tansy Ragwort is a tall (and let it be admitted) handsome weed, with masses of showy yellow "flowers". Often confused with Tansy (*Tanacetum vulgare,* which see), it is superficially very similar in size and manner of growth. However, it can be distinguished at once by noticing that the flower-heads have a ring of conspicuous golden ray-flowers (lacking in *Tanacetum*), and that although the leaves of both plants have similarly lobed and toothed leaves, those of S. jacobaea have terminal segments that are never pointed, but blunt-rounded.

Tansy Ragwort contains a toxic alkaloid, which is cumulative in its effects, and is responsible for considerable loss of cattle and horses.

Apparently in some parts of British Columbia, Senecio jacobaca may survive for several years—but it is usually a biennial. The plant is glabrous. A very curious feature, discernible on considerable magnification, makes identification certain. The seeds (achenes) of the ray-flowers are smooth; those of the disk-flowers densely-haired, and ribbed. There is no beak on either sort and the pappus of both consists of many white hairs.

SENÈCIO TRIANGULÀRIS Hook. *Spear-head Senecio.* [p.559]

It is not possible to exclude, even in the briefest treatment of our Senecio, this abundant and impressive species. It is our tallest representative of the genus; in rich moist soil of the Cowichan Valley we have measured plants that exceeded 7 feet. Triangularis describes the long, pointed-*triangular* leaves that make identification unmistakable. They occur all the way up the tall stems, becoming reduced from about 8 inches in length to about 3 inches. Lower leaves are strikingly notched, with a squared-off base and rather long petioles, but upper ones are only serrate, with a wedge-shaped base and no petiole.

The flattened clusters of yellow inch-wide heads are quite showy. Rays number 5-12, usually 8.

This species is perennial.

Following page: TANACETUM VULGARE ✕1 [p.566]

SALICORNIA RUBRA (HABITAT) ×⅙ [p.112]

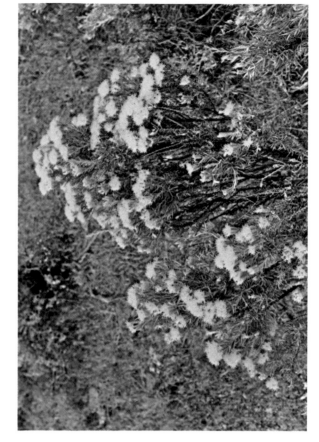

TETRADYMIA CANESCENS ×⅙ [p.568]

TRAGOPOGON PORRIFOLIUS ×⅞ [p.568]

Senecio triangularis ranges through the lower mountain areas of British Columbia, and is quite variable. Small plants with narrower leaves occur at quite low altitudes in boggy areas along the Coast.

SOLIDÀGO CANADÉNSIS L. *Goldenrod.*

Over most of British Columbia the great plumes of Goldenrod wave in the autumn winds. Solidago sums the Latin solidus, *whole,* and ago, to do or *to make,* hence "to make whole", since Goldenrod was once thought to have curative virtues. This *Canada-wide,* highly variable plant, is one of about a hundred (sometimes ill-defined) species of North America. The common name is descriptive, for the rod-like stems serve well to hold aloft attractive sprays of countless tiny golden flowers.

Underground parts, consisting of rhizomes, fibrous roots, and caudex (woody base of leafy stems) must be collected to aid in the difficult identification of about 10 species—or perhaps subspecies—found in our area. In addition a good magnifying glass is needed to study the type of pubescence on stem, leaves, and inflorescence. Much the most common and widespread species is S. canadensis. This perennial grows from creeping rhizomes and is without a well-developed caudex. Stems vary from a modest 10-12 inches to a stately 6 or 7 feet. They vary from nearly glabrous in some varieties, to rather densely short haired, in others. The numerous alternate leaves (carried to the top of the stems) are lance-linear, sharply saw-toothed to entire, and only slightly reduced in size upward. Inflorescence is terminal, and rather like a crowded panicle. Sometimes the branchlets are slightly down-curved, with the flower-heads chiefly on the upper side. Most flower-heads have 10-17 ray-florets. Involucral bracts are thin and overlap only slightly.

[p.559] Most widespread of the forms of Solidago canadensis is var. SALEBRÒSA (Piper) Jones, which has nearly glabrous leaves, few hairs on the stems (especially near the base), and a long spike-like inflorescence. In poor, dry habitats it may be 12-16 inches only, but under more favourable conditions forms very showy clumps 6 feet tall. Var. SUBSERRÀTA (DC.) Cronqu., of the northern Pacific coast, has a shorter inflorescence almost overtopped by the uppermost leaves. The bracts of the involucre are nearly uniform in length, and rather longer, and less closely imbricated (shingled) than those of var. salebrosa. The plants are also smaller, rarely exceeding 3 feet.

A widespread impression that Goldenrod is a hay-fever plant has been discredited by studies that show the pollen is very heavy, and is not wind-borne to any distance. Early ideas of curative properties possessed by the plant are not supported by recent research.

Brilliant contributors to the autumn scene, plumes of the Goldenrod lend a regal touch to the imperial purple of the contemporary tribe of *Asters.*

Season of mists and mellow fruitfulness.
Close bosom-friend of the maturing sun;
Conspiring with him how to load and bless
With fruit the vines that round the thatch-eaves run;
. . . to set budding more,

And still more, later flowers for the bees,
Until they think warm days will never cease. . .

John Keats: To Autumn

SOLIDÀGO SPATHULÀTA DC. (=. S. DECÚMBENS Greene). *Dwarf Goldenrod.* [p.559]

This smaller plant may not exceed 3 inches in poor soil and foot-hill situations, but usually reaches 1-2 feet in the Dry Interior of British Columbia, and adjacent areas north, east, and south. In sand dunes along the Coast is found a form about a foot high that is resinous, especially on the involucral bracts.

Glabrous basal leaves of Dwarf Goldenrod rise from a thickened caudex, and are spatulate, toothed, and persistent; those of the stiff (often reddish) stem are reduced upward and (usually) sparse. The inflorescence of this common plant is variable, though often dense and congested, and never secund (one-sided). The inner bracts of the involucre are much longer than the outer; all are blunt-ended. Most often 8 ray-florets surround 12-13 disk-florets.

SOLIDÀGO MULTIRADIÀTA Ait., *Mountain Golden Rod,* usually of high altitudes from Vancouver Island across the province, may be 2 to 18 inches tall. It is generally very like the lower level *S. spathulata,* but is distinguished by ciliate-margined petioles of the spatulate basal leaves.

SÓNCHUS ARVÉNSIS L. *Sow Thistle.* [p.559]

The generic name is from somphos, *spongy,* the stems being tubular and filled with porous tissues that secrete a bitter, white-milky latex. Arvensis is a very common name, meaning *of the fields,* for this is an extremely abundant and far-ranging weed of our fields and roadsides. The bright yellow "flowers" resemble somewhat those of the Thistles (though much more closely the familiar heads of the Dandelion). Some species have soft spines, never as formidable as those of most Thistles. Apparently pigs are fond of the rather succulent plants.

Sonchus arvensis is much the most impressive of the 4 species that have invaded our area from Eurasia and Africa. It is a perennial, with a semi-taproot and also creeping rhizomes that are partly responsible for its reputation as one of our most troublesome farm-weeds. From the top of its 2-6 foot stem it also launches, all through the summer, huge quantities of parachute-seeds.

Leaves are soft-prickled along the margins, but not hairy. They are pinnately lobed and finely toothed, becoming less deeply lobed but with more clasping bases toward the top of the branched stems. The golden inflorescence often attracts attention by its size, being frequently 2 inches across. The involucral bracts, unlike the remainder of the plant, bear coarse, glandular hairs. All the florets are ligulate (strap-shaped), and all are perfect (i.e. have functioning stamens and pistil). Seeds have 5-10 prominent longitudinal ribs, and no beak (the crowded white pappus being attached directly to the top of the seed).

SÓNCHUS ÁSPER (L.) Hill, *Prickly Sow Thistle,* is an annual like *S. oleraceus* (which see) but is more spectacularly soft-prickled. The auricles (ears of the upper leaves) remain rounded, never becoming pointed. Achenes lack the cross-wrinkling evident in *S. oleraceus.*

SÓNCHUS OLERÁCEUS L. is an annual species, under 3 feet tall, with yellow flower-heads ½-1 inch across. The upper (clasping) leaves develop pronounced "ears", which become acute-pointed. Achenes are rough-ribbed, and also transversely marked with raised wrinkles. This is the species of Sow Thistle best-known as a garden problem.

Sow Thistle, Common Chickweed, *Lactuca* species, *Polygonum convolvulus,* Dandelion (*T. officinale*)—how much simpler life would be if we did not have to contend with these—immigrants all!

One may see in Vienna today perhaps the greatest treasure of botanical literature—a copy made about A.D. 512 of Dioscorides' *De materia medica.* This precious volume is illustrated by amazing drawings apparently derived from Krateuas (or Cratevas, who was physician to Mithridates about 120 B.C.). They are of a quality not rivalled for almost a thousand years. Among the pictures a *Sonchus* (labelled COΓXOC TPAXYC) is clearly recognizable, also several species of *Anemone,* and an *Anagallis.* The two last are named by their modern generic names, which must therefore be at least 1500 years old.

TANACÈTUM VULGÀRE L. *Tansy.* [p.562]

Tanacetum is obscure in derivation, apparently a corruption of the Latin athanasia, *undying,* either from its mediaeval use in medicine, or from the durable flowers. In Middle English the plant was called Tanesey, and in French Tanaisie. Vulgare means *common;* indeed, this stately yellow weed has escaped from the herbalists' gardens, where it was valued for its bitter and aromatic elixir, to line roadsides all round the Northern Hemisphere.

The plant is glabrous, or nearly so, with many stiff stems reaching 3-5 feet. They are clothed with numerous, alternate and attractive leaves. These are pinnate and deeply toothed, almost feather-like, bright green, and about 4-8 inches long. Many bright yellow flower-heads are arranged in a somewhat flattened cluster at the tops of the stems. On closer examination the lanceolate involucral bracts are found to be thin and dry, even chaffy at tips and edges. Only disk-florets are present—the outermost chiefly pistillate, the rest perfect (with anthers as well as pistil). The pappus is reduced to a tiny 5-lobed crown, so small that some authorities state there is no pappus. The receptacle is slightly convex, lacks scales, and is less than ½ inch wide.

Tanacetum vulgare comes into bloom in August and September, when it is quite showy. Tansy is often mistaken for Tansy Ragwort *(Senecio jacobaea,* which see), but the latter has a ring of large and showy ray-florets, and the leaf-segments are blunt or rounded, not sharply-pointed.

TANACÈTUM DOUGLÀSII DC. is a smaller Tansy of the coastal sand-dunes. From 8-24 inches tall, its somewhat hairy leaves are distinctive. They are much more finely-cut than those of its taller relative (in fact, almost like the leaves of yarrow, *Achillea millefolium,* which see), but brighter green. The inflorescence of T. douglasii is flatter-topped, with fewer but larger flower-heads. These are at once distinguished by the presence of a ring of short-strapped ray-flowers. This is a very attractive species. (The valid name may be T. HURONÉNSE Nutt.)

TARÁXACUM OFFICINÀLE Weber. *Common Dandelion.*

We have heard people announce, with something approaching satisfaction, that the only flower they know is a Dandelion. One can regret that they have missed so much pleasure, and be at the same time, a little sceptical. Such persons are amazed to hear that more than a thousand kinds of Dandelions have been described. Most of these are very closely related and excessively difficult to distinguish. For our purposes we can leave the distinctions to the specialists, and illustrate one form of this group of plants that have, perhaps more than any other, conquered a variety of habitat niches the world over. Our word Dandelion is a corruption of the French description of the leaves, le dent-de-lion, which in turn is from the Latin dentem (accusative of dens, a *tooth)* de, *(of),* and leonem (accusative of leo, a *lion.)* Curiously, *Leontodon,* a further variant, is now applied to plants of quite another genus (see *Leontodon autumnalis).*

Taraxacum is thought to be derived from the Greek tarassein, *to stir up,* with reference to medicinal properties once attributed to the root. "Medicinal" in early English usage was equivalent to "officinal", now the specific name.

As with many common flowers, the beauty of this brightest of golden flowers is seldom appreciated.

No lengthy description is necessary. The familiar leaves are more, or less, deeply incised in some varieties. They grow from a caudex at the top of the root, since there is no stem. A most useful recognition feature is the achene. Everyone knows the geometrical perfection of the seed-heads. If seeds of this species are examined with a 10X glass, the achene is found to be olive-green to brown, with a slender "beak" 2½-4 times as long as the achene, and, of course, a terminal tuft of showy hairs forming the pappus (parachute) that spreads the seeds far and wide.

TARÁXACUM LAEVIGÀTUM (Willd.) DC. is another Eurasian import, similar though usually more slender than *T. officinale* and readily distinguished by its reddish or purplish achenes, and shorter beak only 1-3 times as long as the achene.

We have a number of native non-invasive species of this genus, that are usually found in the high mountains. Of these TARÁXACUM ERIÓPHORUM Rydb. has sharply

4-sided reddish achenes, and T. LYRÀTUM (Ledeb.) DC. nearly black achenes. Both are very small plants.

Probably most have heard of Dandelion wine, made from the flowering heads. Less commonly, plants are cased with brown-paper tubes to blanch the leaves, which are used in salads. For centuries the root was employed as a tonic and diuretic.

Dear common flower, that grow'st beside the way,
Fringing the dusty road with harmless gold. . . .

James Russell Lowell:
To the Dandelion

TETRADÝMIA CANÉSCENS DC. *Horse Brush.*   [p.563]

Many of the Tetradymia species have florets clustered in fours, whence the generic name, from the Greek tetradymos, *fourfold.* Canescens, meaning *grey-pubescent,* describes the stems and narrow leaves of this shrub. It is found in very dry, open country, among the foothills of the southern Dry Interior.

Tetradymia closely resembles Rabbit Brush *(Chrysothamnus nauseosus,* which see), and often grows with it. But Rabbit Brush is grey-green, Horse Brush whitish. Tetradymia has linear leaves that are wider and only half as long as the very long, slimmer leaves of *Chrysothamnus.* Finally, the present plant has only 4 involucral bracts, and only 4 florets (none ligulate) in each head.

But both plants are much-branched shrubs about 12-24 inches high, and both are crowned with masses of golden-yellow flower-heads. They are, in fact, so much alike, that many ranchers think they are the same plant.

Horse Brush is often seen above a thin snow-layer, and is then browsed by wild and domestic stock desperate for winter food. A toxic principle inherent in the plant is apparently broken down (possibly by maturation processes, or low temperatures) at that time of year, but in the spring, sheep cropping the young growth develop a malady called Bighead.

TRAGOPÒGON PORRIFÒLIUS L. *Oyster Plant. Salsify.*   [p.563]

Tragopogon is a genus of about 50 species of Eurasia and Africa, 2 of which have extensively invaded our area. The strange name, suggesting some species of prehistoric beast, is derived from the Greek, tragos meaning *goat,* and pogon, a *beard,* in allusion to the long silky pappus of the seed. Porrifolius means with *leaves resembling those of the leek.* People whose original home was the Mediterranean coast, will remember that this big purple-flowered "dandelion" plant is cultivated for its prized fleshy root, which has a very delicate and appetizing flavour.(This is likened by some to that of oysters, but to our taste resembles a mild parsnip.) Salsify or Salsafy is an old name, from the French salsifis, which in turn is derived from the Latin saxifricta, a combination of saxum, a *rock,* plus i—, plus fricta, *rubbed* or abraded. Craighead, Craighead, and Davis point out that this plant, one of those introduced by early settlers in the West, soon escaped. Subsequently it was used by the Indians for food, and also medicinally, as they considered that chewing the coagulated milky juice of the stems provided a remedy for indigestion.

Now common in waste ground and along roadsides, from Vancouver Island across the southern part of the Province, Oyster Plant is conspicuous for the unusual colour of the flower-heads. They are reddish-purple, quite attractively backed by the bright green tips of the long involucral bracts, which project beyond the ray-florets. A glabrous biennial, 16-36 inches tall, T. porrifolius has erect stems clothed with very slender, long-pointed, clasping leaves. The impressive seed-heads resemble gigantic dandelion-puffs. The individual seeds are interesting and beautiful objects to study with the magnifying glass. The achene has a number of raised, and roughened, longitudinal ribs. At the top is a long waist, or beak, which then branches into a fine plume of delicately pinnate-haired pappus bristles. The upper ends of some of these bristles lack hairs, and project above the "parasol"—an arrangement unique among our Composites. All the flowers in a head are ray-florets, and all are fertile, with both stamens and pistil.

TRAGOPÒGON DÙBIUS Scop. is almost exactly similar to *T. porrifolius* (which see), except that the flowers are pale lemon-yellow. Occasionally, sterile hybrids between the two species are found. Ray-florets of the hybrid are purple-tipped, but yellow at their bases.

Both species of Tragopogon are strongly matutinal; that is, they open their flowers at first light, but close them tightly about noon. The plants are then sometimes difficult to find.

Those who have noticed the matutinal habit of the Oyster Plant will read with interest the observation made more than 400 years ago by Petri Andreae Matthioli, in his *Commentaries on the Six Books of Dioscorides:* "The Goatsbeard is sufficiently well-known. . . . Its flower is yellow and somewhat like that of the Dandelion, though larger and enclosed in a sort of button. When the weather is clear it remains wide open; when it is cloudy the flower closes up in its button. . . . From the top of the button hangs a frolicksome beard which is white and rather large and which is, according to Theophrastus, the reason why this herb is called Goatsbeard."

And look—a thousand blossoms with the Day
Woke—and a thousand scatter'd into Clay. . . .

E. Fitzgerald:
The Rubáiyát of Omar Khayyám

ILLUSTRATED GLOSSARY

1. Terms relative to UNDERGROUND PARTS:

Bulb. Underground bud having fleshy scales like an onion.

Corm. Vertical, thickened, solid underground stem, as in gladiolus, or crocus.

Rhizome. Horizontal, elongated, subterranean stem. Too familiar to gardeners in the rhizomes or running rootstocks of quack or couch grass.

Tuber. Thickened solid underground stem with buds ("eyes") as in potato.

Parasitic plant. Fibrous roots replaced wholly or partially with **Haustoria** that penetrate tissues of host plant and draw sustenance from it; often lacks chlorophyll.

Saprophytic plant. Lives on dead organic matter, hence (usually) has no need of green chlorophyll.

2. Terms relative to STEMS:

Herbaceous. Not woody. A stem that dies down to the ground each winter. The stalk may remain but it is dead.

Prostrate. Stem lying flat on the ground, usually rooting at the nodes, as in Twinflower (Linnaea).

Decumbent. Stem that extends along the ground but turns upward near the end, as in Devil's Club (Oplopanax).

Simple. Having no major side branches, as in Hollyhock.

Scape. Flowering stem rising from the ground without true leaves (there may be bracts).

Stolon. Supplementary specialized stem running over the surface of the ground and rooting at the nodes. If only the tip roots, it is generally called a **Runner** (e.g. Strawberry, Fragaria).

3. Terms relative to LEAVES:

A. Arrangement of leaves:

Alternate. Leaves originating one above the other on opposite or nearly opposite sides of the stem; not in pairs.

Opposite. Leaves originating in pairs, opposite each other.

Rosette. Leaves forming a ring at ground level.

Whorl. Three or more leaves arranged wheel-like around the stem.

B. Simple vs. compound leaves:

Simple leaf. One with a single expanded blade. The margins of the blade may be entire or variously notched or lobed, but never divided quite to the mid-rib.

Compound leaves. Those with a number of leaflets arranged either:

(a) Palmately compound—like the fingers and thumb radiating from the palm; i.e. with 3 or more leaflets arising from a common centre.

Some of the more important variations in these parts (one or several of which may be rudimentary, or even apparently missing) are shown:

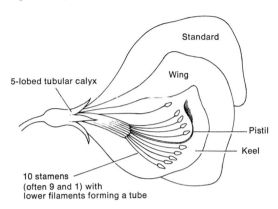

Leguminosae (e.g. Pea)

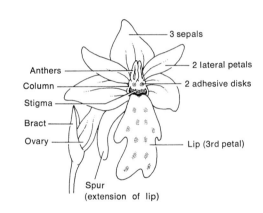

Orchidaceae (e.g. Spotted Orchis)

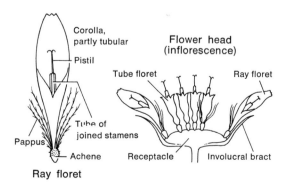

Compositae (e.g. Dandelion)

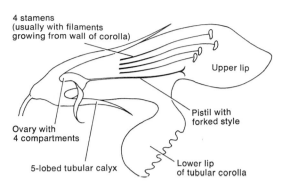

Labiatae (e.g. Mint)

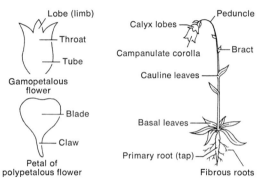

Details of inflorescence

Polypetalous —petals distinct, not at all united.

Gamopetalous—petals united, at least at the base.

Monoecious—flowers of one sex, but both pistillate and staminate ones appearing on the same plant.

Dioecious—flowers of one sex, the pistillate carried by one plant, the staminate by another.

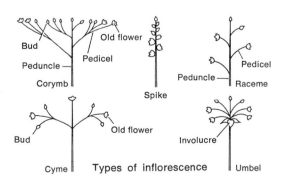

Types of inflorescence

BIBLIOGRAPHY

"Some of them will saye, seeing that I graunte that I have gathered this booke of so many writers, that I offer unto you an heape of other mennis laboures, and nothing of mine owne . . . To whom I answere that if the honye that the bees gather out of so many floure of herbes, shrubbes and trees, that are growing in other mennis meadows, feldes, and closes may justelye be called the bee's honye . . . so maye I call that I have learned and gathered of so many good autoures . . . my booke."

William Turner, 1551

ABRAMS, L., An Illustrated Flora of the Pacific States, Washington, Oregon and California (4 vols.), Stanford University Press, 1940-1960.

ANDERSON, A. W., How We Got Our Flowers, Dover Publications, Inc., N.Y., 1966.

ANDERSON, J. P., Flora of Alaska, Iowa State University Press, 1959.

ARBER, A., Herbals: Their Origin and Evolution, Cambridge University Press, new edn., 1938.

BAGER, BERTEL, Nature as Designer, Frederick Warne & Co., London, 1955.

BAILEY, L. H., How Plants Get Their Names, Dover Publications, New York, 1963.

BILLINGS, W. D., Plants and the Ecosystem, Wadsworth Publishing Co. Inc., Belmont, Cal., 1964.

BOIVIN, BERNARD, Flora of the Prairie Provinces (in 3 parts), Faculté d'Agriculture, Université Laval, 1967.

BRITTEN, J., HOLLAND, R., Dictionary of English Plant Names, Collins, London, 1878-1880.

BROCKMAN, C. F., Flora of Mount Rainier National Park, U.S. Government Printing Office, 1947.

BROWN, ANNORA, Old Man's Garden, Gray's Publishing, Sidney, B.C., 1970.

BUDD, A. C., and BEST, K. F., Wild Plants of the Canadian Prairies, Canada Department of Agriculture Publication No. 983, 1964.

CALDER, J. A., and SAVILE, D. B. O., Studies in Saxifragaceae I. The Heuchera cylindrica complex in and adjacent to British Columbia. (1959). Brittonia, 11, 49-67. II. Saxifraga trachyphyllum in North America. (1960). Brittonia 11, 228-249. III. Saxifraga odontoloma and lyallii, and North American subspecies of S. punctata. (1960). Canadian Journal of Botany 38:409-435.

CALDER, J. A., and TAYLOR, R. L., Flora of the Queen Charlotte Islands, Pt. 1, Research Dept., Canada Dept. of Agric. Monograph No. 4, Part 1, 1968.

CARL, G. CLIFFORD, Notes on the flora and fauna of the Bunsby Islands, British Columbia., Occasional Papers of British Columbia, Provincial Museum of Natural History and Anthropology, Victoria, B.C., Report for year 1955, pp. 31-44.

CLAPHAM, A. R., TUTIN, T. G., WARBURG, E. F., Flora of the British Isles, Cambridge University Press, 1962.

COATS, A. A., Flowers and their Histories, Hulton Press, London, 1956.

CORE, E. L., Plant Taxonomy, Prentice-Hall, Inc., 1955.

CRAIGHEAD, J. J., CRAIGHEAD, F. C., DAVIS, R. J., A Field Guide to Rocky Mountain Wildflowers, Houghton Mifflin, 1963. (Peterson Field Guide Series).

DAVIS, R. J., Flora of Idaho, Wm. C. Brown Co., 1952.

DAWSON, G. M., Report on an Exploration from Port Simpson on the Pacific Coast to Edmonton on the Saskatchewan; a portion of the northern part of British Columbia and the Peace River country., Part B, 1879-80, Geological and Natural History Survey of Canada, Montreal.

DELEVORYAS, T., Plant Diversification, Holt, Rinehart & Winston, New York, 1966.

DOUGLAS, DAVID, Journal kept by David Douglas during his travels in America 1823-1827. Antiquarian Press, New York, 1959.

DOWDEN, A. O. T., Look at a Flower, Thomas Crowell Co., 1963.

DOWDEN, A. O. T., The Secret Life of the Flowers, The Odyssey Press, New York, 1964.

DUDDINGTON, C. L., Evolution and Design in the Plant Kingdom, Crowell, N.Y., 1970.

DUNN, D. B., and GILLETT, J. M., The Lupines of Canada and Alaska, Canada Dept of Agriculture, Monograph No. 2, 1966.

EASTHAM, J. W., Supplement to Flora of Southern British Columbia (J. K. Henry), Special Publn. No. 1, B.C. Provincial Museum, Victoria, 1947.

EASTHAM, J. W., Observations on the flora of the Southern Rocky Mountain Trench in British Columbia, Transactions of the Royal Society of Canada; XLIII, Series III, Sect. 5, 1949.

EASTHAM, J. W., The flora of Fairmont Hotsprings, Museum and Arts Notes, Series 2, 1(4): pp. 20-25, 1951, The Art, Historical, and Scientific Association, Vancouver, B.C.

FERNALD, M. L., Gray's Manual of Botany, 8th edition, American Book Company, New York.

FRISCH, K. von, Bees: Their Vision, Chemical Senses, and Language, Cornell University Press, Ithaca, 1956.

ENARI, LEONID, Plants of the Pacific Northwest, Binfords & Mort, Portland, 1956.

FEATHERLY, H. I., Taxonomic Terminology of the Higher Plants, Iowa State College Press, 1954.

FRANKTON, C., Weeds of Canada, Plant Research Institute, Canada Dept. of Agriculture Publication No. 948, 1967.

FRÖDERSTRÖM, HARALD, The Genus Sedum L., A Systematic Essay, Göteborg, 1936, Elanders Boktryckeri Aktiebolag.

GABRIELSON, I. N., Western American Alpines, Macmillan, 1932.

GARMAN, ERIC H., Pocket Guide to the Trees and Shrubs of British Columbia, B.C. Forest Service Publication B.28, 3rd (revised) edition, 1963.

GILKEY, H. M., and DENNIS, L. R. J., Handbook of Northwestern Plants, Oregon State University Bookstores, Inc., 1967.

GILLETT, J. M., The Gentians of Canada, Alaska, and Greenland, Canada Dept. of Agriculture Publication 1180, 1963.

GOODWIN, T. W., (edit.), Chemistry and Biochemistry of Plant Pigments, Academic Press, London and New York, 1965.

GRIMM, W. C., The Book of Shrubs, The Stackpole Co., 1957.

HARDY, W. G., (edit.), Alberta: A Natural History, M. G. Hurtig, Publishers, Edmonton, Alta., 1970.

HARRINGTON, H. D., and DURRELL, L. W., How to Identify Plants, Sage Books, Denver, 1957.

HASKIN, L. L., Wild Flowers of the Pacific Coast, Binfords and Mort, 2nd edn., 1967.

HENRY, J. K., Flora of Southern British Columbia and Vancouver Island, W. J. Gage, Toronto, 1915.

HENSHAW, JULIA W., Mountain Wild Flowers of Canada, William Briggs, Toronto, 1906.

HEREMAN, S., Paxton's Botanical Dictionary, New Edition 1868, Bradbury, Evans, London.

HESLOP-HARRISON, J., New Concepts in Flowering-Plant Taxonomy, Harvard Univ. Press, Cambridge, Mass., 1964.

HITCHCOCK, CRONQUIST, OWNBEY and THOMPSON, Vascular Plants of the Pacific Northwest (5 vols.), Univ. of Washington Press, to 1969.

HOLLINGWORTH, BUCKNER, Flower Chronicles, Rutgers Univ. Press, 1958.

HULTÉN, ERIC, Flora of Alaska and Neighboring Territories, Stanford Univ. Press, 1968.

Index Kewensis Plantarum Phanerogamarum Nomina et Synonyma Omnium Generum et Specierum a Linnaeo Usque ad Annum MDCCCLXXXV . . . Subjectis Oxonii - et prelo Clarendoniano, 1960.

JACKSON, B. J., Guide to the Literature of Botany, (supplement to Pritzel's Thesaurus), Hafner Publishing Co., N.Y. and London, 1964.

JEFFREY, C., An Introduction to Plant Taxonomy, J. & A. Churchill Ltd., 1968.

JOHNSON, A. T., and SMITH, H. A., Plant Names Simplified, Collingridge Ltd., London, 2nd edn., 1958.

KEBLE-MARTIN, WILLIAM, The Concise British Flora in Colour, Ebury Press, London, 1965.

KELSEY, H. P., and DAYTON, W. A., Standarized Plant Names, McFarland Co., Harrisburg, 1942.

KINGSBURY, J. M., Poisonous Plants of the United States and Canada, Prentice-Hall, New Jersey, 1955.

KIRK, R., The Olympic Rain Forest, Univ. of Washington Press, Seattle, 1966.

KNUTH, P., Handbook of Flower Pollination (5 vols.), Trans. by R. A. Davis, Oxford Univ. Press, New York, 1906-09.

KRAJINA, V. J., Biogeoclimatic Zones and Classification of B.C., in Ecology of Western North America, Dept. of Bot., Univ. of Brit. Col. Bot. Series No. 1, 1959, Vancouver, B.C.

LAWRENCE, G. H. M., Taxonomy of Vascular Plants, The MacMillan Co., New York, 1951.

LEMMON, R. S., and JOHNSON, C. C., Wildflowers of North America in Full Color, Nelson-Doubleday, New York, 1961.

LUBBOCK, SIR J., British Wild Flowers considered in Relation to Insects, MacMillan, London, 1893.

LYONS, C. P., Trees, Shrubs, and Flowers to Know in British Columbia, J. M. Dent, Toronto, 1952.

LYONS, C. P., Trees, Shrubs, and Flowers to Know in Washington, J. M. Dent, Toronto, 1956.

McCLINTOCK, D., and FITTER, R. S. R., Collins Pocket Guide to Wild Flowers, Collins, London, 1955.

McKELVEY, S. D., Botanical Exploration of the Trans-Mississippi West, 1790-1850, Arnold Arboretum of Harvard University, 1955.

MEEUSE, B. J. D., The Story of Pollination, Ronald Press, New York, 1961.

MILTON, VISCOUNT, and CHEADLE, W. B., The Northwest Passage by Land, 1862-63, Facsimile edition reprinted by Coles Publishing Company, Toronto, 1970.

MOSS, E. H., Flora of Alberta, Univ. of Toronto Press, 1959.

MUNZ, PHILLIP A., A California Flora (1959) also Supplement to A California Flora, University of California Press, 1968.

MUNZ, PHILLIP A., Shore Wildflowers of California, Oregon, and Washington, Univ. of California Press, 1964.

NELSON, A., Medical Botany, Livingstone, 1951.

NEWCOMBE, C. F., (edit.), Menzies' Journal of Vancouver's Voyage, April to October, 1792, Archives of British Columbia, Memoir No. 5, Victoria, 1923.

NOVAK, F. A., Pictorial Encyclopedia of Plants and Flowers, Paul Hamlyn, London, 1966.

PECK, M. E., A Manual of the Higher Plants of Oregon, Binfords and Mort, Portland, 1941.

PORSILD, A. E., HARINGTON, C. R., MULLIGAN, G. A., Germination of Ancient Seeds. Science 158:113. (1967).

PRITZEL, G. A., Thesaurus Literaturae Botanicae, Gorlich, Milan, 1871.

RAUP, HUGH M., Forests and Gardens along the Alaska Highway, Geog. Rev., 35: 22-48, 1945.

REED, H. S., A Short History of the Plant Sciences, Chronica Botanica Co., Waltham, Mass., 1942.

RICKETT, H. W., Wild Flowers of the United States, McGraw-Hill, N.Y., 1966.

ROBINSON, TREVOR, The Organic Constituents of Higher Plants: Their Chemistry and Interrelationships, revised edn. 1967, Burgess, Minneapolis.

SHARPLESS, A. W., Alaska Wild Flowers, Stanford Univ. Press, 1938.

SMITH, A. W., A Gardener's Book of Plant Names, Harper & Row Publishers, New York, Evanston and London, 1963.

STAFLEU, P. A., Taxonomic Literature, Inter-Documentation Co. AG., Zug, Switzerland, 1967.

STANWELL-FLETCHER, JOHN F., and THEODORA C., Some accounts of the flora and fauna of the Driftwood Valley region of North-Central British Columbia, Occasional Papers of British Columbia Provincial Museum, No. 4, Victoria, B.C., 1943.

SZCZAWINSKI, A. F., The Heather Family (Ericaceae) of British Columbia, Handbook No. 19, B.C. Provincial Museum, Dept. of Recreation and Conservation, 1962.

SZCZAWINSKI, A. F., The Orchids of British Columbia, Handbook No. 16, B.C. Provincial Museum, Dept. of Recreation and Conservation, 1959.

TAYLOR, T. M. C., The Lily Family (Liliaceae) of British Columbia, Handbook No. 25, B.C. Provincial Museum, Dept. of Recreation and Conservation, 1966.

THWAITES, R. G. (edit.), Original Journals of the Lewis and Clark Expedition, Dodd, Mead, 1905.

TRAILL, C. P., Studies of Plant Life in Canada, William Briggs, Toronto, 1906.

WENT, F. W., The Plants, Life Nature Library, Time Inc., N.Y., 1963.

WILEY, L., Rare Wild Flowers of North America, Leonard Wiley, Portland, 1968.

YOUNGKEN, H. W., Pharmaceutical Botany, 7th edn., Philadelphia, Blakiston, 1951.

INDEX